Feb. 10th 1976.

Congratulations
on winning
a medal for
Judo.

Jay. B.

dictionary
four

Amy L. Brown
John Downing
John Sceats

Chambers young set dictionaries

© 1973 W. & R. Chambers Ltd.

Second impression 1974

Printed in Great Britain by
T. & A. Constable Ltd., Edinburgh

ISBN 0 550 71193 7 (school edition)

ISBN 0 550 10609 X (trade edition)

Preface

Words

A dictionary is a collection of words listed in alphabetical order, with definitions of their meanings. The English language contains many thousands of words, and no one book can include them all. This dictionary contains most of the words that ten- to twelve-year-olds will want to look up.

Meanings

Many words have more than one meaning or shade of meaning. A dictionary can give you only a few of them – usually those which are most often used. If you come across an unfamiliar word, look it up in the dictionary, and if more than one meaning is given, decide which one fits in best with the rest of the sentence. If none of the definitions makes sense, try a larger dictionary for other possible meanings.

In this book, words which are spelled the same but which have very different meanings are listed one after another, with numbers beside them. For example, look up **air 1, air 2** and **air 3**. Where different meanings of the same word are closely related, they are separated by a semicolon (;), but where the relationship is not as close, a colon (:) is used. Additional information about the word being defined, such as an example of how it is used or how it should be pronounced, is enclosed in brackets (like this).

Word 'families'

Words formed from a 'parent' word (for example, **airport** from **air**) are listed below the definition of the 'parent' word. If the meaning is very different from that of the 'parent' word (for example, **artful** and **art**), it is given a separate entry.

Parts of speech

Many dictionaries describe a word as a noun, an adjective, a verb and so on. This dictionary does not – for two main reasons. One reason is that the way a word is defined shows what part of speech it is. For example, a definition beginning with *to* is always a verb (as, *to run, to air*); a definition beginning with *a* or *the* is always a noun (as, *a run, the air*), etc. The other reason is that words are not nouns or verbs, etc. *in themselves* – they become parts of speech because of the ways in which they are used in a sentence.

There is not enough space in this dictionary to list all the possible ways in which a word may be used in a sentence, so where, for example, the noun meaning can be guessed from the verb meaning, the noun is not defined separately. In the same way, when a word (such as **brightly**) is formed from the 'parent' word (**bright**) in a regular way, it has not been included.

The sign □ in a definition is a signal that the word is about to be defined as a different part of speech.

Spelling

Although most words can be spelled in only one way, some have two acceptable spellings. For such words, both spellings are shown in this dictionary, because both are equally correct. Verbs which end in *-ize* (such as **emphasize**) can also be spelled correctly as *-ise* (**emphasise**), but only the *-ize* ending has been used in this dictionary in order to make room for more words.

Pronunciation

Most of the words in this dictionary are not difficult to pronounce, but help may be needed for some (such as **gnat, bough, fascism,** etc.). For these and other words which may be puzzling, a pronunciation guide is given in brackets after the word, to show how it should be said.

Another difficulty that sometimes arises, especially in longer words, is where to put the stress or emphasis. In this dictionary, the syllable to be stressed is underlined (as, emphasis, fanaticism).

Appendixes

At the end of the Dictionary you will find two appendixes which will help you to use it. Appendix One is a list of irregular verbs which do not follow the usual rules for forming past tenses. This should help you to look up past tenses of verbs, if you can't find them in the dictionary. Appendix Two is a list of all the common prefixes and suffixes with their usual meanings.

The next step

This dictionary lists about 15,000 words, but it does not include very common words, such as *and* and *am,* because everyone knows them already; nor does it include all the technical and specialist terms connected with particular subjects, professions, etc. If you want to know the meaning of a word that is not in this dictionary, or if the definition of a word does not give you all the information you want, go on to a more advanced dictionary, such as *Chambers Compact Dictionary,* or *Chambers Twentieth Century Dictionary.*

To parents and teachers

Guidance on how best to use the *Young Set Dictionaries* with children will be found in *Words Children Want to Use,* the handbook to the series, which also contains an account of the research on which the series is based.

a

abacus a frame with beads on rods or wires, used for counting

abandon to give up; to forsake or desert
abandoned forsaken; left completely alone: given up to wickedness

abashed ashamed or confused

abate to grow less (as when a storm begins to abate)

abattoir *(say abatwahr)* a slaughterhouse where animals are killed for food

abbey a monastery or convent; the church that is or once was attached to a monastery or convent
abbess the female head of an abbey
abbot the male head of an abbey

abbreviate to shorten
abbreviation a short way of writing a word by using only a part of it (such as Mr. for Mister)

abdicate to resign from a position of authority (as when a king gives up his crown)

abdomen the part of the body below the chest; the belly
abdominal concerned with the abdomen

abduct to take away by force or trickery; to kidnap

abet to assist or encourage someone (usually a wrong-doer)

abhor to detest; to loathe
abhorrent hateful; loathsome

abide to remain; to continue: to endure; put up with
to abide by to act according to (as when a person abides by a promise or an agreement)

ability see **able**

abject cowering; miserable

ablaze burning strongly; very bright

able having enough strength, cleverness or skill to do something; skilful, clever
ably skilfully, cleverly
ability enough strength, cleverness or skill to do something

ablution the act of washing (especially the body)

abnormal not normal, very unusual
abnormality something unusual, out of the ordinary

aboard on board or in a ship, train, bus or aeroplane

abolish to do away with, put an end to
abolition the act of doing away with or ending something (such as the abolition of slavery)

abominable hateful; detestable

aborigines *(say aborijinees)* the first people to live in a country; the native inhabitants of a country
aboriginal existing in the early days of history □ one of the aborigines

about nearly; almost (as - He has just about finished the work.); more or less (as - The baby is about six months old.); around (standing about); in the opposite direction (turning about) □ here and there (as - trees planted about the park); concerning (taking action about something)

above higher than; more than □ over; in a higher position

abrasion a grazed or skinned place on the body: the act of rubbing or scraping off
abrasive scraping; rubbing □ something that scrapes or rubs (such as sandpaper)

abreast side by side; with fronts in a line

abridge to shorten something written or printed by cutting down the number of words originally used

abroad in or to another country; out of doors

abrupt sudden; hurried: rude and short in manner of speaking

abscess a collection of pus in a part of the body (such as an abscess at the root of an aching tooth)

absent away, not present

absence being away or missing

absentee someone who is away from school or from work

absent-minded not paying attention

absolute complete; certain: not limited by rules or laws (as, an absolute monarch)

absolutely certainly, without doubt

absorb to suck in or take in; to take up the whole of someone's attention

absorbent able to absorb (as a sponge absorbs water)

abstain to keep oneself from doing something (such as abstaining from consuming alcoholic drinks)

abstinence the act of abstaining

abstract existing only in the mind, not in a concrete form □ a summary

abstruse difficult to understand

absurd ridiculous; silly

abundance more than enough; plenty

abundant plentiful

abuse *(say abewz)* to use wrongly; to injure; to scold angrily □ *(say abewss)* unfair or bad use; rude harsh language

abyss *(say abiss)* a very deep chasm; a bottomless depth

abysmal *(say abizmal)* very deep; bottomless

academy a higher school: a society for the encouragement of science or the arts (such as the Royal Academy of Dramatic Art - R.A.D.A.)

academic concerning an academy; scholarly

accede *(say akseed)* to agree or consent to something

accelerate *(say akselerate)* to increase speed

accelerator anything used to increase speed (such as a lever or pedal in a motor)

accent *(say aksent)* tone of voice; a way of pronouncing words □ *(say aksent)* to put stress on a single word or syllable when pronouncing it

accentuate to emphasize or put stress on

accept *(say aksept)* to take something offered; to agree to

accepted generally approved of or believed in

acceptable satisfactory; pleasing

access *(say aksess)* way or means of approach to a place; entrance

accessible able to be reached

accession a coming to (as, a king's accession to the throne)

accessory *(say aksessory)* anything not essential added to help or adorn something (as, car or dress accessories)

accident *(say aksident)* something that happens by chance; a mishap; a disaster

acclaim to applaud; to greet with enthusiastic approval

acclamation shouts of applause or approval

acclimatize to accustom or become accustomed to a different climate or different surroundings

accommodate to make room for; to adjust or make suitable

accommodating obliging

accommodation lodging; room or space

accompany to go along with; to play a musical instrument while someone else plays or sings

accompaniment music played to help a solo instrument, singer or choir

accompanist someone who plays music to help a soloist or choir

accomplice a helper (usually in crime or wrong-doing)

accomplish to finish; to complete

accomplished completed: well educated; highly skilled

accomplishment achievement; a special skill

accord to agree with; to give or grant

accordingly therefore

according to in agreement with: as told or said by someone

accordion a musical instrument with a keyboard and a bellows that is pushed in and out

accost to go up to and speak to someone (usually a stranger)

account a statement of money owing or spent: an explanation or reason; a story □ to give or to be a reason for something
accountant someone who is qualified to keep and inspect accounts
accountable responsible to someone: able to be explained
on account of because of
on no account not for any reason
to take into account to think about when considering a problem

accredited having authority to act (often on behalf of someone else)

accumulate to pile up; to gather together in a mass; to amass
accumulator someone who collects or accumulates; a battery that can be recharged with electricity

accurate correct; exactly right
accuracy exactness

accuse to blame someone for a wrong-doing; to bring a legal charge against someone
accusation a legal charge brought against a person; blame

accustom to make (someone) used to or familiar with
accustomed usual; used to

ace the playing card, domino, die, etc., that has only one mark; someone who is extremely good at something (as, an ace airman)

ache *(say ayk)* a continuous dull pain □ to have a continuous pain
aching giving continuous pain

achieve to complete what one sets out to do; to gain; to win
achievement something done or completed; something accomplished that makes one feel pleased and proud

acid a sour substance that can burn the skin □ tasting sharp or sour
acidity sourness

acknowledge to admit that something is true; to say that something has been received
acknowledg(e)ment an admission or confession; a receipt

acme the top or highest point (as, the acme of success)

acne a pimple; a common skin ailment with pimples

acorn the fruit or seed of an oak tree

acoustics *(say akoostics)* the qualities which make hearing in a room or hall good or bad; the science of sound
acoustic concerning sound or hearing conditions

acquaint to make known; to make familiar with
acquaintance someone known slightly

acquiesce *(say akwee-ess)* to agree; to accept

acquire to get; to gain
aquisition something acquired
acquisitive eager to get possessions

acquit to free from blame
acquittal a statement that someone is innocent

acre a measure of land equal to rather less than half a hectare
acreage the area of a piece of land measured in acres

acrid bitter; irritating; harsh

acrimonious sharp in manner or bitter in speech
acrimony bitterness of feeling or speech

acrobat someone who performs difficult gymnastic feats
acrobatics acrobatic performances

across from one side of something to the other side; on the other side of

acrostic a poem or word-puzzle in which the first or last letters of each line, taken in order, spell a word or sentence

act 1 to do something □ a deed; the doing of something
action something done; a continuous series of acts
active doing something; being busy or lively
activity activeness; action; occupation

act 2 to pretend to be someone else (as, in a play or film) □ part of a play
actor a man or boy who acts
actress a woman or girl who acts

actual real, not imaginary
actually really, in fact

acute sharp-pointed or sharp; keen; quick to understand

adage an old saying; a proverb

adamant refusing to give way

adapt to fit in with different surroundings or events
adaptable able and willing to adapt

add to put something together with something else; to find the sum of two or more numbers
addition the part of arithmetic to do with adding; something added
additional extra; added to something

adder a viper

addict a person who is enslaved by a habit (such as taking dangerous drugs or drinking too much alcohol)

address 1 the name or number of a house, street, town, etc., where a person lives □ to write an address on an envelope or parcel

address 2 a speech given to an audience □ to make a speech: to speak or write to someone

adenoids two small lumps of fleshy tissue in the space at the back of the nose, which can hinder breathing if they are swollen

adept very skilled

adequate enough; sufficient

adhere to stick to; to remain loyal to a person or cause
adherent a follower or supporter
adhesive a substance (such as glue) for sticking things together

adjacent *(say ajaysent)* lying near to but not touching (as when a garage is adjacent to but not part of a house)

adjective a word which is added to a noun to describe it (as, a *red* dress)

adjoin to lie next to and touching (as when two houses are joined together by a single wall)

adjourn to stop a meeting which will be continued at another time

adjust to arrange properly or put in order; to regulate

administer to manage; to govern
administration the business of management; the departments that carry out the work of the government

admiral a naval officer of the highest rank
admiralty the government department responsible for the navy

admire to look up to or think very highly of someone
admirable very good; worthy of admiration
admiration pleased approval

admit to allow someone to enter: to confess or acknowledge
admission admittance: anything confessed or acknowledged
admittance the right or permission to enter

adolescent *(say adolessent)* growing out of childhood into manhood or womanhood
adolescence the period between being a child and becoming an adult

adopt to choose or take as one's own (as when a person adopts someone else's ideas, or when parents adopt a child who is not their own by birth)
adoption the act of adopting

adore to love very much; to worship
adorable very lovable
adoration great love; worship

adorn to make someone or something beautiful (usually by adding ornaments or decorations)

adrift drifting; floating about

adult a grown-up person □ fully grown

adulterate to make something impure by adding something that doesn't belong (as when water is added to pure milk)

adultery a breaking of the marriage promise to be faithful to one's wife or husband

advance to go forward; to put forward (an idea or plan); to make progress □ a loan of money; a forward move
advanced far ahead; well on (in age, school, etc.)
in advance beforehand

advantage a gain or benefit
advantageous profitable; helpful

adventure an exciting or risky undertaking
adventurer a person who looks for adventure

adverb a word which is added to a verb, adjective or other adverb to modify it - that is to say - how, how much, when, etc. (as driving *carefully, extremely carefully, very carefully*)

adversary an enemy; someone who opposes another

adverse acting against someone or something (as when adverse weather conditions prevent some action)
adversity hardship; misfortune

advertise to make something known to the public
advertisement a public announcement (usually by the manufacturer of the goods advertised)

advice *(say adviess)* something helpful said to a person who is not sure what to do; a recommendation or opinion to someone about what should be done
advise *(say advize)* to give advice to; to recommend
advisable wise or sensible

advocate to speak in favour of; to recommend □ someone who argues in favour of something

aerate to put gas or air into a liquid or solid

aerial a system of metal rods or wires which send or receive radio or television signals

aero- air (when used as part of a word)
aerobatics daring manoeuvres performed by airmen
aerodrome a landing and service station for aircraft
aerofoil an air-resistant flat surface (such as the wing or aileron of an aeroplane)
aeronautics the study or art of air navigation
aeroplane a machine that can fly even though it is heavier than air
aerosol a small container filled with a liquid under pressure from air or a harmless gas, so that it can be released as a fine spray

affable easy to speak to or get on with; polite

affair business; a matter or concern; an event
affairs business dealings

affect 1 to change or act upon (as when plans are upset or affected because of the weather): to touch the feelings (as a sad film does)
affecting touching the feelings

affect 2 to pretend to feel or act in a way that is not natural or usual
affected not natural in manner or speech
affectation an attempt to appear as something other than what one is

affection great liking; fondness
affectionate loving; fond

affirm to state something positively and firmly
affirmative saying *yes* in

answer to a question □ the opposite of negative

afflict to cause continued pain or unhappiness
affliction an ailment; suffering; unhappiness

affluent wealthy; having plenty of money
affluence wealth; riches

afford to have enough money to be able to buy something

affront to insult □ an insult

afloat floating

afraid frightened: rather inclined to think (for example, to be afraid it is going to rain)

afresh again

after behind (in place); after or later (in time); following on
aftermath the bad effects following some event (such as after a war)
afternoon the time following midday, before sunset
afterthought a second or later thought
afterwards at a later time

again once more; in addition; at another time

against in an opposite direction to; on the opposite side to; in collision with

agate a precious stone made of layers of quartz in different colours

age the amount of time something or someone has been alive or has existed; a very long period of time (such as the Ice Age) □ to grow old
aged *(say ayjed)* very old; elderly
aged *(say ayjd)* of a certain age (as, a boy aged ten)
ageless never growing old
of age being old enough, by law, to vote or get married

agent someone who acts for or on behalf of another person
agency the office or business of an agent

aggravate to make worse
aggravating annoying; irritating

aggregate to collect into a mass; to accumulate □ the sum total: a mixture of stones, sand and cement

aggressive being first to start a quarrel or fight
aggressor the first one to start a quarrel or fight

aghast horrified; appalled

agile active; nimble
agility nimbleness

agitate to shake or stir up; to disturb; to excite
agitator a person who tries to create unrest among other people

agnostic a person who holds that no one can prove that God exists
agnosticism the theory that there can be no proof of the existence of God or anything beyond the universe we know

ago past; since

agony extreme pain or suffering
agonizing extremely painful

agree to consent to; to think the same as another person or group of people: to suit (as when it is said that sea air agrees with someone)
agreeable pleasant; in favour of or willing
agreement an agreed bargain or contract; the act of agreeing

agriculture the cultivation of the land
agricultural to do with farming

aground stranded on the sea bed in shallow water or on rocks

ahead in front; in advance; farther on

aid to help or assist □ help or assistance

ail to be ill or worried
ailment disease or trouble

aileron one of the flaps at the back of an aeroplane wing

aim 1 to point a weapon carefully at something or someone

aim 2 a plan or purpose to be achieved; a goal to be reached
aimless without a purpose in life

air 1 the mixture of gases that we breathe; the atmosphere; a slight breeze □to expose to the air; to dry (in warm air)
airy like air; open so that air can pass through: see also **air 2**
airing exposure to air or heat: a short walk or drive in the open air
airless without air; stuffy
airborne transported or carried in the air
air conditioning the process of cleaning and regulating the temperature of air in buildings or transport
aircraft any machine that can fly in the air
airfield a place where aircraft can land and take off
air force aircraft used for fighting and the people who control them
airgun a gun that shoots bullets by means of compressed air
airman a man who flies or helps to fly aircraft
air pocket a thinner part of the air which causes the aircraft going through it to lose height suddenly
airport the place where commercial aircraft arrive and depart
airship an aircraft that is lighter than air
airtight closed so tightly that air cannot get in or out

air 2 appearance, look or manner (as when an old house is said to have an air of neglect)
airy light-hearted; flippant

air 3 a melody; a tune

aisle (say ile) a passage between rows of seats in a church, cinema, theatre, etc.

ajar not quite closed

alabaster a smooth white stone-like translucent substance

alacrity briskness; cheerful readiness

alarm sudden surprise or fear: a warning of danger; something that awakens (such as the bell on an alarm clock) or warns (such as a fire alarm)

alarming frightening; surprising in an unpleasant way

alas a word which expresses dismay or sorrow

albatross a large web-footed seabird of the Southern Hemisphere

albino (say albeeno) a person or animal without normal colouring, so that the skin, hair, feathers, etc. are white, and the eyes pink

album a book of blank pages used for collections of stamps, photographs, autographs, etc.; a book-like container for records

albumen white of egg

alchemy the study of chemistry in the Middle Ages (when the main aim was to try to turn non-precious metals into gold)

alcohol a pure spirit in wine, whisky and other strong drinks, that makes them intoxicating
alcoholic relating to alcohol □a person who is addicted to alcoholic drinks

alcove a small room or part of a room set back in a wall

alder a tree belonging to the birch family (usually growing in moist ground)

alderman a member of a town council, next to the mayor in rank

ale a name given to some kinds of beer

alert wide awake; active or watchful □to warn

algae (say aljee) seaweed and other similar plants

algebra a branch of mathematics in which general symbols (especially letters) are used as well as numbers

alias a false name by which a person is known instead of his real name

alibi an excuse by someone charged with wrong-doing that he was somewhere else when it happened

alien foreign; not in keeping with

(as when a person with a normally gentle manner speaks sharply - that is, in a way alien to his nature) □ a foreigner

alight 1 in flames; burning

alight 2 to get down from something (such as a horse, a bus, etc.)

align *(say aline)* to bring something into line with something else (as when aligning a row of sticks)

alike like (as when twin sisters are said to look alike) □ in the same manner (for example - All members of a family are treated alike.)

alimentary concerned with food
alimentary canal the passage for food through the body

alimony the housekeeping money paid to a wife by a husband after they have been divorced or separated

alive living; not dead: alert

alkali *(say alkalie)* a class of compounds (such as caustic soda and potash) which are the chemical opposites of acids and will neutralize them in solution
alkaline containing or having the properties of an alkali

all the whole of □ everything or everyone
all but very nearly
all in tired out, exhausted
all right good; safe and sound; agreed
all-round having many kinds of abilities
at all in the least degree

allay to calm or relieve; to make less (as, to try to allay someone's fears)

allege to state something as a fact, but without proof
allegation something alleged

allegiance loyalty (especially to a country or sovereign)

allegory a straightforward story that also has a second meaning or hidden message (such as a parable or fable)

allergy unusual sensitivity to

certain foods or substances (as when pollen in the air makes some people cough and sneeze, while others come out in a rash when they eat shellfish or strawberries)
allergic being sensitive to or affected by certain usually harmless foods or substances

alleviate to make less hard to bear or endure

alley a passageway (usually between buildings); a garden path between hedges; a long narrow enclosed space used for games (such as a bowling alley)

alliance, allied see **ally**

alligator a reptile like a crocodile, but with a broader snout

allot to share out; to distribute
allotment a portion: a small piece of land used for growing flowers and vegetables

allow to permit; to grant permission
allowance a fixed sum of money or an amount of something granted for a purpose
to allow for, to make allowances for to take into consideration as an excuse when deciding or judging something

alloy a mixture of two or more metals

allude to refer to; to mention in passing
allusion an indirect or casual mention of something in speaking

alluring charming; temptingly attractive

alluvium alluvial soil, sand, gravel, etc., brought down by rivers and deposited on lower land
alluvial deposited by rivers or floods

ally *(say alie)* to join by friendship, agreement, contract or treaty to a person, country, etc. □ *(say alie)* a helper; a friend: a country or state joined with another for a common purpose
alliance a union by contract or treaty
allied joined by treaty: related

or connected

almanac a calendar (usually in the form of a book) that gives information about the weather and other events that are expected to occur during one year

almighty all-powerful

almond the nut-like kernel inside the fruit of the almond tree

almost nearly

alms money or gifts to the poor; charity

aloft overhead; high in the air: above the deck of a sailing ship

alone all by oneself; solitary

along by the side of: from one end towards the other (as when walking along a road): in company with (as when walking along with someone)
alongside beside; side by side

aloof at a distance; apart from; shy and cold in manner
aloofness reluctance to join in with others; coldness of manner

aloud out loud; so as to be heard

alp a high mountain: a meadow or pasture high up in the mountains
alpine connected with or to do with alps (as, alpine scenery)

alpaca a kind of llama with long silky hair; woollen cloth made from this hair

alphabet all the letters used in a language, arranged in a special order
alphabetical in the order of the alphabet

already sooner than expected; beforehand

alsatian a large wolf-like dog

also as well as; too; in addition

altar a raised table or block on which sacrifices were once offered to a deity; a raised table inside a church where acts of religious worship are performed by clergymen

alter to change; to make different; to become different
alteration a change

alternate *(say* alternayt*)* to do or use something by turns □ *(say* alternet*)* happening or following by turns
alternately by turns
alternative a choice between two or more things; either of two things
alternatively on the other hand; instead
alternating current (A.C.) an electric current that reverses direction at regular intervals, unlike direct current (D.C.)

although even if; in spite of

altimeter an instrument for measuring height above sea level

altitude the height of something above a certain level (especially sea level)

alto the lowest female voice (short for contralto); the highest male voice

altogether completely; entirely

aluminium a lightweight silver-coloured metal

always forever; at all times

amass to accumulate; to gather in large quantity

amateur a person who plays a game or takes part in something for the love of it, and not for money (as a professional does); a person who likes to do something (such as painting or playing a musical instrument) even though he is not very good at it
amateurish not very skilful; unprofessional

amaze to surprise greatly; to astonish

ambassador a minister of the highest rank who is sent to a foreign country to represent the interests of his own country

amber a yellowish-orange fossil resin used for beads and ornaments; the colour of amber

ambidextrous able to use either the left hand or the right hand with equal skill

ambiguous having more than

one possible meaning; not clear in meaning
ambiguity uncertainty of meaning; unclearness

ambition a strong desire to be successful in life (as, an ambition to become a great athlete, an airline pilot, a doctor, etc.)
ambitious having or showing ambition

amble to move along at an easy pace

ambulance a special vehicle used to carry sick or injured people

ambush a hidden group of people waiting to make a surprise attack □ to lie in wait for an enemy and attack by surprise

amen a word meaning *so be it* at the end of a prayer

amenable easily led; ready to take advice or to be persuaded

amend to correct; to improve
amendment a correction or improvement
to make amends to make up for a wrong-doing

amenity pleasantness of surroundings

amethyst a bluish-violet precious stone

amiable likable; having a kindly, pleasant nature

amicable friendly; good-natured

amid, amidst in the middle of; among

amiss wrong; out of order
to take amiss to take offence at something said or done

ammeter an instrument for measuring electric current

ammonia a strong-smelling gas, which can be dissolved in water and used for cleaning

ammunition bullets, shells, grenades and other explosive missiles

amnesia loss of memory

amnesty a general pardon for wrong-doers

among, amongst in the midst of; along with or together with (as when someone is said to be among friends); to each of (as when something is shared among friends)

amorous loving; showing love

amount a quantity; the total sum of a number of things added together □ to add up to

ampere the unit used to measure the strength of an electric current (named after a French physicist, Ampère)

amphibian an animal (such as a frog or a crocodile) that can live in water as well as on land; a vehicle that can be used on water or land; an aeroplane that can take off from and alight on water or land because it has floats as well as wheels
amphibious able to live or be used on water or land

amphitheatre a round or oval building having rows of seats all round the inside, rising from a central open space called an arena

ample large; enough; plentiful

amplify to make larger; to increase
amplification enlargement of sound (by increasing the volume) or of a report or account (by adding details)
amplifier something that enlarges: an instrument for increasing the strength of electric current so that the sound from a radio, etc. is made louder

amputate to cut off (as, to amputate a badly injured or diseased limb)

amuse to entertain pleasantly; to make people smile or laugh
amusement something that amuses or entertains; the feeling of being amused or entertained

anaconda a large snake that crushes its prey

anaemia an illness caused by poor quality of blood or an insufficient quantity of it
anaemic suffering from anaemia; looking pale and listless

anaesthetic a drug, inhaled or injected, that produces unconsciousness or numbness for a time

anaesthesia a temporary state of unconsciousness or loss of feeling

anaesthetist a person (usually a doctor) who gives an anaesthetic to a patient

anagram a word or sentence formed by changing the order of letters of another word or words (for example, *meat* for *team, salt* for *last*)

analysis a breaking down of a thing into its separate parts for examination

analyse to examine something in order to find out what it is made of

analyst a person who analyses

analytical having to do with analysis; analysing

anarchist a person who wishes to do away with government and laws

anarchy absence of government, law and order; a state of confusion and disorder

anatomy the physical structure of a body; the study of this structure after cutting up a body into its separate parts

anatomical having to do with anatomy

anatomist a person who dissects or cuts up bodies in order to study their anatomy

ancestor a person far back in one's family, and no longer alive (such as a great-great grandfather); a forefather

ancestral having to do with ancestors

ancestry all of a person's ancestors or forefathers

anchor a heavy piece of metal, usually with hooked ends, attached to a ship or boat by a chain or cable (It digs into the sea bed when thrown overboard, and keeps the vessel from drifting away.) □ to throw out the anchor from a ship or boat

anchorage a place (usually sheltered) where a ship can anchor

to weigh anchor to take up the anchor so that the ship can move away

ancient (*say aynshent*) very old; belonging to times long past

anecdote a little story about some interesting event or occurrence

anemometer an instrument for measuring the speed of the wind

anemone (*say anemonee*) a flowering plant (One kind of anemone, the windflower, grows wild in the woods in springtime, while others, brilliantly coloured, are garden flowers.) For **sea anemone** see under **sea.**

aneroid using no liquid (as, an aneroid barometer which measures the pressure of air without a column of liquid)

anew again or over again

angel a divine messenger, believed to be sent from God; a person who is considered to be very good and helpful

angelic like an angel

anger a strong feeling of rage or bad temper

angry feeling or showing anger

angle 1 the space between two lines meeting at a point: a point of view

angular having an angle or angles (as, an angular piece of furniture)

angle 2 to fish with rod and line; to try to get something by hinting or scheming

angler a person who fishes with rod and line

anglo- English, when used as part of a word (as in **anglophile**, meaning a foreigner who likes and admires England and English people)

angora a goat, cat or rabbit with long silky hair; wool or fabric made from the hair of an angora goat or rabbit

angry see **anger**

anguish very great pain of body or mind; agony

anguished suffering great pain of body or mind

angular see **angle 1**

animal any living creature (not a plant) which can feel and move itself about; any of the four-footed animals

animation liveliness; vivacity
animate (*say animayt*) to give life to; to make lively □ (*say animet*) living, having life
animated full of life; vivacious

animosity hostility; strong dislike

ankle the joint connecting the foot and leg

annals a history of events, recorded year by year

annexe a building or part of a building that has been added on or attached to a main building
annex to add; to take possession (as when a country annexes territory)

annihilate (*say anie-ilate*) to destroy completely so that nothing is left

anniversary the day in each year on which people remember an event which happened once (such as a birthday or wedding)

announce to make something known publicly
announcement a statement made known to the public
announcer a person who makes announcements (especially on radio and television)

annoy to make someone a bit angry; to tease
annoyance a nuisance; something that annoys people

annual happening once a year; yearly □ a plant that lives only one year: a book that comes out once a year

annul to cancel; to abolish (as, to annul a law or rule)

anoint to smear with ointment or oil; to put holy oil on a person's head in a religious ceremony

anonymous (abbreviated **anon.**) of unknown authorship; without the name of the person who has written something (such as a book, a poem, a letter, etc.)
anonymity state of being anonymous or unknown

anorak a warm waterproof jacket (usually with a hood)

another one more; a different thing or person
one another each other

answer a reply to a question; the solution to a problem; the reply to a letter □ to reply; to be responsible for
answerable able to be answered; responsible for (as when a person is answerable for another's good behaviour)

ant a small insect which lives in a community of ants in a hole in the ground or in an ant-hill above the ground
anteater a South American animal with a long nose and sticky tongue which help it to catch the ants it feeds on

antagonist someone who fights against or opposes another; an opponent
antagonism hostility; opposition
antagonize to make someone feel angry or hostile

antarctic at or around the South Pole

ante- before or ahead, when used with another word (such as **anteroom,** meaning a room leading into a main room)

antelope a swift, graceful wild animal related to the goat

antenna one of the feelers on the heads of insects, spiders, lobsters, crabs, etc.: a radio aerial
antennae (*say antennee*) the plural of antenna

anthem a piece of music to be sung by a choir at a religious service; a patriotic song of praise (The British national anthem is *God Save the Queen.*)

anthology a collection of poems, short stories, etc. by different authors, which have been published in one volume

anthracite a kind of hard coal which burns with little flame or smoke

anthropoid like a human being in shape or looks

anti- against, when used with another word (such as **anti-aircraft**, meaning used to fight against aircraft, or **antifreeze**, a substance added to the water in a car radiator to prevent it from freezing in very cold weather)

antibiotic a chemical substance (such as penicillin) made by bacteria, used to stop the growth of other, harmful bacteria

antic an amusing trick or caper; a ridiculous or grotesque movement

anticipate to expect or look forward to something before it actually happens

anticlimax a dull or disappointing ending to what has been an exciting story or event; the opposite of a climax

anti-clockwise in the opposite direction to the way clock hands move

anticyclone a flow of air coming from an area of high atmospheric pressure, which brings fine weather; the opposite of an area of low pressure, which is associated with unsettled weather

antidote something given to act against poison

antipathy a strong dislike or feeling against
antipathetic feeling great dislike; opposed to

antipodes (*say antipodeez*) the opposite side of the world

antique (*say anteek*) very old; old-fashioned □ anything very old (such as furniture, ornaments, statuary, etc.)
antiquarian or **antiquary** someone who studies or collects antiquities
antiquity ancient times; great age; an object from ancient times

antiquated grown old or out of fashion

antiseptic a substance (such as iodine) that destroys harmful germs (especially in cuts and wounds)

antitoxin a substance formed in the body that fights against disease germs

antler a deer's horn or a branch of it

anvil an iron block on which pieces of metal can be hammered into shape

anxious worried or afraid about something that may happen
anxiety worry; fear of what may happen

any one or some; no matter which
anybody any person
anyhow in any way; no matter what; in an untidy state
anyone any person
anything a thing of any kind
anywhere in any place at all
at any rate whatever may happen or may have happened

apace quickly; fast

apart not together; in pieces; aside from

apartheid (*say apart-hate*) a keeping apart of people of different races, by making them live in different areas, and go to different schools, etc.

apartment a room or set of rooms in a house or building, for people to live in

apathy lack of feeling or interest
apathetic without interest or enthusiasm

ape a monkey, especially a large one with little or no tail □ to imitate or copy what someone else does

aperture an opening; a hole

apex the highest tip of something (such as the top point of a triangle); the peak or summit

apiary a place where bees are kept

apiece to or for each one (as

when several people are given one apple apiece)

apology a statement of regret for something wrong that has been said or done
apologize to say one is sorry for something said or done
apologetic feeling sorry or regretful for some fault

apostle a person sent to preach the gospel (especially one of the twelve disciples of Christ)

apostrophe a mark (') used to show when a letter or letters have been left out of a word (such as can't for cannot) or to show that something belongs to someone (as, the man's hat)

appal to terrify; to fill with dismay

apparatus equipment (such as ropes and bars in a gymnasium); a set of tools or instruments used to do a job of work or in a laboratory, etc.

apparel clothing □ to clothe or dress

apparent easy to see: seeming (as when a person shows apparent sorrow, but does not really feel it)
apparently seemingly; evidently

apparition a sudden appearance of something unusual (such as a ghost)

appeal to ask for help or sympathy; to implore: to be pleasing (as when someone says that a certain kind of music appeals to him) □ a request for help
appealing imploring; earnestly asking: arousing sympathy or liking

appear to come into sight; to seem or look (as - He appears to be worried.)
appearance the act of appearing; the outward look of something

appease to calm or pacify someone (often by giving what was asked for)

appendicitis an illness in which the appendix becomes inflamed

appendix something following at the end of the main part of a book or report, etc.: a small narrow tube attached to the large intestine
appendixes, appendices the plural of appendix

appetite the desire or hunger for food

applaud to praise by clapping the hands or by cheering
applause praise loudly expressed by clapping or cheering

apple a firm, round fruit that grows on a tree

apply 1 to put on, or close to, something (as when ointment is applied to a cut); to put one's mind to something (as - He applied himself to his homework.); to be suitable or intended for (as - These instructions apply to girls as well as boys.)
appliance anything which is applied for a particular purpose (especially an instrument of some kind)
application the act of applying; attentive study
applicable able to be applied; suitable

apply 2 to make a formal request (as when someone applies for a job)
application a formal request

appoint to fix or set (as, to appoint a time for a meeting); to choose a person for a job or official position
appointment a fixed time, agreed beforehand (as, an appointment to see the dentist); a job or office to which a person has been appointed

apportion to divide into shares

appraise to set a price or value on something
appraisal a judgment of the value of something

appreciate to understand; to value highly; to see the value of: to rise in value
appreciable noticeable; large enough to be seen or measured
appreciation gratitude; an

understanding of the worth or value of something

appreciative grateful; showing appreciation

apprehend to seize or arrest; to understand or grasp with the mind; to have fear or dread that something is going to happen

apprehension the arrest or capture of a person: understanding: fear

apprehensive anxious; fearful

apprentice a person (usually young) who learns a trade or craft under the direction of a skilled worker

apprenticeship the time during which a person is an apprentice

approach to come near, to draw close □ a way leading to a place; a coming near (such as the approach of school holidays)

approachable friendly, easy to talk to

appropriate 1 (say approepree-et) suitable; proper (as when one dresses in appropriate [warm] clothes in cold weather)

appropriate 2 (say approepree-ayt) to take for one's own use; to take possession: to set apart for a purpose (as when a local council appropriates a sum of money for building a swimming pool)

approve to speak or think well of; to pass as satisfactory; to give permisson

approval good opinion; permission

on approval on trial (as when a book is sent to a customer to examine before he decides whether to buy it)

approximate (say approximet) nearly correct □ (say approximayt) to come very near (especially to a correct answer)

approximation (say approximayshun) a result or answer that is not exactly correct, but is near enough for the purpose

apricot a small pale orange-coloured fruit, rather like a small peach

apron a sleeveless garment worn on the front of the body to prevent the clothes from becoming wet or dirty

apt suitable: liable to (for example - He is apt to lose his temper over little things.): clever or quick at learning

aptitude cleverness; talent or fitness

aqu(a)- water (when used with another word)

aqualung a light-weight diving apparatus, with a compressed-air supply carried on the back

aquamarine a bluish-green precious stone

aquaplane a plane towed behind a motor boat, for a person to stand on and ride the waves

aquarium a tank or number of tanks for keeping water plants, fishes, etc.

aquatic growing or living in water (plants, fish, etc.); taking place on or in water (Water polo is an aquatic sport.)

aqueduct a bridge with a channel for taking water across a valley; a pipe or canal for carrying water from place to place

aquiline curved or hooked like an eagle's beak

arable fit for ploughing and growing crops (arable land)

arbitration a way of settling a dispute by appointing someone to act as judge to decide who is right or what is the best solution

arbitrate to act as a judge; to decide

arbour a shady place in a garden with trees and climbing plants (often with a seat or bench)

arc a part of a circle; a curved line

arc-light a lamp lit by an electric arc (made by the electricity jumping a gap between two pieces of carbon)

arcade a row of arches supported by pillars: a covered walk with shops on both sides

arch a structure or part of a

structure that is curved at the top; anything curved like an arch (such as the arch of the foot) □ to curve or raise in an arch
archway an arched passageway

archaeology *(say arkiolojee)* the study of objects and remains from ancient times before man began to record history

archbishop a chief bishop

archer someone who shoots with a bow and arrows
archery shooting with a bow and arrows

archipelago *(say arkipelago)* a group of small islands; a sea full of small islands

architect *(say arkitekt)* someone who designs and plans buildings
architecture the art of designing buildings: a style of building (Modern architecture is simple and uncluttered, without much ornament.)

arctic at or around the North Pole; very cold

ardent fiery; passionate: eager
ardour warmth of feeling; eagerness

arduous difficult; requiring much hard work

area the size or extent of a surface; any region or piece of ground; space round the basement of a building, below ground level

arena a sanded open space in an amphitheatre where gladiators fought in Roman times; (nowadays) any place with seats round an open space where public contests or other spectacles take place

argue to dispute; to discuss; to try to prove that something is right by giving all the reasons in its favour
argument a dispute; a heated discussion: the reasons for or against something

arid dry; having little moisture

arise to get up; to rise or move upwards; to come into being (as when a question arises from something that has been said)

aristocracy the government of a country controlled by the nobility: these people in a country who are considered to be superior in rank or personal distinction
aristocrat a member of the aristocracy

arithmetic the science or skill of adding, subtracting, multiplying and dividing by using figures
arithmetical having to do with arithmetic

ark the vessel described in the Bible, in which Noah and his family and the animals were saved from the Flood: a sacred chest containing Jewish holy books

arm 1 the part of the body between the shoulder and the hand: anything resembling an arm (such as an inlet of the sea, a rail at the side of a chair, etc.): power (as, the arm of the law)
armchair a chair with arms or rests at each side
armpit the hollow place under the top of the arm

arm 2 a weapon (a firearm) □ to supply with arms
armament guns or equipment for war
armour protective body covering of metal or chain mail (in olden days): protective steel or iron covering for army vehicles, battleships, etc.
armoured protected by armour
armoury a place where arms are made or kept
army a large body of men and women armed for war: a large number of people organized together for a special purpose (as, the Salvation Army)
to lay down arms to surrender
up in arms defiant; ready for battle (or argument)

armada a great fleet of ships, armed for war (especially Spanish ships in olden days)

armadillo a small American

animal with a covering of bony
plates like body armour

armament see **arm 2**

armistice a short truce or complete stop to fighting in a war,
agreed by both sides

armour, army see **arm 2**

aroma a fragrant or spicy smell
aromatic fragrant; spicy

around on all sides of □ in a
circle

arouse to awaken; to stir someone into action

arrange to put in order; to set in
a special order: to come to an
agreement with someone; to
make plans or to prepare for
some event, etc.
arrangement a setting in
order: a plan

array an orderly arrangement;
clothing □ to dress or adorn

arrear something unpaid or not
done
in arrears not up to date (as, in
arrears with the rent)

arrest to stop (as, to arrest an
illness by medical treatment); to
seize and hold (as, to arrest a
thief) □ seizure or capture

arrive to reach a destination; to
come to (as, to arrive at a conclusion)
arrival the act of arriving; a
person or thing that arrives

arrogant overbearing; haughty
arrogance arrogant behaviour

arrow a straight, stick-like weapon
with a sharp point which is shot
from a bow; a sign shaped like
an arrow (→) to show direction

arsenal a government factory or
large store for weapons and
ammunition

arsenic a greyish-white chemical
which forms highly poisonous
compounds (such as white arsenic [arsenic trioxide])

arson the crime of setting fire to
a house or other property

art drawing, painting and
sculpture: skill (as, the art of
arranging flowers)

artist a person skilled in one of
the arts
artistic having to do with art;
showing good taste
artistry artistic skill
arts learning in certain non-
scientific university subjects

artery one of the narrow tubes
which carry blood from the
heart to other parts of the body
arterial belonging to an artery;
like an artery (as, an arterial
road)

artful cunning; crafty

artichoke a thistle-like plant
with a scaly flowerhead, part of
which can be eaten

article any separate object (as,
an article of clothing): a separate piece of writing in a newspaper or magazine, dealing with
a particular subject: a separate
clause in a legal document

articulate *(say articulet)* distinct
in speech; able to express one's
thoughts clearly and well
articulated *(say articulayted)*
distinctly jointed (as, an articulated doll with jointed limbs, or
an articulated vehicle with two
or more hinged cars)

artificial made by art; not natural
artifice a device; cunning; skill

artillery big guns; the branch of
the army that uses such guns

artisan a skilled workman

artist see **art**

artiste *(say arteest)* someone
who performs in public (especially a singer or dancer)

as like, similar to; for instance
□ while: because: since

asbestos a general name for
fibrous minerals which can be
made into fireproof boards and
cloth

ascend to go up or move upward;
to climb
ascent the act of ascending; a
slope upwards

ascertain *(say assertain)* to find
out; to make certain

ash 1 the substance that remains
after anything is burned

ashen pale; ash-coloured

ash 2 a hardwood tree with greyish bark

ashamed feeling shame

ashore on shore

aside on or to one side; apart □words spoken (especially by an actor) which other nearby persons are supposed not to hear

ask to put a question in order to get information; to inquire: to invite

askance sideways; with a side glance

askew to one side; obliquely

asleep sleeping, not awake

asp a small poisonous snake

asparagus a plant whose young shoots are eaten as a vegetable

aspect look; view; direction in which something faces

asphalt a tarry mixture used to make a smooth hard surface on roads and paths

aspidistra a pot plant with large tapering leaves

aspire to aim at high things (such as a prize or a good job) **aspiration** ambition; eager desire

aspirin a common trade name for a pain-killing medicine

ass a donkey: a stupid person

assail to attack suddenly **assailant** someone who attacks

assassin someone who kills by treachery **assassinate** to murder by sudden and secret attack **assassination** a violent murder (especially of a ruler or important politician)

assault a sudden attack □to make an assault

assemble to meet together; to collect or put together **assembly** a meeting of persons for a particular purpose

assent to agree □agreement or saying *yes*

assert to say firmly **assert oneself** to insist on one's right to speak and be heard **assertion** a strong statement

assess to fix an amount to be paid; to estimate the value of something (for tax purposes, etc.) **assessment** the amount or value that has been fixed or estimated

assets the money and goods which are available to a person to pay any debts

assiduous hard-working; persevering

assign to give to someone as his share or as his task: to decide upon (as, to assign a date for a meeting) **assignment** a task or duty to be carried out

assimilate to digest (food); to take in (information)

assist to help: to be present at **assistance** help or aid **assistant** a helper; someone who serves in a shop □helping (as, assistant master)

assizes courts of law held at intervals in English counties

associate to join with one or more persons as a friend or partner; to keep company with □a friend, partner or companion □connected or allied **association** a society or union of people organized for a common purpose

assort to separate into different kinds **assortment** a variety

assume to suppose to be true: to take for granted; to take upon oneself (as, to assume responsibility) **assumption** the act of assuming; something assumed

assure to make sure; to tell someone positively **assurance** a feeling of sureness; a positive statement **assured** certain; confident

aster a plant with star-like flowers

asterisk a star-shaped mark (*)

used in printing to draw attention to a special note in the margin or at the foot of the page

astern (of a ship) behind or in the rear; backwards (as, full speed astern)

asthma (say _asma_) an illness which affects the tubes of the lungs and makes breathing difficult
asthmatic (say _asmatic_) suffering from asthma; breathing with gasps

astonish to surprise greatly; to amaze
astonishment amazement

astound to shock with surprise; to amaze

astral connected with the stars

astray straying; away from the right path or way

astride with the legs on each side of (as, astride a pony)

astrology the study of the influence which the stars are supposed to have on the lives of people
astrologer a fortune teller who studies astrology

astronaut a traveller in space

astronomy the scientific study of the stars and other heavenly bodies
astronomer a scientist who studies astronomy
astronomical concerned with astronomy: enormous (of numbers or distances, because distances between stars are enormous)

astute shrewd; cunning

asunder apart; into parts

asylum a place of refuge or safety: an institution for the mentally ill (now known as a mental hospital)

at a word indicating where (as, at the seaside) or when (as, at ten o'clock), or some similar relation (as, good at games)

atheist someone who believes that there is no God
atheism the belief that there is no God

athlete a competitor in physical sports that involve speed, strength and agility
athletics sports (such as running, jumping, etc.)

atlas a book of maps

atmosphere the mixture of gases (called the air) that surrounds the earth: any surrounding feeling or influence (as, a friendly atmosphere)
atmospheric concerned with the atmosphere
atmospherics crackling noises that interfere with radio communication, due to electric disturbances in the atmosphere

atoll a ring-shaped coral island enclosing a lagoon

atom one of the tiny particles, too small to be visible, of which all matter is made up; anything very small
atomic relating to an atom or atoms
atom(ic) bomb a bomb in which the explosion is caused by splitting the atoms of certain elements (such as uranium)
atomic energy nuclear energy (see **nucleus**)
atomic power power for making electricity, etc., derived from nuclear energy

atomizer a device for reducing liquids to a very fine spray (It works with high pressure like an aerosol.)

atone to make up for wrongdoing

atrocious extremely cruel or wicked; very bad
atrocity an extremely cruel deed

attach to fasten or tie to; to join together
attached joined to; fond of
attachment something attached; a fondness for

attack to fall upon suddenly; to start a fight; to speak or write very critically □ the act of attacking; the onset of an illness (as, an attack of influenza)

attain to reach or gain after

making an effort

attainment the act of attaining; the thing attained

attainments personal accomplishments

attempt to try; to make an effort □ an effort, an endeavour

attend to be present; to wait on or accompany: to pay attention

attendance the act of attending; all the persons present

attendant a helper or servant in a public place □ accompanying

attention notice, heed (as, to attract or pay attention); care: an erect, military position with hands at sides and heels together

attentive listening or observing (as, an attentive attitude); courteous (as, an attentive hostess)

attic a room just under the roof of a house

attire clothing □ to dress

attitude a posture of the body; a way of behaving; a state of thought or feeling

attorney *(say aturnee)* a person who has legal power to act for another

attract to draw to or towards; to arouse pleasurable feelings in a person

attractive able to attract; pleasing; charming

attraction the art of attracting; something which attracts people

attribute *(say atribute)* to consider as belonging to or as caused by (as - He attributed his success to careful training.) □ *(say atribute)* a quality which is natural to a person or to an object

auburn reddish brown (especially of hair)

auction a public sale where articles are sold to the person who bids (offers) the highest price □ to sell goods by auction

audacious *(say audayshus)* bold; daring; impudent

audacity *(say audassity)* boldness; impudence

audible able to be heard

audience an assembly of people who listen or watch (especially at a theatre or other place of entertainment): a ceremonial interview (as - The ambassador had an audience with the queen.)

audio-visual having to do with sound and vision (as, audio-visual aids, which are films, recordings, etc. used in teaching)

audition a hearing (especially to try out a performer, such as an actor, singer, musician, etc.)

auditorium the part of a theatre or other building which is occupied by the audience

augment to increase in size or in number

aunt a father's or a mother's sister; an uncle's wife

aurora the dawn

aurora borealis the northern lights (see **north**)

auspicious favourable; promising success

austere stern; strict; severely simple

austerity severe simplicity of habits or living

authentic genuine; true without any doubt

author the writer of a book, play, article, etc.; the creator of anything

authority the power or right which a person may have and exercise because of his position and responsibilities (as, the authority of a headmaster in a school or of a judge in a court of law); an expert: formal permission

authorize to give a person authority or permission

authoritative very reliable; coming from someone who has authority or special knowledge

autobiography the story of a person's life written by himself or herself

autocrat a ruler or other person who has absolute power

autocratic expecting to be obeyed without question

autograph a person's own signature or handwriting □ to write one's name

automatic self-moving; working of itself: mechanical; without thinking (as when a person acts automatically)
automation the automatic control of machines in a factory by means of other machines (especially computers and similar electronic devices)
automaton a machine that appears to move of itself and may act rather like a human being; a person who seems to act like a machine and without human intelligence

automobile a motor car

autonomy the right of self-government
autonomous having self-government

autumn the third season of the year, following summer
autumnal related to autumn (as, autumnal colours)

auxiliary helping; additional □ a helper

avail to be of use, help or value
available within reach; able to be used

avalanche a mass of snow and ice sliding quickly down from a mountain

avarice the eager desire for riches
avaricious extremely greedy for wealth

avenge to take revenge for some injustice, insult, etc.
avenger someone who avenges

avenue a wide street (usually bordered by trees); a tree-lined approach to a large country house

average the arithmetical mean value of any quantities or amounts, that is, the result obtained by dividing their total by the number of items (for example, the average of 15, 20, 40 and 45 is [15 + 20 + 40 + 45] ÷ 4 = 30.) □ of medium size, ordinary value; standard □ to find the average

aversion dislike

avert to turn from or aside (as when someone averts his eyes): to prevent (as, to avert an accident)

aviary a place for keeping birds

aviation the art and science of flying in aircraft
aviator an airman

avid greedy; eager

avoid to keep clear of; to shun; to escape
avoidable able to be avoided

avoirdupois (say averdepoiz) the method of weighing pounds and ounces (lbs. and oz.) as distinct from the metric system (kilos and grammes)

await to wait for; to expect

awake not asleep; watchful □ to rouse from sleep
awaken to awake; to rouse into interest or attention

award to give or grant something to a person because he has won a contest or is especially deserving in some other way □ a prize or honour; a judgment

aware knowing of; informed or conscious of

away not near; at a distance from a place or person; absent
straight away at once
to do away with to abolish

awe wonder mixed with fear or reverence
awful inspiring awe; terrible; very bad (in conversation, very great, as, an awful bore)
awfully in an awe-inspiring manner (in conversation, very, as, the programme was awfully good)

awhile for a short time

awkward clumsy; embarrassing; difficult to deal with

awning a covering (usually of canvas) to give shelter from the sun's rays

axe a tool with a long handle and a blade which is used for chopping wood, etc.

axiom an accepted principle or rule; a statement that needs no proof

axis a real or imaginary line through the middle of an object around which it rotates (as - The earth rotates on the axis joining the North and South Poles.)

axes *(say ackseez)* the plural of axis

axle the rod or pin on which a wheel turns

aye yes; indeed □a vote in favour of something

azalea a flowering shrubby plant like a small rhododendron

azure sky-blue in colour; cloudless

b

babble to talk or utter sounds in an indistinct way; to reveal secrets: to make a murmuring sound (as water does over stones in a brook)

babel a noisy confusion of sounds or languages

baboon a large monkey with a long face and short tail

baby a very young child or infant
babyish like a baby

bachelor an unmarried man

bacillus *(say basillus)* one of a kind of bacteria, shaped like a rod
bacilli the plural of bacillus

back situated behind; the opposite of front □the back part of the body or of anything (such as the back of a house or book); a position in a football team □towards the rear or an earlier position (as when a person goes back) □to move back: to help or support
backer a person who helps someone (especially by providing money for an undertaking)
backing help or support
background the back part of a scene or picture, as opposed to the foreground
backhand done with the hand turned backwards (as, a backhand tennis stroke) or sloping in a backward direction (as, backhand writing)
backward(s) towards the back;

the opposite of forward
backwash a retreating wave; a backward current
backwater a quiet part of a river which is out of the main stream
backwoods a part of a country which has not been cleared of forests or cultivated in any way

bacon pork which has been salted and dried

bacteria microscopic organisms, some of them harmful, which are present everywhere, including the human body

bad the opposite of good; wicked; hurtful; unwell

badge a special mark or emblem which is worn to distinguish the wearer in some way (for example, to indicate his rank or his membership of a school or club)

badger a grey-coated, burrowing, hibernating animal which gets its food by night

badminton a game rather like tennis played with a shuttlecock instead of a ball

baffle to hinder in a perplexing way
baffling very puzzling or difficult

bag a sack or pouch: the quantity of fish or game caught by a fisherman or huntsman □to put into a bag; to seize or secure; to claim first

baggage another word for luggage

bagpipe a wind instrument which consists of a bag and several pipes

bail 1 the money put down in a court of law to obtain the temporary release of a prisoner who has not yet come to trial □ to get such a prisoner released or bailed out

bail 2 in cricket, one of the cross-pieces on top of a wicket

bail 3 to take water out of a boat with a bucket or other container

bailiff one who acts as manager for the owner of a farm or estate: a sheriff's officer

bait food put on a hook to make fish bite, or in a trap to attract animals □ to set bait: to annoy or worry

bake to cook (usually in an oven), without using fire in direct contact
baker a person who bakes bread and cakes for a living

balalaika a Russian musical instrument rather like a guitar with a triangular body

balance to hold or keep something steady without letting it tip over; to keep oneself from falling □ a small weighing machine (usually) consisting of two dishes suspended from either end of a horizontal beam which is itself supported exactly in the middle: steadiness

balcony a platform jutting out from the wall of a building (usually with railings or a low parapet around it): an upper floor in a theatre or cinema

bald lacking hair on the head

bale a large bundle of goods (such as cotton or hay, usually tightly bound)

ball 1 anything round or nearly so; the round object used in many games
ballbearings in machinery, a device to reduce friction by making a revolving part turn on small metal balls lying loosely in a groove
ballpoint a pen containing a special kind of ink and with a tiny ball instead of a nib

ball 2 a formal dance
ballroom a large room where dances are held

ballad a simple song (usually with sentimental words); a simple poem made up of short verses telling a story

ballast some heavy substance (such as sand or gravel) placed in a ship to keep it steady when a normal cargo is not being carried

ballerina a female ballet dancer

ballet *(say balay)* a dancing performance to music on the stage of a theatre (A ballet often tells a story in mime, but there is no singing as in an opera.)

ballistics the science of projectiles
ballistic missile a missile which is guided over part of its course but falls like an ordinary projectile

balloon a round bag made of thin rubber or silk and filled with air or a light gas (such as hydrogen or helium) which enables it to float high in the air
balloonist a person who goes up in the air in a balloon

ballot a way of voting (as in an election) by marking a paper and putting it in a special ballot box □ to vote by ballot

balm a sweet-smelling soothing ointment; anything that soothes pain
balmy fragrant; mild

balsa a tropical American tree with very light wood used in model-making

balsam an aromatic, resin-like substance obtained from certain trees

bamboo a kind of giant grass with woody hollow stems used for canes and for making articles of furniture

bamboozle to trick; to mystify

ban an order forbidding something □ to make such an order, to prohibit

banana the long yellow-skinned fruit of a tropical tree

band 1 a strip of cloth or other material which may be used to hold things together or to bind round anything (as, a hat-band)
bandage a strip of cloth or lint used to bind up a wound or sore

band 2 a group of persons gathered together for any purpose; a group of musicians playing together

bandana, bandanna a brightly-coloured silk or cotton kerchief

bandit an outlaw who robs people (usually in lonely country)

bandy to give and take (for example, people bandy words or blows with one another)

bandy-legged having bow legs bent outward at the knees

bang a sudden loud noise; a severe blow □ to beat or to slam something hard

bangle a large ring worn on the arm or leg

banish to drive away; to exile
banishment exile

banisters the posts and handrail of a staircase

banjo a musical instrument like a guitar but with a longer neck and a circular body

bank 1 a ridge or mound of earth; the edge of a river

bank 2 a place where money is deposited for safety
banknotes paper money issued by a bank
bankrupt a person who fails in business through lack of money

banner a flag which can be carried between two poles

banns a public notice that a marriage will soon take place

banquet a feast; a large ceremonial dinner

banter to tease in fun □ teasing in fun; joking

baptize to give a name to; to christen
baptism the act of baptizing (usually with water) as a religious ceremony

bar a long piece of anything solid; a hindrance; a counter at which drinks are served; the wooden rail at which prisoners stand for trial; the lawyers (barristers) in a law-court □ to shut out or hinder

barb a backward-pointing spike (as, of an arrow or fish-hook)
barbed having barbs
barbed wire wire with sharp points used for fencing

barbarous brutal; not civilized
barbarian a brutal or uncivilized person
barbaric the same as barbarous
barbarism a lawless, uncivilized way of living

barbecue a framework for smoking or roasting meat over a fire; an open-air party at which meat is cooked in this way

barber a men's hairdresser; a person who shaves and trims beards and hair

barbican a projecting watch-tower or watch-towers (especially for the defence of a bridge or gate)

bard a minstrel in olden times; a poet

bare uncovered; naked; empty
barely not quite; scarcely
barefaced undisguised; impudent

bargain something bought cheaply; an agreement about the terms of a sale □ to argue about such terms (especially the price to be paid)

barge a flat-bottomed boat used on rivers and canals
bargee a person who owns or works on a barge

baritone a male singer with a deep-toned voice between tenor (high) and bass (low)

bark 1 outer covering of the trunk and branches of a tree

bark 2 the loud sharp noise made by dogs, wolves and foxes □ to utter a bark

barley a kind of grain which is used for food and for making beer and whisky

barn a farm building used mainly for storing grain and hay

barnacle a small shellfish which clings to rocks and the bottoms of ships

barometer an instrument which measures the pressure of the air and indicates changes of weather

baron a nobleman's title
baroness a baron's wife
baronet the lowest British title that can be passed on to an heir
baronial concerning a baron

barque a three-masted sailing vessel; a small ship

barrack(s) a building or buildings where soldiers live

barrage an artificial bar across a river to make the water deeper: heavy gunfire (usually continuous) which acts like a barrier

barrel a wooden container with curved sides held together with hoops: the metal tube of a gun

barren unable to produce fruit or vegetation; unable to have children

barricade a barrier put up quickly to block a street etc. □ to block by means of a barricade

barrier any obstacle (like a fence or a wall) which stands in one's way

barrister a lawyer who is qualified to plead in a law-court: see also **bar**

barrow 1 a small wheeled cart that is pushed by hand

barrow 2 an ancient grave-mound

barter to exchange goods without any money payment

basalt a dark-coloured rock of volcanic origin

base 1 the lowest part of anything; the foundation
baseless without foundation; without reason
basement the lowest storey of a building (especially one below ground level)

base 2 low in moral value; worthless; mean

baseball an American ball game, something like rounders

bash to beat or smash in □ a heavy blow

bashful shy; lacking confidence

basin a wide, open dish: any large hollow place containing water

basis the same as base or foundation, but used in a figurative way (as, the basis of their friendship)
bases the plural of basis (as, the bases of their agreement)
basic fundamental; essential (as, basic argument)

bask to lie in warmth or in the sun

basket a container woven out of thin strips of wood, cane or other material

basketball a team game in which a large leather ball is thrown into a raised net

bass 1 (say bayss) the lowest part sung or played in music; a bass singer □ low or deep-sounding

bass 2 a fish of the perch family

bassoon a wind instrument which produces low notes

baste 1 (say bayst) to apply fat to roasting meat to keep it from burning

baste 2 (say bayst) to sew loosely with big stitches

bastion a kind of tower which sticks out at the corner of a fortification

bat 1 a shaped piece of wood used for striking the ball in cricket or baseball □ to use a bat

batsman the player who wields the bat at cricket

bat 2 a night-flying mammal with a body like a mouse and wings which are an extension of its fingers

batch a number or quantity of the same kind of things (especially of bread from one baking)

bath a large vessel in which the body can be washed; the water in a bath □ to wash someone else in a bath
bathroom a room where a person can have a bath
baths a building where baths are provided for the general public

bathe to take a bath or a swim □ a swim or dip in the sea, lake or river

bathysphere an airtight metal chamber which is lowered into the sea, from which people can study marine life

batman an army officer's servant

baton a light stick used by the conductor of a band or orchestra

battalion a large number of soldiers; part of a regiment

batter to beat something repeatedly □ a thin paste made by beating together cooking ingredients (such as flour and milk)

battery 1 a number of electric cells joined together to store electricity

battery 2 an artillery unit including guns, men and their supporting vehicles

battle a fight (especially between two armies)
battle-axe a weapon formerly used in battle
battlefield the place where a battle is fought
battleship a heavily armed and armoured warship

battlement a wall on a building with openings for guns

bauble a trifling ornament; a child's plaything

bauxite a clay-like aluminium ore (originally found at Les Baux in southern France)

bawl to shout or cry out loudly

bay 1 a wide inlet of a sea or lake

bay 2 space between two columns or walls; a recess
bay-window a window which juts out, forming a recess

bay 3 the laurel tree

bay 4 a reddish-brown colour

bay 5 the barking or baying of hunting dogs
to hold at bay to keep an enemy just out of reach

bayonet a steel dagger which can be fixed to the muzzle of a rifle

bazaar a fair where various articles are sold, usually for charity; in Eastern countries, a market place or shopping street

bazooka a rocket-gun used mainly against tanks

be to live or exist; to have a certain quality or state

beach the shore of a sea or lake

beacon a signalling light, like a fire on a hill (in former times); a lighthouse

bead a small ball of coloured glass, wood or other material with a hole through it

beadle an officer in a church or college

beagle a small stocky hound

beak the hard pointed outside of a bird's mouth

beaker a large cup (often without a handle); a glass vessel used by chemists

beam 1 a long straight piece of timber or metal used in building, ships' frames, etc.

beam 2 a ray of light

bean the name given to several plants whose seeds grow in pods, such as the broadbean; the bean-like seeds of some other plants (such as coffee)

bear 1 a large heavy wild animal with thick shaggy fur

bear 2 to carry something; to endure or put up with something

bearable not too hard to bear; endurable

beard the hair that grows on the chin and cheeks of a man

bearing 1 the part of a machine which bears the friction of another part that is moving

bearing 2 behaviour; manner

beast an animal: a brutal person
beastly behaving like a beast

beat 1 to strike again and again
beaten made smooth by beating or treading

beat 2 to defeat; to do better than an opponent or an opposing team in a game
beaten defeated

beat 3 to mark time in music

beautiful lovely; very pleasing to the eye, or ear, etc.
beauty a quality that gives pleasure to the sight, hearing, etc. (as, beauty of appearance, musical sounds, etc.)
beautify to make beautiful

becalmed unable to move through lack of wind (especially of a sailing ship)

because for the reason that; on account of

beckon to summon a person, or call his attention, by nodding or making a sign

become to come to be; to grow or change into
becoming suitable to, or looking well on, a person

bed 1 something to sleep on (usually with a mattress, bedclothes and a pillow)
bedclothes the sheets and blankets for a bed
bedding a mattress and bedclothes
bedroom a room with a bed
bedside the space beside a bed
bedspread the cover kept on a bed during the day
bedridden confined to bed by sickness or old age

bed 2 a small piece of garden (such as a flower bed)

bed 3 the bottom of a river or sea

bedlam a very noisy place: a madhouse

bedraggled dirtied as if by dragging in the wet or dirt

bedrock the solid rock which lies underneath the soil and small rocks

bee a four-winged insect that makes honey and wax
beehive a special kind of box in which bees live
bee-line the shortest distance from one place to another
beeswax the wax made by bees to form the cells of a honeycomb

beech a large tree with smooth silvery bark

beef the meat from a cow or bull
beefsteak a thick slice of beef for grilling or frying
beefy like beef; muscular

beefeaters a name given to guards of the Tower of London

beer an alcoholic drink made from barley flavoured with hops

beetle an insect with four wings (The front pair form hard covers for the back wings when folded.)

beetroot a dark red, root vegetable

befall to happen

before in front of: earlier or sooner
beforehand before the time; in advance

befriend to act as a friend to

beg to ask earnestly or humbly for something
beggar someone who lives by begging for food and small sums of money

begin to start or commence
beginning the start or first part of something

begonia a garden and greenhouse plant with bright showy flowers and leaves

begrudge to feel discontent or envy

beguile to deceive someone: to take the attention of someone away from anything dull or from the slow passage of time

behalf in the interest of; for the sake of (as when someone acts or speaks on behalf of another person or group of people)

behave to act well, or to act in some other manner
behaviour a person's conduct or manners; the way in which he behaves

behead to cut off the head of

behind at the back of □ in the rear

behold to see; to look at

beholden indebted to; under an obligation to

beige *(say bayzh)* a very light pinkish-brown colour

belated happening, or arriving, late

belch to let out wind noisily from the throat

beleaguer to besiege a town

belfry the part of a tower or steeple in which the bells are hung

believe to accept something as true; to have faith; to think or suppose
belief what is accepted as true; faith

belittle to make something look small or unimportant; to speak of something in a depreciating way

bell a hollow metal vessel which rings when struck; a device that makes a ringing sound

bellicose warlike; quarrelsome

belligerent warlike; carrying on war

bellow to roar like a bull; to shout loudly

bellows an instrument for blowing air on to a fire or through the pipes of an organ or accordion

belly the part of the body below the chest, which contains the stomach and the bowels

belong to be the property of; to go along with
belongings things which belong

to a person; his possessions

beloved much loved □ a person very dear to someone

below beneath; at a lower level

belt a band of leather or other material which is worn round the waist; an endless strap connecting one moving wheel to another; anything resembling a belt

bench a long seat; a work-table

bend to curve or make crooked □ a curve

beneath under something

benediction blessing or the saying of a blessing

benefactor a person who helps another in a friendly way; someone who gives to a charitable cause

beneficial useful; bringing good results
beneficiary someone who receives a gift (especially a legacy)

benefit an advantage or favour received □ to gain advantage from; to do good to

benevolent generous; kindly
benevolence a desire to do good; a feeling of generosity

benign gentle; gracious

benzene a clear liquid which evaporates quickly and easily catches fire (It is usually made from coal tar and is used in making chemicals and dyes.)

bequeath to leave something (money, property, etc.) to someone by a will
bequest a legacy

bereaved deprived by death of a dear relative or friend
bereavement a loss by death

beret *(say berray)* a flat round cap without a peak

berry any small round juicy fruit (such as a strawberry or raspberry)

berth a bunk or sleeping-place in a ship or train: a ship's place in a port

beseech to ask earnestly

beset to attack from all sides

beside by the side of; next to

besides in addition to; over and above

besiege to surround a town or fortress with armed forces so that no one can get in or out of it

best good in the highest degree; more than better □ someone's greatest effort

bestial like a beast; depraved

bestow to give or confer (upon a person)

bet to risk money on the result of a game or race
betting gambling with money (especially on horse or dog racing)

betray to deceïve: to give away secret information to an enemy or, by treachery, to allow friends or fellow-countrymen to fall into an enemy's hands
betrayal the act of betraying

better good in a higher degree; preferable

between in a space connecting or separating two people, places or times

bevel a slanting edge (Some mirrors have a bevelled edge.)

beverage any kind of drink

beware to be on one's guard against danger

bewilder to puzzle or confuse
bewilderment perplexity or confusion

bewitch to put under a spell; to fascinate
bewitching fascinating; charming

beyond farther than; out of reach of

biannual half-yearly; happening every six months

bias a leaning to one side; prejudice; a cut or stitching in a slanting direction across cloth

bib a piece of cloth tied round a baby's neck to protect the clothes from spilled food

Bible the holy book of the Christian Church, consisting of the Old and New Testaments
biblical concerning the Bible

bibliography a list of books concerning a particular subject or author

bibulous over-fond of alcoholic drink

bicentenary the 200th anniversary of an event

biceps the muscle on the front of the upper arm

bicker to quarrel about trivial matters

bicycle a two-wheeled vehicle driven by pedals or by a motor (motor-bicycle)

bid to make an offer (at a sale); to command a person to do something

biennial lasting two years; happening once in two years

bier a carriage or wooden stand for carrying a coffin to the grave

big large; important

bigamy the crime of having two wives or two husbands at the same time
bigamist a person who commits bigamy

bigot someone who believes something so stubbornly that he will not let anything change his mind

bike a short word for bicycle

bilberry a shrub with a dark blue berry

bile a bitter fluid produced in the liver to help digestion
bilious affected by, or sick because of, the state of the bile

bilge the broadest part of a ship's bottom; the filth that collects there
bilge-water filthy water which lies in a ship's bilge

bilingual speaking two languages equally well; written in two languages

bill 1 an account for money owing

bill 2 a bird's beak

bill 3 a proposed law or draft of an Act of Parliament

billet a lodging (especially for soldiers)

billiards a game played with a cue and ivory balls on a cloth-covered table which has pockets at the sides and corners

billion a million millions (1000,000,000,000 or 10^{12}) in Britain; a thousand millions (1000,000,000 or 10^9) in the U.S.A. and France

billow a great wave swelled by the wind

billy-goat a male goat

bin a container for corn, bread, coal, rubbish, etc.

bind to fasten or tie together
binding the act of binding; the covering in which the leaves of a book are bound

bingo a game of chance using numbers

binnacle the box which holds a ship's compass

binoculars a form of double telescope with eye-pieces for both eyes (also called field-glasses)

biography a written account of a person's life
biographer the author of a biography

biology the science that deals with living things, plants as well as animals
biologist someone who studies biology or is an expert in that science

biped an animal with two feet

birch a tree with a smooth white or silvery bark; a bundle of birch twigs used as a whip

bird any feathered animal
birdcage a small cage for a pet bird

birth the act of being born; coming into the world
birthday the day of the year on which a person was born
birthright a right (as, the right to inherit) which may be

claimed because of one's birth

biscuit a kind of small flat cake which has been cooked until it is crisp

bisect to divide into two equal parts

bishop a high-ranking clergyman

bison a wild ox

bit 1 a small piece

bit 2 the part of a bridle that goes in a horse's mouth

bitch a female dog

bite to cut into, or seize, something with the teeth □ a small mouthful

bitter sharp (especially to the taste): the opposite of sweet; unpleasant

bivouac (say bivwack) a temporary resting place at night in the open air (especially of soldiers without tents)

bizarre strange; fantastic

blab to talk thoughtlessly; to let out a secret

black of the darkest colour (opposite to white): gloomy; sullen
blackberry a small, juicy black fruit that grows wild on brambles
blackbird a very dark songbird with a yellow beak
blackboard a board painted black for writing on with chalk
blackcurrant a very small black berry, harder than the blackberry, which grows on a garden shrub
blackguard (say blaggard) a scoundrel; a wicked person
blackleg a man who continues to work during a strike
blackmail to force someone to pay money by threatening to reveal some secret information about him
blacksmith a man who makes and mends articles of iron

bladder a thin bag of skin or rubber, etc. which is easily stretched by the liquid or air inside; a bag-like inner part of the body that holds urine

blade a single long thin leaf, especially of grass or corn: the cutting part of a sword or knife: the flat part of an oar

blame to find fault with, to criticize
blameless innocent

blancmange *(say blamonzh)* a milk jelly

bland smooth; mild; polite

blank without any writing or marks; empty □ an empty space

blanket a warm bed-covering, usually made of wool; a covering of any kind (for example, of fog or snow)

blare to sound loudly □ a loud sound (especially of trumpets)

blarney flattery; coaxing talk

blaspheme *(say blasfeem)* to speak of God wickedly or without respect; to curse and swear
blasphemer a person who blasphemes
blasphemy *(say blasfemy)* blasphemous speech

blast a strong gust of air; an explosion □ to blow up (especially with explosives)
blast furnace a special kind of furnace for smelting, into which hot air is blown

blatant vulgarly showy; glaring; noisy

blaze 1 a burst of light or flame; a bright fire □ to burn brightly

blaze 2 a white spot on the face of a horse or cow; a mark made on a tree by removing a piece of bark
blaze a trail to mark a forest path by blazing trees

blazer a sports jacket (often of bright colour)

blazon to make known; to proclaim

bleach to whiten something artificially or by exposure to strong sunlight □ a chemical used for whitening or for removing stains

bleak cold and unsheltered; dull and cheerless

bleary sore and red (of the eyes)

bleat the crying sound made by sheep and goats □ to make such a sound

bleed to lose blood
bleeding a flow or loss of blood

blemish a stain; a fault

blench to shrink back in fear

blend to mix together □ a mixture

bless to make holy; to ask God's favour on: to wish happiness to

blight a disease in plants: anything that spoils

blind 1 without sight; unable to understand or look ahead
blindness lack of sight
blindfold having the eyes bandaged, so as not to see
blind alley a passage closed at one end

blind 2 a screen or shade for windows

blink to move the eyelids quickly
blinkers two pieces of leather fixed to a bridle to prevent a horse from seeing sideways

bliss very great happiness

blister a thin bubble on the skin filled with a watery liquid

blithe gay; light-hearted

blizzard a blinding storm of wind and snow

bloated swollen or puffed up

bloater a lightly smoked herring

blob a drop of liquid

block 1 a mass of wood or stone, etc. (usually flat-sided)
blockhead a stupid fellow

block 2 to bar the way, to obstruct
blockade the blocking of every approach to a place, by land or sea, in order to prevent the passage of supplies

blond a boy or man with fair skin and light-coloured hair

blonde a girl or woman with fair skin and light-coloured hair

blood the red liquid which circulates through arteries and veins inside the body
blood donor someone who gives

blood for use in a hospital

bloodhound a large dog with a keen sense of smell, used for tracking

bloodshed the shedding of blood; slaughter

bloodshot spotted with blood; (of eyes) red and inflamed

bloodthirsty eager to shed blood

blood vessel any vein or artery through which the blood flows

bloody stained with blood

bloom to come into flower □ a flower: a rosy or fresh colour

blossom a flower (especially on a fruit tree)

blot a spot or stain (usually of ink)

blotting paper absorbent paper for drying ink used in writing

blotch an irregular discoloured mark (especially on the skin)

blouse a loose outer garment (often tucked in at the waist), which is mainly worn by girls and women

blow 1 to drive air out of the mouth; to be in motion (of wind and air)

blow 2 a hard knock: a sudden piece of bad luck

blubber 1 the fat of whales and other sea animals

blubber 2 to weep noisily

bludgeon a short, heavy-ended stick used as a weapon

blue the colour of a cloudless sky

bluebell a wildflower with blue blossoms shaped like little bells

bluebottle a large fly with a shiny blue abdomen

blueprint a detailed plan of machinery or of work to be carried out

bluetit a prettily coloured small wild bird

bluff 1 to deceive by pretence

bluff 2 outspoken in manner; rough and hearty

blunder a bad mistake □ to make a bad mistake

blunderbuss an old type of short hand-gun with a wide barrel

blunt the opposite of sharp; having a dull edge or point: very plain-spoken

blur to dim or smear □ a smear or smudge

blurt to say something suddenly without thinking

blush to go pink in the face through feeling shy, ashamed or confused □ a reddish glow on the face caused by this feeling

bluster to blow or to speak boisterously □ noisy, threatening talk

boa 1 a kind of large snake that kills by crushing its prey

boa constrictor a species of South American boa

boa 2 a long winding scarf of fur or feathers

boar a male pig

board 1 a broad flat piece of wood: a table to put food on: meals (as, board and lodging)

boarder a lodger who takes his meals in the house where he is staying

boarding school a school where the pupils can live during term time

board 2 to enter a ship, train, aeroplane, bus, etc.

on board on a ship, or in an aeroplane, etc.

board 3 a group of people appointed to look after a business (as, a Board of Directors) or an institute (as, a Board of Governors)

boast to brag or speak too proudly about oneself or one's possessions

boastful fond of boasting

boat a small ship (usually moved by oars)

boatswain (say bos'n or bosun) a ship's officer who looks after boats, rigging, etc.

bob to move up and down

bobbin a spool for holding thread or yarn

bobsled, bobsleigh a short sled; two short sleds coupled together

bode to foretell or be a sign of

bodice the close-fitting part of a woman's dress down to the waist

body the whole, or main part of, a person or animal; the main part of anything; a group of people acting as a whole
bodily having to do with the human body (not the mind)
bodyguard a guard to protect an important person

bog wet, spongy ground; a marsh

bogey, bogy a goblin: something to be feared

boggle to start with fright or hesitate about something

bogie an undercarriage which works on a pivot so as to go round curves (as, on a railway coach)

bogus sham; not genuine

boil 1 to heat a liquid until it bubbles and turns into vapour (as when water turns into steam); to bubble up because of heat; to cook by boiling (as when boiling an egg)
boiler a large metal container for making steam or for heating water

boil 2 an inflamed swelling

boisterous rough; noisy; stormy

bold brave; daring

bole the trunk of a tree

bollard a short post for fastening a ship's mooring rope; a short post on a street island to divert traffic

bolster a long round pillow □ to prop up or support

bolt 1 a metal rod or bar for fastening a door or gate □ to fasten with a bolt

bolt 2 to run away quickly: to swallow hurriedly

bomb a case containing explosive or some other dangerous material
bombard to attack with large guns
bombardier a corporal in the artillery
bombardment an attack with artillery or with naval guns
bomber an aeroplane used for bombing
bombshell a startling piece of news

bond something that binds or joins together
bondage slavery

bone the hardest material in the body of any vertebrate, whose various parts form the animal's skeleton
bony full of bones or with little flesh

bonfire a large fire in the open air

bonnet a hat tied by strings under the chin (now mostly worn by children): the hinged cover over a motor car engine

bonny pretty; healthy-looking

bonus an extra payment which is additional to the normal one

booby a silly person
booby prize a prize given for the lowest score in a contest
booby trap something placed above a door so as to fall on the first person who enters: a bomb or mine which has been disguised to look harmless

book 1 printed sheets of paper bound together in a cover
bookcase a set of shelves for books
bookkeeper a person in an office who keeps accounts
bookmaker a professional betting man (who keeps a record of his dealings in a special book)
bookworm someone whose main interest is reading

book 2 to reserve or order beforehand
booking office a ticket office

boom 1 a deep hollow sound

boom 2 to show a big increase in trade

boom 3 a wooden pole attached to the mast of a sailing boat to stretch the base of a sail

boomerang a curved wooden missile that turns in the air and comes back to the thrower

boon a request; a favour; something to be thankful for

boor a peasant; a coarse or awkward fellow
boorish behaving like a boor

boot a foot covering (usually of leather) that extends above the ankle
bootee a soft woollen foot covering for babies

booth a covered stall in a market; a tent at a fair

booty plunder or gains (usually taken in war)

border the edge or margin of anything: the boundary of a country; a long garden bed □ to be a border to; to adjoin

bore 1 to make a deep hole with a drill or similar tool

bore 2 to weary; to seem dull and uninteresting □ a boring person or thing
boredom the state of being bored

born come into life by birth; brought forth

borough a town which has a mayor and certain privileges granted by royal charter

borrow to take on loan

borzoi a long-haired dog like a large greyhound

bosom the breast □ very close (as, a bosom friend)

boss the master or manager

botany the study of plants

botch to do something badly; to mend clumsily

bother to annoy or be a nuisance to □ a fuss or nuisance

bottle a container with a narrow opening (usually made of glass) for holding liquids □ to put into bottles

bottom the lowest part of anything
bottomless without bottom; extremely deep

boudoir (say boodwahr) a lady's private sitting room

bough (rhymes with cow) a large branch of a tree

boulder (say bolder) a very large rock or stone (especially one rounded by the action of water)

boulevard a broad street bordered with trees

bounce to rebound; to spring suddenly

bound 1 to spring or leap □ a spring forward or upward

bound 2 tied; fastened: sure to (as - He is bound to win.)

bound 3 on the way to (as - He is bound for London.)

boundary a line marking off one area from another

boundless without limits; vast

bounty a gift; generosity in giving

bouquet (say bookay) a bunch of flowers: the perfume of a wine

bout a contest: a period or spell (as, a bout of flu)

bovine having to do with cattle: dull-witted

bow 1 (rhymes with so) a looped knot

bow 2 (rhymes with so) a springy curved stick bent by a string, used for shooting arrows: the rod with stretched horsehair used to play the strings of a violin
bow-legged with legs bent like a bow; bandy-legged
bow window a curved window

bow 3 (rhymes with now) to bend forward, while lowering the head, in greeting a person: to submit or give in □ the act of bowing

bow(s) 4 (rhymes with now) the front part of a ship
bowsprit (say boe-sprit) a strong spar projecting over the bows of a ship

bowels the inmost parts of the body; the intestines

bower a shady spot in a garden

bowl 1 a deep round dish

bowl 2 to throw a ball overarm (as in cricket) or to roll it along

(as in bowling)

bowler 1 the player who bowls at cricket

bowler 2 a hard felt hat with a rounded top

bowls a game played on a bowling green with heavy balls (bowls)

box 1 any container made of wood, cardboard, metal, etc.

Boxing day the day after Christmas when Christmas-boxes (special presents) are given to some employees

box office the ticket office in a theatre or cinema

box 2 to fight with the fists in boxing gloves; to slap someone (usually on his ears)

boxer a man or youth who practises boxing

boxing the sport in which two opponents box one another (usually in a boxing 'ring', which is square!)

boxing gloves padded gloves worn for boxing

boy a male child

boycott to refuse to deal with (usually in business matters)

brace a pair or couple: anything that joins and holds tightly together □ to tighten or strengthen

bracelet an ornamental chain or band worn round the wrist or arm

braces elastic straps for holding up trousers

bracing strengthening; giving energy

bracken a coarse fern found on heathland and hillsides

bracket 1 a support for something projecting from a wall (such as a shelf or a lamp)

bracket(s) 2 marks used in printing to enclose words, letters or figures — ( ) [ ]

brackish salty tasting (of water)

brag to boast

braggart a person who brags a lot

braid to plait or weave lengths of hair or other materials into a narrow band □ a plait of hair; a narrow band made by plaiting

braille special printing for the blind (It consists of raised dots which they read by feeling with their fingers.)

brain the central part of the nervous system situated inside the head (It works rather like a telephone exchange, receiving messages through all the sense organs [sight, hearing, etc.] and controlling a person's actions and thoughts.); the centre of feeling and thinking

brainy clever

brain-washing gradually forcing a person to change his views (by continual interrogation and propaganda)

brainwave a sudden bright idea

brake the part of a vehicle which acts on the wheels to slow them down

bramble the blackberry bush

bran the skin of grain, which is separated from flour after grinding

branch the arm-like limb of a tree: one of a group of shops, offices, banks, etc., under the same ownership or management □ to divide into, or spread out as, branches

brand a mark or name (brand-name) on something to show who made it, or to whom it belongs: a mark stamped with a hot iron □ to make such a mark

brand-new quite new; unused

brandish to wave something which is held in the hand (such as a bat or a weapon)

brandy a strong spirit distilled from wine

brass a yellow alloy of copper and zinc

brat a scornful name for a child

brave daring, courageous □ to face boldly □ an American Indian warrior

bravery courage; daring

bravo! well done!

brawl a noisy quarrel □ to quarrel noisily

brawn muscle; strength: a kind of potted pork
brawny big and strong

bray the cry of a donkey □ to make such a cry or a sound like it

brazen of or like brass: impudent

brazier a pan for holding hot coals or charcoal

breach a break or gap; the breaking of a law or of a promise

bread a food made of flour (usually wheat flour)
breadwinner one who earns a living for a family

breadth broadness; the distance from side to side

break to force apart or into smaller pieces; to damage or spoil: to interrupt or check (a silence, a fall, a habit)
breakage the act of breaking; the thing broken
breakdown an accidental stoppage (as, of a motor car); collapse or sudden failure of health
breaker a large wave breaking on to rocks or beach
breakneck reckless (of speed)
breakwater a barrier built to break the force of the waves

breakfast the first meal of the day □ to take this meal

breast the front part of a person's chest
breastplate a plate of armour for the chest

breath (say breth) the air taken into the lungs and then forced out: a faint breeze
breathless out of breath

breathe (say breethe) to draw air into the body and force it out again

breech the back part of a gun

breeches (say britches) trousers (especially those fastening just below the knee)

breed to produce young ones: to raise or bring up (as, breeding racehorses or pedigree dogs)
breeding producing young: good manners

breeze a light wind
breezy fairly windy: lively

brethren brothers; fellow members of a religious society (brotherhood)

brevity briefness; shortness

brew to make beer; to make tea
brewery a place for brewing beer

briar, brier a wild rose bush: a root from which tobacco pipes are made

bribe a secret gift to persuade a person to do something dishonest or illegal □ to get someone to take a bribe
bribery giving or taking bribes

brick a small oblong block of baked clay used for building

bride a woman on her wedding day
bridal having to do with a bride or a wedding
bridegroom a man on his wedding day
bridesmaid an unmarried woman who attends a bride at her wedding

bridge 1 a road or similar construction over a river or over another road: the captain's platform on a ship: the bony part of the nose □ to build a bridge over; to span

bridge 2 a card game which resembles whist

bridle the leather straps and fittings attached to a horse's head for guidance and control
bridle path a path for people on horseback

brief short; concise □ a short written statement □ to give instructions (especially to a barrister)

brigade a uniformed band of men who operate together (such as a fire brigade, or a body of soldiers made up of several regiments or battalions)
brigadier the commander of

a brigade

brigand a bandit or robber (especially in deserted country)

bright shining; giving out much light; clever
brighten to make, or become, bright

brilliant very bright, sparkling: very clever
brilliance great brightness: outstanding cleverness

brim the edge of something hollow (such as a cup); the projecting edge of a hat
brimful full to the brim
brim over to overflow

brimstone sulphur

brindled brownish or grey and marked with streaks

brine salt water
briny very salt

bring to fetch; to have something or someone with you when you come; to cause to come (as - Dark clouds bring rain.)

brink the edge of a steep place (such as a cliff or river bank)

brisk lively; quick; active
briskness liveliness; quickness

bristle a short, stiff hair (such as is found on a pig's back) □ to stand stiffly as bristles do
bristly having bristles: prickly

brittle easily broken; fragile

broach to begin to talk about: to open up

broad wide; large; full or strong (as, broad daylight, a broad dialect, or a broad accent)
broadbean the common flat bean
broadcast to scatter widely or freely: to send out news, music or other programmes by radio waves □ a message or programme sent out by a radio broadcasting station
broaden to make or become broad
broadside the side of a ship: the firing together of all the guns on one side of a warship
broadsword a sword with a broad blade

brocade a silk cloth with raised patterns

broccoli a hardy variety of the cauliflower family

brochure *(say broshure)* a booklet or pamphlet

brogue 1 a strong kind of shoe

brogue 2 a broad accent (especially Irish)

broil to cook over hot coals; to grill
broiler a quickly-raised young chicken

broker a businessman who buys and sells for others

bronchitis *(say bronkietis)* inflammation of the breathing tubes of the lungs
bronchial having to do with the windpipe and other breathing tubes

bronco a half-tamed horse

bronze a brown alloy of copper and tin □ made of bronze; bronze coloured

brooch *(say broach)* an ornament with a pin for fastening to clothing

brood to think anxiously for some time: to sit (as a hen on eggs which she is hatching) □ the number of young birds hatched in a nest at the same time

brook a small stream

broom 1 a brush with a long handle, for sweeping
broomstick the handle of a broom

broom 2 a type of bush with yellow flowers

broth a kind of thin soup

brother a son of one's own parents
brotherly like a brother; kindly
brother-in-law the brother of a husband or wife; a sister's husband

brow the forehead; the edge of a hill
browbeat to frighten with looks and words; to bully

brown a dark colour between

orange and black; sunburned □ to roast until brown

brownie a junior member of the Girl Guides: a friendly goblin who is supposed to help with housework

browse to feed on the shoots or leaves of plants: to read here and there without a definite intention or plan

bruise a slight injury to the flesh under the skin which has been discoloured, but not broken, by a blow or fall □ to injure by striking or falling hard enough to discolour the skin

brunette a girl or woman with brown or dark hair and complexion

brunt the shock or force of a blow: the chief strain or stress (as, to bear the brunt of)

brush an instrument set with bristles, hair, etc., used for cleaning, scrubbing or painting; a bushy tail: a skirmish or encounter □ to pass a brush over; to touch lightly in passing
brushwood broken or cut branches and twigs; a thicket

brusque *(say broosk)* abrupt or blunt in manner or speech

brussels sprouts a variety of cabbage with buds or sprouts like tiny cabbages on the stem

brute a beast; a cruel person
brutal like a brute; savagely cruel
brutality savage cruelty

bubble a bladder of water or liquid blown out with air or gas □ to rise in bubbles (as when water is boiled)

buccaneer an old-time pirate in the West Indies; an adventurer

buck the male of the deer, goat, hare and rabbit
buckskin a soft leather made of a buck's skin (especially deerskin)

bucket a container with a handle for holding or carrying water, coal, etc.

buckle a fastening for a belt or strap (usually made of metal) □ to fasten with a buckle

buckler a small shield

buckram a coarse linen or cloth which has been made stiff with paste or gum

bud a shoot of a tree or plant before the leaf or flower has fully opened (for example, a rose bud) □ to put forth buds
budding starting to develop

budge to move or stir

budgerigar an Australian bird like a very small parrot which is popular as a pet (often called budgie for short)

budget any plan showing how money is to be spent, in the home (family budget) or by the government, in the country as a whole (national budget), etc. □ to prepare such a plan

buff a light yellow colour: a soft leather of this colour

buffalo a large animal of the ox family

buffers flat metal plates on strong springs to prevent damage to railway carriages from bumping

buffet *(say boofay)* a counter or bar for refreshments

buffoon a clown; a fool

bug any small insect (especially one that infests some houses)

bugbear something especially annoying; something that arouses fear but is generally imaginary

buggy a light horse-drawn vehicle

bugle a small trumpet used in the army for making signals
bugler a soldier who blows the bugle

build to construct or put together the parts of anything
builder a man whose business it is to build houses, etc.
building a construction; anything built

bulb 1 the glass globe of an electric light

bulb 2 the rounded underground part of some plants (such as the tulip)
bulbous like a bulb; growing from a bulb

bulge to swell out □ a swelling

bulk a large quantity; a great size; the greater part
bulky rather large; taking up much room

bulkhead a wall or partition in a ship which divides the interior into compartments

bull the male of cattle and also of elephants, walruses and whales
bulldog a heavily-built, strong dog with a large head, formerly used to bait bulls
bullfrog a large American frog
bullock a young bull
bull's-eye the centre of a target: a round hard peppermint sweet

bulldozer a powerful caterpillar tractor used for shifting masses of earth and for clearing and levelling ground

bullet the shaped piece of metal fired from a rifle or pistol
bullet-proof not able to be pierced by bullets

bulletin a short news report; a statement on the condition of a sick person

bullion gold and silver in the form of bars

bully someone who frightens or torments others smaller or weaker than himself □ to act like a bully

bulrush a tall strong rush which grows in water and on marshy land

bulwark a rampart: the side of a ship above the deck: anything that serves as a defence

bumblebee a large kind of bee which makes a loud humming sound

bump a lump or swelling: a dull-sounding blow or collision □ to knock or strike against with a dull sound, or without sound
bumper a metal bar fixed to the front, and to the back, of a motor car to lessen the shock of collision

bumpkin an awkward country fellow

bumptious self-important in a pushing manner

bun a small soft round cake

bunch a group of things tied or growing together (like a bunch of keys or of grapes) □ to crowd together

bundle a collection of articles loosely bound together (like a bundle of clothes) □ to make up into a bundle

bung a stopper (usually a cork) for the hole in a barrel

bungalow a house of one storey

bungle to do a thing badly or clumsily

bunion an inflamed swelling on the first joint of the big toe

bunk a shelf-like sleeping place (especially in a ship's cabin)

bunker a large box, especially for keeping a supply of coal: a sandy hollow on a golf course

bunting a thin cloth for flags; small flags used as decorations

buoy *(say boy)* a floating marker which has been anchored to the sea bed as a warning or a guide to ships; a mooring marker for small craft; something to keep a person from sinking in water (life buoy)
buoyancy lightness of weight which makes floating easy
buoyant able to float: cheerful

bur see **burr**

burden a load; something difficult to carry or bear
burdensome heavy; wearying

bureau a writing-table with drawers: an office

burglar someone who breaks into a house, etc. to steal (especially at night)
burglary the breaking into a building with intent to steal

burial see **bury**

burlesque *(say burlesk)* a comic and exaggerated imitation of other people

burly big and sturdy

burn to be on fire; to destroy or injure by fire □ an injury or mark caused by burning
burner the part of an oil lamp or gas jet from which the flame rises

burnish to make bright by rubbing

burr, bur the prickly seed-case of certain plants which readily sticks to anything it touches

burrow a hole dug in the ground for shelter by rabbits, foxes, etc. □ to make holes underground

burst to break open suddenly; to break into pieces: to rush into, through, or out of; to break into (as when someone bursts into song or into tears) □ a sudden outbreak or spurt (as, a burst of speed)

bury to put under, or hide in, the ground; to place a dead body in a grave; to put something in a deep place
burial the act of burying something under earth (especially a dead body); a funeral

bus an omnibus or large public vehicle for carrying passengers

busby a tall fur hat worn by some soldiers

bush a shrub with many small branches and twigs, growing close to the ground: wild uncultivated country
bushy like a bush; thick and spreading

bushel a measure (8 gallons) for measuring grain, fruit, etc.

business trade, profession or work; what especially concerns a person (That's *my* business!)
businesslike practical; systematic; prompt

bust a sculpture of a person's head, shoulders and chest; the upper front part of the human body

bustle to hurry about fussily □ a hurried or fussy activity

busy fully occupied; working hard
business see separate definition
busybody a meddlesome person

but only; except that

butcher a person whose business is to cut up meat and sell it □ to kill for food (as in a slaughter-house); to kill cruelly
butchery a cruel or great slaughter

butler the head man-servant in a large household

butt 1 a large barrel for liquids

butt 2 the thick, heavy end of a rifle

butt 3 to strike with the head (as a goat does)

butter a yellow, fatty food made from cream
buttercup a cup-like golden yellow wildflower
butterscotch a kind of toffee which contains butter

butterfly an insect with large pretty wings

buttocks the rump; the two rounded parts of the body on which a person sits

button a round knob or disc used as a fastening on clothes; a small knob which makes something work when pressed (as, a door-bell button)
buttonhole the narrow hole through which a button is pushed to fasten it

buttress a support built on to the outside of a wall; any support

buxom plump and attractive

buy to purchase; to get something in exchange for money
buyer a purchaser

buzz a humming sound like that of a bee □ to make a humming sound

buzzard a large bird of prey

by at the side of; near; secondary to
by-law a law made by a local authority

bypass a road which avoids a busy area

by-product a product formed incidentally during the manufacture of something else (the main product)

bystander someone standing near; a looker-on

byway a side road; a secluded and little-used road or track

byword a common saying; an object of general scorn

bye a run scored in cricket when the ball is not touched by the batsman but goes past him and the wicket-keeper

bygone past

C

cab a taxi: a driver's shelter on a vehicle

cabaret variety entertainment in a restaurant

cabbage a vegetable with green or purple leaves growing tightly together so as to form a head

cabin a small house or hut made of logs or other rough materials: a small room for officers or passengers on a ship or aeroplane

cabinet 1 a piece of furniture (usually a set of drawers or a cupboard) used for holding ornamental objects or papers (filing cabinet)

cabinet 2 a chosen number of the chief ministers who govern a country (Members of the cabinet act as advisers to the head of state.)

cable a very strong thick chain or rope, sometimes made of pieces of wire twisted together: a wire for carrying electric current: a cablegram □ to send a cablegram

cablegram a telegram sent by means of a cable (usually underground or underwater - for example, the cable lying across the sea bed of the Atlantic Ocean)

cacao the tropical tree from whose seeds cocoa and chocolate are made

cache a hiding-place for stores, treasure, ammunition, etc.; whatever is hidden in a cache

cackle the loud excited noise made by hens or geese: chatter or laughter sounding like this noise □ to make a cackling noise

cactus a prickly plant with thick stems and branches which store water

cacti, cactuses the plural of cactus

cadaverous very thin; haggard; corpse-like

caddie someone who carries a golfer's clubs for him

caddy a small airtight box for storing tea

cadence the rise and fall of sound (as when the voice rises at the end of a question and falls when stating a fact): rhythm, or the measured beat of rhythmical motion (such as the cadence of an express train's wheels)

cadet a boy or young man training to be an officer in one of the armed forces

cadge to beg

café (say caffay) a restaurant; a place for a snack or light meal

cafeteria a restaurant where you serve yourself from a counter

caffeine a stimulating substance in tea and coffee

cage a box made of wood, metal, strong wire, etc., or an open room with bars where birds or animals are kept: a cage-like lift in a mine □ to imprison in a cage

cairn a heap of stones set up as a

landmark, a monument, etc.

caisson an ammunition chest or wagon: a watertight structure used in the construction of bridge foundations, etc.

cajole to coax or wheedle; to persuade by flattery or false promises

cake a baked sweet food made of flour, sugar, fat, eggs, flavouring and other ingredients; any small shaped mass (usually flat, as, a fish cake, a cake of soap, etc.)

calamity a great misfortune; a disaster

calcium a metallic substance found in limestone, chalk, marble and coral (Human beings and animals need calcium to make their bones and teeth strong.)

calculate to count or reckon with figures: to think out
calculating selfish or scheming
calculated deliberate, done on purpose
calculation a reckoning; a sum; the working out of a mathematical problem or its result
calculator a calculating machine; a set of tables to help in calculations

calendar a table showing the days, weeks and months in a year; a list or record of events

calf (say cahf) a young cow or bull
calve (say cahv) to give birth to a calf
calves (say cahvz) the plural of calf
calfskin hide or leather of calf

calf 2 (say cahf) the thick back part of the leg below the knee
calves (say cahvz) the plural of calf

calibre the measurement across the opening of a tube or gun: (of a person) degree of excellence or importance (as when someone who has accomplished some difficult feat is said to be of high calibre)

calico a type of cotton cloth

caliph, calif a title taken by rulers who succeeded Mohammed: see also **Mohammedan**

call to shout or cry out (as when someone calls for help); to name or summon (as when a teacher calls the names on a school register, or calls someone to come to the blackboard): to describe (as when a person calls someone silly or stupid) □ an invitation or summons; a telephone conversation; a short visit
caller a person who comes to visit or makes a telephone call
calling a trade or profession
to call up to summon (especially for service in the armed forces)

calligraphy beautiful handwriting or penmanship

callipers, calipers compasses used for measuring the inside or outside diameter of objects
caliper a splint made of two metal rods which is strapped to a weak leg to give support

callous unkind; hard-hearted

callus a thickened, hard part of the skin (often made tough by hard work)

calm quiet; still; not easily upset or disturbed □ the absence of wind

calorie a measure of heat (especially for measuring the value of different foods in producing bodily heat and energy)

calve see **calf**

calypso a West Indian folk song telling about recent events (often made up by the singer as he goes along)

camber a slight downward curve on each side of a road surface, ship's deck, etc., which makes the middle higher than the sides

cambric a fine white linen

camel a big animal with a long curved neck and one hump (Arabian) or two humps (Bactrian), used in desert countries as a beast of burden and for riding

camel('s) hair hair of the camel, used in making cloth; hairs from a squirrel's tail, used to make artists' paint brushes

cameo a design carved or engraved in relief on a gem, stone, etc. (usually of two or more differently coloured layers so that the design stands out from the background)

camera a box-like apparatus which is used for taking pictures by briefly exposing a sensitized film to light
cine-camera a camera for taking moving pictures
in camera (of a law case) tried in secret or in private

camouflage *(say camooflahzh)* to disguise something from the enemy by making it appear to be a part of the surroundings (usually by painting or covering it, as a warship is painted blue-grey to blend in with the colour of the sea and sky)

camp a place where soldiers or other groups of people live in temporary shelters such as tents or huts □ to set up camp; to live in a camp
camp bed, camp chair, camp stool, etc. furniture that can be folded up when not in use

campaign *(say campain)* a series of military operations in one area or period of a war; an organized series of meetings, speeches, etc. for a special cause or purpose (such as a political campaign); a planned series of advertisements in the press and/or television
campaigner someone who takes part in a campaign

campanula a family of plants with bell-shaped flowers

camphor a solid, gum-like oil with a very strong smell, used for medicine and in mothballs

can 1 a word used with other verbs meaning to be able to or to know how to
could past or conditional form of can (as - I could not swim last summer. - I could learn to play the piano if I had lessons.)

can 2 a metal container for food or liquids □ to preserve food and liquids by putting them into air-tight cans
cannery a factory where food is put into cans

canal a man-made waterway for ships and boats, and sometimes for irrigation: a tube-like passage in the body which carries food, liquid, air, etc.

canary a small yellow songbird kept as a pet

cancel to cross out or strike out (with a line or number of lines) something that is printed or written; to withdraw, take back or put off (for example, an order or an appointment); to mark with a postmark
cancellation the act of cancelling

cancer a disease of body cells which grows and spreads

candelabrum an ornamental candlestick made with branches so that it can hold two or more candles
candelabra the plural of candelabrum (but often used to mean only one)

candid frank honest and straightforward in speech and manner
candour frankness; outspokenness

candidate a person who offers himself for a public office or honour or who is proposed for such a position by someone else; a person who sits for an examination or applies for a job

candle a cylinder of tallow or wax with a wick through the middle, which is burned to give light
candlestick a candle holder

candour see **candid**

candy a sweet made by boiling sugar and other ingredients
candied coated with sugar or sugary syrup

cane the hard stem of a small palm tree or a grass-like plant (such as sugar cane or bamboo); a light walking stick □ to beat with a cane

canine having to do with dogs
canine tooth in human beings, one of the four pointed teeth

canker a spreading sore or diseased spot in human beings, animals and plants

cannibal a human being who eats human flesh; an animal which eats others of its own species
cannibalism the practice of eating one's own kind

cannon a large heavy gun, usually fired from a support on wheels or a stationary mount
cannonball a missile, formerly an iron ball, made to be shot from a cannon

canny cautious, careful (especially with money); shrewd

canoe (say ca*noo*) a light boat, narrow at each end, which is moved through the water by means of a paddle

canon 1 a law or rule of the church; a clergyman belonging to a cathedral; a list of saints
canonize to place someone in the canon or list of saints

canon 2 a musical composition in which one voice starts and the others follow in turn with the same tune (*Three Blind Mice* is a canon.)

canopy a covering hung over a throne, bed, etc.; a rooflike projection; an overhanging shelter

cant 1 insincere, hypocritical talk

cant 2 a slope □ to tilt

cantaloup(e) a small melon with a tough ribbed skin

cantankerous quarrelsome, bad-tempered and unreasonable

canteen an eating place in military camps and barracks, factories, office buildings, etc.: a case for cutlery: a small container used for carrying drinking water, etc.

canter an easy gallop □ to ride at an easy gallop

cantilever a large bracket used to support balconies, stairs, etc.
cantilever bridge a bridge supported by giant cantilevers (These are attached to each pair of upright piers and meet at the centre of each span, as in the Forth railway bridge.)

canton a district in a country; one of the federal states in Switzerland

canvas a strong coarse cloth used for tents, sails, awnings, etc., and for painting pictures on
under canvas in tents: with sails spread

canvass to go round a district asking people to support a cause (by voting, giving money, etc.)

canyon a deep gorge or valley with very steep sides (often with a stream or river at the bottom)

cap a small soft hat without a brim (but usually with a peak): a cover or top (as, on a bottle) □ to cover with a cap: to outdo

capable (say *caypabl*) able; clever or strong enough to do something (as when a person is said to be capable of winning a race)
capability the quality of being capable

capacious roomy; able to hold a large amount (as, a capacious shopping bag)

capacity the ability to hold or contain; the amount that something can hold (as, the capacity [in terms of people] of a hall, or the capacity [in terms of fluid ounces] of a jug): position or power (as when a person acts in the capacity of leader)

cape 1 a sleeveless garment (sometimes attached to a coat or cloak) that fastens round the neck and hangs over the shoulders

cape 2 a point of land extending into the sea

caper to leap or jump about in a lively manner □ a prank

capillary one of the thin hairlike tubes in the body which join the veins to the arteries

capital 1 money or goods for carrying on a business; property that brings in an income
capitalism a system in which a country's land and wealth is mainly owned by individual people and not by the state
capitalize to turn something to one's own advantage: see also **capitalize** under **capital 3**

capital 2 chief, principal, of most importance (as, the capital city of a country); excellent □ a chief town or seat of government

capital 3 one of the large letters of the alphabet (as **A,B,C** in contrast to the small letters **a,b,c**)
capitalize to write or print in capital letters: see also **capitalize** under **capital 1**

capital 4 of the head; involving loss of life (as capital punishment) □ the head or top part of a column

capitulate to give up; to surrender
capitulation a surrender under agreed terms

capon a cock bred only for use as food

caprice a sudden change of mind or mood for no apparent reason
capricious changeable; unreliable

capsize to upset

capstan a revolving machine on a ship or quay, used for winding or pulling heavy cables or weights

capsule a dry covering enclosing the seeds of some plants; a small gelatine container for medicine: a self-contained spacecraft or part of one

captain the commander of a ship or aircraft; an officer in an army; the head or leader of a team, club, etc.

caption the heading of a book chapter, or of a story or article in a magazine, newspaper, etc.; a note about an illustration or cartoon (usually underneath); printed matter in a film

captivate to charm; to fascinate

captive a prisoner; someone or something confined or held so that escape is difficult or impossible □ held (as by a rope)
captivity the condition of being a captive
capture to take or seize by force or skill; to attract or hold (the interest or attention of a person, an audience, etc.) □ the act of capturing

car a vehicle on wheels (especially a motor car)

caramel a chewy sweet similar to toffee; sugar which has been melted and browned, used for colouring and flavouring food

carat a measure of weight for gems: a unit used in describing the fineness of gold (22 carat gold is finer in quality than 14 carat gold.)

caravan a covered carriage or cart; a small house on wheels, pulled by a car or horse: a group of people travelling together for safety (especially in the desert)

caraway a plant with spicy-tasting seeds used to flavour cakes or bread

carbine a short, light rifle

carbohydrate a compound of carbon, hydrogen and oxygen (The sugars and starches in foods are carbohydrates.)

carbolic acid an acid made from coal tar, used in disinfectants and antiseptics

carbon the chemical element which occurs in nature as pure charcoal, diamonds, coal, etc.
carboniferous producing coal
carbon paper a kind of paper coated on one side with a black sooty substance (It is used between two pieces of paper so that what is written or typed on the top sheet is copied on to the bottom sheet, making a carbon copy.)
carbon dioxide a gas given out in breathing and produced by plants
carbon monoxide a very pois-

onous, colourless, odourless gas found in the exhaust fumes of motor vehicles, etc.

carbuncle a red gem (formerly any red precious stone such as a ruby, nowadays a garnet): an inflamed swelling like a large boil

carburettor, carburetter the part of a motor engine in which air and vaporized fuel are mixed

carcass, carcase a dead body; a framework or skeleton

card 1 a flat stiff piece of paper or pasteboard with figures (for playing card games), pictures, designs and printing (for greetings, invitations, etc.)
cards games played with cards
cardboard stiff pasteboard, used for making boxes, book covers, etc.

card 2 an instrument for combing wool, cotton and other fibres □ to comb fibres

cardiac having to do with the heart

cardigan a knitted woollen jacket

cardinal principal; of chief importance □ a high-ranking official of the Roman Catholic Church
cardinal numbers numbers showing how many (1,2,3 etc.): see also **ordinal numbers.**
cardinal points the four chief points of the compass (north, south, east and west)

care a worry or trouble: attention (as - Take care crossing the street.); responsibility (as - Take care of the younger children.) □ to be concerned or anxious about: to look after or be responsible for: to be willing (as - Would you care to go to the cinema?): to be fond of (as - She cares a great deal for him.)
carefree without worries, light-hearted
careful giving special attention to what you are doing
careless not taking care; the opposite of careful
caretaker a person who is

responsible for someone else's property (especially a building)
care-worn looking burdened with worries
to take care to be watchful and painstaking
to take care of to look after

career a progressive course through life (especially in business or a profession); a way of earning a living (as - He chose engineering as a career.) □ to move very quickly (as - The driverless bus careered down the hill.)

caress to touch gently and affectionately □ a fond, gentle touch

cargo the goods or freight carried by ships and aeroplanes

caribou a North American reindeer

caricature a likeness of someone or something, so exaggerated that it appears amusing or ridiculous (For example, a caricature of a person who has a big nose may be drawn so as to show it as a huge beak.)

carillon (say carilyon or carilyon) a set of musical bells, usually played by machinery or from a keyboard; a tune played on such bells

carmine a purplish-red colour

carnation a many-petalled flower with a spicy smell

carnelian see **cornelian**

carnival a festival held just before Lent in some countries; a fair-like entertainment

carnivorous flesh-eating

carol a song of joy or praise (especially those carols sung at Christmas)

carouse to take part in a session of heavy drinking

carousel a roundabout at a fair

carp 1 to find fault (usually about unimportant things)

carp 2 a freshwater fish (usually found in ponds)

carpenter a man who works with wood (especially in the building and furniture trades)

carpet a thick woven covering for floors and stairs; anything resembling a carpet (such as a lawn that looks like a carpet of grass)

carriage a wheeled vehicle for carrying people; the act or cost of carrying: a person's bearing or way of carrying himself
carriageway the part of a road used for vehicles

carrier see **carry**

carrion dead, rotting flesh

carrot a vegetable with an orange pointed root

carry to transport or take from one place to another; to bear; to support; to hold oneself (as - He carries himself well.): to travel (as - The sound of gunshot carried across the lake.): see also **carriage**
carrier someone who carries goods, luggage, etc. for money; a container for carrying (as, a carrier bag); something that carries people or goods (such as an aircraft carrier)
carrier pigeon a pigeon trained to carry messages and then to return home
carrycot a bed with handles, used for carrying a baby
to carry on to keep on in spite of difficulties; to continue
to carry out to accomplish or complete
to be carried away to become very excited or emotional

cart a two-wheeled, horse-drawn vehicle (usually used for carrying loads)
cartwheel a wheel of a cart; a sideways somersault with hands on the ground (resembling a cartwheel going round)

cartilage gristle; a flexible bony substance in human beings and animals

carton a pasteboard box or container (such as a milk carton)

cartoon a short funny film (made by photographing a large number of drawings in sequence); an amusing drawing in a magazine or newspaper (making fun of someone or something)
cartoonist someone who draws cartoons

cartridge a case containing the gunpowder and shot for a gun

carve to shape a piece of wood, ivory, etc., or to cut patterns on it with a knife; to cut meat into slices

cascade a waterfall

case 1 a covering or box holding something inside (as, a pillowcase, a bookcase, a suitcase)
casement the box-like frame of a window; a window opening on hinges

case 2 a special instance or example (as - There is a case of measles in the school.); a legal trial (as, a case of robbery to be judged in a court of law); a state or condition of things (as - You said I was late, but that was not the case.)
in any case whatever happens
in case if it should happen (as - In case it rains we'll take our macs.)

cash coins or banknotes; ready money □ to exchange a cheque for ready money
cashier a person who has charge of receiving and paying out money (in a shop, bank, etc.)
cash register a till showing how much money has been put in each time a payment is made
hard cash, spot cash ready money

cashmere very soft silky wool or woollen material

casino a public building with rooms for gambling, dancing, etc.

cask a barrel-shaped container for holding liquids

casket a small case or box for jewels: a coffin

casserole a covered vessel in which food is both cooked and served

cassock a long robe worn by the

clergy, choir and altar servers in some churches

cast 1 to throw, toss or fling; to shed or drop (as when a snake casts its old skin); to mould or shape (by pouring molten metal, etc. into a mould and letting it harden) □ a throw; a piece of moulded metal that has been cast; a stiff plaster dressing on an injured limb, etc.
castaway a person who has been shipwrecked
cast-off discarded; rejected
cast down discouraged, depressed

cast 2 to assign parts in a play, film, etc. to actors □ the actors and actresses who perform in a play, opera, film, etc.

castanets two hollow shell-shaped pieces of wood or ivory which are held in the hand and clicked together as accompaniment to dancing, singing and guitar music

caste *(say cast)* a social class of people (especially in India)

castellated see **castle**

caster same as **castor**

castle a large fortified house or group of buildings, usually having high thick walls with towers (Nowadays many castles are used as large country mansions or as museums and are not fortified.)
castellated having turrets and battlements like a castle
castles in the air, castles in Spain daydreams or imaginary schemes

castor, caster a small wheel on legs of furniture: a small container with holes in the top, used for salt, pepper, sugar, etc.
castor sugar finely ground sugar

castor oil a thick, unpleasant-tasting oil made from the seeds of a tropical plant, used for medicine and as a lubricant

casual by chance; offhand; not formal
casualty an accident; a person who is wounded or killed by accident: a person or thing lost through death, wounds, capture, etc. (especially in war)

cat a small furry four-footed animal (usually domesticated): any large cat-like animal (such as a lion, tiger, etc.)
cat-o'-nine-tails a whip with nine lashes
catcall a loud whistle or noise expressing disapproval
catgut a kind of cord made from the intestines of sheep and other animals, used for the strings of violins, tennis rackets, etc.
catkins small fluffy flowers that grow on some trees (such as hazel and willow)
catty spiteful

catalogue a list of names, books, articles, etc. in a special order

catamaran a raft or float of logs lashed together; a fast sailing boat with two hulls joined together side by side

catapult a Y-shaped stick with an elastic string fastened to each prong, used for shooting small stones, etc.; (in olden days) a war machine of the same design only larger, used for hurling stones, arrows, etc.

cataract a large waterfall: a cloudiness on the lens of the eye leading to partial or complete blindness

catarrh a watery or thick fluid discharged from the nose and throat when the mucous membrane is inflamed (as when a person has a bad cold)

catastrophe *(say catastrofee)* a sudden disaster; a terrible misfortune
catastrophic *(say catastrofic)* disastrous; calamitous

catch to seize and hold (especially something or someone in motion); to be in time (as, for a bus or train); to surprise or detect (as, to catch a person stealing); to trick someone (especially with words); to become infected or affected by something (as, to catch a cold, to catch fire) □ something seized or taken (as, a catch of fish); something that holds fast (such as a door catch)

catcher a person who catches the ball in games

catching infectious (as - Measles is catching.)

catchy attractive; popular (as, a catchy tune)

catechism *(say catakism)* a series of questions on a subject; a book which teaches something (especially religion) by means of questions and answers

cater *(say cayter)* to supply prepared food for a banquet, a party, etc.; to supply what is needed

caterer someone who serves or supplies food, entertainment, etc., for money

caterpillar a grub that becomes a butterfly or moth □ moving on endless belts (as, a caterpillar tractor)

caterwaul the screech or howl of a cat

catgut see **cat**

cathedral the principal church of a diocese

catherine-wheel a firework that turns round and round while burning

cathode ray tube a device like a large glass bulb in which a narrow beam of electrons strikes against a screen to make a tracing or picture (as in a television set)

catholic of the Roman Catholic church: universal; general □ a member of the Roman Catholic church

catkins see **cat**

cattle grass-eating livestock (such as cows, bulls, calves, etc. which are usually kept on a farm or ranch)

cauldron a large heavy iron pot with a lid and hooped handle, used for boiling liquids

cauliflower a cabbage-like vegetable with an edible white middle part like a flower

caulk to fill up a seam or joint to make it watertight (as, to caulk the deck of a ship)

cause the action or thing that makes something happen; a reason or motive (as, a cause for rejoicing); a movement with a special aim or purpose (as, a worthy cause) □ to make something happen; to bring about

causeway a raised road or pathway (especially across water or marshy ground)

caustic burning: severe or cutting (as, a caustic remark) □ a substance that eats into the flesh by chemical action (as, caustic soda)

cauterize to burn with a caustic or a hot iron

caution carefulness; watchfulness: a warning □ to warn

cautious careful; watchful

cautionary containing a warning (as, a cautionary tale)

cavalcade a procession or train of people (especially on horseback)

cavalier *(say cavaleer)* a horseman (especially a knight): a Royalist in the time of Charles I □ haughty or offhand in manner

cavalry mounted soldiers

cave a hollow underground place usually with an entrance in rocks or in the side of a hill

caveman one of the prehistoric or Stone Age men, who lived in caves

to cave in to collapse; to give way

cavern a deep hollow place underground; a large cave

cavernous hollow; full of caverns

caviar(e) the salted roe of sturgeon (It is a great delicacy and usually very expensive to buy.): anything considered too fine or elegant for ordinary people

cavity a hollow place; a hole

caw the loud hoarse cry of a crow

cease to stop; to come to an end

ceaseless continuing without stopping
cessation an end, a ceasing

cedar a cone-bearing evergreen tree with hard, sweet-smelling wood

cede to yield or give something up (as - Territory is ceded to a country by another.)
cession the giving up or yielding of something to another

ceiling the top of a room; an upper limit (as, the highest amount and no more to be paid for something); the upper limit of height at which a particular kind of aeroplane can fly

celandine a yellow-flowered wild plant (There are two kinds, the greater and lesser celandines.)

celebrate to mark a special occasion by festivities, entertainment, etc.: to praise
celebrated famous
celebration the act of celebrating
celebrity a well-known person

celery a vegetable with thick edible stalks (usually kept away from sunlight to make them white instead of their natural green colour)

celestial having to do with the sky; heavenly

celibacy the unmarried state
celibate living single; bound by vow or intention not to marry

cell a very small room (as in a prison or a monastery); a small unit of living matter (such as a blood cell); a unit of an electric battery; a division of a honeycomb
cellular made up of cells or tiny hollow divisions

cellar an underground room where coal, wine, etc. may be stored

cello *(say chello)* a short word for violoncello, a large, deep-toned stringed instrument shaped like a violin, but rested on the floor and held between the player's knees

celluloid one of the earliest transparent plastics, formerly used for films, etc.

cellulose the main substance of the cell walls of plants

cement any substance that makes two things stick together; a greyish building material (mortar) made by mixing together lime, sand and water

cemetery a burial ground

cenotaph a monument to a person or persons buried elsewhere (such as soldiers who have been buried in a foreign country)

censer a container in which incense is burned

censor an official who examines written or printed material or films, and who has the power to decide whether parts are unsuitable for the public and should be taken out

censure to find fault with; to condemn as wrong

census an official counting of the number of people in a country, city, etc.

cent a coin equal to the hundredth part of a larger unit of money

cent(i) (as part of a word) the hundredth part, a hundred (as, centimetre, centigrade)
per cent see **per**

centaur (in Greek mythology) a creature half man, half horse

centenary a hundredth anniversary of some event
centenarian a person who is one hundred years old or more

centigrade divided into a hundred degrees (On a centigrade thermometer, freezing point is shown as 0 and boiling point at 100.)

centigramme the hundredth part of a gramme

centilitre the hundredth part of a litre

centimetre the hundredth part of a metre

centipede a small, crawling

animal with many legs

centre the middle point or the middle part of anything
central having to do with the centre; chief or principal
centralize to bring to one place (usually the middle or most important point) or to the largest or most important centre (as - Government departments are centralized in the capital city of a country.)
central heating the heating of a building from one source

centrifugal moving or flying out from the centre
centrifugal force a force or power that causes objects moving in a circle to fly out from the centre

centripetal moving towards a centre

century a period of hundred years: a hundred runs in cricket

ceramic having to do with pottery

cereal any kind of grain used as food; food produced from such grain (as, breakfast cereal)

ceremony a formal act or series of acts as laid down by custom or law (as, a wedding ceremony or a coronation ceremony); formality or pomp
ceremonial relating to ceremonies □ a system of ceremonies (as in a church service)
ceremonious very formal

cerise a light, clear red colour

certain sure; without any doubt □ some, or one, not named (as, a certain person, certain local people)
certainly surely; *yes* in reply to a request
certainty something that is certain to happen; something that cannot be doubted

certificate a written or printed statement of the truth of a fact (as, a birth certificate or a certificate stating that certain examinations have been passed)
certify to declare formally that something is true

cessation see **cease**

cession see **cede**

cesspool an underground pool or pit for collecting waste matter from houses without main drainage

chafe to make warm by rubbing (as, to rub cold hands together hard); to make sore or worn by rubbing (for example, by harsh material rubbing against the skin)

chaff the husks of grain left after threshing and winnowing □ to tease gently

chaffinch a small songbird of the finch family

chagrin annoyance or vexation (usually because of failure or disappointment)

chain a series of links or rings passing through one another; any series of things joined together as if by links (as, a chain of mountains, a chain of events) □ to fasten with a chain
chain mail armour made of small metal links
chain store a shop linked with a number of others under the same ownership

chair a movable single seat with a back; an official seat or position of authority (held by a university professor, for example, or by a person who conducts a meeting) □ to carry someone in triumph; to preside over a meeting
chairman, chairwoman a person who presides over a meeting or who is the chief official of a committee, board of directors, etc.

chalet (say *shalay*) a small wooden alpine house with overhanging eaves; any house built in this style

chalice a ceremonial drinking cup or goblet

chalk a soft white limestone; a chalk-like substance in crayons used for writing and drawing

challenge to invite someone to

take part in a contest of strength, skill, etc.; to question or doubt something said or done □a summons to a contest; an objection

chamber a room (especially a bedroom); a place where an assembly meets; a lawmaking body (such as the House of Commons): the enclosed space in a gun that holds the charge **chamber music** music to be played by only a few instruments, and therefore more suitable for performance in a large room than in a concert hall

chamberlain an officer who manages the household of a king or nobleman

chameleon *(say cameelyon)* a small lizard which is able to change its colour to match its surroundings

chamois *(say shamwah)* a goat-like wild antelope; *(say shammy)* a soft yellowish leather (originally made from the skin of the chamois, now also from sheep, goats, deer, etc.)

champagne *(say shampain)* a wine (usually white and sparkling)

→ **champion** a person who has defeated all other competitors in a game or sport; someone who fights in defence of himself or someone else; the winner in a competition for the best animal, plant, etc. □to defend or support **championship** the position of being champion

chance something that happens unexpectedly or without being planned; luck or fate (as when two old friends meet by chance in a big city); an opportunity (as, the chance of a good job); a possibility, a risk (as - There's a chance that it may rain.) □to happen; to risk (as - I'll chance it.)
chancy risky; not certain

chancellor a chief minister of government: the head of a university
Chancellor of the Exchequer the chief minister of finance in British government

chandelier *(say shandeleer)* a framework with branches to hold lights (usually hanging from the ceiling)

chandler a dealer in candles, oil, paint and similar supplies

change to make or become different; to exchange or substitute one thing for another (as, to change clothes, to change plans, to change English money for French money, etc.) □the money returned from a larger amount offered in payment (as when one pays with a £5 note for something costing £4.50 and receives 50p change); notes or coins given in exchange for a larger amount (as when coins are given as change for a £1 note)
changeable variable; likely to change
changeling a child taken or left in place of another (especially in fairy stories)

channel the deeper part of a river, bay, seaway, etc., through which ships can pass; the bed of a stream; a strait or narrow sea (such as the English Channel): a path through the air for the transmission of radio and television signals; a means of sending or receiving information

chant to sing a number of words or syllables all on the same note (as when parts of the Bible, prayers, etc. are chanted or recited in a singing manner); to speak in a singsong, monotonous way

chaos *(say kayoss)* complete confusion or lack of order
chaotic totally confused or disordered

chap 1 a boy or man; a fellow

chap 2 to crack or split open in cracks (as the skin often does in cold windy weather)
chapped roughened or cracked (of the skin)

chapel a small church or a

separate part of a large church; a private church in a large building (such as a school, palace, prison, etc.)

chaperon *(say shaperoen)* an older person (usually a married woman) in charge of a young girl or group of young people at a public dance, performance, etc.

chaplain a clergyman officially attached to a college, an institution (such as a hospital, the armed forces, etc.)

chaps *(say shaps)* leather overtrousers worn by cowboys to protect their legs against thorns

chapter a main section of a book (usually numbered 1, 2, 3, etc.)

char to scorch or burn slightly
charred burned, but not to ashes

character all of a person's qualities which, taken together, make him or her different from anyone else; a person in a play or story; an odd or eccentric person: a distinctive mark or sign (such as a letter of the alphabet or a trademark on the bottom of a plate)
characteristic typical □ a typical quality

charade a game in which the syllables of a word are acted out separately, followed by an acting out of the whole word

charcoal the black remains of partly burned wood

charge 1 to command or require someone to undertake a task or duty: to accuse (as when a thief is charged with stealing): to attack with a rush: to load or fill (as, to charge a gun with ammunition, or to charge a battery with electricity) □ a load (of ammunition) or amount (of electricity): a command: an attack: an accusation: someone or something to be looked after (such as a child, a building, etc.)
to be in charge of to be in control of and responsible for

charge 2 the price asked for goods or services □ to ask (an amount of money) as the price of something; to record the amount to be paid for something at a later date

charger a warhorse

chariot an open two-wheeled vehicle pulled by horses, used in wars and races in ancient times
charioteer a chariot driver

charity a feeling of kindness and love towards other people; the giving of money, food, shelter, etc. to people in need (such as those who are poor or ill); a society or fund set up to give such help
charitable generous and kindly towards others; of service to the poor and needy (as, a charitable institution)

charm a spell, words or object believed to have magical powers; a thing worn or carried in the belief that it will ward off evil or will bring good luck, etc.; the power to attract and please others □ to influence or bewitch (as if by magic); to attract
charmed delighted; very pleased
charming attractive; delightful

chart a map of part of the sea, showing coastlines, currents, depths of water, shoals, rocks and other danger spots: an information sheet, containing a diagram or table, etc. □ to make a chart; to plan

charter an official written paper giving rights and privileges (especially one granted by a ruler or government) □ to grant a charter: to let or hire a ship, aircraft, etc. by contract

chase to run after; to pursue; to hunt; to drive away (as, to chase a stray dog away from a private garden)

chasm *(say cazm)* a deep opening or fissure in the earth

chassis *(say shassee)* the framework which forms the base of a car or lorry; the support for the main landing gear of an aeroplane

chaste *(say chayst)* simple in

style; innocent and pure
chastity (say <u>chastitee</u>) purity

chastise to punish

chat to talk with someone in an easy, friendly way

château (say <u>shatoe</u>) a (French) castle or large country house

chatter to talk continuously and quickly (often about meaningless and unimportant things)
chatterbox a person who is always talking

chauffeur (say <u>showfer</u>) a person who is paid to drive someone else's car for him

cheap low in price; of little value

cheat a person who gets something by trickery or deception □ to be dishonest or unfair

check to go over something (such as a sum) to be sure it is correct; to hinder or stop □ a sudden stop: a pattern of squares

cheek 1 the side of the face below the eye
cheekbone the ridge of bone under the eye

cheek 2 impudence
cheeky saucy; impudent

cheer to shout or applaud as encouragement or to show approval; to comfort or make happy □ joy: a shout of encouragement or approval: good food and entertainment
cheerful bright and lively; happy
cheerless gloomy; miserable
cheery gay; cheerful

cheese a food, made from the curds of milk pressed into a solid mass

cheetah a leopard-like animal used for hunting in some Eastern countries

chef (say <u>shef</u>) a cook (especially in a hotel or restaurant)

chemistry the science that finds out what substances are made of and studies the effects of their action on each other
chemical having to do with chemistry □ a substance used in chemistry or in a chemical process used in industry (for example, bleach is a chemical)
chemist a scientist who studies chemistry; a person who is qualified to dispense drugs and medicines

cheque (say <u>check</u>) a written order on a printed form which instructs a bank to pay out a certain sum (from the writer's account) to the person, firm, etc. named on the form
cheque book a book of printed cheque forms

chequer to mark in coloured squares (as, a chess board or draughts board)
chequered, checkered marked with squares (as, the flag used in motor racing)
chequers, checkers another word for the game of draughts

cherish to protect and love; to keep in the mind (as, to cherish a hope or a memory)

cherry a small red or yellow fruit with a stone, which grows in clusters on the branches of the cherry tree

cherub an angelic being (usually portrayed as a winged creature with a child's face); a beautiful young child
cherubic angelic (as, a cherubic expression)
cherubim, cherubs the plural of cherub

chess a game for two people played with 16 pieces (chessmen) each on a chequered board of 64 squares

chest a large strong box (usually with a lid): the upper front part of the body between the neck and the abdomen

chestnut a reddish-brown edible nut; the tree on which these nuts grow; a reddish-brown colour: see also **horse chestnut**

chew to crush or grind with the teeth
chewing gum sweet gum that is chewed but not swallowed

chick a baby bird; a young child

chicken a young hen or cock; the meat from such a bird
chicken-hearted timid; easily frightened; cowardly

chicken-pox a feverish illness with small itchy blisters on the face and body

chicory a blue-flowered salad plant (Its ground-up root can be mixed with coffee.)

chide to scold; to rebuke

chief a leader or person at the head of something (as, chief of police) □ most important or principal (as, the chief port)
chiefly mainly
chieftain the head of a clan, tribe, etc.

chiffon (say shiffon) a thin gauzy fabric

chilblain a painful itchy swelling on the hands and feet in cold weather

child a very young boy or girl; a son or daughter
childhood the time of being a child (between babyhood and youth)
childish acting like a child; foolish or silly
children the plural of child

chill a feeling of coldness; a shivery cold (often with a fever) □ to make cool or cold
chilly uncomfortably cold

chime a musical sound made by a set of bells

chimney a passage for smoke to escape from a fireplace, furnace, etc.
chimney pot an earthenware or metal pipe at the top of a chimney
chimney sweep a person who clears soot from the inside of a chimney

chimpanzee a very intelligent African ape, smaller than a gorilla

chin the part of the face below the mouth

china porcelain or fine earthenware (originally made in China)

chinchilla a small squirrel-like South American animal, valued for its fur

chink 1 a narrow crack or opening

chink 2 a clinking sound (as when coins are jingled)

chip to knock a small piece off something (such as a cup, a stone, wood, etc.) □ the place where such a piece has been chipped out; a small piece of potato fried in deep fat; a counter used in games

chipmunk a small North American animal, like a striped squirrel

chiropodist (say kiropodist) a person who treats ailments of the feet (such as corns, bunions, etc.)

chirp a short shrill sound made by some birds and insects

chisel a tool with a cutting edge at the end, used for shaping wood, stone or metal

chivalry (say shivalree) the customs of mediaeval knights; knightly qualities (such as bravery and courtesy)
chivalrous showing the qualities of a knight; courteous; courageous

chlorine (say cloreen) a yellowish-green poisonous gas with a very strong smell, used in bleaching and sterilizing water supplies, etc.
chloride a compound of chlorine and another element (Common salt is sodium chloride.)
chlorinate to treat with chlorine (as in purifying water)

chloroform (say cloroform) a colourless liquid used as an anaesthetic

chlorophyll (say clorofill) the green colouring matter of plants

chock-full completely full; crammed to capacity

chocolate a paste made from the ground-up seeds of the cacao tree; a drink, sweets, etc. made from this

choice the act or power of

choosing; the thing chosen; an alternative (as - He was offered the choice of a camera or a bicycle as a present.); a number of things to choose from (as, a wide choice of sweets); see also **choose**

choir *(say kwire)* a group of people trained to sing together; the part of a church where the choir sits

choke to seize by the throat so as to hinder or stop breathing; to block up; to find it hard to breathe because of some obstruction in the throat (such as a bone or thick smoke) □ the action or sound of choking: a device in a car to help in starting a cold engine (It provides a richer petrol/air mixture.)

cholera *(say kolera)* a very serious infectious disease

choose to take or decide one thing rather than another; to select
chose, chosen selected (as - She chose a pink dress, but her friend has chosen a red one.)

chop 1 to cut with quick hard blows; to cut into small pieces □ a thick slice of meat on a rib bone
chopper a person who chops; an implement used for chopping
choppy rough or uneven (especially of a lake or sea when the wind has made the waves higher and they move more quickly)

chops 2 the jaws or mouth of an animal (as - The dog licked his chops.)

chopsticks two thin pieces of ivory, wood, etc., used in Far Eastern countries for eating food

choral, chorale see **chorus**

chord *(say cord)* a number of musical notes which make a harmonious sound when they are all played together at the same time

chorister see **chorus**

chorus *(say corus)* a group of singers or dancers: the part of a

song that is repeated after each verse (the refrain) □ to sing or say together
choral *(say coral)* sung by a group or choir (as, a choral service)
chorale *(say coral)* a simple hymn tune, sung in unison
chorister *(say corister)* a singer in a choir

chose, chosen see **choose**

christen to give a first name to by baptism in the name of Christ (as, to christen a baby *Jane*)

Christian a follower of Jesus Christ

Christianity the religion based on the teachings of Jesus Christ

Christmas an annual festival held to celebrate the birth of Jesus Christ, held on December 25
Christmas Eve December 24

chrome *(say croem)*, **chromium** *(say croemium)* a silvery, shiny metal which does not rust or tarnish easily

chronic *(say cronic)* continuing for a long time (usually said of an illness)

chronicle *(say cronicl)* a record of events, arranged in the order in which they occurred, from the earliest date to the latest

chronological *(say cronological)* arranged in the order in which events happened

chronometer *(say cronometer)* a very accurate time-measuring instrument

chrysalis *(say crissaliss)* the case or cocoon in which an insect is enclosed before it turns into a moth or butterfly; the stage in the development of the insect in which it is enclosed in a cocoon

chrysanthemum *(say crissanthemum)* a flower with many brightly-coloured curving petals

chubby plump and rounded

chuck to pat gently under the chin: to throw or toss

chuckle to laugh quietly

chum a close friend or companion
chummy friendly

chunk a thick piece of anything (such as bread or wood)

church a building for public worship
churchwarden a person (not a clergyman) who looks after the interests of a particular church or parish
churchyard the burial ground around a church

churlish (of behaviour) rude, surly

churn a machine which shakes up milk or cream to produce butter; a large metal container for milk □ to stir or shake strongly (as - The wind churned the waves into foam.)

chute *(say shoot)* a sloping channel used to slide coal, water, rubbish, etc. down to a lower level: a short word for parachute

chutney a highly spiced thick preserve (usually eaten with curry)

cider an alcoholic drink made from apple juice

cigar tobacco leaves rolled tightly together (for smoking)

cigarette finely cut tobacco rolled in thin paper (for smoking)

cinder partly burned wood or coal that glows without flames
cinders ashes left when a fire has burned out

cine-camera *(say sinee-camera)* a camera for taking moving pictures

cinema a building for showing moving pictures; the art or business of making moving pictures

cinnamon the bark of an Asian tree, used for making a kind of spice

cipher 1 *(say siefer)* a zero or nought (0)

cipher 2 a secret way of writing that can only be understood by a person who knows the cipher (what the letters and numbers really stand for)

circle a perfectly round closed curve (Every point on the curve is the same distance from the centre.); a ring: a group of people who have a common interest (as, a poetry circle)

circuit *(say serkit)* a moving around as in a circle; a circling (as, the earth's circuit round the sun); a round of travelling from place to place in the course of one's business, profession, etc.: the path of an electric current
circuitous *(say serkewitus)* roundabout; not direct

circular 1 round; going round in a circle

circular 2 a notice, advertisement, etc. sent to a number of people

circulate to move round in a regular path or course (as - Blood circulates round the body.): to spread or pass around (as - Money circulates.)
circulation the moving around of something in a regular path (as, circulation of air in a room): the distribution or sales of books, newspapers, magazines, etc.; the total numbers of such items sold

circumference the outside line of a circle; the distance round something

circumnavigate to sail round (especially to circumnavigate the world)

circumscribe to draw a line round

circumstance a fact or an event
circumstances the conditions, time, place, etc. that could affect or cause an event (as - In the difficult circumstances he could not avoid the accident.): the state of one's finances (as - The family's poor circumstances were due to the father's unemployment.)

circus a travelling show with acrobats, performing animals, clowns, etc. (often held in a circular tent or arena): a round open space with streets leading to it and around it (as, Piccadilly Circus in London)

cistern a tank for storing water or other liquid

citadel a fortress in or near a city

cite to quote (as, from a book): to summon a person to appear in court

citizen a member of a state, who is subject to its government and laws
citizenship the status, rights and duties of being a citizen

citrus fruit grapefruit, oranges, lemons, limes, etc.

city a large important town; the business centre of a large town (as, the City of London)
cities the plural of city

civic of, or having to do with, citizenship
civics the study of the rights and duties of citizenship

civil of the state or community; relating to citizens; ordinary (not relating to the clergy, armed forces or other special groups): polite
civil engineer see **engineer**
civility courtesy; politeness
civilian an ordinary citizen (not a member of the armed forces) □ having to do with a civilian
civil liberties the rights of a citizen of a country
civil service the many, various branches of government service except the armed forces
civil war war between citizens of the same country

civilization an advanced stage of social and cultural development in a community or country; the opposite of barbarism
civilized not savage or barbaric; educated in the arts, sciences, etc.

claim to demand as a right; to state or assert (as - He claimed that he knew the truth of the matter.) □ a demand for something as a right (as - He put in a claim for his share of the treasure.); a piece of land allotted

to a prospector or miner

clairvoyant having the power to see things not present to the senses; having unusual insight □ a person with clairvoyant powers

clam a shellfish with a soft body and a hinged double shell

clamber to climb or crawl upwards with difficulty

clammy damp, sticky, and usually cold

clamour a loud outcry; loud and continued noise
clamorous noisy; making loud demands

clamp a device of iron, wood, etc. used to fasten or hold things together □ to fasten with a clamp
to clamp down on to stop (an activity); to suppress

clan a tribe or group of families under a single chieftain (usually having the same surname)
clannish loyal to and mainly interested in the affairs of the clan or group to which one belongs

clang a loud, deep ringing sound (as, of large bells)

clank a metallic ringing sound, duller than a clang (for example, the sound made by heavy chains)

clap to strike the palms of the hands together in applause; to strike or thrust together; to put or place with some force (as, to clap one's hand on a friend's shoulder, etc.) □ a burst of loud noise (as, a clap of thunder)
clapper the tongue or striker of a bell
clapping applause with the hands

claret a kind of red wine

clarify to make or become clear

clarinet a wind instrument shaped like a long tube with a single reed in the mouthpiece

clarity see **clear**

clash a loud noise (usually a metallic sound, as of weapons): a conflict (of armies) or disagreement (a clash of opinions)

clasp to hold tightly □ a hinged fastening for a brooch, buckle, etc.

class a group of children or older students meeting together regularly for instruction; a group of people or things of the same kind; a group or division of people according to income, social standing, etc.; a division according to achievement or quality (as, first-class or excellent work, first-class postal service, etc.) □ to place in a class
classify to arrange people or things in classes
classification the act of classifying; arrangement of things in order (as, library books, animals, etc.)
classmate a member of the same class in school
classroom a room in which classes are held

classic of high standard or excellence (as - His behaviour was a classic example of courage.); relating to ancient Greek or Roman times □ a book, musical composition, etc. considered to be of a very high standard
classical of first-class excellence (especially in music, literature, etc.); relating to ancient Greek and Roman times (as, an example of classical architecture); following the style of classics in literature, music, etc.
classics classical literature (especially that of ancient Greece and Rome)

clatter a rattling noise (as, the clatter of dishes, etc.)

clause a part of a sentence containing its own subject and predicate (for example - _Although it was raining we decided to go for a walk._ The underlined words form a clause.); a separate part of a will or document

claw the sharp curved nail on the foot of an animal or bird; the pincer-like end of the leg of a lobster, crab, etc. □ to scratch

clay soft sticky earth that becomes hard when baked

clean without dirt or dust; pure or innocent; neat and well shaped (as, The yacht has clean lines.) □ to make clean □ entirely, completely (as - He got clean away.)
cleanly _(say cleenly)_ in a clean way □ _(say clenly)_ clean; anxious or careful to keep clean
cleanliness _(say clenliness)_ the habit of being clean
cleanse _(say clenz)_ to make clean or pure

clear bright, unclouded (as, a clear blue sky); free from obstruction or difficulty (as, a clear road ahead); plain to see, obvious (as - It is clear that he is not coming now.); distinct, not confusing (as, clear handwriting) □ to make clear; to stand or move away from (as, Clear the road!, Clear out!): to pass by or over without touching (as - The horse cleared the fence easily.)
clearly certainly; without doubt
clearness, clarity the state or condition of being clear
clearance the act of clearing: the amount of space between two objects (so that they do not collide or touch)
clearing an area of land cleared of trees and bushes

cleave 1 to split; to divide or separate by force; to chop
cleaver a butcher's meat chopper
cleft 1, clove(n) 1 having been split or divided (as - The rock was cleft [or cloven] apart.)
cleft 2 a split, crack or fissure
cloven hoof a hoof (like those of cows, sheep, goats, etc.) which is divided

cleave 2 to stick to; to remain faithful to

clef one of the musical symbols (𝄢 𝄞) placed at the beginning of the 5-lined staff (or stave) in written music to define the pitch

clench to close tightly (as, to clench one's teeth or fists)

clergy the ministers of the Christian religion
clergyman one of the clergy; an ordained minister
clerical 1 relating to or of the clergy

clerical see **clergy** and **clerk**

clerk a person employed in an office, bank, etc. to attend to letters, filing, accounts, etc.; an official in a court of law or local government (as, Town Clerk)
clerical 2 relating to a clerk or the work of a clerk (as, a clerical error)

clever quick to understand and to learn; skilful

click a short snapping sound (as, the click of a door latch)

client someone who consults and employs the services of a professional person (such as a doctor or lawyer); a customer
clientèle (say cleeontel) a group of clients (as, the clientèle of a restaurant)

cliff a high, steep rock-face

climate the weather conditions of a region, country, etc. (such as the average temperature, rainfall and sunshine over a period of time)
climatic relating to climate

climax the most exciting part (of a book, adventure, film, etc.); the highest point

climb (say clime) to go up or down (usually with some difficulty, often clinging on with hands and feet); to grow upwards (of a plant) holding on to something (such as a trellis, wire, etc.); to go up (as, an aeroplane, etc.)

clinch to settle or confirm (an argument, an agreement): to fasten securely (as, to drive a nail into a board and bend the point over) □ a boxing term (two boxers holding each other closely so that a full-arm blow cannot be struck)

cling to hold on tightly; to stick close to (as, to cling to one's family); to refuse to be parted from (as, to cling to a belief)

clinic a place (usually for outpatients at a hospital) where medical treatment and advice are given (as, a foot clinic, etc.)

clink a small ringing sound, as when coins or glasses are touched gently together

clinker a hard cinder formed in furnaces

clip 1 a fastener (usually small and made of metal) for holding papers, etc. together □ to fasten with a clip

clip 2 to cut or trim with scissors, shears, etc.
clipping the act of cutting or trimming □ the thing clipped off

clipper a large fast ship with many sails

cloak a loose outer garment without sleeves (usually longer than a cape): something that disguises or covers up (as - The thieves worked at night under the cloak of darkness.)
cloakroom a place where outer garments, hats, umbrellas, etc. may be left for a time: a washroom or lavatory

clock an instrument for measuring time
clockwise moving in the direction that clock hands move
clockwork the machinery that makes a clock go; any similar machinery that works regularly and smoothly

clod a thick lump of earth: a stupid fellow
clodhopper a dull, rustic lout

clog to hinder or block up (as - The drains were clogged by leaves.) □ a shoe with a thick sole of wood, cork, etc.

cloister a covered arcade or walk in a monastery, cathedral, convent, college, etc.

close 1 (say cloess) hot and stuffy: near in time or place; near or intimate (as, a close friend): secretive: shut up or shut in with no opening
close-up a photograph or film

taken very near to the person or thing being photographed

close call, close shave a narrow escape

close-fisted stingy; miserly

close 2 *(say cloze)* to shut; to end (as, to close a meeting); to complete (as, to close a bargain) □ the end, the conclusion
closed circuit an electrical circuit with no break in it
to close down to end; to stop

closet a small private room; a recess or a small room (usually adjoining a large room)

clot a mass of a soft or fluid substance, thickened and stuck together (especially of blood) □ to form into clots

cloth woven material from which garments, coverings, etc. are made; a piece of this material (as, a tablecloth)
clothe to put clothes on; to dress or provide clothes
clothes garments; coverings for the bed (bedclothes)
clothing clothes, garments

cloud a mass of tiny particles of water or ice floating in the atmosphere; any similar floating mass (as, a cloud of dust); a great number (as, a cloud of mosquitoes) □ to cover with clouds; to darken or make gloomy
cloudy darkened with clouds; gloomy, not clear or transparent
cloudburst a sudden, violent downpour of rain

clout a blow □ to strike hard (especially with the open hand)

clove(n) 1 see **cleave 1**

clove 2 the dried flower bud of the clove tree, used as spice

clover a wild plant with leaves (usually) in three rounded parts, used for fodder
cloverleaf a traffic arrangement whereby one road crosses above another and short roads connecting the two make the pattern of a four-leaved clover

clown a person who amuses or entertains others with jokes, tricks, and amusing antics (usually in a circus, wearing funny clothes and make-up); a person who behaves foolishly and without any dignity

cloy to weary by too much (especially of sweetness)

club 1 a heavy stick; a bat or stick used in certain games (such as a golf club) □ to beat with a stick or club

club 2 a group of people who meet together regularly for some purpose; the place where these people meet □ to join together for some purpose

cluck the short call of a hen to her chicks; any similar sound

clue anything that helps towards the solution of a problem, a mystery or a puzzle

clump 1 a number of plants or trees growing close together

clump 2 to walk heavily, with a thumping noise

clumsy awkward; not graceful; not skilful
clumsiness awkwardness; lack of skill

cluster a bunch; a group (as, a cluster of flowers)

clutch to grasp or grip tightly with the hands □ a device used for connecting and disconnecting two moving parts of a machine (as in a motor car)

clutter a confused collection of things; an untidy heap

coach 1 a large, horse-drawn four-wheeled carriage; a railway carriage; a large motor vehicle for long journeys

coach 2 a tutor who teaches pupils privately to prepare them for examinations, etc.; a trainer of athletes (as, a football coach)

coagulate *(say co-agulate)* to thicken into a mass or clot (as - Blood from a cut coagulates.)

coal a solid black mineral used as fuel; pieces of this mineral ready for burning
coal face the exposed surface of the coal in a mine

coal mine the mine or pit from which coal is dug

coalesce *(say co-aless)* to grow together; to unite
coalition a union or alliance (particularly of political parties or states)

coarse rough; rude; of poor quality, texture, etc.; made up of large particles (for example, coarse sand)

coast the edge of the land next to the sea □ to sail along or near a coast: to ride or drive a vehicle without using power
coastal on, near or of a coast (as, coastal plains)
coaster a ship that trades along a coast
coastguard an official body of men who keep watch along the coast for smugglers, shipwrecks, etc.

coat an outer garment with sleeves: any outer covering of wool, fur, etc. (as, a dog's coat, a coat of paint) □ to cover with a coat or layer
coating a covering

coax to persuade or try to persuade in a gentle way

cob a strong, short-legged horse: a male swan: a large hazelnut (also called cobnut): the inedible inner part of an ear of maize (usually called corncob)

cobalt a hard silvery-white metal similar to nickel, with compounds that produce a blue colouring substance

cobble 1, cobblestone a rounded stone used in paving

cobble 2 to mend or patch (especially boots and shoes)
cobbler a person who mends boots and shoes

cobra a poisonous snake which swells out its neck so that it looks like a hood

cobweb the fine network made by a spider to trap insects; anything flimsy or of flimsy texture

cocaine a drug used to deaden pain

cochineal a scarlet dye

cock 1 the male of birds (especially the domestic fowl)
cockerel a young cock
cockpit (formerly) a pit or enclosed space where gamecocks fought: (nowadays) a compartment in an aircraft for the pilot, in a racing car for the driver, etc.
cocksure over-confident, too sure of oneself
cocky boastful; conceited

cock 2 the hammer in the lock of a gun: a valve for regulating the flow of a liquid or gas; a tap □ to draw back the cock of a gun; to tilt (as, one's head or hat)

cock 3 a small conical heap of hay

cockade a rosette, knot of ribbon, etc. worn in the hat as a badge

cockatoo a parrot with a large crest

cocker a breed of (spaniel) dog

cockle a small edible shellfish with a hinged heart-shaped shell
cockleshell the shell of a cockle; a small, fragile boat

cockney a Londoner (especially a person born within the sound of Bow Bells in the East End of London)

cockpit see **cock 1**

cockroach a household pest, a beetle-like insect that comes out at night for food

cocktail a mixed drink containing alcohol

cocoa the seed of the cacao tree, from which a powder is made; a drink made from this powder (The same powder is used to make chocolate.)

coconut a large nut (from a palm tree) that contains a white edible lining and a clear liquid
coconut matting matting made from the husk of a coconut

cocoon the silky sheath or case made around themselves by many kinds of insect larvae (such as silkworms) and by spiders for their eggs: see also **chrysalis**

cod, codfish a large edible North Atlantic sea fish

coddle to pamper; to treat with gentle care (as, to coddle an invalid)

code a system of letters, numbers or other symbols which conveys messages (as, the Morse code); a set of rules (usually unwritten) for standards of behaviour (as, the code of a gentleman); a collection or system of laws or rules (as, the Highway Code)

co-education the education of children or older students of both sexes in the same school or college

coerce (say co-*erss*) to compel, to force
coercion control by force

co-exist to exist together with, or at the same time
peaceful co-existence the state of living peacefully alongside people who hold different opinions from oneself (especially of countries which have different systems of government)

coffee a hot drink made from the ground-up beans of the coffee tree (which grows in some tropical countries)

coffer a chest or box for holding money or treasure

coffin a box or chest for a dead body

cog a tooth on the rim of a wheel used in machinery
cogwheel a wheel with teeth

cogitate (say co*jitate*) to consider a thing carefully; to ponder

cognac (say *conyak*) French brandy (so called after the town of Cognac)

coherent clear and logical (as - He gave a coherent account of what had happened.)

coiffure (say *kwaffure*) the style or way in which a person's hair is dressed

coil to wind in rings or circles (as, to coil a rope) □ one of these rings or circles

coin a piece of metal money □ to make metal into money (as in a mint); to make or invent a new word or phrase

coincide (say co-*inside*) to happen at the same time; to occupy the same position; to agree; to be the same as
coincidence (say co-*insidence*) an accidental happening that occurs at exactly the same time as another event (but is surprising because it is unexpected)

coke fuel made from coal that has been heated to a high temperature so as to remove the gases

colander, cullender a bowl-shaped strainer with holes round the sides and bottom (used in cookery for draining off liquids from vegetables, etc.)

cold the opposite of hot; of low temperature: unfriendly, with no warmth of feeling □ lack of heat; low temperature; cold weather: an illness (usually not very serious) with sneezing, coughing, etc.
cold-blooded having a lower temperature than the human body (as, fish and reptiles); (of people) cruel; lacking in human feelings towards others
cold feet lack of courage
in cold blood on purpose; deliberately

colic a severe stomach-ache

collaborate to work together on the same piece of work; to co-operate treacherously with the enemy
collaborator a person who works in combination with another (as, a collaborator in writing a book); a person who associates treacherously with an enemy

collapse to fall or break down □ a falling or breaking down; a failure (as of a business firm)
collapsible able to be folded up (as, a collapsible chair)

collar something worn round the neck; the part of a garment that goes round the neck (as, a shirt collar)

collar-bone either of the two bones joining the breast-bone and shoulder-blade

colleague a fellow-worker

collect to bring together; to gather
collected composed or calm
collection the act of collecting; money that has been collected; a number of things collected (as, a collection of coins).
collective acting together; combined
collector someone who collects tickets, money, stamps, etc.

college a large group of students and lecturers in a university (as, King's College Cambridge); a learned society (as, the Royal College of Surgeons)

collide to come together with great force; to clash
collision a crashing together with force

collie a Scottish breed of sheep-dog

collier a coal miner; a ship that carries coal
colliery a coal mine

colloquial used in informal everyday conversation, but not generally used in writing or in formal speech

colon 1 a punctuation mark (:)

colon 2 the greater part of the large intestine

colonel (say kernel) an army officer who has command of a regiment

colony a group of people (usually of one nationality) who settle together in another country; the settlement so formed
colonial an inhabitant of a colony □ having to do with a colony
colonize to establish a colony

colosseum, coliseum a large place of entertainment (especially, a large amphitheatre, now in ruins, in Rome)

colossus a gigantic statue or person
colossal of giant size

colour the appearance of an object when light falls on it (as, red, green, blue, yellow); paint □ to paint
coloured having colour; not white-skinned
colour blind unable to distinguish certain colours
colourful full of colour; vivid
off colour faded; not feeling at one's best

colt a young horse

columbine a kind of wild plant with blue flowers; a similar garden plant with larger flowers of many colours

column an upright pillar (usually to support or adorn a building); a vertical row of figures; a vertical division of a page of print (as, the columns of a newspaper); a line of soldiers

coma a long-lasting unconscious state (like a deep sleep)

comb (say coam) a toothed instrument for separating and cleaning hair, wool, flax, etc.: the fleshy crest with toothlike points on the heads of the domestic fowl and some other birds □ to arrange or clean with a comb

combat to fight or struggle against □ a struggle

combine to join together; to unite
combination a union of things or people
combine-harvester a machine that both harvests and threshes grain

combustible liable to catch fire □ anything that will catch fire
combustion burning

come to move towards this place; the opposite of go; to draw near or to reach; to amount to (as – The bill comes to £1.50.)

comedy an amusing play or film
comedian an actor who takes comic parts
comic having to do with comedy; causing laughter □ a picture paper with drawings that tell a funny story or adventure
comical funny

comely pleasing; graceful

comet a heavenly body, which looks like a star with a shining tail

comfort ease; a sense of well-being; quiet enjoyment □ to ease someone who is in trouble or in pain; to soothe; to cheer someone up
   comfortable in comfort; at ease; giving comfort (as, a comfortable armchair)

comic, comical see **comedy**

comma a punctuation mark (,)

command to order; to be in charge of: to look over (as - The window commands a fine view.)
   commandant an officer who has command of a place or of a body of soldiers
   commandeer to seize provisions, etc. for an army
   commander someone who commands; an officer below the rank of captain in the navy or air force
   commandment a command (especially of God, as, *The Ten Commandments*)
   commando a unit of the British army specially trained for difficult tasks; a soldier serving in such a unit

commemorate to celebrate the memory of an event
   commemoration a celebration in memory of an event

commence to begin
   commencement the beginning

commend to praise
   commendable praiseworthy
   commendation praise; the act of commending

comment a remark; an explanatory note □ to make remarks; to write explanatory notes
   commentary a series of comments
   commentator someone who makes or gives a running commentary (for example, in a broadcast of a football match)

commerce the interchange of goods between countries or businesses; trade on a large scale
   commercial having to do with commerce or large-scale trading

commiserate to feel or express sympathy with another person

commission, commissionaire, commissioner see **commit**

commit to do something, usually wrong or unfortunate (as, to commit a crime, or a blunder); to entrust or consign
   commission the act of committing; something committed: a document giving authority: a fee paid to an agent: a group of people (as, a Royal Commission) appointed to investigate something □ to appoint someone to perform some task or duty
   commissionaire a doorkeeper in uniform
   commissioner someone commissioned to carry out some task or duty; a member of a commission
   commitment an obligation or a promise
   committee a number of people selected to attend to some special business (as, a local committee on housing problems)

commodious roomy; comfortable

commodity something useful; an article of trade (Tea, cotton and rubber are commodities.)

commodore an officer above the rank of captain in the navy and the air force

common shared by many; often happening or often seen; usual; of little value; ordinary; vulgar □ an open piece of ground used in common by the people of a town or parish
   commoner anyone who is not a noble
   common law the unwritten law based on customs
   commonplace very ordinary or uninteresting □ a common remark
   commonwealth the whole body of the people: a government in which the power rests with the people; an association of states (as, the British Commonwealth)

commotion a disturbance; an excited action; a fuss

commune to talk together □ a small division of a country (especially in France)
communal of a community; shared by many
communism a system of government under which all industry and commerce is owned by the state and there is no private property (as in Russia, China, etc.)
communist one who believes in communism □ having to do with communism

communicate to make known; to send information (as, to communicate by post)
communication a means of conveying information; a piece of information
communicative inclined to give information; not reserved (as, a communicative or chatty neighbour)
communion fellowship (especially religious)
Holy Communion the celebration of the Lord's Supper

communism, communist see **commune**

community a group of people living in one place

commuter someone who travels daily to work in a city from his home in the suburbs or country

compact closely packed or fitted together; firm □ a small flat case for face powder

companion a person who accompanies another; an associate; a friend
companionable pleasant to have as a companion
companionship the state of being companions; fellowship

company a group of people; a business belonging to a group of people; the crew of a ship (a ship's company); part of a regiment

compare to set things together to see how much alike or how different they are (as, to compare the heights of a group of children); to show that one thing is

similar to another (as - He compared his friend's courage to that of a lion.)
comparable similar; worthy of being compared with
comparative involving comparison with something else (as - There is comparative quiet in the side street, where there is much less traffic than in the main street.)
comparison the act of comparing

compartment a separate part or division (as, of a railway carriage)

compass an instrument, with a magnetized needle, which is used to find directions

compasses an instrument with two movable legs, for drawing circles, etc.

compassion sorrow felt for another person; mercy
compassionate sympathetic; pitying

compatible able to agree with; consistent with

compatriot a fellow-countryman

compel to make or force someone to do something

compensate to make up to someone for loss or damage that he has suffered
compensation something given (often a payment) to make up for someone's loss or damage

compère *(say compair)* someone who introduces the different acts of an entertainment programme □ to act as compère for a stage or broadcast show

compete to strive with others to gain something (for example, to compete in a race for a prize)
competition the act of competing; a contest
competitive having to do with, or involving, competition
competitor anyone who competes; a rival

competent capable; skilled; properly qualified (as, a competent legal adviser)

compile to collect together facts or materials from many sources (usually other books) in order to make a new book; to collect items of information and list them
compilation the act of compiling; the thing compiled

complacent satisfied with oneself; showing satisfaction
complacency self-satisfaction; calm pleasure

complain to grumble; to tell someone that something is unfair, wrong, or painful
complaint a statement of one's trouble or sorrow; an ailment

complement that which completes or fills up (as - The aeroplane has a complement of about 100 passengers.); the difference between a given angle and a right angle (as - The complement of $30°$ is $60°$ since $90° — 30° = 60°$.)
complementary completing; together making up a whole, or a right angle

complete whole; with nothing missing; finished □ to finish; to make whole
completion the act of finishing

complex composed of many parts; not simple; difficult

complexion colour or look of the skin (especially of the face)

compliance see comply

complicate to make complex or difficult
complicated complex or difficult to understand
complication a complicated state; a new circumstance making a situation more difficult

complicity the state of being an accomplice in wrong-doing (as - The police proved his complicity in the robbery.)

compliment an expression of praise or flattery; an expression of formal greeting (as, *with my compliments* accompanying a message or present)
complimentary praising; flattering; given free (as, a complimentary ticket to the theatre)

comply to agree to do what someone orders or wishes
compliance acting in accordance with someone's orders or wishes
compliant prepared to comply; yielding; obliging

component forming one of the parts of a whole □ a single part (as - The cathode ray tube is a major component of a television set.)

compose to form something by putting parts together (as, to compose music, or a poem): to set in order or at rest (as, to compose one's thoughts)
composed quiet; calm
composite made up of parts (as - The daisy is a composite flower.)
composition the act of composing; the thing composed (as, a musical composition or a written composition)
compost a mixture (especially for gardener's manure)
composure calmness

compound 1 a substance made up of a number of different elements (for example - The chemical compounds called carbohydrates contain the elements carbon, hydrogen and oxygen.) □ made up of a number of parts; not simple □ to mix or combine

compound 2 an enclosure round a house or factory (especially in some Eastern countries)

comprehend to understand: to include
comprehensible able to be understood
comprehensive taking in, or including, much
comprehensive school a school which combines the features of various types of secondary education
comprehension the act or power of understanding

compress *(say compress)* to press together □ *(say compress)* a pad or dressing to put pressure on a wound or inflamed part of the body

compression the act of compressing; the state of being compressed (as, the compression of the petrol/air mixture in a motor car engine)

comprise to include; to consist of

compromise *(say compromize)* a settlement of differences in which both sides yield something □ to settle differences by yielding something on both sides: to bring under suspicion by some action (as - He was compromised by his rash behaviour.)

compulsion a strong impulse; the act of compelling
compulsory requiring to be done or carried out; obligatory

compute to calculate
computer an electronic machine which carries out many stages of calculations at a very high speed
computation the act of computing; calculation

comrade a close companion

concave hollow or curved inwards (as, the inner side of a spoon); the opposite of convex
concavity the opposite of convexity; a hollow

conceal to hide; to keep secret

concede to admit; to yield (as, to concede a point in an argument)
concession the act of conceding; something given up

conceit *(say conseet)* too high an opinion of oneself
conceited thinking too highly of oneself

conceive *(say conseev)* to form in the mind; to imagine: to become pregnant
conceivable able to be imagined
conception 1 the act of becoming pregnant; fertilization of an ovum; see also **concept**

concentrate to bring to the centre or one place; to direct all one's thoughts on to one thing; to devote all one's energies to one purpose; to make stronger;

the opposite of dilute □ anything concentrated (especially animal feeding stuff)
concentration a bringing together in one place; the state of being concentrated

concentric having the same point for centre (as, concentric circles)

concept a general idea about something
conception 2 the act of forming an idea in the mind; see also **conceive**

concern to have to do with; to make uneasy; to interest or trouble oneself (as, to be concerned about a friend's illness)
concerned anxious
concerning about

concert *(say consert)* a musical entertainment □ *(say consert)* to arrange by agreement
concerted *(say conserted)* arranged or planned beforehand

concertina a small musical wind instrument, with bellows and keys

concerto *(say conchertoe)* a musical composition for a solo instrument (usually a piano or violin) accompanied by an orchestra

concession see **concede**

conciliate to win over someone as a friend; to reconcile
conciliatory intended, or showing a desire, to conciliate

concise brief; in few words

conclude to bring to an end; to finish; to reach a decision
conclusion the end; the result or decision finally reached

concoct to make up (as, to concoct a story, or to concoct a meal, using a mixture of things)
concoction something concocted

concord agreement

concrete a mixture of cement, gravel, etc. used in building □ made of concrete; solid

concur to agree
concurrence agreement to do

something; coincidence

concurrent agreeing; coming or existing together

concussion a violent shock or shaking; unconsciousness caused by a heavy blow, especially on the head

condemn to sentence to punishment; to blame; to declare unfit for use (as, condemned houses)
condemnation the state of being condemned
condemned cell a cell for a prisoner under sentence of death

condense to make smaller in volume or size; to compress; to reduce a vapour to liquid (as, to condense steam by cooling to form water)
condensation the act of condensing; the liquid formed from a vapour
condenser a device for changing a vapour into liquid; a device for collecting and storing electricity (as, the condenser in a radio set)

condescend to act towards a person as if one is better than he is
condescension a patronizing attitude

condiment a seasoning for food (for example, salt, pepper, vinegar)

condition the state in which any person or thing is (as, a second-hand bike in good condition); something that must happen if something else is to be done (as - She was promised a new dress on condition that she practised the piano.); a term in an agreement
conditional depending on certain conditions being fulfilled

condole to express sympathy with a person for his sorrow
condolence an expression of sympathy with another's sorrow

condone to forgive; to overlook an offence

conducive helping, or tending towards (as - Smoking is not conducive to good health.)

conduct *(say conduct)* to lead or guide; to direct (as, to conduct an orchestra); to transmit (as, an electric current conducted by copper wires); to behave □ *(say conduct)* the act or method of conducting; behaviour (as, good or bad conduct)
conduction transmission (usually of heat or electricity)

conductor a person or thing that leads or transmits; a director of an orchestra; a person who sells tickets in a bus, etc.

conduit a channel or pipe to carry water, etc.

cone a solid shape which is circular at the bottom and pointed at the top (rather like a clown's hat); anything cone-shaped (for example, a fir cone, an ice cream cone)
conical cone-shaped

confectionery all kinds of sweets; pastries and cakes (flour confectionery); the business of a confectioner
confectioner someone who makes or sells confectionery

confederate an ally; an accomplice □ allied; joined by a treaty
confederacy an alliance or league
confederation a grouping (especially of states, joined together in a league)

confer to give in a formal way (as, to confer an honour): to consult together; to carry on a discussion
conference a meeting of many people for a discussion

confess to own up to something; to make a confession
confession the admission of a fault or crime

confetti bits of coloured paper thrown at weddings and carnivals

confide to tell secrets or private thoughts; to entrust to someone's care
confidence trust or belief; a secret; self-reliance
confident trusting firmly; very

sure

confidential not to be told to others

confiding trusting

confine to keep within limits (as - The firemen confined the blaze to a small area.); to shut up

confinement the state of being shut up or imprisoned

confirm to strengthen; to make sure; to admit to full membership of a church

confirmation a making sure; a proof; the church ceremony in which persons are confirmed

confirmed settled in a habit or way of life (as, a confirmed bachelor)

confiscate to take away (as a punishment)

conflagration a great fire

conflict (say _conflict_) a struggle or contest □(say _conflict_) to contradict each other (as - The two accounts of the event conflicted.)

conflicting not in agreement; contradictory

confluence a flowing together; a meeting place (especially of rivers)

conform to follow the way of most other people (for example, in religion, in behaviour, etc.); to be similar to

conformation form or shape; structure

conformity agreement with; likeness; compliance

confound to confuse; to surprise greatly

confront to meet or bring face to face

confuse to mix up (especially to mistake one thing for another): to perplex

confusion a mixing up; disorder; embarrassment

congeal to freeze; to become hard by cooling

congenial having the same tastes and interests (as, a congenial companion); pleasant (as, a congenial occupation)

congestion an overfullness or accumulation (as, of blood in one part of the body, or of traffic at a road junction); overcrowding

congested overcrowded; having too much blood in a part of the body

conglomeration a collection; a confused mixture of things

congratulate to express joy to a person for any success he has had; to think oneself lucky (as - The prisoner congratulated himself on his escape.)

congratulations expressions of joy (spoken or written) for a person's success

congratulatory expressing joy for someone's success

congregation people gathered together (especially in a church)

congress an assembly of delegates and people with special interests (for example, in politics or medicine)

congruent coinciding exactly (as, two congruent triangles)

conical see cone

conifer a cone-bearing tree (such as the fir)

conjecture an opinion based on slight evidence; a guess

conjunction a union; a word that connects two sentences, phrases or words (_and_ and _but_ are conjunctions)

conjure (say _cunjer_) to do tricks that seem magical

conjuror someone who does conjuring tricks

conker a horse chestnut

connect to join or fasten together; to link (as when a person's telephone is connected with another number)

connection, connexion something that connects; a connecting train, plane, etc. (as - We missed our connection.)

conning-tower the place on a warship or submarine from which steering orders are given

connive to take no notice of some wrong-doing (as, to connive at

cheating someone)
connivance silent agreement

connoisseur *(say conissur)* an expert; a critical judge (as, a connoisseur of wine)

conquer to gain by force; to overcome
conqueror someone who conquers
conquest the act of conquering; something conquered

conscience *(say conshens)* a person's inward sense of what is right or wrong
conscientious *(say conshee-enshus)* careful; taking care to do what is right

conscious *(say conshus)* aware of oneself and surroundings; able to hear, see, think, etc.: deliberate (as, making a conscious effort)
consciousness the state of the mind when awake (as - The patient recovered consciousness soon after the accident.)

conscript a person called up to serve in the armed forces
conscription the compulsory enrolling of persons for military service

consecrate to set apart for holy use

consecutive following one after the other in order (6, 7, 8 and 9 are consecutive numbers.)

consent to agree □ agreement (as - She gave her consent.)
consensus a general agreement (of opinion)

consequence something which follows as a result (of an action, etc.); importance (as, a small mistake of no consequence)
consequent following as a direct result
consequential *(say consikwenshal)* following as a result (usually an indirect one)

conserve to keep from damage or loss
conservation preservation (as, the conservation of wild life in Africa)
conservative tending to dislike

any great or sudden changes
conservatory a glass-house (usually heated) for plants

consider to think; to think about carefully
considerable fairly large or important
considerate thoughtful about others
consideration careful thought about something or about other persons; a reason to be kept in mind (as - The distances from school and place of work are important considerations when moving house.)
considering taking into account (as - The secondhand bike is not dear considering its good condition.)

consign *(say consine)* to hand over for delivery; to entrust
consignment a load of goods (as, a consignment by rail or by air)

consist to be made of
consistency thickness or firmness (as, the consistency of modelling clay)
consistent unchanging; not contradictory

console to comfort
consolation the giving of comfort

consolidate to strengthen; to unite

consonant a sound of a language which is not a vowel (Consonants are represented by letters other than **a, e, i, o, u.**)

conspicuous clearly seen or noticeable

conspire to plot together
conspiracy a plot by a group of people
conspirator someone who takes part in a conspiracy

constable a policeman
constabulary a police force

constant unchanging; faithful
constancy unchangeableness; faithfulness

constellation a group of stars

consternation dismay; unpleasant

astonishment

constipation insufficient working of the bowels

constitute to form or make up (as - Children constituted the majority of the audience.)

constituency the area of the country, or the voters in that area, represented by a member of parliament (M.P.)

constituent a voter in a constituency; a necessary part □ helping to form or make up

constitution the form in which the parts of something are put together; the natural state of a person's body and mind (as, a fine constitution); the set of rules and laws by which a country is governed

constitutional having to do with the laws of a country (as, a person's constitutional rights) □ a short walk for the sake of one's health

constraint compulsion (as, to act under constraint); a keeping back of one's feelings (so that one acts in an embarrassed or unnatural way)

constrict to press together tightly; to compress

construct to build or put together

construction anything built; the arrangement of words in a sentence

constructive having to do with making (as distinct from breaking); helpful in a positive way (as, constructive criticism)

consul an agent who looks after his country's affairs in another country; a chief magistrate in ancient Rome

consular having to do with a consul

consult to ask someone for advice

consultant a person who gives professional advice

consultation the act of consulting

consume to eat up; to use; to destroy (as - The fire consumed the entire house.)

consumer anyone who eats or uses something; any member of the general public with money to spend

consumption the act of consuming; the opposite of production: a tuberculous infection (especially of the lungs)

contact a touch; a meeting □ to get in touch with

contagious spreading from person to person (as, a contagious disease)

contain to hold inside; to enclose

container a receptacle (such as a box, tin or bottle) for containing something

contaminate to pollute or make dirty

contemplate to look or gaze at; to expect or intend to do something (as - He contemplates going abroad.): to meditate

contemporary living in, or belonging to, the same period of time; present-day

contempt scorn; very low opinion

contemptible deserving contempt; despicable

contemptuous showing contempt; scornful

contend to fight; to state or maintain a belief

contention a dispute; a strong opinion

contentious quarrelsome

content *(say content)* to satisfy □ contentment

contented satisfied; quietly happy

contentment satisfaction; quiet happiness

contents *(say contents)* what is contained inside anything; the list of subjects or chapters in a book

contest *(say contest)* to fight over something □ *(say contest)* a fight; a struggle; a competition

continent one of the great divisions of the world's land surface (Europe; Africa; Asia; North and South America; Australia)

continental of a continent (as, a continental climate);

European

The Continent the mainland of Europe (not including the United Kingdom or Eire)

continue to keep on doing something; to begin again (as - We will continue our talk after lunch.)
continual keeping on; frequent
continuance the state of going on without interruption
continuation the prolonging; the next part of a story, etc.
continuity the state of being continuous
continuous connected without a break; non-stop

contort to twist or turn violently
contortion a violent twisting

contour an outline or shape
contour line a line drawn on a map through all the places having the same height above sea level (as, 1000 feet, or about 300 metres)

contraband smuggled or prohibited goods

contract 1 *(say contract)* to become or make smaller; to shrink
contraction a shortening or shrinking; abbreviation (as, Wilts for Wiltshire)

contract 2 *(say contract)* an agreement in writing □ *(say contract)* to promise in writing
contractor *(say contractor)* a person who contracts to do work or supply goods at an arranged price

contradict to deny; to say the opposite of something
contradiction a denial; a statement which contradicts another one
contradictory denying; affirming the opposite

contralto the lowest singing voice for women

contrary opposite □ the opposite

contrast the difference between two things which are being compared (as, the contrast in the styles of two artists) □ to compare two things closely so as to show how different they are; to show a marked difference

contravene to disregard or break (a law)
contravention the disregarding or breaking (of rules or laws)

contribute to give along with others (for example, to contribute money to a charity); to pay a share: to write for a magazine or newspaper (as - He contributed an article on sport.)
contribution something contributed

contrite very sorry for some action or behaviour

contrive to devise; to invent; to manage to do
contrivance a device (especially mechanical); the act of contriving

control to guide and keep in check (as, to control a vehicle); to have power or command over (as - The police controlled a crowd of hooligans.) □ restraint; power to check (as, control over one's temper); authority
control tower an airport building (with all-round visibility) from which instructions are given for take-off and landing

controversy an argument; a discussion of opposing views
controversial likely to cause argument; debatable

conundrum a riddle; a puzzling question

conurbation a very large built-up area composed of several towns (for example - There are conurbations centred on Birmingham and Glasgow.)

convalesce to regain health after an illness
convalescence the gradual return to health after an illness
convalescent someone who is convalescing □ having to do with convalescence (as, a convalescent home)

convection the passage of heat through a liquid or gas (especially air) by the setting up of currents through that medium
convector a convection, or

space, heater which heats the air passing through it and so warms the room in which it is placed

convene to call people to a meeting; to meet together

convenient easy to use or reach; suitable
convenience handiness; suitableness
at your convenience when it suits you

convent a house for nuns or monks (usually for nuns)

convention a custom, or accepted way of doing things: an assembly of delegates
conventional customary; formal

converge to come nearer together in position or values; to meet in a point

conversation talk between two or more people
conversational having to do with talk; fond of conversation
converse 1 *(say converse)* to talk

converse 2 see **convert** below

convert *(say convert)* to change from one thing into another (as, to convert an attic into a new room); to change someone's religion □ *(say convert)* a converted person
converse 2 *(say converse)* opposite □ the opposite
conversion a changing over; the act of making a convert
convertible able to be changed into something else □ a car with a roof (usually folding) which can be open or closed

convex curved on the outside (like the back of a spoon); the opposite of concave
convexity the outside shape of something that is rounded; the opposite of concavity

convey to carry; to transmit; to transfer property
conveyance the act of conveying; a vehicle of any kind

convict someone serving a prison sentence (usually a long one) □ *(say convict)* to find a person

guilty in court of a crime
conviction the act of convicting: a strong belief

convince to persuade a person that something is true without any doubt
convincing forcing one to believe (as, convincing evidence)

convivial festive; jovial

convoy a fleet of merchant ships, escorted by warships; a line of army lorries carrying supplies □ to escort for protection

convulse to shake violently (as, to convulse with laughter, grief, etc.)
convulsion a violent shaking; a violent disturbance

coo to make a sound like that of a dove; to murmur in a caressing tone □ a dovelike sound

cook to prepare and heat food for eating □ a person who cooks
cooker a stove on which food is heated
cookery the art or practice of cooking

cool slightly cold: calm; indifferent □ to make or grow cool
coolly calmly; in an indifferent manner

coop a wicker basket; a cage or box for fowls or small animals □ to shut in a coop; to confine in a small place

co-operate to work together for a purpose
co-operation a working together
co-operative society a trading company where customers share the profits

co-ordinate to make things work, or fit in, smoothly together

cope to contend, or struggle with successfully (as, to cope with a difficult job)

coping the top layer of stone (usually sloping) on a wall
coping-stone a stone that tops a wall

copious plentiful

copper a reddish-brown metal; the colour of the metal; a coin made of copper or a copper alloy

copperplate a polished copper plate for engraving; very neat, regular handwriting

coppice, copse a small wood of young trees (which are cut from time to time)

copra the dried kernel of the coconut (the source of coconut oil)

copy to make or do something like someone else; to imitate □ an imitation; a duplicate; a reproduction

copyright the legal right of one person only to publish, print or sell copies of his original work, or parts of it

coral a hard substance of various colours found on the bottom of some seas (It is formed in masses by the skeletons of tiny sea animals, sometimes building up into reefs and atolls.)

cord a thin rope

cordite a smokeless explosive (It looks like cord.)

cordial hearty; friendly □ a stimulating drink

cordon a line of guards or police to keep people from entering an area

corduroy a ribbed cloth with a velvety finish

core the inner part of anything (especially of fruit, such as the core of an apple) □ to remove the core

corgi a small Welsh dog

cork the outer bark of the cork tree (an oak found in Mediterranean countries); a stopper, usually of cork, for bottles, casks, etc. □ to stop with a cork

corkscrew a screw-like device for drawing corks from bottles □ shaped like a corkscrew

cormorant a large and voracious sea bird which dives for fish

corn 1 the seeds of grain plants, such as wheat, barley, maize and oats

corned beef cooked, canned beef

cornflakes a crisp breakfast cereal made from maize

cornflour finely ground flour (especially of maize)

cornflower a blue-flowered plant found in corn fields and also grown in gardens

corn 2 a small hard growth on a toe or foot

cornea the transparent membrane that covers the front of the eye

cornelian, carnelian a red semiprecious stone used in jewellery

corner the place where two converging lines or surfaces meet; an awkward position (as - He found himself in a corner.); a free kick from the corner flag in association football □ to drive into a corner from which escape is difficult

cornerstone a stone built into the foundation of a building at one corner; something on which much depends

cornet a brass instrument like a trumpet but more tapering; an ice cream in a cone-shaped wafer

cornice a continuous moulding round a ceiling (usually of plaster)

coronation the crowning of a king or queen

coroner an official whose chief duty is to hold inquiries into the causes of accidental or suspicious deaths

coronet a small crown worn by the nobility on special occasions

corporal 1 a non-commissioned officer ranking below a sergeant in the army or the air force

corporal 2 relating to the body (as, corporal punishment)

corporate joined together to form a united body or corporation; united (as, a corporate effort)

corporation a number of people (such as a town council) to whom legal power has been given to act collectively

corps (say core) a division of an

army; an organized group

corpse a dead body

corpulent fat

corpuscle *(say corpus'l)* a minute body or particle (For example, the blood contains millions of blood corpuscles.)

corral an enclosure for cattle or horses (especially in North America)

correct free from mistakes; right; true □ to put right; to mark for errors; to punish
correction the correcting of something; a correct answer substituted for a wrong one; a punishment

correspond to send letters: to be similar to
correspondence letters: similarity
correspondent the writer of a letter; a contributor (usually regular) to a newspaper, a news programme on radio or television, etc.

corridor a passageway (especially one off which rooms open)

corrode to eat away or be eaten away (as, rust and some chemicals corrode metal pipes, etc.)
corrosion the process of wearing or eating away

corrugated in folds, ridges or wrinkles
corrugated iron sheet iron which has been produced with a wavy surface for greater strength

corrupt to make another person dishonest (especially by bribing) □ dishonest; taking bribes; bad; rotten
corruption rottenness; bribery

corset a close-fitting undergarment worn to support and shape the body

corvette a small fast warship used by the navy as an escort vessel

cosmetics preparations to beautify the face (such as powders, creams and make-up)

cosmonaut an astronaut

cosmopolitan belonging to all parts of the world; containing people from all parts of the world (as, a cosmopolitan city)

cost the price that has to be paid for anything □ to be valued at (as - It costs 40p.): to involve some loss or suffering (as - The civil war cost many lives.)
costly of great cost; expensive; valuable

costume a style of dress; a woman's complete outer dress; an actor's clothes

cosy comfortable; snug □ a covering for a teapot

cot a small bed for a young child

cottage a small house (especially in the country)

cotton thread or yarn made from the cotton plant; cloth made of cotton
cottonwool cotton in a raw or woolly state (especially prepared as soft wadding)

couch a long padded seat with a low back; a bed

cough *(say coff)* a clearing of the throat with a harsh sound when it is sore or blocked by catarrh □ to clear the throat thus

could see **can 1**

council a group of people who meet to talk over questions and then make decisions (as, a town council)
councillor a member of a council

counsel advice: a barrister □ to advise
counsellor someone who counsels or advises

count 1 to number or name numbers in order; to add up □ the act of counting
countdown the counting (in reverse order) of seconds down to zero (0) as a signal for some important action (for example, the countdown for the take-off of a space-rocket)
counter 1 someone who counts: a table (especially in a shop) on which money is counted or

goods are set out: a token of metal, plastic or cardboard (as used in some indoor games)

count 2 a European nobleman equal in rank to an earl
countess the wife or widow of a count or earl; a lady of the same rank

countenance the face; the expression on the face □ to allow; to encourage

counter 2 against or in the opposite direction □ to meet or answer a move by someone else (as, to counter an attack)
counteract to act against; to hinder
counterfeit to copy something illegally (especially money); to imitate □ an imitation
counterfoil a coupon attached to a bank cheque, etc. but retained by the sender
counterpart a person or thing very like another; a duplicate
counter-revolution a revolution which counteracts a previous revolution

counterpane an outer covering for a bed

country the land outside towns and other built-up areas; any separate land or nation (as - France and Spain are two countries in the continent of Europe.)
countryside the fields, woods, hills, etc. which make up the country scene

county a division of a country (Kent, Glamorgan and Ayrshire are British counties.)

couple two of a kind together; a pair □ to join together
couplet two lines of rhyming verse
coupling a link for joining things together (such as railway carriages)

coupon (say coopon) a ticket or printed slip of paper which can be exchanged for something else; an entry or application form

courage bravery; lack of fear
courageous brave; fearless

courier (say coorier) a messenger; a guide on holiday tours

course the path or direction in which anything moves; the ground on which races are run and some games played (as, a race course, a golf course); a number of things following each other (as, a meal of four courses, a course of ten lessons)

court a space shut in by buildings: a king's or queen's residence and the people who attend the sovereign: a meeting of judges and law officers to administer the law: attention or politeness (as, paying court to someone) □ to woo
courteous (say curtius) polite; considerate
courtesy (say curtisy) courteous behaviour; politeness
courtier a member of a sovereign's court; a flatterer
courtly having fine manners
court martial a court held by officers of the armed forces to deal with offences against military or naval laws
courtship courting with a view to marriage; wooing
courtyard a court or enclosed space beside or within a building

cousin the son or daughter of a person's uncle or aunt

cove a small inlet of the sea; a bay

covenant an agreement between two people or parties to do, or not to do, something □ to agree by covenant about some action

cover to put something on or over something else; to hide; to clothe; to be sufficient for (as - 10p should cover his bus fare.); to extend over (as - The forest covers several square miles.) □ something that covers; a shelter or hiding-place
coverlet a bedcover
covert a thicket where animals can hide □ concealed; secret

covet to desire something eagerly (especially something belonging to someone else)

cow 1 the female of cattle and of

some other animals (as, the elephant, whale, seal, etc.)

cowboy a man who herds cattle on an American ranch

cowherd someone who looks after cows

cowshed a farm building where cattle are kept

cow 2 to frighten with threats

coward a person without courage

cower to crouch in fear

cowl a cap or hood (especially that of a monk); a hood-shaped cover for a chimney

cowslip a kind of primrose found in English pastures

coxswain *(say coxwain or cox'n)* the person who steers a boat; an officer in charge of a boat and crew

coy shy; bashful (usually of a girl)

coyote a small prairie wolf (in North America)

crab a shellfish with five pairs of legs (The first pair has large claws.)

crab apple a small bitter apple

crack a split; a chink: a sudden sharp splitting sound: a sharp blow (as, a crack on the head) □ to split or break apart (as, to crack a nut): to give out a sudden sharp sound: to tell something in an amusing way (as, to crack a joke)

cracker a thin crisp biscuit: a small firework

crackle to give out small cracking noises (as, dry sticks crackling in a fire) □ a crisp noise (as, the crackle of parchment)

crackling a continuous crackling noise: the crisp rind of roast pork

cradle a baby's bed with rockers instead of legs □ to hold as if in a cradle (as - The mother cradled the child in her arms.)

craft a skill; a skilled trade: a vessel; boats or ships

craftsman a person who practises a skilled trade

crafty cunning; artful

crag a rough steep rock

cram to fill very full; to stuff: to stuff the memory with facts for an examination

cramp a painful stiffening of the muscles (often when they have been strained) □ to restrict or hamper (as, to cramp one's efforts)

cranberry the red sour berry of a trailing evergreen shrub

crane a machine for raising heavy weights (It has a long arm fitted with a pulley.): a large wading bird, with long legs, neck and bill □ to stretch out (the neck, like a crane)

cranium the skull

crank a person with odd notions or fads: a lever or arm in a machine which changes a to-and-fro motion to a turning round and round (as in a motor car engine) □ to turn a crank

cranny a chink; a small narrow opening (as in a rough wall)

crape see **crêpe**

crash a loud noise (as of things smashing): a collision: the collapse of a business □ to fall or collide with a crash

crash helmet a padded safety helmet worn by racing motorists, motor cyclists and airmen

crate an openwork container usually made of wood, for packing fruit, bottles, etc.

crater the bowl-shaped mouth of a volcano; a hole in the ground made by an explosion

cravat a kind of necktie worn by men

crave to long for; to beg earnestly

craving a longing or desire

craven cowardly

crawl to move slowly with the body on, or close to, the ground; to move on hands and knees; to creep □ the act of crawling: a stroke used in swimming

crayfish a freshwater shellfish which looks like a small lobster

crayon a coloured pencil for

drawing with

craze a foolish fashion or hobby; a mad fancy for something

crazy mad; silly: made of irregular pieces (as, crazy paving)

creak to make a sharp grating sound □ a sharp, grating sound (as of an unoiled door hinge)

cream the fatty substance that forms on milk; anything like cream (as, ice cream, cold cream); the best part of anything

creamery a place where butter and cheese are made or sold

crease a mark made by folding something like paper or cloth; a line showing the position of the batsman or bowler in cricket □ to make creases

create *(say cree-ate)* to make or bring into being

creation the act of creating; something created

creative able to create; having many new ideas

creator one who creates or produces

creature something that has been created (especially an animal, bird or insect)

crèche *(say cresh)* a public nursery for children

credence *(say creedence)* belief; trust

credentials *(say credensh'lz)* evidence (especially written) to show that a person is trustworthy or entrusted with some authority

credible able to be believed (as, a credible story)

credit good reputation; belief; time allowed for the payment of goods (as, a month's credit); money kept in a banking account (as - He has £20 to his credit in the Savings Bank.) □ to believe; to put an amount of money to someone's credit

creditor someone to whom money is owed

credulous believing too easily

creed a summary of beliefs (especially religious beliefs)

creek a small inlet or river estuary; a small stream

creel a basket for carrying fish

creep to move quietly along the ground (sometimes on hands and knees)

creeper a plant (such as ivy) that grows along the ground or up a wall

cremate to burn to ashes (especially a dead body)

cremation the act of burning to ashes (especially the dead)

crematorium a special place where cremation is carried out

creosote an oily liquid obtained from tar (It is painted on wood to prevent rotting.)

crêpe *(say crape)*, **crape** a thin fabric with a wrinkled surface

crescendo *(say creshendo)* growing in loudness or force □ a gradual increase in sound in music

crescent anything shaped in a curve like the new moon

cress a small plant with sharp-tasting leaves used in salads

crest the comb or tuft on the head of a cock or other bird: the top of a hill or wave: a badge

crestfallen dejected

cretonne a strong, printed cotton fabric used for curtains, etc.

crevasse a deep cleft in a glacier

crevice a crack or narrow opening

crew a ship's company; the group of people in charge of an aeroplane, train, etc.: a company or gang

crib a small bed for a child, with high sides and (usually) wooden bars; a barred trough for cattle food □ to copy another's work unfairly

crick a cramping pain (usually in the neck or shoulders)

cricket 1 an outdoor game played between two teams of eleven each, using bats, a ball and two wickets

cricket 2 a jumping insect like a grasshopper, which makes a chirping sound with its wing covers

crier see **cry**

crime a wrong action that can be punished by law; a sin
criminal concerned with crime (as, a criminal offence) □ someone who is guilty of crime

crimson a deep red colour, tinged with blue

cringe to crouch in fear; to behave too humbly

crinkle a wrinkle □ to wrinkle

crinoline an old-fashioned skirt or petticoat on hoops which make it stick out all round

cripple a lame or disabled person □ to make lame: to weaken seriously

crisis the time of greatest danger or importance; a serious happening

crisp dry and brittle (like potato crisps): wavy or curly (of hair): bracing (as, the crisp morning air)

crisscross in lines crossing over each other in opposing directions (as, a crisscross pattern)

critic someone who judges literary or artistic work (such as plays, books, films, concerts); a fault-finder
critical judging good and bad points; fault-finding: very important or serious (as, a critical moment)
criticize *(say critisize)* to give a judgment on, or an opinion of, something; to find fault with
criticism *(say critisiz'm)* a critical saying or piece of writing (often pointing out faults)

croak a low hoarse sound □ to make such a sound (as a frog or raven does)

crochet *(say croshay)* knitting done in loops with a hooked needle □ to do crochet work

crock a pot or jar
crockery china and earthenware dishes

crocodile a large and dangerous reptile with a scaly skin (Crocodiles are found in and beside the rivers of many hot countries.)

crocus a small garden plant of early spring, with bright purple, yellow or white flowers

croft a small farm or enclosed piece of land

crone a withered old woman

crook anything bent or hooked; a staff with a hook at the end: a dishonest person
crooked not straight: dishonest

croon to sing or hum in a low voice; to sing in a very sentimental way

crop 1 grain, fruit or vegetables grown on the land for food or fodder □ to cut short; to raise or gather crops

crop 2 a short whip used in hunting

croquet *(say crokay)* a game in which wooden balls have to be hit with mallets through a series of small hoops set in a lawn

cross anything shaped like an X or a + (as, a Victoria Cross); in bygone times a large wooden frame to which a condemned person was nailed; the symbol of the Christian religion; a lasting cause of grief or unhappiness □ to mark with a cross; to go from one side of something to the other (as, to cross the street); to meet and pass (as - The plane crossed the path of the other.); to annoy or thwart a person □ lying across (as, a crossbeam): somewhat angry
crossing the act of going across; the place where a street, river, etc. may be crossed
crossbones two thighbones laid across each other (With a skull, they form an emblem of piracy or death.)
crossbow a weapon for shooting arrows, with a device for pulling back the string and releasing the arrow
cross-examine to test a person's evidence (especially in a court of law) by detailed

questioning

crosspatch a bad-tempered person

cross-question this has the same meaning as **cross-examine** (see above)

crossword (puzzle) a word-puzzle in which clues are given to find words to fit into a square

crotchet a note in music: an odd idea or habit
crotchety bad-tempered and complaining

crouch to bend down close to the ground

croupier the person in charge of a gaming-table (where there is gambling for money)

crow 1 a fairly large black bird, with a harsh croaking voice
crowbar an iron bar (usually bent at one end) used as a lever
crow's-nest a platform at the masthead of a ship for a lookout

crow 2 the cry of a cock; the happy cry of a baby □ to cry out with such a sound; to boast

crowd a number of people or things gathered together (generally without order) □ to gather into a crowd

crown the circular gold head-dress worn by a king or queen; the top of anything (such as a head, hat, hill) □ to set a crown on; to reward (as - Success crowned her efforts.)

crucial testing; decisive (as, the crucial moment)

crucify to put to death on a cross; to torture
crucifix a figure or picture of Christ on the cross
crucifixion death on the cross (especially that of Christ)

crude in the natural or raw state; not purified (as, crude oil): rough; blunt (as, crude behaviour)

cruel causing pain (with pleasure or indifference); painful (as, cruel sufferings)
cruelty cruel action or behaviour

cruet a small bottle or jar for vinegar, oil, salt, pepper, etc.

cruise a sea voyage for pleasure □ to sail about with no particular destination
cruiser a fast, middle-sized warship

crumb a small bit of bread, cake or biscuit; a morsel
crumble to break or fall into small pieces

crumple to crush out of shape; to collapse

crunch to chew anything hard (such as an apple) and so make a noise; to crush underfoot

crusade in history, an expedition of Christians to win back the Holy Land from the Mohammedans; any movement in support of a worthwhile cause □ to take part in a crusade

crush to squeeze together or squash; to beat down or overwhelm (as, to crush the enemy forces) □ a tightly packed crowd of people

crust the hard outside coating of a well-baked loaf of bread or pie; the solid outer part of the earth
crusty having a crust: irritable or cross (of a person)

crutch a special stick, with a padded top, to help lame people to walk

crux the difficult part of a problem; the essential point

cry to shed tears; to make a shrill loud sound; to call in a loud voice
crier anyone who cries; a town officer who reads out public notices (now uncommon)

crypt an underground vault (often used as a burial-place)
cryptic secret; very difficult to understand (as, a cryptic saying)

crystal a clear transparent mineral like sparkling glass; cut glass; a regularly shaped particle of a substance (as, granulated sugar, salt, quartz, etc.)
crystalline made up of crystals;

as clear as crystal

crystallize to form into crystals: to become clear and definite (as - His thoughts had not yet crystallized.)

cub the young of certain animals such as foxes; a junior Boy Scout (Cub Scout)

cube a solid square (with six equal square faces, such as a cube of sugar); a number multiplied by its square (for example, the cube of $2 = 8$, since $2 \times 2 \times 2 = 8$)

cube root the number of which another number is the cube (for example, 2 is the cube root of 8)

cubic having the shape of a cube

cubicle a small place partitioned off inside a larger room

cuckoo a bird that cries *cookoo* (It lays its eggs in other birds' nests.)

cucumber a creeping plant with a long green fruit used in salads, sandwiches and pickles

cud food brought back from the stomach and chewed a second time by ruminant animals (such as cows and sheep)

cuddle to hug with affection; to fondle

cudgel a heavy staff; a club □to beat with a cudgel

cue 1 a hint (such as telling a person what to do or say next)

cue 2 a tapering stick used to strike the ball in billiards

cuff 1 the end of a sleeve near the wrist

cuff 2 a blow with the open hand □to strike with the open hand

cuisine *(say cweezeen)* a kitchen; a style of cookery

culinary concerned with the kitchen or with cookery

cull to pick out or separate; to select

cullender see **colander**

culminate to reach the highest or most important point

culmination the highest point

of anything; the climax

culpable deserving blame

culprit a person who is to blame; a wrong-doer

cult a system of religious belief; excessive devotion to a person, idea, system, etc. (such as the cult of physical fitness)

cultivate to prepare the land for crops: to develop or improve (as, to cultivate good manners); to encourage (as, to cultivate a person's friendship)

cultivation the practice of cultivating

culture educational or intellectual development; a type of civilization (as, Bronze Age culture); cultivation

cultured well-educated; having refined manners

cumbersome, cumbrous heavy; unwieldy; clumsy

cumulative becoming greater by many additions (as, a cumulative sum of money)

cunning crafty; skilful in a sly way; clever (as, a cunning device) □craftiness; skill; slyness

cup a small container for holding drinks, (usually with a handle); an ornamental vessel used as a prize

cupboard a set of shelves with doors where dishes, food, etc. are kept

cupful as much as fills an ordinary cup

cupidity *(say kewpiditee)* greed

cur *(say ker)* a mongrel dog; a mean cowardly person

curate *(say kewret)* a clergyman assisting a rector or vicar

curator a person who is in charge (especially a keeper or custodian in a museum or art-gallery)

curb to check or hold back □a check or hindrance; a chain or strap attached to the bit for holding back a horse: see also **kerb**

curdle to turn into curd; to thicken

curd(s) the thickened part of milk when it has been separated to make cheese

cure to heal; to make well: to preserve by salting, drying, etc. □ the action of healing; a remedy
curable able to be cured
curative tending to, or likely to cure

curfew (in earlier times) the ringing of an evening bell, as a signal to put out all fires and lights

curio a rare and curious article

curious anxious to find out; inquisitive: strange or odd
curiosity eagerness to find out; inquisitiveness: something strange and rare

curl to twist into ringlets; to be wavy (as - Her hair curls naturally.) □ a ringlet of hair; a wave or twist
curlers rollers or pins used to curl hair

curlew a wading bird with a long slender bill and long legs

currant a kind of small black raisin used in cakes, etc.; the fruit (small berries, usually red or black) of several prickly shrubs, used chiefly in jams and jellies

current flowing; passing from person to person (as, a current news item); present (as, the current month) □ a flow of air, water or electricity (as, direct current [D.C.] or alternating current [A.C.])
currency the fact or state of being current: the money (notes and coins) of a country

curriculum a course of study (especially at a school or university)

curry a kind of stew with a spicy seasoning

curse to swear; to wish evil upon someone □ a swear word; a wish for evil

cursory hasty (as, a cursory glance)

curt short; rudely brief (as, a curt reply)

curtail to cut short; to lessen

curtain a hanging drapery at a window or at the front of a stage

curtsey a bow made by girls and women by bending the knees

curve a bend; a line shaped like any part of a circle □ to bend; to make a curve

cushion a soft pillow with a decorative covering (for resting against on a chair or settee); any soft pad

custard a kind of sweet sauce made by cooking milk, eggs and sugar together

custody a keeping or guarding; imprisonment (as - The prisoner is in custody.)
custodian a keeper; a caretaker

custom what people are in the habit of doing; common usage
customs duties or taxes on exports and imports
customary usual; habitual
customer any person who buys

cut to divide, or make a slit in, something by using scissors or a knife: to reduce (as, to cut a price); to abridge □ a slit or opening made by cutting
cutter a person or thing that cuts; a small boat
cutting a piece cut off a plant, which, when planted, will grow into a new one; a piece cut from a newspaper; a passage cut through rock for a road or railway

cute smart; knowing; quaintly pleasing

cuticle the outermost thin skin

cutlass a short broad sword

cutlery knives, forks and spoons

cutlet a small slice of meat with the rib-bone attached

cycle a bicycle: a period of time when events happen in a certain order and which then repeats itself (as, the cycle of the four seasons) □ to ride on a bicycle
cyclist a person who rides

a bicycle

cyclone a bad storm with strong whirling winds; a system of winds blowing round a centre of low atmospheric pressure; the opposite of an anti-cyclone

cygnet a young swan

cylinder a roller-shaped object, either hollow or solid
cylindrical cylinder-shaped

cymbals a pair of brass plate-like musical instruments which are beaten together

cynic *(say sinic)* a person who takes a pessimistic or poor view of human nature; sneering
cynicism *(say sinisism)* a cynical attitude

cypress a dense evergreen tree

czar, czarina see **tsar**

d

dab to strike or touch lightly and quickly, usually with something soft or moist (as, to dab away tears with a handkerchief) □ a gentle blow

dabble to play in water with hands or feet: to do anything in a trifling way

dachshund *(say daks-hund)* a small dog with a long body and very short legs

daffodil a yellow spring flower shaped rather like a small trumpet

daft silly; reckless

dagger a short sword for stabbing: a printer's mark (†)

dahlia a garden plant with large bright flowers

daily see **day**

dainty small and delicate; pretty; pleasant-tasting □ a choice morsel of food

dairy the place on a farm where milk is kept and butter and cheese are made; a shop which sells milk

dais *(say dayss)* a platform at the end of a hall

daisy a wild flower with narrow white or pink petals and a yellow centre

dale the low ground between hills

dally to idle or waste time by dawdling: to play, or amuse oneself, with
dalliance dallying or trifling

dalmatian a large white dog with black spots

dam a bank or wall to hold back water □ to hold back by means of a dam

damage an injury or loss □ to harm
damages the payment made to a person for an injury or loss caused by someone else

damask a cloth (usually of linen) with a woven design

dame the title given to a lady which corresponds to the rank of knight for a man

damn *(say dam)* to condemn; to sentence to eternal punishment □ a curse
damnable *(say damnable)* hateful

damp moist; rather wet □ the moist air □ to wet slightly: to discourage
dampen to make damp: to discourage

damsel an old-fashioned word for a young woman

damson a small dark plum

dance to move in time to music □ the act of dancing; a social occasion at which people dance

dandelion a common wild plant with a bright yellow flower and leaves with jagged edges

dandruff a scaly scurf on a

person's scalp

dandy a man who pays a great deal of attention to his clothes and general appearance

danger a risk or peril; the opposite of safety
dangerous very unsafe; very risky

dangle to hang loosely; to hold something so that it swings loosely

dank moist; wet

dapper smart and very neat in appearance: little and active

dappled marked with spots

dare to be bold enough; to venture; to challenge
daring bold; courageous □ boldness

dark without light; blackish; gloomy: secret (as, to keep something dark)
darken to make, or grow, dark or darker

darling someone dearly loved; a favourite

darn to mend a hole with crossing stitches of wool or cotton □ a hole which has been so mended

dart a small pointed weapon or toy for throwing with the hand □ to move quickly
dartboard the round target used in the game of darts
darts a game in which small darts are thrown at a board with numbered sections

dash to rush suddenly; to throw with force □ a rush: a mark in printing or writing (−)
dashing spirited: making a show (as when a dancer makes a dashing figure)

data any facts which yield information when studied

date 1 the time of any event; the day, month and year (as, 23rd May 1973) noted on a letter, etc. □ to give a date to
out-of-date old-fashioned; no longer in use
up-to-date in fashion

date 2 the sweet sticky fruit of the date palm

daub to smear; to paint clumsily

daughter a person's female child
daughter-in-law a son's wife

daunt to frighten; to discourage
dauntless fearless; refusing to be discouraged

davy-lamp a safety lamp for miners

dawdle to waste time; to move slowly

dawn the first light of day; daybreak □ to become day; to begin to appear (as when it dawns on a pupil that he may be late for school)

day the time of daylight, between sunrise and sunset: the 24 hours from one midnight to the next
daybreak the first appearance of the morning light
daydream to have dream-like imaginings while awake □ fanciful imagining while awake

daze to stupefy; to stun
dazed stunned; bewildered

dazzle to daze or confuse by shining a strong light: to amaze by beauty or cleverness

de- a prefix, often indicating down, away from (as, **deposit, depart**) or the undoing of an action (as, **decentralize, deodorize**)

deacon a clergyman below the rank of priest; a church officer
deaconess a woman who helps the clergy in social work

dead without life; without the appearance of life: complete (as, a dead loss)
dead-beat having no strength left
dead heat a race in which two or more competitors are exactly equal
deadline the very latest time set for finishing something
deadlock a standstill resulting from a complete failure to agree (as when there is a deadlock between employers and a trade union)
deadly fatal; causing death: very great; extreme (as, to be in

deadly earnest)

deaf unable to hear; refusing to listen
deafen to make deaf
deafening extremely loud; almost loud enough to cause deafness

deal 1 a quantity or amount: a business arrangement □ to trade or do business with; to divide or distribute (as, to deal cards for a card game)
dealer a person who deals; a trader

deal 2 a plank of fir or pine wood

dean a clergyman of high rank in a cathedral: a person with important responsibilities in a university or college

dear 1 much loved □ a loved one

dear 2 high in price

dearth scarcity; shortage

death the end of life: see also **dead, die**

debase to make lower in value or quality
debased made lower in quality; of low character

debate a discussion (especially a formal one, as in Parliament); an argument □ to argue about; to think beforehand about the advantages and disadvantages of some possible action
debatable requiring discussion; open to doubt

debilitate to make weak
debility a weakness (especially of health)

debit something owed, an item of debt □ to enter such an item in an account (especially a bank account)

debonair gay and with a pleasant manner

debris (say debree) ruins; rubbish

debt (say det) a sum of money owed by a person; a duty or obligation (as, a debt of gratitude)
debtor anyone who owes a debt; the opposite of creditor

debut (say daybew) a first public appearance; a beginning

decade a period of ten years

decadence lowering of standards in behaviour or in tastes

decamp to leave camp; to run away (especially without warning)

decant to pour a liquid carefully from one vessel to another so as to leave any sediment behind (especially when decanting an old wine)
decanter an ornamental bottle (often of cut glass) for holding a decanted liquid

decapitate to behead

decay to become rotten; to fall gradually into ruins; to waste away □ a ruined state; a wasting away

deceased dead or recently dead
the deceased a dead person

deceive to mislead by telling lies; to cheat
deceit the act of deceiving or cheating
deceitful deceiving; insincere

decent proper; generally acceptable (of behaviour): fairly good or of fair size (as, a decent helping of pudding)
decency proper behaviour; modesty

deception an act of deceit or cheating
deceptive of misleading appearance

decide to make up one's mind; to settle
decision the act of deciding; a settling or judgment: firmness (as, a man of decision)
decisive showing decision; firm or clear

deciduous shedding leaves in the autumn

decimal numbered by tens and tenths (thus 32.5 = three tens plus two units plus five-tenths)
decimalization the changing of an older counting method to the decimal system (as from shillings and old pence to new pence)

decimal point the point which separates the whole part of a number from the fractional part: see **decimal** above

decimate to reduce greatly in number, usually by war or disease (literally, to destroy one-tenth of the total)

decimetre the tenth part of a metre (almost 4 inches)

decipher to read something written in cipher or a secret code; to make out the meaning of any difficult writing

decision see **decide**

deck a floor on a ship or on a bus, etc. (as, the upper deck of a bus)
deckchair a light, folding chair (usually with a canvas seat) used out of doors

declare to announce; to say clearly and firmly: to end an innings in cricket before ten wickets have fallen
declaration a firm statement; a formal announcement (as, a declaration of war)

decline 1 to refuse

decline 2 to slope or bend down; to weaken or get worse □ a downward slope; a falling away; a loss of strength

decode to turn a coded message into plain language

decompose to break down, or separate something into its basic elements; to rot or decay

decorate to ornament; to make something look beautiful or gay; to pin on a medal or badge
decoration adornment; ornaments; a medal or badge
decorative ornamental; beautiful
decorator a house painter

decorous quiet and dignified; behaving properly
decorum polite and correct behaviour

decoy to lead into a trap or snare □ anything used to decoy

decrease to become less; to make less □ a lessening or reduction

decree an order; a judgment □ to make a decree; to command

decrepit broken-down by old age

decry to belittle

dedicate to devote to some sacred purpose; to devote mainly to a particular purpose (as when a person dedicates his life to social work of some kind); to inscribe a book to a friend
dedication the act of dedicating: an inscription in a book

deduce to draw conclusions from a study of all the available facts
deduction 1 deducing from the available facts; a conclusion: see also **deduction 2** under **deduct**

deduct to subtract
deduction 2 a taking away from, subtraction: see also **deduction 1**

deed an act; something done: a legal document

deem to think; to judge

deep far down or far in (as, deep under the sea or deep in the forest) □ reaching far down (as, a deep well); intense or strong (as, deep colour, deep feelings); low in tone (as, a deep organ note): secretive (as when a person is described as a *deep one*)
deepen to make deep or deeper; to become deeper
depth deepness; intensity or strength

deer a kind of four-footed animal with long legs and antlers (usually in the male only)

deface to disfigure or spoil the appearance (face) of

defame to speak ill of
defamation the act of defaming a person's character
defamatory containing defamation (as, a defamatory statement)

default to fail to carry out a duty or obligation (especially to fail to pay a debt which is due) □ a failure to carry out such a duty

defeat to win a victory over opponents in a battle or in a game; to conquer □ the loss of a fight or of a game

defect a fault; a flaw

defection failure in duty to one's leader or party; a desertion
defective faulty

defence see **defend**

defend to guard or protect against attack
defence a means of protection: a person's argument against an accusation (especially in a law court)
defendant an accused person (especially in a law court)
defensible able to be defended
defensive on guard; resisting attack

defer 1 to put off to another time
deferment postponement

defer 2 to give way to the wishes of another person
deference a yielding to the opinion or wishes of someone else
deferential showing deference or respect

defiant see **defy**

deficient lacking; wanting
deficiency a lack or shortage
deficit the amount of money lacking to make up a required sum

defile 1 a narrow pass through which troops can march only in file

defile 2 to make dirty: to corrupt

define to fix the limits of; to state the exact meaning of
definite having clear limits; fixed; exact
definition an explanation of the exact meaning of a word or phrase

deflect to turn something aside from its target
deflection a turning sideways (as, the deflection of a compass needle by a magnet)

deform to spoil the shape of
deformity an abnormal shape or disfigurement

defraud to cheat; to take something by fraud

deft skilful and quick

defy to challenge; to resist openly
defiant resisting openly; challenging

degenerate (say dejenerit) having lost former good qualities □ (say dejenerate) to become or grow bad; to become less admirable

degrade to lower in grade or rank; to disgrace
degradation the act of degrading

degree 1 a small unit or division (for example, the degrees on a thermometer)
by degrees gradually

degree 2 rank; a university title (usually gained by examinations)

deify to treat, or worship, as a god
deity a god or goddess

deign (say dain) to do as a favour; to condescend to do something (for example, to deign to reply to a request)

dejected made gloomy or dispirited
dejection a gloomy or downcast state of mind

delay to put off to a later time; to hinder □ a postponement; a hindrance

delectable delightful; pleasing

delegate (say deligit) a person chosen as a representative (as, a delegate to a conference, etc.) □ (say deligate) to send a person to speak or act for others: to entrust (for example, to delegate authority to another person)
delegation a group of delegates acting together

delete (say deleet) to rub or blot out (especially in writing)
deletion the act of deleting; something deleted

deliberate (say deliberit) intentional; not by accident: slow and cautious □ (say deliberate) to consider a matter very carefully before deciding
deliberation careful thought; calmness

delicate not strong; fragile or frail: pleasing to the senses (especially the taste)

delicacy fineness; sensitiveness; great tact: a choice item of food

delicatessen delicacies (especially prepared meats and cheeses): a shop selling these foods

delicious very pleasing to taste and eat: giving much pleasure

delight great pleasure or joy □ to please highly
delightful giving or causing great pleasure

delinquent failing in duty; guilty □ someone who fails in his duty; a wrong-doer
delinquency a failure in duty; a misdeed

delirious wandering in mind (usually temporarily): wildly excited

deliver to hand over to someone: to set free: to give out or speak out (as, to deliver a speech)
deliverance a setting free or rescue
delivery the act of delivering; the way a speech is given (for example - The speaker's delivery was excellent.)

dell a small valley (usually among trees)

delta a triangular piece of land formed by two or more branches of a river at its mouth (as, the delta of the river Nile)

delude to deceive
delusion any mistaken belief

deluge a flood; a great quantity □ to flood; to overwhelm with a great quantity

delve to dig

demand to ask sharply or firmly for something: to require (for example - This job demands great skill.) □ an urgent request; an urgent claim (such as the demands on a doctor's time)

demeanour behaviour; bearing

demented out of one's mind

demerit a fault or shortcoming

demi- a prefix meaning half (though **semi-** is more often used)

demobilize to disband (especially troops when a war is over)

democracy a form of government whose members have been freely elected as their representatives by the people
democrat anyone who believes in democracy
democratic of democracy; believing in equal rights for all the people in a country

demolish to destroy; to lay in ruins
demolition the destruction or pulling down of something

demon an evil spirit; a devil

demonstrate to show clearly; to prove: to express one's views publicly (usually by way of protest)
demonstration a practical display or explanation; a clear proof; a display of emotion; a public expression of opinion (as, by a procession or a large meeting)
demonstrative pointing out something: tending to show one's feelings
demonstrator a person who demonstrates (for example, a teacher who shows pupils how a thing works or how to do something): a person who takes an active part in a public demonstration

demoralize to have a bad influence (especially by destroying confidence and courage): to throw into confusion

demur to object

demure shy; modest

den a wild beast's cave or shelter: a meeting place for thieves, etc.: a private room for study or work

denial see **deny**

denomination a name or title; a particular class of units for measuring (as when tons and cwt. are reduced to the same denomination, for example, to pounds - lb.): a body of people belonging to a particular religion (as, the Catholic denomination)

denominator the number below the line in a vulgar fraction

denote to mean; to be the sign of something

denounce to say something against a person; to accuse
denunciation the act of denouncing or accusing

dense closely-packed; thick (for example, a dense crowd or a dense forest): very stupid
density the quality of being dense (for example - The density of the population was 500 persons to the square mile.)

dent a small hollow made by a blow or by pressure □ to make a dent

dental concerned with the teeth
dentifrice a toothpaste or toothpowder
dentist a person who cures toothache and generally cares for the teeth
denture a set of false teeth

denude to make bare or naked (for example - The countryside was denuded of vegetation.)

denunciation see **denounce**

deny to say that something is not true: to refuse a request
denial a statement that something is not true: the refusal of a request

deodorize to take the smell from
deodorant a substance that removes or conceals unpleasant smells

depart to go away or leave
departure a going away or leaving

department a separate part or division
department store a large shop with many separate departments selling a wide variety of goods

depend to rely on; to be decided by or influenced by other conditions (for example - It all depends on the weather.)
dependable reliable: trustworthy
dependant, dependent relying upon □ someone who is kept or supported by another (for example, a sick relative who is a dependant)
dependence the condition of being dependent on someone or on something

depict to represent in drawing or painting; to describe in words

deplete to empty; to reduce in number or quantity

deplore to express regret and disapproval
deplorable sad; very bad

deport to send a person out of a country for wrong-doing
deportation the act of deporting a person

deportment the way a person carries himself or herself; behaviour

depose to remove from a high office or position (as, to depose a ruler)

deposit to put or set something down: to place money for safe keeping in a bank □ something stored away (especially money deposited in a bank): any solid matter that settles down in a liquid
depository a store house (for example, a furniture depository)

depot *(say deppo)* a storehouse: a regiment's headquarters

depraved evil; corrupt

depreciate to lower the value of; to fall in value; the opposite of appreciate
depreciation the lowering or falling of value

depress to press down; to lower a person's spirits or make sad
depression a hollow: low spirits or sadness: a low level of business activity: an area of low atmospheric pressure (A depression often brings rainy weather.)

deprive to take something away from (as, to deprive someone of his freedom)
deprivation depriving; hardship

depth see **deep**

deputy a person acting in place of

another, or someone so appointed

deputation a group of persons chosen to speak for others

deputize to act as a deputy or substitute

derail to cause to leave the rails or railway line

derange to put out of place or order

deranged out of order: insane

derelict abandoned; given up as useless □ anything derelict (especially a ship)

deride to laugh at; to mock

derision mockery

derisive, desisory mocking, jeering

derive to extract or obtain from a source: to trace the origin of something (especially of words): to arise or be descended from

derivation the source; the tracing of a word to its root

derivative derived from something else (and therefore not original) □ a word formed from another word

derogatory harmful to a person's good name or position

derrick a kind of crane for hoisting heavy weights

oil derrick a tall framework erected over an oil well

descend to go down; to climb down; to pass to a lower place or condition

descendant someone who has a particular person as an ancestor (as, a descendant of the Duke of Wellington)

descent the act of descending; a downward slope

describe to give a picture in words; to trace out or to draw (for example, to describe a circle)

description a picture, or account of anything, in words: sort or kind (as, toys of all descriptions)

descriptive containing descriptions

desecrate to treat something without reverence; to use badly

desert 1 (say _dezert_) a region without water where there is little or no vegetation; a desolate place

desert 2 (say _dezert_) to forsake; to run away from

deserter a soldier who leaves his post or his regiment

desertion the act of deserting

desert(s) 3 (say _dezert(s)_) anything that is deserved, either good or bad

deserve to earn something by doing well; to be worthy of reward

deserving worthy

desiccate to dry up; to preserve by drying (as, desiccated coconut)

design (say _dezine_) to make a plan or pattern □ a sketch; a plan in outline; a pattern

designing scheming, artful

designation (say _dezignay-shun_) the act of appointing or naming someone; a name or title

desire to want very much: to request □ a wish

desirable worthy of desire; pleasing

desirous wishful; desiring to have

desist to stop doing something

desk a piece of furniture used for writing or reading

desolate empty of people; feeling very lonely

desolation loneliness; deep sorrow

despair to give up hope □ hopelessness

despairing having no hope

despatch see **dispatch**

desperado a criminally reckless person (like an outlaw)

desperate despairingly reckless; almost without hope (as, in a desperate situation)

desperation a state of despair; recklessness

despicable worthless; contemptible

despise to look down on with contempt; to scorn

despite in spite of

despondent without hope; dejected

despot a ruler with absolute power; a tyrant

dessert *(say dezert)* fruits, sweets, etc. served at the end of lunch or dinner

destine *(say destin)* to mark out for a certain purpose or goal (as, destined to become famous)
destination the place to which anyone is going; a journey's end
destiny an outcome or end that is considered unavoidable; fate

destitute in utter want, without any means of support
destitution a state of being without any resources

destroy to ruin completely; to demolish; to kill
destroyer someone or something that destroys: a small fast warship armed with torpedoes, used especially in defence against submarines
destructible able to be destroyed
destruction the act of destroying; ruin
destructive causing great damage or destruction

detach to separate from; to unfasten
detachable able to be taken off or separated

detail a small part; an item □ to tell about something fully; to give all the facts
detailed giving many details
in detail fully and item by item

detain to hold back; to keep late; to keep under guard
detention the act of detaining; being detained

detect to discover; to find out
detection the act of detecting (as, the detection of a crime)
detective a person who tracks criminals

detention see **detain**

deter *(say deter)* to hinder or prevent something by causing fear (for example, to deter

thieves by keeping a watchdog)
deterrent anything which has the effect of deterring

detergent a substance used for cleaning with water (usually not containing soap)

deteriorate to get worse
deterioration a growing worse (as, a deterioration in health)

determine to fix or settle: to decide to do something
determination a fixed intention: firmness of character
determined fixed or settled: resolute; with one's mind made up

detest to hate very much

detonate to explode or cause to explode
detonation an explosion with a loud noise
detonator a device that sets off an explosion

detour a roundabout way; a deviation from a main route

detract to take away from; to lessen (especially a person's reputation)

detriment damage; disadvantage

devastate to lay waste; to plunder
devastation the state of being devastated; havoc

develop to grow gradually; to make larger; to grow or bring to a more advanced state (as, a developed country): to make a photograph appear (by using a chemical developer)
development the gradual growth, or working out, of anything (including ideas as well as material things): the developing of a photograph

deviate to turn aside from
deviation a sideways turn or movement; a divergence
devious roundabout: rather dishonest

device see **devise**

devil an evil spirit: a wicked or cruel person
devilish like a devil

devious see **deviate**

devise to contrive; to invent;

to plan

device a contrivance; an invention; a plan; a trick: an emblem

devoid empty of; free from

devote to give up fully; to dedicate (as, to devote one's life to helping others)
devoted warmly loyal
devotion strong affection or loyalty

devour to eat up greedily: to take in greedily with the eyes (for example, by reading an absorbing story)

devout holy or religious: earnest

dew tiny drops of moisture which cover the ground in the early morning (They are deposited from the air when it cools during the night.)

dexterity skill (especially with the hands)
dexterous, dextrous skilful

diabolic, diabolical devilish; very wicked

diadem a kind of royal crown

diagnose to say what is wrong with a sick person after examining him
diagnosis the conclusion reached by a doctor after considering a patient's symptoms

diagonal a straight line drawn between opposite corners □ stretching between opposite corners (as, the diagonal stripes on a Union Jack)

diagram an outlined drawing or plan to show what something is like or how it works

dial the face of a watch or clock; anything round with numbers or letters on it (such as a telephone dial or a sundial) □ to turn a telephone dial to obtain a number

dialect a way of speaking used in a particular part of a country, or used by a particular group of people (as, a Cornish dialect or a Cockney dialect)

dialogue conversation; conversation in written form (as, the dialogue in a novel)

diameter a straight line drawn across a circle and through its centre

diamond an extremely hard and colourless precious stone which is a crystal form of carbon: any shape like a diamond (as on a playing card)

diaphragm *(say diafram)* the muscular part of the body that separates the chest from the abdomen: a dividing membrane or thin partition (for example, the metal disc in the earpiece of a telephone)

diary a book in which day-to-day happenings are written
diarist someone who keeps (that is, writes) a diary

diatribe an angry attack in words or writing

dice see **die 2**

dictate to say or read for another to write; to give dictation: to give orders
dictation something said or read for another person to write down
dictator an all-powerful ruler
dictatorial like a dictator; overbearing (as, a dictatorial manner)

diction manner of speaking; choice of words

dictionary a book which lists words in alphabetical order, together with definitions of their meanings

die 1 to lose life: to wither
die away to fade from sight or hearing (as - The music died away.)

die 2 a small cube with numbers on its six sides, used in games of chance
dice the plural of die (as, a pair of dice)

diesel engine an engine in which heavy oil is ignited by heat produced by compression (and not by sparking plugs)

diet the kind of food eaten (as, a stodgy diet); a prescribed course of food (as, a high-protein diet)

□ to eat certain kinds of food only (for example, dieting to reduce weight)

difference anything which makes one thing unlike another; the amount by which one number is greater than another: a quarrel
differ to be unlike; to disagree
different unlike; not the same
differentiate to make a difference between: to see or tell a difference between

difficult not easy; hard to do or understand; hard to please
difficulty anything hard to do or understand; an obstacle or objection

diffident shy; lacking self-confidence

diffuse *(say diffewz)* to spread widely or scatter □ *(say diffewss)* widely spread (as, a diffuse light); wordy (as, a diffuse speech)
diffusion a spreading out; a scattering

dig to make a hole in the ground; to turn up earth with a spade: to poke or push (as, to dig a person in the ribs) □ an archaeological excavation

digest *(say dijest)* to dissolve food in the stomach so that the body can get energy out of it: to think over (for example, to digest a piece of bad news) □ *(say diejest)* a magazine containing extracts or shortened versions of longer articles
digestible able to be digested
digestion the act of digesting; the ability to digest food
digestive concerning, or helping, digestion

digit any one of the numbers 0 to 9: a finger or toe
digital concerning or using digits (as, a digital computer)

dignify to make worthy: to confer honour on
dignified appearing to be of high worth or rank; showing dignity
dignitary a person of high rank
dignity a stately or solemn manner: a high rank

digress to depart from the main subject when speaking or writing

dike, dyke a ditch: a long embankment or earth-bank (The dikes in Holland prevent flooding from the sea.)

dilapidated neglected and needing repair (as, a dilapidated old building)

dilate to swell; to make or grow larger

dilemma the position of having to choose between two things, each of which is unpleasant or unfavourable (for example - The boy was faced with the dilemma of leaving his cap in the stream or of wading in after it.)

diligent working hard and earnestly
diligence steadiness in working

dilly-dally to loiter; to trifle

dilute to lessen the strength of anything (especially liquid, by adding water)

dim not bright or distinct; not seeing, or understanding clearly □ to make, or become, dark

dimension the measurement of anything (as - The dimensions of the plank were 8 ft. long × 1 ft. wide × ¾ in. thick.)

diminish to make, or become, less
diminution a lessening
diminutive very small

dimple a small hollow (especially in the cheek or chin)

din a loud continued noise

dine to take dinner
dinner the main meal of the day

dinghy *(say ding-gee)* a small boat or ship's tender

dingy *(say dinjy)* shabby or dirty looking; not bright

dinner see **dine**

dinosaur a huge four-footed reptile that lived more than a hundred million years ago

diocese a bishop's district

dip to plunge for a moment; to put into a liquid; to lower for a moment (as, a flag); to slope downwards; to look at casually (as, to dip into a book) □ a bathe; a down-slope

diphtheria an infectious disease of the tonsils and throat

diphthong two vowel sounds pronounced as one syllable (for example, *out*)

diploma a statement confirming that a person has passed an examination; a statement conferring an honour or a privilege

diplomacy the art of negotiating with foreign countries; skill in managing people; tact
diplomat an official engaged in diplomacy (such as an ambassador); a skilled negotiator
diplomatic concerned with diplomacy; tactful

dire dreadful

direct straight; not roundabout; straightforward; frank □ to point or show the way; to instruct; to control
direction the act of directing; the way in which anything goes or moves (as, sailing in a southerly direction); an order or command; an instruction
directly in a direct manner; almost at once
director a person who directs; a member of a group of persons (a board of directors) who manage the affairs of a business
directory a book in which names and addresses are listed
direct current (D.C.) an electric current flowing in one direction only

dirge a funeral song; a lament

dirigible an airship that can be steered

dirt mud, dust or loose earth
dirty not clean, soiled □ to soil with dirt

dis- a prefix which often reverses the meaning of the rest of the word (as, **disagree, dishonest**)

disable to take away ability or strength; to cripple
disability a lack of ability or power
disablement a disability; the act of disabling

disadvantage a drawback; an unfavourable circumstance

disagree the opposite of agree; to differ; to quarrel: to cause indigestion (as - Shellfish disagree with me.)
disagreeable unpleasant

disappear to go out of sight; to fade away
disappearance a vanishing; a fading away

disappoint to fall short of one's hopes or expectations
disappointment anything that disappoints

disapprove to have an unfavourable opinion; the opposite of approve

disarm to take away weapons; the opposite of arm
disarmament a reduction of war weapons by a country or group of countries

disaster a great misfortune; a calamity
disastrous very unfortunate; ruinous

disband to break up or disperse a band of soldiers, etc.

disbelieve not to believe

disburse to pay out

disc, disk any flat, round shape; a gramophone record
disc jockey an announcer of recorded music (especially on radio programmes)

discard to throw away as useless

discern *(say disern)* to see; to distinguish by eyesight or understanding
discernible able to be seen
discerning having insight and understanding
discernment the act of discerning; insight

discharge to unload; to set free; to dismiss; to fire a gun: to perform (duties); to pay (a debt) □unloading; setting free; dismissal; firing (of a gun): performance (of duties)

disciple *(say disiepel)* a follower; someone who believes in a person's teaching (especially religious)

discipline *(say disiplin)* the keeping of order by some kind of control; training in an orderly way of life □to bring under control
disciplinarian a person who is strict in keeping order

disclaim to give up a claim; to deny (as, to disclaim responsibility)

disclose to reveal; to expose to view
disclosure the act of disclosing; something that is disclosed (as, a secret)

discolour to spoil the colour of; to stain

discomfiture embarrassment; defeat

discomfort lack of comfort; uneasiness

disconnect to separate; to detach
disconnected separated; rambling (in talking or writing)

disconsolate inconsolable; very unhappy

discontent lack of contentment; dissatisfaction

discontinue not to continue; to leave off or stop

discord disagreement: (in music) an unpleasant sound

discount a small sum of money taken off an account (for prompt payment, etc.) □to leave out of consideration, or out of account, some part of something (as, to discount someone's exaggerated description)

discourage to take courage away; to dishearten; to try to prevent an action (as, to discourage motorists from speeding)
discouragement the act of discouraging; the feeling of being discouraged
discouraging giving little or

no hope or encouragement

discourse a speech; a sermon □to talk in a learned way

discourteous *(say discurtyus)* not polite or courteous; rude
discourtesy the opposite of courtesy; rudeness

discover to find out; to find by chance
discovery anything discovered; the act of discovering

discredit to take away a person's reputation or good name; to disbelieve □loss of good reputation; disbelief
discreditable disgraceful

discreet careful not to say anything to cause trouble; prudent
discretion *(say diskreshun)* prudence; freedom to decide as one thinks best (as, to leave a decision to someone's discretion)

discrepancy an inconsistency; a difference or lack of agreement (for example, between two accounts of the same event)

discriminate to observe a difference between; to distinguish between
discrimination good judgment; the ability to recognize small differences: a difference in the way two persons are treated

discus *(say discus)* a heavy disc thrown by athletes in competitions (such as the Olympic Games)

discuss *(say discuss)* to talk about
discussion a conversation or debate on a subject

disdain to look down on with scorn or contempt □scorn; haughtiness
disdainful showing a scornful or haughty attitude

disease an illness
diseased having a disease

disfavour disapproval; being out of favour

disfigure to spoil the beauty of; to deface

disgrace shame; dishonour □to

bring shame upon
disgraceful shameful; very bad

disgruntled dissatisfied and sulky

disguise *(say disgize)* to change one's appearance by wearing different clothes, etc.; to hide (as, to disguise one's intentions) □ anything which disguises

disgust a very strong feeling of dislike; loathing □ to arouse such a feeling in someone
disgusting sickening: loathsome

dish a plate or other vessel in which food is served; the food in a dish

dishearten to take away a person's courage or hope

dishevelled untidy; with disordered hair

dishonest the opposite of honest; deceitful

dishonour lack of honour; disgrace □ to take away honour; to disgrace
dishonourable disgraceful

disillusioned having been shown that a former belief was really false

disinclined unwilling

disinfect to free from infection (by destroying disease germs)
disinfectant anything that disinfects

disinherit to take away the right to inherit (as when a father disinherits a son or daughter)

disintegrate to fall into pieces; to break up; to crumble
disintegration breaking up into parts or pieces

disinterested unselfish; not influenced by one's private interests or feelings; impartial (This word is sometimes confused with **uninterested**, the opposite of **interested**.)

disjointed not properly connected

disk see **disc**

dislike the opposite of like

dislocate to put out of joint; to put out of order (as when traffic is dislocated by an accident)
dislocation a dislocated joint

(such as an ankle); a disorganization (as of plans)

dislodge to turn out of a hiding-place or defensive position; to remove something from its proper place by accident

disloyal not loyal; unfaithful
disloyalty the opposite of loyalty

dismal gloomy; sorrowful

dismantle to strip off or take down fittings, furniture, etc.; to take to pieces

dismay loss of courage through fear; consternation □ to discourage; to upset

dismiss to send away; to discharge from employment
dismissal the act of dismissing; discharge

dismount to get off a horse, bicycle, etc.

disobey the opposite of obey; to refuse, or fail, to carry out an instruction
disobedient refusing, or failing, to obey

disorder lack of order; confusion; disturbance □ to disarrange
disorderly confused; lawless (as, disorderly behaviour)

disorganize to destroy an organization or system; to throw into disorder

disown to refuse to own or to admit as one's own

disparage to speak slightingly of a person or of some action

disparity an inequality; a difference; the opposite of parity

dispassionate without passion; calm; impartial

dispatch, despatch to send or send away (as, to dispatch a letter); to do something quickly: to put to death □ the act of sending away; promptness; a message or report: a putting to death

dispel to drive away; to make disappear

dispense to deal out; to distribute: to make up (medical) prescriptions

dispensable that can be done without; not necessary

dispensary a place where medicines are dispensed (as in a hospital or a large chemist's shop)

disperse to scatter in all directions; to go away or vanish (as - The crowd dispersed.)

dispirited dejected; having lost heart

displace to put out of place; to disarrange

displacement a putting out of place: the quantity of water displaced by a floating body (for example, a ship with a displacement of 20,000 tons)

display to show; to exhibit □ a show to attract notice; an exhibition

displease to offend; to be disagreeable to

dispose to arrange; to get rid of (as - He disposed of his old bike.): to incline in feeling (as - Her mother was disposed to forgive her.)

disposal arrangement; a geting rid of; the right to use (as - A car was placed at his disposal.)

disposition arrangement: natural tendency or attitude (as - The pony had a gentle disposition.)

dispossess to take away some possession; to deprive

disproportionate too large or too small compared with something else; lacking in proportion

dispute an argument between people; a quarrel □ to argue about

disputable able to be disputed; not certain

disqualify to take away a qualification; to pronounce unqualified or unfit because a rule has been broken (as when a jockey is disqualified in a race)

disquiet uneasiness; restlessness □ to make uneasy

disregard to pay no attention to □ lack of attention; neglect

disrepair a state of needing repair

disreputable having a bad reputation; disgraceful

disrespect lack of respect; rudeness

disrobe to undress

disrupt to break up; to throw into disorder

disruption a sudden break-up or division (as, disruption in a political meeting)

dissatisfied not satisfied; discontented

dissect to cut into parts

dissection the cutting into parts or pieces for examination (as, the dissection of a frog)

dissemble to disguise (feelings or intentions)

disseminate to spread widely (especially news or information)

dissent to have a different opinion; to refuse to agree □ difference of opinion; a refusal to agree

dissension a bad feeling caused by differences of opinion

disservice an ill turn; an injury

dissimilar unlike, not the same

dissimulate to pretend about, or to hide, one's true feelings

dissipate to squander or waste; to dispel; to scatter

dissipated with wasted strength or looks through too much alcoholic drinking, bad living, etc.

dissipation wasteful spending (of money or energy); bad living habits

dissociate to separate (in thought or in action)

dissolve to melt in solution (as, to dissolve salt in water); to break up; to put an end to (as, to dissolve Parliament)

dissolution a breaking-up or ending

dissuade to persuade or advise a person against doing something

dissuasion persuasion against doing something

distance the space between two places; a far-off place or point (as, a ship visible in the distance)

distant far off; not close; reserved in manner

distaste dislike
distasteful disagreeable; unpleasant

distemper 1 a kind of paint used chiefly on walls □ to paint with distemper

distemper 2 a disease which affects dogs

distend to swell; to stretch outwards

distil to purify a liquid by turning it first into vapour by means of heat, and then by turning the vapour back into a liquid by cooling (Whisky and gin are distilled spirits.); to let or cause a liquid to fall in drops
distillation the act of distilling
distillery a place where alcoholic spirits are distilled

distinct separate; different; clearly seen or heard
distinction a difference: outstanding merit
distinctive different in a distinguishing way; characteristic (as, the distinctive sound of a jet aeroplane)

distinguish to recognize something as different from something else (as, to distinguish a swallow from other birds by its forked tail); to recognize (as, to distinguish a person's face in the dark): to gain distinction or prominence (as, to distinguish oneself by winning a race)
distinguished marked out by some behaviour or ability (as, for courage in an emergency); famous

distort to twist out of shape; to misrepresent
distortion the twisting of anything out of its natural shape or form

distract to draw a person's attention away
distracted having one's attention or mind drawn aside: almost crazy (as, distracted with grief)

distraction a diversion; something that takes one's mind off normal affairs; an amusement; perplexity

distress a feeling of great pain, sorrow or worry □ to cause pain or sorrow

distribute to divide among several; to deal out; to spread widely
distribution distributing; dealing out: the widespread selling of goods by manufacturers, merchants and shops

district an area or region; a part of a county or town □ relating to a district

distrust a lack of trust; suspicion □ to have no trust in

disturb to agitate; to bother; to interrupt
disturbance an act of disturbing; a disorder; an interruption

disused not used; no longer used

ditch a narrow trench dug in the ground (especially for draining water)

ditto (often shortened to **do.**) the same thing as already written (a word used in tables of figures, etc. to avoid writing the same figures or words many times)

ditty a short and simple song

divan a low couch without back or sides

dive to plunge into water or down through the air □ a plunge; a swoop
diver a person who dives into deep water (especially one who works under water on wrecks, etc.)

diverge to separate and go in different directions
divergent going a different way

diverse different; of various kinds
diversify to make different; to give variety to
diversity a different kind; a variety

divert to change direction; to turn aside (as, to divert a blow): to amuse

diversion a turning aside; a different way (as when there is a traffic diversion because of road works): an amusement
diverting amusing

divide to separate into parts; to share; to find out how many times one number contains another
dividend a number that is to be divided (*12 ÷ 6 = 2*): a share of profit from a business
divisible able to be divided
division the act of dividing; a barrier: a section; an army unit
divisor the number by which the dividend is to be divided (*12 ÷ 6 = 2*)

divine belonging to a god; holy □ a clergyman □ to foretell
divination foretelling the future; insight
divinity the nature of a god: a god

division see **divide**

divorce the ending of a marriage by law □ to dissolve the marriage of a husband or wife; to separate

divulge to let out (a secret); to make something known

dizzy giddy; confused

do to perform or carry out any action; to arrange (as when a girl does her hair); to prepare (as - I will do you some bacon and eggs.)

docile easy to manage (especially of animals)

dock 1 a large artificial basin where ships are unloaded or repaired: the place in a law court where the accused person stands
docker a man who works in the docks
dockyard an enclosure with docks, stores, etc. (especially one used by the navy)

dock 2 a weed with large leaves and a long root

dock 3 to clip or cut short

docket a label; a short note attached to a document to indicate its contents

doctor a person trained in healing sick people: a person who has received the highest degree from a university □ to treat a patient as a doctor does

doctrine a set of beliefs on a particular subject

document a paper with written information or evidence
documentary in the form of a document □ a television programme or film which deals with interesting facts about a subject

dodder to shake or tremble

dodge to avoid someone or something by moving quickly □ an act of dodging; a trick

dodo a large bird now extinct

doe the female of the fallow deer, hare or rabbit

doff to take off (especially one's hat or gloves)

dog a four-footed flesh-eating animal often kept as a pet □ to follow closely as a dog does (as, to dog a person's footsteps)
dogged keeping on at what one is doing; persistent

doggerel poorly written or trivial poetry

dogma a doctrine laid down by authority (especially by the Church); an opinion that will not stand contradiction
dogmatic arrogantly authoritative

doldrums parts of the ocean near the equator where there is little wind (so that sailing ships are frequently becalmed): low spirits

dole a payment by the state to an unemployed person □ to give out in small portions

doleful very sad; full of grief

doll a toy in the form of a human being

dolphin a very intelligent sea animal about 8 to 10 feet long, rather like a porpoise (It is friendly towards human beings and can be taught to do tricks.)

during throughout; in the course of

dusk twilight; the time of evening when it is partially dark
dusky dark-coloured; shadowy

dust powdery dirt carried in the air; fine grains of any solid matter (as, coal dust) □ to free from dust; to sprinkle with powder
dustbin a bin for household rubbish
duster a cloth for removing dust

duty anything a person ought to do, or has to do (as - Her office duties are light.): a tax on goods (as, customs duty)
dutiable liable to be taxed
dutiful obedient; attentive to duty

dwarf an animal, plant or person much below ordinary size □ to make look small

dwell to live, or have one's home in a place: to speak for some time about (as, to dwell on a subject)
dwelling the house in which a person lives

dwindle to get less in size; to waste away

dye a substance used to change the colour of cloth or other material □ to change the colour of a material by means of a dye

dyke see **dike**

dynamic concerned with force; (of a person) forceful or very energetic
dynamite a powerful explosive
dynamo a machine for producing electricity

dynasty *(say dinasty)* a succession of rulers of the same family

dysentery *(say disentree)* an infectious disease of the bowels

e

each every one of two or more

eager anxious for, or to do, something; keen

eagle a large bird of prey, with a sharp curved beak and keen eyesight
eaglet a young eagle

ear 1 the part of the head through which sounds are heard
earache a pain in the ear
eardrum the membrane in the middle part of the ear
earmark an owner's mark; a distinctive mark □ to mark something for future attention
earring an ornament attached to the ear
earshot the distance at which a sound can be heard
earwig a brown winged insect with pincers (formerly supposed to creep into the human ear)

ear 2 a spike of grain (as, an ear of wheat)

earl a British nobleman ranking between a marquis and a viscount
earldom the lands or title of an earl

early in good time; at or near the beginning (as, early in his life) □ happening in the near future (as, to fix an early date for an appointment)

earn to gain money, etc. by work; to deserve
earnings wages; salary

earnest serious

earth the planet we live on; the world; soil; dry land; a burrow; an electrical connection with the earth □ to connect something to earth electrically
earthenware pottery (as distinct from china)

earthquake a shaking of the earth's crust

earthwork a fortification made of earth

earthworm the common worm

ease freedom from pain or difficulty; rest from work □ to free from pain, difficulty or pressure

easily with no difficulty

easy not difficult; not hard to do or understand

easel a stand for a blackboard, or for a picture on which an artist is working

east the direction in which the sun rises; the opposite of west

eastern, eastward towards the east

easterly coming from the east (as, an easterly breeze); looking towards the east

Easter a religious festival commemorating the resurrection of Christ

eat to chew and swallow food

eaves the edges of a roof overhanging the walls

eavesdrop to listen in order to overhear secrets

ebb the going back of the sea after high tide; a decline □ to flow away

ebony a very hard, black wood □ made of, or as black as, ebony

eccentric odd; not normal (as, eccentric behaviour): not having an axis or support in the centre (as, an eccentric device in an engine)

eccentricity oddness of behaviour; the state of being eccentric

ecclesiastic(al) having to do with the church or clergy

echo *(say ecko)* a sound that is thrown back by a surface which it strikes (as, echoes in a tunnel or cave) □ to send back sound: to imitate

eclipse (of the sun) a cutting off of light from the sun when the moon comes between it and the earth; (of the moon) a cutting off of light from the moon when the earth's shadow falls on it □ to darken: to surpass

economy the management of money or of financial affairs (as, the economy of a country); a saving (as, a housewife making weekly economies)

economical careful in spending; not wasteful

economics the study of the production and selling of goods for money

economist a person who studies, or is an expert in, economics

economize to be careful in spending

ecstasy a very great joy; a mad delight

ecstatic madly delighted; rapturous

eczema a disease of the skin

eddy a back-current of water or air □ to move round and round (as, smoke eddying in the air)

edge the border of anything (as, the edge of a table); the cutting side of a knife □ to border; to move little by little (as, to edge away from a person)

edgy, on edge uneasy; nervous; irritable

edible fit to be eaten

edict a decree or order by someone in authority

edifice a large building

edit to prepare something written, recorded or filmed (by correcting, shortening, revising, etc.) for printing or broadcasting

edition the number of copies of a book or newspaper printed at one time (as - 5000 copies of the 2nd edition were printed.)

editor someone who edits; a person who selects, and is responsible for, the contents of a newspaper, periodical, etc.

editorial concerned with an editor □ an article written by an editor or leader writer

educate to help people to learn things

education the process of educating people (usually in schools and colleges)

eel a very long, snake-like fish

eerie, eery weird; causing fear (as, an eerie feeling when one is alone in an old house)

efface to rub out; to make seem unimportant (as - He tried to efface the memory of his failure.)

effect the result of an action; the impression produced by something (as, the dramatic effect of the stage-lighting); the meaning of a statement (as - His remarks were to the effect that a rescue attempt should not be delayed.) □ to bring about
effective able to produce a desired result; powerful (as, an effective weapon)

effervescent frothing up; lively (as, an effervescent mood)

efficient (of a person) competent; skilful; (of an instrument or method) satisfactory in use; very practical

effigy a dummy figure of a person (as, an effigy in a waxworks or on a tomb)

effort a strong attempt

effusive gushing; emotional (as - She was effusive in her welcome.)

egg 1 an oval object with a thin shell, laid by birds, insects, etc. (The embryo chicken, etc. lives inside the egg until it is hatched, or born.)

egg 2 (followed by **on**) to urge a person to do something

egoism self-interest; selfishness
egoist a self-centred or selfish person
egotism speaking too much of oneself
egotist a boastful person

eider *(say ieder)* **(duck)** a northern sea duck, valued for its fine down
eiderdown a quilt filled with the downy feathers of the eider duck or a similar material

either the one or the other; the one and the other (as, trees

on either side of the road)

ejaculate to utter, or exclaim, suddenly

eject to throw out
ejector-seat a seat in an aeroplane that can be shot clear with its occupant in an emergency

elaborate *(say elaborait)* to work out in detail; to explain very fully □ *(say elaborit)* very detailed (as, elaborate preparations); highly decorated or finished (as, an elaborate design)

elapse (of time) to pass (as - A week elapsed before he came.)

elastic a material containing rubber which stretches easily □ able to stretch and spring back again
elasticity springiness

elated in high spirits; joyful

elbow the joint where the arm bends; any sharp bend □ to push with the elbow; to jostle

elder 1 a large shrub which produces purple-black berries
elderberry the fruit of the elder, from which wine can be made

elder 2 older; senior □ an older, experienced person
elderly oldish or getting old
eldest oldest

elect to choose by voting; to select □ chosen
election the choosing (usually by voting) of public representatives to sit in parliament, or in a town council, etc.
elector a person who has a vote at an election

electricity an invisible form of energy used to make light and heat and to drive machinery
electric(al) having to do with electricity
electrician a person who installs, operates or repairs electrical appliances and wiring
electrify to give, or adapt to, electricity (as, to electrify the railways)
electrocute to kill by an electric current
electrode one of the two con-

ductors, or poles, of an electric battery

electro-magnet a piece of iron made to act like a magnet by means of electricity (An electric current is passed through a coil of wire wound round the iron.)

electron a minute particle, smaller than an atom, charged with electricity

electronic having to do with electrons or electronics

electronics a branch of science, based on the use of electrons (It is concerned with the conduction of electricity in a vacuum, a gas, etc. and such devices as cathode-ray tubes and transistors.)

electron microscope see **microscope**

elegant graceful; refined; tasteful

element a necessary part of anything; any substance which cannot be broken up or separated into substances different from itself (Examples of these chemical elements are silver, mercury, hydrogen, oxygen and carbon.)

elements the first things to be learned in any subject (as, the elements of arithmetic); the forces of nature (as, the wind and rain)

elementary simple; at the first stage

elephant the largest four-footed animal, which has very thick skin, a trunk and two ivory tusks

elephantine big and clumsy

elevate to raise to a higher position; to improve in thoughts or behaviour

elevation the act of raising; rising ground; height

elevator a lift for raising people or goods to a higher level

elf a tiny, mischievous fairy

elicit to draw out from a person (as, to elicit information from a prisoner)

eligible qualified or worthy to be chosen

eliminate to get rid of; to remove

elimination removal; expulsion

elixir (say *elixer*) a supposed magic drink which people once thought would give lasting life

elk the largest kind of deer, found in the North of Europe, North America and Asia

ellipse an oval shape

elliptical oval

elm a tall tree with corrugated bark and notched leaves

elocution the art of speaking clearly and effectively

elongated stretched out; long and (usually) narrow

elope to run away secretly to get married

eloquent expressing oneself fluently and persuasively; good at speaking in public

else otherwise; if not □other (as, someone else)

elsewhere not here; in another place

elude to escape or avoid by skill or by a trick

elusive hard to catch or grasp

emaciated (say *emayshee-ayted*) very thin or lean; with little flesh

emancipate to set free (especially from slavery)

embalm to preserve a dead body from decay by treating it with drugs; to perfume with balm

embankment a bank of earth or stone to keep water back, to carry a railway, etc.

embargo an order to stop trade (especially ships from entering or leaving a port)

embark to put, or go, on board a ship; to start on anything (as, to embark on a career)

embarkation the act of embarking

embarrass to make someone feel awkward or upset; to put difficulties in someone's way; to hinder

embarrassment the state of being embarrassed

embassy an ambassador and his staff; an ambassador's official residence

embellish to make beautiful with ornaments

ember a glowing cinder

embezzle to spend on oneself money that has been entrusted to one by others

embitter to make bitter; to cause ill-feeling

emblem a badge; a sign (as - The dove is the emblem of peace.)

embolden to make bold; to give courage

emboss to ornament with a raised design (especially metal or leather, but also paper)

embrace to take in the arms with affection; to hug; to include (as - The term American embraces all the countries in the Western Hemisphere.) □ a clasping in the arms or hug

embrasure an opening in a thick wall, with its sides slanting outwards (as, embrasures for cannon in a castle wall)

embrocation a lotion for rubbing on the body (especially to ease stiff muscles)

embroider to ornament with designs in needlework
embroidery embroidering; ornamental patterns in needlework

embryo a young animal or plant in its earliest stage of growth inside the egg, womb or seed; the beginning stage of anything
embryonic in an early stage of development

emerald a bright green precious stone □ green in colour like an emerald

emerge to rise, or come, out
emergency an unexpected happening; a sudden event requiring immediate action

emery a very hard mineral used as a powder for polishing (as, emery paper for smoothing a rough surface)

emigrate to leave one's country and settle in another
emigrant anyone who emi-

grates from his country

eminent rising above others; famous
eminence a rising ground or hill; a title of honour (as, His Eminence)

emit to give, or send, out (as - Fires emit heat.)
emissary someone sent out on a mission (often secret)
emission the act of emitting

emotion any strong feeling (as, the emotions of fear or love); an agitation of the mind
emotional of the emotions; (of a person) easily moved by joy, love, fear, etc.

emperor the male head of an empire

emphasis *(say emfassis)* a stress put on one or more words when speaking (as - Do NOT go near the river.); importance given to something
emphasize to lay stress on anything (as - His report emphasized the need to work harder.)
emphatic expressed with emphasis or force; firm and definite

empire a group of countries or states under one ruler

employ to use or make use of; to give work to someone (usually for payment) □ employment; service
employee anyone who works for an employer
employer anyone who gives people work to do (generally regular work for a salary or wages)
employment the act of employing; the state of being employed; an occupation (in trade, industry, a profession, etc.)

empress the female head of an empire, or an emperor's wife

empty having nothing, or no one, inside; unoccupied (as, an empty house); useless (as, an empty threat) □ an empty bottle, etc. □ to make or become empty (as - The cinema emptied quickly.)
emptiness the state of

being empty

emu a large Australian bird, rather like an ostrich

emulate to try to do as well as, or better than, someone else; to imitate

emulsion a milky mixture of an oil and water

enable to make able

enact to act the part of; to make a law

enamel the hard, shiny coating on baths, cookers, refrigerators, etc.; a glossy paint; the smooth coating of the teeth □ to coat or paint with enamel

encampment a place where troops have made their camp

encase to cover in a case

enchant to put a charm or spell on; to delight
enchanter a magician
enchantress a female enchanter

encircle to enclose with a circle; to surround

enclose to close or shut in; to surround; to put inside an envelope or package
enclosure something enclosed (as, land surrounded by a fence)

encompass to surround

encore (say ongkor) a call from an audience for the repetition of a performance □ to call performers back for a repetition of their act or part of it

encounter to meet (especially unexpectedly) □ a meeting; a fight

encourage to give courage to someone; to urge someone to do something
encouragement the act of encouraging; something which encourages

encroach to trespass; to intrude into, or interfere with, another person's land or rights

encumber to hamper with a burden or difficulty

encyclopaedia (say encyclopee-dia) a reference work containing much information of general knowledge or of a particular subject

end the last point or part; the finish; the death; the aim or purpose (as, the end which he had in view) □ to bring to an end; to destroy

endeavour to try; to strive to do □ an attempt

endorse to write on the back of something (as, to endorse a cheque or a motor licence); to give one's approval to something
endorsement the act or the fact of endorsing

endow to leave money to maintain an institution or a part of one (as, to endow a ward or a bed in a hospital); to give a special talent to someone (as - Nature endowed her with a gift for music.)
endowment money left to endow a hospital, school, etc.

endure to bear with patience; to remain firm; to last
endurance the power of bearing hardship, pain, etc. without giving in

enemy someone who is hostile or fights against one; a force or country armed to fight against another
enmity a state of hostility; ill-will

energy the habit or power of vigorous activity
energetic very active; vigorous

enforce to do by force; to put into force (as, to enforce a law)

engage to bind by a promise; to hire a person to do work; to take hold of (as, to engage a person's attention); to take part in (as, to engage in a sport)
engaged bound by a promise (especially of marriage): occupied or busy
engagement a promise of marriage: a conflict with an enemy (as, a naval engagement)

engine a machine in which energy is used to produce motion (Aeroplanes, cars and diesel-electric locomotives are all moved by engines which get their energy from fuel oils.); a railway locomotive

engineer a person who designs or makes machinery; an officer who manages a ship's engines □ to arrange by careful planning

civil engineer a person who designs or constructs roads, railways, bridges, dams, etc.

engrave to cut a design or letters into a hard surface such as metal, wood or stone

engraving an engraved pattern or plate; a print taken from an engraved surface

engulf to swallow up wholly

enigma a puzzling statement; anything puzzling

enjoy to find pleasure in; to experience pleasure; to get benefit from (as, to enjoy good health)

enjoyable giving pleasure; able to be enjoyed

enjoyment the state of enjoying; pleasure

enlarge to make larger; to make a larger copy

enlargement an increase in the size of anything

enlighten to give information to someone

enlist to join a public service (especially the armed forces); to obtain or make use of (as, to enlist another person's help in some cause)

enliven *(say enliven)* to put life into; to make active or cheerful

enmity see **enemy**

enormous very large; immense

enough sufficient; just as much as is needed

enquire, enquiry see **inquire, inquiry**

enrage to make angry

enrich to make rich

enrol, enroll to enter a name in a roll, register or list

en route *(say on root)* on the way to a place

ensign the flag of a nation, regiment, etc. (The White Ensign is the flag of the Royal Navy.)

enslave to make a slave of someone

ensue to follow or come after; to result

ensure to make sure

entangle to make tangled; to involve in difficulties

entanglement a tangled obstacle (as, a military barrier of barbed-wire); a difficult situation

enter to go or come into a place; to put into a list or record (as, to enter a name or a figure)

entry the act of entering; an entrance; something entered in a record

enterprise an undertaking; some project that is being attempted; a willingness to undertake new things

entertain to amuse; to have as a guest; to hold or turn over in one's mind (as, to entertain a new idea)

entertaining amusing

entertainer a person who performs in some way to amuse an audience

entertainment the act of entertaining; any kind of enjoyable or amusing recreation

enthral(l) to give great delight; to hold as by a spell

enthrone to place (someone) on a throne

enthusiasm keenness; eagerness; intense interest in something

enthusiastic acting with enthusiasm; greatly interested

entice to tempt; to lead astray

enticement a bribe; a promise of reward

entire complete; whole

entirety completeness; the whole

entitle to give a title or name to (as, a book, a poem, etc.); to give a right to a person (as - He is entitled to a place in the team.)

entity something that really exists; existence

entrails the internal parts of an

animal's body; the intestines

entrance 1 (*say* _entrance_) a place of entering; a doorway or gateway; the act of entering
entrant someone who enters (especially one who enters a competition, examination or profession)

entrance 2 (*say* _entrance_) to put into a trance; to overwhelm with delight

entreat to ask earnestly
entreaty an earnest request

entrust to trust something to the care of someone else

entry see **enter**

entwine to twine or twist round

enumerate to count the number of; to name over (as, to enumerate a person's faults)
enumeration the act of numbering; a detailed naming or accounting

enunciate to pronounce distinctly; to express something in a formal way

envelop (*say* _envelop_) to cover by wrapping; to surround entirely
envelope (*say* _envelope_) a folded cover or wrapping (especially for a letter)

enviable, envious see **envy**

environment surroundings (especially as they affect living conditions, such as housing, transport, etc.)
environs the outskirts of a city or town

envisage to picture in one's mind and consider; to think of

envoy a messenger (especially a government representative sent to a foreign country)

envy a grudging feeling about another person's success or good fortune; □ to grudge another person his success or good fortune and desire it for oneself
enviable worth envying; worth having
envious feeling, or showing, envy

epaulet(te) an ornamental

shoulder piece on a uniform

epic a long poem telling of great deeds □ heroic; grand

epidemic an outbreak of a disease which spreads to affect large numbers of people

epilepsy a brain disease which is sometimes accompanied by convulsions
epileptic a person subject to epilepsy □ of epilepsy (as, an epileptic fit)

epilogue the concluding section of a play or book, etc.

episode an event or series of events, happening in a story, in history or in life

epistle a letter (especially one from an apostle, as, the epistles of St. Paul)

epitaph an inscription on a tombstone

epithet a describing word or adjective (as, a *green* field)

epoch (*say* _eepok_ or _epok_) a period in history notable for important events
epoch-making marking an important point in history (as - The aeroplane was an epoch-making invention.)

equable (*say* _ekwable_) uniform; temperate (as, an equable climate); not easily annoyed (as - She has an equable nature.)

equal of the same size, quantity or value (as, an equal share) □ a person of the same age, rank, etc. □ to be the same as; to do as well as
equalize to make equal
equality the state of being equal
equation a statement in which two things are looked on as being equal ($4x + 2 = 14$ is a simple equation in algebra)

equanimity calmness; evenness of temper

equator an imaginary line making a circle round the earth, halfway between the North and South Poles
equatorial of, or near, the

equator

equestrian having to do with horse-riding □ a person riding on horseback

equi- *(say ekwi)* a prefix meaning equal
equidistant equally distant
equilateral having all sides equal
equilibrium equal balance (between weights or forces or between opposing powers, etc.)
equivalent equal in value or meaning

equinox the time in each year when the sun crosses the equator, making night and day equal in length (about March 21st and September 23rd)
equinoctial of about the time of the equinoxes

equine having to do with horses; like a horse

equip to fit out with everything needed
equipment an outfit; the act of equipping (as, the equipment of an expedition)

equity fairness; justice
equitable fair; just

equivalent see **equi-**

era a period of years starting from a particular date (as, the Christian era); an historical period or age

eradicate to root out; to get rid of completely

erase to rub out
eraser something which erases; a rubber
erasure a rubbing out

erect to set upright; to construct (as, a building) □ upright

ermine *(say ermin)* the stoat; its white winter fur (which is used in the robes of judges and peers)

erode to wear away (as, rocks eroded by the weather); to eat away (as - Acid erodes metal.)
erosion a wearing down; an eating away

err to go astray; to make a mistake; to sin
erratic wandering; irregular;

not dependable in behaviour
erroneous mistaken, wrong
error a mistake; a blunder

errand a short journey to take a message or to deliver or collect something

erroneous, error see **err**

erupt to break out; (of a volcano) to throw out lava, etc.
eruption a breaking out or bursting forth (as, an eruption of pimples on the skin)

escalator a moving staircase

escape to get free; to run away; to manage to avoid (as, to escape punishment); to leak (as - The gas was escaping.) □ the act of escaping
escapade a mischievous adventure

escort *(say escort)* an attendant or attendants acting as protector(s) or guide(s); an accompanying ship or ships, for protection or guidance □ *(say escort)* to attend as escort

especial particular; exceptional (as, an especial favour)
especially particularly; most of all; notably

espionage *(say espeeonahzh)* spying; the use of spies

esplanade a level road (especially at the seaside) for walking or driving

espouse *(say espowz)* to take as a wife: to support (a cause)

espresso a coffee-making machine which forces steam through the ground coffee

espy *(say espie)* to catch sight of

esquire *(usually shortened to Esq.)* a title of politeness used after the surname when addressing a letter (instead of Mr. before the name)

essay an attempt: a written composition □ to attempt
essayist a writer of essays

essence the concentrated, pure part of anything (for example, vanilla essence); the most important part of anything, disregarding any details (as, the essence of an argument)

essential absolutely necessary; containing, or relating to, the essence of something

establish to settle firmly; to set up or found (as, to establish a business)

establishment the act of establishing; something established (such as a shop or residence): the permanent staff of a government department, commercial firm, etc.; the number of men in a military force

estate a large piece of land owned by a person or company; the total possessions of a person

esteem to think highly of; to value □ favourable opinion; respect

estimable deserving people's good opinion

estimate to judge the worth of something; to calculate approximately □ an approximate judgment of a value, amount or quantity

estimation judgment; opinion; reckoning

estuary the wide lower part of a river, up which the tide flows

et cetera (usually written **etc.**) a Latin phrase meaning *and the rest* or *and so on*

etch to make designs on metal, glass, etc. by eating out lines with acid

etching the picture from an etched plate

eternal lasting for ever; unchanging

eternity time without end, or seemingly without end; the time or state after death

ether *(say eether)* the clear upper air beyond the clouds: a colourless, volatile liquid used as an anaesthetic and as a solvent of fats

ethereal airy; heavenly

ethical having to do with morals and right behaviour; morally right

etiquette *(say etiket)* the unwritten rules of correct behaviour in polite society; the code of behaviour observed by a particular profession (as, medical etiquette)

eucalyptus *(say yewkaliptus)* a large Australian evergreen tree, valued for oil, gum and timber

euphemism *(say yewfemizm)* a mild name for something that is unpleasant (as - *To pass away* is a euphemism for *to die.*)

evacuate to leave, or withdraw from, a place; to empty out

evacuation a withdrawal (especially of troops, or of civilians from a dangerous place); an emptying out

evade to escape, or avoid something by a trick or skill

evasion a clever escape or avoidance; an excuse

evasive intending to evade; not straightforward (as, an evasive answer)

evaluate to find the value of

evangelist a preacher of the gospel: one of the writers of the four gospels

evaporate to turn into vapour (Water evaporates as steam when it is boiled.); to vanish

evasion, evasive see **evade**

eve evening; the day or night before a festival or event (as, Christmas Eve, the eve of the battle)

even level; smooth: not odd but divisible by two without a remainder □ to make level or smooth □ still (and other uses for emphasis as: even better - Even his friends do not trust him. - The boys take cold showers even in winter.)

evening the close of day, between afternoon and night

event something that happens (as, the chief events of the year); an item in a sports programme

eventful full of events; exciting

eventual happening as a result; final

ever always; at all times (and for

emphasis, as, ever so fast)

evergreen always green □ a shrub or tree that stays green all the year

everlasting lasting for ever; endless

evermore for ever

every each one of a number without exception

everybody, everyone every person

everyday daily; usual; of weekdays, not Sunday

everything all things; all

everywhere in every place

evict to turn out or expel (especially from house or land by force of law)

evident easily seen or understood; obvious

evidence a clear sign or indication; information given in a law court

evil wicked; very bad □ wickedness; sin

evince to show or make evident (as, to evince surprise)

evoke to draw out or bring forth (as, fine acting which evoked much applause); to call up in the mind (as, to evoke happy memories)

evolve to develop (as, to evolve a plan); to come as a result very gradually (as - Mankind has evolved over millions of years.)

evolution a gradual development

ewe *(say yew)* a female sheep

exact accurate □ to compel someone to pay (as, to exact a fine for an offence)

exactly just right; correctly

exacting severe; demanding much from a person (as, an exacting job)

exactitude, exactness accuracy; correctness

exaggerate *(say egzajerate)* to make something seem greater than it actually is; to overstate

exaggeration an overstatement; an extravagant representation

exalt to raise in rank; to praise highly

examine to test; to put questions to; to look at closely

examination, exam a test of knowledge or ability; a close inspection

example a sample or specimen; one case given to help make other cases clear (as, an example of a problem in arithmetic); a person or thing that serves as a pattern or a warning (as - He set a good example to his small brother.)

exasperation a state or mood of extreme irritation or anger

excavate to dig or scoop out a hole; to uncover buried ruins by digging

excavation the act of excavating; a hollow or cavity made by excavating

excavator a machine for excavating; someone who excavates

exceed to go beyond what is allowed (as, to exceed the speed limit); to be greater or better than (as, to exceed one's expectations)

exceedingly greatly

excel to be better than; to be very good at

excellence great merit

Excellency a title of high honour (as, His Excellency, the French Ambassador)

excellent unusually good

except leaving out; apart from □ to leave out

exception something left out; something different from the rest (as, an exception to the rule)

exceptional unusual; standing out from the rest

to take exception to to object to

excerpt a passage taken from a book, play, etc.; an extract

excess a going beyond what is usual or desirable; the amount by which one thing exceeds another □ beyond the amount allowed (as, excess baggage)

excessive beyond what is right and proper (as, excessive prices)

exchange to give one thing in return for another □ the act of exchanging; the exchanging of one country's currency for another's (as, francs for pounds); a building where business transactions take place (as, the Stock Exchange); a building where telephone lines are connected (a telephone exchange)

exchequer *(say ekscheker)* the government department in charge of the country's money affairs

excise a tax on certain goods made inside a country

excite to make a person feel strongly; to rouse or stir up
excitable easily excited
excitement the state of being excited; agitation
exciting producing excitement (as, an exciting football match)

exclaim to speak or cry out suddenly
exclamation a sudden utterance or cry which expresses surprise, etc.
exclamation mark the punctuation mark which follows and indicates a written exclamation (!)
exclamatory expressing exclamation

exclude to shut out; to prevent from sharing; the opposite of include
exclusion the act of excluding; the state of being excluded (as, the exclusion of a country from the United Nations)
exclusive shutting or keeping unwanted people out (as, an exclusive club); not including

excrement see excrete

excrescence any abnormal outgrowth (such as fungus on a tree trunk)

excrete (of animals or plants) to separate and expel waste matter
excrement waste matter expelled from the body; dung

excruciating *(say ekscrooshiayting)* extremely painful

excursion a pleasure trip; a trip by train, bus, etc. at a reduced fare

excuse *(say ekskewss)* a reason given for failing to do something, or for doing something wrong □ *(say ekscuze)* to overlook a fault; to free from an obligation (as, to excuse a pupil from doing homework)
excusable pardonable
Excuse me ... *I beg your pardon* (a mild apology)

execute to perform; to carry into effect (as, to execute a plan): to put to death by law
execution performance; carrying out: putting to death by law
executioner a person appointed to carry out a death sentence
executive *(say eksekutiv)* having power to act or carry out laws □ a person in business or government service who directs or manages; the branch of a government that puts laws into effect
executor *(say eksecutor)* a person appointed to see that a will is carried into effect

exemplary worth following as an example (as, exemplary behaviour); serving as a warning (as, exemplary punishment)

exemplify to be an example of; to show by example

exempt to free from some duty or payment (as, to exempt from military service) □ freed from a duty, etc.

exercise the training of body or mind; a task for practice □ to train by using one's faculties (physical or mental); to use (as, to exercise great care)

exert to bring into action (as, to exert force)
exertion the act of exerting; striving

exhale to breathe out; the opposite of inhale
exhalation a breathing out; a puff of breath

exhaust *(say egzawst)* to use up (as, to exhaust one's supplies); to tire out (as - The runner was exhausted.); to say or do all that can be said or done (as, to exhaust the subject) □ the pipe from an engine which lets out waste, gas, steam, etc.

exhausted tired out; used up

exhaustion extreme tiredness; loss of strength

exhaustive treating very thoroughly (as, an exhaustive description)

exhibit to show or display (often in public) □ something shown or displayed (as, an exhibit in a museum)

exhibition a public show (especially of works of art or of manufactures)

exhilarating enlivening; cheering

exhort to urge strongly (as, to exhort people to vote)

exhortation the act of exhorting

exile a person who has been forced to stay away from his own country; the stay of such a person in a foreign country □ to expel from one's own country; to banish

exist to live; to be

existence the state of existing or being

existent, existing actual; in being at the present time

exit a way out; a going out or off (especially of an actor from the stage)

exodus a going away or out of a large number of people (especially of the Israelites from Egypt, as told in the book of Exodus in the Bible)

exonerate to free from blame

exorbitant going beyond what is reasonable (as, an exorbitant price)

exorcise to drive away an evil spirit

exotic introduced from a foreign country (as, an exotic plant)

expand to spread out; to make or grow larger

expanse a wide area (as, an expanse of ocean)

expansion the act of expanding; the state of being expanded

expansive able or tending to expand; extensive

expatriate *(say expaytree-ate)* to banish or exile a person from his native country; to withdraw oneself from living in one's native country □ expatriated □ an expatriated person

expect to think something will happen; to look forward to

expectant waiting; looking forward to

expectancy the state of expecting; hopefulness

expectation something expected; the state of expecting

expectorate to expel phlegm by coughing or spitting

expedient suitable or advisable for a particular occasion □ an action taken to get out of an awkward or embarrassing position

expedite to hasten; to speed up

expedition an organized journey with a purpose (as, a Mount Everest expedition); promptness; speed

expeditious speedy; swift

expel to drive or force out; to turn out in disgrace (as, to expel a pupil from school)

expulsion the act of expelling

expend to spend (as, to expend money, time or energy on building a boat)

expenditure money spent; the act of expending

expense a cost

expensive costly; dear

experience knowledge gained, not from books, but from actual happenings in life; any happening which affects a person (as, an unpleasant experience) □ to go through; to undergo; to meet with (as, to experience a setback)

experienced skilled as the result of experience

experiment a test or trial (especially one carried out in the hope of discovering something, as, a scientific experiment) □ to carry out experiments; to try things out

experimental based on experiment; used for experiments

expert having a special knowledge or skill □ a person possessing a special knowledge or skill

expire to die; to come to an end; to breathe out
expiry the end or termination of something (as, the expiry of an agreement)

explain to make clear or easy to understand; to give a reason for
explanation the act of explaining; a statement, spoken or written, that explains something difficult to understand
explanatory intended to explain or make clear (as, an explanatory leaflet supplied with a new game)

expletive a meaningless exclamation or swear word

explicable capable of being explained

explicit plainly stated (as, explicit instructions)

explode to blow up with a loud noise; to burst out (as, to explode into loud laughter): to prove wrong (as, to explode a belief or theory)
explosion the act of exploding; a sudden blow-up with a loud noise; an outburst (as, an explosion of anger)
explosive liable to explode; hot-tempered □ something that will explode (as, the high explosive in a bomb)

exploit 1 *(say exploit)* a heroic deed; a remarkable feat

exploit 2 *(say exploit)* to work or turn to use (as, to exploit a nickel mine); to make use of selfishly (as, to exploit another person's skills without fair payment)
exploitation the act of exploiting

explore to search or travel for the purpose of discovery; to search or examine thoroughly
exploration the act of exploring

explosion, explosive see **explode**

exponent someone who demonstrates a skill or interprets the work of others (as, an exponent of the art of boxing, or of the works of a famous musician)

export to send goods out of a country □ the act of exporting
exports the goods sent out of a country for trade purposes; the opposite of imports

expose to lay open for everyone to see; to leave unprotected (as, to expose to wind and rain)
exposition a public exhibition: a detailed explanatory statement
exposure the act of exposing; the direction which a place faces (as, a garden with a southern exposure); the exposing of photographic film to light, or the time taken by such an exposure

expostulate to protest or object in a friendly way

expound to present in detail (as, to expound a theory); to explain fully

express 1 to press or force out; to put one's thoughts or feelings into words, or into music or art □ clearly stated (as, her express wish)
expression the showing of thoughts or feelings by means of language, some form of art, or by the look on one's face (as, the anxious expression on his face)
expressive expressing; full of meaning or feeling

express 2 a very fast train □ fast; special (as, express delivery)

expropriate to take property away from its owner

expulsion see **expel**

expunge to wipe out; to rub out

exquisite *(say ekskwizit or ekskwizit)* of extreme beauty or excellence; (of pleasure or pain) extreme

extant still existing

extend to stretch out; to make

longer (as, to extend the time of an interview)

extension the extending of anything; an added part (as, an extra room built on to a house)

extent the length, area or size of anything (as, the extent of a journey, of a forest); reach or range (as, the full extent of his arm)

extensive wide; large (as, extensive mining operations)

extenuating making something seem less bad (as, extenuating circumstances for the theft)

exterior outer; outside □ the outside of something; the opposite of interior

exterminate to destroy completely (as, to exterminate an insect pest)

external lying on the outside; outside; the opposite of internal (as, a lotion for external application, that is, to the skin, and not to be taken internally like a cough mixture); foreign (as, external trade, that is, exports and imports)

extinct no longer existing (as, an extinct animal, such as the mammoth); no longer active (as, an extinct volcano)

extinguish to put out (as, to extinguish a light, a fire); to put an end to (as, to extinguish a person's hopes)

extinguisher a device which sprays chemicals to put out a fire

extol to praise highly

extort to obtain something by threats or force (as, to extort money)

extortion the obtaining of money, promises, etc. by threats

extortionate much too high (of a price or charge)

extra more than is usual or necessary; additional □ unusually (as, extra careful) □ something additional or unusual

extract *(say extract)* to draw or pull out (as, to extract a tooth, a confession) □ *(say extract)* a

part of something that has been taken out (as, an extract from a book)

extraction the act of extracting: descent or ancestry (as, a boy of French extraction)

extraneous coming from outside and not belonging (as - The music was spoiled by the extraneous sounds of traffic.)

extraordinary beyond the ordinary; unusual; surprising; wonderful (as, a sunset of extraordinary beauty)

extravagant going beyond reasonable limits; spending too freely; wasteful

extravagance lavish expenditure

extreme farthest from the ordinary or normal (as, extreme temperatures, whether hot or cold); very great (as, extreme pain) □ the farthest point; the limit

extremist a person who has extreme ideas or is ready to take extreme actions

extricate to free; to disentangle

exuberant showing high spirits or great happiness; overflowing

exude to give off or discharge by, or as if by, sweating (as, the resin exuded by pine trees)

exult to rejoice greatly; to boast about a victory

eye one of the two bodily organs of sight; a hole like an eye (as, the eye of a needle); a bud on a potato tuber □ to gaze at or look at

eyeball the whole rounded part of the eye

eyebrow the curve of hairs above each eye

eye-glasses a pair of glass lenses to correct faulty eyesight; spectacles

eyelash one of the small hairs that grow along the edge of each eyelid

eyelid the lid or cover of an eye

eyepiece the glass lens of a telescope or microscope to which the eye is applied

eyesight the power of seeing
eyesore anything unpleasant to look at
eyewitness someone who actually sees a thing happen

eyrie, eyry the nest of any bird of prey (especially an eagle)

f

fable a short story intended to teach a moral lesson (especially with animals speaking and acting as humans); an untrue story
fabulous extraordinary; marvellous; almost unbelievable
fabric cloth: the framework, structure or walls of a building, etc.
fabricate to construct or make; to invent or make up (an untrue story or lie)
fabrication a falsehood; a made-up story or excuse
fabulous see **fable**
facade *(say fassahd)* the front of a building (facing towards the street)
face the front part of the head; an expression (as, a happy face); the surface of anything (such as a rock face, the face of the earth) □ to stand opposite to (as - The house faced south.); to resist or stand up to (as, to face danger bravely)
facial having to do with the face
facet *(say fasset)* a side or surface of something that has many sides (such as a cut diamond, crystal, etc.)
facility easiness and quickness (in doing something)
facilitate to make easier
facilities things that make an action possible or easier (as, cooking facilities)
fact anything known to be true or to have happened; something accepted as real and true
factual relating to facts; containing facts
factor a person who does business (usually buying or selling) on behalf of someone else: one

of two or more numbers which have a given product when multiplied together (as, 2 and 4 are both factors of 8): any thing or circumstance that leads to a result or affects the progress of events
factory a building where goods are manufactured
faculty an ability, talent or knack (as, the faculty of making friends easily): a department of study in a university; the academic staff in any of these departments: a natural power of the body (such as hearing) or mind (such as reasoning)
fad a popular fashion or craze
fade to lose colour or freshness; to die away; to go from sight or view (usually used with **out** or **away**)
fag to become weary (fagged out); to work hard □ hard work done unwillingly: a schoolboy made to do work for an older boy
faggot a bundle of sticks
Fahrenheit a temperature scale having the freezing point of water marked at 32 degrees (32°) and the boiling point at 212 degrees (212°)
fail to be unsuccessful in something attempted; to grow weaker or less efficient (as, failing eyesight); to neglect to do something (as - He failed to keep the appointment.): to become bankrupt
failing a fault; a weakness
failure the act of failing; lack of success; a person who has not done what was expected of him
faint lacking in strength; dim or

pale; without courage (as, faint-hearted) □ to lose consciousness; to swoon

fair 1 bright and clear; beautiful; light in colour (as, fair hair): just or equal (as, a fair division of work); neither good nor poor but in between
fairly rather; quite (as - He did fairly well.): justly; equally

fair 2 a large market held at fixed times (often with amusements); an exhibition of goods from different firms, foreign countries, etc.; a bazaar or sale of work to raise funds for a church, charity, etc.

fairy an imaginary small creature in human form (supposed to have magical powers)

faith trust; belief (especially religious belief); confidence
faithful loyal; keeping one's promises; believing; true (as, a faithful account of the event)
faithless not believing (especially not believing in God); not to be trusted; disloyal

fake a cheap imitation of something valuable (as, a fake piece of jewellery); an impostor □ to pretend that something or some action occurred (as, to fake a burglary); to counterfeit (as, to fake a signature)

falcon a long-winged bird of prey (especially a hawk trained to hunt game)
falconry the sport of hunting with trained hawks

fall to drop down; to collapse (as when the wall of a ruined building falls down); to go lower (as, when the price of something falls); to be killed or badly wounded (in battle); to be captured (as, a fort falls in war); to pass into a state of mind or body (as, to fall in love, to fall asleep, etc.); to occur (as - Christmas falls on a Wednesday this year.) □ the act of falling (as - The pony stumbled and had a bad fall.); something that falls (such as a waterfall); a decrease or lessening (as, a fall in temper-

ature, a fall in value, etc.)
fall-out radioactive dust from a nuclear explosion or an atomic power plant
to fall out to quarrel: to leave ranks (a military term)
to fall through to come to nothing; to fail
to fall to to begin with eagerness (as - Here is your breakfast, so fall to!)

fallacy an argument or opinion that is not soundly based, although it may appear so; a false idea or belief
fallacious misleading; not well reasoned

fallible liable to make mistakes or to be mistaken

fallow ploughed land that is left unseeded and uncultivated for a period (usually a year)

false wrong; disloyal; untruthful; not real (as, false teeth)
falsehood a lie; lying
falsify to alter (a document, accounts, etc.) deliberately, so as to deceive
(to bear) false witness (to make) a deliberately untrue statement

falter to stumble; to walk unsteadily: to speak with hesitation

fame reputation (usually good); renown
famed, famous well known to the public; renowned
famously very well (as, to get on famously with a person)

familiar close; intimate; well-known (as, a familiar scene); too intimate or too informal (as, a too familiar manner towards an acquaintance)
familiarize to make (someone) well-acquainted with something (as, to familiarize oneself with the history of ancient Rome)

family parents and their children; all the persons living together in one household; all the people who are descended from one ancestor; a group of people who are related to each other (such as parents, children,

grandparents, aunts, uncles, cousins): a group of animals, plants, languages, etc. which are related (as - Tigers and lions belong to the cat family.)
family tree a chart showing the ancestry and relationship of members of a family

famine great scarcity of food in an area or country; hunger
famished starving; extremely hungry

famous see **fame**

fan 1 a mechanical device with rotating blades that cools the air; a device of paper, silk, etc. made in the shape of a partial circle and moved back and forth by the hand to give a cool breeze to the face □ to cool the air by means of a fan; to clean grain by blowing away the chaff with a fan
fanlight a window above a door (usually in the shape of a half circle)
fantail a pigeon with tail feathers spread out like a fan

fan 2 (short for **fanatic**) an enthusiastic supporter or follower of a public entertainer, a sport, a hobby, etc.
fanatic a person who is over-enthusiastic about something (especially religion)
fanaticism (say *fanatisism*) excessive enthusiasm

fancy a power of the mind to imagine things (especially things that are not likely to happen in real life); a liking for, or attraction to, something (as - She has taken a fancy to antique jewellery.) □ ornamental (not plain or simple) □ to imagine; to think without being sure; to have a liking or inclination for
fanciful imaginative; inclined to have fancies
fancy dress a special costume worn to a party or ball (representing a character in fiction, history, etc.)

fanfare a great flourish blown on trumpets or bugles (often at a solemn ceremony)

fang a long pointed tooth; a poison-bearing tooth of a snake

fanlight, fantail see **fan 1**

fantasy fancy; an imaginative image or idea not based on reality
fantastic unreal; extraordinary; unbelievable

far distant in space or time (as, far away) □ to, at, or over, a great distance (as - The explorers had travelled far.); very much (as, a far greater distance)
farther more distant (as, the farther shore of a lake): see also **further**
faraway distant; dreamy or absent-minded
Far East China, Japan and other countries of East and South-East Asia
far-fetched exaggerated, not reasonable
far-flung extending over a great distance
far-sighted able to see distant things; the opposite of near-sighted; prudent; planning in advance for things that may happen

fare to get on (well or badly); to journey; to be fed or to feed oneself □ the price paid for travelling on a bus, train, aeroplane, etc.; food (as, a menu, or bill of fare)
farewell goodbye □ well-wishing at parting

farm an area of land used for cultivating crops, raising cattle, sheep, etc. □ to cultivate land; to carry on a farm business
farmer a person who owns or manages a farm
farmhand a worker on a farm
farmyard a yard surrounded by farm buildings

farther see **far** and **further**

fascinate (say *fassinate*) to attract greatly; to charm
fascinating very charming; irresistibly attractive

fascism (say *fashism*) a system of government (often ruled by a dictator) which controls everything in a country and which suppresses all public criticism or opposition

fascist a person who supports fascism □ sympathetic towards fascism

fashion the make or cut of a thing; the shape, length, etc. of some item of clothing that is popular during a particular period (as - Knee breeches were the fashion for men in the 18th century.); a custom or way of doing a thing □ to make; to shape
fashionable following the fashion in use at a particular time; in the latest style

fast 1 quick; rapid; (of a clock) ahead of correct time □ quickly

fast 2 firm; fixed (as, stuck fast in the mud)
fasten to fix securely; to attach; to join together
fastening, fastener something that closes or secures (such as a clip, buckle, door catch, etc.)

fast 3 to go hungry; to go without food or certain kinds of food (especially as a religious duty)

fastidious difficult to please; very particular (about cleanliness, etc.)

fat plump; fleshy; oily or greasy; (of land) fertile □ solid oil or grease under the skin of humans and animals
fatted made fat
fatty containing fat (Cream is the fatty part of milk.)
fatten to make or grow fat

fate a supposed power that is beyond human control, so that things that are destined to happen will always happen; fortune; destiny: ruin; death
fatal causing death (as, a fatal accident)
fatalism a belief in fate or destiny; a conviction that all events are prearranged, and nothing anyone does can change things
fatality a death caused by accident
fated doomed; destined to (as - He seemed fated to get the blame, even if it wasn't his fault.)
fateful controlled by fate; lead-

ing to an important decision (as - The fateful day of the interview had arrived.)

father a male parent; an ancestor or forefather; a monk; a priest; one of the oldest, most respected members of a community, a society, parliament, etc. (as, the father of the House of Commons); the inventor or founder of something (as, the father of television)
father-in-law the father of one's husband or wife
fatherland one's native country

fathom a unit (6 feet) used in measuring depth (usually for soundings in water) □ to understand or puzzle out some problem; to get to the bottom of (a mystery)

fatigue weariness; great tiredness (caused by hard work or exertion): weakness (of metals) caused by long use □ to weary

fault a mistake or error; a flaw or defect: responsibility for a mistake (as - It was his fault that the tent collapsed.)
faultless perfect
faulty imperfect; having defects
faultfinder one who constantly criticizes and blames others
at fault wrong

faun a rural Roman god supposed to be part man and part goat

fauna the animals (of all kinds) belonging to a region or to a period of time (as - The fauna of Australia include the kangaroo and the koala bear.)

favour an act of kindness; goodwill; approval; a state of being approved (as, in favour with the voters) □ to prefer; to help towards (as - The breeze favoured the yacht's chances of winning the race.)
favourable helpful; likely to be of advantage
favoured preferred; having special (sometimes unfair) advantages
favourite well- or best-liked (as,

a favourite tune, dress, etc.) □ a person or thing much liked by others

favouritism unfair preference in favour of one person although others have equal claim

in favour of in support of; on the side of

fawn 1 a young deer; a light, yellowish-brown colour (like the coat of a fawn)

fawn 2 (of animals, especially dogs) to show affection and joy by tail-wagging, crouching, licking the hand, etc.; (of humans) to flatter someone or to try to beg a favour by showing too much humility, etc.

fear a strong feeling of alarm at the thought of an approaching danger or difficulty □ to be afraid; to feel fear or fright

fearful full of fear; timid; afraid that something bad may happen; dreadful; frightening (as, the fearful howl of a wolf)

fearless brave; daring

feasible possible; able to be done

feast a large special meal, with many kinds of rich and delicious foods; a festival (especially religious) celebrated with joy or solemnity □ to eat an especially large and sumptuous meal; to see with enjoyment (as - She feasted her eyes on the beautiful scenery.)

feat an act of great skill, strength or daring

feather one of the growths that form the covering of bird's wings and bodies: anything resembling a feather □ to cover or adorn with feathers

feathery like feathers (as, feathery clouds in a blue sky)

featherbed a mattress filled with feathers

featherweight a boxer weighing not more than 9 stone

birds of a feather people of the same sort

feature a part of the face (as, the mouth, eyes, etc.); a quality or characteristic (as - Informality is a feature of the school

dances.); a special article in a newspaper; the main film in a programme □ to give prominence to (as - The theatre company will feature plays by Shakespeare this season.)

federal relating to a union of states or nations which run their own home affairs, but act together in affairs of national or international importance

federation a group of such states or nations (The United States of America and the Union of Soviet Socialist Republics are federations.)

fee a price paid for professional services (as, a lawyer's fee) or for a privilege (as, an entrance fee)

feeble weak; not strong or loud

feed to give food to; to put food into someone's mouth (as, to feed a baby); to supply something necessary (as, to feed a fire with coal, etc.) □ food (especially for cattle)

fed up disgusted and weary

feel to touch; to examine something by handling it; to experience or know something through the senses (as, to feel cold) or through the emotions (as, to feel love for)

feeler an organ on the heads of some insects or animals used for finding food, testing their surroundings by touch, etc.; antenna

feeling a sense of touch; a sensation; an inner thought or idea (as - He had a feeling that things would work out well.) □ experiencing or showing emotion (as, feeling angry)

feet see foot

feign *(say fain)* to pretend to feel (as, to feign interest in something that is dull and boring); to sham

feint *(say faint)* a pretence; a movement intended to deceive (as when a boxer appears to be about to strike a blow but does not carry it through)

felicity happiness: a knack of thinking of the right word or phrase for any occasion
felicitous happy; appropriate
felicitations congratulations

feline of, or like, a cat

fell to cut down (as, to fell a tree); to knock down by striking (a person, an animal, etc.)

fellow a man; a companion or comrade; one of a pair □ belonging to the same group, class, etc. (as, a fellow-countryman)
fellowship friendliness; an association or society: money left to a college or university for the support of graduates (called Fellows)

felon a person who has committed a serious crime
felonious criminal; wicked
felony a serious crime

felt heavy cloth made by rolling and pressing wool or fur fibres together

female one of the sex that produces young; the opposite of male

feminine of or like a woman or girl; the opposite of masculine
feminism belief in the claims of women for equal rights with men
feminist a supporter of women's rights

femur the thigh bone

fen low-lying marshy land (often covered with water)

fence 1 a barrier enclosing an area of land (used to keep animals or people in or out)
fencing 1 wood or other material used in making a fence

fence 2 to practise the art of fencing
fencing 2 the art or skill of fighting with blunted swords, foils, etc.

fend to ward off; to turn aside (as, to fend off a blow): to provide or look after (as, to fend for himself)
fender something that guards or protects against collision; a

low metal or stone guard around a hearth

ferment to cause fermentation in a substance by adding something (such as yeast) that produces chemical changes
fermentation a slow change in a substance, brought about by adding micro-organisms or bacteria (as, if yeast is added to dough, a gas is gradually produced, causing the unbaked bread to rise and expand)

fern a plant which has lacy, feathery leaves but no flowers

ferocious fierce; savage
ferocity savage cruelty

ferret a partly-tamed small animal like the weasel, used to hunt out rabbits, etc. □ to hunt or search out the facts or truth about something

ferry to carry over water (usually a river or lake) by boat or aeroplane; to fly an aircraft from the place of manufacture to an airfield □ a boat which ferries people or goods; a place where ferries operate

fertile able to produce seeds or plants abundantly; fruitful: inventive (as, a fertile imagination)
fertilize to make fertile
fertilizer any substance used to make the soil more fertile

fervent, fervid very enthusiastic; intense; warm in feeling
fervour great warmth of feeling; zeal

fester to give out pus and poisonous matter (from a sore or wound): to rankle

festival a joyful celebration; a season or series of performances (as, a music festival)
festive having to do with a feast or festival; joyful; gay
festivity merrymaking; gaiety

festoon a garland hung between two points □ to decorate with festoons

fetch to go and get: to bring in a price (as - The picture fetched £2000.)

fetching charming

fête *(say fate)* a large outdoor entertainment (often organized to collect money) □ to entertain lavishly

fetish a charm worshipped by some primitive people; something regarded with too much reverence

fetlock the part of a horse's leg just above the hoof

fetter a chain or shackle for the feet □ to put fetters on

feud *(say fewd)* a long-lasting quarrel (especially between families, clans or tribes)

feudal having to do with the feudal system in the Middle Ages, under which the tenants on an overlord's land had to fight for him when needed
feudalism the feudal system

fever an illness accompanied by a rise in temperature and a rapid pulse
feverish having a slight fever: very excited

few a small number of; not many

fez a red, brimless hat (shaped like a flower-pot) with a black tassel

fiancé *(say feeahnsay)* a man engaged to be married
fiancée a woman engaged to be married

fib a small lie □ to tell a fib

fibre any fine thread or thread-like material
fibrous composed of, or like, fibres

fickle inconstant; not dependable

fiction a made-up story; books about people and events that are not really true
fictitious imaginary; false

fiddle a violin □ to play on a fiddle: to play about with something in an aimless way

fidelity faithfulness; truth or exactness in reproducing (as, fidelity in the copying of a painting)

fidget to be restless; to move un-

easily □ someone who fidgets

field a piece of land enclosed for farming or for sport; an expanse of country associated with some event, or with some natural product (as, a battlefield, a coal field); an area of interest, knowledge, etc. (as, the field of politics) □ to stand ready in a cricket field to stop (and return) the ball
field-glasses a small telescope with two eyepieces
field marshal an army officer of the highest rank

fiend *(say feend)* a devil; an extremely wicked person

fierce angry; violent

fiery like fire; blazing: spirited (as, a fiery temper)

fife a small flute

fig the soft, pear-shaped fruit of the fig tree, which grows best in warm countries

fight to struggle with; to contend in a war or in single combat □ a struggle; a battle
fighter someone who fights: a very fast aeroplane used for aerial combat in time of war

figure a number: a shape or form in outline; a drawing or diagram □ to mark with a design: to imagine
figurative of words used imaginatively and not in their true sense
figurehead a decorative figure under a ship's bowsprit: a person who appears as a leader but has no real power
figure of speech see **speak**
figure out to find the answer to a problem by hard thinking

filament a thread-like object (as, the filament of a light bulb)

filch to steal things of little value; to pilfer

file 1 a steel tool with a rough surface for smoothing metal, etc. □ to smooth or cut with a file

file 2 a line of persons one behind another (as, in single file); a folder or other device in which letters and papers are placed in order □ to walk or march in a file (as, to file past); to put in an office file

filial *(say fill-yal)* concerning a son or daughter

filigree very fine ornamental work made from gold or silver threads

fill to make, or become, full (as, to fill a jug with water); to satisfy (as, to fill a person's requirements)
filling anything used to fill up a hole or cavity (as, a filling for a hollow tooth)
filling station a roadside place where motorists can buy petrol and oil

fillet a narrow piece of wood, metal, etc.; a head-band: a slice of meat or fish from which the bones have been removed □ to remove the bones from meat or fish before cooking

filly a young mare

film a thin skin or coating (as, a film of oil on water); a strip of plastic material for taking photographs; a moving picture □ to make a moving picture of (as, to film one of Shakespeare's plays)

filter a device for straining or purifying water and other liquids by separating out dirt and impurities □ to pass through a filter

filth dirt; foul matter
filthy very dirty; foul

fin one of the wing-like parts of a fish which help it to balance and swim

final *(say fienal)* very last; coming at the end; not open to further argument (as, a final decision) □ the last game or contest in a competition
finally at last; at the end

finale *(say finahlay)* the last item in a programme; the end; the last movement in a musical composition

finance money affairs (especially in business and government) □ to provide money for
financial concerned with finance
financier a person skilled in finance

finch one of a family of small birds (including sparrows, chaffinches and bullfinches)

find to come upon or meet with; to discover
finding something found: a judgment in a law court
found discovered; met with; regained

fine 1 excellent or very good (as, fine work, fine weather); thin or slender (as, fine thread); pure (as, fine gold)
finery fine or showy things (especially clothes and jewellery)

fine 2 a sum of money to be paid as a punishment □ to impose a fine on someone

finger one of the five branches of the hand □ to touch with the fingers
fingerprint an ink impression of the ridges of the fingertip (It can be used to identify criminals.)

finish to end or complete □ the end; the last touch (as, a shiny finish to paintwork)

finite having an end or limit

fir a cone-bearing tree, valuable for its timber

fire the heat and light caused by burning; destructive burning (as, of a house); the discharge of firearms (as - The soldiers ceased their fire); spirited enthusiasm □ to set on fire; to discharge a firearm: to arouse strongly (as, to fire the imagination)
firearm any weapon discharged by an explosion (such as a gun)
fire brigade a company of firemen
fire-engine a motor vehicle with equipment for fire fighting
fireman a man whose job it is to help in putting out fires and

in rescuing any people in danger

fireplace the place in a room (under the chimney) where a fire is burned

fireproof proof against fire

fireworks exploding devices (such as squibs, rockets, etc.) which are set alight after dark on special occasions to produce a display of lights

firm 1 strong and not easily moved; with one's mind made up (as, a firm decision)

firm 2 a business partnership or company

firmament the whole vault of the sky, including the stars

first before all others (in place, time or rank); at the beginning

first aid treatment of a wounded or sick person before the doctor's arrival

firth an arm of the sea (especially a river mouth)

fish a vertebrate animal that lives in water and breathes through gills □ to catch, or try to catch, fish; to search for or seek (as, to fish for compliments)

fisherman someone who fishes

fishery the business of catching fish; a place for catching fish

fishing the art or practice of catching fish

fishing-rod a long tapering rod used with a line and hook for catching fish

fishmonger a dealer in fish

fishy like a fish; suspicious or doubtful

fission a splitting or division

fissure a crack; a narrow opening

fist a tightly closed hand (with fingers doubled under the palm)

fisticuffs a fight with the fists

fit 1 suitable or proper (as, fit for a king); in good health □ to be suitable; to be of the right size or shape

fit 2 a sudden attack of illness (especially epilepsy); a sudden emotional outburst (as, a fit of anger)

fitful coming in bursts or short spells

fix to place or attach firmly; to settle definitely (as, to fix a price); to direct steadily (as, to fix one's eyes on the blackboard); to mend

fixture anything firmly fixed (especially furniture attached to the floor or wall): an event (such as a football match) arranged for a fixed date

fizz to make a hissing, bubbling sound □ a frothy drink (such as ginger ale or champagne)

flabbergasted overcome with surprise

flabby soft and yielding to the touch; hanging loose

flag 1 a piece of thin cloth with a special design to show nationality, rank, etc.; a piece of cloth used to give information (as, a red flag for danger)

flagship (in a fleet) the admiral's ship which flies his flag

flag 2 to become tired or weak

flag 3 a flat stone for paving

flagon a large vessel for liquids, with a narrow neck and handle

flail an implement for threshing corn by hand

flair a natural talent; an aptitude

flake a small thin piece of anything (as, a flake of pastry, a snowflake) □ to form into flakes

flamboyant gorgeously coloured; very showy

flame the leaping light or blaze of a fire; the smaller light of a candle or gas-burner: the heat of passion □ to break out in flame

flaming brilliant; violent (as, a flaming temper)

flammable, inflammable easily set on fire

flamingo a water bird which has a long neck and long legs, and is deep pink in colour

flan an open tart with fruit or other filling

flank the side of an animal; the side, or wing, of an army □ to pass round the side of

flannel a warm soft cloth of wool

flannelette a cotton imitation of flannel

flap to move up and down (as - A bird flaps its wings.) □ such a movement; anything which hangs loose or is hinged (as, a table flap)

flare to blaze up; to burn with a glaring unsteady light: to widen out in a bell shape (as, flared trousers) □ a sudden bright light (especially one used as a signal)

flash a momentary burst or gleam of light (as, a flash of lightning); a sudden burst of some emotion (as, a flash of anger) □ to shine out suddenly (as, to flash a torch)
flashlight a sudden artificial light used to take photographs; an electric torch
flashy showy; trying to be smart

flask a narrow-necked bottle of metal or glass

flat smooth; level: tasteless; uninteresting; below the right pitch (as, singing flat); downright (as, a flat lie) □ a private apartment on one floor of a building with several storeys: a sign in music which lowers a note by half a tone (♭)
flatten to make, or become, flat

flatter to praise a person without really meaning it; to represent someone or something as better than is really the case (as, a flattering photograph)
flattery false praise

flaunt to show off

flavour a distinctive taste (as, different flavours of ice cream) □ to give a flavour to (as, to flavour a pancake by adding lemon juice)
flavouring any substance used to give a flavour (as, vanilla flavouring)

flaw a defect; a crack or break

flax a plant whose fibres are woven into linen cloth
flaxen of, or like, flax; light yellow (as, flaxen hair)

flay to strip the skin off

flea a small jumping insect

fleck a spot or speckle

fledgling a young bird just feathered and ready to fly

flee to run away (especially from danger)

fleece a sheep's coat of wool □ to clip wool from; to rob a person of money or belongings
fleecy soft and woolly

fleet 1 a number of ships or vehicles that belong together; a division of the navy, commanded by an admiral

fleet 2 swift; nimble
fleeting passing quickly (as, a fleeting glance)

flesh the soft substance (muscle, etc.) which covers the bones of human beings and animals; the soft, edible part of fruit
fleshy plump; fat

flex to bend □ a length of insulated wire for electricity
flexible easily bent; adaptable; not stiff

flick to strike lightly □ a light tap

flicker to flutter; to burn unsteadily □ a flickering movement

flier see **fly**

flight 1 the act of flying through the air; the distance flown: a series of steps or stairs
flighty changeable; fanciful

flight 2 the act of fleeing or escaping

flimsy thin; easily broken or torn; weak

flinch to shrink back in fear

fling to throw; to toss □ a throw: a lively Scottish dance

flint a hard kind of stone (Sparks can easily be struck off it with a piece of steel.)

flip to toss lightly; to flick (as, to flip a coin) □ a light toss; a flick
flipper a limb adapted for swimming (as, the flippers of seals)

flippant frivolous in speech; not serious

flirt to play at courtship; to trifle with □a person who is in the habit of flirting
flirtation a mock courtship

flit to move about lightly and quickly; to fly away silently or quickly

float to stay on the surface of a liquid (as, a boat floating on water); to stay up in the air (as, a balloon floating near the clouds) □a raft; a cork on a fishing line: a platform on wheels, used in parades, etc.

flock a large group of birds or of sheep □to gather, or go, together in a crowd

floe a field of floating ice

flog to beat; to lash

flood an unusually great flow of water; any great quantity (as, a flood of words) □to overflow
flood-lighting strong lighting from special high-powered lamps
flood-tide the rising tide

floor the part of a room which is walked on; a storey of a building (as, a skyscraper with 50 floors) □to make a floor in: to throw, or knock down on the floor: to puzzle (as - The question floored him.)

flop to fall down suddenly; to fail badly □a collapse; a failure

flora all the plants growing in a region; a descriptive list of these
floral of flowers
florid flowery; of ruddy complexion
florist a person who grows or sells flowers

floss a fluffy substance from some plants, or from the outside of a silkworm's cocoon; silky thread used for embroidery

flotilla a fleet of small ships

flotsam floating articles washed overboard from a ship or wreck: see also **jetsam**

flounce 1 a hanging strip of gathered material sewn to a skirt

flounce 2 to move abruptly or impatiently □a sudden or impatient movement

flounder 1 to struggle awkwardly; to stumble or make mistakes in speaking or thinking

flounder 2 a small flat fish

flour the finely-ground grain of wheat or other cereals; any fine soft powder □to sprinkle with flour

flourish to prosper; to grow luxuriantly (as, flourishing crops) to wave something (as, to flourish a sword) □the waving of a weapon, etc.; an ornamental stroke with a pen (as, to sign a letter with a flourish)

flow to move along smoothly like water in a river or electricity along a wire □a stream or current

flower the blossom of a plant (the part which changes later into fruit or seed): the best of anything □to blossom; to bloom
flowery full of, or decorated with, flowers; full of fine words (as, flowery language)
flowerpot a pot in which one or more plants are grown

flu an abbreviation of **influenza**

fluctuate to move up and down or to and fro; to vary

flue a pipe to carry away smoke and hot air from a stove; a small chimney

fluent able to express oneself easily and quickly (as, a fluent speaker)
fluency ease and readiness in using words

fluff any soft downy stuff (as, the fluff from a blanket)
fluffy soft and downy (as, a fluffy kitten)

fluid flowing; not solid or firm □something which flows, like liquid or gas

fluke a success that happened by chance

fluorescence the property which some substances possess of giving out light under certain conditions

fluorescent lighting brighter electric lighting obtained by having a fluorescent material in the lamp

fluorine a pale greenish-yellow gas

fluoridate, fluoridize to add a fluoride to drinking water (The purpose is to improve dental health.)

fluoride a compound of fluorine with another element

flurry a gust or blast; an agitation □to agitate

flush 1 a flow of blood to the cheeks; a fresh glow □to become red in the face: to clean by a rush of water □well supplied with money

flush 2 having the surface level with the surface alongside (as, a door flush with the door frame)

fluster excitement from hurrying; a flurry □to make confused and nervous

flute a pipe-like musical wind instrument (The hole for the mouth is in the side.)

flutter to move the wings quickly; to move or beat in a quick uneven way (as, a fluttering pulse)

fly to move through the air (especially on wings or in an aircraft); to move or pass very quickly; to run away □a common flying insect

flyer, flier a person who flies; an airman

fly-over a road (or railway) crossing above another one

flywheel an especially heavy wheel which keeps a machine running at a steady speed

flying fish a leaping fish with long fins which help it to stay in the air for a short time

flying squad a body of police with fast cars

foal a young horse □to give birth to a foal

foam froth; bubbles on the surface of a liquid □to produce, or come out in, foam

focus to get a clear picture (by adjusting the lens of a camera,

etc.); to direct or concentrate one's attention on one point or subject □a meeting point for rays of light; any central point

fodder food for cattle (such as hay, oats, etc.)

foe an enemy

fog a thick mist □to cover in fog

foggy very misty

foghorn a horn sounded as a warning signal to ships in foggy weather

foil 1 to defeat; to puzzle □a light, blunt sword, with a button on the point, used in fencing

foil 2 a thin leaf or sheet of metal (as, tin foil)

foist to pass off as genuine; to palm off something unwanted upon someone

fold 1 to double something over; to lay in folds (as, to fold a blanket); to bring close to the body (as, to fold wings, or arms) □a doubling of anything upon itself; a crease

folder a folded leaflet or booklet; a folding case for loose papers

fold 2 an enclosure, especially for sheep

foliage the leaves on trees and plants

folk people

folklore the old customs and traditions of people in a particular region or country

folksong, folktale a song or story which has been handed down to people by their forebears; a modern imitation of such a song or story

follow to go or come behind; to result from; to understand (as, to follow an explanation); to act on (as, to follow advice)

following a group of supporters

folly foolishness; silly conduct

fond very affectionate; foolishly loving and tender; liking (as, fond of dogs)

fondle to caress

font a basin, usually of stone, holding water for baptism

food the things people eat; nourishment: anything which promotes activity or growth (mental or physical, as food for thought)

fool a silly person; a court jester □ to play the fool; to deceive

foolish silly; lacking common sense; ridiculous

foolhardy foolishly bold; rash

foolproof unlikely to go wrong even if clumsily handled

foolscap a large size of writing or printing paper

foot the part of the body on which a man or an animal stands or walks; the lower part of anything; a measure of 12 inches or approximately 30 centimetres □ to pay (a bill)

football a large ball for kicking; a game played with it

foothills the lesser heights below high mountains

foothold a place on which to stand (especially when climbing)

footing a foothold; a foundation

footlights a row of lights along the front edge of a stage

footman a servant in livery

footnote a note at the bottom of a page

footpath a path or way for pedestrians

footprint the mark made by a foot

footstep the sound or mark made by a foot when walking

for because of; on account of (as - He did it for his father.); in return for (as, a reward for his hard work); in preparation or with a purpose towards (as, laying the table for dinner); during (as, for two hours); considering (as, warm weather for the time of year) □ because (She remained indoors, for it was cold.)

forage to go about searching for provisions □ food for horses and cattle

forbear to hold back from (as, to forbear from striking someone)

forbearance control of one's

temper; patience; restraint

forbid to command not to

forbidden prohibited; unlawful

forbidding unpleasant; stern (as, a man of forbidding appearance)

force strength; power; violence; a body of men prepared for action (as, the police force) □ to compel; to push or open by force; to cause a plant to grow or ripen quickly

forced done by great effort (as, a forced march); unnatural (as, a forced smile)

forceful powerful; vigorous

forcible having force; done by force

armed forces the defence forces of a country (soldiers, sailors or airmen)

forceps a pincer-like instrument for gripping and holding

ford a shallow place where water may be crossed on horseback or in a vehicle □ to cross a ford

fore front or in front

foremost first in place or rank

fore- a prefix meaning before

forearm 1 the part of the arm between elbow and wrist

forearm 2 (say fore*arm*) to arm or prepare beforehand

forebear an ancestor

foreboding a feeling that something bad will happen

forecast to tell beforehand; to predict □ a prediction (as, a weather forecast)

forecastle, fo'c'sle (say foaks'l) the forepart of a ship under the main deck

forefather an ancestor

forefinger the finger next to the thumb (the first, or index, finger)

forefoot one of the front feet of a four-footed animal

foregoing something already mentioned

foregone conclusion a conclusion which has been come to before the evidence has been examined; an inevitable result

foreground the part of a picture or view nearest the observer's eye (the opposite of background)

forehead the part of the face above the eyes

foreign (say *forin*) belonging to another country; strange
foreigner a native of another country

foreleg a front leg

foreman an overseer of workmen; the leader of a jury

foremast the ship's mast nearest the bow

foremost see **fore**

forerunner a person or thing that goes, or happens, before

foresee to see or know beforehand
foresight the act of foreseeing; wisdom or care in thinking about the future

foreshore the part of the shore between high and low water marks

forest a large area of land covered with trees
forester someone who has charge of, or works in, a forest
forestry the art of cultivating forests

forestall to act before someone else does, and so hinder his plans

foretaste a taste beforehand; a sample experience beforehand

foretell to prophesy

forethought thought or care for the future

forever for ever; for all time

forewarn to warn beforehand

foreword a preface

forfeit (say *forfit*) a penalty for a fault □ to lose a right by some fault or wrong conduct
forfeiture the act of forfeiting or giving up something as a penalty

forge 1 a smith's workshop, with a furnace for heating metal □ to hammer hot metal into shape: to imitate for fraud (as, to forge someone else's signature)
forgery the imitation of writing, or of a picture, for fraud

forge 2 to move steadily on (as, to forge ahead)

forget to fail to remember
forgetful apt to forget
forget-me-not a low-growing plant with small blue flowers

forgive to pardon; to overlook a fault
forgiveness pardon

forgo to give up; to do without

fork an implement with a handle and two or more prongs, used in cooking or to pick up food; a similar, longer implement used as an agricultural tool; anything resembling a fork (as, a tuning fork) □ to divide into two branches (as - A road forks.)

forlorn forsaken; wretched

form shape; arrangement: a paper with blank spaces in which to write answers to questions or detailed information (as, an application form): a long seat; a class in school: a system (as, a form of government) □ to give shape to; to conceive or develop (as to form an opinion): to take up position in (as, to form fours)
formal according to rule; (of a person's manner) coldly correct
formality a formal act
formation the act of forming; an arrangement or a prearranged order (as, aeroplanes flying in formation)

former past; before in time; the first-mentioned of two (the second-mentioned is the latter)
formerly in former or past times

formidable difficult to deal with (as, a formidable obstacle); causing fear (as, a formidable enemy)

formula a set form of words or signs which is used to express briefly a rule or idea (as, in chemistry, H_2O = water)
formulate to express in a

definite form

forsake to desert; to give up

forsythia a garden shrub with small bright yellow flowers in spring

fort a small place or building specially strengthened for defence against an enemy
fortification the art of strengthening a military position; walls, trenches, etc. built to strengthen a position
fortify to strengthen against attack
fortress a fortified place or stronghold

forte (*say forty*) (music) loud
fortissimo (music) very loud

forth forward; out (as - Come forth!)
forthcoming happening soon
forthwith immediately

fortitude courage in bearing misfortune, pain, etc.

fortnight two weeks (fourteen nights)

fortune whatever comes by chance or luck; wealth; success
fortunate lucky
fortune teller a man or woman supposed to be able to foretell the future by means of playing cards, a crystal ball, tea leaves, etc.

forum (in Roman times) a market place or public place; (nowadays) any meeting place for a general discussion

forward(s) towards, or near, the front (as, to go forwards; a forward movement) □ a player in a forward position □ to send on (as, to forward a letter)

fossil the remains, impression or trace of an animal or plant found preserved in rock
fossilize to change into a fossil

foul very dirty; filthy; stormy (as, foul weather) □ to make foul: to collide, or become entangled, with (as, a ship's propeller fouled by rope) □ a breaking of the rules of a game (as, a foul in football)

found 1 to lay the base or foundation of; to set up or establish (as, to found a school)
foundation the act of founding; the base of a building below ground; the basis of anything
foundation stone one of the stones forming the foundation of a building
founder 1 someone who has founded or established: see also **founder 2**
well founded based on fact; reasonable

found 2 see **find**

founder 2 to collapse in ruins; (of a ship) to fill with water and sink

foundling a small child found deserted

foundry a workshop where metal is melted and shaped by casting it in a mould (as, a brass foundry)

fountain water spouting up into the air continuously from one or more jets; the structure (usually ornamental) which produces the jets of water

fowl a bird (especially one of the poultry kind)

fox a reddish-brown dog-like wild animal with a bushy tail (The female is called a vixen.)

foxglove a plant with tall spikes of flowers, each shaped like the fingers of a glove

foyer (*say fwahyay*) a large lobby in a theatre for the use of the audience during intervals

fraction a fragment; a part of a whole (such as $1/2$, $2/3$)

fracture the breaking of a bone or something hard □ to break or crack something hard

fragile easily broken or damaged; delicate

fragment a piece broken off; a very small part

fragrant sweet-scented
fragrance a sweet scent; a perfume

frail weak; very easily broken
frailty weakness

frame a border or structure around something (as, a picture frame); the skeleton or main parts of anything (as, the frame of a bicycle): a state (as, a frame of mind) □ to put a frame round; to put together; to plan

framework the outline or main part of something that the rest is built on to

franc the unit of money in France, Belgium and some other countries

frank outspoken; open □ to mark a letter by machine to show that postage has been paid

frankincense a sweet-smelling resin, burned as incense

frantic mad; desperate

fraternal brotherly

fraud dishonesty; deceit

fray 1 a fight; a brawl

fray 2 (of cloth, etc.) to wear out by rubbing

freak an abnormal or unusual person, plant or animal (for example, extraordinarily large or small in size); a monstrosity □ unusual, out of the ordinary (as, a freak snowstorm in late spring)

freckle a small brown spot on the skin (especially of the face, neck and arms) □ to be or become spotted with freckles

free not bound or hampered; not imprisoned or enclosed; able to do and say what you like (so long as it does not interfere with the law or with the freedom of others) □ to make or set free

freedom liberty; independence; being without restraint

freehand (of a drawing) done entirely by hand

freehold (of property, especially land) belonging to the owner without any restrictions

freelance independent, not exclusively employed by one firm or person (as, a freelance journalist)

freeman one who is not a slave; a person who has been made an honorary citizen (as, a freeman of the City of London)

free trade international trade without customs duties or other restrictions

free will freedom of choice; the power to act independently

freeze to become ice; to cool to freezing point; to become hard and solid from cold; to feel very cold

freezer a refrigerator or part of a refrigerator that keeps food frozen

freezing point the temperature at which a liquid becomes solid (Water freezes at 32° Fahrenheit or 0° centigrade.)

frozen hardened by cold

freight the load or cargo carried by ships, aeroplanes, trains, lorries, etc.

freighter a ship or aeroplane designed to carry freight

frenzy wild excitement; a fit of madness

frenzied frantically agitated

frequent (*say freekwent*) happening often □ (*say freekwent*) to visit often

frequency repeated occurrence; rate of vibration (as, radio wave frequencies)

fresco a painting made on walls covered with fresh, damp plaster □ a painting so made

fresh new; the opposite of stale; not tired; without salt; (of food) not preserved or frozen

freshen to make or become fresh

fret 1 to wear away or fray by rubbing; to be annoyed or discontented

fretful irritable; peevish

fret 2 to carve or make a design of short straight lines (joined at right angles) on something: a ridge on the fingerboard of a guitar, banjo, etc.

fretsaw a narrow saw with fine teeth

fretwork ornamental woodwork (especially plywood cut with a fretsaw into an open pattern)

friable crumbly; easily reduced to powder

friar a member of a Roman Catholic monastic order

friction rubbing of the surface of one object against another; disagreement or differences of opinion

fridge an abbreviation of **refrigerator**

friend someone known well and much liked; a supporter or helper
friendly amiable; pleasant; kindly
friendship a friendly feeling between people

frieze (*say freez*) an ornamental strip at the top of the walls in a room; a decorative band (of sculpture, etc.) on the outside walls of a building

frigate a fast-sailing warship
frigate-bird a large, swift marine bird of prey, found in the tropics

fright sudden fear; terror; alarm
frighten to make (a person or animal) afraid; to scare
frightful dreadful; awful; shocking; great (as - It is a frightful pity.)
frightfully awfully; greatly; very (as - He was frightfully sorry to be so late.)

frigid cold; frozen with cold; very cold and unfriendly in manner

frill a trimming made from a strip of light material or lace, gathered on one edge and used as decorative edging on clothing, curtains, etc.

fringe hair cut short across the forehead; a border of loose threads used as edging on rugs, lampshades, etc.; anything resembling a fringe

frisky lively; playful

fritter 1 to waste, a little at a time (usually on unimportant things); to squander

fritter 2 a piece of fruit or other food fried in batter

frivolous not serious in attitude; silly; trifling; fond of gaiety
frivolity gaiety; lack of seriousness

frizzy, frizzly tightly curled

fro away; back (as in *to and fro*, meaning to a place and back again, or first in one direction, then in another)

frock a girl's or woman's dress

frog a small, tailless webfooted animal that lives partly in water and partly on land
frogman a diver with foot coverings like a frog's webbed feet and other equipment that enables him to swim about easily in deep water
frog-in-the-throat a hoarse voice caused by catarrh or inflammation of the mucous membrane

frolic to have fun; to play pranks □ a merrymaking

from out of (as - The fine was taken from his weekly pay.); beginning at (as - From tomorrow fares will be increased.); departing from or coming from (as - The train leaves from this station.)

frond the leaf of a fern or palm

front the forward-facing or foremost part of anything (as, the front of a building, of a train, etc.); the land or shore facing the sea, a lake, etc. □ to stand in front of or opposite to
frontal of, or in, the front

frontier the boundary of one country with another; the border between settled and unsettled country (especially in pioneering days)

frontispiece an illustrated page at the front of a book, just before the title page

frost a temperature at or below that at which water freezes (32° Fahrenheit or 0° centigrade); tiny particles of ice on a surface (as, ground frost, frost on roofs and roads, etc.) □ to cover with frost or something that looks like frost (as, icing on a cake)
frosted looking like frost (as,

frosted glass)

frostbite the freezing of a part of the body by exposure to extreme cold

froth foam □ to cause froth on (as - Beer froths when poured into a glass.); to give out froth (as - A racehorse froths at the mouth after a hard run.)

frown to wrinkle the forehead and draw the brows together when displeased or when concentrating or worrying

frozen see **freeze**

frugal wasting little; scanty (as, a frugal meal)

fruit the part of a plant or tree which contains the seeds; the product or result (as, the fruit of their efforts)

fruiterer someone who sells fruit

fruitful producing much fruit; producing good results

fruitless without results; useless (as, a fruitless expedition)

frustrate to bring to nothing; to thwart (as, to frustrate a person's hopes)

frustration a strong feeling of discouragement and disappointment

fry to cook in fat or oil

frying-pan a shallow pan used for frying

fuchsia (*say fewsha*) a shrub with drooping flowers (often purplish-red)

fudge a soft sweetmeat made of sugar, butter, milk and (often) chocolate and nuts: nonsense □ to cheat or fake

fuel any substance used to make heat (such as coal, wood, oil and gas) □ to supply with fuel

fugitive (*say fewjitiv*) someone who is running away □ fleeing; lasting a short time

fugue (*say fewg*) a musical composition in which the theme or melody is taken up in turn by a number of different parts or voices

fulcrum the prop or fixed point

on which a lever rests or turns

fulfil to carry out fully (as, to fulfil a promise); to realize fully (as - His hopes were fulfilled.)

full holding as much as can be contained; holding plenty (as, a purse full of money); complete (as, a full year of 365 days) □ fully or directly (as, a blow full in the face)

fully completely

full-length of the whole or actual length (as, a full-length portrait)

full stop a single point marking the end of a sentence

fumble to grope about awkwardly; to handle awkwardly; to fail to catch a ball

fume(s) smoke or vapour □ to give off fumes: to be in a rage

fumigate to disinfect by means of fumes

fun merriment; amusement; joking

funny full of fun; laughable: odd

funny bone a bone at the elbow (A blow on a nerve at this point produces a funny, tingling sensation in the forearm.)

function a proper or expected activity (as - The function of the eyes is to see.); any formal social gathering (such as a public dinner) □ to perform a function; to work (as, an engine which functions properly)

fund a sum of money set aside for a special purpose: a store or supply (as, a fund of stories); (plural) money available for spending

fundamental underlying or basic (as, a person's fundamental beliefs) □ an essential part; (plural) the first stages or groundwork (as, the fundamentals of arithmetic)

funeral the burial or cremation of a dead person, with any associated ceremony

funereal (*say fewneerial*) concerned with a funeral; dismal; mournful

fungus a plant without chlorophyll (for example, mushrooms and moulds)

funicular (railway) a mountain railway in which the carriages are pulled by a steel cable

funnel a passage or tube for the escape of smoke, etc.; a tube with a wide opening, for pouring liquids into bottles

funny see **fun**

fur the soft, fine hair of certain animals (such as cats and rabbits); animal skins with the hair attached used for trimming or for whole garments (as, a fur collar, a fur coat); a fur-like coating
furry covered with fur; like fur

furious see **fury**

furl to roll up (as, to furl a sail)

furnace an enclosed structure, like a very big oven, in which great heat is produced (as, a furnace for making steel)

furnish to fit up (as, to furnish a house); to supply or provide (as, to furnish a friend with a list of books); to equip
furnishings fittings of any kind (especially furniture)
furniture the movable articles in a house (such as tables, chairs and beds)

furrow the narrow trench made by a plough; a groove; a wrinkle □ to form furrows in; to wrinkle (as, to furrow the brow)

further to a greater extent or distance; in addition (as, a further reason) □ to help on (as, to further a plan)
furthermore in addition to what has been said; moreover
furthermost, furthest farthest; most remote

furtive stealthy; secret

fury rage; violent anger
furious extremely angry; violent

fuse 1 a length of some combustible material which is attached to ignite an explosive charge; any similar device for causing an explosion after a certain time

fuse 2 a short, easily melted piece of wire inserted as a safety device against fire in electrical circuits) □ to melt; to join by melting together; to fail through the melting of a fuse (as - The electric lights fused.)
fusion the act of melting; a merging of things

fuselage the body of an aeroplane

fuss an unnecessary bother or agitation □ to bustle, or be agitated, about unimportant things
fussy making a fuss; too particular

fusty having a mouldy, musty smell

futile useless; having no effect

future the time to come □ that is to come (as, in future years)

fuzzy covered with tiny hairs or fluff: blurred

g

gabble to talk very quickly □ fast, confused talking

gable the triangular, upper part of the end wall of a building

gadget a small device or object (often clever and useful)

gag to stop a person's mouth and so silence him □ something pushed into a person's mouth to silence him: a joke or hoax

gaiety see **gay**

gain to earn; to win; to reach (as - The swimmer gained the bank of the river.) □ something obtained as an addition; a profit

gait way of walking (as, an

awkward gait)

gaiter a covering for the ankle, or for the leg below the knee

gala a festivity or fête

galaxy a vast system of stars (such as The Galaxy, or Milky Way): a splendid gathering of people

gale a strong wind

gall 1 bile: bitterness of feeling
gall bladder a bladder in the body, containing bile
galling annoying

gall 2 a growth on trees (especially oaks) caused by an insect

gallant brave; noble: attentive to women □ (*say gallant*) a man of fashion
gallantry bravery: courteous attention to women

galleon (in former times) a large Spanish sailing ship

gallery a long room or passage (as, a picture gallery); the highest floor of seats as in a theatre

galley (in olden times) a long, low ship moved by oars and sails: a ship's kitchen
galley slave a person forced to row in a galley

gallon a measure for liquids equal to 8 pints (appoximately 4¼ litres)

gallop the fastest speed of a horse □ to go at a gallop

gallows a wooden framework for hanging criminals

galore in abundance

galosh, golosh an overshoe (usually of rubber) worn in wet weather

galvanize to stimulate by an electric current; to rouse suddenly (as, to galvanize someone into action)
galvanized iron iron coated with zinc (by means of electricity) to prevent rusting

gambit an opening move in chess in which one player gives up a piece in order to improve his position later; an opening move

in anything (especially a cunning one)

gamble to play for money; to take big risks □ a risky transaction

gambol to leap playfully (as, lambs in a field) □ a playful leaping about

game an amusement or sport with rules: animals and birds hunted for sport; the meat of some of these, which may be eaten (for example, hare, pheasant, venison) □ plucky
gamekeeper someone employed in the country to look after game birds, fish, etc.)
gaming gambling
big game large animals which are sometimes hunted (such as lions and tigers)

gammon smoked or cured ham; the lower part of a side of bacon including the hind leg

gamut the whole range of a voice or musical instrument; the full range of anything (as, the gamut of emotions)

gander a male goose

gang a number of labourers working together; a band of people going about together (especially for criminal purposes)
gangster a member of a criminal gang

gangrene the decay or death of part of the body due to lack of circulation

gangway a passageway (especially between rows of seats, as in a cinema, or a movable one from ship to shore)

gantry a platform for a travelling crane; a structure supporting railway signals; a stand for barrels

gaol, gaoler see **jail, jailer**

gap an opening or break in something (as, a gap in a hedge)

gape to open the mouth wide (as, in surprise); to be wide open (as, a gaping chasm)

garage (*say garij or garahzh*) a

building or shed for storing one or more motor cars; a large workshop where motor cars are repaired

garb dress or costume □ to clothe

garbage rubbish; refuse

garble to mix up so as to mislead; to pick out certain parts (from a story, etc.) unfairly to suit one's own purpose (as, a garbled account of what happened)

garden a piece of ground on which flowers or vegetables are grown □ to work in a garden

gargle to wash the throat with a bubbling sound, without swallowing the liquid □ a liquid used for gargling

gargoyle a spout jutting out from a roof gutter (often carved like a grotesque human or animal head)

garish showy; gaudy

garland a wreath, or chain, of flowers or leaves

garlic a bulbous plant with a strong smell and pungent taste, used in cooking

garment any article of clothing

garnet a precious stone (usually dark red in colour)

garnish to adorn; to decorate (a dish of food) □ something (such as parsley) used to decorate a dish for the table

garret a room just under the roof of a house

garrison a body of soldiers for guarding a fortified place □ to supply with troops for the defence of a place

garrulous talkative

garter an elastic band to keep a stocking up

gas a substance which is in the form of vapour, neither solid nor liquid (Some gases, like coal-gas, burn; others, like nitrous oxide, deaden pain; many others are poisonous.); an abbreviation for gasoline □ to poison with gas
gaseous in a state of gas
gassy containing gas

gasoline, gasolene an American word for petrol
gas holder, gasometer a large tank for storing gas

gash a deep, open cut or wound □ to make a deep cut

gasp to struggle for breath; to catch one's breath □ the act or sound of gasping

gastric having to do with the stomach
gastronomy the art of good eating

gate a door in a fence, wall or hedge: the number of people at a football match, etc.; the total money paid by them for entrance
gateway the opening or structure for containing a gate; an entrance

gather to collect; to pick (as, to gather flowers); to come to one place (as - The crowd gathered quickly.); to draw together (as, to gather cloth into folds): to learn or conclude (as, to gather from someone's comments that the game had been disappointing)
gathering a crowd; a meeting

gaucho (*say gowcho*) a cowboy of the pampas in South America

gaudy showy; vulgarly bright

gauge (*say gage*) to measure; to estimate □ a measuring device (as, a rain gauge for measuring rainfall); the distance between the rails of a railway line (as, broad or narrow gauge which is greater or less than the standard gauge)

gaunt thin; haggard

gauntlet (in former times) the iron glove of armour, which was thrown down as a challenge; (nowadays) a glove of strong material, with a flared cuff covering the wrist and part of the arm

gauze a thin transparent fabric

gavotte (*say gavot*) an old-fashioned lively dance

gawky awkward; ungainly

gay lively; happy in a light-hearted way; bright (as, gay colours)
gaiety the state of being gay; merrymaking

gaze to look steadily or fixedly at something □a steady or fixed look

gazelle a small graceful antelope with soft, dark eyes

gazette a newspaper (especially an official one)
gazetteer a dictionary of geographical place-names

gear equipment; anything needed for a purpose (such as tools, clothes, etc.); the part of a motor or bicycle which transmits motion to the wheels and enables the speed to be varied

geese see **goose**

Geiger counter an instrument used to detect the presence of radioactivity

gelatine a transparent, tasteless substance obtained from animal bones, hides etc. (used in the manufacture of table jellies, photographic film, glue, etc.)

gelignite a kind of explosive

gem a precious stone or jewel; anything of beauty or value which is greatly admired (as - This painting is one of the gems of the collection.)

gender (in grammar) one of the classes of nouns and pronouns which distinguish sex (namely: masculine [for boy, he, etc.], feminine [for girl, she, etc.] and neuter [for table, it, etc.])

genealogy *(say jeenialogy)* the history of the descent and relationship of families; the list of forefathers of a particular person or family

general 1 the chief commander of an army; the chief or head of a large department or organization (as, director-general, postmaster-general, general manager)

general 2 not special; relating to the whole or to all or most; usual or widespread (as - The general opinion is that milk is good for children.); not in detail (as, general instructions for building a model ship); including, or dealing with, several different things (as, a general store)
generalize to make a general statement (which may or may not cover all cases)
general practitioner (G.P.) a doctor who helps patients with all kinds of ailments and does not specialize in any particular type of disease
in general in most cases

generate to produce; to bring into being (as, to generate electricity)
generation production or formation; a single stage in family descent (as - Son, father and grandfather together represent three generations.); people of roughly the same age or period
generator a producer; an apparatus for producing electricity, gas or steam

generous liberal in sharing or giving things to others; noble-minded
generosity liberality or goodness of nature; willingness to share

genesis the beginning or origin

genial cheering; good-natured and kindly

genius very unusual powers of mind; a person having such powers (the plural is **geniuses**): a good or evil spirit (the plural is **genii,** *say geenee-eye)*

genteel *(say genteel)* well-bred; (sometimes) too refined in manners

gentile anyone who is not a Jew

gentle mild and kind in manners and action: gradual (as, a gentle slope)
gentility good birth; polite manners
gentleman a man of good birth or high social standing; a courteous and honourable man

genuine *(say jenyewin)* real; not

artificial or fake

geography the science that describes the surface of the earth and its inhabitants
  geographer an expert in geography
  geographic(al) having to do with geography

geology the science that describes the history and development of the earth's crust (especially the changes in the various layers of rock over millions of years)
  geologic(al) having to do with geology

geometry the branch of mathematics which deals with lines, angles and figures (such as quadrilaterals, triangles and circles)
  geometric(al) relating to geometry; having a regular shape (like any geometrical figure)

geranium the popular name for a garden and house plant (pelargonium) with showy scarlet, bright pink, or white flowers

germ a very tiny form of animal or plant life that can only be seen under a microscope (Some germs cause disease.): the tiny beginning of anything (as, the germ of an idea)
  germicide a substance that destroys disease germs
  germinate to begin to grow or sprout (especially of a seed)

gesticulate to move the hands and arms about vigorously (especially when speaking)
  gesticulation the making of vigorous gestures
  gesture any movement of the body expressing some feeling (The feeling may not be strong as, a gesture of distaste.); an action of courtesy or tact (as, a gesture of friendship)

get to obtain; to fetch; to receive; to become (as, to get better); to make ready (as, to get dinner); to move into a position (as, to get up, down, etc.); to arrive at (as - We got to the station at 9 o'clock.)

to get away with to do something without being blamed or punished for it
to get off to be let off punishment
to get on with to be friendly with; to make progress with
to get over to recover from
to get round to avoid (a difficulty); to coax a person

geyser a natural spring which shoots out hot water and steam; a water-heater

ghastly horrible; death-like

gherkin a small cucumber, often used for pickling

ghetto (formerly) the Jews' quarter in some cities; (nowadays) a part of a city where people of one race or nationality live

ghost a spirit (especially of a dead person); a faint suggestion (as, a ghost of a chance)
  ghoulish (say goolish) gruesome; fearful

giant an imaginary huge man-like creature; an unusually big person, animal or plant
  gigantic huge; of giant size

gibber to utter sounds which have no sense
  gibberish rapid gabbling talk; nonsense

gibbet (in former times) a gallows on which criminals were hung up after execution

gibbon an ape with very long arms

gibe see **jibe**

giblets the edible parts of the inside of a fowl

giddy dizzy; unsteady: flighty (as, a giddy young girl)
  giddiness the state of being giddy

gift something given; a present: a natural quality or ability
  gifted very talented

gig a light, two-wheeled carriage: a long light boat

gigantic see **giant**

giggle to laugh in small bursts in a silly manner □ a laugh of this kind

gild to cover with gold leaf or imitation gold
gilding, gilt a thin covering of gold or imitation gold

gill an organ for breathing (like an opening) in a fish's skin

gilt see **gild**

gimlet a small tool, with a screw point, for boring holes

gimmick an unusual device or idea to catch attention (especially when selling things)

gin 1 a strong alcoholic drink (It is distilled from grain and flavoured with juniper berries.)

gin 2 a trap or snare: a machine for separating cotton from its seeds

ginger the underground stem of a tropical plant (It has a hot, spicy taste.) □ containing ginger: reddish brown in colour
ginger ale, ginger beer an effervescent soft drink flavoured with ginger
gingerbread a cake flavoured with treacle and (usually) ginger

gingerly with soft steps; very carefully

gingham a cotton cloth (usually with stripes or checks)

gipsy, gypsy a member of a wandering people who originally came from India (Gipsies usually have no permanent home.)

giraffe an African animal with a very long neck and forelegs

gird to bind round; to fasten with a belt (as, to gird on a sword)
girdle a belt or cord round the waist; anything that encloses like a belt

girder a large beam of iron or steel used to support floors, etc. in buildings and bridges

girl a female child; a young woman
girlish of, or like, a girl

girth a measurement round the middle; the belly-band of a saddle

gist (say jist) the main point(s) of a matter (as, the gist of a story)

give to hand over; to provide; to do suddenly (as, to give a shout); to render (as, to give thanks); to pronounce (as, to give a decision); to yield or break (as - The river bank gave under the pressure of water.)
to give in, give up to yield; to hand over
to give way to yield; to fall back

glacier (say glassyer) a huge mass of ice that moves extremely slowly down a mountainside
glacial (say glayshal) icy or very cold; relating to ice or glaciers

glad pleased; cheerful
gladden to make glad; to cheer

glade an open space in a wood

gladiator (in ancient Rome) a man who was trained to fight in an arena with other men or animals

glamour fascination or charm (often only superficial)
glamorous having glamour

glance a quick look; a quick slanting movement or impact □ to take a quick look at; to be hit obliquely off (as - The ball glanced off the edge of the bat.)

gland an organ of the body which secretes substances from the blood or ejects them from the body
glandular relating to glands (as, glandular fever)

glare a dazzling light; an angry look □ to give a dazzling light; to stare angrily
glaring fiercely bright; very obvious (as, a glaring mistake)

glass a hard (usually breakable) material through which light can pass; an article made of glass (especially a mirror or a drinking vessel) □ made of glass
glasses eyeglasses
glassy shiny and smooth (like glass)
glasshouse a greenhouse

glaze to fit with glass; to put windows in (as, to glaze a new house); to cover with a thin coating of anything glassy (as, to glaze pottery) □ a glassy coating; a shiny surface

glazier a person who sets glass in window-frames

gleam to glow or shine faintly □ a small beam of light; a glow

glean to gather by hand what grain remains in a cornfield after the reapers have passed; to collect bits of information (as, to glean snippets of news)

glee joy; gaiety

glen a narrow valley with a stream

glib fluent or ready with insincere talk or chatter

glide to move smoothly and easily; to flow gently □ the act of gliding

glider an aircraft without an engine, which flies by means of upward air currents

glimmer to shine faintly and unsteadily □ a faint gleam (as, a glimmer of light, of hope)

glimmering a glimmer; a faint idea

glimpse a very brief look (as, to catch a glimpse of an aeroplane) □ to get a brief look at

glint to gleam or glitter □ a gleam or glitter

glisten to shine faintly or gleam by reflected light (as - The pavements glistened after the rain.); to sparkle

glitter to sparkle with light (as, glittering diamonds); to be splendid in a sparkling way (as, a glittering evening dress) □ sparkle or showiness

gloat to gaze at, or think about, something with greedy or malicious joy

globe a ball or sphere; the earth; a map of the world on a sphere

global world-wide

globular spherical

globule a drop; a little globe

gloom partial darkness; dimness; dismalness

gloomy dimly lighted; dismal

glory great honour or fame; splendour □ to pride oneself in (as - He gloried in his success.)

glorify to make glorious; to praise highly

glorious splendid; noble

gloss the brightness of a polished surface □ to give a polish to

glossy shiny and smooth

glossary a list of difficult or unusual words with their meanings

glove a covering for the hand (especially with a sheath for each finger)

boxing gloves see **box**

glow *(say gloe)* to burn without a flame; to give out a steady light; to tingle with warmth □ a glowing state; a feeling of warmth

glowing that glows: very enthusiastic (as, a glowing description)

glowworm a beetle whose larvae and wingless females give out light

glower to stare angrily; to scowl

glucose a kind of sugar (generally manufactured from starch)

glue a kind of fluid gelatine used to stick or join things together □ to join with glue or some other adhesive

glum sullen; sad

glut too great a supply (as, a glut of plums) □ to overstock the market; to overload with food

glutton someone who eats too much

gluttonous fond of overeating

gluttony overeating

glycerine a colourless, thick liquid with a sweet taste, used in ointments, medicines, etc.

gnarled *(say narld)* twisted; knotty (as, a gnarled old tree)

gnash *(say nash)* to grind (the teeth) in rage

gnat *(say nat)* a small flying insect which bites

gnaw *(say naw)* to bite in a continuous scraping manner (as, a dog gnawing a bone); to wear away gradually

gnome *(say nome)* a dwarf; a goblin

gnu *(say new)* a large African antelope

go to move or start off; to act or work (as, to make a watch go by winding it up); to turn out or happen (as - Things should go very well.); to become (as, to go mad); to lead to (as - That road goes to London.); to intend or be about to (as - They said they would go for a walk.)
  go-ahead eager; enterprising
  go in for to take up (a particular activity)
  go on to continue
  go with to accompany; to match or be suitable (as - The red gloves go with the red hat.)

goad a sharp-pointed stick for driving oxen □ to drive with a goad; to urge on; to torment

goal the two upright posts between which the ball has to be sent in football, hockey, etc.; a score for doing this; a winning-post; any aim or objective (as, his goal in life)

goat a hairy animal related to sheep (usually having horns and a little beard)

gobble to swallow food quickly

goblet a large drinking-cup without a handle

goblin a mischievous sprite or fairy

god a superhuman being and object of worship; in the Christian and Jewish religions, the creator of the world (God)
  godly keeping God's laws; holy
  goddess a female god
  godfather, godmother a person who, at a child's baptism, promises to see that the child will receive education in the Christian faith
  godsend a very welcome piece of good fortune

goggles large spectacles worn to protect the eyes

gold a precious yellow metal (now mainly used for rings and jewellery); riches or anything very precious
  golden of, or like, gold; very fine (as, a golden opportunity)
  goldfinch a small black and white bird with a crimson face and yellow wing markings
  goldfish a small fish, usually reddish-gold in colour, which is often kept in a garden pond or aquarium
  gold leaf gold beaten into extremely thin leaves, used in decorating fine leather goods, etc.
  goldmine a mine which produces gold; a source of great profit
  goldsmith a worker in gold and silver

golf a game which is played with a small white ball and a set of long-handled clubs (The ball has to be struck repeatedly over a prepared stretch of land, in a series of little holes, using as few strokes as possible.)
  golf course, golf links the large piece of ground over which golf is played (usually with 18 holes.)

golosh see **galosh**

gondola *(say gondola)* a long narrow boat used on the canals of Venice
  gondolier a boatman who propels a gondola

gong a large metal disc which makes a deep ringing sound when it is struck

good having the right qualities (the opposite of bad); well-behaved; kind; pleasant (as, a good time); considerable (as, a good supply) □ goodness; the opposite of evil; advantage or benefit (as, for their good)
  goods movable belongings; merchandise or freight (as, a goods train)
  goodness the quality or act of being good; excellence
  goodbye a word said to someone who is just going away (originally - *God be with you*)
  good afternoon, good day, good

evening, good morning, good night a shortening of - *I wish you a good afternoon,* etc.

good-humoured showing a cheerful mood

good-natured showing kindness

goose a web-footed bird like a duck, but larger; a silly person

gooseflesh a puckering of the skin caused by cold or fear

geese the plural of goose

gooseberry the edible, greenish fruit of the gooseberry bush

gore 1 blood (especially when clotted)

gory covered with blood

gore 2 to pierce with horns or tusks

gorge the throat; a deep, narrow opening between hills □ to swallow greedily

gorgeous splendid; showy

gorilla the largest kind of ape, which lives in Africa

gorse a prickly shrub with yellow flowers

gosling a young goose

gospel the teachings of Christ; His life story as told by Matthew, Mark, Luke or John; anything told or believed as the absolute truth

gossamer fine spider-threads floating in the air or lying on bushes; any very thin fabric

gossip idle talk about others; someone who gossips □ to indulge in idle talk about others

gouge (*say gowge*) a chisel with a hollow blade □ to scoop out; to force out

gourd (*say goord*) a large fleshy fruit with a hard rind; its hollowed-out rind used as a bottle or drinking vessel

gourmand (*say goormahnd*) a glutton

gourmet (*say goormay*) a person with a delicate taste in food and drink; a connoisseur of food and drink

gout acute and painful inflammation of the smaller joints (especially of the big toe)

gouty relating, or subject, to gout

govern to rule with authority; to control; to direct

governess a woman who teaches young children in their home

government the body of persons appointed to rule a country; the ruling or administration by such statesmen; a system of governing (as, democratic government)

governor a ruler; the head of an institution: a regulator that controls the even speed of a machine

gown a woman's dress; a long loose-fitting robe or cloak

grab to seize or grasp suddenly □ a sudden grasp or clutch

grace easy elegance in the shape or movement of a living creature; a pleasing quality; mercy; a delay granted as a favour (as, three days' grace); a short prayer before or after a meal; a ceremonious title (as, His Grace the Archbishop)

graceful elegant in an easy manner; done pleasingly (as, a graceful movement)

graceless without grace; in bad taste

gracious kind; courteous

grade a step in a scale of quality or rank (as, top grade apples) □ to arrange according to grade

gradation arrangement by grade or degree (as, the gradation of colours or shades from dark to light)

gradient the amount of slope in a road or railway (as, a steep gradient)

gradual happening or advancing gently and slowly

graduate to divide into grades (as - A thermometer scale is graduated in degrees.): to receive a university degree □ a person who has a university degree

graft to fix a shoot or twig of one plant on to another so that it joins with it and grows there; to put skin from one part of the body on to another damaged part □ a small piece of a plant or animal which is joined to another individual or part

grain a single small seed; corn in general (wheat, barley, oats, etc.); a hard particle (as, a grain of sand); a very small amount; the pattern of the fibres in wood or leather □ to paint wood in imitation of the natural grain

gramme the unit of weight in the metric system (1000 grammes = 1 kilogramme)

grammar the study of the proper use of words in speaking and writing; a book which describes this
grammatical according to the rules of grammar

gramophone an instrument for reproducing sounds from a revolving grooved disc

granary a storehouse for grain

grand great; very important; noble; splendid: of the second degree of parentage (as, grandfather, grandmother, grandchild)
grandeur (*say grandyur*) splendour of appearance
grandiose grand or imposing; pompous

granite a hard rock, much used in building

grant to give; to allow as a favour; to admit (as, granting that he made a mistake) □ something given; an allowance of money

granule a small grain (as, instant coffee in granules)
granular made up of granules
granulated broken into granules (as, granulated sugar)

grape a fruit that grows in bunches on vines, and from which wine is made
grapefruit a sharp-tasting citrus fruit like a large yellow orange
grapeshot shot which scatters when fired

graph a diagram (usually on squared paper) that shows changes in one or more kinds of measurement (for example, in temperature over a certain time)
graphic relating to drawing, painting, etc. (as, the graphic arts); relating to writing or describing; vivid (as, a graphic story)
graphite a mineral form of carbon used in pencils

grapnel a small anchor with several claws

grapple to seize and hold (as, with a hook or grappling iron); to struggle with (as, to grapple with a problem)
grappling iron an instrument for hooking and holding

grasp to seize and hold; to understand (as, to grasp an idea) □ a grip; a power of understanding (as, a grasp of a subject)
grasping greedy

grass plants with long narrow leaves and a tubular stem which make up the green covering of fields and lawns (Cereals, reeds, bamboo and sugar cane are also grasses.)
grasshopper a jumping insect that makes a chirping sound by rubbing its wings or legs together
grass-snake a small and harmless snake

grate 1 a framework of iron bars for holding a fire
grating a frame of iron bars used to cover an opening

grate 2 to rub, or wear away, with anything rough (as, to grate cheese into particles); to make a harsh sound; to irritate (as - The quarrel grated on her nerves.)
grater a utensil with a rough surface for grating a substance

grateful thankful; expressing gratitude
gratify to please; to satisfy
gratitude thankfulness

gratuity a money gift in return for something done; a tip; a payment made to soldiers, etc. on their retirement

gratuitous (say gratewitus) done or given for nothing; uncalled for (as, gratuitous insult)

grave 1 a hole dug in the earth for the burial of a dead person
graveyard a burial ground; a cemetery

grave 2 of importance; very serious (as, a grave responsibility); solemn

gravel very small stones

graven engraved or carved (as, a graven image)

gravity 1 great seriousness

gravity 2 the force of attraction towards the earth or between heavenly bodies, which varies with their size and distance from one another
gravitate to move or tend towards by the force of gravity; to be strongly attracted towards (as, to gravitate towards the legal profession)

gravy juices from cooked meat

gray see **grey**

graze 1 to feed on growing grass (as, sheep grazing in a field)
grazing the feeding or raising of cattle

graze 2 to pass lightly along the surface of (as, to graze the kerb with a bicycle wheel); to scrape the skin lightly □ a light touch; a slight scrape

grease (say greess) any thick oily substance; softened animal fat □ to smear with grease
greasy of, or like, grease; smeared or coated with grease

great very large or big; very important or famous (as, Alexander the Great); much more than is usual (as, great pain); indicating one degree more in parentage, etc. (as, great-grandfather, great-uncle)

greed too great a desire (especially for food or money)
greedy wanting too much

green of the colour of growing grass and most leaves; unripe: inexperienced or easily taken in □ a grassy plot (as, a village green)
greenery green plants; foliage
greengage a greenish-yellow variety of plum
greengrocer a dealer in fresh vegetables
greenhorn an inexperienced person easily cheated
greenhouse a building with roof and sides of glass for growing plants indoors
greens green vegetables for food (especially cabbage)

greet to meet someone with kind words; to welcome; to send kind wishes
greeting(s) words on meeting; a welcome; a friendly message (as, a greetings card)

gregarious living in flocks, herds or communities; fond of company

grenade a small bomb for throwing by hand or for firing from a rifle

grey, gray ash-coloured (white mixed with black); dull (as, a grey day); greyhaired □ a grey colour; a grey horse
greyhound a tall, slender dog used for dog-racing

grid a grating; a gridiron; a network of wires carrying electric power to different parts of the country
griddle a flat iron plate for cooking pancakes, etc.
gridiron a frame of iron bars for cooking food over a fire

grief sorrow; great sadness
grievance a real, or imagined, wrong or injustice
grieve to feel sorrow; to cause sorrow to
grievous causing sorrow; painful

griffin, griffon, gryphon an imaginary animal with a lion's body and the beak and wings of an eagle

grill to cook food on a gridiron or under a gas or electric grill: to cross-examine severely □ a gridiron; a part of a gas or electric cooker used for grilling; a grilled dish

grille a lattice or grating in a door (for observing without opening), or covering a window (for protection and decoration)

grim stern; cruel; unyielding (as, grim determination)

grimace a twisting of the face (whether in pain or in fun)

grime dirt (usually from soot or coal dust)
grimy very dirty

grin to smile broadly □ a broad smile

grind to crush to powder; to sharpen by rubbing (as, grinding a knife); to grate or rub together (as, grinding the teeth) □ continued hard work at a job or in studying
ground 1 the past of grind
grindstone a circular revolving stone for sharpening tools

grip to hold something tightly with the hand(s); to hold fast the attention or interest □ a firm hold with the hand(s) or mind

grisly frightful; hideous

grist corn for grinding

gristle a tough elastic substance in meat; the cartilage in animal and human bodies

grit hard particles of dirt or sand: firmness of character; courage
gritty having hard particles; sandy: determined

grizzled grey, or mixed with grey
grizzly of a grey colour □ short for grizzly bear, a fierce, North American bear

groan a deep moan □ to utter a deep, moaning sound (from pain or sorrow)

grocer a dealer in tea, sugar and ready-packed foods, also common household supplies (such as soap-powders)
groceries the articles sold by grocers

grog a mixture of spirits and cold water, without sugar
groggy slightly drunk; weak

and dazed from illness, or from blows

groin the part of the body where the thighs join the trunk

groom a person who has charge of horses: a bridegroom □ to look after a horse (clean its coat, etc); to make smart and neat (as, a well-groomed appearance)

groove a furrow or long hollow (usually cut into wood or metal) □ to cut a groove in

grope to search by feeling (as, to grope in the dark)

gross 1 coarse; very fat: glaring (as, a gross mistake)

gross 2 total, without any deductions (thus, a gross price of £27 might consist of a net price of £25 plus a carriage cost of £2.)

gross 3 twelve dozen (144)

grotesque (*say grotesk*) very odd; fantastic (as, a grotesque carving)

grotto a cave; an imitation cave

ground 1 see **grind**

ground 2 the solid surface of the earth; land □ to run (a ship) aground; to bring to the ground; to issue an order that an airman or an aeroplane must not fly
grounding a foundation of learning in a subject
groundless without foundation or reason
groundnut the peanut, a tropical plant with pods that ripen under the earth
grounds 1 the land attached to a large house
grounds 2 dregs or sediment (as, coffee grounds)
grounds 3 good or sufficient reasons (as, grounds for making a complaint)
ground-sheet a waterproof sheet spread on the ground by campers

group a number of persons or things together □ to form into one or more groups

grouse 1 to grumble □ a grumble

grouse 2 a game bird found on moors and hills

grove a small wood

grovel to crawl on the ground (especially in fear); to make oneself too humble

grow to become larger; to develop; to have life; to cultivate (as, to grow plants or trees); to become (as, to grow angry)
grown-up an adult
growth a growing; development

growl to utter a deep, rough sound like an angry dog; to grumble in a surly way □ a deep, snarling sound

grub 1 the larva of an insect

grub 2 to dig in the dirt
grubby dirty

grudge a feeling of ill will against someone for a particular reason (as, to bear someone a grudge) □ to be unwilling to give or acknowledge (as, to grudge a person his success)
grudging reluctant

gruel a thin food made by boiling oatmeal in water

gruelling exhausting

gruesome horrible

gruff rough or abrupt in manner

grumble to murmur with discontent, to complain □ a murmur of discontent

grumpy surly; cross

grunt to make a sound like a pig □ such a sound

guarantee a promise that something undertaken will be carried out (as, a guarantee that a new watch is waterproof and shockproof) □ to give a guarantee

guard to protect from danger or attack; to prevent from escaping; to take precautions against (as, to guard against thieves) □ one or more men stationed for guarding purposes; an official in charge of a railway train; a position of defence (as - The boxer kept up his guard.)
guardian a person who guards or takes care of someone or something

guerrilla describes a method of fighting in which an army is harassed by small bands of men □ a member of such a small band

guess an opinion or an answer to a question, given without any real knowledge or evidence □ to give such an opinion or answer

guest a visitor; a person invited by someone to his house or to some entertainment

guffaw to laugh loudly □ a loud laugh

guide to lead or direct □ a person who points out interesting things, to travellers or tourists; anyone who guides or instructs; a book giving information to tourists
guidance explanation or advice; directions; leadership

guild (in the Middle Ages) a union of merchants or of craftsmen in a particular trade; nowadays) an association of people with common aims or interests

guile cunning; deceit

guillotine (*say giloteen*) an instrument for beheading; a machine for cutting paper □ to behead, or cut short, by using a guillotine

guilt the state of having done wrong, or having broken a law
guilty having done wrong; to do with wrong-doing (as, a guilty conscience)

guinea £1.05; (in former times) an English gold coin

guinea fowl a bird of the pheasant family, grey with white spots

guinea pig a small furry rodent, often kept as a pet

guitar a stringed musical instrument which is plucked or strummed

gulch a narrow, rocky valley

gulf a large inlet of the sea; a very deep place; (between persons) a deep division

gull a web-footed sea bird with long wings, usually coloured grey and white

gullet the tube by which food passes from the mouth to the stomach

gullible easily deceived

gully a channel worn by running water

gulp to swallow eagerly, or with difficulty □ a swallow (of food, drink or air)

gum 1 a sticky substance used as a kind of glue; chewing gum; a fruit-flavoured chewy sweet □ to stick with gum

gum 2 the firm fleshy tissue that surrounds the bases of the teeth
gumboil a small boil or abscess on the gum

gumption shrewdness; common sense

gun any weapon firing bullets or shells (as, a rifle, cannon, etc.)
gunner someone who loads or fires a gun; a private in the artillery
gun carriage a carriage on which a cannon is mounted
gunfire the firing of guns
gunman an armed criminal
gun-metal a dark grey alloy of copper and tin
gunpowder an explosive mixture of potassium nitrate, sulphur and charcoal

gunwale, gunnel (*say gun'l*) the upper edge of a boat's or a ship's side

gurgle to flow with, or make, a bubbling sound □ a bubbling sound

gush to flow out suddenly, or in a strong stream; to talk or behave too enthusiastically □ a sudden, or strong, flowing out

gust a sudden blast of wind; a sudden burst (of laughter) □ (of wind) to blow in gusts
gusty stormy

gusto enthusiasm; enjoyment

gut part of the alimentary canal in the body; a cord made from the intestines of some animals (used for violin strings and fishing lines) □ to remove the inner parts of; to reduce to a shell (as - The house was gutted by fire.)
guts the intestines

gutter a narrow channel for draining off water (especially at the side of a street or from a roof)

guttural (of sounds) formed in the throat (as, *g* in the word *guttural*)

guy 1 a rope or chain to steady a tent or hold anything in position

guy 2 an effigy of Guy Fawkes dressed up on 5th November (the anniversary of the Gunpowder Plot)

guzzle to drink or eat greedily

gymkhana (*say jimkahna*) a meeting for sports and games

gymnasium (*say jimnayzium*) a large room or hall fitted with all kinds of equipment for physical exercises
gymnast someone skilled in gymnastics
gymnastics exercises to strengthen the body; feats of agility

gypsy see **gipsy**

gyrate to spin; to whirl
gyration a whirling motion
gyroscope an apparatus with a heavy fly-wheel, used to keep something pointing in the same direction (for example, a compass)

h

haberdashery items needed for sewing or mending (as, needles, thread, etc.)

habit a person's usual custom, practice or behaviour (as, a habit of rising early); (of animals, plants, etc.) the ordinary way of behaving and developing; an action repeated so often that it is done almost without thinking (for example, brushing one's teeth): a form of dress (as, a nun's habit)

habitual usual; customary

habituate to accustom someone to something

habitable fit to be lived in (especially of houses)

habitat the natural home of a plant or animal (as - The habitat of the Giant Panda is in the mountains of Tibet.)

habitation dwelling place

habitual, habituate see **habit**

hack 1 to chop or cut roughly

hacksaw a small saw set in a frame, used for cutting metal

hack 2 (short for hackney) a horse let out for hire; a carriage or other vehicle for hire: a person who does poorly paid hard work for another (as, a hack writer)

hackneyed (*say hacknid*) used too much (for example, a hackneyed phrase such as *un-accustomed as I am to public speaking*)

hackles the hairs on the back of a dog's neck, which rise when he is angry

haddock a sea fish, rather like a small cod

haemoglobin, hemoglobin the red oxygen-carrying pigment in red blood cells

haemorrhage, hemorrhage (*say hemorij*) bleeding

hag an ugly old woman; (formerly) a witch

haggard care-worn; wild-looking from the effects of worry or suffering

haggle to bargain; to argue about the price of something

hail 1 to call out in greeting □ a call from a distance; earshot (as, within hailing distance)

hail 2 frozen rain which falls as small particles of ice; a storm of

hail □ to shower down as hail

hailstone a single piece of hail

hair a very thin threadlike growth from the skin of humans and animals; a mass of such growth (as, hair on the heads of humans and on animals)

hairbreadth or **hair's breadth** a very small distance; a narrow margin (as - He avoided the accident by a hairbreadth.)

hairbrush a brush for tidying and arranging the hair

hairdresser a person who cuts and arranges hair

hair spring a very fine spring inside the balance wheel of a watch

hake a sea fish of the cod family

hale robust and healthy

half one of two equal parts of a whole

halve to divide into halves

halves two equal parts of anything

half-and-half equal parts of two things (as, a half-and-half drink of orange juice and soda water)

half-back one of the players (behind the forwards) in the game of football

half-brother, half-sister a brother or sister by one parent only (as, when a father dies and the mother later marries again, her children of the second marriage are half-brothers or half-sisters to children of her first marriage.)

halfway up to, or at, half the distance from either end or side of anything □ equally distant from two points

half-wit an idiot

halibut the largest of the flat-fishes

hall the space inside the entrance to a building; the main room inside a great house or palace; a manor house; a large building for public or official functions (as, a concert hall, a Town Hall); the main building or dining room of a college

hallelujah, halleluiah (*say halli-*

looya) an expression of praise to God (meaning *Praise ye the Lord*)

hallmark the mark stamped on articles of gold or silver to show their quality

hallo, halloa see **hello**

hallow to make holy; to treat as sacred
hallowed made, or honoured as, holy
hallowe'en the evening of October 31st (the eve of All-Hallows or All Saints Day)

hallucination an illusion; an impression of a sight or sound that does not exist in reality

halo a ring of light around the sun or moon; a circle painted or drawn round the heads of holy people in pictures

halt 1 to make or cause a temporary stop □ a stopping place; a standstill

halt 2 (in olden days) lame, crippled
halting hesitant; going on with frequent stops (as, halting speech)

halter a rope or strap for leading or tying up a horse, donkey, etc.

halve, halves see **half**

halyard a rope for raising or lowering sails, flags, etc.

ham the back of the thigh; the thigh of a hog (prepared for cooking and eating): an amateur (as, a radio ham)

hamburger chopped, seasoned beef (usually shaped like a round flat cake) fried, and put into a soft bread roll

hamlet a very small village

hammer a tool for driving nails into wood or for beating or breaking hard substances (such as metal or coal); anything resembling a hammer in appearance or use □ to beat or strike with a hammer

hammock a swinging bed or couch of netting or canvas, hung up by the ends

hamper 1 a large basket with a lid (often used for carrying laundry or food, as, a picnic hamper)

hamper 2 to hinder or obstruct (as, to hamper progress)

hamster a small gnawing animal with large cheek-pouches

hand the part of the arm below the wrist, used for grasping and holding; anything resembling the hand in appearance or use (as, the hands of a clock); a worker or helper (as, a farm hand); the cards held by one player in a game of cards □ to pass or give (something) with the hand
handy skilful with the hands; useful: readily at hand
handbag a small lightweight bag (usually carried by girls and women)
handbook a small book or pamphlet giving guidance and information on a subject
handcraft handicraft
handcuffs metal rings (joined by a chain) which are fastened around a prisoner's wrists to prevent him from escaping
handful as much as the hand will hold; a small number or quantity
handicraft a skilled occupation or hobby in which things are made by hand
handiwork something made or done by hand; something done or brought about by a particular person or group of people
handspring a cartwheel or similar kind of somersault
handwriting style of writing by hand; a person's own style of writing by hand
at first hand directly from the person concerned (as - He heard at first hand what had happened.)

handicap something that makes life more difficult for a person (such as the handicap of being lame, blind, etc.) □ (in a race or contest) to make things more difficult for the best performers so as to give the others a fair chance
handicapped at a disadvantage

compared to others

handkerchief a small piece of cloth (usually square) used for wiping the nose or eyes

handle to touch, hold or use with the hand; to manage or control (a situation, a person, etc.) □ the part of an object by which it is held (as, the handle of a cup) **handlebar** the curved steering bar of a bicycle, motorcycle, etc.

handsome good-looking: generous (as, a handsome present); ample (as, a handsome income)

handspring, handwriting see **hand**

hang to fasten something firmly from above so that it can swing freely (as, window curtains) but cannot fall; to suspend (as, to hang a picture on a hook); to put someone to death by suspending him by a rope tied around his neck; to droop (as, to hang the head in shame or sorrow) □ the way in which anything hangs (as, the hang of a skirt) **hanger** a shaped piece of wood, metal or plastic on which clothes are hung **hanging** death by suspension by the neck **to hang out, to hang around** to loiter; to stay near **to hang back** to hesitate **to hang fire** (of firearms, etc.) to be long in exploding or going off; (of plans, etc.) to delay or be delayed

hangar a large shed for aircraft

hank a coil, loop or skein of rope, yarn, etc.

hanker to yearn for; to have a longing for

haphazard not planned

happen to take place; to occur by chance; to chance (as - We happened to be going your way.) **happening** an event

happy glad; joyful; pleased; well-chosen (as, a happy phrase) **happiness** gladness; joy; pleasure

happy-go-lucky trusting to luck

harangue a loud speech addressed to a crowd □ to deliver such a speech

harass to worry with repeated attacks (as, to harass the enemy); to annoy; to pester

harbour a port for ships; any place of refuge or shelter □ to shelter: to store in the mind (as, to harbour a grudge)

hard firm; solid; the opposite of soft; difficult (as, a hard question to answer); strenuous (as, hard work); severe or strict (as, hard rules); (of water), difficult to make a lather in with soap because of the mineral salts in solution **harden** to make, or become, hard **hardly** scarcely; only just **hardship** things or conditions which are hard to bear (such as poverty, hard labour) **hardware** ironmongery **hardwood** hard timber obtained from slow-growing deciduous trees

hardy daring; brave; tough; (of plants) able to grow in the open throughout the year **hardiness** robustness; the ability to endure severe weather

hare a timid animal with long hind legs, which looks like a large rabbit

harem *(say hairem or hareem)* the women's rooms in a Mohammedan house; the women themselves

hark to listen

harlequin a pantomime character who wears a multi-coloured costume

harm injury; wrong □ to injure or hurt **harmful** doing harm **harmless** doing no harm; the opposite of harmful

harmony a pleasing combination of musical tones, colours, etc.; a friendly state of agreement (as - Their views were in complete harmony.) **harmonic** in harmony; having to do with harmony

harmonica a mouth-organ

harmonious pleasant sounding; pleasant to the eye; with good feeling

harmonize to be in harmony; to agree; (in music) to provide the different parts for the melody of a song, etc.

harmonium a small organ

harness the straps and other equipment worn by a horse □ to put harness on a horse

harp a large musical instrument with a triangular frame, played by plucking the strings

harpist a person who plays the harp

harpoon a long, barbed dart, used especially for catching whales □ to strike with a harpoon

harpsichord a keyboard instrument something like a piano, but smaller

harrow a frame with metal spikes, used for breaking up and smoothing ploughed land, and for covering seeds □ to use a harrow on (a field): to distress or hurt (someone's feelings)

harrowing distressing (as, a harrowing experience)

harsh rough; very strict or severe (as, a harsh judgment); jarring to the ears or eyes

harvest the time of gathering in ripened crops; the yield of grain, fruits, etc. □ to reap or gather in crops or fruits

harvester a reaper; a machine for gathering in crops: see also **combine harvester**

harvest moon the full moon nearest to 23rd September

harvest mouse a very small field mouse that builds its nest on stalks of growing grain

hash to chop into small pieces; to mince □ a mixture of meat and vegetables chopped small and (usually) fried

to make a hash of to make a mess of something; to botch or spoil

hashish the leaves, etc. of the Indian hemp plant, which are intoxicating when chewed or smoked

hasp a hinged metal fastening for a door, box-lid, etc. (usually fitted over a staple and secured by a padlock)

hassock a thick, firm cushion used for kneeling or resting the feet

haste hurry; rash speed

hasten to hurry; to move with speed

hasty quick; hurried; too quick (as, a hasty temper)

to make haste to hasten

hat a covering for the head (usually with a crown and brim)

hatter a maker or seller of hats

hatch 1 (of a bird) to be born by breaking out of an eggshell; to produce young from eggs: to concoct or think up a plot or plan

hatchery a place for hatching eggs (especially of fish)

hatch 2 an opening in a ship's deck, or in a floor or roof of a building, etc.; the covering of such an opening

hatchet a small axe

hate to dislike intensely

hateful causing a feeling of hate against someone or something

hatred very great dislike

haughty full of pride; contemptuous of others

haul to drag; to pull with force □ an amount of anything obtained all at once (as, a haul of fish)

haunch (of a person) the hip and buttock together; (of an animal) the leg and loin together

haunt to visit a place very often; to inhabit or appear often in a place (as - A ghost is said to haunt the castle.) □ a place often visited (as - This is one of his favourite haunts.)

haunted inhabited or visited by ghosts

have to own or possess; to be

compelled to (as - You have to leave before dark.); to hold in the mind (as - We have a good idea.) (The word is also used with other verbs to show that action has already taken place, as - We have come to see you.)

haven a harbour; a shelter or place of safety

haversack a bag for food (usually carried on the shoulders)

havoc very great damage; extensive destruction (such as is caused by an earthquake)

hawk 1 to carry goods about the streets, offering them for sale
hawker a street seller

hawk 2 a bird of prey that hunts small birds and animals □ to hunt, using trained hawks

hawser a small cable; a thick rope, used for towing or mooring boats and ships

hawthorn a small thorny tree with pink or white blossoms in spring, and red berries in the autumn
haw(s) the fruit of the hawthorn tree

hay long grass which has been cut and dried for animal fodder
haycock a small conical pile of hay
hay fever an irritation of the nose, throat and eyes, caused by pollen

hazard a risk; a danger
hazardous dangerous; risky

haze thin mist or vapour
hazy misty; dim; not clear in the mind (as, a hazy memory)

hazel a small nut-bearing tree; a light-brown colour like that of the hazelnut
hazelnut the edible nut of the hazel tree

H-bomb a hydrogen bomb

he a male person or animal already referred to (as - The man said he would come soon.)

head the part of the body above the neck; the brain, understanding or comprehension (as - *Use your head!*); the front or top of

anything: the chief or leader; an individual animal or person among a number (as - Three hundred head of cattle were rounded up.) □ to lead or be in charge (as - He headed the expedition.); to go straight to a place (as - The horse headed for home.) □ (used with other words) chief or top-ranking (as, headmaster, head waiter, etc.)

heady intoxicating; impetuous; rash

header a fall or dive, with the head foremost

heading something at the top (as, the heading for the chapter of a book)

headache a pain in the head

headdress a decorative covering for the head (as, a crown or the feathered headdress formerly worn by American Indians)

headland a point of land extending into the sea; a cape

headlight a light at the front of a vehicle or ship

headline the line of larger print at the top of a page or at the beginning of an article in a newspaper or journal; (in plural) the chief points of the news on radio or television

headlong hastily; without proper thought beforehand (as, to rush headlong across the road)

headphones telephone receivers that fit on the ears, used for listening to radio messages, etc.

headquarters a building or central place from which official orders are issued (as, army headquarters, police headquarters, etc.); a central or chief office (as, the headquarters of a large business)

headstone a stone that stands at the head of a grave; the principal stone in a building (the cornerstone)

headstrong wilful; not easily controlled

headway forward movement (especially of a ship)

head wind a wind blowing in the direction opposite to the one in which a ship or vehicle is moving

heads or tails an expression used when tossing a coin to see whether it falls with one side or the other uppermost

heal to make well again; to restore to health

health wholeness or soundness of body; the general state or condition of the body (as, to be in good health)

healthy in good health; encouraging good health (as, a healthy diet)

heap a pile of things; a mound or piled-up mass; (in plural) a great number (as - She had heaps of birthday cards.) □ to pile up (as - His plate was heaped with food.)

hear to take in sound through the ears; to listen to; to be told (as - She heard the news from her neighbour.)

hearsay gossip; a rumour; a spoken account of some event

hearken *(say harken)* to listen carefully (used in former times)

hearse *(say herse)* a special car for carrying the dead

heart the hollow organ of the body that works like a pump to keep the blood circulating; the centre or core of anything; (poetic) the source of love and other human emotions (such as courage)

-hearted used with another word to describe a person's nature (as, soft-hearted)

hearten to encourage, to cheer up (as - She was heartened by the thought of the good times to come.)

hearty warm-hearted; strong; sincere (as, a hearty welcome); large; substantial (as, a hearty meal)

heartless cruel; without pity

heartbreak deep grief

heartbroken terribly distressed by grief

heartburn a painful burning feeling caused by indigestion

heartfelt deep and sincere (as, heartfelt thanks)

heart-rending causing feelings of great sorrow and distress

heartsick very unhappy and depressed

at heart in reality (as - He is a good man at heart.)

by heart from memory (as, to learn a poem by heart)

heart-to-heart frank; honest

to take heart to cheer up; to feel hope

to take to heart to be upset by

hearth the floor of a fireplace in a house; the house itself

heat a feeling of warmth; a high temperature; a time of hot weather (as, the heat of summer); anger or excitement (as - In the heat of the argument, he banged the table.): a part of a race; a division of a contest from which the winner goes on to take part in the final □ to make something hot (as, to heat soup); to become hot: see also **hot**

heater something that heats (as an electric, gas or oil heater)

heat barrier the high temperature of the surrounding air caused by the friction of aircraft, etc. at very high speeds

heat unit the amount of heat necessary to raise the temperature of a pound (0.45 kilogramme) of water one degree Fahrenheit (0.55° centigrade) - B.T.U. = British Thermal Unit

heat wave a period of very hot weather

heath an area of barren open country where little grows except small shrubs; a hardy, evergreen low-growing shrub

heathen a person who does not believe in the God worshipped by Jews, Christians and Mohammedans; a pagan

heather a small evergreen shrub with white or purple bell-like flowers

heave to haul or lift something up with great effort; to throw; to force (air) from the lungs (as, to heave a sigh of relief); to rise and fall (as, the chest heaves when one is out of breath)

heaven the sky; the dwelling

place of God; (in plural) the upper regions of the atmosphere; (poetic) a place or state of bliss
heavenly relating to heaven or the heavens (The stars are heavenly bodies.): beautiful; delightful
heaven-sent very fortunate; opportune

heavy weighty; difficult to lift or carry; loaded down; deep-toned; dull or dark (as, heavy skies); great or large in quantity (as, a heavy shower of rain)
heavily ponderously; weightily; greatly
heavy-handed clumsy, awkward
heavy water a kind of water heavier than ordinary water, used in nuclear reactors
heavyweight a boxer (weighing not less than 175 lb. [about 79 kilogrammes] professional or 178 lb. [about 81 kilogrammes] amateur); any person or thing well above average weight

Hebrew a Jew; the language of Jews or Hebrews □ of, or concerning, Hebrews or Jews

heckle to ask askward questions (especially, to interrupt a public speech at election time)

hectare a measure of land equal to 10,000 square metres or almost 2^1/$_2$ acres

hectic excited; agitated (as, a hectic rush); feverish

hedge a row of bushes or small trees growing closely together like a fence or barrier □ to enclose a piece of land with a hedge: to avoid giving a straight answer or a direct promise
hedgehog a small nocturnal wild animal having a coat of spines mixed with hair
hedgerow a line of hedge (often with trees)

heed to pay attention to; to take notice of

heel 1 the back part of the foot; the part of footwear that covers or supports the heel

heel 2, to heel over (of a ship) to tilt over on to one side

hefty rather heavy and muscular

heifer a young cow

height *(say hite)* the measure of a person or thing from bottom to top; the distance to the top (as, the height of a skyscraper); the utmost degree (as, the height of stupidity)
heighten to increase; to make greater or higher (as, to heighten interest in a subject by showing a film about it)

heir *(say air)* a male who is entitled to receive money, property, etc. on the death of the present owner
heiress *(say airess)* a female who inherits money, property, etc.
heirloom something (usually of value) which is inherited by successive members of a family (as - The vase is an heirloom that belonged to her great-grandmother.)

helicopter a flying machine that moves in the air by means of power-driven propellers turning on a vertical axis

helium a very light, not inflammable, gas used in balloons and airships

hell the opposite of heaven; a place for the wicked after death; a state of misery or extreme wickedness

hello, hullo, hallo, halloa a word used to greet people, or to call attention, to express surprise, etc.

helm the steering apparatus of a ship
helmsman a person who steers

helmet a covering, usually made of metal, that protects the head (Helmets are worn by soldiers, firemen, racing drivers, motor cyclists, deep-sea divers, etc.)

help to do something to make things easier or better for another person; to make less bad; to aid or assist (as - The medicine helped him to recover from his illness.); to prevent oneself from (as - She could not help crying when she heard the sad news.)

helping a serving of food

helpless unable to help or look after oneself (because of weakness or lack of skill, etc.)

helter-skelter in a hasty confused manner □ a spiral slide in an amusement park or fairground

hem the bottom edge or border of a garment, curtain, etc., turned back and sewn into place □ to make a hem on

to hem in to enclose; to surround; to shut in without a way of escaping

hemisphere half of a sphere; half of the earth or half of a globe representing the earth

hemlock a poisonous wild plant with spotted stems; a poisonous drink made from the plant; an evergreen North American tree (hemlock spruce)

hemoglobin see **haemoglobin**

hemorrhage see **haemorrhage**

hemp the name for several different kinds of plant which produce (1) a coarse stringy fibre used for rope, matting, etc.; (2) vegetable oil; (3) a drug (known as hashish, marijuana, etc.)

hen the female of any bird (especially the domestic fowl)

henpecked (of a husband) ruled over by his wife

hence from this place (poetic, as - Get thee hence!); from this time (as, a year hence); therefore (as - This is a dangerous corner - hence the warning sign.)

henceforth, henceforward from now on

her the female already mentioned (as - We are going to see her.) □ belonging to a female (as - This is her book.): see also **she**

hers belonging to a female (as - This book is hers.)

herself her and no one else

herald (in ancient times) an officer who made public procla-

mations or arranged state ceremonies (such as a coronation); (from mediaeval times) an officer responsible for records of the ancestry and coats of arms of noble families; (nowadays) a person who reads proclamations and announcements □ to show the approach of something (as - The first snowdrops herald the coming of spring.)

heraldic concerning heralds or heraldry

heraldry the study of coats of arms and the genealogy of noble families; the pomp and ceremony of heraldry

herb a plant that does not have a woody stem or trunk (as shrubs and trees have); a plant used in medicine; a plant with spicy or scented leaves and stems used for flavouring in cooking

herbaceous herb-like because the leaves and stems die down in winter (as - Hollyhocks and peonies are herbaceous plants.)

herbivorous feeding on plants only (Cows are herbivorous animals.)

herd 1 a number of animals of one kind that keep or are kept together (as, a herd of cows) □ to keep or drive together a number of animals of the same kind

herd 2, herdsman a person who looks after a herd of animals

here in, or to, this place; now, or at this point

hereabouts near this place

hereafter in the future; in the world to come

hereby by means of this (as, in a letter - I hereby renounce all claim to the estate.)

herewith with this (as, in a letter - I enclose herewith a cheque for the amount required.)

heredity the passing on of physical and mental qualities and tendencies from ancestors to their descendants

hereditary inherited from ancestors (as - Red hair is

hereditary in his family.)

heritage something that is inherited

hermetically sealed completely closed (as, a glass bulb or tube which can only be opened by breaking the glass)

hermit a person (especially in early Christian times) who went to live by himself in a cave, etc.; a person who lives apart from other people

hero a very brave man or boy; a person greatly looked up to for courage or other admirable qualities (as, a national hero); the principal character in a book, film or play
heroine the female of hero
heroic very brave; concerning a hero (as, heroic deeds)
heroism great bravery
hero worship very great admiration for a person considered to be a hero or heroine

heroin a drug produced from opium

heron a large wading bird, with long legs and a long neck

herring a small North Atlantic sea fish, much used for food
herringbone a pattern resembling the small bones in a herring's spine

hers, herself see **her**

hesitate to pause or delay in some action (usually because of uncertainty or doubt)
hesitancy, hesitation the act of hesitating
hesitant showing or feeling hesitation

heterogeneous the opposite of homogeneous; made up of things or people of many different kinds (as, a heterogeneous crowd)

hew to cut or chop with blows (as, to hew a path through the woods with an axe)

hexagon a flat figure with six sides and six angles
hexagonal six-sided

hey an expression used to show

surprise or joy, or to attract attention

heyday the time of greatest vigour, prosperity, ability, etc.

hiatus a break or gap in continuity where something is missing (as, a hiatus in a story between the end of one chapter and the beginning of the next one)

hibernate to spend the winter in an inactive state resembling sleep, as some animals do

hiccup, hiccough the sharp, gulping sound caused by a sudden spasm of the diaphragm followed by the closing of the top of the windpipe

hickory a North American tree of the walnut family, which bears edible nuts; the strong wood of this tree

hid, hidden see **hide 1**

hide 1 to put out of sight; to conceal; to keep secret (as, to hide a fear of the sea); to go into or stay in a place where one cannot easily be seen or found
hid the past of hide (as - He hid the money yesterday.)
hidden concealed; not known
hiding 1 concealing; putting (something) or staying in a secret place
hiding-place a secret place where a person or thing is hidden

hide 2 the skin of an animal (for example, cowhide)
hiding 2 a whipping; a thrashing

hideous extremely ugly; horrible; frightful

hieroglyphic *(say hyroglific)* one of the pictures or word-symbols used in ancient picture-writing (as in Egypt, before letters were invented)

hi-fi see **high fidelity**

higgledy-piggledy in complete confusion; without any sort of order

high tall; a long way up from; reaching up from something (such as the ground, zero on a scale, etc.); the opposite of low (as, high tide); great (as, high hopes); important or principal (as, high-ranking official); excellent (as, high quality); (of sound) shrill, pitched above middle tones

highly very (as, highly dangerous); in high rank (as, highly placed)

highness the state of being high: see also **height**; the title given to some princes and princesses

highborn of noble birth

highbrow a person with intellectual tastes in music, literature, etc.

highly-coloured exaggerated (as, a highly-coloured account of the party)

high-fidelity (hi-fi) true or very good in reproducing sound as nearly like the original as possible

high-handed acting in an overbearing way without considering other people's feelings or opinions

highlands a hilly or mountainous district

highlight any bright spot in a picture or photograph; (in plural) the most outstanding or interesting points in a talk, an experience, etc. □ to draw attention towards; to emphasize

high-minded having high ideals and principles

high-octane (of petrol) of high octane number, and therefore of high efficiency

highroad a highway

high seas the open seas beyond the territorial waters immediately surrounding individual countries

high-spirited bold; full of life

high(ly)-strung sensitive and nervous; easily upset

high water the time when the tide is highest

highway a public road (especially a main road)

highwayman (in former times) a man (usually on horseback) who held up and robbed travellers on the road

hike a long walk in the country (sometimes carrying camping equipment or food supplies) □ to take such a walk

hilarious very merry (usually with noisy laughter)
hilarity joyous behaviour

hill a high mass of land, lower than a mountain; a small mound
hillock a small hill

hilt the handle of a sword or dagger

him the male already mentioned (as - We went to see him.): see also **he**
himself him and no one else
his belonging to a male (as - This bat is his; this is his ball.)

hind 1 *(say hiend)* a female deer (especially the red deer)

hind 2 *(say hiend)* placed at the rear or back (as, the hind legs of a dog)
hindquarters the rear parts of an animal

hinder to delay or prevent the start or progress of something
hindrance a person or thing that hinders

hinge a joint (usually of metal) on which a door, a gate, or a lid turns

hint to give information indirectly; to suggest something without actually saying it in so many words (as - He gave a hint that helped her to answer the question correctly.) □ an indirect suggestion

hinterland a region lying inland from the coastline of a country

hip 1 the part of the body below the waist that projects on each side, including the upper part of the thigh bone

hip 2 the fruit of the wild rose

hippopotamus a large African animal with very tough thick skin (It lives in or near rivers or lakes).
hippopotamuses, hippopotami the plural of **hippopotamus**

hire to pay for the use of something for a certain length of time (as, to hire a taxi, etc.); to agree to employ and pay someone as a worker

hire purchase an arrangement by which a person hires something and, after paying off the total price in small amounts, becomes the owner (as - They bought their refrigerator by hire purchase, over a period of twelve months.)

hirsute hairy; shaggy

his see **him**

hiss a noise that sounds like *s-s-s-s-s* (as, the hiss of geese, escaping steam, etc.) □ to make sounds of disapproval (as - The audience hissed to show their poor opinion of the performance.)

historian, etc. see **history**

history an account of past events (especially those that make up the story of a nation); a series of events that have happened to a person or thing (as - This jade carving has a romantic history.)
historian a person who writes histories, or about historical events
historic concerned with history; important or memorable in history (as, an historic old castle)
historical based on facts recorded in history

hit to strike; to reach with a blow or missile; to affect the feelings (as - The dog's death hit him badly.); to come upon by chance (as - He hit upon the solution) □ a successful shot or stroke; a play, musical composition, performance, etc. that is a popular success

hitch to move or pull with a jerk; to fasten securely (by means of a knot, etc.) □ a knot or noose (usually of rope)

hitch-hike to travel by asking for free rides in vehicles

hither to this place; here
hitherto until now; up to this time
hither and thither here and there; in various directions

hive a box or basket-like container where bees live and store up honey; a place where people work very busily (as, a hive of industry)

hoary white or grey with age; old
hoar-frost white particles on lawns, etc. formed by frozen dew

hoard a store or stock of something (usually hidden away) □ to store up supplies, etc. in secret

hoarding a temporary fence of boards around a place where a building is being constructed; a screen of boards where advertisements or notices are displayed

hoarse having a rough, husky voice; harsh and croaking (as, the hoarse cry of a raven)

hoax a trick or joke, intended to deceive or mislead □ to trick or deceive (often meant in fun, but sometimes causing mischief, as when a false alarm is given to hoax the fire or police force)

hob a shelf or other surface next to a fireplace, used to keep things hot

hobble to walk with difficulty; to limp; to fasten together the legs of a horse, donkey, etc. to prevent it from straying

hobby a favourite interest or pastime, outside one's main work

hobby-horse a stick with a horse's head (which children can pretend to ride); a rocking-horse; a wooden horse on a roundabout

hobgoblin a mischievous fairy

hobnail a short nail with a large thick head (often used in the soles and heels of heavy boots)

hock the joint on an animal's hind leg, which is similar to the ankle joint in man

hockey a team game played with a stick curved at one end, and a ball which the players on each side try to hit into their opponents' goal
ice hockey a similar game,

played on ice with a small rubber disc (called a puck) instead of a ball

hocus pocus the nonsense words spoken by a conjurer when performing a trick; trickery or deception

hod a small, v-shaped trough on a pole, used for carrying bricks or mortar; a coal scuttle

hodgepodge see **hotchpotch**

hoe a long-handled garden tool for clearing weeds and loosening the earth

hog a full-grown pig; a greedy, coarse-mannered person □ to grab or take more than one's proper share
hoggish coarse-mannered; greedy
road hog a selfish motorist who shows no patience or consideration towards other motorists
to go the whole hog to do something thoroughly

hogshead a measure of $52^1/_2$ imperial gallons (= 239 litres); a large cask

hoist to lift or heave upwards (especially with a pulley or other tackle) □ a lifting apparatus for heavy goods

hold 1 to keep or grasp in the hand; to keep or have in one's possession; to keep control of (as - They continued to hold the fort.); to contain (as - This bottle holds a pint of milk.); to have a strong opinion about something (as - She holds that smoking should not be allowed in cinemas.); to make someone keep to an agreement (as - We will hold him to his promise.); to carry on or carry out some action (or to hold a meeting) □ the act of holding; a grip or grasp; a thing to hold on to for support or for carrying something
holding (in agriculture) a piece of land held (owned) or rented by a farmer
hold-up a forcible stopping of a person, vehicle, etc. in order to commit robbery; a delay or stop-page (as - We were late because of a hold-up in the traffic.)
to hold forth to speak forcefully and at length
to hold one's own to defend oneself successfully, without giving way
to hold over to postpone
to hold water (of an explanation, theory, etc.) to be soundly reasoned or sensible

hold 2 the storage space below decks in a ship, where cargo is carried

hole an opening in or through something; a hollow space

holiday a time of freedom from work or school

hollow having a space or hole inside; empty (as a hollow victory; (of sound) deep and echoing □ a place which is lower than the land surrounding it

holly an evergreen shrub or tree with prickly leaves and bright berries (usually red)

hollyhock a tall garden plant with large, brightly-coloured or white flowers on each stalk

holster a leather case for a pistol (worn on a belt or attached to a saddle)

holy religious; sacred; saintly; set apart for use in worshipping God
holiness the state of being holy; religious goodness

homage great respect shown publicly (as, to pay homage to a national hero); (in feudal times) a pledge of service by a vassal to an overlord

home the place where a person lives, or where his family lives; one's native country or place of origin; a place where people who are not able to look after themselves are cared for (as, an old people's home, a nursing home, etc.) □ to the place where it belongs; to the point aimed at (as - The nail was hammered home.)
homing a returning home □ trained to return home (as, a homing pigeon)

homely home-like; simple

Home Counties the counties around London

homeland one's native land

homemade made at home, not in a factory

homesick longing to be home again

homestead a house with land and outbuildings around it

at home in one's own house; at ease

to bring home to to make a person understand or believe (a fact, etc.)

homicide the killing of one human being by another

homogeneous of the same kind; made up of parts or types that are similar (the opposite of heterogeneous)

homogeneity the state of being homogeneous

homogenize to break up the fatty part of milk and blend it with the rest, so that the cream is evenly distributed instead of rising to the top

homonym a word that is pronounced in the same way as another, but has a different spelling or meaning (as, *hare* and *hair*)

hone a smooth stone used for sharpening razors, knives, etc. □ to sharpen

honest truthful and trustworthy; not deceitful or thieving

honesty truthfulness and straightforwardness

honey a sweet thick fluid made by honeybees from the nectar they collect from flowers

honeycomb a mass of wax cells made by bees, in which they store their honey: any structure like a honeycomb in appearance

honeymoon a holiday taken by a husband and wife immediately after their wedding

honeysuckle a climbing shrub with sweetly scented flowers

honk the cry of a wild goose; the noise made by a motor horn □ to make such a noise

honour high esteem; great respect; a formal sign of respect (as - The dinner was held in his honour.); truthfulness and integrity □ to have great respect for a person

honourable worthy of honour; honest and high-principled; a title (The Honourable or The Hon.) given to sons and daughters of some peers and to certain other people (such as high-ranking judges, etc.)

honorary given as an honour; (of a title, such as honorary president) without any duties (of an office, such as honorary secretary of a club) without any payment

hood a loose cloth covering for the head and neck (often attached to a coat, etc.); anything that resembles a hood in appearance

hoodwink to deceive

hoof the horny part of the feet of certain animals (such as cattle, horses, deer, etc.)

hoofs, hooves the plural of hoof

hook a piece of metal or other material, curved or bent back at one end, and used to catch, hold or pull things □ to catch or fasten with a hook

hooligan a rough, noisy person (usually a member of a gang who bully people and damage property)

hoop a circular band of wood or metal, used to hold the staves of a cask together, or as a toy, or (in former times) to make a woman's skirt stand out stiffly; an arch in the game of croquet

hoot to shout scornfully; to sound (a motor horn, etc.) □ the cry of an owl (or similar noise)

hooter a steam whistle; a siren

hop 1 to jump on one leg; to move in short jerks (as some birds and animals do)

hopper a person or thing that hops: a bin or funnel-shaped container through which grain, etc. is passed into another container; a barge with an opening at the bottom for emptying out waste materials

hop 2 a climbing plant, trained to grow up poles; (in plural) the fruit cluster of the hop plant, used to flavour beer

hope the wish or desire for something together with the expectation that it will probably come (as - She has every hope of success.) □ to wish for something which may or may not come (as - They hoped for a peaceful solution to the problem.)
hopeful confident for the future; full of hope
hopeless without hope; useless

horde a tribe or group of nomadic people; a great number or crowd

horizon the line at which sky and earth appear to meet
horizontal parallel to the horizon; at right angles to the vertical; lying flat; on a level

horn one of the hard bony outgrowths on the heads of some animals (such as cattle, deer, etc.); something made of, or like, horn; a wind instrument (once made from a horn - nowadays usually of brass or other metal); a device for giving a warning sound (in a vehicle, etc.)
hornbill a bird with a horny growth in its beak

hornet a large kind of wasp which can give a severe sting

hornpipe a lively dance (usually associated with sailors and performed by one person); a tune for this dance

horoscope an observation of the sky and planets as they were at the moment of a person's birth, from which an astrologer foretells his fortune; a general prediction in a newspaper, magazine, etc. of the fortune of people born under the same sign of the zodiac.

horrible, horrify etc. see **horror**

horror a very great fear or loathing; something that causes such feeling
horrible causing a feeling of horror; dreadful; terrible
horrid shocking; frightful; unpleasant
horrific terrifying
horrify to cause a feeling of horror; to shock

horse a large, four-legged, hoofed animal with a long mane and tail, used to pull vehicles or for riding; a frame used as a support for drying clothes, sawing wood, etc.; a piece of equipment in a gymnasium, used for vaulting exercises.
horsy horse-like; very much interested in horses
horse chestnut a tree with large divided leaves and cone-shaped clusters of white or pink flowers; the inedible shiny brown nut of the tree, that grows inside a prickly green covering (a conker)
horsehair the hair from a horse's mane or tail; strong shiny material woven from this hair (used for upholstery, etc.)
horseman, horsewoman a rider skilled in managing horses
horsemanship the art of riding, controlling and training horses
horsepower the average power a horse can exert, used as a unit for measuring the power of engines (as - This car has a 9-horsepower engine.)
horseradish a plant with a sharp-tasting root, used as a condiment (horseradish sauce)
horseshoe a curved iron shoe which is nailed to the bottom of a horse's hoof (to prevent the hoof from being worn down); anything shaped like a horseshoe
on horseback riding or sitting on the back of a horse

horticulture the art of cultivating gardens and orchards
horticultural concerned with gardening and the raising of garden produce

hose socks or stockings; a flexible

pipe used to convey water or other liquids

hosiery knitted goods (especially socks and stockings)

hospitable generous and welcoming to guests or callers
hospitality a kindly welcome and the provision of food, drink and other comforts for guests

hospital a place where the sick and injured can be treated and looked after until they recover

host 1 a crowd; a very large number

host 2 a boy or man who has other people as his guests in his home or in a restaurant, etc; an old-fashioned word for an inn-keeper (mine host)
hostess the female of host

hostage a person who is held captive as a guarantee that promises made by the enemy will be carried out

hostel a place of residence for young people who are studying or working away from home; a place where hikers, etc. can stay overnight (as, a youth hostel)

hostile warlike; unfriendly; of an enemy (as, a hostile army)

hot very warm; the opposite of cold; of high temperature; sharp or biting to the taste (as, mustard, pepper, etc.); excitable or quick to show anger (as, hot-tempered)
hothead a person who acts impulsively (often in anger)
hothouse a heated greenhouse, for growing tender plants

hotchpotch, hotchpot, hodgepodge a confused muddle; a mixture of a number of cooking ingredients all jumbled together

hotel a house (usually large) which provides accommodation, food, etc. for the public (especially travellers); an inn

hound a dog used in hunting □ to pursue someone from place to place

hour 60 minutes; one of the 24 divisions of a day; a fixed time for some service or action (such as a lunch hour, a bank's business hours, etc.)
hourly happening or done every hour
hour-glass an instrument for measuring hours by the running of sand from one glass through a narrow opening into another glass. (It takes exactly one hour for the sand to run through.)

house a building for living in; a business firm; a body of people who are responsible for making the laws of a country (as, the House of Commons); a building for a special purpose (as a store-house, a lighthouse); a section of a school □ *(say howz)* to provide houses for people, animals, etc.
housing houses, flats or other accommodation; provision of these (often by a local authority, as, council housing)
house agent a person who arranges the sale or renting of accommodation
houseboat a large flat-bottomed boat used to live in
household all the people living together in one house (usually a family)
householder the owner or occupier of a house
housekeeper a person in charge of running the domestic affairs of a house (such as cooking, cleaning, etc.)
housekeeping the management of the domestic affairs of a house
housewife the mistress of the house; a woman (usually married) who looks after the domestic affairs of a house
housework the work of cleaning, etc. in a house.

hovel a small (usually poor and tumbledown) cabin or hut

hover to float or stay suspended in the air without moving forward; to linger about
hovercraft a vehicle without wheels which can move at a short distance above the surface of sea or land because it is

supported by a down-driven blast of air

how in what way; to what extent; in what condition; by what means
however nevertheless; in whatever manner; to whatever extent

howl a long, loud whining noise (as, the howl of a dog) □to make such a sound

hub the centre of a wheel

hubbub an uproar; a confused noise

huddle to crowd closely together (usually in disorder); to draw oneself together (as, to be huddled up with cold, to huddle close to the fire)

hue 1 colour

hue 2 a shouting (used in the phrase *hue and cry,* a loud calling out to try to stop a criminal from getting away)

huff a fit of bad tempered sulkiness
huffy touchy; easily offended; sulky

hug to hold someone or something closely in one's arms; to keep close to (as - The boat hugged the shore.)
to hug oneself to be very pleased with oneself

huge enormous; very large
hugely very greatly (as - He enjoyed himself hugely.)

hulk an old, useless ship; the wreck of a ship; a bulky clumsy person, or an unwieldy mass of something
hulking big and clumsy

hull the frame or body of a ship

hullo see **hello**

hum to make a musical sound with the lips closed (as though singing *m - m - m*); to make a soft murmuring sound; to be busy and active (as, to make things hum)
humming a low murmuring sound (as made by bees)
humming-bird a very small, brilliantly-coloured tropical bird (Its wings move so rapidly that

they make a humming sound.)

human of, or to do with, people; relating to man and mankind (in contrast to animals) □a human being
humane kindly; merciful
humanitarian a person who wishes to make better conditions for other human beings by means of new laws, etc.
humanity kindness; generosity; mankind

humble meek; lowly; the opposite of proud and boastful □to defeat or bring low (as, to humble one's enemies); see also **humility**.

humbug a fraud; a person who pretends to be something he is not; nonsense

humdrum dull; dreary

humid moist; damp
humidity moisture (especially the amount of moisture in the air)

humiliate to humble; to make someone feel loss of dignity (especially in front of other people)

humility modesty; the opposite of pride and boastfulness

humour a person's state of mind or mood (as - He is in a good humour.); the ability to see the funny side of things (as, a sense of humour); the quality of being funny (as - He saw the humour of the situation.) □to try to please (as, to humour a sick child)
humorist a person who amuses others by pointing out the funny side of things
humorous amusing; having a good sense of humour
humourless lacking a sense of humour; glum

hump a rounded lump on the back (as, a camel's hump); a mound of earth
humpback having a lump on the back □a small bridge in the shape of a hump

humus decomposed vegetable or animal matter in the soil

hunch a hump; a lump: a strong feeling that something is going to happen □ to pull or bend one's shoulders forward
hunchback a person with a hump on his back

hunger a desire or need for food; any strong desire or yearning for something □ to feel a desire for food; to long for
hungry feeling or showing hunger
hunger strike refusal to eat (as a form of protest against prison conditions, unjust laws, etc.)

hunt to chase or go in search of animals for prey or sport; to search for something (as, to hunt for a lost coin) □ a search; a group of huntsmen
hunter a person who hunts; a horse used in hunting
huntsman a hunter; the person in charge of a pack of hunting hounds

hurdle a movable frame of intertwined twigs or branches, etc. often used as temporary fencing; a barrier, like a wooden frame, to be jumped over in races; a difficulty or obstacle to be overcome □ to jump over hurdles in a race

hurl to throw something violently; to utter with great force (as, to hurl abuse)

hurrah, hurray a shout of joy or triumph

hurricane a violent tropical storm; a violent storm of wind (over 75 miles, or 120 kilometres, per hour)

hurry to move or act quickly (sometimes too hastily) □ haste, rush (as - What's the hurry?)
hurried moving or acting quickly; done too quickly

hurt to cause or give pain; to damage; to wound the feelings □ a wound; an injury

hurtle to rush or dash with great force and speed

husband the man to whom a woman (his wife) is married

husbandry farming; the careful management of money, property, etc.

hush *Silence!; Be quiet!;* to quieten □ a silence (as, a sudden hush)

husk the dry, thin covering of some fruits and seeds □ to remove the husk from
husky 1 like, or full of, husks; dry and hoarse (as - a husky voice caused by a sore throat, etc.): big and strong

husky 2 an Eskimo dog (used to pull sledges)

hustle to hurry; to push someone along roughly and quickly

hut a small, roughly-made house or cabin

hutch a small coop for rabbits or other pets; a hut or small house

hyacinth a bulbous plant which has spikes of fragrant bell-shaped blossoms (white, blue, pink or yellow) that flower in the spring

hybrid an animal or plant whose parents are of different breeds, species, etc. (as, the offspring of a horse and an ass [a mule], a hybrid rose, etc.)

hydr(o)- a prefix meaning water
hydrant a water plug (usually in the street) to which a pipe or hose can be attached to draw water from main pipes
hydraulic worked by water or other liquid
hydraulics the study of fluids in motion (as, of water in pipes)
hydrochloric acid an acid formed from hydrogen and chlorine
hydroelectricity electricity produced by means of machinery driven by water-power (for example, from a large waterfall)
hydrogen a colourless, tasteless, odourless gas which produces water when combined with oxygen (Hydrogen is the lightest substance known, and is highly inflammable.)
hydrogen bomb a very powerful bomb which is exploded by turning hydrogen into helium at a very high temperature
hydrophobia a dread of water (especially as a symptom of

rabies, when the sufferer cannot swallow water); rabies
hydroplane an aeroplane with floats instead of wheels, to enable it to take off from, and to land on, water

hyena a wolf-like animal with a howl that sounds like hysterical laughter

hygiene *(say hyjeen)* the study of rules of health and cleanliness
hygienic of, or relating to, hygiene

hymn a song of praise (usually religious)

hyphen a short dash (-) used to join words that are linked together (as, tug-of-war) or to join two syllables together when a word has to be divided at the end of a line of print or writing
hyphenate to join by a hyphen

hypnosis a sleep-like state in which the person who has been hypnotized speaks or acts as directed by the hypnotizer

hypnotism the practice or art of producing hypnosis
hypnotize to put someone into a state of hypnosis

hypocrisy pretending to be what one is not; pretending to feel other than one really does
hypocrite a person who pretends to be different from what he really is

hypodermic a syringe used to inject medicine under the skin

hypotenuse the side of a right-angled triangle opposite to the right angle

hypothesis a supposition; an assumption made as a starting-point in an argument or discussion

hysteria wild excitement; a nervous illness
hysterical wildly excited; very emotional
hysterics a fit of hysteria (often laughing and crying by turns)

i

I the word used by a speaker or writer in mentioning himself or herself

ibex *(say iebex)* a wild mountain goat with large horns that curve backward

ice water which has been made solid by freezing □ to cover with ice or icing
icing a sugar coating for cakes
icy very cold; slippery with ice
icicle a hanging, pointed piece of ice (formed by the freezing of dropping water)
ice age a far-off time when a large part of the earth's surface was covered with ice
iceberg a huge mass of floating ice
ice cream a flavoured creamy mixture which has been frozen
ice floe a large sheet of ice floating in the sea
ice skates skates with blades instead of rollers

icon, ikon an image; (in the Greek Church) a painting, etc. representing Christ or a saint

idea a picture, or a plan, in the mind; a thought or opinion
ideal existing in the imagination only (the opposite of real); perfect □ what is considered highest and nearest perfection
idealize to regard as nearly perfect or very fine, etc. (as - She idealized her dancing teacher.)
idealist someone who has extremely high standards and aims; a person who tends to imagine things as he thinks they ought to be, rather than as they really are

identify to recognize, or claim to recognize (as, to identify a person)
identical the same in every detail
identification the act of identifying
identity a state of exact sameness; who or what a person is (as - The real identity of the spy was kept a secret.)

idiom a phrase or sentence which has a different meaning from the actual words (as, *jumping out of the frying pan into the fire*)

idiosyncrasy a peculiar or characteristic way of acting or thinking

idiot a very feeble-minded person; a foolish or unwise person
idiotic foolish; stupid

idle doing nothing; not working; lazy; useless (as, idle threats) □ to be doing nothing

idol an image worshipped as a god; any person or thing loved or honoured too much
idolatry the worship of idols
idolize to make an idol of; to love excessively

idyllic happy and simple (as, an idyllic holiday)

igloo an Eskimo's snow hut (usually dome-shaped)

igneous having to do with fire or great heat (as, igneous rock which has been produced by volcanic action within the earth)

ignite to set on fire; to catch fire
ignition the act of igniting; the electrical device in a motor car which, by producing sparks, starts the engine and keeps it running

ignoble of low birth or reputation; dishonourable (as, an ignoble act)

ignominious humiliating; disgraceful

ignore to take no notice of
ignoramus an ignorant person
ignorance lack of knowledge

ignorant without knowledge or information; not knowing

iguana a large tree-lizard found in tropical Central and South America

ill not well, sick; evil; bad; unlucky; unfriendly (as - There was an ill feeling between them.) □ a harm; a misfortune
illness sickness
ill-bred badly brought up; rude
ill-natured cross; peevish
ill-treat, ill-use to treat badly
ill-will unkind feeling; dislike

illegal against the law

illegible not legible; impossible or very hard to read

illegitimate not according to law; born of unmarried parents

illicit not allowed by law

illiterate unable to read and write; uneducated

illogical not logical, not showing sound reasoning

illuminate to light up: to decorate with ornamental lettering or designs (as an old illuminated manuscript)
illumination lighting; bright lights; ornamental lettering and decoration, painted in gold and brilliant colours (often found in valuable old manuscripts)

illusion a false idea, impression or belief
illusory deceptive; false

illustrate to make clear by means of pictures; to explain or decorate with pictures; to make clear by using examples
illustration a picture; an example
illustrative making clear; explanatory

illustrious very distinguished; famous

im- a prefix with the same meaning as **in-**

image a likeness; a copy; a statue or idol; a picture in the mind (something imagined)
imagery mental pictures; word-pictures that make a writer's descriptions more realistic

imagine to form a picture in the mind; to think; to suppose

imaginable able to be thought of

imaginary existing only in the mind; not real

imagination the power of forming images in the mind

imaginative having a lively imagination (often of things or events not actually seen or experienced)

imbecile a person who is feeble-minded

imitate to try to be the same as; to copy

imitation a copy; something not genuine

immaculate spotless

immaterial not important

immature not ripe; not fully developed

immediate having nothing, or no one, coming between (as, his immediate neighbour); with no time between; without delay (as, an immediate reply to a letter)

immediately at once

immemorial going back beyond living memory or written records (as, from time immemorial)

immense so great that measurement seems impossible; vast; very large

immensity an extent not to be measured; vastness (as, the immensity of the ocean)

immerse to plunge completely into water or other liquid; to involve oneself deeply (as - He immersed himself in his book.)

immigrate to come into a country to settle there

immigrant a person who immigrates (He is an emigrant from the country which he left.)

immigration the entry into a country of people from other countries

imminent impending; likely to happen very soon (especially of something unpleasant)

immobile not able to move or be moved; motionless; fixed

immoral not moral; wicked

immortal never dying; never to be forgotten (as, an immortal poem)

immovable impossible to move or change; unyielding

immune free or exempt from; protected from a disease (as, immune to typhoid fever)

immunize to make immune (especially from disease by inoculation)

immunity freedom or exemption; protection from a disease

imp a mischievous child; a little devil or wicked spirit

impish like an imp; mischievous

impact the blow of a moving body striking another (as, the impact of a ball on a bat); a collision

impair to weaken

impale to pierce with something sharp; to fix on a stake

impart to make known (as, to impart a secret)

impartial not favouring one more than another; just

impassable not able to be passed through or over (as, an impassable road)

impasse a difficult situation from which there is no escape

impassioned afflicted by, or showing, strong feeling

impassive not showing, or feeling, any emotion

impatient not patient; restless

impatience lack of patience; restlessness

impeccable faultless

impecunious having no money; poor (often through one's own fault)

impede to hinder; to obstruct

impediment a hindrance; a small defect in speech (especially a stutter)

impel to push forward; to drive on

impend to be about to happen

impenetrable not able to be entered or passed through (as, an impenetrable jungle); impossible to understand (as, an impenetrable mystery)

imperative obligatory; urgent

imperceptible not able to be seen; too small to be noticed

imperfect not perfect; having a fault or defect

imperial connected with an empire, or an emperor or empress
imperialism the policy of having, or extending, an empire over many countries
imperious showing off one's power; haughty

imperil to put in peril or danger

imperishable everlasting; not perishable

impermeable not allowing fluids to pass through (as - A raincoat should be impermeable to rain.)

impersonal not connected with a person; not showing a personal feeling or interest
impersonate to act the part of, or pretend to be, another person
impersonation the act of impersonating
impersonator someone who impersonates another

impertinent not pertinent to the subject which is being considered: impudent
impertinence an intrusion; impudence

imperturbable not able to be upset; always calm

impervious not easily penetrated or affected by (as, impervious to insults)

impetuous impulsive; acting suddenly and rashly
impetus a moving force; an impulse; an encouragement

impinge to strike or touch upon (as - The noise impinged on their ears.)

implacable not able to be appeased or satisfied

implant to plant in; to insert (as, to implant an idea by teaching or argument)

implement a tool or instrument (as, agricultural implements) □ to carry out (a task); to fulfil (a promise)

implicate to involve; to entangle (as - The evidence showed that several people were implicated in the crime.)
implication the act of implicating or implying; something that is implied (meant, though not actually said or written)
implicit, implied meant, though not put into actual words (as, an implicit agreement); the opposite of explicit
imply to express indirectly; to mean (as - Writing a cheque implies that the writer has money in his bank account.)

implore to ask earnestly for

imply see **implicate**

import *(say import)* to bring goods into a country from abroad; the opposite of export
imports goods brought into a country from abroad for trade purposes

important of great consequence or value; having influence or power
importance the fact of being important (as, the importance of the steel industry)

impose to make compulsory (as, to impose a tax, a customs duty, a condition): to take unfair advantage of (as, to impose on a friend's good nature).
imposing making a show; impressive
imposition the act of imposing; a burden; a punishment task

impossible not possible; not capable of being done or being true
impossibility anything that is not possible

impostor a person who pretends to be someone else in order to deceive
imposture a fraud committed by deceit

impoverish to make poor (as, a small country impoverished by war, a soil impoverished by poor farming methods)

impracticable not able to be done or put into practice (as, an impracticable scheme)

impractical not practical; not able to be done without undue trouble

impregnable (of a fort or stronghold) too strong to be captured

impress to mark by pressing in or upon; to fix deeply on the mind
  impression the act or result of impressing; a single printing of a book; an idea or emotion left in the mind by any experience
  impressionable easily impressed or influenced
  impressive making a deep impression on the mind or feelings

imprison to put in prison; to shut up
  imprisonment the act of imprisoning or shutting someone up

improbable unlikely

impromptu made or done without preparation beforehand (as, an impromptu speech)

improper not suitable; wrong; indecent

improve to make, or become, better
  improvement the act, or result, of improving

improvident not providing, or taking thought, for the future; not thrifty

improvise to compose and perform without preparation (as, to improvise on the piano); to use whatever materials are at hand to make a substitute for the real thing (as, to improvise a bed from two or three chairs)

imprudent not showing prudence; unwise

impudent having no shame; insolent
  impudence insolence; an in-

solent act; shameless boldness

impulse a sudden force; a push; a sudden wish (as - He had an impulse to run away.)
  impulsive inclined to act suddenly without careful thought; done on impulse (as, an impulsive action)

impure mixed with something else
  impurity anything mixed with something pure which makes it impure (as - Stone is an impurity if it is mixed with coal.)

in a word which expresses position or inclusion (as, in the house, in early times, in summer, in fashion, etc.)
  inner farther in
  innermost, inmost farthest in

in- a prefix which often means not (as, **inactive**); in (as, **inborn**); into (as, **insight**)

inaccessible not accessible; not able to be approached or reached

inaccurate not accurate; not correct

inactive not active; not working

inadequate not adequate; not enough

inadvisable not advisable; unwise

inane silly; meaningless (as, an inane remark)

inanimate without life

inappropriate not appropriate; not suitable

inarticulate not articulate; unable to express oneself clearly and fluently

inartistic not artistic; lacking in appreciation of art

inattentive not paying attention

inaudible not able to be heard

inaugurate to make a formal beginning of (as, to inaugurate a new parliament after a general election); to open formally to the public (as, to inaugurate a new public library)
  inauguration a formal beginning or opening

inborn born in one; natural (as, an inborn ability to swim well)

incalculable not able to be calculated or measured; very great

incandescent glowing white with heat (as, an incandescent light)

incantation words said or sung as a spell

incapable not capable; unfit

incapacitate to make incapable; to make unfit; to disable

incarnation the taking of human, bodily form by a divine being

incautious not cautious; not careful

incendiary used for setting on fire (as, an incendiary bomb)

incense 1 *(say incense)* to inflame with anger; to enrage

incense 2 *(say incense)* a material burned (especially in religious ceremonies) to produce sweet-smelling fumes

incentive anything that encourages a person to do something (as - His interest in the work was a greater incentive than the money he was paid to do it.)

inception a beginning

incessant unceasing; going on without stopping

inch the twelfth part of a foot (approximately 2·5 centimetres)

incident a happening; an event
  incidental casual or occasional, but not essential (as, incidental holiday expenses such as money spent on drinks, ice creams, postcards, etc.); happening at the same time as something more important (as, incidental music in a play or film)
  incidentally by chance; (in conversation) *by the way*

incinerate to burn to ashes
  incinerator a furnace for incinerating

incipient beginning to exist or appear (as, an incipient cold)

incision the act of cutting into something; a cut; a gash
  incisive cutting into; penetrating; sharp and clear (as, an incisive manner, incisive words)

incite to urge on

incivility rudeness

inclement (of weather) severe; stormy

incline *(say incline)* to lean or slope towards; to have a tendency (as, someone who is inclined to talk a lot); to have a slight desire (as, to be inclined to go to the cinema) □ *(say incline)* a slope
  inclination *(say inclination)* a slope; a bending (as, an inclination of the head or body); a slight desire

include to take in, or count in, with others
  inclusion the act of including
  inclusive including everything mentioned or understood (as, 2nd to 4th July inclusive = 3 days)

incognito *(say incognito)* under a false name (as - The actor travelled incognito, so as to conceal his identity.)

incoherent *(say incoheerent)* not coherent; (of talking or thinking) unclear

incombustible not able to be burned by fire

income money that is paid to a person regularly, as a salary, wages, pension, etc.
  incoming coming in (as, the incoming tide)
  income tax a tax paid on income over a certain amount

incomparable matchless; without equal

incompatible not in agreement; opposite in character; contradictory (as, two separate descriptions of an event which are incompatible)

incompetent lacking in ability to do one's job

incomplete not complete; not finished

incomprehensible impossible to understand

inconceivable not able to be imagined; unthinkable

inconclusive having no definite conclusion or result (as - The evidence at the trial was inconclusive.)

incongruous out of place; not suitable or harmonious

inconsequential of no consequence or importance

inconsiderate not considering, or showing, thought for the feelings or rights of other people

inconsistent not consistent; contradictory in some way (as, inconsistent statements, inconsistent behaviour)

inconspicuous not noticeable (as - They missed the turning because the street-name was inconspicuous.)

inconvenient causing some difficulty or trouble; awkward

incorporate to unite in one body or society

incorrect wrong; not accurate

incorrigible too bad to be corrected or reformed; uncontrollable

increase to grow, or to make greater, in size or amount (as, to increase savings by adding a little money every month) □ growth; the amount added by growth (as, an increase of 20 pence)

incredible impossible to believe (or, seeming so, as, an incredible story)

incredulous not believing; showing disbelief (as - He told the story to an incredulous audience.)

incriminate to show that someone has taken part in a crime

incubate to hatch eggs
incubator an apparatus for hatching eggs by artificial heat (that is, without hens sitting on them); an apparatus for rearing premature babies

incur to bring upon oneself (as, to incur a debt, to incur blame)

incurable not able to be cured (as, an incurable disease)

incursion a hostile raid; a sudden attack

indebted being in debt; being obliged (as, indebted to a person for his help or kindness)

indecent offending against proper conduct; immodest

indecision inability to decide; hesitation
indecisive not having a definite result (as, an indecisive battle); not making firm decisions (as, an indecisive person)

indeed in fact; in truth; really

indefensible unable to be defended; not able to be justified or excused (as - His conduct was indefensible.)

indefinite without a definite, or clear, outline or limits (as, an indefinite area, an indefinite period)
indefinable not able to be defined or clearly described

indelible unable to be rubbed out (as, an indelible pencil mark or an indelible memory of some happening)

indelicate coarse; immodest

indent to make a dent in; to make notches in: (in printing or writing) to begin a new paragraph farther in from the margin
indentation a notch or recess (as, an indentation in a coast-line)

indenture a written agreement or contract (especially between an apprentice and his employer)

independent free from control by others (as, an independent country); thinking or acting for oneself; not depending on others for one's livelihood
independence the state of being independent

indescribable not able to be described (because too vague or too great as, indescribable disorder)

indestructible not able to be destroyed

index an indicator or pointer; an

alphabetical list of names and subjects mentioned in a book (usually placed at the end); the forefinger

indicate to point out; to show
indication the act of indicating; a mark or sign (as - The gift was an indication of her generosity.)
indicator a pointer

indictment *(say indítement)* a formal accusation against a person

indifferent showing no interest or feeling: rather poor in quality or performance (as, an indifferent game of tennis)
indifference lack of feeling or interest

indigenous *(say indíjinus)* growing or produced naturally in a country (as - Oranges are indigenous to Mediterranean countries.)

indigestion discomfort or pain caused by food that has not been properly digested
indigestible not easily digested

indignant annoyed or angry because of hurt feelings or a sense of injustice
indignation an angry feeling caused by a sense of injustice
indignity undeserved rude or contemptuous treatment

indigo a purplish-blue colour; a dye of that colour

indirect not direct or in a straight line; roundabout (as, an indirect route to a place)

indiscreet not discreet or cautious; giving away too much information
indiscretion lack of discretion or caution; an indiscreet act

indiscriminate not making any difference or distinction between one thing and another, or one person and another (as, giving indiscriminate praise)

indispensable not able to be done without; necessary

indisposed slightly ill; not disposed or willing to do something

indisposition a slight illness; unwillingness

indisputable not able to be disputed or denied; certainly true

indistinct not distinct or clear; dim

individual belonging to one only; single; separate □ a single person or animal
individuality separate and distinct existence; distinctive character

indivisible not able to be divided or separated

indolent lazy

indomitable not able to be overcome; unyielding

indoor the opposite of outdoor (as, indoor work)
indoors inside a building

indubitable *(say indewbitable)* not to be doubted; certain

induce to persuade; to bring on (as - Boring talk induces sleepiness.)
inducement something which persuades; an incentive

induction the formal introduction of a person into a new position or office: the production of an electrical charge in one body by simply placing another one near to it, without actual connection

indulge to give way readily to one's own wishes, or to those of another person
indulgent ready to yield to the wishes of others

industry steady attention to work; any branch of production which is concerned with the preparation of materials or goods for sale (as, the coal industry, the fishing industry, the chemicals industry)
industrial having to do with a country's industries
industrious hard-working; diligent

inebriate a drunkard

inedible not fit to be eaten

ineffective not having the desired effect; not working effectively (as, an ineffective law)

ineffectual without any effect; fruitless (as, ineffectual efforts)

inefficient not efficient; not good enough to do the work well (as, inefficient workers, inefficient tools)

ineligible not eligible; not suitable or qualified to be chosen for something

inept not suitable; out of place; foolish (as, an inept remark)

inequality lack of equality; unevenness

inert unable to move by itself (as, an inert body); without any active properties (as, an inert gas)
inertia *(say inershia)* the state of inertness (a property of all matter unless it is changed by some outside force)

inestimable too great to be estimated or valued (as, a medical discovery of inestimable worth to humanity)

inevitable not able to be avoided; certain to happen

inexact not exact; not quite correct

inexcusable not to be excused or justified (as - The behaviour of some of the spectators at the football match was inexcusable.)

inexpedient not advisable, or suitable, in the circumstances

inexpensive not costly; cheap

inexperienced lacking in experience or knowledge

inexplicable not able to be explained or understood

inextricable not able to be disentangled

infallible never making a mistake; certain to succeed (as, an infallible remedy)

infamous *(say infamus)* having an evil reputation; disgraceful
infamy an infamous act; an evil reputation

infant a baby; a very young child □ of, or for, infants
infancy the state or time of

being an infant or very young

infantile babyish (as, infantile conduct); having to do with infants (as, infantile diseases)

infantry foot soldiers

infatuation a foolish love or passion

infect to pass on a disease to; to pass on a feeling or quality (as, to infect the spectators with enthusiasm)
infection the act or means of infecting; an infectious disease
infectious apt to spread

infer to conclude, or judge, from facts or evidence (as - They inferred from the weather forecast that the game might have to be postponed.)
inference *(say inference)* a conclusion or deduction from something written or said

inferior lower in place or in rank; less important; of poor quality (as, inferior goods)

infernal devilish; belonging to hell

infest to swarm over (as, a dog infested with fleas)

infiltrate to filter into or through; (of soldiers) to get through the enemy lines a few at a time

infinite without end or limits; very great (as, infinite mercy)
infinitesimal *(say infinitesimal)* extremely small
infinity infinite space or time (so great as to be beyond human imagination); an infinitely distant place or point

infirm feeble; weak
infirmary a hospital
infirmity a weakness; a physical ailment

inflame to cause to flame; to make hot or angry
inflammable easily set on fire; easily excited to anger: see also **flammable** under **flame**
inflammation heat in a part of the body, with redness, swelling and (often) pain
inflammatory tending to arouse anger or excitement (as, an inflammatory speech)

inflate to swell with air or gas (as, to inflate a balloon); to puff up with pride (as - He had an inflated idea of his own importance.)
inflation the act of inflating: (in a country's economy) the circulation of too much money in proportion to the goods being produced, causing too great a rise in wages and in prices

inflexible not bending; not yielding

inflict to give or impose (as, to inflict a wound, punishment, etc. on someone)
infliction the act of inflicting; a punishment

influence a power to affect other people or things (as - The boy's companions had a bad influence on him.) □ to have or to use influence on (as - The quality of the wheat harvest is influenced by the weather.)
influential having much influence (as, an influential member of the government)

influenza an infectious illness whose symptoms are rather like those of a feverish cold, with aching limbs

influx a flowing in (as, an influx of people, or of goods, into a place)

inform to tell; to give knowledge to; to give information against (as - The burglar informed against his accomplice.)
informant someone who informs or gives news
information facts told to others; knowledge about something
informative giving information
informer someone who gives information; someone who tells on another (especially to the police)

informal not formal; without ceremony

infrequent not frequent

infringe to break a rule or law

infuriate to make very angry

infuse to pour in; to instil or inspire with (as, to infuse some spirit into the tired players); to steep or soak (as, to infuse the tea for five minutes)

ingenious skilfully designed or thought out (as, an ingenious plan); skilful in inventing (as, an ingenious young man)
ingenuity ingeniousness; cleverness

ingenuous frank; free from deception; innocent

ingot a lump of metal cast in a mould (as, gold or steel ingots)

ingratitude lack of gratitude or thankfulness

ingredient one of the things that goes into a mixture

inhabit to live in (a country, a region, etc.)
inhabitant a person who lives permanently in a place (as, the inhabitants of France, of London, etc.)

inhale to breathe in

inherent inborn or natural (as, an inherent characteristic)

inherit to receive property, etc. as an heir; to possess certain qualities that belonged to one's forebears (as - She inherited her mother's good looks.)
inheritance anything which is inherited

inhuman not human; cruel

inimical not friendly; hostile; unfavourable

inimitable not able to be imitated

iniquity wickedness; a sin

initial the first letter of a name or word □ at the beginning or first (as, the initial performance of a play) □ to write the initials of one's name on
initiate to begin; to introduce to some kind of knowledge; to admit into a secret society, club, etc.
initiation the beginning of, or introduction to (as, a pupil's initiation into the French language)

initiative the first step or lead (as - The leader of the expedition naturally took the initiative.); enterprise or eagerness to make progress

inject to force a liquid (usually medicine) into the body by means of a syringe with a hollow needle
injection the act of injecting; the liquid injected

injure to harm; to damage; to wrong
injurious harmful; hurtful
injury a hurt; damage; a wrong

injustice a wrong; an unfair act

ink a coloured liquid used for writing or printing

inkling a hint; a slight indication

inlaid decorated with pieces of fine material which have been inserted into the surface (as, inlaid with ivory, etc.)

inland towards parts of a country away from the coast □ distant from the sea (as; an inland town)

inlet a small narrow bay; an entrance

inmate a resident (especially in an institution)

inn a small country hotel; a public house providing food and lodging for travellers
innkeeper the owner or manager of an inn

innate inborn; natural

inner, innermost, inmost see **in**

innings a team's turn to bat in cricket, etc.; a turn or spell

innocent not guilty; free from, or ignorant of, evil
innocence absence of guilt; harmlessness

innocuous harmless

innovation something new

innumerable not able to be numbered; countless

inoculate to give a person a mild form of a disease by injecting viruses or germs into the bloodstream (This prepares the body against a real attack of the disease and so acts as a safeguard against infection.)

inoffensive giving no offence; harmless

inopportune coming at the wrong time; inconvenient

inquest a legal enquiry into a sudden death

inquire to seek information; to ask
inquiry a search for information; an investigation; a question
inquisitive eager to know; fond of asking questions (especially about other people's affairs)

insane not sane or of sound mind; mad; senseless
insanity lack of sanity; madness

insanitary not sanitary; dangerous to health

inscribe to write in or on (as, to inscribe a name in a book)
inscription something inscribed in a book or on a monument

inscrutable not able to be scrutinized or understood; mysterious (as, an inscrutable person)

insect a very small animal which has six legs and is divided into three sections, the head, thorax and abdomen (for example, ants, bees and beetles)
insecticide a substance for killing insects

insecure not secure or safe

insensible not having any feeling; unconscious: too small or gradual to be noticed
insensitive not sensitive; not having feelings that are easily touched

inseparable not able to be separated or parted (as, inseparable friends)

insert to put in □ something extra put in (as, an insert in a magazine, such as a leaflet)
insertion the act of inserting; something inserted

inset an insert; a small picture, map, etc. set within a larger one

inshore near or towards the

shore of the sea

inside the side or part within (as, the inside of a box, etc.); the opposite of outside (as, inside the house, an inside job, coming inside out of the rain)

insight the power of seeing into a matter and understanding it

insignia badges worn to show that the wearer has some honour or authority

insignificant not signifying anything; having no meaning; unimportant

insincere not sincere

insinuate to introduce in a sly way (as, to insinuate doubts into someone's mind); to hint (especially at a fault)

insipid tasteless; dull

insist to urge or maintain strongly (as - He insisted on being given a better room in the hotel.); to go on saying (as - He insisted that his story was true.)
insistent insisting; urgent

insolent insulting; rude
insolence insulting behaviour; rudeness

insoluble (of a substance) not able to be dissolved; (of a problem or difficulty) not able to be solved

insomnia sleeplessness

inspect to look into carefully; to examine
inspection the act of inspecting; a careful examination
inspector an officer appointed to inspect (as, a tax inspector); a police officer next above a sergeant

inspire to influence the mind in an encouraging way (as, to be inspired to greater effort by a friend's encouragement); to animate with a divine or noble emotion (as - She felt inspired to write a poem.)
inspiration something which gives great encouragement; someone who inspires (as - Nelson was an inspiration to his

officers.); the influence that motivates the creators of great works of art or literature

instability lack of stability or steadiness

install to fix in position for use (as, to install new electrical wiring in a house); to place in an official position (often with some ceremony as, to install a new mayor)
installation the act of installing; something installed (as, a lighting installation)

instalment one part of a serial story or film; one part of the money owed for a purchase which is to be paid for over a period (for example, twelve monthly instalments over a year)

instance an example; a particular case (as, in this instance)

instant immediate □ a moment of time
instantaneous done or happening in an instant
instantly at once; without delay

instead in place of; as a substitute (as - His brother came instead.)

instep the arched upper part of the foot

instil to introduce little by little into the mind (as, to instil ideas, to instil hatred)

instinct a natural tendency in human beings or animals to do some things without being taught or learning from experience (For example, young birds are able to fly by instinct.)
instinctive due to instinct or natural impulse; not reasoned out

institute to set up; to establish □ a society, or the building used by it (as, a Workers' Institute)
institution a society for a particular purpose (as, the Royal National Lifeboat Institution); a residential establishment for a particular purpose (such as a prison, a mental hospital, an in-

stitution for old people); an established custom, law, etc.

instruct to teach; to order or command
instruction teaching; a command; (plural) special directions or commands
instructive giving knowledge or information

instrument a tool: something for producing musical sounds (such as a piano, violin, trumpet)
instrumental for musical instruments (as, instrumental music): helpful (as - He was instrumental in getting the invention patented.)
instrumentalist someone who plays a musical instrument

insubordinate disobedient; rebellious

insufferable not able to be endured; unbearable

insular belonging to an island or islands

insulate to cover or separate with a material (like rubber or plastic) that does not conduct electricity or that does not allow heat to pass (Electrical wires are insulated; refrigerators have an insulated lining.)
insulation, insulator a material that does not conduct electricity; a material that prevents heat from passing through; a material (such as cork) which prevents sound waves from passing (as, the insulation of a soundproof broadcasting studio)

insult to treat with contempt or rudeness □ something said or done that is insulting to a person

insuperable not able to be got over or overcome (as, an insuperable difficulty)

insure to guard against loss by fire, accident, burglary, unemployment, etc. by making payments to an insurance company (The company makes charges according to the amount of risk.)
insurance the act of insuring against anything; a system of insuring (as, National Insurance)

insurgent rising in rebellion □ a rebel
insurrection a rising or revolt

intact undamaged; whole

intangible not able to be felt by touch; not clear and definite to the mind

integer any whole number (that is, not a fraction)
integral necessary to complete the whole of something (as - The back is an integral part of a chair.)
integrate to make up into a whole (by combining parts together); to enable one racial group to live in harmony with another group (the opposite of segregate)
integrity the state of being whole or complete; honesty (as, integrity of character)

intellect the thinking power of the mind
intellectual showing intellect (as, intellectual ability) □ a person of superior intellect
intelligent clever; quick in mind
intelligence ability to learn and understand: knowledge; information specially collected
intelligible able to be understood (as, an intelligible message)

intend to mean to; to plan to
intent a purpose or intention □ determined (as, to be intent on finishing the project)
intention what one means to do; a purpose or aim
intentional done on purpose

intense very great (as, intense heat, intense desire)
intensify to make more intense or greater (as, to intensify one's efforts)
intensity strength or intenseness (as, the intensity of her feelings)

inter (*say inter*) to bury
interment burial

inter- a prefix meaning between or among

intercede to try to act as a peace-maker between two people or groups of people
  intercession the act of interceding or pleading for another

intercept to stop or seize something (or someone) on the way from one place to another

interchange to exchange; to put each into the place of the other (as, the interchange of two pictures on the wall)
  interchangeable able to be changed one for the other without making any difference (as - The two kinds of torch battery are interchangeable.)

intercourse communication or dealings between people, nations, etc.

interest curiosity and attention (as, an interest in wild animals); anything which produces these feelings (as, a story of great interest); advantage or benefit (as - It is in his interest to join in the project.): a sum paid for the loan of money (as, £5 interest on a loan of £100) □ to hold someone's attention
  interesting arousing or holding someone's attention and curiosity (as, an interesting television programme)

interfere to meddle (as, interfering in another person's affairs); to hinder by getting in the way (as, hooligans interfering with a game of football)
  interference the act of interfering; the spoiling of radio reception by another station on a similar wavelength or by natural disturbances (for example, lightning)

interim the time between; the meantime (as, in the interim) □ temporary (as, an interim payment to be followed by a final payment)

interior inner; inside (as, the interior woodwork of a house) □ the inside of anything; the inland part of a country

interject to throw in a remark or exclamation, interrupting someone who is speaking
  interjection one or more words of exclamation (such as *Oh dear!*)

interlock to lock or clasp firmly together

interlude a short piece of music played between the parts of a play, etc.; an interval

intermediate placed or coming between
  intermediary a go-between; someone who acts between two persons (as, an intermediary in a dispute)

interment see **inter**

interminable endless; tiresomely long (as, an interminable speech)

intermission an interval; a pause
  intermittent stopping at intervals and then starting again (as, an intermittent pain)

intern to hold a person prisoner without trial while a country is at war or involved in civil conflict
  internment the act of interning people

internal inside the body (as, the internal organs); the opposite of external (as, the internal trade of a country)

international between, or concerned with, different nations (as, international trade) □ a match between the teams of different nations

interplanetary among the planets

interpret to explain the meaning of something; to translate a foreign language orally
  interpretation the meaning given by someone who is interpreting; an actor's way of playing a part; a musician's way of playing a piece of music
  interpreter a person who translates aloud for the benefit of those speaking different languages

interrogate to question or examine thoroughly (especially in a formal way)

interrogation the act of interrogating; a question; the mark placed after a question (**?**)

interrogative asking a question (as, an interrogative remark)

interrupt to make a break in some action (such as a speech, work or a game); to block or cut off (as - The new building interrupts their view of the sea.)

interruption a sudden break in some action (as, an interruption of classwork)

intersect to divide by cutting or crossing (as, where the two lines intersect one another)

intersection the point where two lines cross; a crossroads

intersperse to scatter between or among; to scatter here and there (as, open country interspersed with trees)

intertwine to twine or twist together

interval a time or space between (as, an interval of ten minutes, ten years or ten metres)

intervene to come or be between (as, to intervene between two persons, nations, etc. who are in dispute, in the hope of settling matters between them)

interview a meeting (usually between two people) for the purpose of obtaining information (as, an interview by a news reporter with a member of the public); a formal meeting between a candidate for a job and his prospective employer(s) □ to have an interview with

intestines the part of the digestive system below the stomach (It comprises an upper, small intestine and a lower, large intestine.)

intimate 1 *(say intimet)* close (as, an intimate friend); private or personal (as, intimate thoughts); detailed (as - He has an intimate knowledge of the country.)

intimacy a close familiarity

intimate 2 *(say intimayt)* to hint;

to indicate; to announce

intimation a hint; an announcement

intimidate to make someone afraid (generally with threats of violence)

intimidation the use of threats to influence another person's actions

into to the inside (as, into the house); to a different state (as, making cloth into a coat); noting parts made by dividing (as, 3 into 6 goes twice)

intolerable not able to be tolerated or endured

intolerant not able or willing to tolerate something; not willing to consider opinions, etc. different from one's own

intone to chant

intonation the rise and fall of the voice in speech

intoxicate to make drunk: to excite greatly

intoxicant an intoxicating drink

intoxication drunkenness; great excitement

intrepid fearless; very brave (as, an intrepid explorer)

intricate complicated; having much detail (as, an intricate design)

intrigue underhand scheming; a plot □ to plot: to arouse one's curiosity (as - The story intrigued her.)

intrinsic naturally belonging to a thing; inherent; genuine (as, the intrinsic value of an heirloom, as distinct from its sentimental value)

introduce to bring in or forward; to bring to notice (as, to introduce a new idea); to make two persons known to one another by telling each the other's name when they meet for the first time (as - The host introduced Mr. A to Mrs. B.)

introduction the act of introducing something (as, the introduction of the metric system); the act of presenting one person to another; something written at the beginning of a book to introduce the story or subject

intrude to thrust oneself in where one is unexpected or unwelcome

intruder someone who intrudes

intrusion the act of intruding

intuition the power of sensing the truth directly without reasoning; a truth perceived in this way

inundate to flood

invade to enter like an enemy

invader a hostile person, army, etc.

invasion the act of invading; an attack on the rights or privacy of another

invalid 1 *(say invalid)* a person who is ill or disabled □ ill or sick □ to put on the sick list (as, to invalid a wounded soldier out of the army)

invalid 2 *(say invalid)* without validity or legal force (as, an invalid hire-purchase agreement); not sound (as, an invalid argument)

invaluable too valuable to be estimated (as, invaluable help)

invariable not varying, not changing

invasion see **invade**

invent to make for the first time (for example, a new machine or a new method); to make up (as, to invent a story or an excuse)

invention something entirely new that has been invented (For example, nylon is a 20th century invention.)

inventive quick to invent; ingenious

inventor a person who has produced one or more inventions (as - Dunlop was the inventor of the pneumatic tyre.)

inventory *(say inventry)* a detailed list of articles (as, an inventory of the furniture in a house, or of the stock in a warehouse

invert to turn upside down; to reverse the order of

inverse opposite; reverse

inversion a turning upside down

invertebrate (of an animal) not having a backbone

invest 1 to put money into a business, etc., with the expectation of making a profit (as, to invest in a new housing estate or stocks and shares)

investment the investing of money for profit

investor anyone who invests

invest 2 to place someone formally in an important office (as - He was invested with a Lord Mayor's authority.)

investiture the ceremony of investing a person

investigate to inquire into with care

investigation a thorough inquiry

investigator someone who investigates

invigorate to give vigour or energy to (as - Sea air invigorates the body.)

invincible not able to be defeated or overcome

inviolable not to be broken or misused (as, an inviolable oath or right)

inviolate not violated or disturbed

invisible not visible; not able to be seen

invite to ask someone to come to one's home or to go somewhere else (as, to invite people to a meeting); to ask for (as, to invite suggestions)

invitation the act of inviting; a request (whether written or oral)

inviting attractive; tempting (as, an inviting display of food)

invocation see **invoke**

invoice a note sent with goods, listing the quantities and prices □ to make out such a list

invoke to call upon earnestly or solemnly; to call upon

(God) in prayer
invocation the act of invoking; an earnest appeal to God

involuntary not done willingly; unintentional

involve to concern; to bring a person into some activity (as, to involve a friend in plans); to include or require (as - Taking part in a play involves learning some lines by heart.)
involved complicated (as, an involved story or plot)

invulnerable not able to be wounded or harmed

inward being or placed within; the opposite of outward; in the mind or soul

iodine a chemical element used in medicine

irate angry
irascible easily angered; irritable
ire anger

iris 1 the coloured part of the eye

iris 2 a plant with sword-shaped leaves and large, showy flowers in various colours
iridescent having rainbow-like colours which change as their position changes

irk to weary; to annoy
irksome tiresome

iron a common metal from which steel is made; a tool or instrument made of iron or steel (such as an electric iron for ironing clothes; a golf club; a branding iron) □ made of iron; as strong as iron (as, an iron will) □ to smooth clothes with an iron
irons fetters or chains
ironmonger a dealer in ironmongery
ironmongery articles of metal (such as tools, locks, nuts and bolts)

irony a way of mocking a person by saying to him the exact opposite of what one means (as - *How clever of you!* - meaning the opposite)
ironical said in irony (as, an ironical statement)

irrational not rational or reasonable

irregular not regular; not according to rule; uneven (as, an irregular surface)
irregularity something which is irregular or against the rules

irrelevant not relevant; not having anything to do with the subject which is being discussed

irreligious not religious

irreparable *(say irreparable)* not able to be repaired or made good (as, an irreparable loss)

irrepressible not able to be repressed or kept in check

irresistible not able to be resisted; extremely charming

irrespective of without regard to (as, irrespective of the weather)

irresponsible not having a sense of responsibility or of duty (as, irresponsible conduct)

irreverent having no reverence or respect

irrevocable *(say irrevocable)* not able to be revoked or changed (as, an irrevocable decision)

irrigate to water land by means of canals, etc.
irrigation the irrigating of land (by natural or by artificial means, such as water pipes)

irritate to make angry or impatient: to hurt the skin, etc. by rubbing, dirt, etc. (as - His eyes were irritated by the dust.)
irritable cross; easily annoyed
irritation anger: redness or soreness of the skin, etc.

island land surrounded by water; anything isolated and detached from its immediate surroundings (as, a street island)
islander an inhabitant of an island

isle an island
islet a little isle

isobar a line on a map passing through all the places where the atmospheric pressure is the same (for example, all places where the barometer shows 30·0 inches, or 1016 millibars, pressure)

isolate *(say ice-olate)* to place alone; to set apart; to keep an infected person away from others who might otherwise catch his disease
isolated lonely or remote from (as, an isolated village)
isolation the act of isolating; the state of being isolated

isotherm a line on a map joining all places which have the same temperature (for example, where the thermometer shows a level of 10° centigrade, or 50° Fahrenheit)

issue to come out (as - A trickle of water issued from the tap.); to give out or send out; to publish □ the act of coming, giving or sending out (as, the issue of a spring from a hillside; the issue of books to a class); a result or outcome: a problem or question (as - That is the real issue.)
at issue being disputed (as, the matter at issue)

isthmus *(say issmus)* a narrow neck of land connecting two larger pieces

it something already mentioned (as - He heard the aeroplane but did not see it at first.); something being spoken about (as - It is his bat.); also in impersonal or indefinite statements (such as, It is raining.)
itself an emphatic form of **it** (as - The coin is treasured by him, though it is itself of little value.); a reflexive form of **it** (as - The kitten entangled itself with the ball of wool.)

italics a kind of printing type that slopes to the right *(as these words do)*

itch a strong tickling or irritating feeling on the skin: a restless desire □ to have such a feeling
itchy affected with an itch (as, an itchy nose)

item a separate article or detail (especially one named in a list); a separate piece of information (as, an item of news)

itinerant making journeys from place to place (as, an itinerant worker) □ a person who journeys from place to place
itinerary a route followed, or to be followed, on a journey (as, an itinerary for a motor tour)

ivory the hard white substance which forms the tusks of the elephant, walrus, etc. □ made of, or like, ivory

ivy a creeping evergreen plant that grows on trees and walls

j

jab to poke or stab at something with a sudden thrust □ a sudden thrust or stab

jabber to talk very quickly (often in a confused way that does not make sense); to chatter

jack a machine for lifting heavy weights (for example, for lifting part of a vehicle so that the wheel or tyre can be repaired or changed); a playing card (the knave); the small white ball that serves as a marker in the game of bowls; a small flag on a ship (especially showing nationality,

as the Union Jack)
jackboot a heavy boot reaching above the knee
jack-in-the-box a box with a toy figure inside which springs up when the lid is opened
jack-knife a large folding pocket-knife: a fancy dive in which the diver bends double in mid-air, straightening out before entering the water
jack-of-all-trades someone who can turn his hand to any job
jack-o'-lantern a will-o'-the-wisp; a lantern made out of a

pumpkin (usually, with a face carved out to show the light)

jackpot an accumulation of money won in a card game, from a gambling machine, etc.

to hit the jackpot to have a success; to win a large amount of money

jack-rabbit a North American hare with very long ears and hind legs

yellowjack yellow fever (a serious disease in some hot countries)

jackal a doglike wild animal that feeds on carrion

jackass a male ass: a fool; a stupid person

laughing jackass an Australian kingfisher (kookaburra) which makes a laughing sound

jackdaw a small crow

jacket a short coat: a loose paper cover on a book; an outer covering

jade a valuable hard stone (usually green, but also found in pink and other colours) used in jewellery, carved ornaments, etc.

jaded weary; worn out with hard work

jagged having rough, sharp edges

jaguar a large spotted wild animal of the cat family, that lives in America

jail a building where people are held prisoner as punishment or while waiting to come to trial; a prison (The word is sometimes spelled gaol.)

jailer an officer who guards prisoners

jam 1 a preserve of fruit cooked with sugar until it is thick and soft

jam 2 to press or squeeze tight; to block or bring to a standstill (as, to jam a piece of machinery so that it will not work); to crowd or fill up (as, a number of people jammed into the lift); to interfere with a broadcasting transmission by sending out a signal on the same wavelength or frequency; to thrust or push

hard (as - He jammed the brakes on.) □ a crowding together (of people, traffic, logs, etc.)

jamb the sidepiece or post of a door, fireplace, etc.

jamboree a noisy celebration or merrymaking; a large gathering of boy scouts (sometimes from many different countries)

jangle to sound harshly or discordantly (as, a jangle of bells)

janitor a doorkeeper; a caretaker (of a building)

jar 1 an earthenware or glass bottle with a wide mouth

jar 2 to make a harsh or unpleasant noise; to grate on (as - That loud screeching jars on my nerves.); to shake or cause to vibrate suddenly and unpleasantly

jargon confused or meaningless talk; a special vocabulary used by professional or other groups of people interested in a particular subject (as, medical jargon)

jasmine a climbing shrub or bush with ornamental white or yellow flowers (Most jasmine is very fragrant.)

jaundice *(say jawndiss)* an illness which causes yellow colouring of the skin and whites of the eyes

jaundiced suffering from jaundice: taking a rather embittered, pessimistic view of life

jaunt a short trip or excursion (especially one for pleasure)

jaunty lively; gay

javelin a light spear thrown by hand

jaw the two large bones in the mouth from which the teeth grow

jay a brightly-coloured noisy bird of the crow family

jay-walker a careless pedestrian who crosses the street against traffic lights or without proper regard to traffic regulations

jazz lively dance music which features improvisation and syncopated rhythms

jealous wishing to possess something belonging to another person; envious
jealousy envy; the state of being jealous

jeans trousers made of strong cotton cloth (usually blue)

jeep a small powerful motor vehicle used by the army

jeer to make fun of; to scoff at □ a taunting or mocking remark

jelly a transparent wobbly food (usually fruit-flavoured); any jelly-like substance
jellyfish a sea animal with a transparent jelly-like body

jemmy a burglar's short crowbar

jerk a short sudden movement □ to pull or twitch suddenly; to move with stops and starts
jerky moving, coming in jerks

jersey a close-fitting knitted pullover with sleeves; a knitted fabric: a cow of Jersey breed (originally bred on the Channel Island of Jersey)

jest a joke; something said in fun □ to make a joke: to speak in a bantering way
jester a person who makes jokes; (in olden times) a fool at the court of a king or nobleman, employed to amuse his master and guests

jet 1 a hard black mineral used for ornaments; the colour of this mineral (as, jet-black, meaning very black)

jet 2 a rush of liquid or gas through a narrow opening (especially from the end of a pipe or hose): a jet aeroplane
jet aeroplane an aeroplane without propellers, powered by an engine driven by the thrust of heated air forced out of nozzles at the rear

jetsam goods thrown overboard from a ship and washed up on the shore; goods from a wreck that do not float to the surface, but remain under water: see also **flotsam**

jettison to throw overboard; to abandon

jetty a small pier

Jew a person whose forebears were Hebrew or Jewish people
Jewish belonging to the Jews

jewel a precious stone; any ornament, person or thing held to be very valuable
jeweller someone who deals in jewellery
jewellery valuable articles and ornaments made of precious metals, gems, etc.

jib 1 a triangular sail at the front of a sailboat: the jutting-out arm of a crane

jib 2 to refuse to do something (as - He jibbed at having to take part in the school concert.)

jibe a taunt; a jeer □ to scoff (at)

jig a lively dance; the music for such a dance □ to dance a jig

jigsaw a narrow saw (usually power-driven) used to cut curves in wood, thick cardboard, etc.
jigsaw puzzle a puzzle made of odd-shaped pieces that are fitted together to make a picture

jilt to dismiss a sweetheart or suitor suddenly, after leading him or her to suppose they would get married

jingle a clinking or tinkling sound (as when coins, keys, etc. are clinked together): a catchy verse or set of verses (often repeating words, and often set to music) as, a television advertising jingle

job a piece of work done (usually for money); a person's employment (as - He has a job in engineering.); anything that has to be done (as - His job is to collect up the notebooks after class.)
jobbing doing odd jobs for payment (as, a jobbing gardener)

jockey a person who rides a horse in a race (usually as a professional)

jocose given to joking; merry

and humorous
jocular full of jokes
jocund the same as jocose, jocular

jog to give a little shake or push with the elbow; to remind (as, to jog a person's memory): to move along at a pace faster than walking but slower than running: to move up and down jerkily
jog-trot a slow, jolting pace (as, a pony's jog-trot)

join to put together or fasten; to connect; to become a member of (as, to join a club, a business firm, a team, etc.); to unite with or take part in (as, to join a group of friends, to join in community singing)
joiner a person who joins or unites; a carpenter who makes wooden doors, window frames, stairs, etc.
joint the place where two or more things join; a part of the body where two bones are joined, but loosely so that they are able to move (as, the elbow joint, the knee joint); a piece of meat for cooking (usually) containing a joint bone
jointed having joints; made up of segments (Bamboo is a plant with jointed stems.)
jointly together
to join up to enlist (in the armed forces)

joist a beam to which the boards of a floor or the laths of a ceiling are fastened

joke something said or done that raises a laugh; a jest; something done for fun, not seriously □ to make jokes; to speak in a joking way
joker a person who makes jokes: an extra playing card used in some card games

jolly cheerful; full of fun □ very (as, jolly good)
jollification a celebration with feasting and merriment
jollity merriment

jolt to move forward in jerky movements (as, a car jolting along a rough country road); to shake or jar suddenly □ a shock (as - It gave him a jolt when he realized how late it was.)

jonquil a plant of the narcissus family, with clusters of sweet-smelling white or yellow flowers and long narrow leaves

jostle to shake or jar by pushing or elbowing against

jot 1 a very small part or amount

jot 2 to make a note of something (as, to jot down some points made in a talk)

journal a diary; a daily account or record (as, of a business firm's transactions, of parliamentary proceedings, etc.); a newspaper (published daily, weekly, etc.); a magazine
journalism the business of writing, editing or publishing a newspaper or magazine
journalist a person who writes for or edits a newspaper or magazine

journey a distance travelled (as, a day's journey, a twenty-mile journey) □ to travel from one place to another (usually some distance away)

joust (in olden times) a combat at a tournament between two mounted knights with lances

jovial jolly and cheerful; full of good humour

jowl the jaw or cheek; a heavy double chin

joy great happiness; a feeling of great pleasure or gladness; something that makes one glad
joyful, joyous feeling or showing joy

jubilant shouting with joy; rejoicing
jubilation a joyful celebration; a rejoicing

jubilee any season of great rejoicing; a joyful celebration of some event (for example, a wedding) that happened many years ago
silver jubilee 25 years
golden jubilee 50 years
diamond jubilee 60 years and

75 years

judge a public official who hears cases in a court of law and decides what action should be taken; a person who is appointed to decide the winners of competitions, contests, races, etc.; a person who has a good knowledge of some subject or activity (as, to be a good judge of horses.) □ to try and to decide legal questions; to form an opinion or to come to a conclusion (as, to judge the value of something)

judgment, judgement the act of judging; the opinion or decision given; the ability to weigh up all sides of a question or problem (as, good judgment)

judicial having to do with a judge or a court of law; critical

judicious wise; showing good judgment or sound common sense

judo a form of Japanese wrestling (now often taught in western countries as a sport and as a form of self-defence without weapons)

jug a container with a handle (and often with a lip or spout for pouring)

juggle to keep a number of objects moving in the air without letting any fall

juggler a person who entertains by juggling

jugular one of the large veins on either side of the neck

juice the liquid part of fruits, vegetables and meat

juicy having much juice (as, juicy oranges)

ju-jitsu an earlier form of judo

juke-box a coin-operated instrument that plays selected records

jumble a mixture or mass of odd things □ to mix together in a confused mass (as, to jumble things together in a cupboard)

jumble sale a sale of odds and ends (often for charity)

jump to spring up off the ground; to leap or get on to (as, to jump aboard a train, a bus, a boat, etc.); to leap from or over (as, to jump off a fence, over a hurdle) □ a sudden movement (as - She gave a jump of surprise.); a leap or the distance of a leap (as - His long jump measured 20 feet.)

to jump at to seize eagerly

to jump the gun to start before the proper time (thus taking unfair advantage of others)

to jump to conclusions to make a snap judgment or make a quick decision before hearing all the facts to be considered

jumper a loose-fitting knitted upper garment with sleeves (worn by girls and women)

junction a place or point of meeting (such as a railway junction or road junction)

jungle a tropical forest in which the trees and undergrowth are very dense

junior younger in age or rank than others

juniper an evergreen shrub with purple berries which are used in making gin

junk 1 a kind of flat-bottomed Chinese sailing ship

junk 2 articles of no value; rubbish

jurisdiction legal authority or power; the district over which a judge or court has authority

jury a group of persons selected in a court of law to hear a case and to decide whether the accused person is guilty or not guilty (If their verdict is *guilty* the judge decides the punishment.); a committee which decides the winner of a competition, etc.

juror, juryman a member of a jury

just 1 exactly (as, just so, just right); not long ago (as - The train has just gone.)

just 2 right and fair; reasonable; deserved in the light of facts (as, a just punishment)

justice fairness in making

judgments; what is right and just

Justice of the Peace (J.P.) a citizen appointed to act as a magistrate in a county, town, etc.

justification a good reason

justify to prove or show that some act is right and fair

jut to stick out

jute the fibre of plants which grow in India and Pakistan, used for making coarse sacks, doormats, string, etc.

juvenile young; youthful; concerning young people

juvenile delinquency breaking of the law by young people (under the age of seventeen)

k

kale a cabbage with open curled leaves

kaleidoscope a tube-shaped toy with small pieces of coloured glass which change patterns (reflected in mirrors) when the tube is turned round

kangaroo a large Australian animal with a long tail and very powerful hind legs which enable it to leap long distances (The female carries her babies in an abdominal pouch.)

kaolin very fine white clay (also called china clay) used in making porcelain

kayak an Eskimo canoe made of wood and covered all over with sealskin which fits around the waist of the occupant so that water cannot get in

keel a long heavy piece of timber or metal that forms the base of the framework of a boat or ship □ to turn (a ship's) keel upward; to capsize

keen sharp (as, a keen blade); cold and cutting (as, a keen wind); eager; enthusiastic (as - He was a keen footballer.)

keep to look after; to hold on to and care for (as, to keep a pet, etc.); to fulfil (as, to keep one's promise); to stay in the same condition or state (as - This food will keep in the refrigerator.); to delay or detain (as, to keep someone prisoner; to keep someone from going ahead) □

(in olden days) the strongest part of a fortress

keeper a person who looks after or cares for something or someone (as, a keeper at the zoo, a doorkeeper, lighthouse keeper, etc.)

keeping care; custody

keepsake anything kept in memory of the giver

keep up to maintain (as, to keep up prices, or a conversation); to hold one's position

keg a small cask

kelp a large brown seaweed (sometimes used as a source of iodine)

ken understanding; knowledge (as - That is beyond my ken.)

kennel a small house or shelter for a dog; a place for breeding dogs or where dogs are kept or boarded

kerb the edge of a pavement

kerchief a piece of cloth used to cover the head or worn as a neck scarf; a handkerchief

kernel the inner part of a nut or grain (usually edible); the most important part of an argument or lecture

kerosene paraffin oil (for burning in oil lamps and heaters)

kestrel a kind of small falcon

ketch a two-masted sailing boat

ketchup a sauce made from tomatoes, mushrooms, etc.

kettle a metal pot (usually with

spout, lid and handle) used for heating liquids

kettledrum a drum made of a half-globe of brass or copper with stretched parchment fitted over the top

key an instrument (usually of metal) which unlocks or unbolts a fastening on a door, gate, etc.; a device that turns or screws to tighten or loosen (a nut, a string on a musical instrument, a winder on a clock, etc.); a lever on a piano, a typewriter, etc.; the chief note (keynote) of a piece of music (as, a symphony in the key of F major); tone or pitch (as of a voice); the solution or explanation of something difficult (as - The key to this problem is more hard work.) □ most important; essential (as, a key man in a job, key industries)

keyboard an orderly arrangement of keys on one or more levels (as, a piano or typewriter keyboard, etc.)

keyhole an opening specially designed for a particular key to fit (in a door, cupboard, etc.)

keystone the stone at the highest point of an arch, holding the rest of the stones in position

keyed up tightened up; excited

khaki dull yellowish-brown □ cloth of this colour used for soldiers' uniforms

kick to hit or strike with the foot; to resist or object (as - He kicked against having to do the extra work.); (of a gun) to spring back or recoil when fired □ a blow with the foot; a strong protest

kid a young goat; leather from the skin of a young goat

kidnap to steal a child; to carry off a person by force
kidnapper a person who kidnaps

kidney one of a pair of glands in the lower back (one on each side)

kill to cause someone or something to die; to put an end to or destroy

kiln a large oven or furnace used for baking pottery, bricks, etc., or for drying hops, grain, etc.

kilogramme a measure of weight equal to 1000 grammes (about $2^1/_5$ lb.)

kilohertz (kHz) a measure of sound wave frequencies or vibrations equal to 1000 cycles per second; (formerly kilocycle)

kilometre a measure of length equal to 1000 metres (about $^5/_8$ths of a mile)

kilowatt a measure of electrical power equal to 1000 watts

kilt a knee-length, pleated tartan skirt

kimono a loose robe with wide sleeves and a broad sash (worn as an outer garment in Japan); a similar garment worn as a dressing gown in other countries

kin persons belonging to the same family; relatives □ related by common ancestry
kindred kin: having similar feelings or tastes
kinsman, kinswoman, kinsfolk a man, a woman, people related to another person
next of kin nearest relatives
kith and kin friends and relatives

kind 1 friendly; good to other people; gentle
kindly kind (as - She is a kindly person.) □ please (as - Would you kindly wait here for a few moments?)
kindness, kindliness the quality or fact of being kind
kind-hearted kind and generous to others

kind 2 sort, group or type (as, different kinds of birds, the same kinds of people, a kind of fish, etc.)
of a kind of the same sort (as - They are two of a kind - both fascinated by motor cars.); not up to much (as - She gave us a meal of a kind.)

kindergarten a school or class for very young children, who learn through games and toys

kindle to set fire to; to light: to arouse great interest or excitement

kindling sticks of wood, paper and other material used to start a fire

king a male head of a nation who inherits his position by right of birth (succeeding the previous ruler); a person or animal considered to be the strongest, the most important, etc. (as - The lion is king of beasts. Mr. X is called an oil king because he controls several international oil companies.); a playing card with the picture of a king

kingdom a state having a king or queen as its head; a monarchy; one of the three great divisions of all objects in nature (the animal kingdom, the vegetable kingdom, the mineral kingdom)

kingfisher a small, brilliantly-coloured crested bird with a long, sharp beak (It dives for fish in rivers and streams.)

kink a short twist or curl in string, rope, etc.: a peculiarity or odd way of behaving

kiosk an open-fronted stall or booth for the sale of newspapers, magazines, sweets, tobacco, etc.; a public telephone box

kipper a herring which has been split open, seasoned and dried in smoke

kiss to touch with your lips (especially as a sign of love or affection); (poetic) to touch gently (as - The sun kissed the roses in the garden.)

kiss of life a mouth-to-mouth method of restoring breathing to an injured person

kit a complete outfit; all the gear or equipment needed for an activity or job (as, a tool kit, a soldier's kit)

kitbag a strong bag for holding equipment

kitchen a room where cooking is done

kitchenette a very small kitchen (as in a small modern flat where there is not much space)

kite a bird of prey of the hawk family: a light frame, covered with paper or cloth, for flying in the air at the end of a long string

kith see kin

kitten a young cat

kiwi a New Zealand bird that cannot fly (It has no tail and small useless wings.)

kleptomania a compulsive urge to steal

kleptomaniac a person who suffers from kleptomania

knack the ability to do something easily and skilfully

knapsack a case or bag for food, etc. which a hiker carries on his back; a rucksack

knave a dishonest person; a rogue; a playing card having the picture of a servant or soldier (the jack)

knavery dishonesty

knavish cheating; dishonest

knead to press and work together into a mass with the fingers (as, to knead dough)

knee the joint in the middle part of the leg, between the thigh and shin bone

kneel to rest on or go down on bent knee(s)

kneecap the flat round bone on the front of the knee joint

knell a slow tolling of a bell (especially at a death or a funeral)

knickerbockers loose breeches gathered in at the knee

knickers short underpants worn by girls and women

knick-knack a small ornamental object (usually of little value)

knife an instrument for cutting, made of a thin sharp metal blade attached to a handle

knives the plural of knife

knight (in former times) a nobleman who served his king or other superior as a man-at-arms; a man of rank with the title *Sir*; a piece in the game of chess (usually with a horse's head)

knighthood the rank or title of knight (as - He was given a knighthood for his service to the queen.)

knight-errant (in mediaeval times) a chivalrous knight who travelled around in search of adventure

knit to form (fabric or a garment) from yarn or thread by making and connecting loops with knitting needles; (of brows) to pull together in a frown or when thinking hard; to grow or cause to draw firmly together (as - The broken bones in his leg took some time to knit together.)

knitting a garment or fabric that is knitted

knitting needle a thin pointed rod of metal, plastic or wood, used in knitting

knob a rounded lump on the surface of something; a rounded handle on a door, cupboard, drawer, etc.

knock to strike with something hard; to bump or be driven against; to rap for admittance (as to knock on a door) □ a sudden stroke; a rap

knocker a hinged metal device on a door for knocking

knock-kneed having knees that touch in walking

knock out (k.o.) a blow, in a boxing match, that knocks an opponent senseless □ to deliver such a blow

knoll a small rounded hill

knot a tie or join made in rope, string, etc. by intertwining parts together and then pulling them tight; a hard joint or lump in a piece of wood: 1 nautical mile per hour (or about 1840 metres per hour) □ to tie in a knot

knotted containing knots

knotty full of knots; difficult (as, a knotty problem)

know to have learned something and be able to remember it; to recognize (as - He knows my father.); to be aware of or to understand (as - He knows a lot about foreign stamps.)

knowing shrewd; cunning (as, a knowing look)

knowingly intentionally

knowledge what has been learned and understood

know-how the practical knowledge and skill to deal with something

knuckle a finger joint

koala an Australian tree-climbing animal that looks like a small bear

kookaburra see **jackass**

Koran the holy book of the Mohammedans

kudos fame; glory

l

label a slip of paper with writing or printing on it (Labels are attached to bottles, boxes, etc. to indicate what is inside, or on luggage to show the name and address of the owner.) □ to fix a label to

laboratory a place where scientific experiments are carried out

labour hard work; workers considered collectively (as, labour in the steel industry) □ to work hard; to move slowly or with difficulty (as - The old car laboured up the hill.)

laborious requiring hard work (as, a laborious task); wearisome

laboured showing signs of effort

labourer someone who does work requiring little skill

laburnum a kind of small tree

with hanging clusters of yellow flowers

labyrinth a maze; a place full of windings

lace a string for fastening shoes, etc.: a net-like ornamental fabric made of fine thread □ to fasten with a lace

lacerate to tear; to wound

lack to be in need of something; to be without something □ a need or want
lack-lustre without brightness

lackadaisical listless; sentimental in a weak way

laconic using few words (as, speaking in a laconic manner)

lacquer a kind of varnish made from a resin □ to cover with lacquer

lacrosse a team-game something like hockey, but the stick has a shallow net at one end

lactic having to do with milk

lad a boy; a youth

ladder a long frame consisting of a set of steps (called rungs) between two upright pieces of wood or metal, used for climbing up or down: a run in a stocking, etc. caused by broken threads □ to cause such a run

ladle a large, cuplike spoon with a long handle, used for lifting liquid □ to lift in a ladle

lady a woman; a title given to the wife of a lord, a baronet or a knight
ladies the plural of lady
ladybird a tiny round beetle (usually red with black spots)

lag to move slowly and fall behind
laggard someone who lags behind □ slow

lager a light kind of beer

lagoon a shallow pond connected with the sea

lair the den of a wild animal

laity see lay 3

lake a large expanse of water surrounded by land

lamb a young sheep (usually under one year old); the meat of this animal

lame crippled; unable to walk; unsatisfactory (as, a lame excuse) □ to make lame
lameness disablement in a leg
lame duck a helpless, or very inefficient, person or firm

• **lament** to mourn; to show grief □ a show of grief; a mournful poem or song
lamentable sad; regrettable
lamentation the act of lamenting; a lament

laminated made up of thin layers (as, laminated plastics)

lamp a glass-covered light

lance a long spear □ to pierce with a surgical instrument (as, to lance a boil so that the skin can heal up)
lancer (formerly) a soldier armed with a lance
lancet a surgical cutting instrument
lance corporal an acting corporal (one not yet promoted)

land the parts of the earth that are not covered by water; a country; an estate (as, a farmer's land) □ to come down from the air on to land or water; to set foot on land from a ship
landing a coming to shore or to ground; the level part of a staircase between flights of steps
landfall an approach to land after a journey
landlady a woman who keeps a boarding-house or inn, or has tenants
land-locked almost shut in by land (as, a land-locked harbour)
landlord a man who keeps an inn or rents any property to tenants
landlubber (a term of scorn used by sailors) a landsman; a person who lives on land and has little knowledge of the sea
landmark any prominent object on land that serves as a guide to seamen
landscape inland scenery; a picture showing this

landslide a mass of land that falls down from the side of a hill (usually due to the effect of heavy rains)

landward(s) towards the land

lane a narrow road or street; a division of a road for a single line of traffic

language human speech; a distinct variety of speech (vocabulary and usage) used in a country (such as English, French, Spanish, etc.); any way of expressing thought (as, the deaf-and-dumb language)
bad language swearing

languid listless; feeble; spiritless
languish to grow weak or feeble
languor *(say lang-gor)* the state of being languid or listless

lank tall and thin; straight and limp (as, lank hair)
lanky lean, tall and ungainly

lantern a case with windows for carrying or holding a light

lanyard, laniard a short rope used as a fastening on a ship; a cord for hanging a whistle, etc. round the neck

lap 1 the part from the waist to the knees of a person sitting down; a fold; one round of a racetrack

lap 2 to lick up with the tongue; (of water) to wash against the shore

lapel the front part of a coat which is folded back and continues the collar

lapse to fall back through lack of effort; to cease to be of use (as - If a television licence is not renewed it will lapse.) □ a slip or mistake (as, a lapse of memory); a passage of time (as, after a lapse of two years)

lapwing a bird of the plover family (also called the peewit)

larceny the legal term for stealing or theft

larch a kind of deciduous cone-bearing tree

lard the melted fat of the pig used in cooking □ to smear

larder a small room or enclosed place where food is kept

large great in size or quantity
at large at liberty; as a whole (as, the population at large)

lariat a rope for fastening horses; a lasso

lark 1 a kind of small songbird (for example, the skylark)

lark 2 a frolic; a prank □ to frolic

larkspur a tall garden plant which has pink, white or blue flowers

larva a grub or an insect after it has left the egg but before it turns into an adult (for example, the caterpillar of a butterfly)
larvae the plural of larva

larynx the upper part of the windpipe
laryngitis *(say larinjietis)* inflammation of the larynx (which makes the throat feel sore)

laser a device which concentrates light into a very narrow and powerful beam

lash the thong or cord of a whip; a stroke with a whip: an eyelash □ to strike with a lash; to fasten with a rope or cord
lash out to kick or hit out recklessly

lass a girl (the feminine of lad)

lassitude weariness

lasso a long rope with a running loop at the end, used for catching wild horses or cattle □ to catch with a lasso

last 1 coming at the end; final

last 2 to continue or go on (as - The game lasted a long time.); to remain in good condition

last 3 a model of a foot (used by shoemakers and repairers)

latch a wood or metal fastening for a door □ to fasten with a latch
latchkey a small key for a latched door

late behind time; the opposite of early; far on in the day or night: recently dead (as, the late

Mr. Smith)
lately, of late recently

latent lying hidden or undeveloped (as, a latent ability)

lateral from, or placed on, the side

latex *(say laytex)* the milky juice of some plants (especially that collected from the rubber tree)

lath a thin narrow strip of wood

lathe *(say laythe)* a machine for turning and shaping articles of wood, metal, etc.

lather a foam made with soap and water □ to cover with lather

Latin the language of ancient Rome

latitude the distance of a place north or south of the equator (It is measured in degrees, 1 degree representing about 69 miles or 110 kilometres.): freedom from restraint

latter the second-mentioned of two persons or things (the first-mentioned being the former); recent

lattice a network of crossed wooden strips
lattice-work a lattice

laud to praise (used mainly in hymns)
laudable praiseworthy

laugh to make sounds with the voice to show amusement, happiness, etc., but also scorn □ a sound caused by laughing
laughable amusing; ridiculous
laughter the act or noise of laughing
laughing-stock an object of scornful laughter

launch 1 to send forth or start something on its way (as, to launch a ship); to throw or hurl
launching-pad a platform from which a rocket can be launched

launch 2 a large, power-driven boat

launder to wash and iron clothes
launderette a shop with self-service washing machines
laundress a woman who washes and irons clothes

laundry a place where clothes are washed and ironed; a bundle of clothes, etc. to be laundered

laurel an evergreen shrub or tree (sweet bay) with large glossy leaves

lava the substances thrown out in a molten stream from a volcano

lavatory a small room with a washbasin or water-closet (W.C.), sometimes both together

lavender a plant with small flowers of a pale purple colour, from which a perfume is made; a pale purple colour

lavish to spend freely □ too free in spending; extravagant

law the rules for governing a country (some made by Parliament, others established by custom); a statute or particular written rule; (in science) a rule which states that, under certain conditions, the same things always happen (as, Newton's laws of motion)
lawful allowed by law; rightful
lawless paying no attention to the laws; unruly
law-abiding obedient to the law
law court a court of law where persons accused of breaking the law are tried
lawsuit a dispute which has to be taken to a court of law for judgment
lawyer a person who practises law (a barrister, or a solicitor, etc.)

lawn 1 a flat area of well-kept grass
lawnmower a machine for cutting the grass on a lawn

lawn 2 a kind of fine linen

lax slack or loose; not strict in discipline or conduct
laxity, laxness slackness or looseness; carelessness
laxative a medicine that loosens the bowels (thus relieving constipation)

lay 1 to put someone or something down (as, to lay a baby in a cot); to place in position (as when laying a table); (of hens) to produce eggs; to set (as - He laid a trap.)

layer a thickness or covering (as, a layer of soil)

lay-by a parking place at the side of a main road

lay 2 see **lie 2**

lay 3 having to do with ordinary people as distinct from clergymen (as, a lay reader of lessons in a church)

laity lay persons

layman someone who is not of the clergy; someone who is not a member of a particular profession

layette a complete outfit for a newborn child

lazy not wanting to work or make any effort; idle

lead *(say leed)* to show the way by going first; to conduct to a place (as - That road leads to the village.); to guide (as - His action leads me to believe that I can trust him.); to live (as - That beggar leads a miserable life.) □ the first or front place (as, to take the lead); guidance; a leash for a dog, etc.

leader a person who leads; a chief; a newspaper article written by the editor (also called a leading article)

leadership the position of a leader; the ability to lead other people

lead 2 *(say led)* a heavy soft grey metal

leaden made of lead; dull; heavy

lead pencil a blacklead pencil for writing or drawing (It contains graphite, not lead.)

leaf one of the many flat parts of a plant or tree (usually green) which grow out from the stems or branches; anything as thin as a leaf (as, the leaves of a book); a hinged flap (as, the leaf of a table)

leaflet a little leaf; a small printed sheet of paper (as, an instruction leaflet)

leafy full of leaves

league 1 a union or alliance for the benefit of all members (as, the League of Nations 1919-1946); an association of clubs for games (as, the Football League)

league 2 an old measure of length (about 3 miles, or 5 kilometres)

leak an escape of liquid or gas through a hole or crack; the hole or crack itself; an escape of secret information □ to have a leak; to escape through a leak

leakage a leaking; anything that enters or escapes by leaking (as, a leakage of rain through a roof)

leaky having leaks (as, a leaky bucket)

lean 1 to slope to one side; to rest against or on something

leaning an inclination or preference □ not quite vertical (as, the Leaning Tower of Pisa)

lean-to a shed which is propped against a building or wall

lean 2 thin; not fat; bringing little profit (as, a lean year) □ flesh without fat

leap to jump; to rush eagerly (as, to leap forward) □ a jump

leap-frog a game in which one player vaults over another who is bending over

leap year every fourth year (when there are 366 days and February has 29 instead of 28, as, for example 1972 and 1976)

learn to find out about things or how to do something; to memorize (as, to learn a poem by heart)

learned *(say lern-ed)* having much knowledge

learning knowledge; scholarship

lease a contract letting a house, shop, etc. for a number of years □ to let, or rent, for an agreed period

leasehold a letting of property by lease

lessee someone to whom a lease is granted

leash a line for holding a dog, etc. □ to put on a leash

least smallest in size or importance
at least at any rate; in any case

leather the skin of an animal prepared for manufacture into shoes, gloves, etc.
leathery like leather; tough (as, leathery meat)

leave to let something remain in a place (as, to leave a book on a table); to go away from a person or place (as, to leave home on holiday, to leave the younger children with their mother); to allow someone to do something (as - Leave it to me!); to bequeath (as - Her grandmother left her a gold chain.) □ permission (as - He was given leave of absence for three days.); a holiday or period of absence (as, seven days' leave from the army)
leavings things left over

leaven (say lev'n) a substance which makes dough rise

lectern a reading desk in a church

lecture a formal talk on a subject to an audience; a warning or scolding □ to deliver a lecture
lecturer a person who lectures

ledge a narrow shelf or shelf-like projection

ledger the chief book of accounts in an office

lee the side away from the wind; the sheltered side
leeward in the direction towards which the wind blows
leeway the distance of course that a ship or aeroplane is driven to leeward by the prevailing wind

leech a blood-sucking worm

leek a vegetable of the onion family (the national emblem of Wales)

leer a sly, sideways look □ to give such a look

left the side opposite to the right □ on, or belonging to, the left (as - Put your left foot forward.)

left-handed using the left hand rather than the right hand

leg one of the limbs which human beings and animals use in order to walk; the part of a garment that covers the leg; a support (as, a table leg)
leggings outer coverings for the legs below the knees
leggy having long, rather thin legs

legacy something left by will; a bequest

legal allowed by law; lawful; having to do with the law (as, a legal document)

legation a diplomatic minister and his mission to another country; the official residence of a legation

legend a story passed down from generation to generation
legendary told as a legend; not historical

legible clear enough to be read (as, legible handwriting)

legion a large number of soldiers; a large number of people

legislate to make laws
legislation laws; the passing of laws

legitimate lawful; genuine; born of parents who are married to each other

leisure (say lezhure) spare time; time free from employment
leisurely without haste; taking plenty of time (as, a leisurely journey)

lemming a small arctic gnawing animal (rather like a water rat)

lemon an oval citrus fruit with yellow rind and sour juice
lemonade a drink made with lemon juice and sugar

lend to let someone have the use of something for a time (as - He lent some money to his friend until the end of the month.)

length the measurement of something from end to end (as, a ruler whose length is 30 centimetres); an extent of time (as, the length of a school term)

lengthen to increase in length
lengthways, lengthwise in the direction of the length
lengthy of great length (as, a lengthy, often tiresome, speech)

lenient mild or merciful (as, a lenient punishment)

lens a piece of glass with curved surfaces as used in eyeglasses, cameras, telescopes and microscopes

lentil the seed of a pea-like plant used for food (especially in soup)

leopard a large wild animal of the cat family, with a spotted skin

leper a person who has leprosy: an outcast
leprosy a chronic skin disease

less smaller (as, of less importance) □ not so much (as - She now eats less stodgy food.); in a lower degree (as, less often) □ a smaller amount (as, much less)
lessen to make, or become, less
lesser smaller (as, to a lesser extent)

lessee see under **lease**

lesson something to be learned, or to be taught; a passage from the Bible read in church

let to allow or permit; to grant the use of a house or other property in return for payment (rent)
let down to lower; to disappoint
let off to excuse; to allow to go free: to discharge (a gun)

lethal (say leethal) causing death

lethargy heavy drowsiness or sleepiness; lack of energy
lethargic unnaturally sleepy; sluggish

letter a written or printed mark expressing a speech sound (as, the 26 letters of the English alphabet); a written or printed message (as, a business letter)
lettering the way in which letters are printed (as, bold or thick lettering)

lettuce a green plant with large leaves, used as a salad

level flat and even (as, a level piece of ground); horizontal; equal or in the same line (as - The two swimmers were level at the 50 metre mark.) □ to make level; (of a gun) to aim
level crossing a crossing of a road and a railway on the same level

lever a bar of metal or wood placed on a support and pushed down at one end in order to raise or shift a heavy object at the other end □ to move as with a lever
leverage the power gained by using a lever

leveret a young hare

leviathan (say levie-athan) a sea monster; anything of huge size

levity lack of seriousness; frivolity

levy to collect by order (as, to levy a tax) □ money collected, or troops raised, by authority

lexicon a dictionary

liable responsible for something (as, being liable for a debt); apt to (as - That dog is liable to bark at every passer-by.)
liability the state of being liable; a debt

liar see **lie 1**

libel anything printed or written which is damaging to a person's reputation □ to defame by libel: see also **slander**
libellous containing a libel (as, a libellous statement)

liberal generous; broadminded; (of education) not specialized or technical but all-round
liberality generosity

liberate to set free; to set at liberty
liberation a setting free; a release
liberty freedom from captivity; freedom to do as one pleases

library a room or building containing a collection of books; a large collection of books for lending or for reference

librarian the keeper of a library

libretto the words of an opera, oratorio, etc.

lice see **louse**

licence a printed official paper giving legal permission for something (as, television licence, car licence, dog licence, etc.)

license to grant a licence to; to permit

licensee someone to whom a licence has been granted

lichen *(say lieken)* a tiny fungus-like plant which grows on the surface of rocks, tree-trunks, etc. giving them a greenish, grey or yellow colouring

lick to pass the tongue over (as, to lick an ice cream or a stamp) □ an act of licking

licorice see **liquorice**

lid a cover for a container; the eyelid

lie 1 a false statement intended to deceive □ to make such a statement

liar someone who tells lies

lying 1 the habit of telling lies □ in the habit of telling lies (as, a lying rogue)

lie 2 to rest in a flat position (as, to lie in bed); to be in a certain position (as - The village lies two miles to the west.); to remain (as, to lie still, lie hidden)

lay 2 the action of **lie 2** in the past (as - He was so tired he lay down on the ground to rest.)

lying 2 being in a flat position (as - The sick man is lying on the hospital bed.)

lie low to keep quiet or hidden

lieutenant *(say leftenant)* an army officer next below a captain

life the state of being alive; the opposite of death; the period between birth and death; a manner of living (as, the life of a sailor) □ lasting for life (as, life imprisonment)

life belt a cork belt, or one filled with air, for keeping a person afloat in water

life boat a boat for saving ship-wrecked persons

life buoy a cork ring used to keep a person afloat in water

lifeless dead; without vigour (as, a lifeless performance in a play)

lifelike like a living person

lifelong lasting the length of a life

lifetime the length of time a person or a thing lasts (as - This car should have a lifetime of more than ten years.)

lift to raise to a higher position; to take and carry away □ the act of lifting; an enclosed platform that carries persons or goods up and down in a building

ligament a tough fibrous tissue which connects the movable bones of the body

ligature anything that binds; a bandage

light 1 something which shines and allows us to see (as, the light of the sun or moon); the actual source of a light (as, a lamp or a flame); the opposite of the dark (as, standing in the light) □ not dark (as, a light colour); bright □ to give light to; to set fire to (as, to light the gas)

lighten 1 to make, or become, brighter

lighter 1 a small device for lighting cigarettes, etc.

lighthouse a high building with a strong light to guide or warn ships or aircraft

lightship a ship anchored in a fixed position to serve as a lighthouse

light-year the distance light travels in a year (about 6,000,000,000,000 miles)

light 2 not heavy; easy to bear, to do or to digest (as, a light meal); little in quantity (as, a light rain or mist); amusing (as, light reading)

lighten 2 to make, or become, less heavy

lighter 2 a large open boat used in unloading and loading ships

light-hearted cheerful
lightly gently; slightly

lightning a large electric flash during a thunderstorm (either between two clouds or from a cloud to earth)

like 1 the same as; similar
likely probable; promising (as, a likely candidate)
likelihood the state of being probable
likeness a resemblance; something that is like a person or some other thing (as - That photo is a good likeness.)
likewise in like manner; also

like 2 to be pleased with; to be fond of
likable, likeable of a pleasing nature; amiable
liking a fondness or a taste for

lilac a garden shrub with cone-shaped clusters of sweet-smelling white or light-purple flowers □ light purple in colour

lilt a cheerful tune or song

lily a tall garden plant with large showy white or brightly-coloured flowers
lily of the valley a small plant with white bell-shaped flowers which have a sweet scent

limb an arm or leg: a branch

limber supple; flexible
limber up to make the body supple by doing some exercises

lime 1 the white substance (calcium oxide) left after heating limestone and used in making cement
limelight a strong white light obtained by heating lime in a special way: the glare of publicity
limestone a kind of rock composed chiefly of calcium carbonate

lime 2 a greenish sour fruit something like a small lemon
lime juice the juice of the lime sweetened and used as a drink

lime 3 see **linden**

limerick a humorous verse in a five-line jingle

limit a boundary; the farthest point □ to restrict or keep to a limit (as, to limit pocket money to a fixed amount each week or month)
limitation a restriction; a shortcoming

limousine a large closed motor car

limp 1 the opposite of stiff; drooping

limp 2 to walk lamely □ a lame walk

limpet a small shellfish that clings to rocks

limpid clear or transparent (as, a limpid stream)

linden, lime 3 the European lime tree

line 1 any long narrow mark; a thread, cord or rope; a wire (as, a telephone or telegraph line); a row of persons or things (as, a line of soldiers, of trees); a railway or underground track; a shipping or aircraft service; a class of goods (as, a shop stocking many lines); a kind of occupation or interest (as - That is not in my line.) □ to make a line or lines on something
lines the plural of line; a written punishment or task
lineage (say lineeaj) one's ancestry
lineal (say lineeal) (of ancestry) in a direct line (as from grandfather to father and from father to son)
linear (of measurements) in one dimension only (that is, length alone, but not length and breadth)
liner a large ship sailing on a regular shipping line

line 2 to cover on the inside
lining an inner layer or covering (especially material used to line a garment)

linen cloth made of flax; articles made of linen (such as sheets and tablecloths)

linger to loiter; to stay about

linguist (say lingwist) someone who studies, or is skilled

in languages
linguistic having to do with languages

liniment an oily liquid for rubbing on the skin (It helps to ease aching muscles, sprains, etc.)

link a ring in a chain □ to connect as by a link
missing link any point or fact needed to complete a series

links a golf course

linnet a small songbird of the finch family

linoleum a smooth floor covering manufactured from jute, linseed oil and powdered cork

linotype a machine which produces solid lines of type for printing (as distinct from the individual letters produced by a monotype machine)

linseed flax seed
linseed oil oil from flax seed

lint a soft woolly substance for dressing sores or wounds

lintel the timber or stone support over a doorway or window

lion a large yellowish-brown flesh-eating animal of the cat family
lioness a female lion
lionize to treat a person as a celebrity
lion's share the largest share

lip one of the soft, fleshy edges of the mouth; the edge of anything (as, the lip of a jug)
lip service saying that one approves of someone or something without meaning it
lipstick rouge in crayon form (used by girls and women to colour their lips)

liqueur *(say leeker or likyour)* a strong alcoholic drink, usually sweet and strongly flavoured

liquid a flowing substance; a fluid, such as water, which is not in gas form □ able to flow; (of sound) soft and clear
liquefy to make or become liquid
liquidate to clear or settle up affairs, pay debts, etc. (as, to

liquidate a bankrupt company)
liquid oxygen oxygen converted to a liquid condition at a very low temperature

liquor any alcoholic drink; the liquid product of cooking, etc.

liquorice a plant with a sweet root used in some medicines and sweets

lisp to speak imperfectly, pronouncing the sounds *s* and *z* like *th* □ the habit of lisping

list 1 a series of words or numbers written down one after another in a column (as, a list of names) □ to write down in a list

list 2 (of a ship) to lean, or heel over to one side □ such a leaning over

listen to give attention so as to hear something; to follow advice

listless without energy or interest; languid

lists (in olden times) an enclosed ground for jousting between knights

literal according to the plain, exact meaning with no exaggeration (as - That is the literal truth!)
literally exactly as stated

literary having to do with literature or learning
literate able to read and write
literacy the ability to read and write
literature verse and prose compositions (especially those of fine quality); the whole body of such compositions in a language (as, English, or French, literature)

lithe *(say lieth)* supple; flexible

lithography a method of printing from a flat surface

litigation the settling of a dispute by law

litre a measurement of capacity (1 litre = about $1^3/_4$ pints)

litter 1 rubbish or waste paper left lying about; a heap of straw, etc. for animals to lie on □ to scatter about carelessly

litter 2 all the young of an animal born at the same time (as, a litter of puppies)

little small in size or quantity □ a small amount □ not much

live 1 *(say liv)* to have life; to continue to be alive; to dwell (as - He lives next door.)
livelong *(say livlong)* whole, entire (as, the livelong day)
living having life □ an occupation or means of keeping oneself alive (as, a good living)
living room a sitting room for general use

live 2 *(say liev)* having life; not dead; active (as, live bullets, a live electric wire); (of a broadcast or telecast) as actually heard or seen, not recorded beforehand
livelihood a person's means of living or daily occupation
lively full of life or high spirits; active
liven to make lively; to brighten up
live rail a rail carrying an electric current
livestock farm animals

liver a large gland in the body (One of its main functions is to purify the blood.)

livery a uniform worn by menservants

livid black and blue; of a bluish, lead colour; pale, ashen: extremely angry

lizard a scaly reptile with four legs and a long tail

llama a South American animal of the camel family, but without any humps

load a burden; as much as can be carried at one time (as, a load of bricks) □ to put a load on to something or someone: to charge a gun with bullets, or a camera with film

loadstone a piece of iron ore which acts like a magnet

loaf 1 a shaped mass of bread
loaves the plural of loaf

loaf 2 to loiter; to pass time idly

loam a fertile soil containing some vegetable matter

loan anything lent for a time, especially money at interest □ to lend

loath, loth unwilling (to)

loathe to dislike greatly
loathing extreme dislike or disgust
loathsome causing loathing; horrible; disgusting

lobby an entrance hall; a passage serving as an entrance (usually) to several rooms

lobster a shellfish with large claws, used for food

local of or belonging to a particular place or district (as, the local public house, cinema, etc.)
localize to restrict to one place or area
locality a district
locate to find where something is (as, to locate a buried treasure, or a town on a map)
location a situation; the act of locating

lock 1 a strong fastening for a door or gate that can only be opened with a key; an enclosure in a canal for raising or lowering boats from one level to another; a tight hold in wrestling □ to fasten with a lock
locker a small cupboard for sports gear, personal belongings, etc.
lockjaw tetanus (a disease which stiffens the jaw muscles)
lockout (in a trade dispute) the act of locking out employees by an employer
locksmith a smith who makes and mends locks

lock 2 a curl or tuft of hair

locomotive a railway engine □ moving from place to place
locomotion movement from place to place

locust an insect like a large grasshopper (Locusts move in swarms, feeding on and destroying all vegetation and crops.)

lodge a small house at the entrance to a park or at the gates of a large house in the country; a house usually only occupied during the shooting or hunting season □ to live in someone else's house as a lodger; to become fixed in (as, a stone lodged in one's shoe)

lodger a person who pays to live in someone else's house

lodgings one or more rooms occupied by a lodger or lodgers

loft a room or space just under a roof which can be used for storing things

lofty very high (as, a lofty tree); proud; haughty (as, a lofty manner)

log a part of a felled tree; a thick piece of unshaped wood: a logbook □ to write down events in a logbook

logbook a daily record of a ship's or aeroplane's progress, kept by the captain

loganberry a dark-red fruit like a large raspberry

logic the science and art of reasoning

logical according to the rules of logic; according to sound reasoning

loin a cut of meat from the back of an animal used for food (as, loin chops)

loins the lower part of the back

loincloth a piece of cloth worn round the hips (especially in south-east Asia)

loiter to linger

loll to sit or lie about in a lazy way

lollipop a large sweet on a stick

lone by oneself; solitary

lonely alone; without friends; isolated (as, a lonely spot)

loneliness the feeling or state of being lonely

lonesome feeling lonely; solitary

long the opposite of short (as, a long distance, a long time, etc.); taking a considerable time to utter, to perform, etc. □ to wish for something very much

longing an eager desire

longbow a large bow drawn by hand

longhand the ordinary way of writing (as, distinct from short-hand or typewriting)

long-playing (of a gramophone record) playing for a long time because of an extremely fine groove

long-range able to reach a long distance (as, a long-range gun); covering a relatively long future time (as, a long-range forecast)

long-sighted able to see distant things very well, but not those which are close; having foresight

long-suffering putting up with troubles patiently for a long time

long-winded able to run far without resting: speaking or writing at tiresome length

longevity (*say* lon*jev*ity) great length of life

longitude (*say* lon*ji*tude) the distance of a place east or west of the Greenwich meridian (measured in degrees on a map; see also **latitude**)

look to direct the eyes so as to see someone or something; to seem (as - She looks happy.); to face (as, a room looking towards the sea) □ the act of looking; appearance (as - The office had an untidy look.); a facial expression (as, an angry look)

looking-glass a mirror

lookout a careful watch; an observation post or the person posted there as watcher (as, the lookout in a ship's crow's-nest)

Look out! Be careful!

loom 1 a machine for weaving thread into cloth

loom 2 to appear dimly (often in a magnified, threatening way, as, a ship looming through the fog)

loop a piece of string, ribbon, wire, etc. twisted into a ring; a closed, or nearly closed, bend or curve

loophole a hole or slit in a wall; a means of escape

to loop the loop to fly an aeroplane in a complete vertical loop or circle

loose *(say looss)* slack; the opposite of tight; not tied; not closely packed
loosen to make loose

loot plunder □ to plunder

lop to cut off the top or ends of (as, to lop a tree)

lope to run with long strides

lop-sided leaning to one side more than to the other

loquacious *(say lokwayshus)* talkative

lord a titled nobleman; part of an official title (as, Lord Mayor): (the Lord) God, Christ
lordly dignified; haughty
lordship a word used when addressing, or referring to, a lord (as, Your Lordship, His Lordship)

lore learning (especially of a traditional kind)

lorry an open motor vehicle used to transport heavy loads

lose *(say looz)* to be unable to find something; to mislay; to have taken away from one by accident, theft, etc.; to miss (as, to lose a train); the opposite of win (as, to lose a race)
loser someone who loses
loss the act, or fact, of losing; something that is lost
lost missing; thrown away (as, a lost opportunity, a lost cause)

lot a large number or quantity (as, a lot of money); one's fortune in life (as - His lot is a sorry one.)

loth see **loath**

lotion a soothing or healing liquid to be applied to the skin

lottery a sharing out of money or prizes won by chance

lotus an African or Indian water-lily: a legendary tree

loud making a great sound; the opposite of quiet; showy
loudspeaker an instrument for reproducing sounds so that they can be heard at a distance

lounge to move about lazily □ a sitting room (especially a large one in a hotel)
lounger an idler
lounge suit a man's ordinary suit for daily, informal wear

louse a small wingless insect which is a kind of parasite
lice the plural of louse

love great fondness or affection; a devoted attachment to someone of the opposite sex; a loved person: (in tennis, etc.) a score of nothing □ to have the feeling of love for someone; to enjoy very much
lovable worthy of love
lovely beautiful; attractive
lover someone in love with a person of the opposite sex; a person who loves something (as, a lover of the theatre)
loving very affectionate

low 1 not high (as, a low building, a low price); not lying or reaching far up (as, low clouds); not loud (as, speaking in a low voice); sad (as, feeling in low spirits)
lower less high □ to make less high; to let down (as, to lower a flag)
lowlands relatively low-lying country (as, the Lowlands of Scotland)
lowly humble in rank

low 2 to make the noise of cattle; to moo
lowing the noise made by cattle

loyal faithful

lozenge a diamond shape; a kind of small sweet or medicine of this shape

lubricate *(say loobricate)* to oil or grease (as, to lubricate an engine)
lubricant an oil or grease used to reduce friction
lubrication the application of lubricants

lucid *(say loosid)* easily understood; clear-minded

luck fortune, good or bad; chance; good luck (as - Wish

me luck!)

lucky having good luck; fortunate

lucre *(say looker)* money (especially money gained selfishly)
lucrative profitable

ludicrous *(say loodicrus)* absurd; silly enough to be laughed at

lug to pull along or drag with effort
luggage a traveller's baggage

lugger a small vessel with square sails

lugubrious mournful; dismal

lukewarm slightly warm; half-hearted (as, lukewarm interest)

lull to soothe or calm □ an interval of calm (as, a lull before a storm)
lullaby a song to lull young children to sleep

lumbago *(say lumbaygo)* a painful condition in the lower part of the back
lumbar of, or in, the lower part of the back

lumber timber which has been sawn up or split: useless old furniture and other bulky objects □ to fill with useless things: to move heavily and clumsily
lumberjack a man employed in felling, sawing and shifting timber

luminous giving light; shining; clear

lump a small shapeless mass (as, a lump of clay, coal, etc.); a swelling □ to throw together and treat alike (as, to lump together all the vegetables in one basket)
lumpy full of lumps; like a lump

lunar having to do with the moon (as, a lunar crater)

lunatic an insane person; a madman □ extremely foolish; affected with lunacy
lunacy insanity; a kind of madness

lunch, luncheon a midday meal □ to take lunch

lung one of the two main organs inside the chest which are used

for breathing air in and out

lunge a sudden thrust or push □ to make such a thrust (as, to lunge forward)

lupin a garden plant with long spikes of brightly-coloured flowers

lurch to pitch forward suddenly, or roll to one side □ a lurching movement

lure to tempt away; to entice □ something which entices or tempts away

lurid glaringly reddish-yellow in colour; ghastly; highly sensational (as, a lurid cinema film)

lurk to lie in wait in a hidden position

luscious very sweet; especially juicy and delicious (as, a luscious fruit)

lush green and luxuriant (as, a meadow of lush grass)

lust a depraved desire; an excessive desire (as, a lust for power for its own sake) □ to have depraved or excessive desires
lusty vigorous or healthy

lustre brightness; gloss; splendour
lustrous bright; shining

lute (in olden times) a stringed musical instrument shaped like a half pear

luxury something pleasant and often expensive, but not necessary in everyday life (for example, costly foods, very fine clothes and furniture, expensive holidays); indulgence in these things
luxuriant showing abundant growth of leaves and branches (as, a luxuriant forest)
luxurious given luxuries and great comfort (as, a luxurious way of life)

lying 1 see **lie 1**

lying 2 see **lie 2**

lynch to judge and put to death without a legal trial

lynx a wild animal of the cat family, noted for its sharp sight lyre (in ancient times) a musical instrument like a small harp

lyric a short poem expressing the personal feelings of the poet; the words for a song

lyrical, lyric expressing individual feelings or great enthusiasm

m

mac an abbreviation of **mackintosh**

macaroni a food made of stiff tubes of wheat paste that become soft when cooked

macaroon a small sweet cake or biscuit made of crushed almonds, sugar and white of egg

macaw a brilliantly-coloured, big tropical parrot with long tail feathers and a harsh cry

mace 1 a staff with an ornamental metal top, once used as a weapon, but nowadays carried on ceremonial occasions as a sign of authority

mace 2 a spice made from the outer covering of nutmeg

machine a combination of parts (such as wheels, levers, etc.) which work together to do a job (as, a sewing machine, an adding machine) or to make something move (as, a motor cycle); an engine □ to use machinery for (as, to machine a dress); to make something with a machine tool

machinery machines in general; the working parts of a machine

machinist a person who makes or who operates a machine

machine-gun an automatic gun, mounted on a portable stand, which fires bullets rapidly one after another

machine shop a workshop where metal, etc. is shaped by machine tools

machine tool a power-driven machine that shapes metal, wood, plastic, etc. by cutting, pressing, etc.

mackerel a sea fish used for food, bluish green with wavy markings above, and silvery below

mackintosh a raincoat made of waterproof material (named after the man who patented the material, Charles Macintosh)

mad insane; out of one's mind; crazy; very foolish or unwise (as - That was a mad thing to do.); angry or furious; frantic (as, mad or maddened with pain); suffering with rabies (as, a mad dog)

madden to make (someone) mad or furious (as - The unnecessary delay maddened him.)

maddening irritating; very annoying

madness insanity; reckless or wild behaviour

madcap a reckless, impulsive person

madhouse (in former times) a lunatic asylum where insane people were kept; (nowadays) a place or situation full of noise and confusion

madman, madwoman a person who is insane

like mad with great energy; furiously

madam a polite form of address to a lady (for example, in a shop - Madam, may I help you?)

madonna the Virgin Mary (especially as shown in paintings and other works of art)

maelstrom a whirlpool; any place of confusion or disturbance

magazine 1 a storehouse for military supplies; the gunpowder room in a ship; a compartment in a rifle for holding extra cartridges

magazine 2 a publication issued weekly or monthly, with stories, articles and (usually) illustrations by various people

magenta a reddish-purple colour

maggot a small worm or grub found in bad meat, cheese, fruit, etc.

magic the art or power which is said to produce marvellous results with the help of the forces of nature or of supernatural beings; any unexplained influence that brings about surprising results; sorcery □ having to do with magic (as, a conjuror's magic wand)
magical produced by, or as if by, magic; mysteriously wonderful
magician a person who is skilled in magic; a conjuror
black magic magic done for an evil purpose
magic lantern an early device for projecting pictures on to a screen

magistrate a person who has the power to enforce laws (especially a Justice of the Peace, or a magistrate in a police court)

magnanimity nobleness of character; generosity
magnanimous generous; not petty-minded

magnesium a silvery-white metal that burns with a dazzling white light

magnet a bar or shaped piece of iron, steel, etc. which has the power to attract other pieces of iron, etc.; any person or thing that attracts strongly (as - The theatre was always a magnet to her.)
magnetic having the powers of a magnet; strongly attractive (as - She had a magnetic personality.)
magnetism the power or quality in the magnet that causes it to attract; the branch of science concerned with magnets; an unusually strong personal attraction or influence
magnetize to make (something) magnetic; to attract or influence strongly
magnetic ink ink with a magnetic quality, used to print cheques, etc. that are to be sorted by machine
magnetic needle a slender bar of magnetized steel (especially used in a mariner's compass) which always points to the magnetic north
magnetic north a northerly direction which is usually either to the east' or west of the geographical pole (the true north)
magnetic tape plastic tape coated on one side with magnetic material on which television pictures, sound, computer data, etc. can be recorded
magneto a small electric generator with a permanent magnet, used to ignite the fuel in a car engine

magnificent splendid in appearance; great or noble in deeds
magnificence splendour; grandeur

magnify to make something appear greater (as by looking at it through a magnifying glass); to exaggerate (as - She was apt to magnify her troubles.); (religious) to praise highly
magnitude greatness (of size); extent; importance (as - This is a discovery of the first magnitude.)

magnolia a tree or shrub with large glossy leaves and showy white, pink or purple flowers (usually fragrant)

magpie a noisy white and black bird of the crow family (It is well known for its habit of collecting bright, shiny objects.)

mahogany a tropical American tree; the hard reddish-brown wood of this tree, much used for furniture

maid an unmarried woman (especially a young one); a maiden; a female servant
maiden an unmarried girl □ first (as, a maiden speech, a maiden voyage, etc.)

maiden name the family name of a woman before her marriage (as - Mrs. Smith was Miss Jones before she was married.)

maid of honour an unmarried woman who attends a queen or princess; the chief woman attendant of a bride at her wedding

maidenhair a kind of fern with delicate stems and finely divided leaves

mail 1 anything that is sent through the post (such as letters and parcels) □ to post or send by post

mailbag a bag in which letters, parcels, etc. are sent or carried

mail order an order for goods to be sent by post (Payment is usually made with the order or on delivery.)

mail 2 body armour made of interlinked steel rings; armour in general

maim to cripple; to deprive (a person or animal) of the use of a limb, a foot, a toe, etc.; to wound or hurt seriously

main chief; principal; most important □ the principal pipe or tube in a system of pipes for carrying water, gas, etc. (as - Turn the water off at the main while the leak is mended.); strength or power (as - They fought with might and main.); the high sea (as, the Spanish Main)

mainly chiefly; mostly

maindeck, mainmast, mainsail, etc. the most important deck, mast, sail, etc. on a ship

mainland a large extent of land (in contrast to nearby islands)

mainspring the chief spring in a mechanism (such as a clock or watch) that causes movement

mainstay a rope on a ship stretching forward from the mainmast: the chief support (as - His cheerful help was the family's mainstay during a difficult time.)

maintain to keep a thing in good condition (as, to maintain a car in working order); to continue or keep up (as, to maintain an attack); to provide for the expenses of (as, to maintain a household)

to maintain that to continue to argue a point of view; to insist (as - He maintained that what he had written was absolutely true.)

maintenance (financial) support; means of support (food, clothes, etc.); upkeep

maize Indian corn; an American cereal with large ears of yellow seeds growing on tall stalks

majesty greatness (of rank) and glory (of God); a title used in addressing kings and queens (Your Majesty, Her Majesty, His Majesty, Their Majesties)

major great or greater in size or importance (as, a meeting of major government officials, a major catastrophe, etc.) □ a person of full legal age; an army officer next in rank above a captain; anything that is major (greater) in contrast to minor (lesser)

majority the greater number (more than half of a quantity of things, number of people, etc.); the difference between a greater and a smaller number of votes (as - He had 24 votes, a majority of 5 over the other candidate's 19 votes.)

make to construct or produce (as, to make a dress, to make a table); to earn (as, to make money, to make a living); to carry out or perform (as, to make a journey; to make an attempt); to compel (as, to make someone obey); to cause (as, to make trouble); to prepare (as, to make a meal, to make a bed) □ kind or brand (as - What make of car does he own?)

made-up invented (a made-up story); wearing make-up

makeshift something used temporarily because the real thing or preferred thing is not available

make-up the way parts of

something are put together to make a whole: face powder, lipstick, eye colouring, etc.; cosmetics, false hair, etc. used by an actor to portray a character

to make believe to pretend □ **(make-believe)** imaginary; pretended

to make good to do well; to carry out a promise; to make up for a loss

to make light of, to make little of to treat as unimportant

to make much of to flatter or fuss over; to treat as important

to make nothing of not to understand (as - I can make nothing of this letter.): to treat as unimportant (as - He made nothing of his bad luck.)

to make off to run away

to make out to see, but not very clearly (as - They could just make out the tower in the fog.)

to make up for to compensate for

maladjusted not well adjusted; not content or comfortable in one's home, work or surroundings

malady an illness; disease

malaria a fever caused by tiny parasites carried by a certain type of mosquito

male of the sex that is able to father offspring; the opposite of female □ a boy or a man

malice (*say maliss*) spite; ill-will **malicious** spiteful; feeling ill-will towards others; wishing to harm others (as, by malicious gossip, etc.)

malign (*say maline*) to speak evil of others (especially falsely); to slander

malignant showing or feeling hatred: (of disease) very serious (often likely to cause death)

malinger to pretend to be ill in order to avoid work or some duty

mallard the male of the common wild duck

malleable (*say mal-eeable*) able to be rolled or beaten into a new

shape (as, malleable metals); (of a person) easily influenced or impressed by others

mallet a small wooden hammer; a long-handled hammer used in croquet or polo

malnutrition lack of food or of enough nourishing food

malt barley or other grain, soaked in water until it has sprouted, and then dried for use in brewing beer, etc. □ containing or flavoured with malt

malted milk powder made from dried milk and malted cereals; a drink made from this powder (usually dissolved in milk)

maltreat to treat roughly or unkindly (as - The cat had been maltreated by its former owners.)

mammal any of the animals whose females have milk to feed their young

mammoth a kind of huge hairy elephant now extinct □ huge; very large (as - The advertisement said: Come to see the mammoth circus.)

man a human being; human beings or people in general; a male human being when he is grown up □ to supply men for service or defence (as, to man the boats, man the guns, etc.)

men the plural of man

manly brave and straightforward

mannish (of a woman) like a man in appearance or manner

manhood the state of being a man; manly quality

mankind the human race

man-at-arms a soldier (especially one who is mounted and heavily armed)

man-of-war a warship

manslaughter the killing of a person (against the law) without meaning to

manage to control or be in charge of (a business, a household, a shop, etc.); to succeed in doing something (as - He just managed to catch the train. She managed without help.)

manageable able to be controlled or handled (as - They reduced the amount of their luggage to a manageable size.)
management the act or art of managing; the managers of a firm, a football club, etc.
manager, manageress the person in charge of a business, etc.

mandarin (in former days) an official of high rank in China; the standard national language of China: a flattish fruit resembling a small orange

mandate a command or order (especially from a higher authority): power given to a nation or person to act in the name of another □ to give (a territory, etc.) into the charge of a nation

mandible a jaw or jawbone (especially the lower); (in birds and insects) one or both jaws or biting organs

mandolin, mandoline a round-backed musical instrument played by plucking the metal strings

mane long hair on the back of the neck of some animals (such as horses and lions); (sometimes of a person) a thick bushy head of long hair

manger (say *maynjer*) an open box or trough for animal food (such as for horses and cattle)

mangle 1 a machine with heavy rollers for squeezing water from clothes, or for smoothing them when dry

mangle 2 to tear, cut or crush something to pieces; to spoil something (a speech, a song) by mistakes and generally poor performance

mango an Indian tree; the oblong yellowish-red fruit of this tree

mangold, mangel wurzel a root vegetable, rather like a beetroot, used for feeding animals

mangrove a low shrub or tree that grows on swampy shores, coasts or river banks in tropical countries (Roots grow from the trunk above ground in a tangled mass.)

mania madness; a craze; an excessive enthusiasm or desire for something (as - He has a mania for horse-racing.)
maniac a madman; an over-enthusiastic or reckless person (as - Some people drive like maniacs.)

manicure the care of hands and fingernails

manifest easily seen or understood □ to show plainly
manifestation the act of showing plainly; a display or showing (as - His broad smile was a manifestation of his goodwill.)

manifesto a public written declaration of intentions (especially by a head of state or a political party)

manifold many and varied (as - Her duties were manifold.)

manipulate to handle something with skill (as, to manipulate a bicycle in traffic); to manage (a person, a situation) skilfully (sometimes by trickery or deceit)

mannequin (say *manikin*) a person (usually female) who is employed to wear and display clothes to possible buyers

manner a way of acting or behaving (as, an offhand manner, a gentlemanly manner); the way in which anything is done (as, a careless manner, a considerate manner)
manners behaviour towards others (as, good manners at table)
mannerly showing good manners
mannerism a habit or style of expression or speech peculiar to a person (as - She has a mannerism of tugging at her hair when trying to work out a problem.)

manoeuvre (say *manoover*) a skilfully planned movement of troops, ships or aircraft; a clever trick or manipulation □ to manage skilfully (as - He manoeuvred the car into a limited parking space.)

manoeuvres large-scale practice battles for troops, ships, etc.

manor (in feudal times) the land belonging to a nobleman
manor house the house of a lord of the manor

mansion a large, grand house

mantel, mantelpiece, mantelshelf a narrow shelf or ornamental piece of wood, etc. above a fireplace

mantilla a large piece of lace or veiling draped over a high comb at the back of the head and covering the shoulders (worn by Spanish women on festive occasions)

mantis an insect resembling a grasshopper with long forelegs which are held doubled up as though in prayer

mantle a cloak or sleeveless loose outer garment; a covering (as, a mantle of snow)

manual of the hand; done by or with the hands (as, manual work) □ a handbook or book of instructions; the keyboard of an organ (played with the hands)

manufacture to make by hand (in former times, but nowadays mainly by machinery) □ the process of manufacturing
manufacturer a person who owns or controls a factory

manure something (animal excrement, compost, etc.) put into the ground to fertilize crops and plants; a fertilizer

manuscript written by hand (as, a manuscript copy of a report) □ a book or document written or typed (not printed); an author's copy of a book, etc. in writing or typescript (before printing)

many a large number □ the opposite of few; numerous

map a drawing or outline showing the main features of the surface of the earth, a country, etc. (or a part of it); a similar plan of the stars in the sky

to map out to plan in detail (as - He mapped out the year's work. They spent several hours mapping out the route of their journey.)

maple a tree, some kinds of which are valued for their attractive foliage, their timber or for the sugar obtained from the sap (The maple leaf is the national emblem of Canada.)

mar to spoil; to ruin (as - Their picnic was marred by a thunderstorm.)

marathon a long-distance footrace (now usually about 26 miles, or 42 kilometres); any contest requiring endurance

marauder a person who roams about in search of plunder

marble a kind of white or coloured limestone that can be highly polished, much used for decorating fine buildings, for ornamental sculpture, etc.: a small round ball of glass or clay (originally of marble) used in the game of marbles □ made of, or like, marble (as, a marble statue)

march to walk in time with a regular step (as, soldiers marching on parade) □ steady progress (as, the march of events); the marching distance covered at one time (as, a day's march); a regular rhythmic walk (especially by troops); a piece of music for marching

marchioness see **marquis**

mare the female of the horse

margarine a substitute for butter which is made mostly from vegetable oils

margin an edge; a border; the blank edge on the page of a book, newspaper, etc. where nothing is printed: something extra allowed (beyond what is necessary) in case of emergencies (as - He allowed a margin of ten minutes in case of traffic hold-ups.)

marginal placed in the margin (as, marginal notes); close to the

age or limit; barely enough (as -
The chairman was elected by a
marginal vote of 21 to 20.)

marigold a strong-smelling garden plant with orange or yellow
flowers

marijuana, marihuana the dried
flowers and leaves of hemp used
to make doped cigarettes

marine having to do with the sea
or ocean (as - Sharks are marine
animals.); done or used at sea
(as, marine stores or ships' supplies) □ a soldier serving on a
ship; all the ships of a country
(as, the British mercantile marine)

marina a dock or small harbour which provides moorings
and other services for yachts
and small boats

mariner a sailor; a seaman

marionette a puppet made to
move by pulling strings attached
to its arms and legs and head

marital having to do with a husband or with marriage

maritime having to do with the
sea; related to shipping and sea
trade (as - Britain is a maritime
country.)

marjoram an aromatic herb used
for seasoning in cooking

mark a written or printed sign or
figure (as, a pricemark, a trade
mark); a target, etc. to be aimed
at; a spot or stain; a point given
for good work, such as in an
examination, etc. □ to make a
mark on something; to pay close
attention to (as, to mark well
what is being said)

marked having marks: striking
or noticeable (as - Her health
shows a marked improvement.):
watched or suspected (as - He
was a marked man after taking
part in the riot.)

markedly noticeably

marker a person who marks or
records the score at games

marksman a person who
shoots well

to mark time to move the feet
up and down as if marching, but
without moving forward

up to the mark up to standard;
in good health

market a gathering of people in a
public place to buy and sell
(food, animals, flowers, etc.); a
demand for (as - This wet summer has created a market for
umbrellas.); an area or country
where there is a good prospect
for selling goods (as - There is a
good market for citrus fruits in
Northern European countries.)
□ to sell; to put on sale

marketable fit to be sold; in
demand

market garden a large garden
where fruit and vegetables are
grown for marketing

market place an open space
where markets are held

marmalade a thick jam made
from sugar and oranges or other
citrus fruit

marmoset a small bushy-tailed
monkey that lives in Central and
South America

marmot a thickset burrowing
rodent (also called woodchuck)

maroon 1 a dark brownish-red
colour

maroon 2 to put someone on a
desolate island or shore and
leave him there (usually as a
punishment)

marquee *(say mar*kee*)* a large
tent

marquis, marquess *(say mark-
wiss)* a title of nobility next
below that of duke

marchioness *(say marshon-
ess)* the feminine of marquis;
the wife or widow of a marquis

marriage see **marry**

marrow the soft substance in the
hollow parts of bones: a vegetable marrow: see under **vegetable**

marry to take (a person) as husband or wife (as - Joan is going
to marry John.); to perform the
marriage ceremony (Clergymen
and registrars are authorized to
marry people.)

married the past of marry

marriage the ceremony by

which a man and woman become husband and wife

marriageable suitable or old enough to be married

marriage lines a certificate stating that a marriage has taken place

marsh a piece of low-lying wet land; a swamp

marshy swampy

marsh mallow a marsh plant with pink flowers; **(marshmallow)** a sticky white or pink sweet (originally made from the root of this plant)

marshal a high-ranking officer in the army or air force; an officer who arranges ceremonies, official parades, etc.; (in the United States) a civil officer who performs duties similar to those of a sheriff (also a court officer, the head of a police or fire department, etc.) □ to arrange in order (as, to marshal troops, to marshal facts to support an argument, etc.); to usher (as - The delegates to the conference were marshalled into the hall.)

marshalling yard a place where railway wagons are sorted out and made up into trains

marsupial an animal that carries its young in a pouch (as, the kangaroo)

mart a market; a trading place

martial warlike; belonging to, or associated with, war (as, martial music, martial uniform)

martial law military government of a country in time of war, or in a time of national emergency (when civil law is temporarily replaced by martial law)

martin a bird of the swallow family (One kind is called the house martin because it builds its nest on house walls, under eaves, etc.)

martyr *(say marter)* a person who has suffered great hardship or even death, rather than give up his beliefs (usually religious) □ to cause a person to suffer or die for his beliefs

martyrdom the sufferings or death of a martyr

marvel to wonder (how, why); to be amazed or astonished (at some event, etc.) □ something amazing or astonishing

marvellous wonderful; splendid; almost unbelievable

marzipan a sweet food made of crushed almonds and sugar

mascot a person, animal, charm, etc. that is supposed to bring good luck

masculine of or like a man or boy; the opposite of feminine

mash a mixture of boiled grain, meal, vegetables, etc. used to feed animals; a pulpy mass made by crushing or pounding (as, mashed potatoes) □ to crush or pound something into a pulpy mass

mask a cover for hiding, disguising or protecting the face; a face that shows nothing of what the person is feeling □ to hide or disguise something (especially the face)

mason a skilled worker or builder in stone

masonry the work of a mason; stonework

masquerade *(say maskerade)* a party (usually a ball or a dance) where the guests wear fancy-dress costumes and masks □ to pretend to be someone other than oneself; to act or live under false pretences

mass 1 a lump of matter (as, a mass of granite); a large number or quantity (as, a mass of people in the street); the main part or bulk of something □ to bring together or form into a mass (as - Troops were massed for manoeuvres.)

massive bulky and heavy; large and impressive; very great in numbers or quantity

mass meeting a large meeting (usually to discuss some political or community problem, etc.)

mass production the production of very large quantities of articles by machine to exactly the same pattern

mass 2 celebration of communion in the Roman Catholic church; music written specially to accompany this ceremony (Some of this music is performed without the ceremony in concert halls as well as churches.)

massacre *(say massaker)* a great slaughter; the killing of a large number of people (especially with cruelty and violence) □ to slaughter; to kill (many people) with violence

massage *(say massahzh or massahzh)* the rubbing, kneading, etc. of parts of the body to relieve pain or stiffness □ to treat by massage
  masseur, masseuse *(say masser, massez)* a man, a woman who gives massage to others

mast a long upright pole that supports the sails and rigging of a sailing vessel; any tall upright pole (as, a television mast)
  masthead the top of a mast

master a person who controls or commands; an owner (of an animal, or, in former times, a slave); an employer; a male teacher; a person very skilled in a profession or trade (as, a master builder, a master carpenter); an artist, musician, etc. whose work is greatly admired □ chief; most important; controlling (as, master key, master switch) □ to control or overcome (as, to master a feeling of shyness); to become skilful in (as, to master the violin)
  masterful showing power or determination to be in control
  masterly skilful; showing the skill of a master
  masterpiece a painting, musical composition, piece of work, etc. that is worthy of a master
  mastery victory (over); control (of); great skill in or knowledge of
  master of ceremonies (abbreviated **M.C.**) a person who directs and announces the programme of speakers, entertainers, etc. at a public function

masticate to chew

mastiff a large thick-set powerful dog (often used as a watch-dog)

mat 1 a piece of material made from coarse fibres, plaited rushes, carpet, etc. for wiping shoes on, for covering the floor, for sleeping on, or for other purposes; a small piece of material placed under hot plates, vases, ornaments, etc; a tangled or interwoven mass (as, a mat of hair, a mat of undergrowth) □ to cover with mats; to interweave or tangle
  matted thickly tangled or intertwined (as, matted hair)
  matting material used as mats (especially coconut fibre, rushes, etc.)

mat 2, matt having a dull surface without gloss or shine (as mat paint)

match 1 a short thin piece of wood, pressed paper, etc. tipped with a substance that easily catches fire when rubbed; a wick or cord made to burn at an even rate of speed (formerly used to fire cannon and some firearms)
  matchbox a box for holding matches

match 2 a person or thing equal to, or as good as, another (as - In an argument, John is a match for James.); the same (as - The colour of this ribbon is a perfect match for her pink dress.); a marriage (as - She has made a good match.); a contest or a game between teams (as, a tennis match, a football match) □ to be of the same size, colour, ability, etc.; to arrange to compete against (as, to match the East and the West football teams); to hold one's own against
  matchless better than anything else of the same kind; unequalled
  matchmaker a person who tries to bring about a marriage between others

mate a companion; a friend; a fellow-worker; a husband or wife; one of a pair of birds or animals (usually a male and a female); the officer on a merchant ship ranking next below the captain □ to pair; to marry

material the substance of which anything is made; cloth or fabric □ physical, not spiritual; consisting of matter: essential or important (as, material evidence)
  materialize to take bodily form; to become fact; to appear or turn up (as - The expected supplies materialized at last.)

maternal having to do with a mother; suitable to a mother (as, maternal love for a child); motherly; related through one's mother (as - He had one maternal uncle, his mother's brother John.)
  maternity the state of being a mother; motherhood; relating to motherhood (as, a maternity ward in a hospital)

mathematics the science or branch of knowledge dealing with numbers, measurements, quantities and the relationship between these
  mathematical of, or done by, mathematics; very accurate; exact (as - The machine works with mathematical precision.)
  mathematician a person who has a good knowledge of, and ability to work in, mathematics; an expert in mathematics

matinée (say matinay) an after-. noon performance of a show

matriarch (say maytriark) a woman who is head and ruler of her family and descendants; an elderly woman who dominates her family and friends
  matriarchy a form of social organization (especially in some primitive tribes) in which the mothers are heads of the families

matrimony the state of being married; the act of marrying
  matrimonial of, or relating to, marriage

matrix something in which another thing is formed or is embedded (as, the mass of rock in which gems, precious metal, etc. are found); a mould for casting metal, etc. (especially printer's type)
  matrices (say maytrisseez) the plural of matrix

matron a married woman; an, elderly lady; a woman in charge of nursing and domestic arrangements in a hospital, school or other institution
  matronly elderly and sedate

matter something that takes up space and that can be seen, handled, etc.; a physical substance (not mental or spiritual); what anything is made of (as, colouring matter); the subject being talked, written or thought about (as - He gave the matter serious consideration.); the trouble, problem, etc. (as - What is the matter with you?): pus (the yellowish matter that comes out of a boil, etc.) □ to be of importance, concern, etc. (as - This is something that matters to us all.)
  matters affairs; business (as - He has great ability in financial matters.)
  a matter of course a thing to be expected
  matter-of-fact realistic; down-to-earth; not imaginative
  as a matter of fact in reality
  no matter never mind; it makes no difference

mattress a part of a bed made of a large flat bag stuffed with horse-hair, cotton, feathers or other soft material (Mattresses usually have springs inside, or rest on a framework of springs.)

mature fully grown or developed; ripe; ready for use □ to grow to maturity; to bring to maturity (as, to mature cheeses before putting them on sale)
  maturity full growth or development; ripeness

maul to hurt badly by rough

or savage treatment

mausoleum a very fine tomb or monument

mauve a delicate shade of purple

maxim a general truth or rule (especially as a guide to conduct)

maximum greatest (as - This machine works with maximum efficiency.); the greatest number, quantity, degree, etc. possible (as - The maximum number of people allowed in the lift is eight.)

may 1 generally used with another verb to express permission (as - You may go now.); possibility (as - We may go if the rain stops.); to express a wish (as - May you always be as happy as you are today.)
might 1 the past of may (as - I might have gone, but the weather was too bad.)

may 2 the pink or white blossom on a hawthorn tree

maybe perhaps

mayonnaise a thick sauce made of yolk of egg, oil, vinegar or lemon and seasoning, used with salads, cold meat, fish, etc.

mayor the chief public official of a city or borough
mayoress the wife of a mayor, or other lady who carries out the social and ceremonial duties of a mayor's wife

maypole a pole for dancing around (On the first day of May the pole is decorated with flowers and ribbons.)

maze a network of winding paths and passages; a labyrinth; a state of puzzlement or confusion

mazurka a lively Polish dance; the music for such a dance

me the person who is speaking (as - Give it to me.)
mine, my belonging to me (as - This book is mine. This is my book.)
myself me and no one else

mead 1 (*say meed*) an alcoholic drink made of fermented honey and water

meadow (*say meddoe*) **mead 2** (poetic) a field (especially one where grass is grown to make hay for animals); a rich pasture-land near a stream

meagre having little flesh; lean; scanty (as - Their meagre supplies of food barely lasted out the winter.)

meal 1 food eaten at certain times of the day (as, breakfast, dinner, etc.)

meal 2 grain or seeds ground to a coarse powder
mealy like meal; crumbly or powdery (as, mealy potatoes)
mealy-mouthed not completely frank or sincere; speaking with excessive delicacy or smoothness, avoiding plain, simple terms

mean 1 (of actions, thoughts, etc.) not honourable; not generous or kindly; stingy; (formerly) low in rank or birth; humble or shabby (as - When he was a child his family lived in mean surroundings.)

mean 2 average; having the middle position
meantime, meanwhile in the interval between two happenings

mean 3 to have in mind; to intend (as - I mean to finish this piece of work.); to indicate or signify (as - The word *exit* means a way out.); to be important to (as - His kindness means a great deal to me.)
meaning what is intended to be expressed or signified; the sense or explanation of something said or written
meant (*say ment*) the past of mean (as - She meant well.)

meander (*say meeander*) to flow in a winding course (as - The river meandered along the valley.); to wander about without any particular destination (as - They meandered through the streets of the picturesque old town.)

means a method, instrument, action, etc. which brings about some result (as - He used every possible means to get there on time.); wealth (as, a man of means); money, resources or income (as - It was beyond his means to buy a new suit.)

by means of through the use of

by all means certainly; yes indeed; at any cost; in every way possible

by no means certainly not; not at all

measles an infectious disease which produces high fever and red spots on the skin

measure the dimensions, size or quantity of anything as measured; something by which length, amount, etc, is judged (as, a cup or vessel for measuring liquids, a rule for measuring inches, centimetres, etc.); an amount, an extent, a degree (as - There was some measure of agreement between us.); a step or action (as - They took measures to prevent the crowd from rushing on to the pitch.); a legislative bill or act □ to find the size or amount of anything; to mark off, weigh out, etc. (as, to measure off a length of cloth); to compare (as - He measured his strength against his friend's.); to take measurements (as - The tailor measured him for a suit.)

measurable able to be measured (as - They have arrived within measurable distance of their home.)

measured slow and rhythmical (as - The soldiers walked with measured steps to the memorial.); slow and deliberate (as - He spoke in measured tones.)

measurement the act of measuring; the size, amount, etc. found by measuring

meat the flesh of animals used for food; (formerly) anything eaten as food

mechanic a skilled worker with tools or machines

mechanical having to do with machines; worked or done by machinery; done automatically or almost without thinking (as - Brushing one's teeth becomes a mechanical action.)

mechanics the science of the action of forces on objects; the skill of constructing machinery

mechanism all the parts of a machine together; the working parts of something (as, the mechanism of a clock)

mechanize to equip (a factory, etc.) with machinery; to equip (troops) with armed and armoured vehicles

medal a piece of metal shaped like a coin, cross, star, etc. with a design or inscription that shows why it was given to the owner (for bravery, service to his country, outstanding ability in sport, etc.)

medallion a large medal; anything resembling a round or oval medal (such as a portrait)

medallist a person who has won a medal (as, a gold medallist in the Olympic Games)

meddle to interfere with what someone is trying to do; to concern oneself too much with other people's affairs; to tamper with (as, to meddle with machinery)

meddlesome fond of meddling

mediaeval, medieval *(say medieeval)* of, or having to do with, the Middle Ages

mediate *(say meediate)* to act as peacemaker between enemies who are fighting, or two people who are quarrelling; to try to bring about a settlement of an industrial dispute, etc. by getting the two sides together

medicine any substance used to prevent or treat disease; the science of treating people who are ill by means of drugs, special foods, etc.

medical having to do with medicine or with doctors

medicate to put medicine into something

medicinal having power to heal or help recovery from illness

medicine man (in some primitive tribes) a witch doctor or magician

medieval see **mediaeval**

mediocre *(say meedy-oker)* middling; neither very good nor very bad (as, a mediocre performance)

meditate to think deeply (about a subject, especially religious); to consider carefully; to plan
meditation deep and continued thought; contemplation

medium 1 middle-sized; of middle quality (between the two extremes)

medium 2 something through which an effect is produced (for example - Air is the medium through which sound is carried.); the means by which, or channel through which, something is done (as - The news reached all parts of the world through the medium of radio.): a person through whom spirits of the dead are said to speak (The plural for this meaning is **mediums**.)
media the plural of medium (as - Newspapers and television are media for advertising.)

medley a mixture; a jumble; a musical composition made up of parts of other pieces (as, a medley of tunes from an operetta; a medley of popular songs)

meek gentle and patient; submissive, not aggressive

meet to come face to face with someone (as, to meet a friend on the street); to come into the company or presence of someone for discussion, combat, competition, etc. (as - The two teams are to meet on Saturday.); to come to a place where something is, or soon will be (as, to meet a train); to join or cross (as - A crossroads is where two roads meet.); to fulfil or satisfy (as, to meet requirements, to meet a demand for money); to come together; to assemble
met the past of meet
meeting a coming together (of

two or more people); an assembly or gathering

megahertz (MHz, formerly **megacycle**) a measure of radio wave frequencies or vibrations (1000 kHz or kilocycles per second)

megaphone a trumpet-shaped device which amplifies sound (Megaphones are used in speaking to crowds out of doors, to carry the sound over a greater distance.)

melancholy *(say melankoly)* lowness of spirits; deep sadness □ sad; gloomy

mellow (of fruit) ripe; juicy; sweet; (of wine) matured and full-flavoured; (of sound, colour, light) soft and rich - not harsh; (of a person's character) softened and made gentler by age and experience □ to soften or ripen with time

melodic, melodious see **melody**

melodrama a sensational drama in which the situations and emotions are exaggerated
melodramatic exaggerated in behaviour

melody a musical air or tune; a pleasing series of musical notes; sweet music
melodies the plural of melody
melodic having to do with melody (the tune only, as distinct from harmony)
melodious pleasing to the ear (as, a melodious speaking voice); tuneful

melon a large sweet fruit with much juice and many seeds (It grows on a trailing vine, like cucumbers, pumpkins, etc.)

melt to become liquid (usually by heating); to dissolve or disappear (as - The mist melted away as the sun rose higher.); to soften in feeling; to become kinder and more affectionate (as - Her heart melted when she saw how sorry he was.)
molten (of metal) melted (as, molten steel)

member a person who belongs to

a special group (as, a member of a club, a Member of Parliament, a member of the human race - as distinct from animals); a part of a person's body (especially a limb)

membership the state or fact of being a member (of a club, a team, etc.); members as a whole (as - The entire membership voted for him.)

membrane a thin flexible layer of tissue in the body of a human being, an animal or a plant, which acts as a lining or connecting tissue, forms the outside covering of cells, etc.

memento something kept to remind one of an occasion, a place once visited, a loved person, etc.; a keepsake; a souvenir
mementos the plural of memento

memoirs (say _memwahrs_) an autobiography which gives a personal account of important events in which the writer was concerned (as, memoirs of an ex-prime minister, an ex-president, etc.)

memorandum a note of anything to help one to remember; a brief summary of a meeting, etc. to remind one of what was discussed
memorandums, memoranda the plural of memorandum

memory the power or ability to remember anything; all the things that can be remembered by people; the length of time that events can be remembered (as, things that have happened within living memory); something or someone remembered (as, a happy memory of the holiday)
memorable worth remembering; unforgettable
memorial something (such as a building, a monument, etc.) which is built to honour the memory of someone or some event (as, a war memorial) □ honouring the memory of a person or event

(as, a memorial service)
memorize to learn by heart; to commit to memory

men see under **man**

menace a threat (as, to demand money with menaces); something that threatens to cause harm or damage □ to threaten
menacing threatening

menagerie a collection of caged wild animals; a place where such animals are kept

mend to repair; to put something damaged right again; to improve (in health); to correct or improve (manners, behaviour, etc.)

menial (say _meenial_) a servant (especially one employed to do domestic work) □ (of work) lowly; suitable for a household servant

mensuration measuring; the methods for finding the lengths, areas, volumes, etc. of objects

mental having to do with the mind; done in the mind and not written down (as, mental arithmetic); suffering from illness in the mind (as, a hospital for mental patients)
mentally in the mind
mentality mental power; intellectual ability

menthol a strong-smelling substance obtained from oil of peppermint, used to relieve inflammation of the nasal passages in colds, etc.

mention to refer to, or speak about something briefly (as - He mentioned the play, but did not say what it was about.); to name (as, a soldier mentioned for bravery in dispatches) □ a brief reference or remark

menu a list of dishes to be served at a meal, or that can be ordered for a meal (as, a restaurant menu)

mercantile having to do with merchants or with trading
mercantile marine the ships and sailors which carry on a country's trade with other countries

mercenary working or doing something only for money or reward ☐ a soldier hired to fight in a foreign army

merchant a trader (especially one who has a large business, or who buys and sells foreign goods)
merchandise goods that are bought and sold in trade
merchantman a ship used in trading (especially with foreign countries)
merchant service, merchant navy the mercantile marine

merciful, merciless see **mercy**

mercury a heavy silvery metallic element that is liquid at ordinary temperatures (also called quicksilver)
mercurial changeable; (of a person's nature) bright and lively

mercy kindness and pity towards others (including enemies and those who have done one harm); a willingness to forgive
merciful willing to forgive or to let someone off with a lighter punishment than he deserves
merciless without mercy; cruel
at the mercy of in someone's power; likely to be harmed by (as - The small boat was at the mercy of the storm.)

mere nothing more than (as, a mere mention, a mere scratch)
merely simply; only

merge to mingle with; to blend with; to be absorbed into (something greater)
merger a joining together of business firms into one large firm

meridian an imaginary circle (or half circle) passing through the North and South Poles and any other given place on the earth's surface (The prime meridian [0°] passes through Greenwich.); the highest point (of the course of the sun, of success, etc.)

meringue *(say merang)* a light sweet food made of beaten white of egg and sugar baked until firm and crisp

merit something (such as bravery) which deserves reward or recognition; excellence or worth (as, an award of merit) ☐ to deserve (as a reward or punishment)
merits the rights and wrongs (of an argument, a legal case)
meritorious deserving reward or praise (as, meritorious conduct)

mermaid an imaginary sea creature, supposed to be half woman and half fish, with a fish's tail instead of legs
merman the masculine of mermaid

merry cheerful and happy; joyful; slightly drunk
merrily happily; joyfully
merriment fun; gaiety with laughter and noise
merry-go-round a roundabout
merrymaking a joyful festivity or entertainment

mesh the space between the threads of a net or the thin wires of a sieve, etc.; a net or network ☐ (of machinery) to interlock or fit together (as - The teeth of the gears meshed.)

mesmerize to hypnotize

mess 1 an untidy muddle (often unpleasant to see or smell); confusion or disorder (as - These office papers are in a mess.)
messy untidy

mess 2 a number of people who take their meals together (especially in the armed forces)
messmate a member of the same mess (usually a ship's)

message a piece of news, information, instructions, etc. sent or passed from one person to another (Messages can be oral or written.)
messenger a person who carries messages

met see **meet**

metabolism the sum of the chemical changes in the cells of a living body which provide energy

metal a substance (such as gold, silver, tin, iron) which is usually shiny or lustrous, which conducts heat or electricity, and which can be hammered into shape or moulded (when molten): broken stones used for mending roads, etc.

metallic made of metal; like metal

metallurgy *(say metallurgy or metallurgy)* the study of metals; the art or science of extracting metals from ores and preparing them for use

metamorphosis change of form, substance, character, etc. through natural development, or by magic (as, in mythology and fairy stories, people are supposedly changed into stones, animals, plants, etc.); the marked change which takes place in some living beings during growth (as, the metamorphosis of a caterpillar into a butterfly, a tadpole into a frog, etc.)

metaphor a way of describing someone or something by giving it a quality belonging to something else, to make the description more interesting, clear or poetic (as - Her hat was a picture. He is a tiger when someone angers him.)

metaphorical expressing in metaphors; not literal fact

mixed metaphor the using of two or more metaphors that, taken together, are confusing or contradictory (as - When you embark on the sea of life, put your best foot forward!)

meteor any one of an infinite number of small masses of matter travelling in space at great speed (They are seen as shooting stars or fiery streaks in the sky because friction makes them glow brightly when they enter the earth's atmosphere.); anything brilliant or dazzling that does not last long

meteoric like, or having to do with, meteors; atmospheric; bright, and rapidly successful for a short time (as - He was completely unknown before his meteoric rise to fame.)

meteorite a meteor (of stone or metal) which has fallen to earth

meteorologist a person who studies the weather; a weather forecaster

meteorology the study of the earth's atmosphere, weather and climate

meter an instrument for measuring (and usually recording) the amount of gas, water, electricity, etc. used in a building

parking meter a meter for measuring the time that a car is parked

method an orderly way of doing something (such as the way a person regularly goes about a job of work, etc.); a planned series of actions (as, a method of teaching people to drive)

methodical arranged or done in an orderly way, according to a plan or system (as - She goes about her household tasks in a methodical way.)

methylated spirit(s) an alcohol, unsuitable for drinking, which is used as fuel in spirit lamps, etc.

meticulous very careful and accurate about small details; too particular and fussy about appearance, neatness, etc.

metre 1 (in poetry) the regular arrangement of groups of stressed syllables; rhythm (as, *tum* ti *tum* ti *tum* ti *tum,* ti *tum* ti *tum* ti *TUM*)

metrical having a regular pattern of stressed syllables

metre 2 the chief unit of length in the metric system (almost $1^1/_{10}$ th yards)

metric having to do with the metric system

metric system an international system of weights and measures based on tens (for example, 1 metre = 100 centimetres; 1 kilometre = 1000 metres)

metronome an instrument with a rod that marks musical time with a loud tick at regular variable intervals

metropolis *(say metropolis)* the chief city of a country; a chief centre
metropolitan *(say metropolitan)* having to do with a metropolis

mettle courage; pluck
mettlesome high-spirited

mew the crying sound made by a cat or kitten □ to make such a sound

mews a street or yard once used for stabling horses, nowadays often converted into living accommodation or garages

mica *(say mieka)* a glittering mineral that is easily divided into thin, semi-transparent sheets

mice see **mouse**

microbe a very tiny living thing; a germ (especially causing disease)

microfilm a very narrow photographic film of documents, books, etc.; which can be enlarged by projection on a screen

micrometer an instrument for measuring very small distances or angles

microphone an instrument for picking up sound-waves and turning them into electrical energy for broadcasting, tape recording, etc.

microscope an instrument which magnifies tiny objects so that details invisible to the naked eye can be seen
microscopic seen only with the aid of a microscope; very tiny

mid- a prefix meaning at, in, or the middle of, etc. (as, **at midday**, in **midocean**, **midstream**, **midterm**)
midday the middle of the day; noon
midland in the middle or interior of a country, away from the coast
midnight the middle of the night (12 o'clock at night; 24.00 hours)

midshipman a young man training to be a naval officer
midst the middle or central part □ among (as, in the midst of the crowd)
midsummer the middle of summer (the period about June 21)
midway in the middle of the distance (between two points); halfway
midwinter the middle of winter (the period about December 21)
in mid air in the air; well above the ground

middle halfway; at equal distance from each end □ the middle point; the centre or central point
middling of middle or average size or quality; not very good or very bad
middle-aged between youth and old age
Middle Ages the period of time between the fall of the Roman Empire and the Italian Renaissance (the 5th to 15th centuries A.D.)

midge a small fly; a gnat

midget a person who is much smaller than average, even when fully grown; anything much smaller than the average of its kind

midst see **mid**

midwife a woman who helps at the birth of children

might 1 see **may 1**

might 2 power; strength
mighty having great power; very large (as, a mighty army)

migrate to go regularly from one region to another (as certain birds and animals do, for food, warmer climate, etc.); to move from one country to another, or from one part of a country to another
migrant a person, bird, animal, etc. who migrates
migratory migrating; wandering

mild gentle; kind and amiable; not sharp or hot-tempered; (of weather) pleasantly warm (not very hot or cold)

mildew a disease on plants, leather, cloth, etc. which leaves greyish marks caused by the growth of tiny fungi

mile a distance of 1760 yards (1·61 kilometres)
mileage distance measured in miles (as, the mileage from London to Edinburgh); miles travelled
milestone a stone set up by the roadside to show the distance in miles to a place; some important event in history or a person's life (as - Magna Carta was a milestone in British history.)
geographical, or **nautical mile** a unit of distance at sea (6080 feet or 1·85 kilometres)

military having to do with the army or with warfare □the army; soldiers
militant warlike; fighting
militate to fight against; to work, or exert force against (as - They tried hard, but outside influences militated against their success.)
militia a body of men trained to fight for their country if necessary in time of emergency (not regular soldiers)

milk a white liquid produced by female mammals as nourishment for their young; this liquid drawn from cows and goats, and used by humans for a drink or for dairy products; any milk-like fluid □to squeeze or draw milk from (cows, goats, etc.)
milky made of, or resembling, milk; (of liquid) cloudy, not clear
Milky Way a vast number of stars stretching in a luminous band across the sky; The Galaxy (of stars to which the solar system belongs)

mill a machine for grinding (coffee, grain, pepper, etc.) by crushing between rough, hard surfaces; a building where grain, etc. is ground; a place where certain manufacturing processes

are carried on (for example, a steel mill, a paper mill, a cotton mill) □to grind; to move aimlessly around in a group (as - The sheep milled about in the pen.)
miller a person who owns or works in a grain mill
millrace the current of water that turns a mill-wheel or the channel in which it runs
millstone one of the two heavy circular stones between which grain is ground in a mill; a heavy burden (of responsibility, etc.)
mill-wheel a water-wheel that drives the machinery of a mill

millet a grain plant used for food or fodder

millibar a unit of barometric (atmospheric) pressure (1000 millibars = 29·53 inches of mercury.)

milligramme a weight of one thousandth of a gramme

millimetre a measure of one thousandth of a metre in length

million a thousand thousands (1,000,000)
millionaire a very rich man who has a million pounds or more

milliner a person who makes and sells hats for women

millipede, millepede a small worm-like animal with many pairs of legs

mime a play without any spoken parts, in which the actors tell the story by gestures and facial expressions; an actor in such a play □to act or mimic without words
mimic to imitate or copy someone (especially in a mocking way) □a person who imitates or copies
mimicking imitating
mimicry the act of mimicking

minaret a slender tower on a mosque (from which the call to prayer is sounded)

mince to chop or grind something (usually meat) into small pieces; to speak or walk in a prim, affected way □ chopped or ground-up meat

mincer a machine for mincing

mince meat anything cut or ground into small pieces; a mixture of chopped-up fruit, nuts, raisins, etc., usually cooked in pastry (mince pie)

not to mince matters, words to put (usually unpleasant) facts in a blunt, untactful way, regardless of people's feelings

mind the power of a person to think, reason, feel emotions, etc.; the intellect or intelligence (in contrast to feelings, emotions, etc.); remembrance or memory (as, to keep in mind); opinion, intention, inclination, etc. (as, to change one's mind, to have a mind to do something) □ to pay attention to, to obey (as, to mind one's parents); to watch out for, to take care (as, to mind the step); to be in charge of or look after (as, to mind the shop, to mind the baby); to be upset by (as, to mind losing an argument)

mindful bearing in mind; aware (as, mindful of the dangers)

mindless stupid; without reason or thought

in two minds undecided

of one mind in agreement

to be out of one's mind to be insane

to lose one's mind to become insane

mine 1 see me

mine 2 a place (usually a pit or tunnel) from which minerals are dug out; (in war time) a heavy charge of explosive placed underground, under a ship, etc. to destroy enemy troops and supplies □ to dig out minerals from the earth; to lay mines; to blow up with mines

miner a person who works in a mine (as, a coalminer)

minefield an area containing explosive mines

minelayer, minesweeper a ship used to place mines in, or remove them from, the sea

mineral any substance in the earth that can be dug out and used (for example, coal, iron ore, gold, diamonds) □ of, or having to do with, minerals

mineralogy the study of minerals

mineral oil an oil (especially petroleum) obtained from minerals

mineral water spring water containing traces of minerals; a soft drink (usually fizzy)

mingle to mix; to go about among (as - They mingled with the other guests.)

mini- (as part of a word) small or miniature (as, minibus, miniskirt)

miniature a small copy of anything; a very small painting of a landscape or (especially) a portrait □ on a small scale (as, a miniature poodle, which is much smaller than the French poodle)

minimum the smallest possible quantity or number; the lowest point or degree recorded (as - The minimum temperature today was 10° centigrade.) □ smallest; least

minima, minimums the plural of minimum

minimize to reduce or make as small as possible (as, to minimize the dangers of rock-climbing by taking proper equipment)

minister a clergyman; the political head of one of the ministries or departments of government (as, the Minister of Education, of Health, etc.); a representative of a country's government in another country □ to be of service, or to give help (to); to supply necessary things (to)

ministerial having to do with a minister; having to do with a ministry or government department (as, a ministerial decision to raise the school-leaving age)

ministration(s) the act of giving aid, care, religious service, etc.

ministry the profession or duties of a minister of religion; a department of government or the building in which it works

mink a small weasel-like animal, valued for its fur

minnow a tiny freshwater fish

minor less in importance, size, value, etc.; the opposite of major: a person under the age when he legally becomes an adult (18 in Great Britain)
minority the smaller number (less than half the total); the political party with the fewest members; the opposite of majority; the period during which a person is under age

minstrel (in mediaeval times) a travelling musician; (in modern times) one of a group of entertainers who black their faces in imitation of negroes

mint 1 a place where metal coins are made (under government authority); a large sum (as - He won a mint of money on the Pools.)
in mint condition unused; undamaged

mint 2 a plant with strongly aromatic leaves, used for flavouring; a mint-flavoured sweet

minuet (in former days) a slow, graceful ballroom dance with short steps; the music for this dance

minus a preposition used to show subtraction (as - Six minus four equals two [6 − 4 = 2]); without (as - He arrived minus one glove.) □ (a quantity) less than zero (as - The temperature was minus 3°, that is to say, 3 degrees below zero.); the sign (−) for subtraction

minute 1 *(say minet)* the sixtieth part of an hour; (in measuring an angle) the sixtieth part of a degree: a very short time (as - I'll be there in a minute.)
minutes 1 the plural of minute (as - There are fifteen minutes in a quarter of an hour.)
minutes 2 the notes recording what was said at a formal meeting

minute 2 *(say mynewt)* very small; paying attention to the smallest details (as - He examined the watch with minute care.)

miracle an act or happening beyond human power; a fortunate or wonderful thing or event that has no natural cause or explanation; a marvel; a wonder
miraculous of, or like, a miracle; marvellous

mirage *(say mirahzh)* something a person imagines he sees although it is not really there (especially the imaginary appearance of a lake in the desert, which is really the effect of shimmering sunlight on the sand)

mire deep mud; wet swampy ground

mirror a piece of glass backed with some reflecting substance (such as mercury); a looking-glass; a surface that reflects □ to reflect as a mirror does (as - She could see her reflection mirrored in the pond's calm surface.)

mirth merriment; laughter

mis- a prefix added to a word to mean wrong(ly) or bad(ly), for example: **misapply; misbehave; miscalculate; misconduct; misdeed; misfortune; misgovern; mishandle; misinform; mismanage; misplace; mispronounce; misspell; mistrust; misunderstand; misuse**

misadventure an unlucky happening; an accident

misanthrope, misanthropist a person who hates mankind
misanthropic hating or distrusting mankind
misanthropy a hatred or distrust of mankind

misapprehend to misunderstand or take a wrong meaning from (something said or done)
misapprehension misunderstanding of meaning or mistaken belief (as - He thinks I don't like him, but he is under a misapprehension.)

miscarriage failure (of a plan or scheme); failure to get the right

result (as - By a miscarriage of justice the wrong man was sent to prison.); the birth of young so long before the proper time that their survival is not possible
miscarry to fail or be unsuccessful; to have the wrong result; (of a female) to have a miscarriage

miscellaneous *(say misselaynius)* mixed; made up of several different kinds (as, a miscellaneous collection of coins)
miscellany *(say missellany)* a mixture of different kinds; a collection of writings on different subjects or by different authors

mischance bad luck; a mishap

mischief *(say mischif)* harm; evil; damage; behaviour or conduct that causes trouble or annoyance to others
mischievous *(say mischivus)* causing mischief; teasing; likely to annoy or cause trouble

misconception a false idea or a misunderstanding

misconstruction a wrong meaning or interpretation

misdemeanour a misdeed or offence (especially against the law)

miser *(say miezer)* a person who hoards all his money and lives in a very poor way so as to save still more money

miserable wretched; very unhappy; very poor in quality or quantity (as, a miserable wage, a miserable meal)
misery great unhappiness (often because of poverty, pain, etc.)

misfire to fail to explode or catch fire; to fail to have an effect or to succeed (as - It seemed a good idea, but it misfired.)

misfit a thing that does not fit well; a person who does not fit in well with the people around him, or who is unhappy in the work he does, etc.

misgiving a feeling of fear or doubt about some action (as - I have misgivings about the whole plan, and I do not think it will work.)

mishap an unlucky accident (usually not serious)

misinterpret to take a wrong meaning from; to explain incorrectly

misjudge to judge wrongly (as - He fell into the water because he misjudged the distance from the boat to the jetty.); to have an unjust opinion of a person (as - She was sorry afterwards that she had misjudged her teacher.)

mislay to lay (something) down and then forget where it was put; to lose
mislaid the past of mislay

mislead *(say misleed)* to give someone a wrong idea (by passing on false or mistaken information); to cause (someone) to make a mistake, or go wrong
misled *(say misled)* having been made to believe something that is not true (as - I thought he was here, but I was misled.)

misogynist *(say missojinist)* a hater of women

misprint a mistake in printing (as, *weeding* instead of *wedding*)

misquote to make a mistake in repeating what someone has said or written (for example, *Money is the root of all evil* when it should be *The love of money is the root of all evil.*)

miss 1 a young woman or girl; (with a capital letter, **Miss**) a form of address or courtesy title used before the name of an unmarried girl or woman (as - May I introduce you to Miss Jones?)

miss 2 to fail to hit, catch, find, hear, see something or someone; to fail to keep (an appointment) or take advantage of (an opportunity); to feel the want or absence of (a person, a possession) □ a failure to hit (the bull's eye, the jackpot, etc.) or catch (a ball, etc.)
missing not in its usual place; not able to be found; lost; lacking

missile any weapon, or object used as a weapon, for throwing or shooting
guided missile a jet or rocket-propelled missile directed to its target by a built-in device or by radio control, etc.

mission a delegation sent by a government to a foreign country to carry out negotiations, establish trade relations, etc.; a group of people sent out to spread a particular religious belief; the purpose or duty for which a messenger, delegate, etc. is sent out (as - His mission was to find out whether a peaceful settlement was possible.)
missionary a person sent on a mission (especially religious)

mist a cloud of moisture hanging in the air (like very thin fog or drizzle); anything that blurs (physical) vision or (mental) understanding or judgment □ to form a mist: to become misty
misty full of mist; hazy or blurred

mistake to make an error; to misunderstand □ an error, wrong action or statement; an error of judgment (as - It was a mistake to think I could manage this alone.)
mistaken wrong; in error (as - You are mistaken in thinking she will help you.); showing poor judgment (as - It was a mistaken idea to come so far in one day.)

mister (abbreviated **Mr.**) a form of address or courtesy title used before the name of a man (from the word master)

mistletoe an evergreen plant with pearly white berries, which grows on the trunks and branches of trees, and is much used for Christmas decorations

mistress (feminine of master) a woman who controls or has authority; a female head of a family or household; a woman teacher; (abbreviated **Mrs.** - say missez) a form of address or courtesy title used before the name of a married woman

mite anything very small (as - That baby is a dear little mite.); (in olden times) a small coin of little value; a small bit or amount

mitigate to make (pain, suffering, punishment, anger) less great or severe

mitre (say mieter) a tall pointed headdress worn by archbishops and bishops

mitten a glove-like covering for the hand, with (usually) a separate division for the thumb, but not for each of the four fingers

mix to combine or blend several things together into one mass by stirring or shaking (as, to mix cement, to mix ingredients for a cake, etc.); to muddle or confuse (as, to mix up the details of one event with another); to associate or get along with others (as - They mix well with other children in the neighbourhood.)
mixed made up of different kinds (as, mixed sweets); of different sexes (as - The litter of puppies was mixed, three males and two females.); muddled or confused
mixer a mixing machine; a person who makes a mixture; a person who gets on well or badly with others (as - He is a good mixer. She is a bad mixer.)
mixture a blend or mass formed by mixing
mixed-up confused; (of people) bewildered; not feeling secure or happy in one's surroundings

mizzen-mast the rear mast of a sailing vessel with two or three masts

mnemonic (say nemonik) something that helps one to remember (often a rhyme or jingle, such as - Thirty days hath September, etc., which is a mnemonic for the number of days in each month of the year.)

moan a low sound of grief or pain □ to utter a moan

moat a deep trench round a

castle, etc. (in former times, usually filled with water)

mob a noisy or disorderly crowd □ to crowd round in a disorderly way (as - The players were mobbed as they left the field.)

mobile easily moved; able to move quickly (as, a mobile squad); (of face) changing easily in expression
mobilize to call (troops, etc.) into active service

moccasin a heelless soft leather shoe worn by North American Indians

mock to laugh at; to make fun of □ sham or false (as, a mock battle)
mockery the act of making fun of something
mocking-bird a North American bird of the thrush family which imitates the notes of other birds

mode a fashion; a manner of acting or doing (as, a mode of travel)

model a small copy of something; something to be copied (as, the model or design for a new aeroplane); a person who poses for an artist; a person employed to wear and show off new clothes □ acting as a model; fit to be copied

moderate *(say moderet)* fair; not unreasonably great (as, a moderate price, a moderate speed); of medium quality or worth □ *(say moderate)* to keep within bounds; to reduce in intensity, etc. (as, to moderate one's speed in a car)
moderately fairly; reasonably

modern belonging to the present time or age; not old
modernize to bring up to date

modest not boastful or vain; not very large (as, a modest income)
modesty the quality or fact of being modest

modify to change; to alter slightly (as, to modify one's opinion)

modulate to vary or soften the tone of (as, to modulate the

voice)

module a self-contained unit forming part of a spacecraft; a self-contained electronic unit; (in architecture) a standard for measuring

mohair the long silken hair of the Angora goat; cloth made of it

Mohammedan having to do with the religion established by Mohammed (A.D. 570 - 632) in Arabia □ a follower of this faith

moist slightly wet; damp
moisten to wet slightly
moisture moistness; slight wetness

molar a back tooth with a flat surface which grinds food

molasses a thick syrup that is left when sugar is manufactured

mole 1 a small burrowing animal with very small eyes and soft fur
molehill a little heap of earth cast up by a mole

mole 2 a small (usually dark) spot on the skin

molecule *(say mollecule)* the smallest particle of any substance that has the properties of that substance
molecular *(say molecular)* of, or having to do with, molecules

molest to meddle with; to annoy

mollusc a soft animal without a backbone, and (usually) with a hard shell (for example, shellfish, snails)

molten see melt

moment a very short space of time; an instant: importance or value (as - Nothing of moment has happened.)
momentary *(say momentary)* lasting for a moment
momentous *(say momentous)* of great importance

momentum *(say momentum)* the force of anything that is moving (as - He couldn't stop the bicycle and his momentum carried him on to the pavement.)

monarch a king, queen, emperor or empress
monarchy a kingdom; govern-

ment by a monarch

monastery a building where monks live

monastic having to do with monks, monasteries, etc.

money the coins and banknotes used in paying for things; wealth

monetary having to do with money (as, a monetary reward for returning someone's lost property)

mongoose a small weasel-like animal of India that kills snakes

mongrel an animal (especially a dog) of mixed breed □ mixed in breed

monitor a pupil chosen by a teacher to help in certain ways (such as seeing that school rules are kept, etc.): a kind of instrument for checking the quality or production of some manufactured goods □ to use a monitor; to listen and check on foreign radio broadcasts

monk a member of a male religious group living in a monastery

monkey a lively animal, like a small ape but with a long tail, which lives in trees in tropical countries; a mischievous child □ to meddle with

monkey nut the peanut or groundnut

monocle a single eyeglass

monogamy the rule or custom of marriage to one wife or one husband only at a time: see also **polygamy**

monogamous having to do with monogamy

monogram two or more letters intertwined into a single design (for example, someone's initials)

monologue a speech (usually long) by one person

monoplane an aeroplane with one pair of wings (Many early aeroplanes had two pairs of wings, and were called biplanes.)

monopoly the sole right of making or selling something (as -

The XYZ Company has a monopoly in the manufacture of nylon fibre.); sole possession of (as - No political party has a monopoly of wisdom.)

monopolize to have the sole right of anything; to take up completely (as - She was very talkative and monopolized the conversation.)

monosyllable a word of one syllable only

monotone a single, unchanging tone of voice

monotonous in one unchanging tone; dull

monotony lack of change; dullness

monotype a machine with a keyboard that casts and sets type for printing one letter at a time: see also **linotype**

monsoon a wind that blows in the Indian Ocean; the rainy season in summer caused by the southwest monsoon

monster an imaginary creature (usually very large and terrifying); a plant or animal of unusual appearance □ huge (as, a monster wedding-cake)

monstrosity something not natural

monstrous huge; horrible

month one of the twelve divisions of the year, each lasting about four weeks (namely, January, February, March, April, etc.)

monthly happening once a month □ a paper or magazine published once in a month

monument a statue, building, etc. put up in memory of a person or event (such as a war memorial)

moo the sound made by a cow □ to low like a cow

mood the state of a person's feelings, temper or mind (as, to be in a good mood, or a bad mood)

moody often changing one's mood; gloomy

moon the heavenly body that moves round the earth once a month and at night reflects light from the sun □ to wander about; to gaze dreamily

moonbeam a beam of light from the moon

moonlight the light of the moon □ happening in moonlight (as, a moonlight bathe)

moonshine the shining of the moon: nonsense

moor 1 a large stretch of open land with poor soil (often covered with heath)

moorhen a female coot or waterfowl

moorland a countryside made up of moors

moor 2 to fasten or secure (of a ship, etc.) by cable or anchor

moorings the place where a ship is moored

moose the largest deer of North America

mop a bunch of coarse yarn, or pieces of sponge, fixed on a short handle for washing dishes, or on a longer handle for cleaning floors, etc.; a thick mass of hair like a mop □ to rub or wipe with a mop

mope to act in a listless way and look sad

moral having to do with character and good or bad behaviour (as - Human beings, unlike animals, have a moral sense.) □ the practical lesson to be learned from a story or a personal experience

morals a person's moral standards and conduct

morale *(say morahl)* the level of courage and confidence (as - The morale of the troops was high [or low].)

moralize to draw a lesson from a story or happening

morality moral principles or conduct

morass *(say morass)* a marsh

morbid not healthy; thinking too much about sickly or gloomy things (as, morbid thoughts, a morbid person)

more a larger quantity or number of (as - Jane has more apples

than John.) □ to a greater degree (as, more difficult, more beautiful)

moreover besides

morning the first part of the day (between dawn and midday) □ taking place in the morning (as, a morning lesson)

morn (poetic) morning (as, one fine September morn)

morocco fine goatskin leather (first made only in Morocco)

moron an adult of low mental ability

morose sullen or gloomy

morphia *(say morfia)*, **morphine** *(say morfeen)* a habit-forming drug obtained from opium and used mainly to deaden pain

morse a code for signalling and telegraphy in which the letters are represented by dots and dashes or short and long flashes (named after its inventor, Samuel Morse)

morsel a small piece of something (especially food)

mortal liable to die; causing death (as, a mortal blow); deadly (as, a mortal enemy, mortal fear) □ a human being

mortality the state of being mortal; the number of deaths in a period (as, a high mortality, or mortality rate)

mortar a mixture of lime, sand and water used in building to hold bricks or blocks together

mortar-board a college cap with a square flat top

mortgage *(say morgij)* a legal agreement by which a sum of money is loaned to buy a house, land, etc. (The borrower has to give up the property if he fails to repay the loan.) □ to pledge property as security for a loan

mortify to annoy or make someone ashamed by humiliating him

mortuary a place where bodies are kept before burial

mosaic *(say mozayic)* a design made by arranging lots of small pieces of marble, coloured glass, etc.

Moslem a Mohammedan □ of, or belonging to, the Mohammedans

mosque *(say mosk)* a Mohammedan place of worship

mosquito *(say moskeeto)* a small flying insect that bites (Some kinds of mosquito transmit diseases, such as malaria.)

moss a tiny green flowerless plant that grows in patches in moist places, such as tree trunks, old stones, etc.

most the largest quantity or number of (as - John scored most runs in the first innings.); the majority (as - Most people like ice cream.) □ in the highest degree (as - That is what upsets him most.)
mostly chiefly or mainly

motel a motor hotel, used mostly by motorists for overnight stops

moth one of a family of insects rather like butterflies which are seen mostly at night (The larva of the clothes moth eats holes in cloth.)
mothball a small piece or ball of camphor or similar substance used to keep moths from eating clothing, etc.
moth-eaten eaten and partly destroyed by moths; old and worn

mother a female parent; the female head of a convent (as, the Mother Superior) □ to care for, as a mother does
motherly like a mother
motherhood the state of being a mother
mother-in-law the mother of one's husband or wife
mother-of-pearl the shining iridescent substance found on the inside of certain shells (especially of pearl oysters)
mother tongue a person's native language

motion the act or state of moving; the movement from one place to another: a proposal put before a meeting □ to make a movement or sign (as - The farmer motioned the boy to come nearer.)
motionless without any movement (as, standing motionless)

motive causing motion (as, a motive force or power) □ a thought or emotion that makes a person act in a particular way (as - His motive for refusing cigarettes was his wish to do well at sports.)
motivate to supply a motive or reason for some action (as - He was motivated by ambition.)

motley of many different colours; mixed (as, a motley crowd) □ the coloured clothing of a jester

motor a machine which makes something work or move (as, an electric motor, a petrol motor) □ driven by a motor (as, a motor car, motor bicycle, motor boat, etc.) □ to travel by motor vehicle
motorist someone who drives a motor car, especially for pleasure
motor bike, motor cycle a motor bicycle
motorway a dual carriageway for fast motor traffic with no crossings on the same level

mottled marked with spots or blotches of many colours

motto a short sentence or phrase which expresses a guiding idea (as - *Be prepared!* or *Honesty is the best policy.*)

mould 1 a shape into which a liquid substance is poured so that it takes on the same shape when it has cooled or set (as, a jelly mould) □ to form in a mould; to shape
moulding a decorated border (as, the moulding on a picture frame)

mould 2 a fluffy growth on stale bread, cheese, etc.

moult (of birds) to shed feathers

mound a bank of earth or stones; a small rounded hill

mount 1 to go up (as, to mount the stairs); to get up on (as, to mount a horse or a bicycle); to fix something in a holder (as, to mount a photograph in an album, to mount a jewel in a brooch) □ a riding animal (especially a horse); a support or backing (as, for a photograph)

mountain a very high hill; anything very large (as, a mountain of work to be done) □ of, or relating to, a mountain (as, mountain goats)

mount 2 a mountain

mountaineer a mountain climber

mountainous full of mountains (as - Switzerland is a mountainous country.); huge (as, mountainous seas)

mourn to be sorrowful; to grieve

mourner someone who mourns (as, a mourner at a funeral)

mournful sad; causing, or showing, sorrow (as, a mournful face)

mourning the act of showing grief; the dark clothing of mourners

mouse a small gnawing animal, sometimes found in houses and sometimes in fields

mice the plural of mouse

mousse (say mooss) a light whipped-up dessert, sometimes frozen like ice cream

moustache, mustache (say mus-tash) the hair on a man's upper lip

mouth the opening in the head through which a person or an animal eats and utters sounds; any opening or entrance (as, the mouth of a river, of a cave, of a bottle, etc.) □ to speak or pronounce words in an exaggerated manner

mouthful as much as fills the mouth

mouth organ a small musical instrument played by the mouth

mouthpiece the part of a musical instrument, or tobacco pipe, which is held in the mouth

down in the mouth sad; out of spirits

move to go, or to change some-

thing, from one place to another; to change homes (as - They moved from London to the country.); to arouse (as - The team's foul play moved the crowd to anger.) □ the act of moving; a single movement (as, a move in chess)

movable able to be moved; not fixed

movement the act of moving; a change of position; a group activity intended to bring about a change of some kind (as, a movement to improve international understanding)

moving in motion; causing emotion (especially pity)

movie, moving-picture a cinema film

mow to cut grass with a machine or scythe (as, to mow a lawn, a meadow); to cut down in great numbers (as - The infantry were mown down by machine-gun fire.)

mower someone who mows; a machine for mowing

much a great quantity of □ to a great degree (as, much louder); nearly (as, much the same): see also **more** and **most**

muck dirt; dung

mucus (say mewcus) the slimy fluid from the nose

mucous like mucus

mucous membrane the thin lining of the nose, etc. that is in contact with the outside air

mud wet soft earth

muddy covered with, or containing, mud

mudguard a piece of metal to catch mud splashes from the wheels of a road vehicle

muddle to make a mess of; to bungle; to confuse (as, muddled thinking) □ a mess; a confusion

muff 1 a tube-shaped cover (usually of fur) for keeping the hands warm

muff 2 to fail to catch a ball (as, in cricket); to do something clumsily

muffin a soft, bread-like cake,

toasted and eaten with butter

muffle to wrap up for warmth: to deaden sound (as, to muffle an alarm clock with a pillow)
muffler a scarf for the throat

mug a large heavy cup with straight sides

muggy (of weather) close and damp

mulberry a tree with purple berries and with leaves on which silkworms feed

mule an animal whose parents are a horse and a donkey: a stubborn person
muleteer someone who drives mules

mullet a type of small edible seafish

multi- a prefix meaning many or much
multi-coloured many-coloured
multifarious of many kinds (as, multifarious activities)
multimillionaire a person with property worth several million pounds
multiracial of many races (as - Brazil has a multiracial population.)

multiple having many parts □ a number that contains another an exact number of times (as - 24 is a multiple of 2, 3, 4, 6, 8, and 12.)

multiply to increase; to take a number any number of times (twice, three times, four times, etc.) and find the total (as - 6 multiplied by 4, or 6 × 4 = 24.)
multiplication the act of multiplying
multiplier the number by which another is to be multiplied

multitude a great number; a crowd

mum silent; not speaking
mummer an actor in a dumb show

mumble to speak indistinctly with the lips nearly closed □ indistinct speech

mummy a human body pre-served inside wrappings by the ancient Egyptians, etc.
mummify to make into a mummy

mumps a disease of the glands of the neck, causing an uncomfortable swelling

munch to chew with a crunching sound

municipal (say mewnisipal) having to do with a city or town
municipality a city or town with local self-government

munitions weapons and ammunition used in war

mural having to do with a wall; on a wall □ a painting or design on a wall

murder to kill on purpose and unlawfully □ the act of murdering
murderer someone who kills another person on purpose
murderous capable of, or guilty of, murder; deadly

murky dark; gloomy

murmur a low continuous sound (as, the murmur of waves lapping a shore) □ to make a murmur; to speak in a low voice; to grumble

muscle (say muss'l) a fleshy bundle of fibres (in the arm, leg, etc.) which causes movements by alternately contracting and stretching out
muscular having to do with the muscles; strong

muse 1 to think over a matter quietly

muse 2 one of the nine Greek goddesses of poetry, music, dancing, etc.

museum a building where interesting collections of historic, scientific, etc. objects are set out for visitors to see

mushroom a type of fungus which is (usually) small and umbrella-shaped (especially one that can be cooked and eaten)

music any arrangement of sounds that are pleasing to the ear; the art of combining, or

composing, such sounds; the score of a musical composition
musical having to do with music; pleasing to the ear
musician *(say mewzishan)* a person skilled in performing music

musket an old-fashioned gun once carried by foot soldiers
musketeer a soldier armed with a musket

muslin a fine soft cotton cloth resembling gauze

mussel a shellfish enclosed within a shell in two parts, used for food

must an auxiliary verb, used with other verbs to indicate that something or some action is necessary (as - We must get home before it gets dark. The lost purse must be found.)

mustache see **moustache**

mustang the wild horse of the American prairies

mustard a brownish-yellow seasoning made from the seeds of the mustard plant (It is eaten with meat and has a hot, strong taste.)

muster to gather together (as, to muster troops); to summon up (courage or strength)

musty mouldy; stale in smell or taste

mute dumb; silent; not sounded (as - The letter *k* in *know* is mute.)

mutilate to maim; to deform by cutting off a limb, etc.; to damage badly
mutilation the act of mutilating

mutiny to rise against officers in the armed forces; to refuse to obey any recognized authority □ a rebellion in the army or navy
mutineer someone who mutinies
mutinous inclined to mutiny; rebellious

mutter to utter words in a low voice; to murmur; to grumble

mutton the meat from sheep

mutual (of actions or feelings) given and received by each to the other(s) (as, mutual help, mutual friendship); shared (as, a mutual friend)

muzzle the jaws and nose of an animal; an arrangement of straps, etc. fastened round the jaws and nose to keep it from biting (as, a dog muzzle): the open end of a gun barrel □ to put a muzzle on; to gag or silence

myopia shortness of sight
myopic short-sighted or near-sighted

myriad a very great number □ numberless (as, myriad stars)

myrrh *(say murr)* a kind of resin with a bitter taste, used in some medicines, etc.

myrtle an evergreen shrub with beautiful, fragrant leaves

mystery something that cannot be (or has not been) explained; a deep secret
mysterious difficult to understand; secret
mystic(al) having a sacred or secret meaning
mystify to puzzle greatly; to confuse

myth a story about heroes or gods of ancient times; a fable; some imagined person or thing
mythical told of in a myth; imaginary
mythology a collection of myths; the study of myths

n

nab to seize; to catch suddenly

nag 1 to find fault with constantly
nagging persistent (as, a nagging pain)

nag 2 a horse (especially a small one or one in poor condition)

nail the horny part at the end of a finger or toe: a thin pointed piece of metal for joining pieces of wood together □ to fasten with nails

naïve *(say na-eev)* simple in thought, manner or speech

naked without clothes or covering

name the word or words by which a person, place or thing is known or called; character or reputation (as, to have a name for fair dealing) □ to give a name to; to mention (as - The newsreader named several villages affected by the earthquake.)
nameless without a name
namely that is to say (as - Two boys volunteered, namely Peter and John.)
nameplate a metal plate having a person's name on it (as, for example, one fixed outside a doctor's surgery)
namesake someone having the same name as another

nanny-goat a female goat

nap 1 a short sleep □ to take a short sleep

nap 2 a woolly surface on cloth

nap 3 a card game

napalm an inflammable jelly used in some bombs

nape the back of the neck

napkin (table napkin) a square piece of linen or paper used at the table for wiping the mouth and fingers; (nappy) a small towel which is pinned round a baby

narcissus a bulbous plant with narrow leaves and white or yellow fragrant flowers

narcotic a drug that eases pain or makes one sleep

narrate to tell a story (as, to narrate one's adventures)
narration the telling of a story
narrative a story □ telling a story
narrator someone who tells a story

narrow not wide; with little to spare (as, a narrow escape); limited in outlook or opinions (as, narrow-minded) □ to make or become narrow
narrows a sea or river passage of little width

nasal of the nose; sounded through the nose (as - He has a nasal voice.)

nasturtium *(say nasturshum)* a plant with round flat leaves and orange, yellow or red flowers

nasty very disagreeable; the opposite of nice; difficult to deal with (as, a nasty problem)
nastiness great unpleasantness

natal *(say naytal)* having to do with birth

nation all the people living in one country, or under the same government; a race of people (as, the Jewish nation)
national belonging to one nation □ a person belonging to a particular nation (as, a British national)
nationalist someone who seeks to unite the people of a nation under their own independent government (as, a Scottish or a Welsh nationalist)
nationality membership of a particular nation (as - He has American nationality.)
nationalize to make something the property of a nation (for example - Coalmining is a nationalized industry.)
National Anthem the special song or hymn of a country (for example, in Britain *God save the Queen.*)
nation-wide covering, or taking place throughout, the

whole nation

native a person born in a particular country or place (as, a native of France, of Edinburgh); one of the original inhabitants of a country (as - The natives of Australia are called aborigines.) □ having to do with one's place of birth or origin (as, a person's native land)
the Nativity the birth of Christ

nature all the world around us that is not man-made (such as plants, animals, streams, mountains, etc.); (human nature) the qualities that are characteristic of a person or thing (as - She has a gentle nature. The nature of the country is mountainous.)
natural having to do with nature (as, the natural, not man-made, features of a landscape); born in a person (as, a natural gift for music); unaffected or without airs (as, behaving in a natural manner) □ a sign (♮) in music to show that a note is not sharp or flat
naturalist a person who studies animals and plant life
naturalize to give the rights of a citizen to someone born in another country
naturally of course; simply
natured having a certain temper (as, good-natured)
natural gas gas suitable for burning which is found naturally in the earth or under the sea
natural history the study of animals and plants
natural resources the natural wealth of a country (such as forests, minerals and water for power)

naught *(say nawt)* nothing: see also **nought**

naughty bad; misbehaving
naughtiness bad behaviour

nausea *(say nawsia)* a feeling of sickness
nauseate to make sick; to fill with disgust

nautical having to do with ships or sailors
nautical mile see **mile**

naval see under **navigate**

nave the middle or main part of a church

navel the small hollow in the centre of the belly

navigate to direct or manage a ship or aircraft on its course
navigable able to be used by ships (as, a navigable river)
navigation the art of directing ships, etc.
navigator a person who directs the course of a ship, etc.
navy a nation's fleet of fighting ships; the men serving on these ships
naval having to do with the navy
navy blue dark blue

nay no

near close to □ not far away in place or time; close in relationship (as, a near relative or friend) □ to approach
nearly almost; closely
near side (of vehicles, etc.) the left-hand side
near-sighted short-sighted

neat trim; tidy; skilfully done (as, a neat job)

nebula a misty appearance in a clear night sky produced either by a huge number of very distant stars or by a great mass of gas and dust
nebulae the plural of nebula
nebulous hazy; vague

necessary not able to be done without; needed; not able to be escaped (as, a necessary duty) □ something that cannot be done without (as - Food and clothing are basic necessaries of life.)
necessitate to make necessary (as - Competing in a sports contest necessitates training beforehand.)
necessity something that cannot be done without; a great need

neck the part between head and body; anything shaped like a neck (as, the neck of a bottle, a neck of land)

necklace a string of beads or a thin chain worn round the neck

necktie a tie or scarf for the neck

neck and neck exactly equal (as, two horses racing neck and neck)

nectar a sweet liquid collected by bees from flowers to make honey; the supposed drink of the ancient Greek gods; a delicious drink

nectarine a kind of smooth-skinned peach

née *(say nay)* the French word for born, used chiefly of married women to indicate their surname before marriage (as, Mrs. Knight, née Brown)

need a necessity; a lack; poverty □ to be in want of

needful necessary

needless unnecessary

needy poor

needle a small sharp piece of steel used in sewing (with an eye at the blunt end for the thread); a longer similar object, without an eye, used in pairs for knitting; a pointer (as, a compass needle); the long pointed leaf of a pine, fir, etc.

needlework embroidery or sewing done with a needle

negative meaning or saying no (as, a negative answer) □ a word or words denying something (as - The answer is in the negative.); (in photography) an image on film in which the lights and shades are the opposite of those in nature

neglect to treat carelessly; to fail to give proper attention to; to fail to do □ want of care or attention

neglectful careless

negligence carelessness

negligent careless

negligible not worth considering; very small

negotiate to bargain with; to discuss something in order to reach agreement; to get past an obstacle or difficulty

negotiable able to be arranged or negotiated

negotiation a discussion aimed at reaching an agreement (as - Negotiations were opened between the employers and the trade union.)

negotiator a person who negotiates

negro a member of an African race with a dark skin; a person descended wholly or partly from this race

neigh *(say nay)* to utter the cry of a horse □ such a cry

neighbour someone who lives near another

neighbourhood this district (as - They live in the neighbourhood.); a district near a place (as, in the neighbourhood of Oxford)

neighbouring near in place; adjoining (as, neighbouring countries)

neighbourly friendly

neither not one or the other (as - Neither of the two answers is correct.); not either (as - Neither the first nor the second answer is correct.)

neon a colourless gas (as, in neon lighting, where an electric current lights up the gas in a glass tube)

nephew the son of a brother or sister

nerve one of the great number of long fibres in the body which carry sensations (such as heat, cold, pain) from all parts of the body to the brain and transmit messages back causing action; courage or coolness (as, to keep one's nerve in a difficult situation)

nerves the plural of nerve; nervousness (as - She suffers from nerves.)

nervous, nervy easily excited or frightened; timid

nervousness the state of being nervous

to get on one's nerves to irritate one

nest a place or structure in which

birds, and some small animals and insects, live and bring up their young (as, a robin's nest) □ to build or occupy a nest

nestle *(say nes'l)* to lie close together, like young birds in a nest; to settle comfortably

nestling *(say nes'ling)* a young newly hatched bird

net 1 cord or twine knotted so as to form a loose arrangement of crossing lines with many spaces in between, used for catching birds, fish, etc. □ to catch as in a net

netting a net material (as, wire netting)

netball a team game in which a large ball has to be thrown into a high net

network any system of lines like a net (as, a network of roads)

net 2, nett remaining after any expenses, charges, etc. have been deducted (as, net profit, net price)

nettle a weed with prickly hairs which sting the skin □ to sting; to annoy

nettle rash a skin rash that looks like the effect of nettle stings

neuralgia a pain in the nerves, especially in those of the head or face

neurotic in a constantly nervous state (and often over-anxious without good reason)

neuter (in grammar) neither masculine nor feminine (the pronoun *it* and the noun *desk* are neuter); (of animals) neither male nor female; unable to reproduce

neutral not taking sides □ a country or person not taking part in a war or dispute

neutrality the state of being neutral

neutralize to make neutral; to make something useless or harmless by having an opposite effect (as, to neutralize an acid poison with an alkali)

neutron one of the particles

(with no electrical charge) which together with protons, make up the nucleus of an atom

never not ever; not at any time

nevertheless in spite of that

new recent; not seen or known before (as, a new teacher); not used or worn (as, a new dress)

newly very recently (as, newly arrived)

newborn just born

newcomer a person who has recently arrived

newfangled (of things or ideas) new, but not thought much of

New Year a fresh calendar year starting on January 1st

news a report of a recent event; new information (as, waiting for news of a hospital patient)

newsagent someone who sells newspapers

newspaper printed sheets of paper containing news (as, daily or weekly newspapers)

newt a small animal, rather like a lizard, that lives both on land and in water

next nearest in place or time (as, the next person in a queue, the next bus) □ following after someone or something (as - His brother came next.)

nib the writing point of a pen that is not a ball point

nibble to take very small bites of something □ a little bite

nice agreeable; friendly; pleasant: exact or careful (as, a nice sense of timing)

nicely very well (as - That will suit me nicely.)

niche a hollow in a wall for a statue or ornament

nick a notch; a little cut □ to cut notches; to make a little cut

nickel a greyish-white metal used in alloys and for plating (as, nickel-plating)

nickname an added name (usually given in fun or affection, but sometimes in contempt)

nicotine a poisonous substance

contained in tobacco

niece the daughter of a brother or sister

niggardly mean (as, a niggardly ungenerous person)

nigh near

night the time between sunset and sunrise; darkness □to do with the night (as, night-time, a night worker)
nightly every night; by night
nightdress, nightgown a garment worn in bed
nightfall the beginning of the night; dusk
nightmare a frightening dream
nightshade a plant with poisonous berries
night shift a turn of duty or work at night
night watchman a man who looks after a building during the night

nightingale a small bird which sings beautifully at night as well as by day

nil nothing

nimble quick in moving; quick in thinking (as, a nimble mind)

ninepins a bowling game in which players try to knock down nine bottle-shaped pins

ninny a foolish person

nip to pinch; to cut or bite off a bit of something □a pinch; sharp coldness (as - There's a nip in the air.)

nipple the part of the breast from which a baby, or baby animal, sucks milk

nit the egg of a louse or other small insect

nitrate a chemical fertilizer

nitrogen a colourless, odourless gas, forming nearly four-fifths of the air we breathe
nitro-glycerine a powerful explosive

nitwit a very foolish person

no the opposite of yes; a denial or refusal □not any (as - They have no bread.)
no one not any person

noble of high birth or rank; great in character □a man of high rank
nobly in a noble manner (as, to behave nobly under difficult conditions)
nobility nobleness of character; all the nobles of a country
nobleman a man of high rank

nobody no one; a person of no importance

nocturnal active or happening at night (as, a nocturnal animal)
nocturne a dreamy piece of music (usually for the piano)

nod to bend the head forward quickly (often as a sign of agreement); to let the head fall forward in weariness □a quick forward movement of the head

node a knob or swelling, especially where a leaf stalk joins a branch or twig
nodule a little rounded lump

Noël *(say no-el)* Christmas

noise a sound (often a loud or disturbing sound)
noisy making a loud sound (as, noisy traffic)

nomad one of a group of people without a fixed home, who wander with their animals from place to place; a wanderer

nominal in name only; unimportant (as, a nominal fine of 25p)
nominate to name, or mention by name; to propose someone's name for a position or for election
nomination the act of nominating; the state of being nominated
nominee someone who is proposed for a position, etc.

non- a prefix which usually changes the meaning of a word to its opposite
non-committal unwilling to take sides or to express a definite opinion
non-conductor any substance which does not readily conduct heat or electricity (such as plastic)
non-conformist a person who

does not agree with those in authority, especially with the established Church

non-existent not existing, not real (as, a non-existent monster)

non-resident not living in the place mentioned (as, a hotel restaurant open to non-residents)

non-stop going on without a stop

nonagenarian someone who is ninety years old or more

nonchalant casual in manner; not easily upset

nondescript not easy to describe or classify; characterless (as - He wore rather nondescript clothes.)

none not one; not any □ not at all (as, none the worse)
none the less nevertheless; in spite of this

nonentity a person of no importance

nonsense words that have no sense or meaning; foolishness
nonsensical silly

noodle a food similar to macaroni, but usually made with egg and cut into long flat strips

nook a corner; a recess

noon midday, twelve o'clock
noonday the time about midday

noose a loop in a rope or cord with a slip-knot which enables the loop to be pulled tight

nor and not: see also **neither**

norm a standard or pattern to judge other things by
normal ordinary; usual

north in the direction opposite to south (to the left of a person facing the rising sun in the east) □ a region in this direction
northern, northerly of, or towards, the north
North Pole see **pole**
northern lights the aurora borealis (greenish lights sometimes seen in the northern sky at night)

nose the part of the face through which we breathe and smell; a jutting-out part of anything (as, the nose of an aeroplane) □ to make a way by feeling and pushing (as, a ship nosing its way between ice-floes); to track by smelling

nosey, nosy having a large nose; fond of prying

nose-dive a dive head first □ to dive head first (as - The aeroplane nose-dived into the sea.)

nosegay a small bunch of fragrant flowers

to poke one's nose into to pry into; to meddle in

to turn up one's nose at to show disdain or contempt for

nostalgia a sentimental longing for past times

nostril one of the openings of the nose

not expressing refusal or denial

notable, notability see **note**

notary an official who is authorized to certify legal statements and documents (for example, contracts and deeds)

notation a system of signs for showing numbers, musical sounds, etc. (as, the decimal notation, the sol-fa notation)

notch a nick; a small v-shaped cut □ to make a notch

note a sign or short piece of writing to draw someone's attention to something; a short explanation; a short letter: a piece of paper used as money (as, a pound [£] note): (in music) a single tone (as, a high note, a low note); a sign that shows the pitch and duration of a tone according to its shape and position on the staff; a key on the piano, etc. □ to make a note of; to notice

notable worth noting; memorable; important

notability notableness; a notable person

noted well-known

notebook a small book in which to make notes

noteworthy notable

of note distinguished (as, an author of note)

nothing no thing; not anything

notice an announcement or statement made, or shown, publicly; attention (as - She attracted notice.); a warning that an agreement is ending (as - The manager gave the employee one month's notice.) □ to see; to take note of
noticeable likely to be noticed (as, a noticeable difference)
to take notice to pay attention

notify to inform; to give notice or warning of something
notifiable (of diseases) that must be reported to the public health authorities
notification the act of notifying; a notice given

notion an idea; a fancy or vague belief

notorious well known in a bad way (as, a notorious criminal)

notwithstanding in spite of □ nevertheless

nougat *(say nooga)* a thick sweet paste containing chopped nuts (usually in the form of a bar)

nought *(say nawt)* naught; nothing; the figure 0

noun (in grammar) a word used as the name of a person or thing (For example, the words *boy, James, person* and *thing* are all nouns.)

nourish to feed; to encourage the growth of any living thing (as, to nourish a plant); to keep in the mind (as, to nourish the hope of success)
nourishing (of food) giving the body what is necessary for health and growth
nourishment anything that nourishes

novel 1 new and different; unusual
novelty something new or unusual

novel 2 a long story which is based on fiction and not facts
novelist a writer of novels

novice *(say noviss)* a beginner

now at the present time
nowadays at the present day
now, now that since, because (as - I can go now that my father has come home.)
now and then from time to time; sometimes

nowhere not anywhere; in or to no place (as - He's going nowhere.)

noxious *(say nokshus)* harmful to living things (as, noxious gases)

nozzle a spout fitted to the end of a pipe or hose

nuance *(say newans)* a very small shade of difference in meaning, opinion, colour, etc.

nucleus the central part around which something collects, or from which something grows (as, the nucleus of a nebula); the part of a plant or animal cell that controls its development; the central part of an atom, consisting of two kinds of particle (the neutron and proton)
nuclear having to do with a nucleus, especially of the atom
nuclei *(say newclee-ie)* the plural of nucleus
nuclear energy the atomic energy released by splitting of certain kinds of atoms (uranium and plutonium)
nuclear fission the splitting of the nuclei of atoms
nuclear reactor apparatus for producing atomic energy

nude naked, without clothes □ an unclothed human figure or statue
nudist a person who approves of going without clothes
nudity the state of being nude; nakedness

nudge a gentle poke (especially with an elbow) □ to poke gently (especially with an elbow)

nugget a lump (especially of gold)

nuisance a person or thing that is annoying or troublesome

null of no value or effect

nullify to undo the effect of something; to make useless

null and void having no legal force

numb having lost the power to feel or move (as - Her fingers were numb with cold.) □ to make numb

number a word or figure showing how many (6, 36 and 216 are numbers); the place of anything in a series (as, the house with number 7 in a street); a collection of things or persons (as, a number of books, of people); one issue of a newspaper or magazine □ to count; to amount to in number (as - The class numbers 24.)

numeral a single figure used in making up a number (as, 2 or 3, III or IV)

numerator (in fractions) the number above the line

numerical in numbers (as, a secret message written in a numerical code)

numerous very many (as, a numerous gathering of people)

numismatics the collection and study of coins and medals

numbskull a stupid fellow

nun a member of a female religious group living in a convent

nunnery a convent for nuns

nuptial having to do with marriage

nuptials a wedding ceremony

nurse a person (usually a woman) who has been trained to help doctors to look after sick or injured people □ to look after invalids, especially in hospital: to give babies milk from the breast: to hold, or to manage, with care

nursery a room for young children to sleep or play in; a place where young plants and trees are raised

nursery school a school for children under five

nursing home a small private hospital

nurture the bringing up of young children; nourishment □ to bring up; to nourish

nut a fruit or seed consisting of a kernel inside a hard shell: a small piece of metal with a hole in it, through which the end of a bolt can be screwed

nutcrackers a pair of hinged metal arms used for cracking nuts

in a nutshell (of arguments, opinions, etc.) expressed very briefly

nutmeg a hard East-Indian seed, used as a spice to flavour food

nutrient one of the substances in foods which provide nourishment □ giving nourishment

nutriment nourishment; food (as - The prisoners did not get enough nutriment from their meagre rations.)

nutrition the science or study of food values and of the nutrient requirements of human beings or animals; the process of providing nourishing foods

nutritious nourishing

nuzzle to press, or rub against, with the nose (as - The dog nuzzled my hand.)

nylon a kind of man-made material obtained from petroleum (Nylon is used for stockings, shirts, ropes, brushes, etc.)

nymph *(say nimf)* a Greek goddess of the rivers, trees, etc.; a beautiful girl

O

O, Oh an exclamation expressing surprise, admiration, pain, etc.

oaf a stupid fellow; an awkward lout

oak a large tree having acorns as

its fruit; its hard wood
oaken made of oak

oar a pole with a flat end (the blade) for rowing a boat
oarsman a rower

oasis *(say o-aysiss)* a place in a desert where there is water and vegetation
oases the plural of oasis

oath a solemn promise to speak the truth, to keep one's word, or to be loyal to someone; a swear word

oats a kind of grain used to make porridge and to feed animals
oatcake a thin hard cake of oatmeal
oatmeal a meal made by grinding oats

obedience, obedient see **obey**

obelisk a tall, four-sided pillar with a pointed top

obese *(say obeess)* very fat

obey to do what one is told to do (as, to obey an order, to obey one's father)
obedience the act of obeying; willingness to obey (as - He showed obedience.)
obedient obeying; ready to obey

obituary a notice (usually in a newspaper) of a person's death

object 1 *(say object)* any material thing that can be seen or felt; an aim or purpose (as - His object in life was to become a doctor.); (in grammar) the word(s) standing for the person or thing on which any action is done (as *the ball* in *He kicked the ball.*)
objective an aim or goal □ without prejudice; fair (as, an objective opinion of someone's character)
object lesson an example that should act as a warning

object 2 *(say object)* to express disagreement or disapproval (as, to object to a referee's decision)
objection the act of objecting; the reason for objection (as - My objection is that not enough time has been allowed.)
objectionable disagreeable;

nasty (as, an objectionable smell)

oblige *(say obliej)* to force or compel (as - The motorist was obliged to stop when he ran out of petrol.): to do a favour or service for someone
obligation *(say obligayshun)* a promise or duty (as, to have, or be under, an obligation to another person)
obligatory *(say obligatree)* necessary; required as a duty
obliging *(say obliejing)* ready to do a good turn; helpful

oblique *(say obleek)* slanting; sloping

obliterate to blot out; to destroy completely

oblivion forgetfulness; a state of being forgotten
oblivious forgetful; unaware (as, oblivious of the crowd around him)

oblong a shape in the form of a rectangle with two opposite sides longer than the other two

obnoxious objectionable; causing dislike or offence

oboe a double-reed woodwind instrument with a high pitch

obscene *(say obseen)* indecent; offensive to morals

obscure dark; not clear or easily understood; unknown □ to darken; to make less clear
obscurity obscureness; an obscure point

obsequious *(say obseekwiyus)* trying to win favour by being excessively agreeable and humble to another person

observe to watch with attention; to notice; to obey (as, to observe the rules)
observance the keeping of a rule, a special day, etc. (as, Sunday observance)
observant quick to notice (as, an observant policeman)
observation the act of observing; a remark
observatory a building with telescopes for making observations of the solar system, stars,

etc.

obsess to fill the mind of; to worry continually (as, to be obsessed with the fear of losing one's job)
obsession an idea or emotion which occupies the mind continually

obsolete gone out of use (as, an obsolete model of a car)

obstacle anything that stands in one's way or hinders progress

obstinate stubborn; unyielding
obstinacy stubbornness

obstreperous noisy; boisterous or unruly

obstruct to block up; to hinder from passing
obstruction the act of obstructing; an obstacle

obtain to get; to gain (as, to obtain a certificate or diploma)

obtuse blunt, not pointed; stupid
obtuse angle an angle greater than a right angle

obverse the side of a coin bearing the head or main design

obvious evident; easily seen or understood

occasion a particular time (as, on this occasion); a special event (as, a grand occasion); an opportunity
occasional happening now and then
occasionally now and then; not often

occult mysterious; supernatural; secret

occupy to live in (as - The Jones family occupied flat No. 6.); to take up space (as - The bed occupied most of the space in her small room.); to take up time (as - On holiday they occupied themselves mostly in playing games and swimming.); to capture (as, a town occupied by the enemy)
occupancy the act or fact of occupying a house, office, etc.
occupant, occupier anyone who has possession of a house, office, etc.

occupation a person's usual job, trade or profession

occur to happen; to appear or be found (as - Hurricanes often occur in the Gulf of Mexico.); to come into the mind (as - An idea occurred to him.)
occurrence a happening or event

ocean one of the five vast expanses of salt water which cover most of the earth's surface (namely: Atlantic, Pacific, Indian, Arctic, and Antarctic)

ochre *(say oker)* a kind of pigment varying in colour between yellow and red (It consists of fine clay and iron oxide.)

o'clock the time by (originally, of) the clock (as, 7 o'clock)

octagon a shape with eight sides and eight angles
octagonal shaped like an octagon

octave (in music) a series of eight notes (as, from middle C to the C next above)

octogenarian someone who is eighty years old or more

octopus a sea creature with eight arms covered with suckers

oculist a doctor who specializes in eye ailments

odd (of a number) not even (that is, leaving a remainder when divided by 2): unusual or strange
oddity a strange person or thing
oddments, odds and ends objects, scraps, etc. of different kinds; bits and pieces
odds chances or probability (as - The odds are in his favour.); difference (as - It makes no odds.)
at odds quarrelling; opposed to one another

ode a poem, usually of some length, addressed to some person or thing (as, *Ode to a Skylark*)

odious hateful

odour a smell (which may be

pleasant or unpleasant)
odorous emitting an odour (usually fragrant)

of a connecting word with several meanings, examples being: belonging to (as, the house of a friend); from (as, within 50 kilometres of Paris); made from (as, a house of bricks); from among (as, one of my friends); about (as, to talk well of a person); with or comprising (as, a man of character, a city of two million inhabitants)

off away from a place or position (as - The jet plane took off from the airport.); away from a usual state or condition (as - The shop's sales fell off. The driver shut off the engine.) □ the opposite of on (as - The electricity is off.); farther away (as, the off side of a car)
off-and-on occasionally
off-colour not feeling very well
offhand casual; lacking in politeness (as, an offhand manner); without previous preparation
off-licence a licence for selling alcoholic drinks for drinking off the premises (unlike a public house where customers drink on the premises)
offset to make up for
offshoot a small branch of something
off side (in football) the position of a player who finds himself between the ball, or the last player who played it, and the opponents' goal
offspring a child or children

offal waste or parts of dead animals considered unfit to use as human food; but also certain nutritious parts (such as the heart, kidneys and liver) cut off in trimming a carcase and sold by butchers

offend to displease; to make angry; to act wrongly
offence any cause of anger or hurt feelings; a crime
offender someone who offends
offensive causing displeasure or hurt; disgusting (as, an offensive odour); used in attack (as, an offensive weapon) □ an attack (as, a military offensive)

offer to hold out, or put forward, something (as, to offer a gift, offer goods for sale, to offer a suggestion); to say that one is willing (as, to offer help) □ an act of offering (as, the offer of a new job)
offering a gift; a collection of money at a church service

office a place where most of the paper work (letters, accounts, etc.) of a business is carried on; a position of authority, especially in the government (as, the office of Prime Minister)
officer a person holding a commission in the army, navy or air force; a person who carries out a public duty (as, a local government officer)
official having to do with a position of authority (as, an official notice) □ a person holding a position of trust in the service of the government, etc. (as, a customs official, a bank official)
officiate to perform a duty or service (as - The priest officiated at the funeral.)
officious interfering; fussy

often many times; frequently

ogre an ugly giant or monster in fairy tales

oil a greasy liquid of vegetable, animal or mineral origin (as, olive oil, whale oil, or petroleum oil) □ to smear with oil or apply oil to
oils the plural of oil; oil paint
oily like oil; greasy
oilcake a cake or mass of linseed, etc. from which the oil has been pressed out, used as fodder
oilfield an area where mineral oil is found underground (as, the oilfields of the Middle East, etc.)
oil painting a picture painted in oils
oilskin a cloth or garment made waterproof by means of oil
oil well a hole drilled into the earth's surface or sea bed to obtain petroleum

ointment a greasy substance put

on the skin to heal hurts or sores

old advanced in age (as, an old man); having a certain age (as, ten years old): not new (as, an old coat, an old castle, etc.)
olden belonging to long ago
older having lived longer than someone else
old-fashioned out-of-date

olive a tree with silvery-green leaves which is grown in Mediterranean countries for its oily fruit; the fruit of this tree; a brownish-green colour like the unripe olive; (of the skin or complexion) yellowish-brown
olive branch a symbol of peace
olive oil the oil pressed from the fruit of the olive tree

omelet(te) eggs beaten with milk or water and cooked in a pan until semi-solid, then folded over before serving

omen a sign of a future event
ominous having to do with an omen; suggesting future trouble

omit to leave out; to fail to do
omission an act of omitting; something omitted

omnibus a large public road vehicle for passengers (now generally shortened to **bus**)

omnipotent *(say omnipotent)* all powerful; having unlimited authority

omniscient *(say omnishent)* all-knowing; knowing everything

omnivorous feeding on all kinds of food, both vegetable and animal

on touching the upper or outer surface of (as, on the table, on the wall of a house); showing where, generally (as, on the opposite side, on the Continent); showing when (as, on the 25th December); also many other uses (as, goods on sale, being on guard; money spent on clothes, having pity on a beggar; a book on foreign travel □ to move on, putting on one's clothes, the play went on, etc.)
onward going forward (as - March onward!) □ towards a

place or time ahead (as, moving onward[s])

once for one time only (as, once not twice); at some time in the past (as - We lived there once.)
at once without delay

oncoming approaching (as, the oncoming bus) □ an approach

one a single person; a person or a thing (as - One cannot be sure whether it will rain tomorrow.) □ united (as - They acted together as one party.)
one another each other
oneself the reflexive and emphatic form of one
one-sided limited to one side; unfair (as, a one-sided argument)
at one in agreement

onerous see **onus**

onion a bulb-like vegetable with a strong smell and flavour

onlooker a spectator (especially one who looks on by chance)

only one and no more of the kind (as, an only son or daughter) □ not more than (as, only ten players); merely (as - It will only upset him.); alone (as, a present for John only) □ except that (as - She would like to go, only she feels unwell.)

onset a fierce attack; the beginning (as, the onset of a cold)

onslaught an attack

onus a burden; a responsibility
onerous burdensome; needing much work or effort (as, an onerous task)

onward(s) see **on**

ooze to flow or leak out very slowly

opal a milky-white precious stone with changing rainbow colours
opalescent pearly-white with changing rainbow colours

opaque *(say opayk)* not letting light pass through

open not shut; not closed or covered; free to be entered, etc. (as, open to the public); free from obstruction or trees (as, an open space)

opening an open place; a gap; an opportunity

open air the fresh air out of doors

open-minded willing to consider new ideas

opera a play in which the words are sung and accompanied by an orchestra

operetta a short light opera with gay music

operate to act or work (as, a man operating a machine); (in surgery) to perform an operation

operation an action; a military campaign; (in surgery) the cutting of a part of the body in order to restore health)

operative working; having effect (as - The new rule is operative.) □ a factory worker

operator someone who operates a machine, etc. (as, a calculating-machine operator)

opinion what one thinks or believes about something; a general view or belief (as, public opinion); a professional judgment (as, to seek a doctor's, or a lawyer's opinion)

a matter of opinion a matter on which several different views may be held

opium a narcotic drug derived from the white poppy

opponent see **oppose**

opportune coming at the right moment (as - His arrival was opportune.); convenient (as, an opportune moment)

opportunity a chance to do something

oppose to fight or go against (whether by force or argument)

opponent someone who fights or resists a person or a course of action

opposite (say opposite) as different as possible (as - He turned round and went in the opposite direction.); in a facing position (as, the opposite side of the table) □ something as different as possible (as - Up is the opposite of down.)

opposition the act of opposing; those who resist or oppose; (with a capital letter) the political party opposed to the party in power

oppress to govern or treat people harshly; to weigh down (as - She was oppressed by worry.)

oppression the act of oppressing; a feeling of being weighed down

oppressive harsh; heavy; (of weather) heavy or tiring

optic, optical having to do with sight or with optics

optician a person who makes or sells optical instruments (especially spectacles)

optics the science of light

optimism the habit of taking a bright, hopeful view of things generally; hopefulness; the opposite of pessimism

optimist someone who is always hopeful; the opposite of pessimist

optimistic inclined to be hopeful

option a choice

optional left to one's choice (as, an optional subject at school, as distinct from a required subject)

oracle (in ancient times) the supposed answer from a god in reply to a difficult question; a person of great wisdom

oral spoken, not written (as, an oral exam)

orange a juicy round fruit grown in warm countries; the reddish-yellow colour of this fruit

orang-utan a large man-like ape, reddish-brown in colour, which lives in parts of the East Indies

oration (orayshun) a formal public speech

orator (say orator) an eloquent public speaker

oratory the art of public speaking; eloquent public speech

oratorio (say oratorio) a sacred story (usually Biblical) set to music

orb a globe or sphere; a

heavenly body

orbit the path in which one heavenly body moves round another (as, the earth's orbit round the sun); the path in which a spacecraft goes round the earth, moon, etc. □ to go round in orbit

orchard a large enclosure with fruit trees (as, an apple orchard)

orchestra *(say orkestra)* a group of musicians playing together under a conductor
orchestral (of music) composed for, or played by, a whole orchestra
orchestrate to arrange a piece of music for a whole orchestra to play

orchid *(say orkid)* a plant with showy flowers

ordain to appoint a person to be a priest or clergyman by means of a church ceremony

ordeal a hard trial or test; a painful experience

order 1 a command; a rule; a direction to supply goods □ to command; to give an order for (as, to order the coal or oil)
ordinance a law
orderly 1 a soldier who carries the orders and messages of an officer; a hospital attendant

order 2 the regular arrangement of things in space or time (as, the names printed in order of merit); system; peaceful condition (as, keeping law and order); an honour given by a monarch, etc. (as, the Order of the Garter) □ to arrange
ordinal showing order in a series (The ordinal numbers are: first, second, third, etc. - see also **cardinal**)
orderly 2 in good order; well-behaved (as, an orderly crowd)
in order correct according to the regular method or rules
in order to for the purpose of

ordinance see **order 1**

ordinary usual; common; normal; not special □ the common run of things

ordnance military supplies, such as big guns and ammunition; a government department concerned with these
ordnance survey a series of official maps of the United Kingdom (prepared by the Ordnance Survey Department)

ore rock or mineral from which metals can be obtained (for example, iron ore)

organ 1 a large musical instrument consisting of pipes played by means of a keyboard (There are also smaller pipeless organs).
organist someone who plays an organ

organ 2 any part of the body which does a special job (such as the heart, lungs, liver, etc.)
organic having to do with the organs of living things
organize to plan and arrange many parts (with their various functions) so that together they form a working whole; to get a group of people to act together for a particular purpose (as, to organize a youth club)
organization the act of organizing; a large body of people working together for a purpose (as, the World Health Organization - W.H.O.)
organism a living animal or plant
organic chemistry the chemistry of compounds containing carbon

organdie, organdy a fine thin stiffened muslin used for dresses, curtains, etc.

orient, orientate to find one's position or the direction one is facing
oriental eastern □ a native of the Far East
orientation the act of finding one's position (especially with regard to the points of the compass)

origin *(say orijin)* the beginning or source of anything (as, *The Origin of Species* by Charles Darwin)

original *(say orijinál)* existing at, or from, the beginning (as - The original church on this site was built in the seventh century.); new and different (as, an original idea) □ any actual painting by an artist as distinct from later copies

originality the ability to think, or to do things, without copying others

originate to bring into being; to begin

ornament anything that adorns or is supposed to add beauty □ to adorn or decorate

ornate ornamented elaborately

ornithology the science and study of birds

ornithologist someone who makes a special study of birds

orphan a child whose parents are dead

orphanage a home for orphans

orthodox holding the views and beliefs (especially in religion) that are most usually held

orthography the correct spelling of words

orthopaedics *(say orthopeedics)* the prevention, or correction, of deformities (especially in childhood)

oscillate *(say ossilate)* to swing to and fro; to fluctuate

ossify to turn into bone

ostentation the making of a great show to impress people

ostentatious making a great show to impress or attract attention (as, a lady who dresses or furnishes her home in an ostentatious manner)

ostrich a very large, long-legged bird which cannot fly but is able to run swiftly

other the second of two (as, the other shoe); the remaining (as, the chairs, tables, beds, and other furniture); different (as - It was some other boy.) □ another

otherwise if not; in another way; in other circumstances

every other each alternate or

second (as, every other weekday - Monday, Wednesday and Friday or Tuesday, Thursday and Saturday)

otter a furry swimming animal of the weasel family, which lives on fish

ought *(say awt)* an auxiliary verb used with other verbs: to express a duty (as - We ought to return home now.); to refer to something expected or desirable (as - Our team ought to win on Saturday.)

ounce a weight equal to one-sixteenth of a pound (or approximately 28 grammes)

our belonging to us (as, our shoes, our school, etc.)

ours belonging to us (as - These shoes are ours.)

ourselves the emphatic reflexive form of we and us (as - We ourselves want to go. We hid ourselves in the garden.)

oust *(say owst)* to drive out of a place or position (as - The rebels ousted the president of the republic.)

out not inside or within; the opposite of in; not at home; in or into the open air (as - We're going out.); to, or at, an end (as - The light went out.)

outer more out or without

outing a trip, journey, etc. for pleasure out of doors

outward(s) on the outside or surface □ towards the outside

out-and-out thorough; complete (as, an out-and-out scoundrel)

out-of-date old-fashioned

out of doors outside the house; in the open air

out-patient a hospital patient who is living at home

out- a prefix meaning away from, outwards, beyond, etc.

outbid to offer a higher price

outbreak the breaking out or beginning (as, the outbreak of a disease, of war, etc.)

outbuilding a building separate from a main building; a shed

outburst a bursting out (as, an

outburst of cheering)

outcast a person who has been driven away from home and society

outclassed appearing to be in a lower class; poor in comparison

outcome the result (as, the outcome of a discussion)

outcry a loud cry of anger, distress, etc.

outdistance to leave behind in a race, etc.

outdo to do better than

outdoor done out of doors (as, outdoor games)

outfit a set of clothing or equipment for some purpose (as, a camping outfit)

outfitter someone who sells outfits, but especially men's ready-made clothing

outflank to pass round the side of an opposing force and get beyond it (as, to outflank a regiment)

outgrow to grow larger than

outgrowth an offshoot

outhouse an outbuilding or shed

outlast to last longer than

outlaw a lawless person; a bandit □ to place someone beyond the protection of the law

outlay money paid out

outlet a way or passage outwards; a means of letting out one's emotion or energy (as - Sports are a good outlet for energy.)

outline a line drawn round the outside edge to show the shape of something; a rough plan or sketch; the main ideas of a story, speech, book, etc. □ to sketch the main lines of a drawing; to give the main points of a story, book, etc.

outlive to live longer than

outlook a view (as, the outlook from a window); what is likely to happen in the future (as, the weather outlook)

outlying lying at a distance (as, an outlying village)

outnumber to be greater in number than

outpost a military post or a place in the wilds

output the goods produced by a machine, a factory, or even by industry as a whole (as, the national output)

outrage a wicked and violent act; an act that offends feelings very much □ to injure by violence; to insult

outrageous violent; very wrong

outright direct (as, an outright win) □ completely

outrun to run faster than

outset the beginning

outside the outer side or surface; the opposite of inside; the farthest limit □ on the outside □ not in (as, outside the field)

outsider someone considered to be outside a particular social group, profession, etc.; a horse not expected to win a race

outsize over normal size

outskirts the outer border (as, the outskirts of a town)

outspoken expressing one's thoughts frankly or boldly

outstanding excellent; (of debts, etc.) not yet paid or done

outstrip to leave behind in running

outwit to be too clever for

oval egg-shaped

ovary the part of the female body in which egg cells are formed
ovary an egg or egg cell

ovation an outburst of cheering and applause

oven a. closed space (as in a stove) for cooking and baking

over higher than; above; on parts of (as - He spilled paint over the table.); across (as, to walk over a bridge); about (as, to quarrel over a trifle) □ above (as, aged twelve and over): to express movement towards, downwards, etc. (as, to come over, to knock over) □ (in cricket) a fixed number of balls bowled at one end before changing to the other end

over and above in addition to
over and over again and again
all over at an end (as - It's all over.)

over- a prefix meaning above,

across, upper, beyond, etc.

overall a simple garment worn over other clothes to keep them clean □ including the whole, or everything

overawe to make silent by fear or wonder

overbalance to lose balance and fall; to cause this to happen

overbearing haughty; domineering

overboard over the side of a ship (as - Man overboard!)

overburden to burden with too heavy a load, work, etc.

overcast (of the sky) cloudy

overcharge to charge too high a price

overcoat an outdoor coat worn over all other clothes

overcome to get the better of; to defeat □ helpless from any cause (as, overcome by fumes from a fire, overcome by emotion)

overcrowded with too many people (as, overcrowded slums)

overdo to do too much (as, to overdo physical training for a sport); to cook too long

overdone done too much; cooked too much

overdose too great a dose of medicine

overdraft the amount of money overdrawn from one's bank account

overdraw to draw more money from a bank than one has in one's account

overdue behind the stated or agreed time (as, an overdue train)

overeat to eat too much

overflow to flow or spill over □ a flowing over

overgrown covered over with spreading plants (as, a garden overgrown with weeds); grown too large

overhang to hang, or stick out, over

overhaul to catch up with; to examine and repair thoroughly □ the action of overhauling (as, the overhaul of a ship or car)

overhear to hear something that was not meant to be heard

overjoyed filled with joy; extremely glad

overland going across land and not by sea

overlap to cover anything partly with another (as, to overlap tiles on a roof)

overleaf on the other side of the page

overload to load or fill too much

overlook to look over from a higher position: to fail to notice; to excuse (as - The teacher decided to overlook the mistake.)

overnight during, or throughout, the night

overpass a road going over another road, railway, etc.

overpower to overcome by greater strength

overpowering unable to be resisted

overrate to rate or value too highly

oversea(s) beyond the sea; abroad

oversee to look over; to be in charge of

overseer someone who oversees or supervises

overshadow to throw a shadow over; to seem more important or greater than

oversight a mistake or omission

overtake to catch or come up with

overthrow to upset; to defeat completely

overtime time spent in working beyond usual hours

overturn to upset; to destroy the power of (as, to overturn a government)

overwhelm to cover completely and crush (as - The great waves overwhelmed the small boat.); to defeat utterly

overwork to work so hard or so long as to affect one's health

overt openly done; not hidden

overture an offer or proposal intended to open discussions (as, a peaceful overture to a former enemy); a piece of music played as an introduction to an opera, etc.

ovum see **ovary**

owe to be in debt to (as - He owes his friend £1.); to be under an obligation to (as - He owes his friend an apology. He owes his success to his own efforts.)
owing to because of

owl a nocturnal bird of prey with large eyes and a curved beak

own to have or possess something: to admit or confess something (as - The car driver owned to having made a mistake.) □ belonging to oneself (as, my own, his own)
owner a legal possessor (as, the farm owner)
ownership legal possession

on one's own without the help of others; alone
to get one's own back to get even

ox the male of the cow used for drawing loads
oxen the plural of ox

oxygen a gas without colour or smell which forms about one-fifth of the air we breathe (Oxygen is essential for life and for burning anything.)

oyster a shellfish with a flat shell in two parts, used as a food

ozone a form of oxygen with a peculiar smell; (often used to mean) pure, healthy air

p

pace a single step; the length of one step; the rate or manner of walking (as, a quick pace, a leisurely pace) □ to measure by steps

pacify to bring peace to; to calm
pacific peaceful; tending towards peace
pacifist a person who believes all war to be wrong or who is opposed to war

pack to put (clothes, etc.) into a bag or other luggage; to put (goods) into a container; to press closely together □ a bundle to be carried on the back (as, a soldier's pack); a complete set of cards; a number of animals (as, a pack of hounds); a kind of packing for food, etc. (as, a vacuum pack)
package a bundle; a parcel
packet a small package
pack horse (formerly) a horse used to carry packages
pack-ice a mass of large pieces of floating ice in the sea

pact an agreement or contract; a treaty

pad 1 any soft cushion-like mass to prevent jarring or rubbing; many sheets of paper fastened

together at one end: a rocket-launching platform: the paw of a fox, hare, etc. □ to stuff with anything soft; (in writing) to fill out an essay or story with useless or irrelevant material just to make it longer
padding stuffing material; (in writing) useless matter put in just to fill space

pad 2 to trudge along; to walk with a soft, dull-sounding tread

paddle to wade about in shallow water; to propel a boat with a paddle (as, paddling a canoe) □ a short oar with a broad blade used in canoes; one of the boards of a paddle-wheel
paddle steamer a ship driven forward by two large paddle-wheels instead of propellers
paddle-wheel a wheel with boards fixed horizontally all round the outside (which act as paddles while the wheel is turning)

paddock a small closed-in field (usually near a house or stable)

paddy-field a muddy field in which rice is grown

padlock a detachable lock with a

hinged hook or link which can be fixed to gates, and outside doors, etc. □ to fasten with a padlock

pagan *(say paygan)* a heathen

page 1 one side of a sheet of paper, whether printed, written on, or blank

page 2 a young boy attendant at a ceremony; a boy who does errands in a hotel; (in mediaeval times) a boy training to be a knight

pageant *(say pajent)* a show or parade (usually in costume to illustrate the history of a place)
pageantry splendid show or display

pagoda an Eastern temple, especially in the form of a tower of many storeys with projecting roofs

pail a bucket

pain suffering; a hurt feeling in body or mind
pains the plural of pain: care (as - He took pains with his homework.)
painful causing pain; full of pain
painless without pain (as, a painless tooth extraction)
painstaking taking great care
under, or **on, pain of** liable to the punishment of (as, under pain of death)

paint to put colour on; to make a picture with colours □ a substance for colouring (as, oil paints, which are pigments ground up finely in oil)
painter 1 an artist in painting; a house decorator
painting a painted picture

painter 2 a rope used to fasten a boat

pair two of the same kind (as, a pair of shoes, etc.); a set of two similar things which form one article (as, a pair of scissors, of tongs, etc.); a couple □ to join in pairs or couples

pal a partner or mate; a chum

palace a royal residence; any splendid official residence
palatial like a palace; splendid

palaeolithic belonging to the early Stone Age (when man used primitive stone tools)

palate *(say palat)* the roof of the mouth; a sense of taste (as - He has a fine palate where wines are concerned.)
palatable *(say palatab'l)* pleasant to the taste

palatial see **palace**

pale whitish in colour; wan □ to lose colour or turn pale

palette a piece of thin board on which a painter mixes his colours

paling a fence made of wooden stakes; a wooden stake

palisade a fence of stakes, especially for defence purposes

pall 1 *(say pawl)* the cloth covering a coffin at a funeral; a cloak; a curtain or haze (as, a pall of smoke hanging over an industrial area)
pall-bearer a person who attends or helps carry the coffin at a funeral

pall 2 *(say pawl)* to become dull or uninteresting

palliative something that lessens pain, or the symptoms of a disease □ making less severe

pallid pale; sickly looking
pallor unnatural paleness

palm 1 the inside of the hand, between the fingers and the wrist
palmist a person who claims to tell fortunes by looking at the lines of the palm
to palm off to pass off, or give something with the intention of cheating (as - He palmed off a bad 10p piece on me.)

palm 2 a kind of tall tree with large fan-shaped, divided leaves growing mainly in hot countries (There are coconut palms and date palms.)

palpable able to be touched or felt; easily noticed (as, a palpable lie)

palpitate (of the heart) to throb; to beat rapidly
palpitation a throbbing or fast beating of the heart

palsy *(say pawlzy)* a loss of feeling or control in a set of muscles; paralysis

paltry of little value; worthless

pampas a name for the vast plains in southern South America

pamper to spoil by giving way to (a person's whims or wishes); to indulge too much

pamphlet *(say pamflet)* a small book, whose pages are fastened together but not bound

pan 1 a container used in cooking (usually broad and shallow); anything of a similar shape □ to wash sand containing specks of gold, etc. in a pan; (with *out*) to turn out (well, badly, etc.)
pancake a thin cake of batter fried in a pan

pan 2 to move a television or cine-camera so as to follow an object or produce a wide view (derived from the word **panorama**)

panacea *(say panaseeya)* a remedy for all ills; a cure-all

pancake see **pan 1**

panda a large black and white wild animal, something like a bear (This is the giant panda found in Tibet; there are also smaller raccoon-like pandas in the Himalayas.)

pandemonium an uproar

pander to provide anything that is pleasing to low tastes (as, papers or magazines that pander to a liking for scandal)

pane a sheet of glass

panel a rectangular piece of wood, glass, etc., often with a border (as, the panels in a door): a group of persons chosen for a purpose (such as to serve on a jury, or to answer questions in a television or radio game)

pang a sudden sharp pain

panic a sudden or great fear that affects people and prevents them from thinking reasonably □ to feel or be affected by panic
panicky inclined to panic

panorama a wide or complete view

pansy a small garden plant with velvety flowers, rather like large violets but of varied colours

pant to gasp for breath □ a gasping breath

pantaloons a kind of trousers

pantechnicon a furniture removal van; a furniture store

panther a leopard

pantomime a musical play for children, based on a fairy tale; a dumb show in which the players mime

pantry a small room where food, dishes, etc. are kept

pants underwear; trousers

papal having to do with the Pope

paper a thin material used for writing, printing, wrapping, wall-covering, etc. (generally made from wood pulp, rags, straw, etc.); a newspaper; a document; a set of exam questions □ made of paper (as, a paper doll) □ to cover with paper (as, to paper the walls of a room)
paperback a book with a paper cover

papier-mâché *(say papyay-mahshay)* a substance made of paper pulp that can be moulded into shapes

papoose a North American Indian baby

papyrus *(say papierus)* a reed which the Egyptians and others used in olden times to make a kind of writing paper

par an equal value; a normal state or standard (as - He was feeling below par, so his mother kept him in bed for a day.)

parable a fable or story told to teach a lesson

parachute a contrivance made of fine nylon which opens like an umbrella to enable a person or object to come down to earth safely from an aeroplane □ to descend by parachute

parade a show or display; a procession of people, sometimes in costume; an orderly arrangement of troops for inspection or exercise □ to march in a procession

paradise heaven; any place of great happiness

paraffin an oil used mainly for burning in heaters, etc.

paragon a pattern or model of perfection

paragraph a division of a piece of writing or printing

parallel (of lines) going in the same direction and remaining the same distance apart (like railway lines) □ a parallel line; a similarity □ to be similar to or to match (as - His efforts could not be paralleled.)
parallelogram a four-sided figure whose opposite sides are equal and parallel

paralyse to affect with paralysis; to make helpless
paralysis a loss of the power to move and feel in some part of the body
paralytic suffering from paralysis □ a paralysed person

paramount above all others in rank or power; the very greatest (as, a matter of paramount importance)

parapet a low wall on a bridge, balcony, etc.

paraphernalia *(say parafernaylia)* a person's belongings; equipment

paraphrase to put into other words

parasite an animal or plant that lives on another without giving any benefit in return (such as the flea, mistletoe, etc.); anyone who lives entirely at the expense of others

parasol a kind of umbrella to shade the head and face from the sun

paratroops troops carried by air, to be dropped by parachute

parcel a package (especially one wrapped in paper) □ to divide out into portions

parch to dry up; to scorch
parched dried up; very thirsty

parchment the skin of a goat, sheep, etc. after it has been scraped, cleaned and dried; strong paper resembling this

pardon to forgive; to free from punishment; to excuse □ forgiveness
pardonable excusable; able to be forgiven

pare to peel (as, to pare an apple); to cut off the outer surface of something

parent a father or mother
parentage birth; family (as, of noble parentage)
parental having to do with parents (as, parental care)

parish a subdivision of a county (in England and Wales); a district with its own church and clergyman
parishioner a member of a church parish
parochial relating to a parish

parity the state of being equal (in amount, quantity, rank, etc.)

park an open space with grass, trees, etc. for the recreation of the public; an enclosed piece of land surrounding a mansion; a piece of ground where motor cars may be left for a time (car park or parking place) □ to put a vehicle in a parking space
parking meter see **meter**

parliament the law-making body of Great Britain, consisting of the House of Commons and House of Lords (Some other countries also have parliaments.)

parlour a sitting-room

parochial see **parish**

parody an amusing imitation of another person's style of writing □ to make a parody of

parole the conditional release of a prisoner; a word of honour (especially given by a prisoner of war that he will not escape)

paroxysm *(say paroksizm)* a fit of acute pain or of some strong emotion (as, a paroxysm of rage)

parquet *(say parkay or parket)* a floor covering of wood blocks set in a pattern

parrot a brightly coloured bird with a hooked bill found in some hot countries (Parrots are sometimes kept as pets and are able to imitate human speech.)

parry to keep off or turn aside (as, to parry a blow, a question, etc.)

parse to name the kinds of words in a sentence (nouns, pronouns, verbs, etc.) and say how they are connected with each other

parsimony excessive care in spending money, etc.; stinginess **parsimonious** mean; stingy

parsley a small herb with bright green tightly-curled leaves, used in cookery

parsnip a vegetable with a thick whitish root shaped rather like a carrot

parson a clergyman

part something less than the whole; a portion, piece or share of something (as, a spare part for a machine); a character in a play; (in music) a series of notes for a particular voice or instrument (as, a soprano part, a cello part) □ to divide into parts; to separate; to go in different ways (as - They parted good friends.) **parting** the act of separating; a line of division **to part with** to give up **to take part** to have an active part or share in **to take someone's part** to side with someone

partake (with *of*) to eat or take some food or drink; (with *in*) to take part in

partial *(say parshal)* in part only, not total or complete (as, a partial success); showing favour to one person or side; fond of (as - She was partial to folk music.)

participate to take a share or part in (as, to participate in a discussion, in team games, etc.) **participant, participator** someone who participates

participle an adjective formed from a verb, and ending in -*ing* or -*ed* (for example, a runn*ing* commentary on a football match; a bak*ed* apple)

particle a tiny bit of matter (as, a particle of dust); any of the parts of an atom: a small connecting word (such as: *on, in, by, to, and*)

particular single or special (as, a particular person in a crowd, a particular article in a shop window); very careful or difficult to please (as - She is particular about her choice of shoes.) □ a single point or detail **particulars** the facts or details of anything (as, the particulars of a burglary)

parting see **part**

partisan a devoted follower, or member of a party or side; a guerrilla fighter

partition a division; a thin wall between rooms

partner a person who shares with another or others (as, a partner in a business): one of a pair in dancing or in playing a game (as, a tennis partner); a husband or wife □ to accompany someone as a partner **partnership** two or more people working, or playing together

partridge a plump wild bird of the pheasant family

party a gathering of guests for an entertainment or celebrations (as, a birthday party); a large group of persons who have united for political or other action (as, the Conservative, Labour or Liberal Party)

pass to move ahead of something in front of one (as, to pass a

crossroads or another car); to send from person to person, place to place, etc. (as, to pass a note in a classroom); (of time) to go by (as - The afternoon passed quickly.); to be successful (as, to pass an exam, a test, etc.) □ a narrow way through mountains; a ticket of admission or for free travel; the transfer of the ball to another player in a team game; success in an examination
passable fairly good; (of a road, river, etc.) able to be passed through or over
passage a long narrow way (especially between rooms in a building); a journey in a ship; a portion of a book or a piece of music; the act of passing
passenger anyone who travels, but especially by public transport such as a bus, train, ship or aeroplane
passer(s)-by any person (or people) passing near
passport a government document giving permission to travel abroad
password a secret word which allows those using it to pass a sentry into a military camp, etc.

passion a strong feeling (especially of anger, or of love); a great liking (as - She has a passion for strawberry jam.)
passionate showing or easily moved to show strong feelings; intense (as, a passionate devotion to a charitable cause)

passive not resisting; not active

Passover an annual feast of the Jews in memory of their deliverance from Egypt

passport see **pass**

past having happened at an earlier time (as, past events) □ the time that has passed (as – In the past there were many more workers on the land.) □ beyond; farther than (as, going past the house)

paste any soft mixture; a sticky, whitish liquid for sticking papers, etc. together; a food spread (as, meat paste)

pasteboard a kind of cardboard made by pasting sheets of paper together
pasty like paste; pale □ a kind of meat pie

pastel a coloured chalky crayon

pasteurize to heat milk to a temperature of 65° centigrade for half an hour so as to kill many harmful germs (named after the French scientist L. Pasteur)

pastille a small sweet (often medicated, as a cough pastille)

pastime something that helps to pass the time pleasantly; a recreation

pastor a clergyman; (in ancient times) a shepherd
pastoral having to do with shepherds or with country life in general (as, Beethoven's *Pastoral Symphony*); having to do with the work of a clergyman in helping people

pastry a mixture of flour, water and fat, rolled flat and baked to form the crust of pies, tarts, etc.; an article of food made wholly or partly from pastry

pasture a piece of land with growing grass for cattle and sheep to feed on
pasturage grazing land for cattle, etc.

pat 1 a gentle tap (as with the palm of the hand): a small lump (of butter, margarine, etc.) □ to strike gently; to tap

pat 2 exactly right; quite ready (as - He had his answers pat at the oral exam.)

patch a piece of material put on to mend or cover a hole; a small piece of ground (as, a cabbage patch) □ to mend with a patch
patchy uneven; mixed in quality

pate the top of the head

patent an official document giving one person or firm the sole right to make or sell a new invention □ to obtain a patent for □ protected by patent (as, a patent razor): easily seen; obvious

paternal fatherly; on the father's side of the family (as, one's paternal grandmother, or father's mother)

path, pathway a narrow way for persons on foot; a track

pathetic causing pity; touching
pathos *(say paythos)* the quality in anything (speaking, writing, etc.) that causes pity or sadness

patience *(say payshens)* the ability to wait quietly; the ability to put up with pain, delays and other setbacks calmly: a card game (usually played by one person)
patient *(say payshent)* enduring delay, etc. without complaining □ a person under medical treatment

patriot anyone who truly loves and serves his country
patriotic like a patriot; inspired by love and devotion to one's country
patriotism devotion to one's country

patrol to keep guard or watch by going the rounds of a camp, the streets of a town, etc. □ the body of soldiers, police, etc. who do this; a small group of boy scouts or girl guides; the act of patrolling

patron *(say paytron)* a protector; an influential supporter
patronize to act as a patron towards someone; to encourage: to treat a person as an inferior

patter to pat or tap quickly (as, rain pattering on a roof) □ the sound so made (by rain, footsteps, etc.): chatter; many words spoken or sung very quickly

pattern a decorative design (as, the pattern on a carpet or on wallpaper); an example or model to be copied (as, a dress pattern)

paunch the belly; a large belly

pauper a person without money or possessions

pause a slight hesitation; a short stop □ to stop for a moment

pave to lay flat stones, concrete, etc. to form a level surface (as, to pave a street)
pavement a paved surface (especially for pedestrians at the side of a street)

pavilion a large tent; a clubhouse for changing on a sports ground: an ornamental building

paw an animal's foot with claws □ to scrape with the forefoot; to handle roughly or clumsily

pawn 1 to hand over an article of value (to a pawnbroker) for a loan of money (The article will be given back when the loan is repaid with interest.)
pawnbroker a person who lends money for pawned articles

pawn 2 (in chess) one of the eight small pieces of lowest rank; a person who is considered unimportant and is made use of by someone else

pay to give money for goods or services (as, to pay a shopkeeper or a hairdresser); to return money which is owed; to reward or punish (as - He will be paid for his trouble.); to give (attention, etc.); to be worthwhile (as – It pays to be polite.) □ money given as wages, salary, etc.
payable that should be paid; due
payee anyone to whom money is paid
payment the act of paying; money paid

pea one of the edible round green seeds which grow in the pods of a climbing plant

peace a state of quiet or calm; absence of war
peaceful quiet; calm
peacemaker someone who brings about peace between enemies

peach a juicy, velvety-skinned fruit with a stone-like seed

peacock a large bird noted for its beautiful tail feathers, which can be spread out like a fan
peahen the female of the peacock

peak the pointed top of a mountain or hill; the highest point (as, the peak of a famous man's career); the jutting-out brim of a cap
peaked pointed

peal the ringing of a set of bells; a loud sound (as, a peal of laughter or of thunder) □ to sound loudly

peanut another name for the groundnut, which grows underground in pods

pear a juicy fruit rather like an apple, only softer and narrower towards the stem

pearl a small round white gem used in necklaces and other jewellery (Pearls grow inside some oysters and other shellfish.); a pearl-like object or something very precious

peasant a countryman or worker on the land

peat a kind of turf, dried and used for fuel

pebble a small, roundish stone

peck to strike, or pick up, with the beak

peculiar special; odd; strange
peculiarity something special or odd about a person

pedal any lever pressed by the foot (as, a piano pedal) □ to work the pedals of

pedant someone who shows off his learning

peddler, pedlar someone who goes about with a pack of goods for sale
peddle to go from house to house selling small articles

pedestal the base of a pillar or statue

pedestrian anyone who goes on foot □ going on foot

pedigree a list of a person's or animal's ancestors

peel to strip off skin or bark from □ rind (as, orange peel)

peep to look through a hole or narrow opening □ a glimpse

peer 1 a nobleman; a member of the House of Lords

peer 2 to look closely or searchingly (as, to peer in the dark)

peerless unequalled; matchless

peevish irritable; cross

peg a small wooden, metal or plastic pin (Some pegs are used for hanging up washing, other larger kinds are for fastening down tent ropes.) □ to fasten with a peg

pekinese a small pug-nosed dog of Chinese breed

pelican a large water-bird with a huge, pouched bill for storing fish

pellet a little ball (of paper, clay, lead, etc.)

pelt 1 to throw things repeatedly; to fall heavily (as, the rain pelted down)

pelt 2 a raw skin or hide

pen 1 an instrument used for writing in ink

pen 2 a small enclosure for fowls, sheep, etc.

penal *(say peenal)* having to do with punishment
penalize to punish
penalty a punishment; a fine; a free kick at goal for breaking a rule in football
penance punishment accepted willingly by a person

pence see **penny**

pencil a thin wooden rod containing graphite or coloured crayon for writing or drawing

pendant anything that hangs (especially an ornament on a chain)
pending awaiting a decision
pendulum a weight that swings freely to and fro at the end of a rod (as in some clocks)

penetrate to pierce; to enter

penguin an Antarctic seabird which is unable to fly and walks upright on very short legs

penicillin an antibiotic substance, obtained from a mould, which kills many disease bacteria

peninsula a piece of land that is almost surrounded by water

penknife a small pocket knife (originally used to mend quill pens)

pennant a long narrow flag with a pointed end

penny a small bronze coin now equal to one hundredth of £1 (Formerly there were 240 old pence in £1.)

pension a sum of money paid regularly to a person because of past services or retirement
pensioner a person who receives a pension

pensive thoughtful

pentagon a figure with five sides and five angles

penthouse a shed, with a sloping roof, joined to a building; a flat built on the roof of a building

penultimate last but one

peony a garden plant with large red, pink or white flowers (usually double)

people men, women and children; persons generally; a nation or race □ to fill with people or animals (as, to people a new land)

pepper a spicy powder with a hot taste which is used to season food; a bright green or red vegetable that grows in hot countries

peppermint a kind of mint used for flavouring; a sweet with a strong minty taste

per for each (as, the price per bunch, or per dozen)
per annum for each year
per cent for each hundred (often written %)
percentage the rate per hundred

perambulator a baby-carriage (often abbreviated to **pram**)

perceive to notice; to see; to understand
perceptible able to be seen or heard (as, a perceptible murmur)

perception the act or power of perceiving

perch 1 a stick or rod on which birds stand or sit; any high position □ to rest on a perch

perch 2 a kind of freshwater fish

percolate to strain or filter

percussion the striking of one thing against another; all musical instruments played by striking (as, drums, cymbals, the piano, etc.)

perennial (of plants) growing year after year without replanting or sowing new seeds

perfect *(say perfect)* without any faults; accurate; complete □ *(say perfect)* to make perfect; to finish
perfection the state of being perfect

perfidious treacherous; untrustworthy

perforate to pierce; to make one or more holes through

perform to do or act; to play a part on the stage, etc.; to play on a musical instrument
performance the carrying out of some task (as - The racehorse gave a very satisfactory performance.); any entertainment (in a theatre, circus, etc.)
performer someone who performs

perfume a pleasant scent (usually liquid in a bottle); a fragrance □ to scent (as - The jasmine perfumed the night air.)

perhaps possibly; maybe

peril a great danger
perilous very dangerous

perimeter the outside boundary of a figure or area (as, the perimeter of a field)

period a length of time (as, a period of two hours, or of fifty years); a stage in history: a full stop (.)
periodic(al) happening at regular intervals □ a magazine which comes out every week, or every month, etc.

periscope a tube-like instrument,

with mirrors or lenses, which is used in submarines and trenches to see what is going on above

perish to die; to decay or waste away

perishable liable to go bad quickly (as, perishable foods)

perjure to tell a lie after swearing to tell the truth

perjury the act of perjuring oneself or swearing to false evidence

permanent lasting an extremely long time; the opposite of temporary

permeate to pass or spread right through something (as, water permeating sand, a smell of cooking permeating a room)

permeable able to be passed through (as, a membrane that is permeable to water)

permit *(say permit)* to allow; to give permission to ▢ *(say permit)* a written permission (as, a permit to visit an exhibition)

permissible allowable

permission freedom given to do something

permissive allowing much freedom

permutation arranging a set of things in every possible order (For example, there are six ways of arranging the three letters A, B, and C: ABC, ACB, BAC, BCA, CAB and CBA)

pernicious (of behaviour and disease) very harmful; destructive

perpendicular vertical; standing upright ▢ a line at right angles to another

perpetrate to commit (a crime, a sin, etc.)

perpetual never ceasing; everlasting

perpetuate to cause something to last for a very long time

perplex to puzzle or bewilder

persecute to harass; to hunt down and cause suffering to (especially for religious beliefs)

persevere to continue steadily with some task in spite of difficulties

perseverance the habit of persevering

persist to keep on doing, asking, thinking, etc. (as, to persist in coming back again and again: to persist in believing that ghosts exist)

persistent persisting; obstinate

person a human being

personal belonging or relating to oneself; private

personality all the characteristics that make up an individual person as he appears to other people (as, a pleasant personality)

perspective the art of drawing so that all the objects in a scene look as though they are of the right size and in the right position (for example, appearing smaller because they are farther away)

perspire to sweat

perspiration sweat

persuade to cause a person to do or think something by advising or arguing with him; to convince

persuasion the act of persuading

persuasive having the power to persuade people

pert saucy; cheeky

pertain to belong to; to have to do with

pertinent closely connected with the subject being discussed; relevant

perturb to disturb greatly; to make anxious

peruse to read carefully

pervade to go or spread through (as - A fishy smell pervaded the market.)

perverse obstinate in doing wrong; stubborn

perversion a turning away from what is normal

pervert *(say pervert)* to turn to a wrong or abnormal use; to corrupt ▢ *(say pervert)* someone who has been perverted

pessimism the habit of thinking that things are likely to turn out badly; the opposite of optimism
pessimist a person who usually takes a gloomy view of things

pest any insect, animal, etc. that is destructive of growing crops or of food; a troublesome person or thing

pester to annoy someone continually

pestle *(say pess'l)* a thick rounded tool used by chemists to pound substances into powder

pet a tame animal kept at home (such as a dog or cat); a favourite person □ to treat as a pet; to fondle

petal one of the leaves of a flower or blossom

petition a special request to a person or group in authority (especially one signed by many people) □ to address a petition to; to ask as a favour

petrel a small seabird with long wings

petrify to turn into stone: to stiffen with fear (as - He was petrified by the lion's roar.)

petroleum a mixture of mineral oils found under the earth's surface and reached by sinking oil wells
petrol refined petroleum used as fuel in motor cars, aeroplanes, etc.

petticoat a woman's underskirt

petty trifling; of little importance

petulant peevish; fretful

pew one of the wooden benches with backs used by the congregation in church

pewter an alloy of tin and lead (used for making ornaments, mugs and tableware)

phantasy see **fantasy**

phantom a ghost

pharmaceutical having to do with the preparation of medicines and drugs
pharmacy the art of preparing medicines; a chemist's shop

phase one of a series of changes (as, the phases of the moon - full, half, etc.): a stage in development (as, a new phase in his life)

pheasant a long-tailed, handsome game bird

phenomenon *(say fenomenon)* any person, thing or event that is very unusual or remarkable (Rainbows and comets are natural phenomena.)
phenomenal very unusual or remarkable (as, a phenomenal success)

philanthropy the love of doing good to mankind generally
philanthropist a person who tries to benefit mankind (by doing welfare work, giving money, etc.)

philatelist a stamp collector

philosopher a person who studies philosophy; a lover of wisdom
philosophic(al) having to do with philosophy; calm
philosophy the study of what is really known about the principles of human behaviour and the universe and its basic laws; true reasoning about the nature and value of things

phlegm *(say flem)* the thick slimy matter brought up from the throat by coughing; calmness
phlegmatic *(say flegmatic)* calm; not easily excited

phlox *(say floks)* a garden plant with clusters of very fragrant white, purplish or reddish flowers

phoenix *(say feenix)* (in old fables) a bird supposed to burn itself and afterwards rise afresh from the ashes like a young bird (It is therefore an emblem of everlasting life.)

phone short for telephone

phonetic having to do with the sounds of language; spelled in the same way as it is sounded (as - Fotograf is a phonetic spelling of photograph.)

photography the art of taking pictures with a camera (The film used has a chemical coating which is sensitive to light.)
photograph, photo a picture made by means of a camera □ to take such a picture

phrase a small group of words expressing a single idea (usually part of a sentence) □ to express in words

physical having to do with material and not mental things (as, a physical force); having to do with the body, and not with the mind (as, physical exercises)
physician a doctor
physicist *(say fizisist)* a person who studies, or specializes in, physics
physics the branch of science which deals with such properties of matter and energy as heat, light, sound, magnetism and electricity

physiology the study of the ways in which animals and plants grow and live

physique *(say fizeek)* the build or type of a person's body (as, a boxer with a powerful physique)

piano, pianoforte a large musical instrument with a keyboard (Pressing the keys causes felt-covered hammers to strike wires of different lengths, producing musical sounds.)
pianist someone able to play the piano

piccolo a small flute with a higher pitch than an ordinary flute

pick to choose; to gather (fruit, flowers, etc.): to open a lock without a key □ a kind of large, pointed axe used to break hard ground: the best parts of something (as, the pick of the bunch)
pickaxe a kind of pick, pointed on only one side
pickpocket a thief who picks, or steals from, people's pockets

picket a pointed stake which is knocked into the ground (for example, they are placed side by side to make a fence): a group of men on guard or on some special

duty □ to set a picket or guard

pickle to preserve cooked vegetables in vinegar □ vegetables so preserved

picnic an outing during which a meal is eaten out of doors □ to have a picnic

picture a drawing, painting or photograph; a portrait; a cinema film □ to form a picture in the mind; to imagine
pictorial having pictures
picturesque *(say picturesk)* like a picture; such as would make a striking or beautiful picture (as, a picturesque landscape)

pie meat or fruit baked in a crust of pastry

piebald black and white in patches; of two colours (as, a piebald horse)

piece a part of anything; a single article (as, a piece of paper); a composition (as, a piece of music, of poetry, etc.)

pier a platform of stone, wood, etc. stretching from the shore into the sea, etc., and used as a landing place for ships and boats

pierce to make a hole through; to penetrate
piercing very sharp; penetrating (as, a piercing scream)

pig a fat farm animal (The chief pigmeats are pork, bacon and ham.)
piggery, pigsty places where pigs are kept
pig-headed stubborn
pigskin leather made from the skin of a pig
pigtail a braid or plait of hair

pigeon a plump bird of the dove family (sometimes kept as a pet, or for racing)
pigeon-hole a small division in a desk, etc. for storing papers

pigment paint; the colouring substance in the skin

pigmy, pygmy one of a tribe of very small people found in some hot countries; a dwarf

pike a large greedy, freshwater

fish with a pointed head: a weapon like a long spear formerly used by foot-soldiers

pilchard a sea-fish like a small herring

pile 1 a heap of things (as, a pile of clothes, of crockery, etc.) □ to heap up

pile 2 one of many large stakes (of wood or metal) driven into the earth as a foundation for a large building or bridge

pile 3 the soft raised surface on carpets and some cloths

pilfer to steal in small amounts

pilgrim someone who makes a long journey to a holy place
pilgrimage a journey to a holy place

pill medicine in a little ball or tablet

pillar a large post or column supporting or decorating part of a building
pillar box a postbox shaped like a short pillar

pillion a passenger seat on a motor cycle

pillory (in olden times) a wooden frame (with holes for the head and hands) used to punish wrong-doers □ to mock in public

pillow a cushion for the head used in bed □ to rest on a pillow
pillowcase a loose covering for a pillow

pilot a person who steers a ship into harbour; a person who controls an aircraft □ to steer or guide

pimple a small pointed swelling on the skin

pin a short pointed piece of wire used for fastening papers, etc. together □ to fasten with a pin; to hold fast (as - The bully pinned him to the ground).

pinafore a loose covering worn to protect the front of a dress; a sleeveless dress worn over a blouse, etc.

pinch to squeeze (especially between finger and thumb); to nip □ an act of pinching; a very small amount (as, a pinch of salt)

pincers a gripping tool used for pulling out nails, etc.

pine 1 a cone-bearing evergreen tree with needle-like leaves
pineapple a yellowish fruit, shaped like a large pine cone, growing in hot countries

pine 2 to waste away (with grief, suffering, etc.): to long for

pink a pale red colour: a spicily-scented garden flower (like a small carnation but [usually] with fewer petals)

pinnacle a high point (like a spire or slender turret); the highest point

pint a liquid measure equal to $1/8$th of a gallon (or just over $1/2$ litre)

pioneer someone who goes ahead to prepare the way for others; an explorer □ to be the first in any enterprise

pious acting in a religious or devout manner

pip a fruit seed; a spot on dice, playing cards, etc.; a short note given as a time signal (on the radio or telephone)

pipe a tube (of metal, plastic or earthenware) for carrying water, gas, etc.; a small tube with a bowl at the end for smoking tobacco; a tubular musical instrument played by blowing through the end or a hole in the side □ to play (a tune) on a pipe
pipe line a long line of pipes to carry oil from an oil field, etc.

pique (say peek) a feeling of annoyance; resentment

pirate a sea robber or buccaneer □ to take without permission
piracy robbery at sea

pirouette to spin round on the tips of the toes while dancing □ such a dance movement

pistil the seed-bearing part of a flower

pistol a small hand-gun that can be carried in the pocket

piston a round piece of metal that slides up and down inside a hollow cylinder in motor car engines, pumps, etc.

pit a hole in the ground; a large hole dug in the earth to extract minerals (as, a coal pit); the ground floor of a theatre
pitfall a trap; a hidden danger

pitch 1 to throw or fall forward; to put up (a tent, stall, etc.) □ the level of a musical note (high or low): (in cricket) the ground between the wickets
pitchfork a large fork for pitching hay

pitch 2 a thick black substance obtained by boiling down coal tar

pitcher a large jug for liquids

piteous see **pity**

pith the soft part inside the stems of plants; the important part of anything
pithy full of meaning (as, a pithy remark)

pittance a very small allowance or income

pity a sympathetic feeling for other people's sufferings; something unfortunate or regrettable (as - That's a pity!) □ to feel pity for
piteous, pitiable to be pitied; miserable
pitiful sad; contemptible (as, a pitiful excuse)

pivot the pin or centre on which anything turns or depends

pixy, pixie a mischievous fairy

placard a written or printed poster (usually an advertisement) placed on a wall, etc.

place any part of space with room for someone or something; an area set aside for a special purpose (as, a place of worship); a person's home (as, his place); a person's seat or position (as - Keep my place.); a particular spot (as - She lost her place in the book.) □ to put or set down anywhere

placid (say plassid) calm; not easily disturbed

plague (say playg) a deadly disease that spreads quickly among people; many troublesome things (as, a plague of locusts, mice, etc.) □ to pester or annoy

plaice a broad, flat fish with yellow spots

plaid (say plad) a piece of woollen cloth (usually) in a tartan pattern

plain simple or ordinary; without ornament; level; clear or frank (as, plain speaking) □ a level expanse of land

plaintiff a person who takes action against another in the law courts

plaintive sorrowful

plait (say plat) hair or ribbon twisted together over and under rather like a piece of rope □ to braid or twine together

plan an outline drawing (of a building, town, etc.) as though seen from above; a scheme or arrangement to do something □ to think out beforehand how to do something; to make a plan of

plane 1 a carpenter's tool for smoothing wood: a level surface □ to make smooth □ perfectly level (as, a plane figure or surface)

plane 2 a large tree with broad leaves

plane 3 an aeroplane

planet a heavenly body (such as the earth) which revolves round the sun or any other star

plank a long flat piece of timber

plant anything growing from the earth having a stem, root and leaves: a factory or machinery used in a factory □ to put into the ground for growth; to set down firmly
plantation a place planted (especially with trees)

plaster a mixture of lime, water and sand which is applied to walls and ceilings where it hardens to a smooth surface: a piece of sticky tape to hold a bandage in place

plastic a chemical compound (such as nylon, polythene, etc.) which can be moulded when soft or converted into artificial (man-made) fibres □ easily moulded or shaped (as, clay, wax, molten glass, etc.)

plasticine a soft clay-like substance used for modelling

plate a round, flat dish for food; a flat piece of metal; gold and silver articles □ to cover one metal with a coating of another (for example, nickel, chrome or silver)
plating a thin metal covering (as, nickel-plating)
plate-glass a fine kind of glass used in thick sheets for large mirrors and windows

plateau *(say plattoe)* a tableland; a broad level expanse of high land

platform a raised level surface (as, a railway platform, a platform for speakers, etc.)

platinum a heavy steel-grey metal that is more valuable than gold

platitude a commonplace remark made to sound important

platoon a subdivision of a company of soldiers

plausible seeming to be true or reasonable (as, a plausible explanation)

play to take part in a game or to amuse oneself; to perform on a musical instrument or on the stage; to gamble □ a story acted on the stage; the playing of a game; an amusement; gambling; a way of acting (as, fair play)
player a sportsman; an actor; a musician
playful fond of playing; frolicsome (as, a playful kitten)
playmate a companion in play
playground a place for playing in, especially at school or in a park
playtime a time set aside for playing

plea an excuse; an urgent request
plead to beg earnestly; to argue in support of a cause (especially in a law court)

please to give pleasure to; to like or think fit (as - Come as often as you please!); (in polite conversation) if you are willing (as - Please sit down.)
pleasant nice; agreeable
pleasure joy or enjoyment; delight

pleat a fold in cloth which has been pressed or stitched down (A kilt has many pleats.)

pledge a solemn promise (to do something); something given as security for a loan, etc. □ to give as security; to make a solemn promise

plenty a full supply (as, plenty of food for everyone)
plentiful much more than enough; abundant

pliable flexible; easily folded; easily persuaded

pliers small pincers for bending wire, etc.

plight condition or situation (usually bad, as, in a sad plight)

plimsolls light canvas shoes with rubber soles

plod to walk heavily and slowly; to work on steadily

plot a small piece of land: the main theme of a story, play, etc.: a secret plan (usually something evil, like the Gunpowder Plot) □ to plan secretly (usually something evil); to conspire

plough a farm tool pulled by a tractor, to turn up the soil □ to turn up the ground in furrows; to force a way through

pluck 1 courage; bravery

pluck 2 to pull or pull out (as, to pluck the strings of a guitar; to pluck the feathers of a fowl)

plug a peg or stopper for a hole (as, a bath plug); a connection with prongs that fit into an electric light or power socket

☐ to stop with a plug

plum a smooth-skinned, juicy stone-fruit

plumage see **plume**

plumber *(say plummer)* a man who fits and mends water and gas pipes, cisterns, etc.
plumb *(say plum)* a lead weight hung on a string (or plumbline) to test that a wall is being built vertically ☐ standing straight up
plumbing the plumber's trade; the system of pipes fitted by a plumber

plume a feather (especially a large ornamental one)
plumage feathers

plump rather fat and well-rounded ☐ to grow plump; to swell

plunder to carry off people's belongings by force; to loot ☐ goods seized by force

plunge to throw oneself (into water, the sea, etc.); to rush forward suddenly ☐ a dive

plural more than one (as - The plural of *mouse* is *mice*)

plus with the addition of; the sign (+) between numbers (as, 6 + 3 = 9)

plutocrat a person who is powerful because of his wealth

ply to work at steadily or continually; to make regular journeys or voyages (as, a ferry boat which plies between Dover and Calais)

plywood boarding made by gluing thin layers of wood together

pneumatic *(say newmatik)* filled with air; worked by compressed air (as, a pneumatic drill)

pneumonia *(say newmoania)* inflammation of the lungs

poach 1 to cook an egg without the shell in boiling water

poach 2 to trespass on someone's property in order to catch fish or other game illegally

pocket a small bag or pouch (especially one sewn into clothes) for carrying things ☐ to put into a pocket; to steal
pocket money an allowance of money for personal expenses

pod a long seed-case or shell containing peas, beans, etc.

podgy short and fat

poem a piece of writing in verse as distinct from prose, expressing one's thoughts and imaginings (usually in lines with a regular beat, which rhyme at the end)
poet, poetess a writer of poetry
poetic having to do with poetry and the language used in it
poetry the art of writing poems; poems

poignant *(say poinyant)* sharp; very painful or sad (as, a poignant farewell)

point a sharp end of anything (as, the point of a pencil); a dot on paper (as, a decimal point); an exact place or spot; a moment in time; one of the questions in an argument or discussion (as, the main point of his argument); a mark in a competition or game ☐ to aim; to draw attention to (as, to point out a person, a mistake, etc.)
pointed sharp; keen
point-blank (of a shot) fired at close range; direct
pointless without point or meaning

poise a state of balance; a dignity of carriage or manner ☐ to balance; to hold still, or hover, in the air

poison any substance which, when swallowed or otherwise taken into the body, seriously harms or even kills ☐ to injure or kill with poison
poisonous having the effect of poison; harmful (as, poisonous slander)

poke to thrust at (as, to poke a fire); to prod or push into something ☐ a thrust or prod
poker a metal rod for poking a fire: a card game

pole 1 a long rounded wooden

rod or post (as, a flag pole)

pole 2 the north or south end of the world's axis; one of the opposite points of a magnet or electric battery (+ or −)
polar having to do with the regions around the North or South Poles

polecat a large member of the weasel family

police the body of men and women whose main duties are to keep order and see that a country's laws are obeyed □ to control with police

policy 1 an agreed course of action (as, government policy)

policy 2 a written agreement with an insurance company

polio, poliomyelitis *(say poliomielietis)* a virus infection of the spinal cord which results in paralysis or weakness of the muscles

polish to make smooth and shiny by rubbing □ a gloss or shine; a liquid or paste used for polishing: fine manners

polite courteous; showing good manners

politics the study of government; political affairs (as, party politics)
political having to do with government or with politicians
politician *(say politishan)* someone whose business is politics; an active member of a political party (Conservative, Labour, Liberal, etc.)

polka a lively dance; the music for this

poll *(say pole)* a counting of voters at an election; a total number of votes (as, a poll of 10,000) □ to receive (a number of votes, as - He polled 6000 votes.)

pollen the fertilizing powder in flowers
pollinate to fertilize with pollen

pollute to contaminate or make impure; to make dirty
pollution contamination; dirt

polo a game rather like hockey,

played on horseback with long-handled mallets

polygamy *(say poligamy)* the custom of having more than one wife (or, less commonly, husband) at the same time

polygon a figure of many angles and sides (such as a pentagon or hexagon)

polytechnic a school in which many subjects are taught (especially technical ones such as engineering)

polythene a type of plastic used for domestic buckets, bowls, etc.

pomegranate a large round fruit with a thick reddish skin and many seeds

pommel the knob on a sword-hilt; a knob sticking up from the front of a saddle

pomp a magnificent display; splendour (as, the pomp and ceremony of a coronation)
pompous boastful and self-important

poncho a South American cloak like a blanket with a hole in the middle for the head

pond a small lake

ponder to think over; to consider
ponderous weighty; not easy to handle

pontoon a flat-bottomed boat; a floating platform

pony a small horse

poodle a curly-haired dog (The hair is often clipped in an elaborate pattern.)

pool 1 a small area of still water; a deep part of a stream

pool 2 the total money played for in a game or gamble (as, a football pool) □ to put together money, or other resources, into a pool

poor having little money or few belongings; not good (as, meat of poor quality, poor soil)

pop 1 a sharp quick sound (as, the pop of a cork) □ to make such a sound; to move suddenly (as, to pop out)

pop 2 short for **popular** (as, pop music)

popcorn a kind of maize that pops open when heated

pope the head of the Roman Catholic Church, who lives in Rome

poplar a tall, narrow, quick-growing tree

poplin a strong, lustrous cotton material used for shirts, dresses, etc.

poppy a hairy-stemmed plant (usually with large red flowers)

populace the ordinary people of a country

popular liked by most people; common (as, a popular belief)
popularize to make popular; to make generally known
popularity the state of being popular (as, the popularity of a well-known singer)

population the people, or number of people, who live in a place
populate to fill with people
populous full of people (as - Belgium is a populous country.)

porcelain white glazed china of especially fine quality

porch a covered entrance to a building

porcupine a gnawing wild animal covered with bristling quills

pore 1 a tiny hole, especially the opening of a sweat gland in the skin
porous having pores which allow a fluid to pass through

pore 2 to look at closely (as, to pore over an interesting book)

pork the meat of the pig, especially when fresh

porpoise a blunt-nosed sea animal of the dolphin family, about 2 metres long

porridge a hot breakfast food made from oatmeal and water or milk

port 1 a harbour; a town with a harbour; the left side of a ship
porthole a small window (usually round) in a ship's side

port 2 a strong fortified wine (usually dark red) from Portugal

portcullis a large grating that can be let down quickly to close a gateway (as in old castles)

porter a man who carries one's luggage (at a station, hotel, etc.): a doorkeeper
portable easily carried (as, a portable television set)

portfolio a flat case for carrying papers or drawings

portion a part or share; a helping of food

portly stout; large and dignified

portrait a painting, drawing or photograph of a person
portray to paint or draw a person; to describe in words

pose an attitude (often assumed, as, for a photograph) □ to take up an attitude; to pretend to be someone else (as - She posed as a famous film actress.): to puzzle with a question or problem

position situation or place; rank or job (as, a good or a high position)

positive definite; certain; (in electricity) the opposite of negative □ (in photography) the print made from a negative

posse (say possee) a body of men authorized to enforce order

possess to own or to have
possessed dominated by an evil spirit
possession something owned

possible able to happen; able to be done
possibility something that may happen, or may be done
possibly perhaps

post 1 a pole (of wood, metal, or concrete) fixed upright in the ground □ to fix (a notice) on a post or board
poster a large notice or placard

post 2 the carrying of letters and other mail: any place of duty (as, a military post); a job in an office, etc. □ to put (a letter, etc.) in a postbox for collection: to station (as, to post a sentry)

postage the money paid for sending a letter, etc.

postcard a card (usually a picture postcard) on which a message may be sent by post

postman a man who delivers letters

postmark a mark, showing the date, stamped on a letter at the post office

post office an office for receiving and dispatching letters, etc. by post (It also sells stamps, television licences, etc.)

post- (before another word) after or behind (as, **post-war; post-mortem** [after death]; **postscript** or **P.S.** [a short part added to a letter after the signature])

posterior coming after or later

posterity descendants; future generations

postpone to put off to a future time

posture the way a person holds or carries his body

posy a small bunch of flowers

pot any deep dish for cooking; a round container of clay or plastic for plants □ to plant in a pot

potato a common vegetable which grows under the ground in the form of tubers (potatoes)

potent strong; powerful (as, a potent medicine)

potentate a powerful person; a prince

potential possible but not yet real (as, the potential sales of a product)

potter 1 to do small odd jobs; to dawdle

potter 2 someone who makes articles of baked clay

pottery articles of baked clay; a place where these are made

pouch a pocket or bag (as, a tobacco pouch, a kangaroo's pouch)

poultry domestic fowls (such as chickens, ducks, turkeys)

pounce to spring or swoop suddenly □ a sudden spring or swoop

pound 1 a measure of weight (just under half a kilogramme): a measure of English money (£1 = 100 pence)

pound 2 to beat into small pieces or powder; to thump

pour to make a liquid flow (as, to pour out a cup of tea); to flow strongly or rain heavily

pout to push out the closed lips to show displeasure □ a pushing out of the lips

poverty the state of being poor; want or need (especially of money)

powder any substance as fine as dust (such as flour, face powder, etc.) □ to make into a powder; to sprinkle or apply powder

power strength or force (as, electric power); the ability to do anything; a strong nation or authority

power station a place where electricity is produced

powwow a discussion among or with North American Indians; a friendly talk

practice the repetition of an action to gain skill (as, practice at cricket, on the piano, etc.); a usual action or habit; a professional man's business (as, a doctor's practice)

practicable able to be used or done

practical learned by practice (as, practical, not theoretical, knowledge); efficient in actual use

practise to put into practice or action (as, to practise on a musical instrument)

practitioner a person who practises a profession (especially medicine, as, a general practitioner or G.P.)

prairie a vast, grassy plain without trees

praise to speak highly of (a person or thing); (religious) to glorify by singing hymns □ an expression of approval or honour

praiseworthy worthy of praise

pram see **perambulator**

prance to walk or dance about proudly

prank a mischievous trick

prattle to talk a lot about nothing much □ empty talk

prawn a shellfish like a large shrimp

pray to ask earnestly; to speak to God; to beg humbly
prayer an earnest request; any act of prayer (especially in worship)

pre- (in front of a word) before (as, in **pre-war, prearrange**)

preach to give a sermon (usually religious)
preacher one who preaches; a clergyman

preamble a preface or introduction

precarious uncertain; depending on chance

precaution care taken beforehand (as, to wear warm clothes as a precaution against catching cold)

precede to go before in time or importance
precedent (say _pressedent_) a past action which may serve as an example for future action

precept a rule to guide a person's action; a commandment

precinct (say _preesinkt_) the enclosed space around a building (as, the cathedral precincts)

precious very valuable; of high price

precipice (say _pressipis_) a steep cliff
precipitous very steep

precipitate to throw down headlong; to hasten or bring about suddenly (as, to precipitate a ruler's fall from power) □ a powdery substance which settles at the bottom of a liquid
precipitation great haste: rainfall

precise definite or exact (as, precise instructions)

precision exactness

precocious (say _precoeshus_) showing unusually early development (especially mentally)

predatory living by plundering or preying upon others (as - Tigers are predatory animals.)

predecessor (say _preedecessor_) a former holder of a job or position

predicament an unfortunate or difficult situation

predict to foretell

predominate to be dominant; to be the stronger, or the greater in number
predominant ruling; superior in position

preen to arrange feathers with the beak as birds do; to make oneself neat and tidy

preface (say _preffis_) a short introduction to a book; a foreword □ to say by way of a preface (as - He prefaced his remarks by a reference to the recent bad weather.)

prefect someone given authority over others; (in schools) a senior pupil with certain powers

prefer to like one thing better than another
preference the choosing of one thing rather than another

prefix a syllable placed at the beginning of a word to change its meaning (as - _un_ before the word _important_ changes the meaning to _not important_.)

pregnant carrying an unborn baby in the womb

prehistoric(al) belonging to the period before history was recorded

prejudice (say _prejoodis_) an unfair opinion or feeling about anything (often through lack of careful thought) □ to bias a person's mind; to spoil (as - The whistling and shouting of the home crowd prejudiced the visiting team's chances of winning.)
prejudicial detrimental; harmful

preliminary introductory; preparatory

prelude a short musical piece (especially an introductory section); an action or event that serves as an introduction to something longer or more important

premature ripe, or coming, before the proper time

premier first; chief □ a prime minister

première *(say premyer)* the first performance of a play, etc.

premises a building together with any outer buildings and grounds

premium a reward; a regular payment (usually yearly) on an insurance policy

preoccupied lost in thought

prepare to get ready; to train or equip for (as, to prepare for a race)
preparation the act of preparing; study for a lesson in class (shortened to prep); something prepared or made up (as, cosmetic, or medicinal, preparations)
preparatory preparing; introductory (as, a preparatory school)

preposition a short word placed before a noun or pronoun to show how it is related to another word (for example: *on, under, to, from, in, out, by, for*)

preposterous against common sense; quite absurd

prescribe to lay down as a rule; to order the use of a medicine
prescription a doctor's written direction or order for preparing a medicine

present 1 being in a place; the opposite of absent; at this time □ the time now (not the past or future)
presence the state of being present
presently soon; before very long

present 2 a gift (as, a birthday present) □ *(say preezent)* to give formally (as, to present prizes); to introduce one person to another
presentable fit to be presented or seen
presentation the formal presenting of a gift or prize; a showing (as, of a school play)

preserve to keep safe from harm; to maintain or keep in existence; to keep (food, etc.) from going bad □ something preserved (as, a game preserve); preserved fruit or jam
preservative a substance that preserves food, etc.

preside to act as chairman in charge of a meeting
president the chief executive officer of a republic; the head of a college, club, institution, etc.

press to push against (as a button) or down (as, flowers in a book); to squeeze; to smooth out or iron (clothes); to urge (a person) □ a crowd: a printing machine; newspapers and magazines collectively
pressure the act of pressing; a pressing force; a strong influence (as, the pressure of events)

prestige *(say presteezh)* reputation; influence due to a person's rank

presume to take for granted; to do something without having the right
presumption something taken for granted
presumptuous arrogant; taking for granted

pretend to make believe; to feign (as, to pretend one is ill)
pretence, pretension a real or false claim to something
pretentious claiming too much; over-assuming; showy

pretext an excuse

pretty attractive (especially to the eye or ear); neat □ fairly (as, pretty difficult)

prevail to gain victory (over or against); to persuade (as, to prevail on a friend to go fishing); to be usual

prevailing usual or most common (as - The prevailing winds blow from the southwest.)

prevalent widespread; common

prevent to keep from happening; to hinder

previous (in time) before; former

prey animals and birds that may be killed by others for food □ to seize and eat (as - Owls prey upon small rodents.)

price the amount of money that has to be paid for something bought (as, a price of 25 pence each); something that has to be given up or done for something desired (as, to pay a high price for freedom)

priceless of very great value

prick to pierce slightly with a sharp point; to give a feeling of pricking □ an act, or feeling, of pricking

prickle a little prick; a sharp point growing on a plant or an animal's skin

prickly full of prickles; tingling (as, a prickly feeling)

pride too great an opinion of oneself; haughtiness; a feeling of pleasure after doing something well □ to be proud of (as - She prides herself on her auburn hair.)

priest a person authorized to conduct religious services; a clergyman or minister

prig a smug or conceited person

prim (of a person's behaviour) formal; excessively neat and correct

prima ballerina *(say preema ballereena)* the leading female dancer in a ballet company

prima donna the leading female singer in an opera

prime first in rank or importance (as, prime minister); first-rate or excellent (as, prime quality beef)

primary first; at, or of, the first stage

primate 1 an archbishop

primate 2 a member of the highest order of mammals

primer a first reading book; a simple introductory book

primeval *(say prymeeval)* belonging to the first age of the world

primitive of very early times; out-of-date; crude

primrose a pale yellow wildflower that blooms early in the spring □ pale yellow in colour

prince a high-ranking nobleman (usually) the son of a king or queen

princess the wife of a prince; the daughter of a king or queen

principal highest in rank or importance; chief (as, the principal town) □ the head of a college or school: a sum of money (in a bank, etc.) on which interest is paid

principality a state ruled by a prince (such as Monaco)

principally chiefly; mainly

principle a basic general truth or law; a rule to guide one's conduct (as, acting in accordance with high, or with sound, principles)

print to mark words and pictures on paper with a machine (a printing press); to write in capital letters; to stamp a pattern on; to make a finished photograph □ printed lettering; a photograph made from a negative

printer someone who prints books, newspapers, etc.

prior earlier or former □ the head of a priory

priority the right to be first (as - An ambulance has priority in traffic.)

priory a monastery or convent

prism a solid body whose two ends are the same shape and size (as, a glass prism with triangular ends, which splits light into separate rainbow colours)

prison a building where criminals are kept locked up for varying periods; a jail

prisoner someone under arrest,

or locked up in prison

private *(say pryvate)* belonging to one person or group of people, not to the general public; personal (as, his private opinion); secret □ an ordinary soldier
privacy seclusion; secrecy

privation poverty; hardship

privet a bushy shrub used for hedges

privilege *(say privilej)* an advantage enjoyed by only one person or a few people

prize 1 a reward for good work, or for success in a competition; a ship captured in war □ worthy of a prize (as, a prize bull) □ to value highly

prize 2, prise to force open with a lever or tool

pro- (before a word) favouring, or on the side of (as, pro-British)

probable likely to happen or to be true
probability likelihood; (in mathematics) the chance of a particular thing happening (as - The probability of a tossed coin falling either heads or tails is one in two.)

probation a testing; the suspending of an offender's sentence by the courts on condition that he behaves himself

probe a long thin instrument used to examine a wound □ to examine closely

problem a question or matter which is difficult to resolve or understand

proceed to go on; to continue
procedure a method of doing business, etc.
proceeding an action; (in plural) a legal action; a record of the matters dealt with at a meeting
proceeds the money taken at a sale, concert, etc.
procession a large number of people or vehicles proceeding in a line

process a series of actions producing changes (especially a

method of operation in manufacturing goods)

proclaim to announce publicly; to cry aloud
proclamation an official announcement

procure to get or obtain

prod to poke; to urge on

prodigal spending very wastefully

prodigy *(say prodijy)* a person who is exceptionally clever in some way (as, a child prodigy)
prodigious enormous; astonishing

produce *(say prodewce)* to make or bring into being; to cause or bring about □ *(say prodewce)* farm products; crops
producer someone who produces; someone responsible for bringing out a play, film, etc.
product something produced or manufactured (as - The products of Australia include wool and butter.): (mathematics) the result obtained by multiplying numbers together
production the act or process of producing; what is produced (as, the production of a factory, a mine, etc.)
productive having the power to produce; bringing results

profane not sacred; showing contempt of sacred things
profanity bad language or swearing; lack of respect for sacred things

profess to declare openly or strongly; to pretend (as - She professes to be an experienced rider.)
profession an occupation requiring special knowledge (as, the medical, legal, etc. professions); an open declaration
professional having to do with a profession: playing football, boxing, etc. for money (unlike unpaid amateurs)
professor a university teacher of the highest rank

proficient skilled; expert

profile a side view of a head or

face

profit gain; the difference between the selling price of anything and its cost (including selling expenses); benefit or advantage □ to gain; to get some benefit (as, to profit from one's mistakes)
profitable bringing profit or advantage
profiteer someone who makes excessive profits

profound very deep; deeply felt (as, a profound grief); intellectually deep (as, a profound thinker)

profuse *(say profewss)* excessive; extravagant (as, profuse thanks)
profusion a great abundance

programme a printed sheet or booklet listing the items of some entertainment; a scheme or plan; the instructions for an electronic computer □ to write such instructions in computer language

progress movement forward; advance; improvement □ to go forward; to improve
progressive going forward; advancing by stages

prohibit to forbid; to prevent
prohibitive tending to prevent or make impossible

project a scheme or plan; a special task or piece of research □ *(say project)* to throw or put forward; to use a beam of light to throw a picture on a screen; to jut out
projectile a missile
projection the art of projecting; something which juts out
projector a device for projecting pictures onto a screen

prolific very fruitful or productive

prologue introductory lines to a play or poem

prolong to make something last longer (as, to prolong a discussion)

promenade *(say promenahd)* a walk or ride for pleasure; an esplanade or public walk □ to walk about for pleasure

prominent standing out; easily seen; famous

promiscuous *(say promiskewuss)* not discriminating; being casual in relations with other people (especially those of the opposite sex)

promise to give one's word or make a promise (to do, or not to do, something) □ a statement assuring another person that one will do, or not do, something: a sign of future success (as, a boy or girl who shows promise)
promising likely to turn out well; full of promise

promontory a headland or high cape jutting into the sea

promote to raise to a higher rank or position; to encourage (as, to promote a worthy cause; to promote sales)
promotion an advancement in rank or grade; encouragement; advertising (as, sales promotion)

prompt quick; at once; without delay □ to move to action (as - His anger prompted him to hit back.); to help (an actor or speaker by reminding him of forgotten words or lines)
promptitude, promptness quickness; readiness

prone lying face downward: inclined to (as, prone to forgetfulness)

prong the spike of a fork

pronoun a word used instead of a noun (such as: *you, he, she, me, it, who, that, them*)

pronounce to speak or utter words or sounds; to give a judgment formally
pronounced easily noticed (as, a pronounced improvement)
pronouncement an announcement or declaration
pronunciation the way a word is said

proof see **prove**

prop a support of any kind (as, a clothes prop to keep up a line of washing); short for propeller (as, a turbo-prop aircraft); □ to hold up by means of a support

propagate to spread (as, to propagate news, or a rumour); to increase by natural means (as, to propagate seedlings, young plants, etc.)
propaganda any activity for spreading particular opinions or ideas (as, anti-war propaganda)

propel to drive forward
propeller a set of specially shaped blades on a shaft, which revolves to drive forward a ship or aircraft
propulsion a driving forward

proper right or fitting; correct; suitable
properly in the right way

property something that is owned by a person, school, government, etc.; land or buildings: a quality of a substance (as - Whiteness is a property of chalk.)

prophesy *(say professie)* to foretell the future
prophecy *(say professee)* a prediction; something foretold
prophet someone who makes prophecies; someone who announces a message from God

proportion a part, or share, of the whole (as - Only a small proportion of people are left-handed.); the ratio or size or quantity of one thing compared with another (as, a mixture of margarine and butter in the proportion of 1 to 9)
proportional, proportionate in proportion
in (out of) proportion suitable (or not) in size, etc., when compared with something else (as - A pig's tail seems out of proportion to its body.)

propose to suggest, or put forward, for consideration (as, to propose a new plan); to intend; to offer (especially marriage)
proposal an act of proposing; anything proposed; an offer

(especially of marriage)
proposition a formal statement; a suggestion or plan (as, a business proposition)

proprietor an owner (especially of a shop, hotel, etc.)

propriety rightness or fitness; correctness of behaviour

propulsion see **propel**

prosaic *(say prozayic)* dull; uninteresting

prose any writing that is not in verse

prosecute to bring legal action against a person
prosecution the act of bringing a law court action; the person or persons bringing such action
prosecutor the officer who prosecutes (especially in a criminal court)

prospect a likely result or outlook for the future (as, an election candidate faced with the prospect of defeat; a job with good prospects); a wide view or scene (as, a pleasant prospect) □ *(say prospect)* to make a search for minerals
prospective expected; likely to be, or to happen
prospectus a booklet giving information about a school, a new business or a new book, etc.

prosper to succeed; to get on well
prosperity material success; good fortune
prosperous successful; thriving

prostrate *(say prostret)* lying flat (especially with face to the ground); worn out or exhausted □ *(say prostrate)* to throw down on the ground; to bow (oneself) low in reverence

protect to defend or guard (from danger, loss, etc.); to keep safe
protective giving safety or cover (as, protective clothing)
protector a guardian; a person who protects from harm or injury

protégé *(say protayzhay)* a person who is helped in his career by someone important and influential

protein any of a large number of substances (found in milk, eggs, meat, etc.) essential to the growth and health of people and animals

protest *(say protest)* to object strongly; to state or declare solemnly (as - The accused man protested his innocence.) □ *(say protest)* a strong declaration of disapproval or disagreement

Protestant a member of one of the Christian churches other than the Roman Catholic or Greek Orthodox churches

proton a minute particle with a positive electrical charge that forms the nucleus of the hydrogen atom and part of the nucleus of all other atoms

protoplasm a semi-fluid substance contained in all living cells

prototype the first or original model from which anything is copied (as, a prototype of a new car, aeroplane, etc.)

protract to draw out or lengthen in time (as, a protracted committee meeting)
protractor an instrument for measuring and drawing angles on paper

protrude to stick out; to thrust forward

proud having a feeling of pride or great satisfaction about a skill, a possession, one's appearance, etc.; having a feeling that one is superior to others; haughty

prove to show that something is true; to test or try (as, to prove the strength of something); to show correctness (as, of a problem in arithmetic); to turn out to be (as - Eventually he was proved to be right.)
proof a test which shows that something is true; evidence strong enough to clear up any doubts □ able to keep out (as, bullet-proof, waterproof)

proverb a well-known and wise saying (usually meant to have a moral, as - It's no use crying over spilt milk.)
proverbial well-known; spoken about by many people

provide to supply; to give what is needed; to get ready what is needed (as, to provide food for a camping trip)
provided (that) if; on condition (that)
provision the act of providing; a condition laid down in a contract, agreement, etc.
provisions a stock of food
provisional temporary; for the time being
proviso a condition in a document, etc.

providence foresight; thrift; God's foresight and care for all creatures
provident showing forethought in planning for the future; thrifty
providential fortunate; coming as if by God's care or divine help

province a division of a country; the extent or limit of one's knowledge (as - Higher mathematics is outside my province.); (in plural) the parts of a country away from the chief city
provincial belonging or having to do with a province or the provinces; narrow and limited in experience or attitude

provision, etc. see **provide**

provoke to cause anger, annoyance, impatience, etc.; to bring about or stir up (as, to provoke a person into action)
provocation the act of provoking; a cause of anger
provocative causing anger or annoyance; stimulating thought or action

prow the front part of a ship

prowess bravery; great courage (especially in battle); great skill or ability

prowl to move about quietly and stealthily (especially in search of plunder)

proximity nearness (in time, place, etc.)

prudent careful and wise (in

action and conduct); the opposite of reckless

prudence caution; wisdom in practical matters

prune 1 a dried plum

prune 2 to trim or cut off unnecessary twigs and branches from trees and shrubs to encourage new growth; to cut out unnecessary parts of a manuscript, a speech, etc.

pry to peep or peer (especially into secret or personal matters)

psalm (say sahm) a sacred song or hymn

pseudo- (say suedoe) (as part of a word) false; sham
pseudonym (say suedonim) a false name used by an author (Lewis Carroll was the pseudonym of the Rev. Charles L. Dodgson.)

psychic, psychical (say sykik, sykikal) having to do with the mind or soul; sensitive to non-physical or spiritual forces

psychology (say sykology) the science that studies the human mind and mental processes
psychologist someone who studies or practises psychology

pub short for public house

public open to or belonging to people in general; the opposite of private; generally known or spoken about □ people as a whole; a certain section of the population (as, the cinema-going public)
publican the owner or manager of a public house or inn
publication the publishing of books, magazines, etc. □ something printed and published (such as a book or magazine)
publicity a kind of advertising which makes a person or thing known to the public
publish to put (a book, magazine, etc.) on sale to the public; to proclaim or announce publicly (as, to publish the true facts)
public house a place where beer and other alcoholic drinks are sold and drunk

puck a hard rubber disc used in the game of ice hockey

pucker to gather into wrinkles or folds

pudding any soft sweet food eaten at the end of a meal (usually made with flour, milk, eggs, sugar, etc.); other soft flour and fat mixtures (as, Yorkshire, suet, etc. puddings); a type of sausage (as, black pudding)

puddle a small muddy pool

puff to blow air or smoke out of the mouth in small gusts; to breathe heavily (as, after running or strenuous exercise); to blow out steam, smoke, etc. (as, from a steam engine); to swell up or out (as, to puff out one's cheeks, one's chest, etc.) □ a sudden gust of air, wind, smoke, etc.; a pad for applying powder; a kind of very light pastry
puffy swollen; flabby; breathing in puffs

puffin a sea bird with a short, thick, brightly-coloured beak

pug a type of small, thickset dog with a blunt nose
pug nose a short, thick nose with a slightly up-turned tip

pugnacious fond of fighting; quarrelsome

puke to vomit

pull to move or bring something towards oneself; to pluck or draw out (as, to pull a tooth); to tear apart □ the act of pulling

pullet a young hen

pulley a wheel with a grooved rim in which fits a cord, chain, etc., used for lifting heavy objects

pullover a knitted garment (usually with sleeves)

pulp the soft fleshy part of a fruit or vegetable; a soft moist mass (especially of wood, rags, etc.) used for making paper □ to reduce to a pulp

pulpit a raised structure (especially in a church) from which a preacher delivers a sermon

pulse 1 a regular beat or throb

(as, of the heart and arteries)
pulsate to beat or throb

pulse(s) 2 beans, peas and similar edible seeds

pulverize to pound or grind into powder or dust

puma a large catlike American animal

pumice *(say pumiss)*, **pumice stone** a piece of light, hardened lava, used for removing stains or smoothing rough surfaces

pummel to beat with the fists

pump a machine used to raise water from a well or for transferring or compressing liquids, gases, etc. □ to raise or force with a pump

pumpkin a large yellow- or orange-coloured fruit that grows on a trailing vine

pun a play on words in which the same word (or a word that sounds the same as another) is given two different meanings (as - Why do lords catch cold easily? Because peers [piers] are nearly always standing in water. - or - Which fruit do you choose? Any, so long as I get a pair [pear].)

punch 1 a drink made of various juices, water, spice, sugar and (usually) alcoholic spirits

punch 2 to strike hard with the fist; to pierce or stamp by using a tool or machine □ a tool for punching holes (in paper, leather, etc.)

punctual on time; prompt; not late
punctuality promptness; arrival on time

punctuate to add punctuation marks to a piece of writing; to divide up (as - The speech was punctuated by applause.)
punctuation the system of using punctuation marks in writing to make it easy to read and understand
punctuation marks all of the symbols used in writing, other than letters (especially commas, full stops, question marks, etc.)

puncture to pierce or prick with a sharp point □ the act of piercing or pricking; a small hole; a hole in a tyre

pundit a learned man

pungent sharp to taste or smell (as, mustard); biting or stimulating (as, comments, remarks)

punish to make a person suffer for a fault or crime; to inflict punishment (on someone)
punishment the act of punishing; the penalty to be paid for a fault or crime
punitive inflicting punishment; intended to have a punishing effect

punt 1 a small, flat-bottomed boat with square ends □ to move a punt by pushing with a pole

punt 2 to kick a dropped football before it touches the ground

puny small and weak; undersized

pup, puppy a young dog

pupa a stage (often in a cocoon) in the growth of an insect (as, when a caterpillar becomes a pupa before emerging as a butterfly) .

pupil 1 a person who learns from a teacher

pupil 2 the round dark centre of the eye through which the light passes

puppet a doll which can be moved by strings, or by putting the hand inside it; a person who unthinkingly does what another person tells him

purchase 1 to buy something □ something bought
purchase tax a tax on certain goods sold within a country

purchase 2 any extra power gained in lifting or moving by using a lever, a capstan, etc.

pure clean; not mixed with anything else; free from dirt or contamination; without faults; innocent; utter or absolute (as, pure nonsense)
purely in a pure manner; merely; entirely (as, purely

by accident)

purification the act of purifying

purify to make pure

purity the state of being pure; freedom from contamination

purée *(say puray)* food boiled to a pulp and pushed through a sieve

purge to make clear or pure; to clear out (waste material) from the bowels
purgative a medicine that clears out waste matter from the bowels

puritanical very strict and (often) narrow-minded

purl a knitting stitch; the opposite of plain stitch

purple a colour made by mixing red and blue together

purport meaning; gist (as, the purport of a message) □ to mean; to appear to be (as - The message purported to come from him.)

purpose *(say purpus)* an aim or goal towards which one's thoughts and efforts are directed; the reason or idea behind some action; use or object (as - What is the purpose of the invention?)
purposeful knowing what one wants to do
purposely, on purpose deliberately; intentionally

purr the murmuring sound made by a contented cat

purse a small bag for carrying money □ to draw the lips tightly together

pursue to follow (especially with the intention of overtaking or capturing); to chase after; to be engaged or occupied in (as, to pursue a course of studies)
pursuit the act of pursuing; anything pursued (as, an occupation, hobby, etc.)

purvey (of food, provisions, etc.) to supply or provide (usually as a business, as to purvey meat)
purveyor supplier (as - A butcher is a purveyor of meat.)

pus thick yellowish matter produced in wounds, boils, etc.

push to thrust or move something away with force; to shove; to press hard against; to make an effort; to urge on (as - They pushed him into accepting the responsibility.) □ a thrust; an effort
pushing aggressive; too sure of oneself

put to place, lay or set something in position; to cause to be, or to bring into a certain state (as, to put things right); to express (as, to put the argument clearly); to drive or force (as, to put the enemy to flight)

putrefy to rot; to decay
putrid rotten; foul; stinking

putt to hit a ball lightly across a green on a golf course
putter a golf club used for putting

putty a soft cement of powdered chalk and linseed oil, used for fixing glass into window frames, etc.

puzzle to worry or perplex with a difficult question; to be difficult to understand (as - His behaviour puzzles me.) □ a problem, situation, etc. that is difficult to solve or understand; a riddle, game or toy that tests one's mental powers

pygmy see **pigmy**

pyjamas a sleeping suit

pylon a high tower-like structure of light steel, used to support electric power cables; a guiding mark at an airfield

pyramid a solid shape with a triangle on each of three sides and a base, meeting in a point at the top; any structure of this shape (especially those built to enclose tombs in ancient Egypt)

pyre a pile of wood for burning a dead body

python a large and powerful snake which crushes its prey by coiling around it

q

quack 1 the cry of a duck □ to make this sound

quack 2 a person who pretends he has skill and knowledge (especially medical) that he does not really possess

quadrangle a plane figure with four angles (and therefore four sides): a four-sided open space with buildings around it (as in a college)

quadrant $1/4$ of the circumference or area of a circle □ an instrument (shaped like a $1/4$ circle) used in navigation, astronomy, etc. for measuring altitudes

quadruped a four-footed animal

quadruple made up of four parts; four times as much
quadruplets four babies born to one mother at one birth

quaff to drink deeply and in large quantities

quail 1 to lose courage; to shrink back in fear

quail 2 a small wild bird of the partridge family

quaint pleasantly odd or unusual (especially in an old-fashioned way, as, a quaint old village)

quake to tremble or shiver (with fear, cold, etc.) □ a shudder; an earthquake

qualify to prove oneself fit, competent or skilled enough to carry out an activity, to follow a profession, a trade, etc. (as - Before he can qualify as a doctor, he has to pass all his exams.); to make a statement weaker by adding something to make it less positive (as - At first, he said *I never wear a hat,* but qualified this by adding *except in winter.*)
qualified competent; skilled; having qualifications
qualification the act of qualifying; the skill or attainment that makes a person qualified to fill a position, enter a trade or profession, etc.

quality the real nature or charac-

ter of a person or thing; the degree of goodness or badness of something (as - These shoes are of better quality and will last longer.)

qualm a sudden attack of faintness or sickness; an uneasy feeling or fear (as a result of a guilty conscience, etc.)

quandary a state of uncertainty about what to do in a puzzling situation

quantity an amount (especially a large amount)

quarantine (a period of) compulsory isolation to keep a person who has a contagious disease (such as smallpox) from passing it on to others; the place where the isolation period is spent

quarrel an angry dispute or argument; a disagreement □ to dispute angrily; to break off a friendship; to complain about or find fault with (as - Most people would quarrel with his extreme ideas.)
quarrelsome inclined to quarrel or find fault

quarry 1 an open excavation from which building stone, slate, etc. is cut or blasted

quarry 2 a hunted animal or bird; prey; a victim

quart a measure of liquid, equal to two pints or $1/4$ gallon

quarter a fourth part of anything (as, a quarter of an hour, the last quarter of the year, etc.); a district or direction (as, the business quarter of a city, attacks from all quarters); mercy granted to an enemy □ to divide into four equal parts
quarters lodgings for soldiers, staff, etc.
quarterly occurring once every three months □ a magazine, etc. published once every quarter (of a year)
quarter-deck the rear part of the upper deck of a ship

quartet, quartette a set or group of four; a musical composition for four voices or instruments; the performers of such music

quartz the commonest rock-forming silica, found in transparent crystals (sometimes coloured, such as amethysts)

quatrain a stanza or poem of four lines

quaver to tremble or shake; to speak or sing in a shaky, tremulous voice; (in music) to trill

quay *(say kee)* a landing place for boats and ships to load or unload

queasy nauseated, feeling sick; squeamish

queen the female ruler of a country; the wife of a king; the only egg-bearing female in a colony of bees, ants, termites, etc.; a playing card; a chess piece
queen mother the mother of a reigning king or queen

queer odd or strange; not ordinary: not well

quell to overcome or subdue (protests, a revolt, an outburst of shouting, etc.)

quench to put out (a fire); to satisfy or slake (as, to quench one's thirst)

querulous complaining; peevish

query a question; a question mark (**?**) □ to question or inquire about something

quest a search after or pursuit of something (as - The early explorers went in quest of gold.)

question an inquiry; the act of asking (usually for information); something asked (expecting an answer); a problem or puzzle □ to inquire; to ask questions; to doubt or disagree (as - I question their legal right to take such action.)
questionable not trustworthy; doubtful; not sure or decided; (as, a person of questionable character)
questionnaire a set of written questions to be answered by a number of people to obtain information about their opinions, expenditure of money, etc.

queue *(say kew)* a line of people waiting their turn (to board a bus, enter a cinema); a pigtail

quibble to evade the real point of a discussion by clever use of words, by bringing up other questions, etc. □ a trivial objection

quick fast; speedy; happening in a very short time; responding rapidly (as, a quick temper) □ a very sensitive part of the body (as, to bite one's nails to the quick)
quicken to make alive; to hurry or hasten
quicksand wet, loose sand into which a person is likely to sink
quicksilver mercury
quick-witted responding or thinking quickly

quiet not noisy; at rest; calm; not moving □ rest; peace □ to make quiet or to calm
quieten to make, or become, quiet

quill the stiff hollow part of a feather; a large feather; one of the sharp spines on some animals (such as the hedgehog or porcupine)

quilt a thick padded bedcover

quince a hard yellow fruit with an acid taste, used in making jellies, marmalade, etc.

quinine a bitter medicine made from the bark of a South American tree, used in treating malaria and other fevers

quintet, quintette a set or group of five; a musical composition for five voices or instruments; the performers of such music

quintuplets five babies born to one mother at one birth

quire 24 sheets of paper, a twentieth part of a ream

quit to leave; to go away; to give up or discontinue something (as, to quit a job)

quitter a person who gives up easily

quite completely; entirely; *yes indeed*! □ rather or fairly (as - I pass quite near the shops every day.)

quiver 1 a case for arrows

quiver 2 to tremble, to shake or shiver

quiz a set of questions to be answered (usually as a competition before an audience); a short test of knowledge
quizzical questioning or gently mocking (as, a quizzical look)

quoit *(say koit)* a heavy flat ring of metal, rope, etc. which is aimed at a peg in the game of quoits

quorum the smallest number of people who must be present at a meeting before business can

officially be done

quota a part or share to be given (or received) by each member of a group, community, nation, etc. (as - The United Kingdom agreed to import a quota of bacon from Denmark.)

quote to refer to (something read, spoken, etc.); to repeat exactly (something someone has said or written)
quotation the act of quoting; something quoted (as, a quotation from one of Shakespeare's plays)
quotation marks the double or single marks used at the beginning and end of something quoted (written or printed " " or ' ')

quotient the result of dividing one number by another (for example, the quotient of 16 ÷ 2 is 8)

r

rabbi a Jewish priest or teacher of the Jewish law

rabbit a small furry, burrowing animal with long ears

rabble a noisy, disorderly crowd; a mob

rabies a serious brain disease (usually fatal) of dogs and other animals, which can be passed on to humans through a bite from a rabid animal
rabid having rabies; violent; extreme in attitude; mad

race 1 living beings of the same kind (descended from the same ancestors, having a similar skin colour or other physical attributes, etc.)
racial having to do with race

race 2 a competition between people, animals, vehicles, etc. to see who or which is the fastest; a swift current of water (as, a mill race) □ to take part in a race; to

rush or hurry (as - He raced for the bus.)
racecourse, racetrack the ground or course over which races are run

racial see **race 1**

rack a framework to keep things in or on (as, a hat rack): (in olden times) an instrument of torture on which people's limbs were stretched

racket 1, racquet a bat with a network of strings stretched on an oval frame, used in playing tennis and other games

racket 2 a din; an uproar; a loud and continued noise (as, from a crowd of people)

radar a radio device used to locate aircraft, ships, etc. in darkness or fog (Their distance and position can be found by studying the picture shown on a radar screen. The word radar comes from the words **ra**dio **d**etecting and ranging.)

radiant sending out rays of heat or light; shining; bright; beaming with joy (as, a radiant smile)
radiance brilliance; brightness

radiate to send out rays of heat or light; to spread out in many directions from a centre

radiation the act of sending out rays (of light, electricity, etc.); the giving off of dangerous rays from a radioactive substance

radiator a set of pipes or other apparatus used to heat a room by electricity, hot water or steam; the part of a car that holds water to cool the engine

radical belonging to the principle or root of something (as - A radical change of design is needed before the machine will work efficiently.); extreme; complete (as, a radical change in the political system) □ a person who wants great changes (especially in the system of government)

radio a system of broadcasting or receiving people's voices, music, etc. without a connecting wire (wireless); a wireless receiving set □ having to do with radio or with electrical energy emitted in wave form

radioactive giving out energy in the form of dangerous rays

radish the sharp-tasting red or white root of a small garden plant, eaten raw in salads, etc.

radium a radioactive metallic element which gives out rays used in treating certain diseases

radius a straight line from the centre of a circle to its circumference; the area (roughly circular) within a given distance from a central point (as, a house within a radius of five miles from the station)
radii *(say raydee-ie)* the plural of radius

raffia strips of palm fibre used for making mats, baskets, etc.

raffle a lottery in which numbered tickets are sold for a prize or prizes given to the holder of the winning number(s)

raft a number of logs or planks fastened together as a floating platform

rafter one of the sloping beams supporting a roof

rag an old piece of torn cloth; (in plural) clothes that are old, worn and shabby
ragged torn; tattered; rough or jagged

rage great anger; fury; violence (as of the wind, sea, etc.): something very fashionable or in demand (as - Surfing is all the rage this summer.) □ to be furiously angry

raid a quick surprise attack (as, an air raid, a police raid, etc.)

rail a wooden or metal bar used as part of a fence; one of the metal bars that are used to form a railway track
railing a fence of rails and supporting posts
railway, railroad a track of parallel metal rails on which trains run

raiment an old-fashioned word for clothing

rain water falling in drops from the clouds; anything that falls like rain □ to fall, or send down like rain
rainbow a brilliantly coloured arch appearing in the sky opposite the sun, caused when the sun's rays shine through raindrops or mist
raincoat a coat made of some waterproof material
rainfall the amount of rain that falls in a certain period (measured by depth, as, an average of 25 inches a year)

raise to lift up; to cause to rise; to grow or breed (plants, animals, etc.); to bring up (a family); to collect (as, to raise money); to cause (as, to raise a laugh, a protest, etc.); to increase (as, to raise prices)

raisin a dried grape, used in cakes, puddings, etc.

rake a garden tool with a long handle and a bar with teeth at the end, used for smoothing, gathering dead leaves, etc. □ to smooth or collect together with a rake

rally (military) to gather together again (as - The general tried to rally his troops after their retreat.); to revive or pull together (one's wits, strength, etc.,); to come together to support (as - The whole school rallied to cheer on their team.)

ram 1 a male sheep

ram 2 a device used in olden days for battering down walls, etc. □ to push, cram or press (into); to crash hard into (a ship, a vehicle, etc.)
    ramrod a rod for ramming down the charge into a muzzle-loading gun; a rod for cleaning a gun barrel

ramble to walk about for pleasure; to wander aimlessly; to talk in a confused, disconnected way (as - He rambled on about events in his childhood.) □ a long walk

ramp a slightly sloping passageway, road surface, etc. connecting two levels

rampart a flat-topped mound or wall built as a defence

ramshackle badly made; falling to pieces

ranch a very large farm where cattle, sheep or horses are raised

rancid *(say ransid)* smelling or tasting stale (as, rancid butter)

rancour a feeling of anger or ill-will

random aimless; by chance (as, a random shot)
    at random without any plan or purpose

range to set in a row; to place in a certain order or position; to wander (as - The sheep ranged over the hills.); to extend; to vary (as - The temperature ranges between 7° and 15° centigrade.) □ a line or row (of mountains, etc.); a variety (as, a wide range of goods); distance or space that can be covered (by a shot, a sound, etc.); a practice ground for shooting (as, a rifle range); an open stretch of ground (especially for grazing); a flat-topped cooking stove

ranger a forest or park keeper; (in North America) a member of an organized patrol

rank 1 a line or row (as, of soldiers); the order or position of a person (in the armed forces, in society, etc.); (in plural) soldiers who are not officers □ to arrange in lines or in a certain order; to be classed, or have a certain position, according to merit (as, to rank high, or above others)
    rank and file ordinary troops; ordinary people

rank 2 growing freely and strongly (especially coarse grass, weeds, etc.); unpleasantly strong-smelling; rancid; extreme (as, rank stupidity)

rankle to cause annoyance or irritation (as - The unjust accusation rankled in her mind for days.)

ransack to plunder; to search thoroughly (as, to ransack a desk for missing papers)

ransom a sum of money paid in return for the freeing of a captive

rant to talk or scold for a long time in a noisy manner

rap a sharp blow; a knock □ to strike a hard sharp blow; to knock or tap (as, a rap on a door)

rapid quick; speedy; very fast
    rapids a place in a river (usually steep and rocky) where the water flows very quickly

rapier a long thin sword used in fencing

rapt completely absorbed or lost in thought, wonder, etc. (as, to listen with rapt attention)
    rapture great delight; ecstasy

rare 1 (of meat) lightly cooked; underdone

rare 2 unusual; uncommon; exceptionally valuable or good

rascal a dishonest person; one who makes mischief or cannot be trusted

rash 1 red spots or redness on the skin (as, in measles, chicken pox, etc.)

rash 2 acting hastily or impulsively, without forethought

rasher a thin slice of bacon

rasp a coarse file □ to speak in a rough, grating voice

raspberry a small soft red fruit, containing tiny seeds

rat a gnawing animal like a large mouse

rate payment per hour or per week (as, a higher rate of pay); speed (as, a rate of 50 miles per hour); (usually in plural) a yearly tax on the value of property, paid by the owner towards the cost of providing public services; rank or quality (as, first-rate, second-rate)

rating grade or position; a sailor below the rank of officer

rather somewhat; to some extent; preferably or more willingly (as - Would you rather come with us?)

ratify to agree to; to confirm (as, to ratify an international treaty)

ratio *(say rayshio)* the proportion of one thing to another (as - The boys outnumbered the girls by a ratio of 3 to 1.)

ration *(say rash'n)* a fixed or measured amount (of food, etc.) given out (to members of the armed forces, civilians in war time, etc.)

rational *(say rashional)* reasonable; sensible; having the ability to reason

rattle to give out short sharp sounds (as when hard objects are shaken together); to clatter; to speak or recite quickly (as, to rattle off a poem) □ a child's toy that makes a rattling sound

rattler, rattlesnake a poisonous American snake with horny rattling rings on its tail

raucous hoarse; harsh (as, a raucous voice)

ravage to lay waste and plunder; to ruin (as - The enemy ravaged the countryside.)

rave to talk wildly or as if mad; to praise extravagantly (as, to rave over a singer's performance)

raven a large, glossy black bird of the crow family □ glossy black (as, raven-haired)

ravenous very hungry

ravine a deep, narrow gorge

ravish to carry away by force; to plunder: (of beauty) to fill one with delight or pleasure

raw not cooked; in the natural state (before being prepared or manufactured, as raw sugar); (of skin) rubbed and sore; chilly and damp (as, a raw windy day); inexperienced (as, raw recruits to the army)

rawboned skinny; gaunt

rawhide the untanned skin of cattle, etc.

ray 1 a narrow beam of light, heat, etc.; a faint gleam or glimmer (of hope, of light, etc.); (in plural) lines, petals, etc. going out from a centre

ray 2 a large flat fish (often with a whiplike stinging tail

rayon a silky material made from wood pulp

raze to knock down or ruin (a city, a building) by destroying everything above ground level

razor a sharp-edged instrument used to shave off hair

re- a prefix meaning again (as, to **reappear,** to **reconsider,** etc.)

reach to stretch out or extend as far as (as - The river reaches the sea.) □ extent or distance (as, within reach of home)

react *(say ree-act)* to act or respond to some action, statement, situation, etc.; to undergo chemical change (by the action of one substance on another)

reaction response to a situation, an experience, etc.; a chemical change

reactionary wishing to return to a former, less progressive state of things (especially in government)

read to understand written or printed words; to say aloud what is printed or written; to study (as, to read a book on biology)

reader a person who reads; a school book for learning or practising reading

to read between the lines to see a hidden meaning in what is actually written or printed

to read up to study

ready prepared; willing and able to do something at once; quick to act; available (as, ready money)

readily willingly; easily; quickly

ready-made manufactured; not made to order (as, ready-made clothes)

real actually existing; true (not imaginary or imitation)

really in fact; truly

realist a person who takes a practical view of life (in contrast to a romantic)

realistic facing reality; seeing things as they are; (in art, literature) true to life (as - That picture is so realistic, you can almost smell the flowers.)

reality what is real; what actually exists

realize to come to understand; to achieve (as - He realized his ambition.); to make real or true (as - Her worst fears were realized.)

realization understanding; comprehension

realm kingdom; a part or section of human knowledge, action, experience, etc. (as, the realm of sport, the realm of music)

ream 20 quires (of paper); (plural) large quantities of paper or writing (as, reams of poetry)

reap to cut and gather in crops of grain; to gain or obtain (a reward, benefit)

reaper a person who reaps; a reaping machine

rear 1 the back part; a position at the back or behind; the last part of an army or fleet

rear 2 to raise (cattle, horses, pigs, etc.); to bring up (children); (of a horse) to rise up on the hind legs

rearm *(say ree-arm)* to supply arms again (usually new and better)

rearmament the act of rearming

reason a cause; an explanation or excuse (for some action); the mental ability or power to form opinions, to think things out; good judgment or common sense □ to try to persuade others by reasonable argument; to think things out clearly

reasonable sensible; fair

reassure to remove (a person's) fears or doubts; to comfort

reassurance the act of reassuring or comforting

rebel *(say rebel)* to oppose someone in authority (especially to use force against a government) □ *(say rebel)* a person who opposes those in power

rebellion an uprising against authority; open opposition to those in power (especially armed revolt); refusal to obey

rebellious inclined to rebel or disobey (as, to be in a rebellious mood)

rebound to spring back (after hitting something); to bounce back

rebuff a snub; a blunt refusal

rebuke to scold; to find fault or criticize

recall to call back; to remember

recapitulate to summarize again or restate briefly the chief points (of an argument, a debate, a speech)

recede to move or go back; to become more distant

receding sloping backward; becoming more distant (as, a train receding into the distance)

receipt see **receive**

receive to take or accept something that is given or sent (as, to receive a gift, a compliment, a letter, etc.); to welcome or meet (as, to receive guests)
receiver a person who receives (especially a person who knowingly accepts stolen goods); a radio or television set that receives broadcasts; the part of a telephone through which sounds are heard
receipt *(say reseet)* the act of receiving; a written or printed note stating that something has been paid for or that something has been received; (plural) amount of money received (as - The football club's receipts were up on last year's.): a recipe
reception the act or way of receiving (a thing, a person, a speech, etc.); a formal social gathering (as, a wedding reception after the ceremony)
receptive able to understand and accept ideas, information, etc. quickly; willing and ready to listen.

recent happening or made a short time ago; new or fresh

receptacle anything that holds or contains (as, a box, a dustbin, a bucket)

recess 1 a part of a room set back in a wall; an alcove; a niche

recess 2 a short rest from work or school

recipe *(say ressipee)* the ingredients and directions for preparing something (especially food); a prescription or remedy (as - A recipe for good health is fresh air, regular exercise and a balanced diet.)

recipient a person who receives

reciprocate to give or have a similar feeling (as, to reciprocate a kindness by doing a kindness)
reciprocal shared; given and received mutually (as, a reciprocal agreement between two countries)

recite to repeat aloud something that has been memorized (such as a poem, part of a play, etc.); to go over details in order (as, to recite the particulars of an illness)
recital the act of reciting; a public performance (of music, dancing, etc., usually by one person or one person at a time)
recitation a poem, part of a play, etc. repeated aloud from memory; the act of reciting

reckless rash; not thinking or caring about what may happen (as, a reckless driver)

reckon to count or add up; to consider; to think or believe
reckoning a bill or account to be settled; a calculation

reclaim to make productive or useful again (as, to reclaim land from the sea by building dikes and draining the water out)

recline to lean on one's back or side (as, to recline on a bed)

recognize to know something because it has been seen before; to know a person because of a previous meeting, etc.; to admit or acknowledge (as - They recognized how much he had done for them.)
recognition the act of recognizing; acknowledgment (as - A medal was presented in recognition of his bravery.)

recoil to draw or shrink back in horror, fear, etc.; to spring back (as a gun recoils after firing)

recollect to remember; to call to mind
recollection memory; a thing remembered (as, recollections of childhood)

recommend to advise; to praise or speak well of (as - I can recommend this book.)
recommendation an act of recommending; a favourable statement about a person or thing

recompense to repay or reward (a person for a service, a piece of work, etc.) □ a reward or compensation

reconcile to bring people together again in friendship (often after a quarrel or disagreement); to come to accept (as - They eventually reconciled themselves to losing the championship.); to adjust or settle (as, to reconcile two opposing points of view or two seemingly contradictory statements)
reconciliation a renewing of a broken friendship; the act of reconciling

reconstruct to build again (a place or thing that has been destroyed or badly damaged); to go over carefully in detail (as, to reconstruct the way a crime may have been carried out)

record *(say record)* to set down (in written or printed form) events at the time of happening; to copy (by means of a machine) voices, musical instruments, etc., which can later be reproduced (as, to record a speech, a song, etc.) □ *(say reckord)* a written or printed account of events or facts; a disc on which a speech, music, etc. is recorded (a gramophone record); the best that someone has ever done (as, a world record for the high jump, the fastest time for a race, etc.)
recorder 1 a person who records; an instrument for recording: see **tape recorder**
recorder 2 a musical instrument, played by blowing into a mouthpiece
recording the process of making a record (as, a recording [of sound] on a gramophone disc or magnetic tape); the sound record so made
record-player an electrically-powered gramophone

recover to find or get back again, something that has been lost, misplaced, etc.; to regain (health, one's self-control, etc.)
recovery a return to health, prosperity, etc.; the act of recovering or finding a lost object

recreation *(say rekreeayshun)*

rest or relaxation from work or study; a hobby or pastime (such as a sport, gardening, painting, reading)

recruit a newly-enlisted member of an organization (for example, the army) □ to reinforce or add to the strength of the armed forces, an organization, etc. by getting new members to join

rectangle a four-sided figure with opposite sides equal and four right angles
rectangular shaped like a rectangle; having four right angles

rectify to correct; to put right (as, to rectify an error)

rector a clergyman (in the Church of England) in charge of a parish; a title given to some headmasters in Scotland and to some heads of colleges
rectory the house of a rector

recumbent lying down

recuperate to recover (strength or health)

recur to occur or happen again (as, an illness that recurs)

red the colour of blood: (political) a person who has radical or revolutionary ideas (especially a communist)
redden to make or become red (as - His face reddened with embarrassment.)
Red Cross an international organization for relieving suffering in war time or in times of disaster (such as a great flood)
redskin a North American Indian
redwood a very tall North American timber tree; the brownish-red wood of this tree

redeem to buy back; to pay back a loan and get back something left as a guarantee (with a pawnbroker); to fulfil (a promise); to compensate for (as - He redeemed his earlier mistakes by scoring the winning goal.)
redemption the act of redeeming; (religious) salvation; atonement

redress to set right or make up for (a wrong, an unkindness, etc.) □ relief; compensation

re-dress to dress again

reduce to make smaller in quantity, size, extent, etc.; to make less (as, to reduce prices); to weaken; to change into other terms or into another form
reduction the act of reducing; the amount by which something is reduced

redundant more than is necessary; (of workers) no longer required

reed a tall stiff grass that grows in or near water; a vibrating part of some musical instruments (such as the clarinet, oboe, pipe organ); a musical pipe made of a hollow reed

reef a chain of rocks at or near the surface of water

reek smoke; unpleasant fumes □ to give off smoke, fumes or an unpleasant smell (as - The room reeked of stale tobacco.)

reel 1 a lively dance; the music for this

reel 2 to whirl or be in a dizzy whirl (as - My head is reeling.); to sway or walk unsteadily; to tell something rapidly (as, to reel off a story)

reel 3 a bobbin or cylinder of wood, metal or plastic on which thread, wire, fishing lines, etc. may be wound; a length of cinema film wound on to a spool □ to wind on a reel; to draw or pull in by means of a reel (as, to reel in a fish)

refectory a dining hall (especially in a school or in a monastery)

refer to direct or send someone who is seeking information or help to a particular person, place, authoritative book, etc. (as - For information about early aeroplanes, the teacher referred him to an encyclopaedia.); to look up information in a book; to mention or speak of (as, to refer to a piece in a newspaper); to concern or relate to (as - His remark referred to a holiday we spent together.)

referee a person to whom something is referred for a judgment or decision; an umpire in certain sports and games

reference the act of referring; a mention (as - He made a reference to the school in his speech.); a letter or statement about a person's character, quality of work, etc.; a person who gives such a reference
reference book, reference library a book or a library to be consulted for information

refill to fill again □ a replacement or duplicate for filling again (as, a refill for a loose-leaf notebook, a refill for a lipstick)

refine to purify; to clarify; to make less coarse or crude; to improve by making more elegant, delicate, etc.
refined freed from impurities; cultured and well-mannered
refinement good taste and elegance; good manners
refinery a place where refining is carried out (as, an oil refinery, a sugar refinery)

reflect to throw back (light, heat, etc.); to show an image or likeness (as, in a mirror or the smooth surface of a pond); to think carefully and deeply
reflection the act of reflecting or throwing back light; an image or likeness produced by a mirror, etc.; careful thought; a remark or observation made after careful thought; criticism or fault-finding (as - My remarks were not intended as a reflection on his conduct.)
reflector something with a reflecting surface

reflex an involuntary action or movement (such as the leg jerking when the knee-cap is struck)
reflexive referring back (as, a reflexive pronoun such as *herself* in *She dressed herself.*)

reform to make better or improve by removing faults; to abandon bad habits, evil ways,

etc. for a better way of living; to change from bad behaviour to good conduct □ an improvement; change for the better
reformation a radical change for the better; the act of reforming
reformer a person who wishes to bring about improvements

re-form to form again

refract to change the direction of a ray of light (as when a slanting ray is refracted or bent by passing from air into water)

refrain 1 to hold oneself back or to keep from doing something (as - Passengers must refrain from smoking while the aeroplane is taking off.)

refrain 2 a chorus coming at the end of each verse of a song; a line or phrase repeated at intervals in a poem or song

refresh to make or become fresh again; to renew strength or energy (as - A good night's sleep will refresh you.)
refreshment something which refreshes (as, a cooling drink)

refrigerate to make cold; to preserve (food, etc.) by freezing
refrigerator a cold box or room where food is stored to keep it fresh

refuge a shelter (from attack, danger, etc.)
refugee a person who seeks shelter in another country (especially to escape political or religious persecution)

refund to pay back or repay (as, to refund a deposit)

refuse 1 *(say refewz)* to say one will not do, accept, or take part in, something
refusal the act of refusing

refuse 2 *(say refewss)* rubbish; waste material to be thrown away

regain to win back; to recover (health, good spirits); to get back to (as, to regain the shore when swimming)

regal royal; kingly

regard to look at carefully; to consider (as, to regard something as a nuisance); to think well of (as, to regard a person highly) □ an attentive look; concern (for); affection; respect; (plural) good wishes (as - Please give my regards to your family.)
regarding with, or in regard to; concerning
regardless without concern or consideration (as - He said he would come regardless of the weather.)

regatta a race or series of races for yachts or other boats

regenerate to produce, or make, anew; to restore to a former condition; to reform (character, behaviour)

regent a person who rules in place of a king or queen
regency (period of) rule by a regent

régime *(say rayzheem)* system of government

regiment a body of soldiers under the command of a colonel

region a large area of land; a district; a part of the body (as, a pain in the region of the left lung)

register a written list of names and other information kept as a regular record (as, a register of pupils, a register of voters); the range of a voice or musical instrument □ to make an entry in a register (as, to sign a hotel register); to show or record (as - The thermometer registers 7° centigrade.); to pay extra at a post office for special care of a parcel or letter
registrar an official who keeps records of births, marriages and deaths
registry an office where registers are kept
register office, registry office an office where records of births, marriages, etc. are kept, and where marriages take place

regret to feel sorry about something □ a sorrowful feeling of loss or unhappiness; a wish that something had happened differently, or that one had not acted in a certain way

regretful feeling regret

regrettable to be regretted; deserving regret; unfortunate (as, a regrettable incident)

regular usual; always happening at the same time or at fixed intervals; done according to rule; even (as, regular teeth); belonging to the permanent army (as, a regular soldier)

regulate to control by rules; to keep or put in good order (as, to regulate a clock)

regulation a rule or order

regulator a person who regulates; a device for controlling speed (especially of a clock or watch)

rehearse to practise for a performance of a play, a concert, etc.; to tell or repeat details in order (as - He rehearsed the events of their day in the country.)

rehearsal a rehearsing or practice for a performance

dress rehearsal the final practice of a play, opera, etc. with all the costumes, make-up, scenery, etc.

reign *(say rain)* the period of time that a king, queen or emperor rules □ to rule

reimburse to repay or pay back

reimbursement the act of paying back

rein one of the two leather straps used to guide and control a horse □ to control or check by reins (or as if by reins)

reindeer a kind of large antlered deer that lives in some northern regions

reinforce to strengthen (troops) with new forces or supplies; to add new material to make something stronger (as, to reinforce concrete by adding metal bars or mesh to it)

reinforcements fresh troops, supplies, etc.

reinstate to put back into a former position or into power

reiterate to repeat again and again

reject to throw away; to refuse to accept, acknowledge, admit or agree to (as, to reject a request)

rejection a refusal (to take, to admit, etc.)

rejoice to feel full of joy; to give joy or make a person joyful (as - They rejoiced at the good news.)

rejoin to join again; to come back to (as, to rejoin a ship after shore leave); to give an answer to a reply

rejoinder an answer to a reply; a retort

rejuvenate to make young again

relapse to fall back (into former bad habits, ill health, etc.)

relate to tell (a story); to show how one thing is connected with another (as - Poor health is often related to bad housing conditions.)

related connected; of the same family; having the same origins

relation, relative 1 a person connected with another by being born into the same family, or by marriage

relative 2 concerning; belonging to; referring to; comparative

relationship a connection; the way people are related (as - Their relationship is that of mother and daughter.)

relax to loosen (a tight grasp, muscles, etc.); to make (rules and regulations) less severe; to rest from work and take things easily

relaxation the act of relaxing; entertainment or recreation (as, a way of relaxing)

relay a fresh set of men or animals to relieve others □ to send out a broadcast message received from another station

relay race a race in which members of a team take turns in running a part of the total distance

release to set free; to let go; to relieve (as, from pain or suffering); to allow to be made public (as, to release a news item, an important public announcement, a film or book) □ a setting free

relent to become less severe or cruel; to become gentler and more forgiving
relentless without pity

relevant having to do with, or relating to, a subject being discussed or considered

reliable, reliance see **rely**

relic something remaining from an earlier time or connected with a dead person (especially a saint)

relief a lessening of pain or anxiety; release from a post or duty; help given to people in need (as, famine relief): (of carving or sculpture) a design raised above the background
relief map a map which shows (usually by colour) which areas are higher than others
relieve to ease or lessen pain, anxiety, worry, etc.; to give help to (people in need, a besieged town); to take over a duty (from someone)

religion a belief in, and worship of, God or gods; a system of faith and worship (as, the Christian, the Jewish and the Mohammedan religions)
religious concerned with, or devoted to, religion

relinquish to let go; to give up (any claim to something)

relish to enjoy; to like the taste of □ a flavour; something that gives a flavour to food

reluctant unwilling

rely to trust completely; to depend on (as, to rely on a person's help, honesty, confidence, etc.)
reliable trustworthy
reliance trust; dependence

remain to stay, or to be left, behind; to stay in the same place; to continue without change
remainder the part that remains after the removal of the rest
remains what is left (after a meal, a fire in a building, etc.); a

dead body

remand to send a person awaiting trial back to prison until further evidence is obtained

remark to notice or observe; to comment; to say □ a comment; something said
remarkable deserving of notice or comment; unusual

remedy a cure for an illness or difficult problem; a medicine; a means of righting a wrong □ to cure; to put right
remedial *(say remeedial)* able, or helping, to cure or put right

remember to keep in the mind; to recall to the mind (something that may temporarily have been forgotten); to show that one has not forgotten (a person's birthday, a special occasion, an anniversary)
remembrance the act of remembering; memory

remind to make a person remember or think of something (such as an appointment that might otherwise be forgotten); to make one think of (as - That tune reminds me of a holiday in Italy.)
reminder something (such as a note in a diary) that reminds

reminisce *(say reminiss)* to talk about things remembered
reminiscence a remembering or telling about past events
reminiscent reminding one of (things past; a person once known, etc.)

remit to pardon or forgive (a wrong); to send (money); to hand over (as, to remit a prisoner to a higher court)
remission forgiveness; pardon
remittance money sent (especially to a distant place)

remnant something remaining or left over from a larger piece (as, a remnant of cloth)

remonstrate to make a protest or speak against some action or proposal

remorse sorrow for a wrong action; repentance for an action that has harmed another

remote far off in time or place; out of the way (as, a remote village); slight (as, a remote chance, a remote resemblance)

remove to take away; to take off (clothes, covers, etc.); to put in another place or position; to move house; to go away
removal the act of taking or moving away; a change of residence

remunerate to pay (someone) for a service, a job done, etc.

rend to tear or split apart with great force
rent 1 a tear or rip

render to give or to deliver (thanks, a bill, etc.); to cause to be or make (as, to render a person speechless); to translate (as, to render French into English); to perform (as, to render a piece on the piano)
rendition a rendering; a performance

rendezvous (say rondivoo) a meeting place; a planned meeting

renew to make new again; to repair; to begin again (as, to renew a friendship, to renew a lease)
renewal a renewing

renounce to give up or reject publicly (a title, a claim, a position)
renunciation the formal act of giving (something) up (as, a king's renunciation of his throne)

renovate to repair; to make like new again (as, to renovate an old house)

renown fame

rent 1 see **rend**

rent 2 money paid for the use of someone else's property (as, for a house, a car, etc.) □ to hold or use (property) in return for payment of rent; to let or lease for rent

renunciation see **renounce**

repair to mend; to make up for (a wrong) □ an act of mending (as,

car repairs); condition (as, a house in good repair)

repatriate to send or bring (a person) back to his own country

repay to pay back (money borrowed; a kindness; etc.)

repeal to do away with; to cancel (as, to repeal a law)

repeat to say or do (something) again; to say from memory; to tell (something heard or known) to others; to happen over again; □ a second showing or hearing (of a performance)
repetition the act of repeating; something repeated
repetitive repeating something too often

repel to drive back or away; to cause dislike or disgust (as, an insolent manner that repelled everyone)
repellent disgusting □ something that drives or keeps away (as, a fly repellent)

repent to be sorry for something said or done, or for something one has failed to do; to regret

repercussion an echo; an after-effect of some event or action (usually bad)

repertory, repertoire (say repertwahr) a stock of pieces, plays, operas, etc. that a person or company is prepared to perform
repertory theatre a theatre with a permanent company who perform in a series of plays from their repertoire

repetition see **repeat**

replace to put back; to put something in place of (as, to replace a broken gate)
replacement a substitute

replenish to fill up again (as, to replenish a supply of food)

replica an exact copy (especially of a painting, statue, etc.)

reply to answer □ an answer or response

report to pass on news or tell about some person, event, etc.; to take notes or give an account of some happening (especially for a newspaper); to make a formal complaint about someone's action; to present oneself for duty (as - He reports to the office at nine o'clock.) □ an account or description of an event; a factual statement (as, a weather report, a school report); rumour, gossip: a loud noise (as, the report of a gun firing) **reporter** a person who reports (especially for a newspaper)

repose to place (as, to repose confidence in a person): to rest □ rest; sleep

reprehensible deserving blame, (as, a reprehensible act)

represent to speak or act for or on behalf of a person, a company, a country, etc.; to claim (as, to represent oneself as an expert swimmer); to portray (as, to represent a person in a painting or a character in a play) **representation** the act of representing; an image or picture; a strong claim or appeal **representative** typical □ a person in business, government, etc. who represents others

repress to keep or hold down (often by force); to keep under control (especially feelings and emotions)

reprieve to delay the execution of a condemned person; to postpone punishment □ a delay of execution, punishment, etc.

reprimand a severe scolding □ to reprove or scold severely

reprisal the act of paying back one harmful act with another; retaliation

reproach to blame in a sorrowful way; to find fault (with a person's actions or behaviour) □ blame; a cause of shame (as, a reproach to one's family)

reproduce to produce again; to copy; to produce young **reproduction** the act of reproducing; a copy

reproof a scolding or blame; a rebuke **reprove** to blame; to scold; to

rebuke

reptile a cold-blooded crawling or creeping animal with a scaly skin (such as a snake, crocodile, or lizard)

republic a form of government without a king or queen, usually ruled by an elected president (such as that of the U.S.A. or France)

repudiate to refuse to recognize or acknowledge (as, to repudiate a debt, an authority, etc.)

repugnant hateful; very disagreeable

repulse to drive back □ a driving back; a rebuff **repulsive** loathsome; causing disgust **repulsion** a strong dislike; disgust

reputation, repute the general opinion that people have of the character of a person, business, etc; good opinion or respect (as, a firm with an international reputation for goods of high quality) **reputable** *(say repewtable)* well thought of; respectable **reputed** considered or supposed to be (as, a land-owner reputed to be a millionaire)

request to ask, or ask for (as, to request a reply to a letter); to ask as a favour □ the asking of a favour; a thing asked for

require to need; to demand **requirement** a need; a demand **requisite** *(say rekwizit)* something needed for a purpose (as, toilet requisites like soap, a toothbrush, etc.) □ required; necessary **requisition** a formal request or order (as, a requisition for school supplies)

rescue to save; to free from danger or captivity □ an act of saving from danger, etc.

research a careful search or investigation to find out new facts (as, medical research into heart disease)

resemble to be like, or look like

resemblance likeness

resent to feel angry or indignant at
resentment a feeling of indignation

reserve to keep back for later use, or for a special purpose; to book (a seat at the theatre, etc.) □ someone or something reserved (as, a reserve for the first team); shyness (or not showing one's feelings); an area of country kept for the protection of wild animals (as, a nature reserve)
reserved shy: booked in advance
reservation an act of reserving; a condition before agreeing to something; a booked seat, room, etc.

reservoir *(say rezervwahr)* a lake (usually artificial) or tank for storing water

reside to live (in, at, etc.)
residence period of living in a place (as, during their residence abroad); a mansion
resident someone who has his home in a place (as, a local resident □ dwelling (in a place)
residential (of a district, suburb, etc.) containing, or suitable for, private houses

residue what is left over; remainder

resign *(say rezien)* to give up one's position, employment, etc.
resignation *(say rezignayshun)* the act of resigning
resigned not complaining

resilient elastic; springing back easily (to good health or good spirits)

resin a natural substance that oozes out of certain trees; a similar artificial substance (synthetic resin) made from chemicals

resist to struggle against (especially successfully)
resistance the act or power of resisting; the opposition of a country's people to foreign occupation (as, a resistance movement)

resistor a device used to resist the passing of electricity through a circuit

resolute bold; determined
resolution firmness of purpose; determination, a firm decision (as, a New Year resolution not to smoke cigarettes); a proposal put before a public meeting

resolve to decide; to solve (as, to resolve a problem) □ a resolution

resonant resounding; echoing

resort to turn (to) in difficulty □ someone or something resorted to: a popular place, especially for holidays

resound to sound loudly; to echo

resource a source of help; (plural) wealth or other means of helping or defending oneself (as, a country's resources)
resourceful clever in getting out of difficulties

respect to admire or regard someone highly □ high opinion
respectable deserving respect or attention; proper
respectful showing respect or deference
respective relating to each separately (as - The two football teams took up their respective positions.)

respire to breathe
respiration breathing
artificial respiration a method of helping an unconscious person to breathe

respite *(say respit or respite)* a pause or short rest

resplendent very splendid; brilliant

respond to answer; to react (as, to respond to the doctor's treatment)
response an answer or reply; a reaction
responsible trustworthy (as, a responsible worker); requiring the care of persons or important things (as, a responsible position in a hospital, business, etc.); accountable for (as, the hooligan

responsible for breaking the windows)

responsibility anything for which a person is responsible

rest 1 to stop work or any other activity; to be quiet and still; to lean (on or against) □ the state of being still; sleep; peace; a support (as, a book rest); (music) a pause

restful at rest; quiet

restive, restless unable to rest; impatient of control (as, a restive racehorse)

rest 2 the remainder; what is left

restaurant a place where meals are served to customers

restore to put, or give, back; to repair (a painting, a building of historic interest, etc.)

restrain to hold back; to check

restraint the act of restraining; self-control

restrict to limit; to keep within bounds (as - The pupils are restricted to the school premises.)

restriction an act of restricting; a rule or regulation

restrictive limiting

result an outcome or effect of some action; the answer to a sum or calculation □ to end (in) (as - The game resulted in a draw.)

resume to take up, or begin again (as, to resume work)

resumption a new start

résumé *(say rayzhewmay)* a summary

resurrect to bring back into life, or to use

resurrection a rising from the dead (especially the Resurrection of Christ)

retail to sell goods to consumers, or in small quantities; to repeat (a story) in detail □ the sale of goods to actual users or consumers □ concerned with such sales (as, the retail price)

retailer a shopkeeper

retain to keep or continue to hold

retention the act of keeping or holding in

retentive able to keep or hold (as, a retentive memory)

retaliate to hit back; to repay a wrong action with another wrong action

retard to delay or make slow

retention, retentive see **retain**

reticent not saying much; reserved

retina *(say retina)* the thin layer of cells at the back of the eye which are sensitive to differences of light and colour

retinue the attendants who follow a person of high rank or importance

retire to go back; to go to bed; to give up one's regular job, profession or business (generally after the age of 60 or 65)

retired having given up work

retiring going back; giving up work; shy or reserved

retirement the state of having retired (as - He now gets a retirement pension.)

retort to make a sharp or witty reply □ such a reply

retract to take back something said; to draw back (as, a cat's claws)

retractable able to be drawn back or up (as, the retractable wheels of an aeroplane)

retreat to move back or go away (as - The enemy retreated.) □ a withdrawal or movement backward

retribution a deserved punishment

retrieve to search for and fetch

retriever a breed of dog trained to retrieve birds that have been shot

retrograde going backward; getting worse

retrospective looking backward (on past events)

return to come back or go back; to give, send or throw back □ a going, or sending back; a repetition; profit or receipts (as, the box-office returns of a cinema)

by return(of post) by the next

post back

reunion a meeting of relatives, old friends or colleagues (as, a family reunion)

reveal to show something previously hidden; to make known
revelation an act of revealing; a disclosure

reveille (say *revalli* or *revelli*) a bugle call at daybreak to awaken soldiers

revel to make merry; to take great delight in
revelry, revels merrymaking

revelation see **reveal**

revenge an injury or harm done to a person in return for some harm received □ to take or seek revenge on someone

revenue income; money received as payments

reverberate to echo or resound (as, organ music reverberating in a cathedral)

revere (say *reveer*) to regard with deep respect
reverence deep respect
reverend worthy of respect; (abbreviated **Rev.**) a clergyman's title (as, the Rev. James Smith)
reverent showing reverence

reverie (say *revery*) a state of thinking dreamily; a day-dream

reverse to turn the other way round; to back (a car) □ the opposite, or back (as, the reverse of a coin); a defeat or setback
reversal the act of reversing
revert to return to a former subject or topic of conversation

review a display and inspection of troops, etc.; a viewing again or reconsideration (as, a review of the school timetable); a critic's opinion of a new book, film, etc. or a magazine containing many such reviews □ to inspect troops on parade, etc.; to examine again (as, to review the situation); to write a review of

revile to say harsh things about

revise to examine and correct; to change (as, to revise one's opinion)

revision the act or product of revising

revive to bring, or come, back to life, strength, use, etc.
revival (say *revival*) a return to life, strength, use, etc. (as, the revival of an old film); a renewed interest (as, a religious revival)

revoke to cancel (a rule or decision)

revolt a rebellion □ to rebel; to feel disgust
revolting disgusting (as, a revolting taste)

revolution a complete turn (as - The earth makes one revolution round its centre axis every 24 hours.); a great change; the overthrowing of a government by rebels
revolutionary bringing about great changes (in government, ideas, etc.) □ someone who supports a revolution
revolutionize to cause great changes in
revolve to roll or turn round (as, wheels revolve)
revolver a pistol in which the chambers revolve after each bullet is fired

revue a light, theatrical show, often musical and topical

revulsion disgust

reward something given in return for anything done (usually a good service, as, a reward for finding a lost purse) □ to give a reward to

reword to put into different words

rhapsody an extravagant and exciting piece of music or poetry

rhetoric the art of eloquence in speaking or writing; fine but exaggerated or insincere speech

rheumatism a disease causing pain and stiffness in and around the joints

rhinoceros a large wild animal with a very thick skin and one or two horns on its snout

rhododendron an evergreen bush with large showy flowers

rhubarb a plant with thick red stalks used in cooking

rhyme, rime *(say rime)* a word whose ending sounds the same as another (as *blue* and *crew*, *remember* and *December*) □ (of words) to end with the same sound

rhythm *(say rith'm)* a regular beat or pattern in music or verse; a regular (often smooth) pattern of movements
rhythmic(al) with rhythm; smooth-flowing

rib one of the bones which curve from the backbone to protect the chest; a ridge
ribbed raised in ridges (as ribbed cloth)

ribbon a narrow strip of material (often used for ornament)

rice the seeds of a plant grown in hot countries and cooked as a food in most countries

rich wealthy; having plenty (as, a country rich in minerals, etc.); (of land, soil) fertile; (of food) containing much fat, sugar or fruit, etc.
richly greatly (as, richly deserved)

rick a stack of hay, etc.

rickets a children's disease causing softening and bending of the bones
rickety unsteady (as, a rickety chair)

ricochet *(say ricoshay* a glancing rebound (as of a bullet striking a wall or rock at an angle) □ to glance off

rid to free from; to clear of (as, to rid a house of mice) □ riddance (as, to get rid of a pest)
riddance a clearing away

riddle 1 a puzzling question

riddle 2 a kind of sieve with large holes □ to sift with a riddle; to make lots of holes in (as, to riddle a door with bullets)

ride to travel or be carried in a car, on a horse, bicycle, etc. □ a journey in a car, on horseback, etc.

rider someone who rides

ridge a raised strip of earth between furrows; a long narrow top or crest (as, a ridge of hills); a long narrow elevation (as, a ridge of high pressure on a weather map)

ridicule *(say ridicule)* to laugh at; to mock
ridiculous deserving to be laughed at; absurd

rifle a firearm with a long barrel spirally grooved inside to make it shoot more accurately

rift a large crack or fissure

rig to set up or fit out (as, to rig up a shelter or rig out someone with clothes, etc.)
rigging the system of ropes on the masts of a sailing ship

right correct or true; the opposite of wrong; the opposite of left □ the right thing to do; justice; the right side □ to the right side (as, turning right); straight (as, going right on) □ to set right or in order
right angle an angle of 90 degrees (like any angle in a square)
rightful having a right or just claim
right-handed using the right hand to write with, throw with, etc.

righteous just and honourable

rigid stiff; unbending; strict (as, a rigid set of rules)

rigour harshness; severity; strictness
rigorous very strict; severe

rim an outside edge (as, the rim of a cup, or of a wheel)

rind the skin or peel of fruit

ring 1 a circle; a small hoop (of gold, etc.) worn on a finger; any space set apart for boxing, wrestling, circus performances, etc. □ to encircle
ringleader the leader in getting up to some mischief
ringlet a long curl of hair

ring road a road that goes round a town or town centre to avoid crowded traffic

ring 2 the sound of a bell, or a similar sound □ to cause a bell to sound; to make a bell-like sound; to telephone (as, to ring up a friend)

rink a sheet of ice for skating

rinse to wash lightly in clear water (to remove soap or detergent); to take liquid into and let it out of (as, to rinse one's mouth)

riot a noisy disorder caused by a crowd of people □ to take part in a riot
riotous noisy and uncontrolled

rip to tear (open, away, off, up, etc.)

ripe ready for gathering or eating (as, ripe corn, apples, etc.); fully developed or ready for use (as - The time was now ripe for carrying out their plans.)
ripen to become ripe

ripple a little wave or movement on the surface of water

rise to move upwards or go higher; to get up (from bed, or a chair); to come from or have its source in (as - The river Rhone rises in the Alps.); to rebel □ a slope upwards; an increase in wages, prices, etc.
rising coming up (as, the rising sun) □ a rebellion

risk a chance of loss or injury □ to take the chance of (as, to risk one's life)
risky dangerous; liable to go wrong

rissole a fried cake of minced meat or fish

rite a ceremony (especially religious)
ritual concerned with rites □ a set way of performing a religious service

rival someone who tries to equal or beat another; a competitor □ to try to equal; to seem to be equal to
rivalry the state of being, or feeling like, a rival

river a large stream of water flowing across the land

rivet a kind of bolt for fastening metal plates together □ to fasten with rivets; to fix firmly (as, riveted to the spot)

roach a silvery fresh-water fish

road a hard level way for vehicles to travel on

roam to wander about

roar to make a loud deep sound; to laugh loudly □ the sound so made (as, a lion's roar, a roar of laughter)

roast to cook in an oven, or before a fire; to heat strongly □ a roasted joint or one for roasting

rob to steal from (as, to rob a person, a house, etc.)
robber someone who steals
robbery an act of stealing (as, an armed robbery)

robe a long flowing gown or loose outer garment; (plural) official dress (as, of a mayor, judge, etc.) □ to dress (especially in robes)

robin a small songbird with a red breast

robot *(say roebot)* a mechanical man; a person who behaves in a mechanical way

robust *(say roebust)* strong, healthy; vigorous

rock 1 a large lump of stone
rockery, rock garden a collection of small rocks with earth in between for growing small plants

rock 2 to move backwards and forwards, or from side to side (as - Don't rock the boat!)

rocket a kind of firework, signal light, etc. which shoots high into the air; a missile projected into the sky by a backward jet of hot gases (The largest rockets are able to carry and launch spacecraft into outer space at tremendous speeds.)

rod a long thin stick or bar; a fishing-rod

rodent a gnawing animal (such

as a mouse, rabbit, squirrel)

rodeo *(say rodayo)* a round-up of cattle; a show of riding by cowboys

roe 1 the eggs of fishes

roe 2 a small kind of deer; a female red deer

rogue a rascal; a dishonest person
roguish rascally; mischievous

rôle, role a part played (especially by an actor or actress)

roll to move along by turning over like a ball or wheel; to rock from side to side (as, a rolling ship); to wrap round and round (as, to roll up a carpet) □ any material wound up into the shape of a tube (as, a roll of paper, cloth, etc.); a small loaf; a rolling movement: a list of names (as, an electoral roll)
roll-call the calling of names from a list
roller a cylinder-shaped object used for flattening or squeezing; a long heavy wave
roller-skates skates with wheels
rolling-pin a roller for flattening out dough or pastry before cooking

romance any imaginary story which seems better than real life; a love story □ to write or tell romances
romantic full of, or inclining towards, romance

romp to play in a lively way □ a lively game
rompers a young child's overall with short trousers

roof the top covering of a building or vehicle

rook a type of crow: another name for the castle in chess □ to swindle

room space (as, room for everybody); a division made by the inside walls of a house
roomy having plenty of room

roost a perch on which a bird rests at night □ to sit or sleep on a perch
rooster a domestic cock

root the part of a plant or tree that is underground and absorbs food from the soil; the base of a tooth, hair, etc.; the cause or origin of something □ to form or develop a root; (of an animal) to turn up ground, etc. in search of food

rope a thick twisted cord made from hemp, nylon, etc. □ to catch or fasten with a rope

rose a beautiful flower (usually scented) which may be coloured red, pink, yellow or white; the prickly shrub bearing such flowers: a light red colour
rosy light red: hopeful (as, a rosy future)
rosary a rose garden: a string of beads used in saying prayers
rosette a rose-shaped badge made of ribbons

rosemary a small fragrant evergreen shrub

rostrum a platform for public speaking

rot to go bad or decay □ decay
rotten decayed; very bad: spoiled (as, rotten apples)

rotate to turn round like a wheel
rota a list of duties to be repeated in a set order
rotary turning like a wheel
rotation a turning round like a wheel; a repetition in a set order (as, in planting different crops)
rotor the part of a motor, dynamo, etc. which rotates

rotund round; plump

rouge *(say roozh)* a red cosmetic; a fine polishing powder

rough *(say ruf)* not smooth; uneven; coarse; harsh: not exact (as, a rough estimate) □ a hooligan
roughly in a rough way: about (as, roughly in that direction)
roughen to make rough

roulette a gambling game in which a small ball is made to roll inside a revolving wheel

round curved like a circle or the surface of a ball; shaped like a ring, globe, etc. □ around, on all sides (as - The enemy were all round them.) □ a burst of noise (as, a round of applause, of firing, etc.); a single bullet or shell; a stage in a contest (as – There were ten rounds.); a complete game of golf

roundabout a revolving circular platform with wooden animals, etc. for people to sit on; a road junction where traffic has to go round in a circle □ indirect or taking a long way round

rounders a game with bat and ball

round up to drive or gather together

rouse to awaken; to stir up
rousing stirring (as, a rousing cheer)

rout *(say rowt)* to defeat and put to flight □ a disorderly flight

route *(say root)* a road or course to be followed

routine *(say rooteen)* a fixed way of doing things □ regular; unvarying

rove to wander
rover a wanderer; a pirate

row 1 *(rhymes with no)* a line of persons or things

row 2 *(rhymes with no)* to propel (a boat) with oars □ a short trip in a rowing-boat

row 3 *(rhymes with now)* a noisy quarrel; a noise
rowdy noisy and quarrelsome □ a rowdy person

royal having to do with a king or queen (as, the royal family)
royalist someone who supports a king
royalty members of a royal family; the state of being royal: a payment to an author, composer, etc. for every copy of a book sold, or every public performance

rub to move something against the surface of something else; to wipe or clean (as, to rub with a duster); (with *out* or *off*) to erase or remove □ a wipe

rubber an elastic material, either soft or hard, which is manufactured from the sap of the rubber-tree (Tyres, tennis-balls,

etc. are made of natural or artificial rubber.); an eraser made of rubber

rubbish waste material; litter; nonsense

rubble small rough stones used in building

rubicund (of complexion, skin, etc.) red or reddish

ruby a deep red precious stone □ ruby-coloured

rucksack a pack or bag carried on the back by climbers, hikers, etc.; a knapsack

rudder a flat piece of wood or metal hinged at the back of a boat or aeroplane for steering

ruddy red; rosy (as, a ruddy complexion)

rude ill-mannered; not polite; rough

rudiments the first principles or rules of a subject
rudimentary in an early stage of development; elementary

rueful sorrowful

ruff a frilled collar (as worn in the days of Elizabeth I)

ruffian a rough brutal fellow

ruffle to disturb the smoothness of anything (as, ruffled feathers); to annoy (as, to ruffle someone's feelings) □ a frill used as trimming on a dress or blouse

rug a thick floor-mat; a thick covering (as, a travelling rug)

rugby a form of football using an oval ball which may be carried

rugged rough; uneven; sturdy

ruin to destroy or spoil completely; to reduce to poverty □ destruction; downfall; broken-down remains of buildings (as, old ruins)
ruinous ruined; leading to ruin

rule regulation or order; a government's laws (as, under foreign rule): a ruler for measuring □ to govern or be in power; to draw lines on (as, to rule a page)
ruler someone who governs: a strip of wood, plastic, etc. for

drawing straight lines

ruling governing (as, a ruling body of persons); a decision

as a rule usually

rum an alcoholic drink made from fermented sugar-cane juice

rumble a low-pitched rolling sound (as, the rumble of thunder) □ to make such a noise

ruminate to chew the cud: to be deep in thought

ruminant an animal (like the cow) that chews the cud

rumour an unconfirmed story (about a person or an event) which may not be true □ to spread a rumour

rump the hind part of an animal; meat from this part

rumple to make untidy (as, to rumple the hair, the bedclothes) □ a fold or wrinkle

rumpus a noisy disturbance

run to move swiftly on one's feet; to hurry; to race; to go or work (as - The train engine, etc. is running.); to continue (as, a play which ran for six months, a running commentary); to manage or keep something going (as, to run a business, service, etc.); to extend, etc. (as - The lane runs up to the main road.); to flow, drip, etc. (as, a tide running high, a running nose); to incur (as, to run a risk) □ the act of running; a drive or trip; a period (as, a run of luck; in the long run); a unit of scoring in cricket; a rush to obtain something (as, a run on tickets for a show)

runner someone who runs; a messenger; the blade of a skate or one of the metal pieces on

which a sled runs

runner-up someone who comes second in a race or contest

run-down in poor health

run over to overflow; (of a car, etc.) to knock down a person or animal

runway a path for aircraft to take off from and land on

rung a step of a ladder

rupture a breaking (as, of a friendship); a breaking or bursting (as, of a blood vessel) □ to break or burst

rural having to do with the country; the opposite of urban

ruse a trick; a cunning plan

rush 1 to hurry or move quickly □ a quick forward movement; a hurry (as - I'm in a rush.)

rush 2 a tall grasslike plant growing near water

rusk a light crisp biscuit like hard toast

russet reddish-brown

rust a reddish-brown coating formed on iron and steel by exposure to air and moisture □ to get rusty

rusty covered with rust: showing signs of being out of practice (as - Her French is rusty.)

rustic typical of the country or country life; roughly made (as, a rustic seat)

rustle a soft whispering sound (as, the rustle of dry leaves); to make such a sound

rut a deep track made by wheels; a routine or fixed way of doing things

ruthless cruel; without pity

rye a kind of grain

S

Sabbath a day of the week set apart for religious worship and rest (among Jews the seventh day [Saturday]; among most Christians, the first day [Sunday])

sabotage (say *sabotahzh*) deliberate destruction or malicious damage to machinery, property, etc. by workers, enemies in wartime or anyone who wants to destroy or hinder the carrying out of a plan, project or aim

sabre a curved cavalry sword

saccharine an artificial sweetener, used as a substitute for sugar

sack 1 a large bag of paper, cloth, plastic or some coarse material (for holding grain, flour, etc.); the amount held in a standard-sized sack (as, a sack of flour)
to get the sack to be dismissed from a job

sack 2 to plunder (a captured town)

sacred holy; dedicated to the worship of God; connected with religion (as, sacred music)

sacrifice an offering to God or to gods (especially on an altar); the thing offered as a sacrifice; the giving up of something to help another or to achieve some important aim

sacrilege the misuse of a holy thing or place (such as breaking into a church and stealing or breaking holy objects)
sacrilegious profane

sad full of sorrow; unhappy; feeling or showing grief
sadden to make or become sad

saddle a seat (usually leather) for a rider on an animal, bicycle, motorbike, etc. □ to put a saddle on (a horse, a donkey, etc.); to burden or put a load on (as, to saddle a father with his son's debts)
saddler a maker of saddles and harness

safari an expedition (usually) in search of wild animals

safe free from danger; not in danger; unharmed; reliable or able to be trusted (as, a safe bridge, or driver) □ a heavy metal box or chest in which money, valuables and important papers can be protected from thieves, fire, etc.
safeguard anything that prevents danger or gives security and protection (as - A bolt and a chain inside a door are a safeguard against burglars.)
safety freedom from harm or danger □ designed or intended

to keep the user safe (as, safety belts in aeroplane and car seats)

sag to sink down or bend in the middle; to hang or droop limply

saga a story in the ancient literature of Iceland; a legend or collection of legends about heroic deeds, a famous family, etc.

sagacious wise; having good judgment; shrewd
sagacity wisdom; soundness of judgment

sage 1 a man of great wisdom □ wise; prudent

sage 2 a plant with pungent leaves, used for flavouring stuffings, etc.
sagebrush an American shrub with leaves smelling like sage

sago a starchy substance (obtained from the trunks of East Indian palm trees) used to make puddings, etc.

sail a sheet of canvas or cloth, spread to catch the wind, which drives a sailing ship or boat forward; a journey in a sailboat or a ship; an arm of a windmill □ to travel by ship; to glide or float along (in water or in air); to steer or navigate a boat or ship
sailor a person who sails; a seaman
to set sail to set out on a voyage

saint a very good and holy person
saintly very holy; pious

sake cause; purpose; motive or reason (as, for the sake of peace, for the sake of his mother's happiness); benefit or advantage (as - He took on a job with longer hours for the sake of the extra money.)

salad a mixture of raw vegetables (such as lettuce, celery, etc.) and cold cooked vegetables, meat, fish, eggs, etc., usually served with a sauce or dressing
salad cream a kind of bottled mayonnaise
salad dressing a thin sauce made of oil, vinegar and seasoning

salamander a small, lizard-like animal

salary money paid regularly every week or every month for work done

sale the exchange of anything for money; the act or business of selling; a selling of goods at reduced prices; an auction

sal(e)able fit to be sold; able to be sold

salient (of an angle) projecting or pointing outwards; outstanding, principal (as, the salient points of a speech)

saline salty; containing salt

saliva the liquid that forms in the mouth; spittle

sallow (of complexion or skin) pale, yellowish, rather sickly looking

sally a sudden rushing out (as, a sally by besieged soldiers on their attackers); an excursion: an outburst of witty, amusing or angry remarks □ (with *forth* or *out*) to rush out suddenly; to set forth

salmon (*say sammon*) a large fish with silvery scales and pink flesh, much used as food

saloon a large public room; a dining room or lounge for passengers on a ship; a closed-in motor car; (in the United States) a public bar for alcoholic drinks

salt a colourless or white substance (sodium chloride) obtained from rock or from sea water, used for seasoning and preserving food; any other substance formed from a metal and an acid (as salt is); an old sailor; (plural) a medicinal mixture of salts □ to season, treat, preserve, etc. with salt

salty tasting of, or containing, salt

saltcellar a small dish or container for table salt

to take with a grain (or a pinch) of salt to listen to a story, a statement, etc. with a certain amount of doubt or disbelief

salute to greet someone with friendly words, gesture, a kiss, etc.; to honour (an important person) by firing guns, displaying flags, etc.; (in the armed forces) to raise the hand in a formal gesture (such as touching the forehead) when meeting a superior officer

salutation the act or words of greeting; the introductory words of a letter (as, *Dear Sir*)

salvage the saving of a ship (wrecked or in danger) or its cargo, or of goods and property threatened by flood, fire, etc.; the reward paid for this act; the goods saved from a fire, etc. □ to save from complete loss or destruction

salvation the saving of a person from sinning and its results; the means of saving from death, danger, etc.

salve an ointment to heal or soothe sores, wounds, etc. □ to soothe or heal

same exactly alike; not different; unchanged; mentioned before

at the same time nevertheless

sample one of, or a small part of, something that shows what the whole is like □ to take or test a sample (as, to sample a piece of cake)

sampler a piece of needlework which girls used to make as an example of their skill (It often included embroidered figures, the alphabet, names, etc.)

sanatorium a hospital (especially for people suffering from diseases of the lungs)

sanction permission; approval □ to allow; to permit (as, to sanction the use of a playing field for a charity match)

sanctity holiness; sacredness

sanctify to make holy or sacred; to set aside for sacred use

sanctimonious making a show of being, or pretending to be, holy

sanctuary a holy place; the most sacred part of a church or temple; a place where one can be safe from pursuers: a nature reserve where birds and animals are protected (as, a bird sanctuary)

sand small particles or grains of crushed or worn-down rock, found in a mass (sands) by the sea, in deserts, etc. □ to sprinkle with sand; to smooth with sand
sandy like sand; covered with sand
sandbank a ridge or bank of sand formed by tide, wind or currents
sand dune a ridge of loose sand formed by the wind
sandpaper paper with a layer of sand glued on to it, used for smoothing and polishing
sandpiper a wading bird which makes a high piping sound
sandstone a kind of soft rock made of layers of sand pressed together

sandal a light shoe held on the foot by straps

sandwich two pieces of bread with any sort of food between them; anything arranged like this □ to place something between two layers or between two objects

sane mentally sound and healthy; sensible; showing common sense
sanity soundness of mind; the opposite of madness or insanity

sanitary having to do with conditions or arrangements that encourage good health (such as good drainage, disposal of rubbish, cleanliness, etc.); free from dirt, infection, or other conditions harmful to health
sanitation the use of proper sanitary arrangements to protect health

sanity see **sane**

sap 1 the juice in plants and trees
sapling a young tree

sap 2 to destroy or undermine by digging beneath; to weaken (as, to sap a person's strength) □ a trench or tunnel leading towards the enemy's position
sapper a person who saps (especially a private in the Royal Engineers)

sapphire *(say saffire)* a clear deep blue precious stone

sarcasm a cutting, hurtful remark, said in scorn
sarcastic hurtful and contemptuous; often using sarcasm

sardine a small fish, sometimes eaten fresh, but more often preserved in oil and packed tightly in tins

sargasso a kind of greenish-brown seaweed that grows in a large mass in a part of the North Atlantic (known as the Sargasso Sea)

sari a long piece of cloth wrapped around the body and hanging loose over the shoulder, worn by girls and women in India

sarong a skirt-like garment worn by men and women in Malaya

sash 1 a strip of ribbon or cloth worn around the waist or over the shoulder

sash 2 a window frame for panes of glass (especially one that slides up and down)

satchel a small bag (especially for carrying school books)

satellite a planet that revolves around another larger planet (as the moon revolves around the earth); any man-made body launched into space and put into orbit around the earth; an attendant or follower of an important or powerful person; a town, country, etc. that is dependent on, or controlled by, a more important or powerful neighbour

satin a closely woven heavy silk with a shiny surface

satire a piece of ironical or sarcastic writing which makes fun of people (especially their weaknesses and foolish actions)
satirical having to do with satire; containing satire (as, a satirical newspaper article)

satisfy to give what is required or needed; to please (a person); to appease or quieten (hunger, need for sleep, etc.); to convince

(as - His explanation satisfied the headmaster.)

satisfaction the act of satisfying; a feeling of pleasure and content (after a good meal; after accomplishing something difficult, etc.); anything that satisfies

satisfactory good enough; meeting requirements; satisfying; adequate or convincing (as, a satisfactory performance; a satisfactory explanation)

saturate to soak or fill completely (especially with water)

sauce a prepared liquid (usually fairly thick) which is added to food to give flavour (such as mint sauce, apple sauce, tomato sauce, etc.)

saucy cheeky; a bit impudent

saucepan a cooking pot with a handle and (usually) a lid

saucer a small shallow dish used under a cup

saunter to stroll along without hurrying

sausage a finely chopped and seasoned meat mixture, stuffed into a thin bag of animal membrane

savage wild; fierce and cruel; uncivilized □ an uncivilized human being; a brutal or cruel person

savagery the state of being savage; cruelty; fierce brutality

save to bring out of danger; to rescue; to protect from harm, damage, loss; to keep from spending or using (as, to save money, time, energy, etc.) □ except (as - All, save one, were found.)

saving the act of rescuing (as, the saving of many lives) □ redeeming (as - In spite of her many faults, she has the saving grace of kindness.); thrifty

savings money saved and put by (in a bank, etc.) for the future

saviour a person who rescues, saves, protects, etc.; (with capital letter) Jesus Christ

savour to taste (especially with enjoyment, as, to savour the delicious food) □ taste; flavour

savoury having a pleasant taste or smell (sharp or seasoned, not sweet) □ a small tasty dish at the end of a formal dinner

savoy a winter cabbage with a firm head of crinkled leaves

saw a cutting tool with a handle and a wide blade with teeth along the edge; a band or disc with a toothed edge, worked by machinery □ to cut with a saw; to use a saw

sawdust wood-dust made in sawing

sawmill a mill where wood is sawn into boards, planks, etc.

saxophone a wind instrument with a reed mouthpiece and finger keys on a metal tube curved upwards at the end

say to speak; to utter words; to tell; to repeat or recite (as, to say one's prayers) □ a person's right to speak (as - He ought to have a say in deciding what to do.)

saying something often said by people (as, a proverb)

scab the dry crust which forms on a sore or wound when it is healing; a disease of animals and plants (with scabby spots)

scabbard a case or holder for a sword; a sheath for a dagger

scaffold a temporary arrangement of metal supports and raised platforms for men working on buildings; a raised platform for executions

scaffolding scaffolds for men working on buildings; a framework

scald to burn (the skin) with hot liquid or steam □ a burn caused in this way

scale 1 anything marked off in regular divisions and used as a measure (as, on a thermometer); (music) a series of tones going up or down in pitch according to a system of fixed intervals; the dimensions of a picture, model, plan, etc. measured in proportion to the thing itself (as, a model of a building made to scale, a map drawn to a scale of one inch to the mile, etc.) □ to climb up (a mountain, a ladder)

scale 2 one of the small hard flakes that cover the bodies of fishes and snakes; a similar flake or covering which protects the bud of a leaf

scale 3 the dish or pan of a balance; (plural) a weighing machine

scallop a shellfish with a pair of hinged, fan-shaped shells, having a ridged surface and wavy edge □ to embroider or cut an edging with a wavy edge

scalp the skin and hair on the top of the head □ to cut off the scalp

scamp 1 a rascal

scamp 2 to do work in a lazy and careless way

scamper to run away quickly; to run about in a lively way

scampi small North European lobsters used for food

scan to read (verse) emphasizing the rhythm or beat; to examine the metre of a line of verse; to examine carefully; (in television) to pass a beam of light over every part (of a scene, an object) in turn

scandal a disgraceful or shocking action (by an individual or a group of people) of which most people disapprove; talk or gossip that damages a person's reputation

scandalize to shock or horrify (by scandalous behaviour)

scandalous shocking; disgraceful; shameful

scant, scanty barely sufficient; not plentiful (as, a scanty harvest)

scapegoat a person who gets the blame for other people's wrongdoing

scar the mark left on the skin after a sore or a wound has healed; any mark or blemish □ to mark with a scar

scarce (say scairce) not plentiful; not enough; hard to find

scarcely barely; not quite; hardly (as - They could scarcely see the outline of the mountains in the mist.)

scarceness, scarcity shortage; lack or want (of); a very small supply

scare to frighten; to startle □ a sudden fright or alarm

scarecrow a figure (often a crude dummy of a man) set up in a field to scare birds away from the crops

scarf a piece of cloth worn round the neck, head or shoulders

scarlet a bright red colour

scarlet fever an infectious disease which produces high fever, a rash and sore throat

scathing (say scaything) bitter or unkind (as, a scathing remark about someone)

scatter to throw or sprinkle about in all directions (seed, food for animals, etc.); to separate and go away in all directions (as, the crowds scattered)

scatterbrain a person who cannot keep his mind or attention on a subject for long

scavenger a person who cleans the streets or who picks up rubbish; any animal that feeds on decaying matter

scene (say seen) one part of an act in a play or opera (as - There are three scenes in Act I.); the place where something happens or is supposed to happen; an episode or important action in a play, book, etc. (as, the death scene); stage scenery; a view or landscape; an embarrassing show of strong feeling (anger, weeping, etc.)

scenery the painted curtains, screens and general background on a stage; the general appearance of a stretch of country (as, mountain scenery, woodland scenery, etc.)

scenic having to do with scenery (on the stage, as a good scenic effect, or real, as a scenic journey in Switzerland)

scent to discover by the sense of

smell; to get an idea or suspicion of something (as, to scent danger); to give out a smell (as - Lilac blossoms scented the air.) □ a perfume; an odour; the trail of smell by which an animal may be tracked

off the scent on the wrong track

sceptic *(say skeptic)* a person who doubts or questions commonly held opinions, beliefs, etc.
sceptical doubtful; inclined to disbelieve or question
scepticism doubt

sceptre *(say septer)* an ornamental rod or staff carried on ceremonial occasions by monarchs

schedule *(say shedule)* a list of articles (such as an inventory); a timetable or programme setting out the times fixed for certain events; a form with spaces for filling in detailed information □ to form into a schedule or list
scheduled planned or arranged (for something to happen at a certain time)

scheme *(say skeem)* a plan or arrangement; a programme of action to be followed; a project; a crafty secret plan (often dishonest or evil)

scholar a pupil; a student; a person who has an extensive knowledge (of one or more subjects); the holder of a scholarship
scholarly having the qualities of a scholar; showing careful attention to accuracy and detail
scholarship the abilities and qualities of a scholar; learning: a sum of money awarded annually to a student to help pay for further studies
scholastic having to do with schools, studies, scholars, etc.

school 1 a place for learning from teachers; the staff and pupils in a school; a group of people with similar ideas, opinions, etc. (especially in philosophy, art, music, etc., as, a composer of the romantic school) □ to teach or train

school 2 a large number of one kind of fish, whales or other water animals, swimming about together (as, a school of porpoises)

schooner a fast sailing ship with two or more masts

science knowledge obtained by careful study and testing, and arranged so that it can be studied as a whole; a department or branch of such knowledge (as, the science of biology, chemistry, etc.)
scientific having to do with science; applying the results or methods of science (as, a scientific approach to agricultural problems)
scientist a person who studies one or more branches of science

scintillate *(say sintillate)* to sparkle

scissors a cutting tool with two blades fastened together in the middle

scoff to make fun of; to mock

scold to find fault with someone; to speak to someone in a cross or angry way □ a person (especially a woman) who is noisy, rude and fault-finding

scoop a tool shaped like a deep shovel, used to dig up loose earth, stones, coal, etc.; a small shovel-like tool for digging out a measure of sugar, flour, small sweets, etc. □ to dig or lift out, as with a scoop

scoot to move off quickly; to dart away
scooter a small two-wheeled vehicle, moved by pushing with one foot or by an engine

scope area covered, range or extent (of a subject, a scientific report, etc., as - Many scientific terms do not come within the scope of this dictionary.); opportunity or room for growth (as - His present job gives scope for his creative ability.)

scorch to burn slightly; to singe; to dry up with heat

score a gash, notch or line; the number of points gained in a game, test, etc.; an amount (usually of money) owing; a set of twenty (as, a score of volunteers); reason (as, to retire on the score of poor health); a written or printed piece of music showing all the parts (vocal or instrumental or both) on separate staves, one under the other □ to mark with notches and lines; to gain or record points (in a game or examination); to win (as, to score a success)

scorn to look down on; to refuse or reject with contempt; to despise □ a feeling of contempt
scornful contemptuous; feeling or showing scorn

scorpion a spider-like creature, having a long tail with a poisonous sting

scot-free without being hurt or punished, or having to pay (as - He got away scot-free.)

scoundrel a mean rascal; a rogue; a dishonourable man

scour to clean by hard rubbing with something rough (such as steel wool)

scourge *(say scurj)* a whip; an affliction; a means of punishment □ to whip; to punish or afflict

scout a person sent out to bring in information or to spy on the enemy; a member of the Boy Scouts □ to act as a scout

scowl to frown □ an angry or sullen look

scramble to move or climb (up, along) on hands and knees (usually with difficulty, as, to scramble up a steep cliff); to push or struggle for something (as, to scramble for a good place to watch a game); to mix together (as, to scramble eggs); to jumble up a message sent by radio or telephone so that it can only be understood by decoding or through a special receiver □ the act of scrambling; a struggle (with others) for something; a motor cycle trial over rough country

scrap a small piece of something (as, a scrap of cloth, a scrap of paper); bits of iron or other metal no longer useful in their present form (scrap metal) □ to abandon (as, to scrap plans); to throw away as useless
scrapbook a book with blank pages for sticking pictures, newspaper cuttings, etc.
scrap heap a heap of old metal; a heap of rubbish

scrape to rub against with something rough or sharp; to rub against with a grating noise (and usually some damage, as, to scrape the side of a car against a wall); to remove by drawing a sharp edge over (as, to scrape new potatoes, a rusty surface); to manage with difficulty (as, to scrape a living, to scrape up a sum of money) □ the act of scraping; a mark or sound made by scraping; a troublesome situation or difficulty (often caused by a person's own foolishness)

scratch to scrape (and usually mark) a surface with a sharp point; to tear or dig with claws or nails (to relieve itching) □ a mark or sound made by scratching; a slight wound

scrawl to write untidily or hastily □ writing that is untidy and difficult to read

scrawny thin; skinny

scream to cry out in a loud piercing voice (as in pain, fear, anger) □ a loud high-pitched cry of terror, pain, etc.

screech to utter a harsh, shrill scream

screen a movable folding framework or panel, used to protect from heat (a firescreen), draughts, observation, etc.; anything that serves as a screen (as, a high hedge); a partition (especially in a church); the white surface (of a wall, stiff curtain, etc.) on which moving pictures or slides are shown; the part of a television set on which the picture appears □ to shelter or hide (as, with a screen); to put through a coarse sieve

screw a special kind of nail with spiral grooving (called the thread) and a slotted head; a turn or twist (of a screw); a propeller (screw propeller) with spiral blades, used in ships and aircraft □ to fasten or tighten with a screw or screwing movement; to force (as, to screw up one's courage)
screwdriver a tool for putting in (or taking out) screws

scribble to write carelessly □ bad or careless writing; meaningless marks (as made by a young child who has not yet learned to read or write)

script handwriting; handwriting that looks like print or print that looks like handwriting; the text of a play, broadcast, motion picture, etc.

scripture the sacred writings of a religion; the Scriptures (the Bible)

scroll a roll of paper or parchment (usually with writing on it); an ornament made to look like a partly unrolled scroll

scrub 1 to rub hard (usually with a stiff brush and water) in order to clean

scrub 2 a stunted or low-growing tree or bush; an area of country covered thickly with such trees or bushes

scruff the back of the neck

scrum (in rugby) short for scrummage - a struggle for the ball when the rival forwards are bunched tightly round it

scrupulous careful in the smallest details; conscientious

scrutiny a close or careful examination of or look at something
scrutinize to look at carefully and closely

scuffle to struggle or fight in a clumsy, confused way (especially at close quarters) □ a rough confused struggle

scull a short, light oar □ to move a boat with a pair of sculls; to propel a boat by using a scull at the stern

scullery a small room where the rough, dirty kitchen work is done (such as cleaning utensils, preparing vegetables, etc.)

sculpture the art of carving stone and wood, or modelling clay or metal into statues and ornamental designs
sculptor, sculptress an artist in carving or modelling

scum froth or foam on the surface of a liquid; the lowest or most worthless part of anything (as - People who steal from the old and helpless are the scum of the earth.)

scurf small flakes or scales of dead skin (especially on the scalp)

scurry to hurry along; to scamper

scurvy 1 a disease caused by lack of fresh fruit or vegetables (In former times sailors on long voyages often developed scurvy.)

scurvy 2 mean; low-down; contemptible (as, a scurvy trick)

scuttle 1 (also **coal-scuttle**) a metal box or container for coal

scuttle 2 an opening with a lid in the deck or side of a ship □ to sink a ship by making holes in the bottom and sides

scuttle 3 to hurry away; to run off quickly

scythe *(say sieth)* a large curved blade on a handle, used for cutting grass, etc. by hand

sea the mass of salt water that covers the greater part of the earth's surface; a large stretch of salt water smaller than an ocean (as, the Black Sea, the Mediterranean Sea); a heavy swell or wave; rough water; a great number or quantity (as, a sea of faces, a sea of troubles)
sea anemone a small plant-like animal found on rocks at the seaside

sea breeze a wind blowing off the sea towards the land

seafarer a traveller by sea (especially a sailor)

seagull a gull (see separate entry)

seahorse a small fish with a horse-like head and a curly tail that helps it to swim in an upright position

sea legs ability to walk steadily on a ship's deck in rough seas

sea lion a large type of seal (The male has a mane and makes a roaring noise.)

seaman a sailor (especially one who is not an officer)

seamanship the knowledge and skill necessary to handle a ship at sea

seaplane an aeroplane that can take off from and land on the sea

seashell the hard covering on some kinds of fish and sea animals (Empty ones are found in large numbers on the seashore.)

seashore the land close to the sea

seasickness nausea caused by the motion of a ship

seaside a holiday resort near the coast; the seashore

seaweed plant(s) growing in the sea

seaworthy (of boats and ships) well-constructed and equipped and in working order to go to sea

seal 1 a fish-eating furry animal that can live on land as well as in the sea

seal 2 a piece of wax or other material having a raised design attached to an official document to show that it is real and not a forgery; an engraved stone or stamp which makes a raised design when pressed into melted sealing wax; a closure or fastening (such as sealing wax) on a letter, parcel, etc., to ensure that the contents are kept secret □ to mark or fasten with a seal; to close up (as, to seal an envelope); to settle or conclude a business deal or agreement (as - They sealed the bargain with a handshake.)

sealing wax a special kind of hard wax for sealing letters, etc.

seam the line or fold made when two pieces of material are joined together by sewing; a line or layer (in the ground) of coal, metal ore, etc. □ to join with a seam (as, to seam the sides of a skirt)

search to look carefully for something; to examine (a person, his belongings, house, etc.); to try to find something hidden, stolen, etc. □ the act of searching; an attempt to find something

searching looking closely; (of eyes, look, etc.) very observant; (of an inquiry or investigation) very thorough

searchlight a strong beam of light which shows up distant objects at night

search warrant legal permission to search a house (for stolen goods, etc.)

seashore, seaside, etc. see **sea**

season 1 one of the four divisions of the year (spring, summer, autumn, winter); a special period of time for celebrating (as, the Christmas season), or carrying out a particular job (as, the harvest season), etc.; the usual or proper time for something

seasonable suited to the season (as - Cold weather in winter is seasonable.)

seasonal having to do with a season or the seasons; happening at one particular season

season ticket a ticket (especially a railway ticket) that can be used daily for a limited period of time

season 2 to add salt, pepper, mustard, etc. to food to give it flavour; to make ready for use by maturing, drying, etc. (as, to season timber before using it in building)

seasoning something added to food to give it flavour (as, salt, herbs, spices)

seat a piece of furniture for sitting on (such as a chair, bench, etc.); the part of a chair, etc. on which a person sits; the part of the body or a garment on which a person sits (as, the seat of his trousers); a place on, or from, which something is carried on (as, the seat of government, a seat of learning) □ to cause to sit (as - Please be seated.); to have seats for (a number of people)

seating the provision or arrangement of seats (in a theatre, concert hall, etc.)

seat belt a safety belt which can be fastened to hold a person in his seat in a car or aeroplane

seclude to shut off; to keep away (from others or from sight)

secluded hidden; private; away from others

second 1 the 60th part of a minute (of time) or of a degree (in measuring angles)

second 2 next, or following after, the first (in time, place, etc.); another of the same kind, similar (as, a second helping) □ a person, thing, etc. in second place; a supporter or helper (especially for a person who, in former times, fought a duel) □ to make the second speech or statement in support of a proposal or motion

secondary second in position or importance; (of education) between primary school and higher education

second-class, second-rate less than the highest or best; inferior

second-hand not new; previously used or owned by someone else

secret hidden from others; private; not known or told to others □ something known only to one person or to very few people; information kept hidden from others; something not known or fully explained (as, the secrets of the universe)

secrecy the state of being secret; mystery; privacy

secrete to hide or conceal

secret service a government department concerned with espionage

secretive inclined to keeping things secret

secretary a person who deals with correspondence and confidential papers for an employer, a firm, government department, society, etc.

secretarial having to do with a secretary's duties

Secretary of State a cabinet minister who holds one of the most important government positions

section a part or division; the view of the inside of anything (as, an apple, a tree trunk) when it is cut right through; a thin slice of something which can be examined under a microscope

sector a three-sided part of a circle of which two sides are radii; a section (of an army front line, of occupied territory)

secular having to do with earthly things (of the world, not of the spirit); not sacred or religious (Hymns are religious, not secular, music.)

secure safe; free from fear or danger; firmly fastened or fixed □ to make safe or firm; to fasten; to seize; to obtain (information, etc.)

security safety; protection; something given or pledged as a guarantee (that a loan will be repaid, etc.)

sedan, sedan chair an enclosed seat for one person, carried on poles by two bearers

sedate (of a person's manner) calm; serious; dignified

sedative soothing; calming □ a medicine that soothes the nerves

sedentary (of an occupation) requiring long periods of sitting down (as, clerical or secretarial work)

sediment what settles at the bottom of a liquid; the dregs

seduce to lead (a person) away from correct behaviour or conduct; to persuade (a person) to do something against his own feelings of right and wrong

seduction the act of tempting (a person) into wrong-doing

seductive tempting; enticing

see 1 the district over which a bishop or archbishop has authority

see 2 to perceive or look at through the eyes; to understand (as - I see what he means.); to find out; to attend to (as - I'll see to it.); to meet or consult (as, to see a friend, to see a dentist)

seed the part of a plant, tree, etc. from which new plants grow; a seed-like part of a plant (such as a grain or a nut); children or descendants □ to sow or sprinkle with seeds

seedy full of seeds: shabby; uncared for: not feeling very well

seedbed a piece of ground prepared for growing seeds

seedling a young plant just emerging from a seed (especially a young tree)

seek to look or search for; to try to get (as, to seek help, advice, etc.)

sought *(say sawt)* the past tense of seek

seem to appear to be (as - She seems friendly.); to appear (as - She seems to be paying attention.); to appear to exist or be so (as - It seems that there is a difficulty.)

seeming having the appearance of (but not necessarily really so)

seemingly apparently

seemly suitable; appropriate; (of behaviour) correct; decent

seesaw a plank fastened to something heavy in the middle so that it is balanced, allowing one end to go up while the other goes down; an up-and-down movement resembling that of a seesaw

seethe to boil; to be very angry or agitated

segment a part cut off; part of a circle cut off by a straight line; any of the parts into which a jointed thing is divided, which can easily be separated (as, a segment of orange)

segregate to separate from others; to keep in separate groups

segregation the act of segregating

seismic having to do with an earthquake

seismograph an instrument that records and measures the force of an earthquake

seize to take (suddenly) by force; to snatch; to grasp: (of machinery) to become stuck or jammed (as - The car engine has seized up and won't move.)

seizure the act of seizing or capturing: a sudden attack of illness; a fit

seldom not often; rarely

select to pick out (from a number); to choose □ chosen as best; picked out or graded as best

selection the act of choosing; something chosen; a number of things to choose from

self one's own person; a person as an individual (apart from others); one's personality, nature or character

selfish thinking only of oneself and caring little for others

selfless the opposite of selfish; thinking of others before oneself

self- a prefix meaning: of, or acting on, oneself (as, **self-control**); automatic or acting by means of something in itself (as, a **self-winding** watch); in or within oneself or itself (as, **self-centred**, **self-contained**) Examples of the way this prefix is used are as follows:

self-centred selfish; concerned only with one's own interests and affairs

self-coloured of only one colour; of the natural colour

self-confidence belief in one's own abilities

self-conscious thinking too much of oneself and the impression one is making on others

self-denial doing without something in order to give to others

self-evident obvious; not needing any proof or explanation

self-explanatory clear; not needing explanation

self-important full of one's own importance or position in the community

self-indulgent indulging one's appetite, love of comfort, etc. to excess

self-made owing success to one's own efforts, and not to advantages of rank, privilege, etc.

self-portrait an artist's picture of himself

self-possessed calm and controlled in manner

self-preservation a natural instinct to keep oneself from harm, danger, etc.

self-propelled moved by its own motor (not pushed or pulled by anyone or anything)

self-reliance confidence in one's own capabilities

self-righteous thinking very highly of one's own goodness and behaviour.

self-sacrifice giving up one's own possessions, opportunities, even one's life, for the good of others

self-service (of a shop, cafeteria, etc.) in which customers help themselves to what is wanted instead of being waited on

self-sufficient needing no help from anyone else

self-taught taught by one's own study, reading, etc. with no help from others

self-raising flour flour prepared for baking so that there is no need to add baking powder, etc. to make it rise

sell to hand over or provide for money (as, to sell a book, a house, etc.)
seller someone who sells
sold the past tense of sell

semi- a prefix meaning half (as **semicircle, semi-colon(;), semi-detached, semi-final**)

semolina small hard particles of wheat, often used to make puddings

senate the upper house of a parliament in some countries (for example, the U.S.A., Australia); the governing body of some British universities
senator a member of a senate

send to cause or direct (a person) to go somewhere; to cause something to be carried somewhere (as, to send a letter)
sender someone who sends
send-off a friendly farewell or party for someone setting out on a journey, etc.

senile *(say seenile)* showing the weakness of old age
senility old age

senior older in age; higher in rank or more advanced □ someone who is senior
seniority the state of being senior

sensation a feeling through the senses (of sight, touch, etc.); a general feeling of strong excitement (as - The news of the first moon-landing created a sensation.)
sensational causing great excitement

sense one of the powers by which we feel or take notice (seeing, hearing, tasting, smelling and touching); what is wise or reasonable and therefore the opposite of nonsense (as - His action made sense, or good sense.); a special aptitude or quality (as, a sense of humour, a sense of direction); meaning (as - What is the sense of that word as used in that poem?) □ to feel or realize (as - She sensed his disappointment.)
senseless stunned or unconscious; foolish
sensible wise; having good sense (as, a sensible thing to do)
sensitive feeling easily or strongly (as - She is very sensitive to criticism)
sensuous affecting the senses pleasantly (as, the sensuous touch of velvet)

sentence a number of words which together make a complete statement, order or question: a judgment or declaration of punishment by a court or a judge (as, a sentence of six months' imprisonment) □ to pronounce judgment on

sentiment a thought or opinion affected by feelings (as, a romantic sentiment, sentiments of pity, etc.)
sentimental having, or showing, too much emotion (often not wholly sincere)

sentry, sentinel a soldier posted on guard

separate *(say separet)* apart; not connected; divided □ *(say separate)* to set apart; to divide; to go different ways
separation the act of separating

septic (of a wound, cut, etc.) poisoning to the blood (by letting bacteria in)

septuagenarian a person seventy to seventy-nine years old

sepulchre *(say sepulker)* a tomb
sepulchral *(say sepulkral)* having to do with tombs or burials; (of voice) deep or gloomy in tone

sequel a result or consequence; a story which continues an earlier story

sequence a number of things following one another (as, a sequence of events)

sequestered lonely; secluded

sequin a small round shiny ornament used to decorate evening dresses, stage costumes, etc.

serenade a song or music in the open air at night (especially under a lady's window) □ to entertain with a serenade

serene *(say sereen)* calm (as, a serene sea); content (as, a serene mood)
serenity calmness; tranquillity

serf (in former times) a slave to the owner of the land on which he worked
serfdom the state of being a serf

serge a strong cloth, usually woollen, with fine ridges

sergeant *(say sarjent)* a non-commissioned army officer above the rank of corporal; a police officer
sergeant-major an army rank above sergeant

series a number of things or events which follow one another in order
serial a story which is published or broadcast in a series of parts □ in a series

serious thoughtful; earnest; not to be taken lightly (as, a serious matter, illness, etc.)

sermon a serious talk (usually given in church and based on a quotation from the Bible)

serpent a snake
serpentine winding (like a moving serpent)

serve to work for an employer; to hand out food at a meal; to sell things to, or wait on, customers in a shop; to be suitable for (as, to serve a purpose); (in tennis) to throw the ball up and strike it; to carry out duties (as, to serve in the army, navy, etc.)
servant someone who is paid to work for someone else, especially in domestic service (as a cook, etc.)
service *(say servis)* the duties of a servant or of someone who serves; employment in the armed forces or in a government department; the officials in such public departments (the civil service); religious worship or a religious ceremony (as, a marriage service); the supply of public transport, etc. (as, a bus service); help (as - Can I be of service?)
servile like a slave; slavish or cringing
servitude slavery

serviette a table napkin

session a meeting of a court or council

set to place or put; to fix properly (as, to set a broken wrist); to arrange (a table) for a meal; to fix (hair) in a certain style; to make or cause to be (as, to set

free, to set on fire, etc.); to become firm (as, when a jelly, etc. sets); to disappear below the horizon (as - The sun sets.) □ fixed or arranged beforehand □ a group of persons or a collection of things of a similar nature (as, a set of golf clubs); an apparatus (as, a radio or television set)
setback a check to progress; a defeat
set square a ruler shaped like a triangle with one right angle
setting a background
set out (or off) to begin a journey

settee a long seat with a back

setter a breed of hunting dog that can be trained to find and retrieve game

settle to place at, or come to rest (as, to settle in an armchair); to make one's home in a place (as, to settle in another country): to agree upon; to bring to an end (as, to settle a quarrel); to pay a bill
settlement an agreement or settling of a dispute, etc.; a payment (of a bill or account): a small community of people who have settled together somewhere

sever *(say sever)* to cut apart or break off (as, to sever a friendship)

several more than two or three, but not many; a few; various

severe *(say seveer)* very strict or critical (as, a severe master, critic, etc.); serious; distressing (as, a severe pain); harsh (as, a severe winter)
severity severeness (as, the severity of his punishment)

sew *(say so)* to join together, or mend, with a needle and thread

sewer *(say sooer)* an underground drain for receiving and carrying away dirty water and waste matter from houses and streets
sewage the water and waste matter carried off by sewers

sex either of the two groups, male and female, into which animals and human beings are divided
sexual having to do with sex (as, sexual characteristics)

sextant an instrument for measuring angles, used as an aid in navigation

sexton a church officer who attends the clergyman and sees to bell-ringing, grave-digging, burials, etc.

shabby worn-looking; poorly dressed: mean or unfair

shack a roughly built hut

shackle to fasten with chains; to hold in check
shackles fetters or chains used to fasten a prisoner's limbs

shade partial darkness (as, in the shade and out of the sun); the darker parts in a picture (as, more light than shade); a degree of colour (as, a darker shade of red) □ to screen the light away from (as, by a lampshade); to darken (as, to shade parts of a drawing)
shady sheltered from the sun
shadow the dark shape of an object caused when it gets in the way of a light □ to follow (a person) about and watch him closely

shaft the long handle of a spear, axe, golf club, etc.; an arrow; a ray or beam of light; the main part of a pillar or column; a long revolving rod which transmits motion from an engine: a passage in a mine; a vertical passage from the bottom of a building to the top (as, a lift shaft)

shaggy covered with rough hair or wool; untidy or rough-looking (as, shaggy hair)

shake to move, or be moved, up and down or from side to side with quick jerky movements; to tremble or make tremble; to make or be made unsteady, unsure, weak (as, to shake one's faith, confidence, etc.) □ the act of shaking; a drink made by shaking the ingredients (as, a milk shake)

shaky weak; trembling (as from fear, old age, illness, etc.); likely to collapse; not reliable (as, a shaky excuse)

to shake hands to greet a person by clasping right hands (with or without a shaking movement)

shall part of an auxiliary verb used to express the future (as - I shall go tomorrow; we shall arrive home late.)

should the past tense of shall (as - We should have gone.); a conditional form of shall (as - We should like to go if the weather remains fine.)

shallot a kind of small onion

shallow not deep; (of mind) superficial; not feeling or thinking deeply □ (often in plural) a place where the water is not deep

sham not real; imitation; pretended (as, sham jewellery, a sham fight on the stage) □ a fraud; an imitation; something that is not what it appears to be □ to pretend or fake (as - He shammed illness.)

shamble to walk in a shuffling, awkward way

shambles a slaughterhouse: a scene of slaughter and destruction (as - The battlefield was a shambles.)

shame a painful, unhappy feeling caused by guilt, failure or wrong-doing of any kind; disgrace or dishonour □ to make (a person) feel shame

shameful disgraceful; bringing shame, dishonour, etc.

shameless feeling or showing no shame; impudent; brazen

shamefaced ashamed; very shy or bashful

shammy see **chamois**

shampoo to wash the hair □ a soapy preparation for washing the hair

shamrock a kind of clover plant with tiny leaves divided into three sections (the national emblem of Ireland)

shank the lower part of the leg, between the knee and the ankle; the part of a tool joining the handle to the head; a shaft

shanty 1 a roughly built hut; a ramshackle dwelling

shanty 2, chanty a sailor's work-song with chorus

shape the form or outline of anything (as - The shape of a ball is round.); a mould; a jelly, etc. turned out of a mould □ to make or mould into a certain form; to influence or direct (as, an event that shaped his future plans); to take shape or develop (as - Plans for the holiday are shaping up well.)

shapeless having no shape or regular form

shapely well-formed; of attractive shape (as - She has a shapely figure.)

share to divide (something) among several people; to have (something) in common (as - They shared a liking for football.); to receive or take a share □ a portion or part of something divided between two or more people; one of the portions into which the capital of a business is divided

shareholder a person who holds one or more shares in a business

shark a general name for a group of (mostly) carnivorous fishes, some types of which are very large and ferocious with saw-edged teeth

sharp having a thin cutting edge or fine point; cutting or piercing; stinging or hurting (as, sharp winds, sharp words); alert or keen (as, to keep a sharp look-out); (musical) too high in pitch; raised by a semitone □ punctually, precisely (for example, at 9.00 a.m. sharp) □ a sign in music (#) to show that a note is to be raised by half a tone

sharpen to make sharp

sharpener an instrument or device for sharpening (tools, pencils, etc.)

sharpshooter a good (rifle) marksman

sharpsighted having keen eyesight

sharp-witted quick-thinking

shatter to break something into many pieces; to upset or ruin completely (a person's hopes, plans, etc.)

shave to cut off hair with a razor; to scrape or cut away a surface (of wood, etc.); to graze or nearly touch in passing; □ the act of shaving; a narrow escape or miss (a close shave)

shaving a very thin slice or strip (as, a wood shaving)

shawl a piece of cloth worn loosely around the head or shoulders by girls and women

she a female person or animal already referred to (as - Her mother said she would be home soon.)

sheaf a bundle (of corn) or a bunch (of papers) tied together

shear to cut or clip hair or wool (especially the wool from sheep)

shears scissors (especially large ones used to clip wool, hedges, etc.)

sheath a cover for the blade of a sword or knife; a long close-fitting covering

sheathe to put into or cover with a scabbard or sheath

shed 1 to throw or cast off (as, to shed leaves, rain, clothes); to pour out (as, to shed blood, tears); to send forth or out (as, to shed light, cheerfulness)

shed 2 a small structure or outhouse used for storage or shelter (such as a toolshed)

sheen brightness; gloss (as -The dog's coat has a nice sheen.)

sheep a ruminant animal of the goat family, valued for its thick wool, flesh, etc.; a meek and timid person; one who follows others without thinking for himself

sheepish shy; shamefaced; embarrassed

sheep dog a dog trained to watch and control a flock of sheep

sheepskin the skin of a sheep (especially with the wool left on); the leather prepared from it

sheer very steep, almost vertical (as, a sheer rock-face); pure or unmixed with anything else; absolute (as, sheer joy; sheer nonsense); (of cloth) very fine and thin, nearly transparent

sheet 1 a large piece of cloth used under a blanket as bedding; a broad thin piece of anything (such as a sheet of ice, metal, paper, glass, etc.)

sheet 2 a rope attached to the lower corner of a sail (used to adjust the angle at which the sail catches the wind)

sheik(h) (say shake or sheek) an Arab chief

shelf a board or piece of metal fixed on a wall, in a cupboard, bookcase, etc., used to keep things on; a shelf-like ledge or layer of rock; a flat sandbank

shelves the plural of shelf

shelve to put things on a shelf (as, books in a library); to put (a problem, a difficult decision, etc.) aside to be considered later; to slope gently (as - The land shelves towards the sea.)

shell a hard outer covering of a nut, egg, shellfish, turtle, etc.; a husk or pod (as of peas); any framework (of a ship, building, etc.) not yet completed, or burnt out; anything resembling a shell in shape; a metal case, filled with explosive, to be fired from a gun, cannon, etc.

shellfish a water animal that has a shell (as, an oyster, crab, lobster, etc.)

shellac a resin used for making varnish

shelter a building, structure or anything that gives protection and cover against wind, rain, attack, etc.; protection from harm □ to give protection to; to provide shelter for (a person); to take shelter

shepherd *(say sheperd)* someone who looks after sheep

sheriff the chief officer in a county or district

sherry a strong wine (named after the town of Jerez *(say Haireth)* in southern Spain)

shield (in mediaeval times) a broad piece of defensive armour carried on the arm to ward off blows; anything resembling, or used as, a shield to protect oneself □ to protect from harm; to defend

shift to change direction (as - The wind shifted to the southwest.); to change the position of (by moving, as to shift furniture, stage scenery); to transfer (as, to shift blame, responsibility); to manage or get along (as - He must shift for himself.) □ a move; a change; a set of people taking turns with another set (especially at work)
shiftless unreliable; lazy; inefficient
shifty tricky; not trustworthy; (of eyes or expression) not honest and straightforward

shilling a silver-coloured coin worth 5 pence ($1/20$ of a pound)

shimmer to shine with a trembling, quivering light

shin the front part of the leg between the knee and the ankle

shine to give out or reflect light; to be bright; to be good at (as, to shine at mathematics); to cause to shine (as, to shine a light on something); to polish (as, to shine shoes, silver) □ brightness; a polish
shiny bright; glossy; polished

shingle coarse gravel or small rounded stones found at the edge of the sea: a flat piece of wood, used to cover a roof in the same way as slates or tiles

ship a large vessel which travels across the ocean, seas, etc. □ to send (goods) by ship; to take on to a ship
shipmate a fellow sailor on a ship

shipment goods sent by ship
shipping ships considered as a whole (as, the shipping of a country)
shipshape in good order; trim or tidy
shipwreck the wreck or loss of a ship (especially by accident)
shipyard a large yard where ships are built or repaired

shire a county (as, Yorkshire)

shirk to avoid carrying out some duty
shirker someone who shirks

shirt a garment with sleeves worn by men and boys on the upper part of the body

shiver to tremble (with cold, fear, etc.) □ a trembling

shoal a great number of fishes swimming together (as, a shoal of herring): a shallow place; a sandbank

shock a sudden violent blow or collision; unexpected bad news; a sudden shaking (as, in an earthquake); a sudden physical disturbance (caused by electricity, an accident, etc.) □ to give a shock to; to upset or horrify
shocking giving a shock (as, the shocking news of a bad accident); disgusting (as, shocking behaviour)

shod see **shoe**

shoddy of poor quality; cheap and badly made (as, shoddy clothes, furniture, etc.)

shoe a strong outer covering for the foot, not reaching above the ankle; something resembling a shoe (such as a horseshoe) □ to put shoes on
shod wearing shoes (as, well shod)
shoemaker someone who nowadays usually only sells and repairs shoes and boots

shoot to fire a bullet from a gun, or let fly an arrow from a bow; to direct (a ball, etc.) with force (as, to shoot for goal); to move very quickly (as, to shoot out of the door); to put forth in new growth; to photograph or film

□ a new twig or growth

shot the past tense of shoot

shooting star a meteor

shop a place where goods are sold to the public; a workshop in a factory where some kind of industry is carried on □ to visit shops in order to buy things (as, to go shopping)

shoplifter a person who steals things from a shop

shore the land bordering the sea or a lake

short not long; not tall; not sufficient in quantity or weight (as - He is short of money.); (in speaking) sharp or rude

shorts short trousers

shorten to make shorter

shortage a deficiency or lack

shortbread a crisp, crumbly cake made of flour, butter and sugar

short-circuit a short cut in an electrical circuit caused by a fault, which produces heat with a danger of fire

shortcoming a fault

short cut a short way (shorter than usual)

shorthand a quick way of writing down what is heard with strokes and dots to show the different sounds

short-handed having fewer workers or helpers than usual

shortly in a short time; soon

short-sighted seeing clearly only things that are near; being foolish in not foreseeing what may happen

short-tempered easily made angry

shot a single act or sound of shooting; a bullet or other projectile; a marksman; (as - He's a good shot.); a stroke, kick, etc. in a game (as, Good shot!); one scene in a film: see also **shoot**

should see **shall**

shoulder the part of the body between the neck and the upper arm □ to carry on the shoulder

shoulder-blade the broad flat bone of the shoulder

shout a loud cry or burst of voices (as, a shout of laughter, applause) □ to utter a shout

shove *(say shuv)* to push along □ a push or thrust

shovel a broad kind of spade or scoop □ to shift or lift with a shovel

show to point out or make clear; to display □ a display or act of showing; a performance or entertainment; an exhibition (as, a Flower Show, Dairy Show)

showy bright and gaudy

showman someone who owns or exhibits a show (such as a circus)

show off to try to make an impression on other people (as, to show off a new dress, to show off a skill, etc.)

showroom a room where goods are displayed for people to see

shower a short fall (as of rain, etc.); a fall or flight of many things together (as, a shower of bullets, meteors, arrows, blows, etc.); a shower-bath □ to pour (as, to shower confetti on a bride, praise on the winners of a cup-final)

showery raining from time to time

shower-bath a bath with a spray (either overhead or on a flexible pipe)

shrank see **shrink**

shrapnel pieces of flying metal from an exploding shell or bomb

shred a scrap or strip, cut or torn off □ to cut or tear

shrewd showing keen judgment

shriek to utter a high-pitched scream or laugh □ a shrill scream or laugh

shrill high-pitched in tone and piercing to the ears

shrimp a small shellfish with a long tail

shrine a casket for holding holy relics; a holy or sacred place

shrink to grow smaller (as - This shirt may shrink when you wash it.); to draw back (from) in fear or disgust

shrank the past tense of shrink
shrinkage the amount by which anything shrinks
shrunken grown smaller

shrivel to dry up and become wrinkled

shroud a cloth used to cover or wrap round a dead body □ to cover up as with a shroud (as, a river shrouded in mist)
shrouds the ropes from the masthead to a ship's sides

shrub a small woody plant or bush
shrubbery a group of shrubs

shrug to raise one's shoulders, especially to show doubt or lack of interest □ the motion of shrugging the shoulders

shrunken see **shrink**

shudder to shiver or tremble (as, from cold, horror or disgust) □ the act of shuddering

shuffle to move the feet along without lifting them; to mix (especially playing cards) □ an act of shuffling

shun to avoid or keep away from

shunt to shove or move aside; to turn aside (as, to shunt a railway engine, carriage, etc. into a siding)

shut to close something that is open (a door, a window, a book); to keep out or bar entry (as, to shut the gates); to confine (as - Shut the cat in.)
shutter a cover for a window or an opening (as, in a camera)

shuttle (in weaving) a device that carries the thread from side to side through the lengthwise threads; a similar device in a sewing machine
shuttlecock a cork with feathers stuck in one end, struck back and forth in the game of badminton
shuttle service trains, buses, etc. that only run back and forth between two stations or two stopping points

shy 1 to throw or toss □ a throw;

a try

shy 2 (of an animal) timid; easily frightened; (of a person) bashful; self-conscious; not wanting to draw attention to oneself □ (of a horse, etc.) to start back or to one side (from fear)

sick ill; not well; diseased; vomiting or feeling inclined to vomit; weary or tired of (as, to be sick of this damp weather); disgusted (as - It makes me sick to see all this litter thrown about.)
sickness the state of being sick
sicken to make, or become, sick
sickening making sick; disgusting; tiresome
sickly unhealthy; (of colour) pale or weak; feeble (as, a sickly smile)

sickle a tool with a curved blade and a short handle, used to cut grain, grass, etc.

side an edge, border or boundary line; an upright or sloping surface (as, the side of a box, a hill, etc.); the part of the body between the armpit and the hip; either surface of anything (as, a piece of paper, a blanket, a carpet); a region or district (as, the west side of a city); a team; a group of people having a particular point of view (in opposition to another group holding a different point of view) □ at, towards, from or on one side or a side (as, a side door, a side road, a side pocket) □ to take the same side or give support (as - He sided with his friend in the argument.)
sideboard a piece of dining room furniture for holding plates, cutlery, table linen, etc.
siding a short line of rails on which train engines, carriages, etc. are shunted from the main line
sideline a line marking the side of a playing field, tennis court, etc.; the space just outside this line: a line of goods sold in addition to one's main stock; a job carried on outside one's regular work

sidelong from, or to, the side; indirect (as, a sidelong glance)

sideshow a small show outside or at one side of the main show; a less important part of a large show (as, a sideshow at a circus)

sidestep to avoid something by stepping to one side; to avoid (some work, a difficult problem, etc.)

sidetrack to turn or shunt into a siding; to turn a person away from doing something already begun; to turn an argument or discussion away from the main point

sidewalk (in the United States) footpath or pavement

sideways, sidewise with the side turned towards the front (as, to move sideways); from the side (as, to see something sideways)

sidle to go or move sideways; to edge along in a stealthy manner

siege an attempt to capture a town or port by surrounding it, so that no help can reach it

siesta *(say see-esta)* a short sleep or rest taken after lunch (especially in hot climates)

sieve *(say siv)* a container with a mesh or many holes in the bottom, used to separate fine grains of sand, flour, etc. from the coarse ones, solids from liquids, etc.

sift to separate by passing through a sieve (as, to sift flour); to test or examine (facts, evidence) carefully

sigh *(say sie)* to take a long deep breath, breathing out heavily (in sorrow, weariness, etc.) □ the act or sound of sighing

sight the ability to see: the act of seeing; something seen; something unusual, beautiful, etc. that is worth seeing; something terrible, unpleasant, untidy (as - What a dreadful sight!); a device on the barrel of a gun to guide the aim □ to see (as, to sight land from a ship)

sighted having sight, or having a certain kind of sight (as, short-sighted)

sight-reading reading or playing unfamiliar music straight away, without having to study it first

sight-seeing visiting places of interest in a strange country, city, etc.

at sight, on sight as soon as seen

sign a movement (such as a nod, a handwave) which conveys without words what one means; a mark with a meaning (such as a plus [+] sign); an advertisement; a notice that gives information (as, a hotel sign, the name and occupation of a tradesman outside his place of business, a *For sale* sign on a house, a car, etc.); a forecast of something to come (as - A red sunset is often a sign of fine weather.) □ to show or indicate by a sign (a nod, a wave, etc.); to write one's name (on a cheque, at the end of a letter, etc.)

signpost a post with a sign showing directions, distances, etc. or giving information

signal a sign, sound, word of command, etc. that starts some action (as - The train started after the guard blew his whistle as a signal.); a sound broadcast or received (as, a time signal); an information sign (as, traffic signals)

signature *(say signachure)* a signed name (as the signature at the end of a letter); (in music) the flats and sharps that show the key

signatory someone who has signed an agreement

signet-ring a ring with the owner's initials on it

signify to be a sign of; to mean

significance meaning; importance

significant having meaning or importance (as, the most significant features of a country)

silage see **silo**

silence absence of sound or of talking; quietness □ to cause to

be quiet or still (as, to silence a class)
silent not speaking; noiseless

silhouette *(say silooet)* an outline drawing filled in with black (like a dark shadow)

silk the very fine, soft thread spun by silkworms; the cloth woven from this thread □ made of silk
silken, silky made of silk; like silk
silkworm a moth caterpillar which spins silk

sill a ledge or shelf (as, a window sill)

silly foolish; not showing common sense

silo *(say sielo)* a tower-like building for storing grain, etc.; an airtight building or pit for storing green cattle food
silage green crops kept as fodder for cattle

silt fine sand and fertile soil left behind by a river □ to block (up) with silt

silvan, sylvan wooded; living in woods

silver a rather soft greyish-white metal which can be highly polished to make silverware, jewellery and ornaments; coins made of an alloy of silver and nickel □ silvery
silvery made of, or looking like, silver; (of sound) clear and musical
silver-plate dishes, spoons, etc. of silver, or plated with silver
silversmith a craftsman in silver or maker of silver articles
silverware articles made of silver (especially for table use)

similar like, or almost like
similarity a resemblance
simile *(say similee)* a figure of speech used to make a comparison clearer or more striking (as - The kite flew *like a bird;* the east wind cut *like a knife.*)

simmer to keep on the point of boiling (often with a gentle hissing sound); to be on the point of

bursting out (as, simmering with anger, with excitement, etc.)

simper to smile in a silly manner

simple easy; plain or ordinary; foolish or easily cheated
simplicity easiness; plainness
simplification the act of making (a problem, etc.) easier
simplify to make simpler
simply in a simple manner; merely

simulate to pretend to have, feel, etc. (as, to simulate interest in a particular subject)

simultaneous happening at the same time

sin a wicked act, especially against one's religion □ to commit a sin; to do wrong
sinful wicked
sinner someone who sins

since from the time of (as, since term began, since 1970, etc.) □ from then until now (as - He left school early and I've not seen him since.) □ because (as - Since we got home early we can start to make the tea.)

sincere honest in what one says and does; true or genuine (as, sincere friends)
sincerely with sincerity (as, *Yours sincerely* to end a letter less formally than *Yours faithfully*)
sincerity genuineness; frankness; freedom from pretence

sinew a tendon, or tough fibrous tissue, joining a muscle to a bone; (plural) strength; resources

sing to make musical sounds with the voice
singsong monotonous up-and-down tone of voice □ a gathering of people singing together informally

singe *(say sinj)* to burn slightly; to scorch

single one only; not double; not married; one way only (as, a single ticket) □ to pick out (as, to single out one pupil in a class)
singly one by one
single-handed by oneself,

without help

single-minded with one purpose only in one's mind

singular unusual or strange; (in grammar) one only, not plural

singularity strangeness

singularly unusually; strangely

sinister suggesting evil or a threat of evil; evil-looking

sink to go down or downwards into something (especially to sink below the surface of water); to go down gradually into a lower position or less active state (as, the sun, a fire, hope, etc. sinks); to invest (as, to sink all one's money in a business) □ a basin (usually) with running water and a drain for carrying off dirty water

sank, sunk the past tense of the verb sink (as - The ship sank last year. The bathers have sunk up to their knees in quicksand.)

sunken on a lower level than the surroundings (as, a sunken garden); sunk (as, sunken treasure); hollowed (as, sunken cheeks)

sinuous bending or winding in and out (as, a sinuous river); (of a person) smooth or graceful in movement

sinus a hollow or cavity (especially an air cavity in the head)

sinusitis inflammation of one of the nasal sinuses

sip to drink in very small quantities □ the quantity sipped at one moment

siphon (say *siefon*) a tube for drawing liquid out of one container into another lower one; a glass bottle for soda water, etc. which is released under pressure

sir a word of respect used in speaking or writing to a man (as, *Dear Sir* to start a letter); the title of a knight or a baronet

siren 1 a hooter, whistle, etc. used as a signal or warning (as, a factory siren, a fire siren, a police siren)

siren 2 (in mythology) a sea nymph, said to lure sailors and their ships into danger by her beautiful singing; (nowadays) an attractive, charming, but possibly dangerous woman (for example, a beautiful woman spy)

sirloin the upper part of a loin of beef

sisal (say *siessl* or *siezl*) a fibre obtained from the leaves of a plant grown in some hot countries, used in making rope, cord and twine

sister a daughter of one's own parents; a member of a religious community (usually a nun); a nurse of senior rank (usually in charge of a hospital ward) □ closely related; alike in appearance or design (as, sister ships)

sisterly like a sister; kindly; charitable

sister-in-law the wife of a brother, or the sister of a husband or wife

sit to rest or be seated on a chair, bench, the ground, etc.; (of birds) to perch; to rest on a nest (as, to sit on eggs before hatching); to be an official member (as, to sit on a committee, in parliament); to be in session (as - The court is sitting.); to pose (as, a model for an artist)

sat the past tense of sit (as - They sat down.)

sitter a person who poses (for a photograph, a portrait); a sitting bird

sitting seated; resting on eggs □ a session or meeting (of a committee, parliament, etc.); a period of posing (as - The sitting lasted an hour.)

sitting room a room chiefly for sitting in

sit-down strike a strike in which workers stay in the factory, etc. but refuse to do any work

to sit tight to stay where one is; to refuse to move

site an area of ground where a

building, a town, a memorial, etc. was, is at present, or is to be in the future

situated located or placed (as - The house is nicely situated.)
situation a place or location; position or circumstances (as, to be in a difficult or embarrassing situation); employment (as - After leaving school, he will have to look for a suitable situation.)

size 1 the space taken up by anything; the measurements or dimensions of anything; largeness or bulk; a grading or classification according to measurement (such as dress sizes, shoe sizes)
sizable, sizeable fairly large

size 2 a weak glue or gluey material, used for glazing or preparing a surface for painting

sizzle to make a hissing sound of frying or burning (as - Bacon sizzles in the frying pan.)

skate 1 a large flat fish of the ray family, with very wide fins

skate 2 a metal blade or a set of small rollers which can be attached to a shoe or boot and used for gliding on ice (ice skates) or smooth pavement, etc. (roller skates) □ to move on skates; to glide as if on skates

skein a loosely coiled length of thread or yarn

skeleton the bony framework of the body of a human being, animal, fish or bird; the framework or outline of a building, ship, etc.
skeleton crew a set of people who work together, reduced to the smallest possible number
skeleton key a device like a key without the middle bits, used to pick locks
skeleton in the cupboard a closely guarded secret (usually something shameful or embarrassing to a family)

sketch a rough plan, painting or drawing (especially one that will be completed later); an outline for a play, book, etc.; a short play

or scene □ to make a quick rough plan (as for a drawing, a theatrical costume); to tell the main points of a story, film, etc.
sketchy like a sketch; roughly drawn or outlined; incomplete

skewer a long wooden or metal pin pushed through a piece of meat to keep it together while roasting

ski *(say skee)* one of a pair of long narrow strips of wood, metal or plastic, fastened to boots and used for gliding over the snow □ to move on skis

skid a wedge, etc. placed under one of the wheels of a vehicle to keep it from moving down a steep hill; (in plural) logs, planks, etc. used to support something being moved by sliding or pushing; a sideways slip □ to slip sideways (especially of wheels which slip sideways on a wet or icy surface without turning)

skiff a small light boat that can be rowed or sailed by one person

skill cleverness at doing something (either from much practice or natural ability); the ability needed for a craft or profession
skilful having or showing skill; able to do something well
skilled expert, skilful (especially through training, as a skilled musician)

skim to remove the thick surface matter from the top of liquid (as, to skim the cream off milk); to glide lightly and quickly over the surface of (the ground, water, etc.); to read through something very quickly, to get a general idea of what it is about
skim milk milk from which the cream has been skimmed

skimp to give barely enough; to do something without proper care and attention; to be mean and stingy by spending far too little
skimpy scanty; (of clothing) too small or too tight - not cut full enough; stingy

skin the outer covering of the bodies of human beings, animals, birds and fish; the outer covering of fruit, vegetables, etc.; anything resembling skin □ to remove the skin from
skinny very thin
skin-deep no deeper than the skin; not very serious (as - Her sorrow was only skin-deep.)
skinflint a mean, miserly person

skip to jump or hop over a turning rope; to move along lightly with leaps and bounds: to leave out something (as, to skip a meal, to skip a chapter in a book)
skipping-rope a rope held at each end and turned round and round for a person to skip over

skipper the captain of a ship, aircraft or team

skirmish a fight between small groups of soldiers; a short sharp argument or disagreement

skirt a garment that hangs down from the waist; the part of a dress below the waist; □ to be or to pass along the outer edge (as, a wood that skirts the town)
skirting board a narrow board that goes round the walls of a room just above the floor

skit a short piece of writing or a dramatic sketch making fun of a person or group of people, some event, etc. (as, a skit on politicians)

skittish lively; frisky; (of a horse) easily frightened

skittle one of nine bottle-shaped pieces of wood used in the game of skittles

skulk to sneak out of the way; to hide or lurk (usually for a bad purpose)

skull the bony part of the head

skunk a small North American black animal with white stripes and a bushy tail (It squirts out a very unpleasant-smelling liquid when attacked.)

sky (sometimes used in the plural - **skies**) the upper air or atmosphere; the heavens; weather or climate
skylark the common lark which sings while hovering in the air high above the ground
skylarking mischievous behaviour; playing jokes
skylight a window in a roof or ceiling
skyline the horizon; the line made by buildings as they stand out against the sky
skyscraper a very high building

slab a flat thick piece of something (as, a slab of cake, stone, etc.)

slack loose; not tightly stretched; not busy (as, a slack period in a shop's business); lazy and careless □ the loose part of a rope; (in plural) trousers □ to do less (work) than one should
slacken to make or become slower, looser, less active, etc.
slacker a person who slacks or does not do his fair share

slag waste material from melted or refined metal

slake to quench (thirst): to mix lime with water

slam to shut or bang (a door, a lid) with a loud noise; to put (something) down with a bang (as - She slammed the books on the table.)

slander an untrue remark about someone, made with the intention of damaging his reputation and character □ to utter slander

slang words or phrases popularly used in informal talk or writing, but not considered acceptable in formal speech or serious writing (Most slang soon becomes out-of-date and disappears.): see also **jargon** □ to scold or abuse

slant to slope; to place or lie diagonally □ a slope; a sloping surface
slanting diagonal; sloping; not straight up and down

slap a blow with the palm of the hand; to strike with the open hand or anything flat

slapdash off-hand; in a bold and careless way

slapstick comedy boisterous, knockabout comedy

slash to make long cuts in something; to cut by striking violently and at random □ a sweeping blow; a long cut or slit (in cloth)

slat a thin strip of wood, metal or plastic (as, slats in a venetian blind)

slate a fine-grained, easily-split rock, dull grey, blue or green in colour, used for roofing, blackboards, etc.

slaughter (say slawter) the killing of animals (especially for food); a terrible killing (usually of great numbers of people) □ to butcher; to massacre

slaughterhouse a place where animals are killed for food

slave someone who is not free because he is owned by another person; a person who is completely devoted to another; someone who works very hard for little reward; someone enslaved by some interest or habit (as, a slave to fashion, a slave to tobacco)

slavery the state of being a slave; the custom of owning or trading in slaves; drudgery

slavish slave-like; following rules and instructions absolutely (often unnecessarily)

slave driver a person who oversees the work of slaves and urges them on; (nowadays) a hard taskmaster

slay to kill

sled, sledge 1 a vehicle with metal or wooden runners, used to move people or goods over snow-covered ground

sledge 2, sledgehammer a large heavy hammer (usually held with both hands)

sleek smooth and glossy (as, the coat of a horse that has been well fed and well groomed)

sleep to rest with the eyes closed and consciousness relaxed; to be asleep □ the state of not being awake

slept the past tense of sleep (as - They slept well after their long walk.)

sleeper someone who sleeps: one of the heavy wooden or metal beams supporting railway lines: (also **sleeping car**) a railway carriage with berths or beds for night passengers

sleepless not able to sleep; alert and watchful

sleeping bag a large bag made of warm material for a camper, etc. to sleep in (especially out of doors)

sleepwalker a person who gets out of bed and walks about while asleep

sleet rain mixed with snow or hail

sleeve the part of a garment that covers the arm

sleeveless without sleeves

sleigh (say slay) a large sled (usually horse-drawn)

sleight (say sliet) **of hand** skill and quickness in using the hands to perform card and conjuring tricks

slender slim; narrow; not strong or thick in appearance; small in amount (as, slender evidence, income)

slept see **sleep**

sleuth (say slooth) a detective; a tracker

slice a flat (usually) thin piece cut from something (as, a slice of bread, meat, etc.) □ to cut into slices; to cut through

slick sleek and smooth; clever and smooth in speech and manner (sometimes sly and tricky) □ to polish; to smooth or tidy (as, to slick one's hair down) □ an oil-covered area on water

slide to move smoothly down or along on something; to slip or glide (as, to slide on ice) □ a slippery, sloping surface for sliding (as, a playground slide); a loosened mass of earth, rock, etc.; a picture for projecting onto a screen; a piece of glass on which something can be examined through a microscope

slight small in quantity, value or importance; (of a person) slender in build □to treat as unimportant; to insult or snub (a person) by ignoring or being rude to him □an insult; a snub
slightly by a small amount (as, slightly more than half)
slighting insulting; impolite; showing contempt or lack of respect (as, to make a slighting remark)

slim slender; thin; slight □to become slimmer by dieting, etc.

slime thin slippery mud or filth
slimy covered with slime; resembling slime

sling a strap with a string attached to each end for hurling stones, etc.; a catapult; a bandage hanging from the neck or shoulder to support an injured arm or hand; a rope, chain or heavy net used to hoist and lower heavy cargo, etc. □to hurl with a sling; to move or carry in a sling

slink to sneak away; to move or creep as though in fear

slip 1 to slide or glide; to move quietly (as - She slipped away without being noticed.); to give or pass something secretly to someone (as, to slip money into a person's hand); to cause to slide, drop, etc. (as, to let a glass slip from one's hand); to lose one's footing (as, to slip on an icy path) □the act of slipping; a slight mistake; a woman's undergarment, worn under a dress; a covering for a pillow
slipper a soft indoor shoe (easy to slip on the foot)
slippery (of a surface) very smooth (as - Be careful walking on this slippery floor!); (of a person) untrustworthy; unreliable
slip knot a knot made to slip along a rope or string
slipshod having shoes worn down at the heels; (of work, writing, etc.) very careless;

sloppy
slipstream the stream of air forced back by an aeroplane propeller

slip 2 a strip or narrow piece of paper, etc.

slit to make a long cut in; to cut into strips □a long narrow cut or opening

slither to slip or slide about (as, on a muddy pavement)

sliver a small thin (often pointed or sharp) piece of something; a splinter

slobber to let saliva or liquid dribble or trickle from the mouth

slog to hit hard; to work hard; to walk along in a determined, steady way □a hard blow; a long spell of hard work

slogan a word or phrase that encourages people to work for a purpose (political, national, etc.) or that encourages them to buy something (as - *Eat more fruit. Drink more milk.*); (in former times) a warcry to soldiers in battle, etc.

sloop a light sailing boat, having only one mast

slop to spill; to overflow □spilled liquid; (in plural) tasteless semiliquid food; dirty waste liquid
sloppy wet; muddy; careless; untidy: very sentimental (as, a sloppy love story, film, etc.)

slope an upward or downward slant or inclination; a surface higher at one end than the other (as, a roof with a steep slope) □to have, or to place in, a slanting direction or position (as - The road slopes down from the hill.)

slot a small narrow opening (usually in a machine) which is made to receive a coin; a larger narrow opening for posting or delivering letters, etc.
slot-machine a machine which begins to work when a coin is inserted in a slot

sloth *(say sloath)* laziness: a

slow-moving South American animal that hangs down by its feet from branches, and feeds on leaves and fruit

slouch a hunched-up, drooping position of the body in walking, standing or sitting □ to move, walk, or sit with a slouch

slough *(say sluff)* the cast-off skin of a snake □ to cast or shed the skin, a coat, etc.

slovenly careless or untidy in work, appearance, habits, etc.

slow *(say sloe)* not fast; taking a long time to do something; behind in time (as, a clock that is slow); dull (not quick-witted and lively) □ to make or become slow

sludge slimy soft mud

slug 1 an animal like a snail, but without a shell
sluggard a person who is slow and lazy
sluggish slow to move

slug 2 a small lump of metal (especially a bullet for firing from a gun): a heavy blow

sluice an artificial channel for water, with a sliding gate (a **sluice gate**) for controlling the flow or changing the direction □ to flood, or wash out, with a flow of water

slum an overcrowded part of a city (usually occupied by the poorest people, in unpleasant, unhealthy conditions)

slumber to sleep; to doze

slump to fall or sink suddenly; to slouch (as, to slump in a chair) □ a sudden fall in prices, values, etc. (as, a slump in house property values)

slur to pass over lightly or quickly (without giving enough attention or consideration to (as, to slur over one's mistakes); to pronounce or sound words indistinctly; to blame or run down (a person's reputation) □ (music) a mark (⌣) showing that two or more notes are to be sung to the same syllable or played with a gliding effect
slurred indistinct; (of musical notes) played or glided over so that they seem to run together

slush melting snow; soft or liquid mud

slut a dirty, untidy woman
sluttish dirty; untidy; careless

sly cunning; artful; crafty; mischievous (as a sly, joking remark)

smack 1 taste or flavour; a trace □ to have a taste or suggestion of (as - This smacks of conspiracy.)

smack 2 a small fishing vessel

smack 3 to slap or strike sharply; to open and shut (the lips) noisily (as, when eating or drinking with enjoyment); to kiss noisily □ a sharp loud noise; a hearty, noisy kiss; a slap

small little; the opposite of big or large; unimportant □ the smallest or narrowest part of a thing (as, the small of the back)
small hours the hours immediately after midnight (1 a.m., 2 a.m., etc.)
small-minded narrow-minded; limited and petty in interests and sympathies
smallpox a serious contagious disease, with a high fever and skin blisters (pocks) which usually leave permanent scars
small talk chatter; talk about unimportant matters

smart clever; quick to learn; well-dressed; fashionable; trim and neat □ a sharp stinging pain □ to feel such a pain (as - My arm smarts where I grazed it.)

smash to break into pieces (usually with force and a crashing noise); to strike with great force; to ruin or wreck (as, to smash one's hopes, prospects, etc.) □ the act of smashing; an accident (as, a car smash)

smattering a slight knowledge of a subject (as, a smattering of French)

smear to spread or rub (something greasy or sticky); to spread a surface (with something greasy or sticky) □ a smudge or dirty mark

smell the ability to sense or notice something through the nose; an odour, perfume, stench, etc.; the sense that makes one aware of odours, perfumes, etc. □ to use this sense; to give off an odour, fragrance, etc. (as - The linen smells of lavender. The kitchen smells of fried onions.)
smelly having an unpleasant smell

smelt to melt (ore) in order to separate the metal from the other material

smile to show pleasure, amusement, etc. by drawing up the corners of the lips; to look happy □ the act of smiling

smirk to smile in an unnatural, exaggerated manner

smite to hit or strike hard; to affect the feelings (as, to be smitten with love)

smith a person who works in metals (as, a blacksmith, a silversmith)
smithy the workshop of a smith

smock a loose over-garment worn while working to protect the clothes from dirt (as, an artist's smock); any loose full garment resembling a smock
smocking a type of needlework that gathers material in a honeycomb effect (as, the yoke of a smock)

smog smoky fog (The word is made up of the first two letters of **smoke** and the last two letters of **fog**.)

smoke the cloudlike gases and particles of soot that arise from something burning; a column or cloud of smoke □ to give out smoke: to draw in and puff out smoke (as, to smoke a pipe); to dry or cure (as, to smoke fish, ham, etc.)
smokeless not having or giving out smoke (as, smokeless fuel)
smoky giving out smoke; filled with smoke

smoker a person who smokes tobacco; a railway carriage where smoking is allowed

smooth (of surface) not rough or uneven; without lumps or bumps; hairless; (of movement) not jerky; gently flowing □ to make smooth; to calm or soothe (feelings)
smooth-spoken, **smooth-tongued** soft and agreeable in speech (often with the intention of flattery or deception)

smother to kill by covering the nose and mouth with something thick, so as to prevent breathing; to suffocate; to extinguish or hide (as, to smother a fire, a yawn)

smoulder to burn slowly without flame (Damp or green wood smoulders.)

smudge a stain; a smear of dirt □ to stain or soil

smug self-satisfied; pleased with oneself

smuggle to bring something secretly from one country into another, without paying customs duty; to send or take secretly
smuggler a person who smuggles; a vessel used in smuggling

smut soot; a spot of dirt or soot: indecent language
smutty dirty; grimy; (of talk) indecent; obscene

snack a quick light meal (such as a sandwich or biscuits and cheese)

snag a sharp piece of a branch or stump, left sticking out when the rest of the tree has been broken off (especially one embedded in a river or lake where it can be dangerous to boats); an unexpected problem or difficulty

snail a small slow-moving animal with a coiled shell into which it can retreat for protection; a person who is very slow

snake a legless, scaly reptile with a long body (sometimes poisonous); anything resembling a snake in form or movement

snap to break or shut suddenly, with a sharp cracking noise; to bite, or try to bite (as a dog snaps); to seize or grasp (as, to snap up a bargain); to speak sharply or angrily; to take a picture or snapshot (with a camera) □ a small catch or lock (as on a purse); a short spell of cold weather; a snapshot; a kind of card game

snappy full of life and energy; quick (as - Make it snappy!)

snapdragon a garden plant whose many-coloured flowers resemble a snapping mouth when squeezed open and shut

snapshot a photograph (especially one taken with a hand-held camera)

snare a running noose of string, wire, etc. used as a trap; a trap; a trick to catch or tempt (a person); a hidden danger or temptation □ to catch or trap in a snare, or as if in a snare

snarl 1 to make a growling noise, with the teeth showing; to speak in an angry quarrelsome way

snarl 2 to tangle or knot (as, of hair, string, etc.) □ any difficult or complicated situation

snatch to seize or grab suddenly; to take quickly when time allows (as, to snatch a bite to eat) □ an attempt to seize; a small bit (as, a snatch of music)

sneak to move or creep about stealthily; to behave in a mean sly, secretive way; to tell tales about others; to take secretly, or steal □ a mean deceitful person **sneaking** mean; underhand; secret or not openly expressed (as - I had a sneaking feeling that he wouldn't turn up.)

sneer to show scorn or contempt by a mocking expression, tone of voice or sarcastic words □ a scornful smile or remark

sneeze to make a sudden involuntary blowing noise through the nose □ the act of sneezing

snicker see **snigger**

sniff to take in air through the nose in short breaths; to smell a scent (as, to sniff the smell of freshly-cut grass) □ a short breath taken through the nose

snigger, snicker to giggle or laugh in a quiet sly way (usually at someone else's embarrassment or difficulties)

snip to cut off sharply (especially with scissors, as to snip off a lock of hair) **snippet** a small piece cut off

snipe 1 a game bird with a long straight bill, found in marshes

snipe 2 to shoot at an individual from cover (as, to snipe at an enemy soldier) **sniper** a person who makes such a shot (usually with a rifle)

snob a person who admires and tries to make friends with people whom he thinks are of a better class than himself, and who looks down on people he thinks are of a lower class **snobbish** acting like a snob **snobbery, snobbishness** the act of being snobbish or the behaviour of a snob

snooker a game played on a billiard table, using cues and coloured balls

snoop to spy or pry into other people's business in a sneaking way

snooze to doze; to sleep lightly or take a nap □ a nap

snore to make a loud breathing noise through the mouth and nose while asleep

snorkel a tube with the end above water so that air is brought to underwater swimmers and submarine crews, etc.

snort to force air noisily through the nostrils □ the act or sound of snorting

snout the sticking-out nose and mouth of some animals such as pigs and porpoises

snow frozen drops of water or water vapour that fall down through the air in light white flakes (snowflakes) □ to fall down in snowflakes or like snowflakes

snowball a ball made of snow pressed together

snowbound closed in or shut in by snow (so that one cannot move away or go out)

snowcapped (of mountain tops) covered with snow

snowdrift a bank of snow blown together by the wind

snowdrop a small white flower growing from a bulb early in spring (often blooming when snow is still on the ground)

snowflake a flake, or single piece, of snow

snowline a line or level on a mountain above which there is always snow

snowman a figure in the shape of a human being, made of snow

snowplough a machine for clearing snow from roads, railway lines, etc.

snowshoe one of a pair of frames strung with thin strips of leather, worn on the feet to keep people from sinking into soft snow

snub to insult; to treat with scorn or contempt; to cut someone short when he is speaking by ignoring him or making a cutting remark □ an act of snubbing □ (of the shape of a nose) short, broad and slightly upturned at the end

snuff 1, snuff out to nip off the burnt portion of a candle or lamp wick

snuff 2 to sniff; to smell or examine by smelling (as a dog snuffs at a bone) □ powdered tobacco which is snuffed up the nose

snuffbox a small box for holding snuff

snuffle to breathe heavily and noisily through the nose (especially during a cold when the nose is blocked by mucus)

snuffles, sniffles a blocked-up condition of the nose

snug cosy and warm (of a comfortable bed, room, etc.)

snuggle to nestle, cuddle closely

so in this way or that way (as shown or described, as - Stir the milk in slowly - so.); therefore, or for this reason (as - It rained, so we came home.); to such an extent or degree (as - I cannot walk so fast. It is so heavy that I cannot lift it.); staying the same (as - It is cold and likely to remain so.)

soak to become or make wet through; to place in or drench with liquid; to saturate; to absorb or draw in liquid (as, a sponge soaks up water)

soap a substance made of oils, fats and an alkali, used in washing (Soap comes in solid form, and also in liquid, powder or flakes.) □ to rub with soap

soapy like soap; covered with, or containing, soap

soapsuds soapy water worked into a froth of bubbles

soar to fly high into the air (of birds, aircraft); to rise very steeply (as, prices, rents soar)

sob to weep noisily; to cry with deep jerky breaths; to make a sobbing sound (as, the wind in the trees)

sober not drunk; not too emotional or exaggerated (as, a sober account of an event); serious (as - His face wore a sober expression.)

sobriety the state of being sober

sociable enjoying the company of others; friendly; companionable

sociability, sociableness the state of being sociable; an inclination towards being sociable and friendly

social having to do with friendliness and companionship (as, a social club, a social evening at the pub, a social gathering or party at someone's house); having to do with society in any sense (especially arrangements and rules for the welfare and good of people in a community); having to do with divisions, groups or classes of people in society according to rank, position, etc.

socially in a friendly way, not connected with business, etc. (as - I don't know him well socially, although we've worked in the same office for years.)

socialism the belief that a country's wealth (land, industries, mines, etc.) should belong to the people as a whole, not to individual private owners, and that the state should control and decide how these resources should be used

socialist a believer in socialism

social insurance insurance against unemployment, sickness and old age (organized and paid for by employers and employees and the government)

social security the principle or plan of providing social insurance

social service welfare work

society companionship; the community or mankind as a whole; an association or group of people with a common interest (as, a debating society, a dramatic society); the fashionable part of a community (usually wealthy and often of high rank)

sociology the study of the ordinary everyday life of people as members of social groups (in contrast to psychology, which studies the individual person)

sociologist a person who studies sociology

sock a short stocking

socket a hollow place that something is fitted into (as, an electric light socket)

sod a layer of earth with grass growing on it; turf

soda a powdery or crystalline salt used in washing (clothes) or in manufacturing; a powdery white substance used in baking and in medicines

soda water a fizzy soft drink

sofa an upholstered couch with back and arms

soft not hard; easily pushed or pressed out of shape (as, a

cushion, a piece of dough); not loud; gentle and restful (as, soft music, soft colours); not strict or firm; kind and sympathetic (as, soft-hearted); (of drinks) not containing alcohol

soften *(say soffen)* to make or become soft or softer

softwood the soft wood obtained from coniferous trees (such as fir)

soggy soaked with water; damp and heavy

soil 1 the upper layer of earth in which trees and plants grow; loose earth

soil 2 dirt; something that makes a spot or stain □ to make dirty; to stain

sojourn to stay for a while □ a temporary stay (as, a weekend sojourn at the seaside)

solace something that makes pain or sorrow easier to bear □ to comfort or make up for

solar having to do with the sun; affected or influenced by the sun

solar system the sun and the planets (including the earth) which move round it

sold see sell

solder *(say solder or sodder)* an alloy of lead and tin used for soldering □ to join by, or as if by, soldering

soldering the act of joining certain metals by means of melted solder, which, when hard, unites two metals or pieces of metal

soldier a man in military service; a private (not an officer)

sole 1 the bottom or underside of a foot, shoe or boot □ to put a new sole on a shoe, boot, etc.

sole 2 a small flat fish valued for food

sole 3 only; single; alone without anyone else (as, the sole heir to a fortune)

solely only; singly; alone

sol-fa (music) a system of syllables to be sung to the notes of the scale

solemn done with special (often religious) ceremony (as - The queen's coronation was a solemn occasion.); serious or very earnest (as - The judge's face had a solemn expression.)
solemnity a solemn ceremony; great seriousness
solemnize to celebrate or perform (a wedding, etc.) with a religious or special ceremony

solicit to ask earnestly for (as, to solicit a favour)
solicitor someone who asks earnestly; a lawyer who gives legal advice to people and prepares documents for court cases, etc.
solicitous asking earnest or anxious questions
solicitude anxious concern about someone or something (as, showing solicitude about her neighbour's health)

solid hard and firm in shape; not hollow, liquid, or gaseous; strongly made; of a uniform, unmixed substance (as, solid gold) □ a substance that is solid; a figure that has length, breadth, and height
solidify to make or become solid (as - Water solidifies when it turns into ice.)
solidity the state of being solid

soliloquy *(say solilokwee)* talking to oneself; an actor's speech to himself
soliloquize to speak to oneself

solitary alone; by oneself; (of a place) lonely or remote
solitude the state of being alone

solo a musical piece for one singer or one instrument □ performed by one alone (as, flying solo)
soloist someone who plays or sings a solo

solstice *(say solstiss)* the time of longest daylight (summer solstice, about June 21st) or the time of longest darkness (the winter solstice, about December 21st)

solution a liquid with something dissolved in it (as, a saline solution): the answer to a problem or difficulty
solve to find the answer to (a problem, mystery, etc.)
solvent 1 anything that will dissolve, or make a solution with, a substance
soluble able to be dissolved in a liquid (as - Salt is soluble in water.): (of a problem, etc.) able to be solved

solvency the state of being solvent or able to pay all debts
solvent 2 able to pay all debts

sombre *(say somber)* dark; gloomy

sombrero *(say sombrairo)* a broad-brimmed hat (which shades the face from the sun)

some a few; several; a little (as, some cake) □ part of a larger number (as, some of the class)
somebody, someone some person; a person of importance
somehow in some way or other
something a thing not stated (as, something left behind)
sometime at a time not stated or known
sometimes at times; now and then
somewhat rather; a little
somewhere in some place

somersault a leap in which a person turns head over heels

somnolence sleepiness
somnolent drowsy

son a person's male child
son-in-law the husband of a person's daughter

sonata a piece of music (usually composed for one or two instruments)

song a poem or rhyming verse set to music to be sung by one or more persons: the musical notes of a bird
songster a singer; a singing bird

sonic having to do with sound waves; travelling at about the speed of sound

sonnet a poem of fourteen lines with rhymes arranged in a certain way

sonorous giving a deep loud sound (as, a sonorous bell)

soon in a short time from now: early
sooner more readily; rather

soot a black powder (mainly carbon) which is left in chimneys, etc. from burning coal, etc.
sooty covered with soot; like soot

soothe to calm or comfort; to ease (pain)
soothing calming; comforting

sop bread dipped in soup, etc. before being eaten: something given to keep a person quiet □ to soak
sopping soaking wet

sophisticated *(say sofisticated)* made wise by education and experience; no longer satisfied with simple and natural things; (of machinery and equipment) elaborate and up-to-date

soporific causing sleep □ something that causes sleep

soprano a female singer with a voice of the highest pitch; such a singing voice

sorcerer a wizard; a user of magic spells
sorcery witchcraft; magic

sordid dirty or filthy; mean or very poor

sore painful; irritated □ a painful wound, blister, etc.
sorely painfully; very greatly (as, sorely in need of help)

sorrow grief or pain of mind; sadness □ to feel sorrow
sorrowful full of sorrow; very sad

sorry sad because of something said or done, or of some happening; feeling sorrow (either much or little)

sort a kind of class (as - Toffees and fruit-gums are sweets of different sorts.) □ to separate any mixed things into similar lots or sorts (as, sorting letters at the post office according to their addresses)
sorter someone who sorts, especially letters
out of sorts not feeling very well

SOS *(say ess - o - ess)* a code signal calling for help (in Morse • • • - - - • • • •)

sought see **seek**

soul the spirit or non-physical, innermost part of a person (which is believed by many to survive after death); a person (as - She's a nice old soul.)
soulful full of feeling
soulless without animation or fine feeling; dull (as, a soulless task)

sound 1 anything that can be heard (such as talk, music, or any noise) □ to make a sound; to seem to be (as - That sounds like a tall story.)
sound barrier the much greater air resistance which an aeroplane meets at about the speed of sound (about 760 miles per hour at sea level)

sound 2 in good condition; healthy; showing good sense or reasoning (as, sound advice, sound thinking) □ completely (as, sound, or soundly, asleep)

sound 3 a strait or narrow passage of water connecting two seas, etc.

sound 4 to measure the depth of water; to try to find out (people's opinions, etc.)
sounding the measuring of depth (by using a weighted sounding-line)

soup a liquid food, made by boiling meat, vegetables, etc.

sour having an acid taste or smell (like that of lemons, vinegar, etc.); peevish or disagreeable

source the place where something has its beginning (especially a spring as the source of a river)

south the direction opposite to north (where the sun is seen at midday in Great Britain) □ southern (as, a south wind)
southerly, southern of, or

towards, the south

south-east, south-eastern the direction half-way between south and east

south-west, south-western the direction half-way between south and west

sou'wester a wind blowing from the south-west; a waterproof hat which covers the back of the neck

souvenir a keepsake; a memento of a place or event (as, a souvenir of Brighton or Blackpool, or of the Coronation)

sovereign *(say sovrin)* a king or queen; an English gold coin formerly worth one pound (£1) □ supreme or above all others (as, a sovereign remedy); self-governing (as, a sovereign state)

sovereignty highest power

soviet a council of government in Russia (the Union of Soviet Socialist Republics)

sow *(rhymes with no)* to scatter (seed) over, or plant it in, the ground; to spread (as, to sow trouble)

sow *(rhymes with now)* a female pig

soya bean a bean rich in protein and fat, grown mainly in the Far East (A sauce is made from these beans.)

spa a place where there is a mineral spring (as, Bath Spa)

space an empty or open place; a distance between objects; the immense region (where there is no air) between the earth, moon, sun and other heavenly bodies □ to set (things) apart from each other (as, to space out plants in a garden)

spacious with plenty of room; wide

space capsule a capsule-shaped spacecraft

spacecraft, spaceship a rocket-propelled enclosed vessel which can travel far into space

space heating central heating

spaceman a traveller in space

spade a tool with a broad blade

used for digging

spaghetti *(say spagetee)* an Italian food, rather like macaroni, made of wheat paste in very thin string-like pieces

span the distance between the tips of the thumb and little finger when a man's hand is stretched out (nearly 23 centimetres); the full extent (of a bridge, arch, etc.) from end to end; the full time anything lasts □ to stretch across (as, a bridge spanning a river)

spangle a small, thin sparkling ornament for a garment □ to sprinkle with spangles

spaniel a breed of dog with a smooth coat and large floppy ears

spank to strike with the flat of the hand; to smack □ a loud slap, especially on the buttocks

spanner a tool for tightening or loosening nuts

spar 1 a stout pole (especially a ship's mast, boom, etc.)

spar 2 to use the fists as in boxing (usually with a sparring partner)

spare to do without (as - Her mother cannot spare her daughter now as she is helping with the housework.); to afford (as - Can you spare 10 pence for ice cream? Can you spare the time to go with me?); to avoid or use little of (as, to spare no effort, or no expense); to treat with mercy □ extra; not being used at the time (as, a spare tyre)

sparing careful or economical in using something

spark a glowing hot particle (as, sparks from a bonfire); a small electric flash (as produced by a sparking plug in a car engine to explode a mixture of petrol and air); a trace (as a spark of courage, humour, etc.)

sparkle to shine in a glittering way; to effervesce with tiny glittering bubbles (as, champagne sparkles)

sparkler a small firework which gives off lots of sparks

sparrow a common small brown bird

sparse thinly scattered; scanty

spasm a sudden involuntary jerk of the muscles (such as a hiccup); any sudden convulsive movement
spasmodic coming jerkily or not regularly (as, spasmodic efforts)

spate a flood

spatter to splash (with mud, paint, etc.)

spatula *(say spachewla)* a broad blunt blade used for spreading

spawn the clustered eggs of fishes or frogs □ to produce spawn

speak to utter words or talk; to say aloud or tell (as, to speak the truth)
speaker someone who speaks; (with capital letter) the person who presides over meetings in the House of Commons
speech the act or power of speaking; spoken words; a formal talk
speechless unable to speak (because of surprise, rage, etc.)
spoke, spoken past tenses of the verb speak (as - He spoke yesterday. He has spoken already.)
spokesman someone who speaks for others
figure of speech an expression in which words are used in an unusual way, for the purpose of making a striking effect

spear a long weapon with an iron or steel point □ to pierce with a spear

special out of the ordinary, exceptional; meant for a certain purpose (as, a special constable, or special correspondent for a newspaper)
specialize to study, or work in, a single branch of knowledge or business
specialist someone who specializes (as, a heart specialist in medicine)
speciality, specialty a special activity, subject or product

species *(say speeshees)* a group of plants, or of animals, which are alike in certain ways; a kind or sort

specify to say or set down exactly what is wanted; to make particular mention of (as - The builder specified metal, not wooden, window-frames.)
specific giving all the details; definite (as, specific instructions)
specification the act of specifying; a statement containing all the details needed (to build a house, design a new car, ship, etc.)

specimen one example of something; a sample (to be examined or studied)

speck a small spot; a tiny grain (as, a speck of dust)
speckle a speck of colour different from its surroundings
speckled marked with speckles

spectacle an interesting or striking sight (such as a wonderful sunset)
spectacles glasses worn by a person to help his eyesight
spectacular making a great show; dramatic (as - The splashdown of the astronauts was spectacular.)
spectator someone who looks on

spectre a ghost
spectral ghostly

spectrum the band of colours seen in a rainbow or produced by the splitting up of white light when it passes through a glass prism
spectra the plural of spectrum
spectroscope an instrument for viewing the spectra formed by light rays of different wavelengths

speculate to make guesses (about); to buy and sell (shares, etc.) hoping to make a profit but risking a loss

speculative concerned with speculating (as, a speculative business)

speech, speechless see **speak**

speed quickness of moving; rate of motion (as, a speed of 50 miles per hour) □ to move or drive very fast
speedy quick or prompt (as, a speedy delivery)
speedometer an instrument that measures and shows the speed of a vehicle

spell 1 to give in order the letters that make up a word

spell 2 words which are supposed to act like a magic charm
spellbinding holding as by a spell; fascinating
spellbound held as by a spell; fascinated (as - The audience was spellbound by the speech.)

spell 3 a turn at any occupation (as, a spell of work, rest, play); a short time

spend to pay out money; to expend; to pass time (as - He spent a fortnight abroad last year.); to use up
spent the past tense of spend; exhausted (as - He felt spent.)
spendthrift somebody who spends money freely and carelessly

sphere *(say sfeer)* a globe or round ball (In a true sphere any point on the surface is the same distance from the centre.); a circle of society or particular area of activity or influence (as, in the sphere of education, in the sporting sphere, etc.)
spherical having the form of a sphere or round ball

spice a strong-smelling, sharp-tasting flavouring for food, usually powdered (such as pepper, nutmeg, cinnamon) □ to season with spice
spicy tasting or smelling of spices; piquant

spider a small creature, with a body in two sections and eight long thin legs, which spins a web to catch flies, etc.

spidery like a spider; sprawling and very thin (as, spidery handwriting)

spike a thin pointed object (as, spikes on the top of iron railings; a spike-shaped cluster of flowers): an ear of corn □ to pierce, or set with, spikes

spill 1 to let (a liquid, powder, etc.) run out or overflow; to shed (as, to spill blood) □ a fall or tumble

spill 2 a thin strip of wood or twisted paper for lighting a candle, pipe, etc.

spin to whirl round quickly; to make thread out of raw wool, cotton, etc. by drawing it out and twisting it □ a whirling motion; a short ride on a cycle or in a car (as, to go for a spin)
spinning-wheel a simple machine for spinning yarn, worked by hand or by a foot-treadle

spinach a vegetable whose dark green leaves are boiled for food

spindle a thin rod on which thread is twisted and wound in spinning
spindly long and thin, like a spindle

spine the backbone of a person or animal; a spine-like ridge; a thorn; a stiff, pointed part of some animals, fish, etc., growing out of the skin
spinal having to do with the spine (as, a spinal column)
spineless having no spine; weak or lacking in moral courage
spiny full of spines; thorny

spinney a small group of trees; a copse

spinster an unmarried woman

spiral winding round and round in a continuous curve (like the thread of a screw or a spiral staircase) □ a spiral line, movement or object

spire a tall structure on a roof which tapers to a point (especially a church spire)

spirit the soul; the vital principle

that guides a person's emotions and behaviour; liveliness; courage (as - The accused defended himself with spirit.): a ghost: (plural) mood (as, feeling low in spirits); a strong distilled alcoholic drink (especially whisky, gin or brandy) □ to carry off secretly as if by magic (as - She was spirited away.)

spirited lively; courageous

spiritless without liveliness or courage

spiritual having to do with the soul □ an American negro hymn with a strong rhythm

spiritualist someone who believes that the spirits of the dead can communicate with living people

spit 1 the liquid that forms in the mouth; saliva □ to throw spit out of the mouth; to rain slightly

spittle spit or saliva

spit 2 a narrow metal bar on which meat is roasted: a long narrow strip of land sticking out into the sea

spite a grudge; ill-will □ to vex; to annoy out of spite

spiteful showing spite

in spite of in defiance of; without taking notice of; notwithstanding (as, to start out on a picnic in spite of a cloudy sky)

splash to spatter (with water, mud, etc.); to fall or move with splashes (especially in water) □ a noisy disturbance of liquid (especially water); a wet or dirty mark made by splashing

splashdown the landing of a spacecraft on the sea

spleen a soft organ of the body near the stomach: ill-humour; bad temper

splendid brilliant; magnificent; very fine; excellent

splendour brilliance; magnificence

splice to join two ends of rope by twisting the strands together; to join together two pieces of wood by overlapping the ends □ a joint made by splicing

splint a strip of wood, etc. tied to

a broken arm or leg to hold it in position

splinter a small sharp piece of wood, glass, metal, etc. which has broken off □ to split into splinters

split to cut or break something from end to end; to break in pieces or into parts; to divide and separate (as - The crowd split up and went home.) □ a long crack or break

splitting cutting; very bad (as, a splitting headache)

spoil to damage or make useless; to become damaged or useless (as, spoiled fruit): to allow a child to have his own way too much and thus develop a selfish character: to take by force or plunder □ plunder from a captured ship, etc.

spoke 1, spoken, spokesman see **speak**

spoke 2 one of the rods or bars from the centre to the rim of a wheel

sponge the soft porous skeleton of a sea animal which is used for washing because it sucks up and holds so much water; a substitute for this made of foam rubber or plastic; a sponge cake or pudding □ to wipe with a sponge: to live on others by getting money, etc. from them (as - He sponges on his relatives.)

spongy like a sponge; soft and wet

sponsor someone who promises that another person will carry out some duty, etc.; a godfather or godmother □ to support or guarantee

spontaneous (say spontayneus) done or said readily and naturally, of one's own free will (as, spontaneous cheering when a popular singer appears)

spontaneity (say spontaneeity) naturalness of action

spook a ghost

spool a reel for thread, photographic film, etc.

spoon a small hollow utensil

(usually metal) with a handle for lifting liquid and soft foods to the mouth, etc. □ to lift with a spoon

sporadic happening here and there, or now and again

spore one of the tiny seed-like cells of ferns which separate and become new plants

sporran a pouch worn in front of a kilt

sport a game, games or pastime, usually out of doors (such as football, cricket, athletics, fishing, etc.); a sportsman □ to play or have fun
sporting having to do with sport (as, a sporting event); fond of sports
sportive playful; merry
sportsman, sportswoman someone who participates in a sporting activity; someone who believes in fair play and who is a good loser
sportsmanship a liking for fair play and good behaviour in sport

spot a small mark or stain (as, a spot of paint, grease, etc.); a pimple or small blemish on the skin; a place (as, a sheltered spot; the spot where we met) □ to mark with spots; to catch sight of
spotted, spotty marked with spots
spotless without a spot; very clean
spotlight a very bright light that is shone on an actor on the stage

spouse a person's husband or wife

spout a tube-like projection with an opening through which liquid is poured (as, the spout of a kettle, teapot, etc.); a jet or gush of liquid □ to throw out or gush; to talk a lot

sprain to twist or overstrain (a joint, such as the ankle or wrist so that it swells) □ the wrenching of a joint

sprat a sea-fish like a very small herring

sprawl to sit or lie with arms and legs stretched out carelessly

spray 1 a cloud of small flying drops of liquid (as, the spray from a waterfall, or from an aerosol); an instrument for sending it out (as, a scent spray) □ to squirt with a fine mist of liquid

spray 2 a spreading shoot or twig with small, slender branches or flowers

spread to cover a surface with (as, to spread jam); to scatter or distribute widely (as, to spread news); to open out (as, to spread one's arms, or a newspaper) □ the act or extent of spreading (as, the spread of an infectious disease); a cover for a bed; anything (like meat paste, etc.) for spreading on bread; a large meal laid out
spread-eagled with arms and legs spread out

spree a lively frolic

sprig a small shoot or twig

sprightly lively; vivacious

spring to jump or leap; to move or start up suddenly (as - He sprang to his feet.); to produce suddenly (as, to spring a surprise) □ a leap; a coil of wire which springs back into position when pressure on it is released (as, a watch spring); strong metal strips or coils for reducing shocks (as, car springs); a small stream which springs up out of the ground: the season of the year which follows winter, when the young plants begin to grow
springy spring-like or elastic
springboard a springy board from which swimmers jump off or dive
springbok a South African antelope
springtide a very high tide when there is a new or a full moon

sprinkle to scatter in small drops or bits
sprinkler something which sprinkles water (such as may be attached to a garden hose)

sprinkling a small quantity sprinkled; a small number

sprint to run a short race at full speed □ such a run (as, the 100 metres sprint)

sprite a fairy or elf

sprout to begin to grow □ a young shoot or bud; a kind of vegetable: see **brussels sprout**

spruce 1 neat; smart

spruce 2 a type of fir tree with hanging cones

spry lively; nimble

spur a sharp-pointed device worn on a rider's heel and used to urge on his horse; anything that urges a person on to do something □ to urge on
on the spur of the moment suddenly, without thinking beforehand

spurious not genuine; false

spurn to refuse with scorn

spurt to squirt out or spout in a sudden stream □ a sudden gush of liquid; a sudden effort

sputnik a man-made earth satellite

spy a secret agent employed to get information, especially military; someone who watches others secretly □ to act as a spy; to watch secretly; to catch sight of
spyglass a small telescope

squabble to have a noisy quarrel □ a noisy, usually petty, quarrel

squad a small group of soldiers or workmen

squadron a section of a fleet; a division of a regiment; a group of aeroplanes (each of these defence forces being under one commander)

squalid very dirty and uncared-for (as, a squalid dwelling)
squalor the state of being squalid (as, the squalor of the slums)

squall a strong and sudden gust of wind: a loud cry □ to cry out loudly

squander to spend (one's money, strength, etc.) wastefully

square a rectangle whose four sides are equal in length; a large open place in the middle of a town or city (as, Trafalgar Square in London, or Times Square in New York); (in arithmetic) the answer obtained when a number is multiplied by itself ($3 \times 3 = 9$ or 3^2, that is, the square of 3 or 3 squared) □ shaped like a square; fair or honest (as, a square deal); satisfying (as, a square meal) □ to make square; to settle what is owed (as, to square an account); to multiply a number by itself
squarely honestly or fairly
square metre, centimetre, etc. an area equal to a square in which each side is one metre, one centimetre, etc.
square root (of a number) the number which, when multiplied by itself, gives the number of which it is the square root (thus, 3 is the square root of 9 because $3 \times 3 = 9$; 4 is the square root of 16, etc.)

squash to crush or press out of shape; to put down (as, to squash a rebellion) □ a soft drink made from squashed fruit, sugar and water

squat to sit down on the heels; to settle on a piece of land without a legal right □ short and thick
squatter a person who occupies some land or property without authority; (in Australia) a landowner

squaw the wife of a North American Indian

squawk a harsh croaky cry □ to make such a cry (as, a hen that squawks when disturbed)

squeak a slight shrill sound (as, the squeak of a mouse) □ to make such a sound

squeal a loud shrill cry (as, the squeal of a pig) □ to give out such a cry

squeamish a little bit sick; easily sickened or shocked

squeeze to press hard; to grasp,

or press together, tightly (as, to squeeze hands); to force through by pressing (as, to squeeze through a crowd) □ the act of squeezing; pressure

squib a small firework

squid a sea creature with ten arms (especially one of the smaller types which are used for bait)

squint (of eyes) not looking straight; looking in slightly different directions; cross-eyed □ to partly close the eyes (because of a too-bright light, so as to focus clearly, etc.) □ the condition of being cross-eyed

squire (in mediaeval times) a youth who attended and served a knight in preparation for his own knighthood; (in later times) a country gentleman owning an estate; a male attendant or escort to a lady

squirm to wriggle or twist the body (in pain, embarrassment, etc.)

squirrel a small red or grey gnawing animal with a bushy tail (living mostly in trees)

squirt to shoot or force out a sudden rush of liquid

stab to pierce or cut with a pointed weapon, fork or other implement □ the act of stabbing; a sharp pain (physical or mental, as - Her unkind remark was like a stab in the heart.)

stable 1 a building where horses or cattle are fed and kept □ to keep in a stable

stable 2 firm; steady; not likely to change suddenly (as - He is a reliable person of stable character.)
stability steadiness; reliability
stabilize to make steady; to equip a ship, aeroplane, etc. with a device that keeps it steady

staccato (in music) with notes played or sung in a short sharp manner so that each one sounds clear and separate; (in speaking) in a jerky manner, not smooth and continuous

stack a large heap or pile of hay, wood, etc.; a chimney; a collection or group of things standing together (as, a stack of books) □ to pile into a stack

stadium *(say staydium)* an open-air sports ground with rows of seats all round

staff a pole; a stick carried in the hand (often an ornamental one, carried as a sign of authority); a group of people working together in an office, a hospital, a shop, etc.; (in music) the five lines and four spaces on which notes are printed or written (≣): see also **stave**

stag a male deer (especially the red deer)

stage a raised platform or scaffold; a platform in a theatre or hall where people perform a play, perform music, etc.; the theatrical profession (as - Her great ambition was to go on the stage.); the distance between two stops on a journey; a period or step in progress, development, etc. (as, a stage in one's career, life, etc.) □ to put (a play, etc.) on the stage; to organize; to carry out (as, to stage a protest)
stage coach a horse-drawn public coach that used to carry passengers and post from stage to stage
stage fright nervousness when appearing in front of an audience (especially for the first time)

stagger to walk unsteadily, lurching and stumbling; to surprise or shock (as - That news staggers me.)
staggering shocking; overpowering

stagnant (of water) not flowing or moving (often foul or impure); not lively and active; dull
stagnation the state of being stagnant
stagnate to be, or become, stagnant; to be inactive or dull

staid serious in manner

stain to mark or spot; to change

the colour of something (as, to stain woodwork dark brown); to mark or spot with disgrace, shame, etc. (as - That unfortunate event left a stain on his reputation.) □ a spot or mark; a dye or colouring matter; a cause of shame

stainless without stain; not easily soiled or rusted (as, stainless steel)

stained glass glass painted with colours fixed into its surface

stair one of a number of steps for going up or down to different levels; (in plural) the steps in a staircase or stairway

staircase, stairway a number of steps (usually with a rail or rails)

stake 1 a strong stick or post, pointed at one end; (in former times) a post to which witches (and others sentenced to be burned to death) were tied

stake 2 money put down as a bet; something at risk to be gained or lost □ to put down money as a bet; to risk (as - He staked his future on the success of his new invention.)

stalactite an icicle-shaped deposit *hanging down* from the roof or side of a cave (formed by dripping water containing lime)

stalagmite an icicle-shaped deposit *sticking up* from the floor or side of a cave (formed by dripping water containing lime)

stale not fresh; dry and tasteless because of being kept too long; (of news, a joke, etc.) no longer interesting because it has been repeated or performed too often; not able to do one's best because of over-training, etc.

stalemate (in chess) a position in which a player cannot make a move without losing the game; (in a contest) a position in which neither side can win; a draw

stalk 1 the stem of a plant or flower; something resembling a stalk

stalk 2 to walk with slow stiff steps; (in hunting) to creep quietly so as not to be heard

stall 1 a division or place for one animal in a stable, cowshed, etc.; a table, booth, or stand where goods for sale are displayed; a seat in church or in a theatre

stall 2 to avoid or delay coming to an immediate decision; to cause to stop (as, to stall a car engine) without meaning to do so; (of an aircraft) to lose flying speed for a time

stallion a male horse

stalwart strong and brave

stamen *(say staymen)* the central part of a flower that bears the pollen

stamina strength or power to endure (fatigue, disease, etc.)

stammer to repeat syllables or sounds several times before being able to say a whole word or phrase; to stutter

stamp to bring the foot down heavily; to strike (the floor, ground, etc.) forcibly with the sole of the foot; to fix a mark or design on something by pressing or imprinting (as, a post-mark on an envelope); to stick a postage stamp on an envelope, postcard, etc. □ the act of stamping; a small piece of coloured paper, sticky on one side, such as a postage stamp (see **post**), a trading stamp, a national insurance stamp, etc.; a machine or device for stamping

stampede a sudden wild running away of a large number of frightened animals (especially cattle or horses); a sudden rush of a number of people (as, a stampede towards the exits of a football ground)

stance a standing position in playing golf, cricket, etc.

stanch, staunch 1 to stop the flow of (especially blood)

stand to be in an upright position, not lying or sitting down; to get up on one's feet; to be on one's feet without walking (as - Stand still!); to be set or placed (as - The church stands on a hill.); to set upright or on end (as, to stand a trunk on end): to be a candidate in an election □ an act or place of standing; rows of raised seats for people watching sports; a piece of furniture for hanging things on or putting things in (as, a hat stand, an umbrella stand)

stood the past tense of stand (as - The soldiers stood to attention.)

standing upright or erect; not moving; remaining without change □ (of a person) rank, position, reputation (as, a man of good standing in a community)

standby a thing or person ready or available when needed

standing-room places for standing only (as - All the seats are taken, but there is standing-room for twenty people.)

standpoint a position from which a person sees a situation (as - From my standpoint, the plan is a bad one.); a point of view

standstill a complete stop

to stand fast to refuse to give in

to stand for to be a candidate for (as, to stand for Parliament); to be a symbol of or to represent (as - A red flag stands for danger.)

to stand out to be noticeable (as - He stands out in a crowd because he is unusually tall.); to continue to fight or stick out for or against something

to stand up for to stick up for or defend (as, to stand up for one's rights)

to stand up to to endure; to put up with (as, to stand up to pain, hardship); to face bravely (as, to stand up to a bully)

standard a flag, banner or symbolic figure on a pole (especially one carried by a military unit, etc.); a measure of lengths, weights, etc. used as a unit in describing other lengths, weights, etc.; a grade or level of excellence (as, a high standard of work, a low standard of living); an upright support (as, a lamp standard) □ accepted as a standard or model; of a usual or average size, type, etc.

standardize to make something standard or uniform in size, weight, quality, etc. (For example, many machine parts are standardized so that it is easy to replace one that is broken or worn.)

standard bearer a person who carries a standard or banner

stanza a group of lines forming a part or division of a poem

staple 1 a bent piece of wire, pointed at both ends and driven through sheets of paper to fasten them together; a similar piece of metal (usually U-shaped) used to hold wires in place, to hold a bolt, etc. □ to fasten by means of a staple

stapler a machine for fastening with staples

staple 2 a chief product grown or manufactured in an area, a country, etc. (as - Wheat is a staple of Canada. Cotton manufacture is a staple of Manchester.); a main or leading item (as - Bread is a staple of their diet.) □ principal or main (as, a staple crop, a staple industry)

star any of the bright heavenly bodies seen at night (especially those which appear to have a fixed position and which shine with their own light, as the sun does); a star-like object or figure with rays or points (usually five); (in astrology) a planet which is supposed to have some influence on one's life and luck: a person with outstanding ability or talent (as, a tennis star, a football star); the leading actor or actress, singer, etc. in a film, play, opera, etc. □ to take a leading part in a film, etc.

starry full of, or covered with, stars (as, starry skies); like, or shining like, stars

starfish a flat sea animal with five arms resembling the points of a star

starboard the right side of a ship when facing towards the front (the bow)

starch a white flour-like substance found in potatoes, maize, etc.; a preparation from this, used as a stiffener in laundering clothes □ to stiffen (clothes, linen) with starch
starchy stiff with, or containing, starch: stiff and formal in manner

stare to look at someone or something fixedly for some time without blinking or looking away

stark stiff; sheer or utter (as, stark nonsense); completely (as, stark naked); (of dress) simple and plain

starling a bird with glossy, dark greenish-purple feathers speckled with whitish spots

start 1 to begin; to set out on a journey, etc.; to set going (as, to start a clock, to start a car) □ a beginning; the act of starting or setting something going; the place where something begins or sets out; a beginning before others (as, to have a start of fifteen metres in a race before the others begin)

start 2 to move, jump or jerk suddenly (as, with surprise, fear, etc.) □ a sudden movement or jerk of the body (caused by surprise, fear, etc.)

startle to cause (a person, an animal) to start with surprise, alarm, etc.
startling surprising; frightening; upsetting or shocking (as, startling news)

starve to suffer or die from hunger; to cause someone to suffer or die of hunger
starvation the act of starving; the state of being starved

state 1 to tell, say, or set out in writing, formally and in detail
stated fixed; regular (as - The doctor's surgery is held at stated times each morning and

evening.)
statement something stated (especially for official purposes, for financial records, etc.)

state 2 condition (of a thing or person, as, a road in a bad state of repair, a person in an unhappy state of mind) □ ceremonial (as, the state opening of Parliament, a state banquet.)
stately dignified; noble; splendid (as, a stately mansion)

state 3 all the people of a country under one government; a territory or a division of a country joined with others under one government (as, the United States of America, the Union of Soviet Socialist Republics); the government (and its officials) □ having to do with the state or the government (as, offices of state, state ownership of land, etc.)
statesman a person occupied in government affairs (especially one who has proved to be wise and skilled)

stateroom a private cabin on a ship or in a railway carriage

station (say stayshun) a place where trains, buses, etc. stop regularly; a place which is a centre for work or duties of a particular kind (as, a fire station, a radio station, a police station); a situation, position or place (in life, in the scale of nature, etc.) □ to appoint or assign (a person to a particular post or place, as to be stationed at a naval base)
stationary not moving; fixed in a place or position

stationery writing paper, envelopes, pens, pencils and all other articles needed for writing, typing, etc.
stationer a person who sells such supplies

statistics information collected and set out in an orderly way in the form of figures (as, statistics of population, of production, of foreign trade, of road accidents, etc.); the methods of collecting such statistics, analysing them and their underlying causes

statue a figure (often life-size) of a person or animal, carved from wood or stone, or moulded of metal, wax, etc.
statuary statues collectively
statuesque *(say statew-esk)* like a statue in dignity, grace, etc.

stature the height of a person's body (as, a man of average stature)

status *(say staytus)* a person's rank, standing, position, etc. in society, an organization or any group; the state or condition of affairs (as, the financial status of a business)
status symbol a possession which serves as a symbol of a person's social status (such as a large house, car, etc.)

statute a written law of a country
statutory according to law (A statutory offence is one punishable by law.)

staunch 2 firm; steadfast; trustworthy (as, a staunch friend); (of a ship or boat) watertight; sound and sturdy: see **stanch**, **staunch 1**

stave a staff; a strong stick or rod; one of the long pieces of wood that form the sides of a barrel; (music) a staff; a verse or stanza of a poem, song, etc. ▢ (used with *off*) to keep away, or at a distance (as, to try to stave off a cold by taking hot fruit drinks, etc.)

stay 1 a rope used to support a ship's mast; a support; a prop ▢ to support; to secure with stays

stay 2 to remain, or continue to be, in a place for a period of time; to be still; to pause, or to stop (as - Stay where you are!); to remain in the same condition (as - This bread stays fresh for several days.) ▢ a temporary visit or sojourn (as, a brief stay in London)
staying power ability or strength to go on with something without giving up

stead *(say sted)* place (in former times); (nowadays) used as part of a word (such as instead, homestead) or phrase (as - Because I was not well, she offered to go in my stead. This warm sweater will stand you in good stead on cold days.)

steadfast steady; fixed; firm (as, a steadfast look, purpose, faith, etc.); reliable and trustworthy (as, a steadfast friend)

steady firm; not shifting or moving (from a position); not easily upset or nervous; not changing (opinions, employment, etc.); hardworking and reliable; regular (as, a steady pace, pulse, etc.) ▢ to make, or become, steady

steak a thick slice of meat (especially beef) or fish

steal to take something belonging to someone else (especially secretly); to take or get something secretly (as, to steal a look, to steal a nap); to move or go about quietly (so as not to be noticed)
stole 1 the past tense of steal (as - The thief stole a wallet.)
stealth *(say stelth)* a secret movement or action
stealthy acting in a secret or sly manner; done secretly and quietly

steam the cloud-like gas or vapour into which water changes when it boils; power or heat produced by using steam pressure; power or energy (as, to let off steam by running about in the playground) ▢ to **send out** steam; to cook by steam; to become misted (up, over) by steam (as - The windows are all steamed up.)
steamy full of, covered with, steam
steamer, steamboat, steamship a ship or boat driven by steam power
steam engine an engine that works by steam under pressure
steamroller a steam-driven engine with very wide and heavy

wheels (rollers) used to crush and flatten materials used in making and repairing roads

steed a horse (especially one for riding)

steel a very strong metal made from iron hardened by the addition of a little carbon; a cutting tool, weapon, etc. made from steel □ made of or like steel (as, steel wool) □ to harden or strengthen one's courage (as, to steel oneself to endure pain)
steely hard and cold (as, a steely look); resembling steel in hardness, colour, etc.

steep 1 rising nearly straight up, not sloping gradually (as, a steep hill, steep stairs, etc.); too great or too much (as, a steep price)

steep 2 to wet thoroughly; to soak; to saturate

steeple a high (usually) pointed tower on a church; a spire
steeplejack a person who climbs steeples, tall chimneys, etc., to make repairs

steeplechase a race (on foot or horseback) across country, over obstacles such as walls, hedges, ditches, etc.

steer 1 a young male ox raised for beef

steer 2 to guide or control a vehicle's direction by means of a wheel, rudder, etc.
steerage the act of steering: the part of a ship occupied by passengers who pay the lowest fares
steering, steering gear the mechanism or apparatus used in steering a vehicle
steering wheel the wheel which is turned in steering a vehicle
steersman the person who steers a ship or boat
to steer clear of to avoid; to keep out of the way of

stellar having to do with the stars

stem the slender upright part of a plant that grows up from the root; any part of a plant which supports leaves, flowers or fruit;

anything resembling a stem or stalk (as, the stem of a wineglass); the curved prow of a ship □ to grow out of or develop from (as - The plans for a club stemmed from an overheard remark.); to make progress against or in spite of (a strong tide, firm opposition, etc.)
stemmed the past tense of stem (as - The ship stemmed the tide.) □ having a stem

stench a very strong bad smell; a stink

stencil a design or pattern cut out of metal, cardboard, etc.; the design or pattern which is produced by rubbing ink, paint, etc. over the cut-out parts; a thin piece of special material from which many copies of typewriting, etc. can be made □ to cut a stencil

stenography the ability or skill of writing in shorthand
stenographer a shorthand writer

stentorian (of a voice) very loud or powerful

step one movement of the leg in walking, running or dancing; the distance covered by such a movement; a footprint; a manner of walking (as - He has a firm step.); the sound made by a step; a resting place for the foot (as, a step on a ladder, staircase, etc.); □ to take a step (forward, backward, etc.); to walk
stepping stone a stone rising above water, mud, etc., on which one can step in crossing a stream, etc.
stepladder a ladder with steps instead of rungs, and a support to keep it upright
in step (in walking, marching, etc.) putting forward the same foot at the same time as another person or persons
out of step not in step
to step out to walk more quickly
to step up to increase (production); to come forward
to keep step to march in step

(especially to music)

to take steps to take action (as - I shall take steps to prevent such a thing from happening again.)

step- a prefix used as part of a word to show a relationship resulting from re-marriage of a parent, not a blood relationship - for example:
stepfather the husband of one's mother (but not one's own father)
stepsister a daughter of a stepfather or stepmother (by a former marriage)

steppe a great expanse of grassy, almost treeless, plain (in eastern Europe and Asia)

stereophonic giving the effect of music or other sounds coming from more than one direction

stereoscope an instrument with two eye-pieces through which two slightly different pictures blend into one which appears solid or three-dimensional

sterile not producing or not able to produce offspring, flowers, fruit, etc.; the opposite of fertile; barren; without germs (as, a sterile bandage)
sterility the state of being sterile
sterilize to make sterile; to kill germs (as, to sterilize surgical instruments, milk bottles, etc.)
sterilizer an apparatus for sterilizing

sterling British money of standard value (as, a sum of money payable in sterling) □ (of silver) of standard quality (Articles made of sterling silver have a hallmark stamped on them.); (of a person) of good trustworthy character

stern 1 the back part of a ship or boat

stern 2 (of manner, look or voice) angry; displeased; harsh; strict

stethoscope an instrument used by a doctor to listen to a patient's heartbeat, breathing, etc.

stevedore a person who loads and unloads ships' cargo

stew to boil or simmer food (especially meat and vegetables) slowly in liquid □ a dish of food so cooked

steward, stewardess a person who manages someone else's household, estate or property; a person who helps to make arrangements at a race meeting, a dance, etc.; one who is in charge of provisions and serving of meals on a ship, etc.; an attendant on a passenger ship, aeroplane, etc.

stick 1 a small branch or twig; a long thin piece of wood (especially for firewood); a wooden rod, club, staff, etc.; anything resembling a stick in shape (as, a stick of gum, a stick of sealing wax)

stick 2 to pierce or stab with something sharp; to thrust into, up, etc. (as, to stick a pin into a balloon, to stick a hand up); to fix or fasten by means of something pointed or adhesive (as, to stick something with a drawing pin, to stick a stamp); to be caught or fixed (as - This window sticks and can't be opened.); to hold fast or keep close to (as, to stick to one's friends)
stuck the past tense of stick (as - They stuck to the job and finished it at last.)
sticky gluey; adhesive; (of problems, situations, etc.) difficult; (of weather or climate) hot and humid

stickleback a small river-fish with prickles or spines on its back

stiff firm; hard; not easily bent or moved (as, stiff fingers, a stiff lock); thick or not flowing (as, stiff paste); (of manner) very formal, not easy and natural; strong (as, a stiff test, a stiff dose of medicine)
stiffen to make, or become, stiff

stifle *(say stiefl)* to kill by cutting off air supply; to smother; to suppress or hold back (a cry, a yawn); to feel great discomfort or die through lack of air

stifling very close and stuffy

stigma a mark of disgrace or reproach (on one's character or reputation): (in a flower) the knobby top of the pistil which receives the pollen

stile a step or set of steps for climbing over a wall or fence

stiletto a dagger with a narrow blade

still 1 an apparatus for distilling liquids (especially alcoholic, such as whisky)

still 2 without movement; quiet; at rest; calm □ to make or become silent, calm □ nevertheless (as - Although I warned them, they still went out.); continuing until now (as - She still had beautiful auburn hair in spite of her age.); even (as - You will do still better if you work hard at it.)

stillborn born dead (as, a still-born lamb)

stilt one of a pair of tall poles with foot-rests, which a person can stand on and walk above the ground

stilted stiff and formal (in manner, speech, etc.)

stimulant something (such as a drink of brandy) that makes the heart and brain more active; some event or piece of news that makes one feel more active and cheerful

stimulate to act as a stimulant; to rouse to action or effort (as - The offer of a bonus stimulated him to work harder.)

stimulus an incentive; something that stirs one to action or greater efforts

sting a sharp or pointed part of some animals, insects and plants which can prick and cause pain (Some stings are severe and poisonous.); the act of piercing with a sting; the wound or swelling caused by a sting □ to wound or give pain by means of a sting; to feel hurt or pain from, or as from, a sting

stingy *(say stinjy)* mean in spending or giving; the opposite of generous

stink to give out a strong offensive smell □ a stench

stint to limit; to share out a limited amount of something (especially in a stingy way) □ a fixed amount of work that has to be done

stir to move (even slightly); to shake up or mix; to arouse feelings (as, to stir up anger, to stir pity) □ a disturbance; a fuss or state of excitement (as - The news caused a stir.)

stirring lively; exciting (as, stirring music)

stirrup one of a pair of metal loops or rings hanging from a saddle to support the feet when riding a horse

stitch 1 a loop made by thread drawn through material by a needle; a loop made by knitting or crochet □ to sew with stitches

stitch 2 a sharp sudden pain in one's side

in stitches helpless and almost in pain with laughter

stoat a weasel with a black-tipped tail (In winter, when its coat turns white it is called ermine.)

stock a stump, log or block of wood; the trunk or main stem of a tree; the handle or support of a rifle, whip, etc.: the family or ancestors from whom a person is descended (as - He comes from good sturdy stock.): the cattle, horses, etc. kept on a farm or ranch: a supply of goods (especially stock kept in a shop or store): money invested in a business or lent to the government: (in cooking) liquid in which meat, bones and (sometimes) vegetables are boiled as a basis for soup: a shrubby garden plant with small fragrant flowers: (in plural) a wooden frame with holes in which the ankles and (sometimes) wrists of wrong-doers were held as a punishment (in former times): the framework on which a ship is supported while it is being built □to keep a supply of; to supply (a farm, a ranch) with animals

stocky short and rather stout

stockbroker a person who buys and sells stocks and shares for others

stock exchange, stock market a place where stocks and shares are bought and sold

stockstill completely still; motionless

stockade a fence of strong posts fixed in the ground, used as a barrier against attack

stocking a close-fitting knitted or woven covering for the foot and leg

stodge heavy and dull food

stodgy (of food) heavy and indigestible; (of people, writing) dull and uninteresting

stoic *(say stoe-ik)* a person who shows no outward signs of feeling either pain or pleasure

stoical showing no emotion

stoicism indifference to both pleasure and pain

stoke to put fuel on a fire

stoker a person who, or machine which, feeds fuel into a furnace

stole 2 a long narrow piece of material, often made of silk or fur, worn over the shoulders and hanging down: see also **steal**

stolid (of someone's manner or personality)' dull; unimaginative; unemotional

stomach the strong muscular pouch in the body into which food passes after it is swallowed, and where most of it is digested; the belly or abdomen; wish or appetite (as - He had no stomach for the task.) □to put up with or endure (as - He cannot stomach the sight of blood.)

stone a small piece of rock; a shaped piece of stone for a special purpose (as, a milestone, a tombstone); a jewel or gem

(precious stone); the hard seed or kernel in some fruits (cherries, peaches, etc.); a unit of weight (1 stone = 14 pounds or 6·35 kilogrammes.) □made of or like stone □to throw stones at; to take stones out of (fruit)

stony made of, or like, stone; covered with stones (as, a stony beach); hard and unkind (as, a stony expression)

stonily in a hard cold manner (as - He stared at her stonily.)

Stone Age the earliest period in mankind's history, when tools and weapons were made of stone (before the use of metal)

stone-blind, -cold, -dead, -deaf completely blind, cold, dead, deaf

stood see **stand**

stool a seat without back or arms

stoop to bend forward and downward; to lower oneself by doing something mean, beneath one's dignity, etc. (as - He would not stoop to cheating.) □a bending forward of the body

stop to cease some action or leave off doing something; to prevent (as, to stop a car from entering a road); to put an end to something (as, to stop complaining); to cease moving, going forward, etc.; to stuff up and so close a hole or opening □the act of stopping (as, to come to a stop); a halt or pause; a stopping place (as, a bus stop); a punctuation mark; a full stop (.)

stopper something (like a cork or plug) used to close a hole or opening (such as the neck of a bottle)

stopgap a substitute that temporarily fills a need or takes the place of something lacking or missing (especially in an emergency, as to use a piece of sticking plaster as a stopgap to mend a broken spectacle frame)

stop press a space in a newspaper left free for news that has come in at the last minute

stopwatch a watch with a hand or hands that can be started and stopped instantly by pressing a small knob (used especially by time-keepers in athletic and sporting events)

store a shop (particularly one with many departments); a storehouse; a large quantity or supply; (in plural) supplies of food, ammunition, etc. □ to put (goods, supplies) away until needed; to supply or stock up (as, to store a cupboard with food)
storage the act of storing; the state of being stored (as, to keep furniture in storage); the price charged for storing
storehouse, storeroom a building, room or other place where things are stored
in store waiting or intended (for someone, as - There was a great surprise in store for her.)

storey, story 1 a set of rooms occupying all of one floor or level of a building
storeys, stories the plural of storey, story (as, a building ten storeys high)

stork a large wading bird with very long legs and a long bill and neck

storm a sudden outburst of bad weather, with heavy rain, snow or hail, wind and sometimes thunder and lightning; a violent outbreak (of anger, tears, applause, etc.) □ to blow, rain, snow, etc; to rage or show anger; to make an attack (as, to storm a fortress)
stormy having many storms; blowing, raining, etc. (as, stormy weather, stormy seas); violent and noisy (as, a stormy meeting)

story 2 an account of an event or series of events (whether true or imaginary); a tale; a brief anecdote; a joke told in the form of a short story; a falsehood: see also **storey, story 1**

stout strong and tough (as, stout canvas material); brave and sturdy (as, stout fellows); thick or fat and solid (as, a person of stout build) □ a strong kind of beer

stove an apparatus which gives heat for cooking or for warming a room

stow *(say stoe)* to pack or store away in a suitable place (as, to stow things neatly under a berth, to stow cargo in a ship's hold)
stowaway someone who hides himself on a ship, aeroplane, etc. to avoid paying the fare

straddle to stand or walk with the legs straight and wide apart; to stand or sit with the legs on either side of something (a chair, a horse)

straggle to stray from the main line or course (of a march, etc.); to wander off or lag behind others in a group; (of a plant or shrub) to spread or trail untidily
straggler a person who straggles (especially one left behind); a straggly plant

straight *(say strait)* not bent or curved; direct; (of a person) honest and fair; not wandering from the point; level (as - That picture is hanging crookedly - put it straight.); in order, not confused (as, to keep money accounts straight) □ at once (as, straight away)
straighten to put, or make, straight; to tidy or put in order
straightforward direct; uncomplicated; honest and frank

strain 1 to stretch or pull as tightly as possible; to put all one's strength, ability, etc. into doing something; to exert or use to the fullest (as, to strain eyes, ears, every nerve); to injure or damage (through over-exercise, overwork, too great an effort, etc.): to separate solid from liquid by using a sieve □ a great effort; an injury caused by straining (especially muscles); the state of being strained (by overwork, worry, etc.)
strained showing strain; not easy and natural (as, a strained smile, expression); pushed or

stretched to breaking point (as, strained relations between two people, two countries)

strainer something used to strain (as, a sieve or colander)

strain 2 the race, stock or family from which a person is descended (of animals or plants); a quality or streak in a person's character (as, a strain of pessimism); general style or manner (as - He always spoke in the same cheerful strain.): a musical air or melody

strait (often in plural) a narrow strip of sea between two pieces of land (connecting two seas or two lakes): (usually in plural) difficulties; need (as, to be in dire straits)

strait-jacket a jacket with very long sleeves which can be tied behind the back so that the wearer cannot move his arms

strand 1 the shore of a sea or lake □ to run aground on the shore (as, a ship that has been stranded); to place or be placed in a helpless, difficult situation (as, to be stranded without money in a strange city)

strand 2 one of the threads that make up rope, yarn, etc.

strange unusual; not known or familiar; from another country, district, etc.; odd or queer (as, strange behaviour)

stranger someone not known to a person; a foreigner or outsider (as, a stranger in a country not his own)

strangle to kill by squeezing the throat and so stopping the breath; to choke; to smother or suppress (a cry, a sob)

strangulate to compress or constrict (a vein, a part of the intestine, etc.) so as to stop proper circulation or functioning)

strangulation the act of strangling, of being strangled or strangulated

strap a narrow strip of leather, cloth, etc. (usually with a buckle) used for fastening, hold-

ing or binding □ to bind or fasten with a strap; to beat with a strap

strata see **stratum**

stratagem a careful plan or trick, designed to outwit an enemy

strategy the art of planning and carrying out a military or naval campaign; the art of carrying out a plan (as, the strategy used in a political campaign)

strategic *(say strateejik)* having to do with strategy; important or necessary to the successful completion of a plan or stratagem

stratosphere see **stratum**

stratum a layer; a bed of rock or earth made up of layers

strata the plural of stratum

stratify to form or deposit in layers (as, stratified rocks)

stratosphere an upper region or layer of the atmosphere, some miles above the earth's surface

straw the stalk on which grain grows; a number of such stalks (after threshing and drying) used for animal bedding, etc., and for making straw hats and other articles; a straw-like tube used for drinking; something of no value (as - His opinion is not worth a straw.)

strawberry a small juicy red fruit with many seeds, that grows on a low plant

stray to wander away (from the right road or way, from companions, from control) □ an animal that has strayed or become lost □ gone astray (as, a stray dog); single or isolated (as, a stray bullet)

streak *(say streek)* a line, mark or stripe, different in colour from the surrounding background (as, streaks of red in the evening sky); a flash (as, a streak of lightning); a trace or element of character (as, a streak of humour); a thin layer (as, streaks of fat in meat or bacon) □ to mark with streaks

streaked, streaky marked with,

or having, streaks

stream a small river, brook, etc.; a flow of air, water, light, etc.; anything flowing continuously (as, a stream of cars, a stream of words) □ to flow or pour (as - The tears streamed down her cheeks.); to stretch or float out in a line (as - Her long hair streamed in the wind.)

streamer a long narrow ribbon or pennant (that streams in the wind)

streamlined (of a car, boat, aeroplane, etc.) shaped so as to go through air or water easily, with as little air resistance as possible

street a paved road (broader than a lane) with houses, etc. on one or both sides

strength the power or ability to do something (especially something requiring physical or muscular strength); the quality of being strong; toughness (as - Be sure to get a rope of sufficient strength.); the number of men in an armed force (as - The strength of the peacetime army is limited.)

strengthen to make strong or stronger: see also **strong**

strenuous requiring much effort or strength; energetic; vigorous (as, a strenuous protest)

stress force or pressure (of one thing upon another); strain (especially mental or emotional, from worry, overwork, etc.); the accent or emphasis on a syllable in pronouncing a word (In *em*phasis the stress is on *em*.) □ to put emphasis on (as - He stressed the importance of arriving on time.)

stretch to reach out; to extend (as - The forest stretches for many miles.); to draw or pull out to the greatest width or length (as, to stretch out a piece of elastic) □ the act of stretching; the extent to which something can be stretched; a continuous period of time; a straight or unbroken area or space (as, a stretch of country)

stretcher a folding frame for carrying people who are unable to walk because they are sick or wounded

stretcher-bearer a person who helps to carry a stretcher

at a stretch continuously, without stopping (as, to work for several hours at a stretch)

strew to sprinkle or scatter (seeds, straw) loosely

stricken injured; wounded; struck or afflicted by illness, old age, etc.

strict severe; stern; insisting on complete obedience, etc., with no exceptions

stride to walk with long steps □ a long step

strode the past tense of stride (as - He strode along briskly.)

strident (of a voice, musical instrument, etc.) sounding harsh, loud and unpleasant

strife fighting; quarrelling or arguing angrily; conflict

strike to hit or give a blow forcibly; to run into or collide with (as when a ship strikes a rock); to produce fire or a light (as, to strike a match); to find or come across suddenly (as, to strike oil); to make a sound (as, to strike a note on a piano, [of a clock] to strike the hour): to stop work because of workers' complaints (about wages, working conditions, etc.) against the employers; to occur to suddenly (as - It has just struck me that you might be interested in our idea.) □ a stopping of work because the workers have decided to strike; a lucky find or discovery (as, an oil strike)

striking noticeable; attention-getting; remarkable

struck the past tense of strike (as - The clock struck twelve.)

string a thick thread or a cord, used for tying up parcels, etc.; a cord on which things are threaded (such as a string of beads, a string of onions); anything resembling such a string (as, a string of cars, a string of lights); a cord or wire on a musical instrument (as, a piano string, violin string); (in plural) the stringed instruments in an orchestra □ to thread on a string; to take the string from (as, to string beans)

stringed having strings (as, a stringed instrument)

stringy like string; full of strings or tough fibres (as, stringy meat)

strip a long narrow piece of anything □ to tear or pull off in strips; to take the leaves, skin, fruit, etc. from trees or plants; to remove all one's clothes; to remove or take away (furnishings from a room, valuables from a person, etc.)

stripe a line or band (usually long and narrow) different from its background in colour, design, etc. (as, a flag with red stripes on a white background); a chevron or strip of braid worn on a uniform sleeve (showing rank, etc.); a blow with a whip or rod; the bruise or mark from such a blow □ to make stripes on

strive to try hard to do or achieve something (as, to strive for success); to fight or struggle against: see also **strife**

strode see **stride**

stroke 1 to rub gently (as, to stroke a cat)

stroke 2 an act of striking; a blow; one movement of anything (as, a stroke of a pen, a stroke in swimming, tennis, etc.); an unexpected happening (as, a stroke of good luck); a sudden, severe kind of illness which causes loss of movement or paralysis □ to row the stroke oar in a boat

stroke oar the oar nearest the stern in a rowing boat, or its rower (who sets the pace for the others)

stroll (*say* stroal) to walk in a leisurely way; to wander or roam about

strong powerful; firm and sturdy; able to resist attacks; healthy and robust; not weak or mild (as, strong tea, cheese): see also **strength**

strong drink drinks containing alcohol (especially spirits)

stronghold a fortress or other place armed against attack

strong language forceful, emphatic language; swearing

strongroom, strongbox a strongly made room or container for valuables

struck see **strike**

structure a building (especially a large one); the way the parts of anything are built up or arranged; something built or constructed (as, a bridge, a dam)

structural having to do with structure or the way a thing is constructed

struggle to make a great effort (to do or achieve something); to fight (for freedom, against an enemy, etc.); to twist and turn to get free (as - The wrestler struggled to get out of a hold.); to get on with difficulty (as, to struggle against a storm) □ a great effort; a fight

strum to play on an instrument in an unskilful way

strut 1 to walk about in a pompous, vain, self-important manner; to swagger

strut 2 a bar or rod used to resist pressure in the direction of its length

stub a short end of a pencil, cigarette, etc. (left over from a larger piece); a tree stump □ to strike (the foot, the toe) against something hard

stubby short, thick and blunt

stubble the stubs or short ends of stalks left in the ground after grain has been cut; a short bristly growth of beard

stubborn obstinate; unwilling to give way to others; determined (as, a stubborn resistance to changes of any kind)

stucco a plaster of lime and sand used to cover outer walls of houses, etc.

stuck see **stick**

stud a nail with a large head; a double-headed button used for fastening a collar ☐ to fasten studs in; to sprinkle over (as - The Aegean Sea is studded with islands.)

student see **study**

studio the workshop of an artist or photographer; a building or place where films are made; a room from which radio or television programmes are broadcast

study to learn about a subject by giving time and attention to it; to examine closely; to consider (as, to study a guest's needs) ☐ the giving of time and attention in order to gain knowledge; a room used for study; a piece of music, painting, etc., which is partly experimental
student someone who studies
studious earnest and hardworking in one's studies; fond of study

stuff the material of which anything is made; cloth (especially woollen); possessions (as - That's *my* stuff.) ☐ to pack tightly
stuffing material used to stuff; a mixture of breadcrumbs, seasoning, etc., used to stuff a chicken, turkey, etc.
stuffy (of a room) close or badly ventilated

stumble to trip or take a false step; to find by chance (as - They stumbled on a hidden cave.) ☐ a false step

stump the part of anything which is left after the main part has been cut or worn away (as, the stump of a tree, pencil, etc.); (in cricket) one of the three sticks forming a wicket ☐ (in cricket) to knock down a wicket while the batsman is outside his crease: to puzzle completely: to walk along heavily
stumpy short and thick

stun to knock senseless; to amaze or surprise greatly

stunt a daring feat; something done to attract attention

stunted dwarf-like; not fully grown (as, a stunted tree)

stupefy (say stewpify) to make stupid or deaden the feelings (as, stupefied with strong drink, grief, etc.); to make speechless with surprise
stupefaction amazement; astonishment
stupendous amazing; wonderful (usually because of size or importance, as a stupendous achievement)

stupid foolish; dull in understanding or learning
stupidity stupidness; a stupid act

sturdy strong; healthy; firm

sturgeon a large fish from which caviare is obtained

stutter to utter words in a jerky, hesitating way; to stammer ☐ a stammer
stutterer someone who stutters

sty 1 a pigsty or pen for pigs

sty 2, stye a small, inflamed swelling on the eyelid

style the manner in which a person writes or expresses his ideas; a way of doing something (as, a style of dancing, playing a game, etc.); a fashion
stylish fashionable; smart

suave (say swahv) (of a person or his manner) polite or agreeable in a smooth way
suavity a suave manner

sub- a prefix generally meaning under or below or lesser (as, **subdivision, subeditor, subnormal, subsoil, subway**)

subdivide to divide into smaller parts or divisions

subdue to overcome; to make obedient

subject (say subject) something which is being talked or written about (as, the subject set for an essay); a branch of learning (as, the subjects of history, geography, biology, etc.): any citizen under a ruler: (in grammar) the

words in a sentence which are
responsible for the action expressed in it, and which therefore generally come before the
verb (as - *The boys* kicked the
ball. *They* ran away.) □ under
the power of; liable to suffer
from (as, subject to colds); depending upon (as, subject to certain conditions) □ *(say subject)*
to bring under the power of; to
cause to suffer from (as, to subject a prisoner to solitary confinement)

subjugate to conquer; to bring
under one's power

sublime noble; grand (as, sublime thoughts)

submarine a ship which can
travel under water □ found
under the sea

submerge to plunge or sink
under water
submergence, submersion the
act, or state, of submerging

submit to give in; to yield; to put
something before a person for
his opinion or acceptance
submission a surrender: something submitted (as, a plan, a
document)
submissive willing to submit;
yielding easily

subordinate lower in rank or
importance □ someone who is
subordinate to another person

subscribe to give money or help
for some purpose (as, to subscribe to a charity); to agree to
something written by signing
one's name underneath; to agree
to buy a magazine, newspaper,
etc. regularly
subscription money given for
some purpose (such as a charity,
or for the regular delivery of a
magazine, newspaper, etc.)

subsequent following; coming
after

subservient slavish; too willing to
do something for someone

subside to settle down or get less
and less (as - The flood subsided. The storm subsided.)
subsidence a falling down or

collapse (as, the subsidence of
the roof of a mine)

subsidy money paid by a government to help an industry or
service because such aid is in
the interests of the general public (for example, subsidies paid
to farmers to keep food prices
down)
subsidiary of less importance
(as, a subsidiary branch of a
business)
subsidize to provide money in
the form of a subsidy

subsist to have existence; to keep
oneself alive (as - The prisoner
subsisted on bread and water for
several weeks.)
subsistence the state of existing; means of keeping alive

subsoil the layer of earth just
beneath the surface

subsonic relating to any speed
less than the speed of sound

substance anything that can be
seen and felt; the real meaning
of something (as - The substance of his long speech could
be summarized in a few minutes.); wealth (as, a man of substance)
substantial solid; strong; fairly
big or important (as, a substantial sum of money)
substantially in total effect;
essentially (as - His evidence
was substantially correct.)
substantiate to support a statement with evidence; to confirm
or prove

substitute to put in place of another person or object (as, to
substitute one player for another) □ some person or thing
used instead of another
substitution the act of substi-
tuting

subterfuge a trick or scheme to
get out of a difficulty

subterranean under the ground;
hidden

subtitle an additional or explanatory title to a book or film

subtle *(say suttl)* faint; elusive;
difficult to describe (as, a subtle

perfume, a subtle difference)

subtlety *(say suttʼlty)* subtleness; a subtle trick

subtract to take away from another number or quantity so as to find the difference

subtraction the operation of subtracting (for example, 18−12 = 6)

suburb a residential area adjoining a large town

suburban having to do with suburbs (as, a suburban bus route)

subversive tending to overthrow (a government, etc.)

subversion overthrow or destruction

subway an underground way (for pedestrians, traffic, etc.); an underground railway

succeed to manage to do what one has set out to do; to get on well: to follow or to take the place of (as - He succeeded his father as head of the family business.)

success a favourable result after trying to do something; a person or thing that turns out well (as - The outing was a success.)

successful turning out well or as planned; having succeeded (as, a successful candidate in an election)

succession a following after, or coming into another's place; a number (of persons or things) following each other in time or place (as, a succession of visitors, a succession of losses at betting)

successive following in order

successor someone who follows and takes another's place

succinct *(say sucksingkt)* brief; in few words

succulent *(say suckewlent)* juicy

succumb *(say suckum)* to yield; to die

such of this or that kind (as, such people, such a country); so good, so great, etc. (as, such a fine day, of such importance)

suck to draw into the mouth (as,

to suck milk); to hold in the mouth and lick without chewing (as, to suck a sweet) □ a sucking movement

sucker someone who sucks; a pad (of rubber, etc.) which sticks to a surface by suction; a side shoot rising from a plant's root

suckle to give milk to a baby (as, a cow suckling a new-born calf)

suction the act of drawing in something by sucking (as, the suction of a vacuum cleaner)

sudden happening all at once, generally unexpectedly (as, a sudden attack); abrupt (as, a sudden turning)

suddenly all at once; without warning

suds froth or foam on soapy water

sue to start a law case against

suede *(say swayd)* a soft leather with a dull surface, used for making some shoes, jackets, etc.

suet a hard fat obtained from cattle, sheep, etc.

suffer to feel pain; to bear; to undergo (as, to suffer a change, a loss, etc.)

suffering pain; trouble

suffice to be enough, or good enough

sufficient enough; adequate

suffix a small part added at the end of a basic word (as, -ness in good*ness*, -ly in sudden*ly*, -ful in resent*ful*)

suffocate to choke by stopping the breath; to stifle for want of fresh air

suffocation the act of suffocating

suffrage a vote, or the right to vote, in an election

suffuse to spread over or cover (as - Her cheeks were suffused with a warm glow.)

sugar a sweet substance (generally white) obtained mostly from sugar cane and sugar beet

sugary like sugar; sweet

sugar beet a large white, carrot-shaped plant grown in temperate countries

sugar cane a very tall grass-like plant grown in hot countries

suggest to propose or put forward (as, to suggest an idea, a plan, etc.); to hint

suggestion a proposal or an idea put forward

suggestive giving a hint of something (as, a curved nose suggestive of an eagle's beak)

suicide the taking of one's own life; someone who kills himself on purpose

suicidal having to do with suicide; certain to result in personal disaster (as - His attempt to rob a bank was suicidal.)

suit a set of clothes (such as a coat and trousers) intended to be worn together; an action in a law court; a set of one kind of playing cards (as, of spades or diamonds) □ to fit or look well on (as - The hairstyle suits her.); to be pleasing or agreeable (as - The warm climate suited him.); to be convenient (as - The dentist fixed a time to suit me.)

suitable fitting a purpose; convenient

suitcase a medium-sized travelling case for carrying clothes, etc.

suitor a man who is courting a woman

suite *(say sweet)* a number of things making up a set (as, a suite of furniture, of rooms, of music); a number of attendants who accompany an important person

sulk to keep silent because one is displeased or angry

sulky sullen; silent and resentful or angry

sullen gloomy-looking; silent and angry

sully to soil or dirty

sulphur a yellow, non-metallic element, used in making matches, gunpowder, sulphuric acid, etc.

sulphuric acid a strong acid with many industrial uses

sultan the name for a ruler in some eastern countries

sultana the mother, wife, or daughter of a sultan: a kind of raisin

sultry (of the weather) very hot and close

sum the total when two or more things are added together; a problem in arithmetic □ to add together

summarize to make a summary of; to state briefly

summary a shortened story, statement, etc. giving only the main points □ short or quick (as, a summary trial)

summer the warmest season of the year (in northern regions, June, July and August)

summit the highest point (of a hill, mountain, etc.)

summit conference a meeting between the heads of governments

summon to call upon someone to appear (especially in a court of law)

summons a summoning or order (especially to appear in court) □ to serve (someone) with a summons

sumptuous costly; splendid (as, sumptuous furnishings)

sun the heavenly body which shines by day, giving light and heat to the earth and other planets which move in their separate orbits around it

sunny full of sunshine; cheerful

sunbeam a ray of sunlight

sunburn a browning, or reddening of the skin caused by the sun's rays

sunburned, sunburnt browned or tanned by the sun

sundial an instrument on which a shadow cast by the sun indicates the time of day

sunflower a large yellow flower with petals spread out like rays of the sun

sunlight the light of the sun

sunrise the rising of the sun in

the east; the time of this

sunset the setting of the sun in the west; the time of this

sunshine bright sunlight; brightness

sunstroke an illness caused by too much exposure to the heat of the sun

sundae an ice cream served with fruit, syrup, nuts, etc.

sunder to cut apart; to separate

sundry several; various
sundries odds and ends

sunk, sunken see **sink**

sup to eat supper; to eat small amounts from a spoon

super- a prefix meaning above or beyond, in addition or in excess (as, **superabundant, superhuman, supernatural, supertax**)

superb very fine; magnificent

supercilious haughty; looking down on others

superficial of, or near, the surface; not deep or sincere (as, a superficial wound, superficial feelings); not real or thorough (as - The car test was only superficial.)

superfluous *(say superfluous)* beyond what is necessary or enough; unnecessary

superintend to be in charge of, to control or manage
superintendent a person in charge of a building, institution, etc.; a police officer ranking above an inspector

superior higher in rank; better or greater (as, of superior quality, of superior strength) □ a person in a superior position

superlative superior to all others; of the highest quality; (in grammar) an adjective or adverb which expresses the highest degree of a quality, etc. (as, highest, heaviest, best, ugliest, most beautiful, farthest)

supermarket a large, mainly self-service store selling food and other goods

supersede to take the place of (as - Steam trains have been mostly superseded by electric ones.)

supersonic faster than the speed of sound

superstition a misguided belief in magic and supernatural things; a belief or fear which has no real foundation (for example, that it is bad luck to walk under a ladder)
superstitious believing in superstitions

superstructure a structure on the top of something else

supervise to superintend; to see that work is done properly
supervision the act of supervising; inspection
supervisor someone who supervises; an overseer

supper an evening meal

supplant to overthrow and take the place of

supple bending easily (like an acrobat's body); pliable or springy

supplement something added to make up for something lacking (as, a supplement to a prisoner's diet); an extra part added to a newspaper or magazine (as, a colour supplement) □ to make, or to be, an addition to
supplementary additional

supply to provide what is wanted or lacking □ the act of supplying; what is supplied (as - Printers need a regular supply of paper.); the amount of something available (as - Coal is in short supply, or in ample supply.); (in plural) a stock of necessary goods

support to hold up, or bear the weight of, something or somebody; to help or take the side of (as, to support a football team); to provide someone with his or her food, clothing, etc. (as - She supports her disabled sister.) □ the act of supporting; someone or something that supports
supporter someone who supports (especially a football club, etc.)

suppose to imagine or pretend (as - Let us suppose we win a prize.); to be inclined to believe or think (as - I suppose we should return home before dark.)
supposition something that is supposed, or taken to be, true

suppress to crush or put down (a rebellion, etc.); to keep back (some news, a yawn, etc.)
suppression concealment; the act of suppressing

supreme (say supreem) highest; greatest (as, a supreme ruler, a supreme effort)
supremacy (say supremacy) the state of being supreme; the highest authority or power (as, the supremacy of Parliament)

surcharge an additional charge or tax

sure certain; firm or strong; trustworthy or dependable (as, a sure friend, a sure method); without doubt (as - Are you quite sure?)
surely without question or doubt
sure-footed unlikely to slip or stumble

surf the foam made by waves rushing up a beach

surface the outside part of anything (as, the surface of a table, of the earth, of the sea, etc.)

surfeit (say surfit) too much of anything (as, a surfeit of food)

surge a rising or swelling movement (as, the surge of a large wave); a sudden rise or increase (as - She felt a surge of emotion.) □ to make a surge (as - The crowd surged forward.)

surgeon a doctor who treats certain injuries and diseases by means of an operation on the damaged part of the body
surgery a doctor's or dentist's consulting room; the treatment of injuries or diseases by operation
surgical having to do with surgery

surly gruff in manner; rude

surliness gruffness or rudeness of manner

surmise to guess or suppose □ a guessing or supposing

surmount to overcome (an obstacle, difficulty, etc.); to mount above or be on the top of (as, a hill surmounted by a castle)

surname a person's last name, or family name

surpass to go beyond; to be better than

surplice (say surplis) a loose white garment worn in some churches by clergymen and choristers

surplus what is left over after using what is needed; the amount by which income exceeds expenditure

surprise something unexpected □ to cause a feeling of wonder or mild astonishment; to come upon someone without warning □ sudden and unexpected (as, a surprise attack or visit)

surrender to give up or yield; to hand over

surreptitious (say surreptishus) done in a secret stealthy way

surround to go, or to be, all around (as - The army surrounded the town. The sea surrounds Great Britain.)
surroundings the kind of country, conditions, etc. that surround a person or place

surtax an additional tax

surveillance (say survaylance) a close watch; a constant guard

survey (say survay) to look over (especially with care, as to survey a new house); to measure out a piece of land □ (say survay) a detailed examination (as, a national survey of housing conditions); a written report giving the results of such a survey; a detailed map: see also **ordnance survey**
surveyor a person who makes surveys of land, property, etc.

survive to remain alive (as - The shipwrecked men survived.); to live longer than (as - He survived his younger brother.)

survival the state of surviving; anything that remains from earlier times

survivor someone who remains alive

susceptible *(say susseptible)* liable to be affected by (as, susceptible to colds)

suspect *(say suspect)* to have doubts about or distrust; to believe, without being certain, that a person is guilty □ *(say suspect)* a person thought to be guilty

suspicion a feeling of doubt

suspicious suspecting; having a feeling of doubt; causing suspicion (as, a suspicious movement)

suspend to hang up; to stop for a time (as, to suspend play in a football match); to postpone (as, to postpone judgment)

suspender one of a pair of straps to support socks

suspense a time of anxious waiting (for news, etc.)

suspension bridge a bridge, without supports from underneath, which is held up by steel cables stretching between towers on either side

suspicion, suspicious see **suspect**

sustain to hold or keep up; to support; to give strength to (as - A good breakfast sustains one for the morning's work.); to suffer or undergo (as, to sustain an injury, defeat)

sustained (of a musical note, an effort, etc.) continuing without a break

sustenance food or nourishment for the body (or for the mind, such as good literature)

swab a small piece of cotton wool, gauze, etc. (usually on a stick), used to apply medicine to a sore, a wound, etc.; a mop for cleaning ship's decks, etc. □ to use a swab

swaddle to wrap a person (especially a baby) tightly in clothes

swaddling clothes strips of cloth (formerly) used to bind tightly round a new-born baby

swagger to walk proudly, swinging the arms and body; to strut; to boast or brag loudly □ a conceited or insolent manner

swallow 1 to take food or drink into the stomach through the mouth and throat; to accept or believe (as, to swallow an insult, to swallow a tall story); to keep back or suppress (a sob, an angry reply); to take in and cover anything completely (as - The boat was swallowed up in the fog.)

swallow 2 an insect-eating small bird with long pointed wings and a forked tail (Swallows are notable for their graceful flight and for the great distance they cover in migration.)

swamp wet, marshy, low-lying ground, usually with grass and trees but unfit for cultivation □ to fill (a boat) with water; to overwhelm (with too much work, too much opposition, etc.)

swan a large, graceful water bird with a very long curving neck

swap see **swop**

swarm 1 a large number of insects (especially honey bees) or animals moving together; a great number of people together; a crowd

swarm 2 (with *up* or *over*) to climb (a wall, a tree, etc.) by clinging on with arms and legs and pulling oneself up

swarthy dark-skinned

swath *(say swoth)* a strip of grass or grain cut by a scythe; a row or strip

swathe *(say swayth)* to bind or wrap around with bandages, cloth, etc.

sway to swing or move back and forth, to and fro (as - Trees sway in the wind.); to cause to bend or be bent to one side; to influence or be influenced (as - The audience was swayed by his powerful arguments.) □ rule or government; control over (as - The Romans held sway in Britain for more than 300 years.)

swear *(say swair)* to make a solemn promise (to tell the truth) before God; to use profane language; to curse; to bind someone (to secrecy, etc.) by making him take a solemn oath
swore the past tense of swear (as - They swore to be loyal.)
sworn bound by oath (as, sworn evidence); keeping to one's opinion or attitude as if bound by oath to do so (as - The two families had been sworn enemies for years.)
to swear by to put complete trust in (a person, a remedy, etc.)

sweat *(say swet)* the drops of moisture given out by the pores of the skin (when one is hot, nervous, etc.); perspiration □ to give out sweat; to work or labour very hard
sweaty wet or stained with sweat
sweater (originally) a thick jersey worn by athletes, etc.; (nowadays) also a knitted pullover or jumper

swede a large yellow turnip

sweep to clean a floor or other surface by using a brush or broom; to remove or gather up dirt by means of a brush or broom; to move or carry (along, off, away, etc.) with a brushing or sweeping movement (as, to sweep things off a table); to travel or move quickly (as - Fire swept through the hotel. She swept out of the room.) □ a sweeping movement; a chimney sweep
swept the past tense of sweep
sweepstake(s) the gamble on a race, in which a number of people pay for a ticket, and the money goes to the holder(s) of the winning ticket(s); the race itself

sweet tasting like, or of, sugar; not sour, salty or bitter; pleasant to the taste, smell, hearing, etc. (as, sweet perfume, sweet music); (of a person's nature, expression) kind, gentle, pleasant (as, a sweet smile) □ a small piece of sugary food (as, toffee, chocolate); a sweet pudding or dessert served at the end of a meal
sweeten to make sweet (as by adding sugar)
sweetheart a person who loves and is loved in return
sweetmeat a food made mostly of sugar
sweet pea a climbing garden plant with very fragrant flowers of many colours

swell to grow or make larger or louder; (of the sea) to rise in large waves; to increase the number or size of □ a series of long, unbroken waves rolling in the same direction; an increase in size
swelling a lump or swollen part of the body (as, a swelling caused by toothache)
swollen *(say swoelen)* swelled (as, swollen feet); enlarged by swelling

swelter to be faint or limp from great heat; to suffer from intense heat
sweltering very hot

swept see sweep

swerve to turn aside quickly (from a direct course, or a course of action) □ the act of swerving

swift 1 fast-moving; quick; rapid

swift 2 a fast-flying bird resembling a swallow (but not related)

swig a large mouthful of a drink □ to take a deep drink or draught of liquid

swill to drink greedily (usually a great quantity); to rinse or wash out with water □ liquid food for pigs

swim to move along in, or through the surface of, water, using arms and legs, fins, tail, etc.; to cross by swimming (as, to swim a river, a lake, etc.); to be dizzy (as - All this traffic makes my head swim.); to be covered by a liquid (as, meat swimming in gravy) □ the act of swimming (as, to go for a swim)

swimmingly smoothly and easily; successfully (as, to get on swimmingly)

swindle to cheat someone (usually to get money or property) □ a fraud; a dishonest trick (to get money)

swindler a cheat; a rogue

swine a pig

swineherd a person who looks after pigs

swing to move in the air, back and forth, up and down, etc. (as, a pendulum, a gate or door); to move something in a curve or circle (as, to swing a bat, a golf club); to sway (as, branches in the wind, an anchored ship with the tide); to move on a swing; to march or walk with quick swaying movements (as, with arms swinging) □ the act of swinging; a hanging seat, suspended by ropes or chains; the sweep or curving movement of a golf club, bat, etc.

swung the past tense of swing (as - The hammock swung gently in the breeze.)

swipe to strike hard and sweepingly □ a wild and sweeping blow

swirl to move about or sweep along with a whirling, twisting motion

swish a whistling, hissing or rustling sound (as, the swish of a rod or a whip cutting through the air; the swish of silk, taffeta, etc.) □ to strike through the air with a switch, whip, etc.; to rustle

switch a slender, flexible twig, cane or whip; a small lever or handle which turns an electric current on or off; a device used to change trains from one set of rails to another; a change (of opinion, attitude, etc. as, to switch from one point of view to another) □ to strike with a switch; to change over (as, to switch horses, a job); to turn (one's attention to another subject); to turn off, on (as, to switch off a light)

switchback a railway or road with steep ups and downs

switchboard an apparatus made up of a large board or panel with switches for controlling or connecting electric currents, telephones, etc.

swivel a joint with one end mounted on a firm base, enabling whatever is fixed on the other end to move freely (as, a swivel chair, a gun)

swollen see swell

swoon to faint □ a faint

swoop to sweep or come down on with a rush (as, a hawk swoops on its prey) □ a sudden downward rush or attack

swop to exchange something for something else (without paying money)

sword (*say* sord) a weapon with a long pointed blade, sharp on one or both edges

sword dance a dance performed over swords crossed on the ground, or with swords in hands

swordfish a large edible fish, having a very long pointed upper jaw like a sword

swordsman a person skilled in the use of a sword; a fencer

swore, sworn see swear

sycamore (*say* sickamore) a name given to several kinds of large tree (The maple, plane, and some fig trees are called sycamores.)

syllable a sound that makes a word or part of a word (For example, the words *boy* and *girl* each have one syllable, but the words *women* and *children* each have two syllables.)

syllabus a programme or list of a course of talks, lectures, etc.

sylph (in mythology) a spirit of the air; a slender graceful young girl

symbol an object which stands for something else (as - The cross is a symbol of Christianity. The dove is a symbol of peace.); a sign or figure which is a short way of indicating or showing something (as, + is the symbol for addition, ÷ for division, etc.)

symbolic, symbolical having to do with symbols; used as, or standing for, a sign of some principle, organization, etc.

symbolize to be a symbol or sign of

symmetry equality in measurement, shape, position of parts on either side of a dividing line (as, the symmetry of a house with a door in the middle and the same number of windows of the same size on either side)

symmetrical having symmetry; not lop-sided or unequal in appearance

sympathy a feeling of pity and sorrow for someone else in difficulties; a feeling of agreement in outlook, opinions, etc. with another person or group of people (as - I am in sympathy with his point of view.); ability to understand the feelings and opinions of others (even when not agreeing with them)

sympathetic feeling sympathy; favourably inclined towards (as, to be sympathetic towards a plan)

sympathize to feel or show sympathy

symphony a long piece of music for an orchestra (usually divided into three or four parts or movements with different themes, rhythms, etc.)

symphonic having to do with, or like, a symphony

symptom a sign or indication of illness (as, a high fever, a rash); a sign or indication of a state of unrest, rebellion, etc.

symptomatic indicating or pointing to symptoms

synagogue a Jewish place of worship; an assembly of Jews gathered together to worship

synchronize (say _sinkronize_) to take place or to happen at the same time (as - They synchronized their plans so as to meet at exactly three o'clock.); to coincide (as, to synchronize the sound track of a film with the lip movements of the speaker); to make (clocks, watches) agree in time

syncopate (in music) to change the beat so that the emphasis comes on a beat normally not accented

syncopation the alteration of musical rhythm by syncopating

syndicate a council or group of people joined together to manage a large business, group of newspapers, or other important business undertaking; an agency that supplies articles, photographs, etc. to a number of different newspapers (for publication at the same time)

synonym (say _sinonim_) a word having the same (or nearly the same) meaning as another word (as, _ass_ and _donkey_, _courage_ and _bravery_, _small_ and _little_, etc.)

synonymous (say _sinonimous_) having the same meaning as; equivalent (as - His name is synonymous with honesty.)

synopsis a short summary or outline of the plot of a book, a play, etc.

synthetic man-made; artificial; not grown or formed naturally (as synthetic rubber, not real rubber)

syringe a tube with a piston or rubber bulb for drawing liquid in and squirting it out again; a similar device with a needle, used to inject medicine

syrup a thick, sticky liquid made of water, fruit juice and sugar boiled together; treacle, molasses, etc. made pure for table use

system an arrangement of many parts or things which work together for a purpose, or which combine together so as to produce a result (as, a railway system, a tax system, an education system); certain parts of the body working as a whole (as, the digestive system, the nervous system); an orderly way of working or doing something (as

- He does his work more quickly because he has a system.)
systematic having or using a system in work or procedure; thorough and methodical in one's work

t

tab a small tag, flap or loop attached to clothing, a wallet, etc., used for fastening, pulling or hanging up

tabby a striped or brindled cat (especially a female)

tabernacle (in ancient times) a tent used as a place of worship by the Jews during their wanderings in the wilderness; (nowadays) a building used as a place of worship

table a piece of furniture with a flat top on legs (used for meals, writing, playing games, etc.); food on a table (as, to sit down to table): a set of figures or facts arranged in columns (as, a multiplication table, a timetable)
tablecloth a cloth for covering a table (especially for meals)
tableland a level expanse of high land; a plateau
tablespoon a large spoon used at table for serving, and for measuring ingredients in cooking
table tennis an indoor game similar to tennis, played with small bats and light balls on a large table

tablet a small flat cake or piece of something (as, a tablet of soap, aspirin tablets, etc.); a small flat surface on which to write, paint, draw, etc.; a slab of stone, etc. on which a design, inscription, etc. can be carved; a pad of writing or drawing paper

tabulate to arrange information in the form of tables or columns

tacit *(say tassit)* understood, agreed, without saying so aloud (as, to give tacit permission to

do something); silent
taciturn not talkative; silent

tack a short nail with a broad flat head: a zig-zag course taken by a boat or ship when sailing against the wind □ to change sailing direction

tackle the equipment or gear needed for work, games, etc. (especially fishing tackle, such as lines, rods, hooks, etc.); the ropes, rigging, etc. of a ship; ropes and pulleys for hoisting heavy objects □ (in football) to seize a player carrying the ball in an attempt to bring him down, or to obstruct him so as to gain possession of the ball; to make a great effort to carry out a job, solve a problem, etc.

tact the ability to get on with or to deal with other people without upsetting them or hurting their feelings
tactful having the quality of tact (as, a tactful remark)
tactless lacking in tact; likely to say things to upset or offend people

tactics the art or science of manoeuvring troops, warships, etc. to advantage in battle; a way of planning or acting in order to gain advantage or success
tactical having to do with tactics or planning (as, a tactical move)

tadpole a frog in its early form, before its legs develop

taffeta a stiff shiny silk cloth used for dresses, etc.

tag a label; a metal or plastic point on the end of shoe laces, etc.: a children's game in which one person chases and tries to touch another □ to attach oneself to another person or to follow on closely (as, to tag along)

tail the part of an animal, aeroplane, etc. that extends at the rear; anything resembling a tail (as, the tail of a kite, tail of a coat, etc.); the end of (as, the tail of a queue); (in plural, on a coin) the opposite side to heads
tailcoat a coat that is short in the front, with long narrow tails at the back, worn as part of formal full evening dress for men
tail spin (of an aeroplane) a steep downwards spin
tail wind a wind from behind (increasing the speed of an aeroplane, etc.)

tailor a person who makes outer clothing (such as, suits, overcoats, trousers and skirts) □ to make (and fit) outer clothing

taint to spoil; to contaminate; to go bad or become rotten □ a trace of decay or infection; a stain or blemish (on one's character, reputation, etc.)

take to lay hold of; to seize or capture; to grasp; to receive or accept (food, a gift); to use, eat, subscribe to, etc., regularly (as, to take a bus, to take sugar, to take a morning newspaper); to remove or subtract (as, to take 4 from 6); to require (as - This recipe takes four eggs. This job will take a long time.)
took the past tense of take (as - He took the dog for a walk.)
taking pleasing; attractive (as, a taking manner) □ (in plural) the total money taken at a concert, charity performance, etc.
to take after to resemble or be like in appearance, manner, etc. (as - He takes after his father.)
to take in to understand (an explanation, a lecture, etc.): to make smaller (as, to take in a dress because one has got thinner): to deceive or cheat
to take off to remove (hat, coat, etc.); (of aircraft) to leave the surface of land or water

to take part to share or participate (in)
to take place to occur; to happen
to take to to depart for (as, to take to the hills) for safety, refuge, etc.; to be attracted to (a person, a hobby)
to take up to begin to learn something (as, to take up golf)

talc a very soft white powder used in making face powders, talcum powder, etc.
talcum powder a fine powder (used for dusting the body after bathing)

tale a story; an untrue story; a lie

talent a special, natural gift or skill (as, a talent for music, for drawing, etc.); (in ancient times) a measure of weight or the value of this weight in gold or silver

talisman a charm (such as an engraved ring or stone) supposed to have magic powers for the wearer

talk (say tawk) to speak; to utter words; to gossip □ conversation; a speech or lecture; gossip
talkative chatty; fond of talking; the opposite of taciturn
a talking to a scolding

tall high (as, a tall tree, tall building); hard to believe, exaggerated (as, a tall story)
a tall order a difficult or almost impossible task, instruction, etc.

tallow the hard fat of some animals, melted down to make soap, candles, etc.

tally (in former times) a stick with notches cut in it to keep accounts or a score; (nowadays) an account; a label or tag □ to count or reckon up; to agree with or match (as - His account tallies with ours.)

talon the claw of a bird of prey (such as an eagle, a hawk)

tambourine a small one-sided drum with small metal discs around the edge, played with the hand, or shaken to give a tinkling sound

tame not wild; used to living with human beings; uninteresting or dull - not exciting □to make tame

tamper to meddle or interfere with something

tan to make an animal's skin into leather by treating it with tannin; to make (the skin) brown by exposure to the sun; to become tanned □the colour of skin browned by the sun; a yellowish brown or light brown colour
tanned yellowish-brown or light brown (because of exposure to the sun)
tanner a person whose work is tanning hides
tannery a place where hides are made into leather
tannin a substance obtained from plants and tree-bark, used in tanning, dyeing, etc. (One form of tannin is found in tea.)

tandem one behind another (as, horses driven in tandem, a tandem bicycle with two seats)

tang a strong taste, flavour or smell (as, a tang of onion, of sea air)

tangent a straight line that touches a curve but does not cut through it

tangerine a small sweet orange (flat at each end, with a loose skin)

tangible able to be touched; real and solid (as, a tangible object)

tangle to twist, mix, or knot together (as, threads, hair, etc.) □a knot, snarl or confused mass (of wool, hair, problems)

tango a dance, originally from Argentina; music for this dance

tank a large container for holding liquids or gas; a heavy armoured vehicle moving on caterpillar wheels and armed with guns
tanker a ship that carries oil or other liquids in bulk

tankard a large drinking cup or mug (often of metal, with a lid)

tannin see tan

tantalize to tease or torment by displaying or offering something desirable, but keeping it just out of reach

tantrum an outburst of bad temper

tap 1 to strike or knock on something gently □a light knock or blow (as - He tapped on the window pane to get her attention.)

tap 2 a device (usually with a handle or valve) for controlling the flow of liquid or gas □to draw off liquid by opening a tap; to draw on supplies, etc. (as, to tap the resources of a rich part of a country); to attach a receiver to a telephone wire secretly, so as to hear private conversations

tape a narrow strip of strong cloth, sticky paper, plastic, etc. used for tying or binding, for measuring, for recording sound, etc.; a string stretched across the finishing line of a race (The winner breaks through the tape.)
tape measure a length of tape marked off in inches, centimetres, etc. for measuring
tape recorder a machine that records and plays back sounds on magnetic tape

taper a long thin wax candle or light □to grow smaller and smaller towards one end (as, a cone tapers to a point); to grow less and less strong (as when a bad cold gradually tapers off)

tapestry a hand-made decorative covering for walls, chairs, etc., made by weaving a picture or design into the material; a machine-made copy of tapestry

tapioca a white starchy food obtained from the root of a tropical plant, used in puddings

tar a dark, sticky thick substance obtained from wood, coal, etc. □to smear with tar
tarry 1 of or like tar; covered with tar

tarantula a large hairy poisonous spider

tardy late; slow
    tardiness lateness; unpunctuality

target a mark, point or object to be aimed at in shooting, archery, darts, etc.; a person or thing that is made fun of (as - He was the target of their ridicule.)

tariff a list of charges or prices; a list of taxes on goods being imported into a country

tarmac(adam) a kind of road surface made of small broken stones and tar

tarnish to make or become dull or discoloured (especially silver or silver-coloured metal)

tarpaulin a strong waterproofed cloth

tarry 1 see **tar**

tarry 2 to linger or loiter; to be slow or late

tart a piece of pastry containing jam or fruit

tartan a woollen material with a check pattern in different colours and designs, worn originally in the Scottish Highlands (each clan having its own tartan with a unique pattern); any one of the patterns

task a set amount or special piece of work to be done; any work or duty (especially if difficult)
    taskmaster a person who sets a task (and usually sees that it is done)

tassel a tuft of threads or strings tied together at the top and hanging loosely, used as an ornament on clothing, lampshades, etc.; anything like a tassel (as catkins)

taste to try or test the flavour or quality of something by taking a small quantity into the mouth (as, to taste food to see if it is properly seasoned or sweetened, pleasant or unpleasant, etc.); to try by eating or drinking a little; to have a flavour (as - This tastes of garlic, strawberries lemons, etc.); to recognize a kind of flavour or taste (as - She complained that the milk tasted sour.); to experience or enjoy (as, to taste the rewards of success) □ a small bit or piece of food; the sense used in tasting; a flavour; a liking for (as, taste for music); the ability to appreciate or discern what is excellent, beautiful, appropriate, etc. (as, good taste in clothes, design, furnishings, etc.)
    tasteful showing good taste (in choice of clothes, colours, etc.)
    tasteless without flavour; insipid: in poor taste (as - Her remark was unkind and tasteless.)
    taster a person whose profession is to taste and judge the taste of tea, wine, etc.
    tasty appetizing; good to eat

tatters ragged or torn pieces (of clothing, etc.)
    tattered ragged and torn

tattle to tell tales or to gossip about (other people); gossip; idle chatter

tattoo 1 a signal sounded on a bugle and drum to call armed forces to their quarters (especially at night); a parade or marching display with music (usually at night)

tattoo 2 to prick or mark a pattern on a person's skin by inserting colour with a special needle □ a mark or design made in this way
    tattooed marked with a tattoo

taunt to tease unkindly; to jeer at □ an unkind, jeering remark

taut tightly drawn; stretched to the fullest extent (as, a taut rope); (of nerves) tense; strained

tavern a public house; an inn

tawny yellowish-brown (A lion is tawny.)

tax a charge made by the government on incomes, certain products, etc. to provide money for running the state, maintaining the armed forces, public services, etc.: a strain or burden (as - The extra work is a tax on her strength.) □ to require a tax to be paid; to put a strain on (as - Such behaviour taxes a person's patience.)

taxation the act of taxing; the money collected from taxes

tax-free not taxed

taxpayer a person who pays taxes

taxi, taxicab a car (and driver) which can be hired to carry passengers □ (taxi) to go by taxi; (of an aircraft) to run along the ground under its own power

taxidermy the art of preparing and stuffing the skins of animals so that they look lifelike

taxidermist a person who does this work

tea a drink made by pouring boiling water on to the dried leaves of the tea plant; a shrub grown in Asia, cultivated for its leaves from which a drink is made; any beverage resembling tea in appearance or made in the same way (as, beef tea, herbal tea, etc.); an afternoon meal at which tea is served

tea caddy see **caddy**

tea chest a large square container of light wood lined with metal foil in which tea is packed and shipped

tea cosy a cover of thick or padded material put over a teapot to keep the contents hot

teacup a medium-sized cup in which tea is served

teapot a special pot with a lid and spout, used for making tea

teaspoon a small spoon used to stir tea; a measure (teaspoonful) used in cooking, measuring doses of medicine, etc.

teach to show or explain to someone how to do something; to give knowledge or skill to another (as, to teach French, music, etc.): to be a teacher

taught *(say tawt)* the past tense of teach (as - He taught modern languages.)

teacher a person who helps others to learn

teaching the work or profession of a teacher; something that is taught; (in plural) beliefs; rules of conduct; instructions

teak a hardwood tree found in India and Africa, used in making furniture, ships, etc.

team a group of people working or playing together; two or more animals working together (as, a team of horses, oxen, etc.)

teamster a driver of a team or (nowadays) a lorry or truck

teamwork working together as a unit or team; co-operation

teapot see **tea**

tear 1 *(say teer)* a drop of liquid that comes from the eye when one weeps; (in plural) weeping as a result of grief, pain, etc.

tearful weepy; with tears (as, a tearful request)

tear 2 *(say tair)* to pull apart, down, away, with force; to rip; to make a cut in (as, to tear the skin); to pain or hurt the feelings (as, to tear the heart in sorrow, sympathy, etc.) □ a split, cut, etc. made by tearing

tore the past tense of tear (as - He tore my shirt.)

torn having a tear in (as, a torn shirt)

tease to annoy a person by making fun, by joking remarks, by asking the same thing over and over, etc.: to comb or sort out a tangle (of wool, hair, etc.) □ a person who teases

teaser a tricky question or problem

teasel a plant with large prickly flower heads

teaspoon see **tea**

teat the part of the mother's body through which babies and young animals suck milk; the nipple; the rubber end of a baby's feeding bottle

technical having to do with industrial engineering or mechanical skills; having a special skilled knowledge of a practical art or science (as, a technical expert on bridges); belonging to a particular art, profession, trade, etc. (as, a technical article in an engineering journal)

technicality a technical point or detail

technician a person skilled in the practical work of an art, trade, profession, etc. (as, a technician in a laboratory)

technique *(say tekneek)* the way in which a skilled performance is carried out (as - His musical technique has been developed by years of practice.); technical skill

technology (the study of) branches of science which have practical uses (as, the technology of soap manufacture)

tedious tiresome and boring; going on for a long time (as, a tedious speech, a tedious journey)

tediousness, tedium tiresomeness, wearisomeness

tee (in the game of golf) the peg or small heap of sand, etc. used to support the ball for the first stroke at each hole; the levelled ground where this is placed

teem to be abundant; to be full to overflowing; to swarm with

teens the years of a person's life from 13 to 19 inclusive

teenager a person between these ages

teeth see **tooth**

teetotaller a person who never takes alcoholic drinks

teetotal completely abstaining from the use of alcohol

telecast a television broadcast □ to send out a television broadcast

telegram a message sent by telegraph

telegraph an apparatus or system for sending messages to a distant place by means of wires and electricity, or by radio

telegraphy *(say telegrafee)* the art of constructing or using telegraphic apparatus

telepathy the communication of thought between two people

without speech, writing or other physical means

telepathic able to communicate in this way

telephone an instrument that enables one person to speak to another at a distance by means of wires and electricity, or by radio (as, a radio telephone from ship to shore) □ to speak on a telephone

telephonist a person who operates a telephone switchboard

telephotography the taking of photographs of distant objects, etc. by means of a camera with a telephoto lens

teleprinter an electric machine (like a typewriter) that prints out messages sent and received by telegraph

telescope a tube-like instrument fitted with a system of lenses which make distant objects seem larger and nearer □ to push together parts which are shaped to slide inside one another (like the jointed sections of some small telescopes); to crush together in a collision, etc. (as, railway coaches telescoped by the force of a collision with another train)

telescopic of, or having to do with, a telescope (as, a telescopic lens)

television the sending of pictures from a distance and their reproduction on a screen by means of radio waves; a television receiving set

televise to transmit a picture by means of television

tell to say or speak in words (as, to tell a lie, the truth); to give an account or report (as, to tell a story, to tell what happened); to inform (as, to tell someone how to get to a place, the time of a meeting, etc.); to command or order (as - Tell him to come at once!); to recognize or distinguish (as, to be unable to tell the difference between two things); to make known (a secret)

told the past tense of tell

teller a bank clerk who receives and pays out money; a person who counts votes in an election

telling influential; having a great effect

temper a person's mood or state of mind (as, to be in a good temper, a bad temper); anger (as, an outburst of temper); a usual state of calmness and self-control (as, to lose one's temper): the degree of hardness or toughness of metal, etc. □ to bring metal, glass, etc. to the right degree of hardness by a process of heating and cooling: to modify or make less harsh (as, to temper the effect of a criticism by smiling)

tempered having a kind of temper or mood (as, good-tempered): of a certain degree of hardness (as, tempered steel)

temperament an inborn quality of mood and feeling; a person's nature or disposition (as, an aggressive temperament, a nervous temperament)

temperamental showing quick changes of mood; unpredictable; excitable

temperate moderate; not extreme (as, temperate language, a temperate climate); not eating or drinking too much

temperance moderation; self-control; moderation in, or abstinence from, the use of alcoholic drinks

temperature degree of heat or cold (as, the temperature of air, water, etc.); body heat (usually above normal, as - She has a high temperature.)

temperate zones the parts of the earth's surface of moderate temperature, lying between the tropics and the polar regions

tempest a violent wind storm

tempestuous stormy or violent (as, a period in history, a person's nature or mood, etc.)

temple 1 a building in which people pray and worship

temple 2 one of the flat parts at either side of the head between the eye and the top of the ear

tempo the speed at which music is (or should be) played or sung; the rate or speed of any activity (as - The tempo of life in a city is faster than in the country.)

temporary lasting or used only for a limited period of time, (as, temporary employment, a temporary repair)

temporarily for the time being; not permanently

tempt to try to persuade someone to do something (usually bad or wrong); to entice or attract (as, to be tempted to eat more than is good for one)

temptation the act of tempting; something that tempts

tenacious holding tightly; keeping a firm hold (of); stubborn or persistent

tenant a person who rents a house, land, etc. from another

tenancy the occupation of a house, etc. as a tenant

tend 1 to look after; to care for (as, to tend sheep, to tend a furnace)

tender 1 a small vessel that carries supplies, etc. to a larger one; a rail-truck with supplies of coal and water, attached to a steam locomotive

tend 2 to move or turn towards a certain direction; to be inclined or likely (to happen, to result in, etc.); to have a liking for or leaning towards (as - She tends to look on the bright side.)

tendency a natural inclination or leaning towards a kind of action (as, a tendency towards laziness)

tender 1 see **tend 1**

tender 2 to offer; to present formally (as to tender one's resignation from a job); to offer to do something for a certain price (as, to tender an estimate for building a bridge) □ an offer (especially for work)

legal tender coins or notes that must be accepted when offered in payment (Small-value coins are legal tender for small amounts, but not for large sums.)

tender 3 soft; delicate; easily hurt or damaged; painful when touched; not hard or tough (as, tender meat); loving and gentle

tenderfoot a person who is not used to roughing it out-of-doors; a newcomer

tendon a sinew; a tough cord-like tissue joining a muscle and a bone, etc.

tendril a slender curling shoot on some climbing plants which twists itself around a support; something like a tendril (as, a tendril of hair)

tenement a building divided into flats (especially one that houses many families)

tennis a game played by two or four people, using rackets to hit a ball back and forth over a net

tennis court a piece of level ground prepared and laid out for tennis

tenor 1 the highest adult male singing voice; a man who sings tenor parts; the part above bass and below alto in music for four vocal parts

tenor 2 general course or direction (of thought, actions, way of life, etc.); trend or drift (as, the tenor of his remarks)

tense 1 a form of a verb which shows whether an action belongs to the present, past or future time (For example, *I am* [present], *I was* [past], *I shall be* [future])

tense 2 strained; stretched tight; showing strain (especially nervous strain)

tent a portable shelter (usually) made of canvas or some other strong material supported by poles and anchored to the ground by ropes and pegs

tentacle a long slender organ that projects from the heads or bodies of some insects, fish or animals, used for feeling, grasping or moving; anything resembling a tentacle

tentative made or done as a trial, but not definite (as, a tentative offer or suggestion that can be altered or withdrawn if not acceptable)

tenuous thin, slender (as - The threads of a spider's web are tenuous.)

tenure the holding of property, an office, a job, etc.; the conditions or period of this (as - His tenure of office as treasurer was very brief.)

tepee a cone-shaped tent that American Indians lived in

tepid lukewarm; slightly warm

term a length of time (as, a term of office, a school term, etc.); a name or a word used in a special way (as, a scientific term, a technical term); (in plural) conditions, rules, etc. (as, the terms of a contract); charges or financial arrangements (as, terms for a cooker bought on hire purchase); relationship (as, to be on good terms, friendly terms, equal terms) □ to name or call by a term

terminology certain words or expressions used in a particular profession, subject, etc. (as, medical terminology)

to come to terms, to make terms to come to an agreement, an arrangement

terminate to bring to an end; to come to an end or limit

termination the act of ending; end; conclusion

terminal of, or at, the end of something □ an end or ending: the end of an electric circuit to which connections are made; a terminus

terminus the end (of a line, route, railway)

termite a pale ant-like insect that eats wood

tern a sea bird, smaller than a gull, with a long forked tail

terrace a raised level bank of earth like a big step; a flat level space or walk along the top or side of a slope, a hill, etc.; a row of houses joined together

terrain a stretch of land (especially with reference to its physical features, as, a rocky terrain)

terrapin a North American turtle

terrestrial having to do with the earth or the land (not spiritual or heavenly)

terrible, terrify, etc. see **terror**

terrier a name given to several types of small dog (once used for hunting, but now mainly kept as pets)

territory an area of land; a region or district; land under the control of a government or ruler; a part of a country, but not yet admitted to statehood (especially in former times)
territorial of, or belonging to, a territory
territorial waters seas close to a country's shores

terror very great fear; something that causes extreme fear
terrible dreadful; awful; causing great fear
terrify to frighten greatly; to cause terror
terrific fearful; terrifying: very great (as, a terrific wind, a terrific surprise)
terrorist a person who terrorizes others
terrorize to terrify a person or people by violence or threats of violence
terror-stricken seized or struck by terror

terse (of a speech, explanation, etc.) short and well put (not long and rambling); concise

test an examination to find out what a person knows (as at school) or how well he does something (as, a driving test); a trial (as, to test one's strength) □ to try something out to see how well it works, etc. (as, to test an aeroplane, an engine, etc.)
test match an important cricket match between countries

test pilot a person who tries out new aircraft
test tube a glass tube closed at one end, used in chemistry tests

testament a written statement (usually called a will) which sets out what is to be done with a person's property after death; (with a capital letter) one of the two main sections of the Bible (the *Old Testament* and the *New Testament*)

testify to give evidence or information (especially in a court of law); to make a formal statement or declaration of what a person knows to be true; to support or confirm a fact or truth (as - His friends will testify to his devotion to his mother.)
testimony evidence or proof; a public statement of belief or faith
testimonial a written statement telling what is known about a person's character, abilities, efficiency, etc.; a gift or memento presented to a person in appreciation of something he has done

testy irritable; short-tempered

tetanus a serious disease (lockjaw) which stiffens the jaw muscles, caused by a germ which enters the blood stream through a wound

tether a rope or chain, used to tie an animal to a stake, etc. so that it can only move or feed within limits □ to tie an animal in this way

text the main printed part of a book or article (not illustrations, notes, etc.); a verse or quotation from the Bible about which a sermon is preached; the subject or theme of a speech, lecture, essay, etc.
text book a book (usually a school book) which gives basic information about a subject

textile a cloth or fabric made by weaving □ having to do with cloth or weaving (as, the textile industry)

texture the way in which something is made or woven (as, the loose texture, the smooth texture, of woven cloth); the composition or substance of anything (as, rough, coarse, lumpy, etc., texture of paper, wood, stone)

than a word meaning in comparison or compared to (as - This is better *than* that. This mountain is higher *than* the others. The work is harder *than* I had expected.)

thank to say or express in some way how pleased and grateful one is for a gift, for kindness, etc.; to acknowledge that something has happened because of favourable conditions, someone's help, etc. (as - They have the good weather to thank for the success of the fête.) □ (in plural) gratitude; grateful words
thankful feeling or showing thanks
thankless showing no gratitude or thanks; ungrateful
thanksgiving a service or gathering giving thanks (especially to God for favours received)
thanks, thank you I, or we, thank you (for something gratefully received)

that referring to something already mentioned; apart or more distant (as - She said it was *that* one, not this one. *That* is the place. At *that* time, we were very young.); also used instead of who or which (as, records *that* were played, animals *that* are pets); a connecting word (as, to say *that* he is coming, to speak so *that* we can hear); to show a result (as, to work so hard *that* one is exhausted)
those the plural of that

thatch a roof or covering of straw or reeds □ to cover (a house, etc.) with thatch

thaw to melt or become liquid (as, ice or snow thaws); (of manner) to become less cold and formal □ the melting of ice and snow by heat; the change in

temperature that causes a thaw

theatre a building in which plays or other stage entertainments are presented; a room or hall resembling a theatre (as, a theatre for surgery in a hospital); an area or region where something takes place (as, a theatre of war)
theatrical having to do with drama or the theatre; behaving in an unnatural affected way (as, though acting, not as in real life)

thee see **thou**

theft see **thieve**

their(s) see **they**

them, themselves see **they**

theme a subject for talking or writing about; (in music) a principal melody (often repeated, varied and developed in a composition)
theme song a melody or musical composition that introduces and is identified with a particular character, programme, film, etc.

then at that time; afterwards: therefore
thence from that time or place; for that reason
thenceforth, thenceforward from that time on

theology the science or study of God and of man's relationship with God; the study of the doctrines and beliefs of a religion (especially Christianity)
theological having to do with theology (as, a theological college)

theorem something which can be proved to be true by explaining one's reasoning step by step
theory an explanation which one thinks is correct but has not been proved; the principles and main ideas of a subject, art, science, etc.
theoretical having to do with theory, not actual experience (as, to have a theoretical knowledge of the principle of aviation without being able to fly an air-

craft); the opposite of practical

there in that place; the opposite of here, in this place; at that point (as - I must stop you there.); to that place or point (as - We went there.); also used to begin a sentence in which the real subject follows the verb (as - There are good reasons for his decision.)

thereabouts about or near to that place; about that quantity, number, etc. (as, fifty people or thereabouts)

thereafter after that; afterwards

thereby by that means; connected with or resulting from that

therefore as a result; for this or that reason; consequently

therein in that place; in that matter or situation (as - Therein lies a problem.)

thereupon following (some act or circumstance); immediately

therm a unit of heat, used in measuring gas consumption

thermal having to do with heat (as, thermal baths or hot springs)

thermometer an instrument for measuring temperature

thermonuclear having to do with the very high temperature produced by the fusion of atomic nuclei

thermostat a device that automatically controls temperature (of a room, watertank, etc.)

these see this

they, them the people already referred to; the plural of he, she, it; people in general (as - They say that daily exercise is good for the health.)

themselves they or them and no one else

their, theirs belonging to them (as - This is their house. This house is theirs.)

thick not thin or slender (as, a thick slice, a thick branch); dense (as, thick fog, a thick jungle); difficult to see through (as, thick snow); (of a person) stupid or dull □ the most crowded or active part (as, in the thick of a fight)

thicken to make, or become, thick or thicker

thickness the state of being thick; the distance through something (as, the thickness of a book)

thicket a dense planting of trees or shrubs

thick-set closely planted; (of a person) having a solid stocky build

thick-skinned not sensitive; not easily upset by insults

thief a person who steals or takes something that doesn't belong to him

thieves the plural of thief

thieve to steal; to be a thief

theft an act of thieving; stealing

thigh the thick part of the leg above the knee

thimble a metal or plastic cover for the fingertip, worn as a protection while sewing

thin not thick or fat; having little distance through (as, a thin magazine); not crowded or set close together (as, a thin clump of trees); poor in strength or quality (as, thin soup, a thin voice); easy to see through (as, thin material, a thin excuse) □ to make or become thin or thinner

thinning becoming thin or thinner (as, thinning hair)

thin-skinned sensitive; easily offended or hurt

thine see thou

thing an object not living (as, a book, a stone); a living being (as - That kitten is a dear little thing.); a word used to mean a particular object, a fact, idea, circumstance, etc.; anything not named; (in plural) affairs, matters, conditions, etc. (as - Things are bad, improving, in a muddle, etc.); clothing or belongings (as - Take off your things. Pick up your things.)

think to form ideas or pictures in the mind; to reason or work things out in the mind; to have an opinion about (as, to think well of someone); to intend or consider doing something (as, to think of going to see a film)

thought 1 *(say thawt)* the past of think (as - She thought for a long time before deciding.): see also **thought 2**

third next after second; last of three; one of three equal parts, dimensions, etc.

thirst the dry feeling in the throat caused by a need for something to drink; an eager desire for news, information, knowledge, etc. □ to feel thirst
thirsty feeling, or suffering from, thirst; (of earth) parched; needing water

this referring to something or someone near at hand, within sight, etc. (as - *this* ring on my finger, *this* corner we are coming to); the opposite of that
these the plural of this

thistle *(say thissl)* a plant with a prickly stem and leaves, and (usually) purple flowers
thistledown the light feathery parts of thistle seeds

thither to that place: see also **hither**

thong a strip of leather used for fastening; the lash of a whip

thorax the part of the body between the neck and abdomen; the chest; (in insects) the middle division of the body, that bears the wings and legs

thorn a sharp, woody prickle or spike on some plants and shrubs (as, a rose, a hawthorn)
thorny prickly; full of thorns; likely to cause argument (as, a thorny subject)

thorough *(say thurruh)* complete; well done (as, a thorough piece of work); (of a person) paying great attention to detail; very careful (in studying, carrying out a job, etc.)
thoroughbred an animal (a horse, dog, etc.) of pure breed, which is valuable for racing,

jumping or show purposes
thoroughfare a public street or road
thoroughgoing complete; going right through

thou, thee (in former times) you, the person to whom one is writing or speaking (nowadays used only in poetic or religious language)
thy, thine belonging to thee (you); yours (especially in poetic or Biblical use)
thyself yourself and no one else

though *(say thoe)* although; even if; however

thought 1 see **think**

thought 2 *(say thawt)* an idea; the act of thinking; something in the mind (as, a pleasant thought); consideration or attention (as, to give thought to a problem)
thoughtful thinking deeply; taking thought for others; kind; considerate
thoughtless inconsiderate; not considering what the result of an action, behaviour, etc. will be

thrash to beat; to flog; to toss or move about violently (as, to thrash about in the water); (with *out*) to discuss (a matter thoroughly); to thresh grain: see **thresh**
thrashing a beating; a flogging

thread a very thin line or cord (especially one twisted and drawn out) of silk, cotton, flax, etc.; anything resembling a thread (as, the threadlike parts of a spider's web); the ridges or grooves on a screw; the sequence of ideas or happenings in a story that connect the whole (as - He mixed up the order of events in telling what happened so that we lost the thread of the story.) □ to put a piece of thread through the eye of a needle; to put beads on a thread; to find one's way through (as, to thread one's way through a crowd, between trees)
threadbare (of clothes, linen,

etc.) worn thin so that the threads of the material show; (of an excuse, a subject) too often used, discussed, etc., so that it is no longer interesting or convincing

threat *(say thret)* a warning of harm or injury to a person; a warning of punishment or something bad that may happen (as, a result of behaviour, failure to do something, etc.)
threaten to utter a threat or threats; to show warning signs that something unpleasant may happen (as - The black clouds threatened a heavy rainstorm.)

thresh to separate grain from straw by beating with a flail, machinery, etc.
thresher a person or machine that threshes

threshold the piece of stone or timber under the door to a house or other building; a doorway or entrance; a beginning or point of entering (as, to be at the threshold of a new career)

threw see **throw**

thrice three times

thrift spending and managing one's own money carefully in order to save
thrifty careful and economical; the opposite of extravagant
thriftless not thrifty; careless about spending money

thrill a feeling of excitement that may make one tingle or shiver (from joy, fear, etc.)
thrilling exciting
thriller an exciting story, play, film, etc. (usually about detectives, murders, etc.)

thrive to get on well; to be successful; to grow strong and healthy

throat the front part of the neck below the chin; the inside of the front part of the neck, which contains the gullet and windpipe

throb to palpitate or pulsate; to beat hard or fast (as, the heart throbs after a cross-country run) □ a strong beat or pulsation (of the heart, an engine, etc.)

throne a special seat or chair for a king, queen, bishop, etc. on ceremonial occasions

throng a crowd; a great number □ to crowd together; to crowd into

throttle to choke or strangle by squeezing the windpipe; to stop or slow down an engine by closing a valve (thus shutting off the steam, flow of fuel, etc.) □ a device for controlling the flow of fuel to an engine, etc.

through *(say throo)* from one end to the other; from one side to another; into one end and out at the other (as, a road that goes through a village); from the beginning to the end (as, to sit through a performance); because of, or as a result of (as, to get something through knowing the right people) □ going straight through without changing or having to stop (as, a through train, a through road); finished with (as, to be through with playing with dolls)
throughout in every part of; from the beginning to the end of

throw to fling, cast or hurl something (through the air, on the ground, to another person, etc.) □ the act of throwing; the distance to which anything may be thrown
threw, thrown past forms of throw (as - He threw off his coat; he has thrown the ball.)

thrush a brown songbird with a speckled breast

thrust to push with great force; to stab; to pierce □ a hard push; a stab

thud a dull hollow sound (as of something heavy falling to the ground)

thug a ruffian; a cut-throat

thumb the short thick finger of the hand □ to turn over quickly the pages of a book, etc.; to soil by handling with thumb and fingers

thump to strike, fall or move with

a dull heavy sound □ a heavy blow

thunder the loud crashing or rumbling noise heard after a flash of lightning; any loud rumbling noise (as, the thunder of a distant cannon) □ to give out thunder or a sound like thunder (as - It thundered yesterday. He thundered his orders.)

thunderous, thundery of, or like, thunder

thunderbolt a flash of lightning followed by a clap of thunder: a tremendous surprise

thunderclap a sudden peal or roar of thunder

thunderstorm a heavy rainstorm with thunder and lightning

thunderstruck completely stunned or overcome by astonishment

thus therefore; in this way or manner

thwart to hinder or prevent (a person from carrying out a plan); to frustrate or obstruct □ a cross-seat in a rowing boat

thy see **thou**

thyme *(say time)* a small shrubby plant with sweet-smelling leaves used for seasoning when cooking

tiara a crown-like ornament for the head

tibia the shin bone, between the knee and ankle

tick 1 a blood-sucking very tiny animal (which feeds on sheep, pigeons, etc.)

tick 2 a mark used to show that something is correct, or has been dealt with

tick 3 a soft, clicking noise (especially the regular noise made by a clock or watch □ to make such a noise

tick 4 the cloth case or cover of a mattress

ticking the fabric from which ticks are made

ticket a marked piece of paper or cardboard which gives the purchaser the right to travel on a bus, train, plane, etc., or to be admitted to an entertainment, etc.; a price card or label

tickle to touch someone lightly with the fingers, a feather, etc. causing them to laugh or giggle (as, to tickle a person under the arms); to itch or tingle (as, from a dry throat, a cold in the nose, etc.); to please and amuse (as - The comedian's act tickled the audience.)

ticklish easily tickled; sensitive to tickling; (of a situation or problem) difficult to cope with; needing careful handling

tide the rise and fall of the surface of the sea which occurs twice a day, because of the attraction of the sun and moon; the ebb and flow of the tide (as, to be carried away by the tide or brought in by the tide); a season or time of the year (as, Christmastide)

tidal having to do with, or affected by, tides

tidal wave a great sea wave (often caused by an earthquake under the sea)

tidings news (as, to bring tidings of far-away friends)

tidy neat; orderly; the opposite of messy: fairly large (as, a tidy sum of money)

tie to fasten (with rope, cord, etc.); to make a bow or knot in (with ribbon, string, etc.); to be restricted or limited (by responsibilities, duties, etc.): to score the same number of points (in a game, examination, etc.) □ a necktie; a link or connection (as, family ties); an equal number of points, votes, etc.

tier *(say teer)* a row or rank (of seats, benches, etc., especially one of a number of rows raised one behind another)

tiff a slight quarrel or disagreement

tiger, tigress a large fierce cat-like animal found in Asia, having tawny fur striped with black

tight *(say tiet)* packed or fitting closely; the opposite of loose; firmly held or stretched
tighten to make, or become, tight or tighter
tights a very close-fitting garment covering the lower part of the body from waist to toes
tightrope a tightly stretched rope (or wire) on which acrobats perform balancing tricks

tile a flattish piece of baked clay or concrete used to cover roofs, floors, etc. □ to cover with tiles

till 1 to plough the land, plant and grow crops (as, to till the soil)

till 2 up to a certain time (as, to work till 5.30); to a time when (as - We won't meet till Sunday.)

till 3 a drawer or box for money in a shop, bank, etc.

tiller the handle of a boat's rudder

tilt to lean to one side; to slant; to raise or be raised at one end (as, to tilt a platform); (in mediaeval times) to joust □ a slant
full tilt with full speed and force

timber wood for building or carpentry; trees suitable for this use; forests or woods of timber trees; a large beam used in the construction of a house, ship, etc.

time the hour of the day; the moment or period at or during which something takes place (as - It is time for a meal. It is time for my music lesson.); (often plural, often in history) a particular period (as, the time when the Industrial Revolution began, hard times during the war, in future times, etc.); a season of the year (as, springtime, planting time); a suitable period or moment for doing something (as - Now is the time to ask him.); (often in plural) one of a number of single happenings (as, to call three times); (in plural) multiplying a number by another (as, 6×4 = 24); (in music)

rhythm, tempo (as, to beat time to a march) □ to measure seconds, minutes, hours (as, to time a race); to choose the right (or wrong) moment to do something
timely well-timed; at the right moment
timeless not measured by or belonging to any particular period of time; unending
time-honoured thought much of through a long period of time or because of lasting so long
time limit a certain length of time by which something has to stop or to be finished
timepiece a watch or clock
timetable a list showing the times when certain things take place (as, the arrivals and departures of buses, trains, planes, etc.)
the time being the present time (as - This car will do for the time being, but we may want to change it later on.)

timid easily frightened; the opposite of brave; shy; cautious
timorous very timid; very easily frightened

tin a silvery-coloured metal; a box or can made of thin steel coated with tin □ made of tin □ to cover with tin; to pack in tins
tinny like tin; (of a noise) having a thin metallic sound (like that of a tin being struck)
tin foil tin or a similar metal in thin sheets (used for wrapping things)

tinder any very dry material which can easily be set alight, even by a spark

tine a spike of a fork or rake

tinge to give a slight amount (of colour, feeling, etc.) to (as, clouds tinged with pink from the setting sun; a feeling of affection tinged with pity) □ a slight amount (as, a tinge of regret in her voice)

tingle to feel a prickling or stinging sensation; to have a thrilling feeling (as, to tingle with excitement)

tinker a man who mends kettles, pans, etc. □ to repair badly; to meddle with

tinkle to make a little ringing sound □ such a sound

tinsel a shiny, glittering material used for Christmas decorations; anything showy but of little value

tint a light colour □ to give a slight colouring to (as, rose-tinted)

tiny very small

tip 1 the top end or point of anything (as, the tip of one's tongue, the tip of an iceberg)
tiptoe to walk quietly on the tips of the toes
on tiptoe walking on the tips of the toes

tip 2 to tilt or cause to slant; to overturn (as, to tip over a chair); to empty (as, to tip out the ash from an ashtray); to strike lightly (as, to tip and run in cricket): to give a hint; to make a small gift of money (as, to tip a waiter) □ a tap or light stroke; a hint; a small gift of money

tirade a long, scolding speech

tire 1 to make, or become, weary
tired weary; bored with (as, tired of piano practice)
tireless never becoming weary; never resting
tiresome making tired; boring; annoying

tire 2 see **tyre**

tissue a very finely woven material; the substance of which flesh, muscle, etc. is made
tissue paper a very thin soft paper

tit, titmouse any one of a variety of small birds, some of which are brightly coloured (as, blue tit, great tit, coal tit)

tit for tat blow for blow

Titan a mythical giant
titanic huge

titanium a very light, strong metal

titbit a choice little bit or morsel (of food, of gossip, etc.)

tithe *(say tiethe)* a kind of tax paid to the church; a tenth part

titivate to smarten up (one's dress, etc.)

title the name of a book, poem, etc.; a word in front of a person's name to show rank or honour (as, Sir, Lord, General) or as a form of address (Mr., Mrs., Miss); legal right or claim
titled having a title
title deed a document that proves someone is the rightful owner of some property

titmouse see **tit**

titter to giggle or laugh nervously □ a giggle or nervous little laugh

tittle-tattle gossip or idle chatter

to towards; in the direction of; as far as (as, going to the station); showing a connection (as, the answer to a question, the key to a door, etc.); against, compared with, etc. (as, three to one, not up to standard); introducing the person affected by an action (as, giving a present to her friend); as a sign that the next word is a verb (as, to read, to sing, to run, etc.) □ into a place or condition required (as - Pull the door to. Soon after the operation the patient came to.)
to and fro see **fro**

toad an animal like a large frog with a rough skin
toadstool a poisonous fungus shaped like a mushroom
toady to flatter a person just to gain his favour □ a servile flatterer

toast to make bread, etc. brown and crisp by heating it; to warm (the feet, etc.): to drink to the health or success of a person □ toasted bread: the act of toasting a person or persons (for example, a bride and bridegroom)

tobacco a plant whose large leaves are dried, cut up and prepared for smoking in cigarettes, cigars or a pipe

tobacconist someone who sells tobacco, cigarettes, etc.

toboggan a long sled curved up at the front (usually without runners)

today, to-day this day; the present time

toddle to walk with short unsteady steps (like an infant)
toddler a young child just able to walk

toe one of the five finger-like end parts of the foot

toffee a sweet made of sugar and butter

toga the loose outer garment worn by a citizen of ancient Rome

together in, or to, the same place (as - We stayed, or went, together.); at the same time, or in company (as - We arrived together.)

togs clothes

toil to work hard □ hard or tiring work

toilet the act of washing, dressing, etc.; a room with a wash-basin, mirror, etc.; a lavatory or water closet

token a mark or visible sign (as, a book given to someone as a token of the giver's gratitude); a keepsake; a piece of metal, plastic, etc. used in place of a coin or ticket; a voucher (as, a book token, etc.)

tolerable able to be endured or put up with; fairly good
tolerance putting up with people or ideas one does not approve of or agree with
tolerant willing to consider or tolerate ideas different from one's own
tolerate to put up with or endure

toll 1 *(say tole)* to sound (a large bell) slowly and regularly (as, after someone's death)

toll 2 *(say tole)* a tax paid to cross a toll-bridge, or to use a toll-road: the cost in injury and damage (especially of accidents or disasters)

tomahawk a light axe formerly used by North American Indians

tomato a round juicy fruit (usually red) used in salads, soups, etc.
tomatoes the plural of tomato

tomb *(say toom)* a grave or burial place
tombstone a carved stone placed over a grave in memory of the person buried there

tomboy a girl who enjoys energetic boyish games

tomcat an adult male cat

tome a large book

tomfoolery silly behaviour

tomorrow, to-morrow the day after today

tomtit a small bird (the tit or titmouse)

tom-tom a drum beaten with the hands

ton a measure of weight (English long ton = 2240 lb.; American short ton = 1000 kilogrammes, or approximately 2205 lb.)
tonnage a measure of the space in a large ship

tone a sound, usually musical; the quality of a voice or sound (as, a harsh tone, a soft tone, a shrill tone); a shade of colour (as, a bluish tone) □ to blend or fit in (with): to give strength to (as, to tone up the muscles)
tonic a medicine that helps to restore one's energy

tongs an instrument for grasping and lifting (as, sugar tongs, coal tongs)

tongue *(say tung)* the movable organ in the mouth, used in tasting and speaking; a tongue-like leather flap in a shoe; a language (as, the French tongue)
tongue-tied not able to speak easily (from shyness, etc.)
tongue-twister a sentence or phrase which is difficult to say quickly (for example - *Peter Piper picked a peck of pickled peppers.*)

tonight, to-night this night

tonnage see ton

tonsils one of two small pieces of fleshy tissue at the back of the throat
tonsillitis an inflammation of the tonsils

tonsure the shaving of all or part of the head by priests and monks; the part of the head so shaven

too extremely, over (as, too noisy): also (as - His friend came too.)

tool an instrument for doing work (such as a hammer, chisel, screw-driver); a person used by someone else (especially for a wrong purpose) simply to gain the latter's ends

tooth one of the hard bony bodies in the mouth, used for biting and chewing; anything tooth-like (as, the teeth of a comb, of a saw, etc.)
teeth the plural of tooth
toothed having teeth
toothache a pain in a tooth
toothbrush a small brush used to clean the teeth
toothpaste a paste used on a toothbrush to clean the teeth

top 1 the highest place or uppermost part of anything (as, the top of a mountain, of a table); a lid or cover (of a box, of a bottle); the upper edge or end (as, the top of a page); the highest rank or position (as, top of the class, top of the football league) □ highest (as, top price, top score) □ to rise above; to do better than; to take off the top of
topping something put on top to complete it (as, topping on a sweet or pudding); whatever has been removed from something that has been topped (as, toppings of plants, trees, etc.)
topmost highest; uppermost
topcoat an overcoat
top hat a tall, cylindrical stiff hat covered with silk
top-heavy having more weight in the upper part than in the lower

topnotch of highest quality

top 2 a child's spinning toy

topaz a precious stone (often dark orange or yellow)

topic any subject people choose to speak, write or argue about
topical having to do with a topic; having to do with current events, or something everyone is interested in at the moment

topography (the description of) the physical features of an area or region (often shown on a map)

topple to fall forward (usually because of being top-heavy or unsteady); to tumble off or down; to cause something to fall over

topsy-turvy turned upside down; in a confused or disorderly state

torch a light which can be carried in the hand (formerly a flame at the end of a piece of wood, twisted flax, etc.); nowadays, a battery-operated electric light)

torment *(say torment)* to torture; to inflict great physical suffering, or mental distress and worry; to tease or annoy □ *(say torment)* great pain or suffering (mental or physical)

tornado a violent whirling wind that causes great damage

torpedo a cigar-shaped, self-propelled vessel with an explosive warhead, fired from a submarine, ship, etc. or dropped from an aeroplane (It travels through or on the surface of water and explodes on impact with the target.) □ to attack with or damage by means of torpedoes

torpid slow-moving; sluggish; dull or stupid

torrent a rushing stream (as, a torrent of water, lava, etc.); a violent downpour or flow (of rain, words, etc.)
torrential like a torrent (as, torrential rain)

torrid extremely hot; parching or burning (as, a torrid climate)

torrid zone the hottest part of the earth's surface, lying in a broad band on either side of the equator

torso the human trunk, without limbs or head (especially of a statue)

tortoise *(say tortus)* a slow-moving, four-footed animal with a thick shell; a turtle (especially a land or fresh-water turtle)
tortoise-shell the shell of a kind of sea-turtle, valued for its beautiful mottled colouring (black, amber, yellow, etc.)

tortuous winding or twisting (as, a tortuous path); (of reasoning, business methods, etc.) deceitful; not straightforward

torture to inflict great pain on a person, as a punishment, or (especially) to try to force a confession, get information, etc. □ great pain (physical or mental); agony

toss to throw something lightly or carelessly; to fling or throw (about, to and fro, from side to side, etc.); to throw up a coin (to see which side lands uppermost); to be thrown about (as, a ship is tossed in a storm) □ the act of tossing; a throwing back (of the head, in scorn or annoyance)
toss-up the tossing of a coin to decide something; something not yet sure or decided; an equal chance (as - It's a toss-up whether they will come or not.)

tot 1 a small child

tot 2 to add up (as, to tot up one's expenses)

total the sum of; the whole amount □ complete (as, a total eclipse, a total failure); entire (as, the total cost of something) □ to add up (as - The charges for each of them totalled £20.)
totally completely
totalisator (usually abbreviated to **tote**) a machine that works out the amount of money to be shared out to people who have won bets on the races
totalitarian concerning a system of government which is under the absolute control of one party (No opposition is allowed.)

totem *(say toetem)* an animal or plant taken by a tribe, family group, etc. as a symbol or emblem; an image of this
totem pole a pole or post on which totems are carved or painted (often set up in front of the houses of some North American Indians)

totter to walk unsteadily and shakily; to shake as though about to fall

toucan a brightly-coloured tropical bird with a huge beak

touch *(say tuch)* to feel with the fingers or some other part of the body; to come in contact with (as - The two cars just touched in passing); to reach (as far as, as high as); to handle, hit, etc. lightly; to mark or colour slightly (as, to touch up a picture, to add a touch of colour); to border or be adjacent to (as - The park touches the river at one point.); to affect the feelings (causing pity, sorrow, etc.) □ the act of touching or being touched; the sense by which a person feels the hardness, softness, texture, temperature, etc. of things (usually by means of the hands); a small amount, a slight degree (as, a touch of colour, a touch of flu); a light tap (as, a touch on the shoulder)
touching causing pity or sympathy; sad
touchy easily offended
touch-lines (in football) the boundary lines marking the area of play
touch-down (in football) the touching of the ball to the ground behind the opponent's goal line: the alighting of an aircraft

tough *(say tuf)* hard; strong; not easily broken; not easily chewed
toughen to make, or become, tough

tour to travel about from place to place for pleasure (usually returning to the starting place) □ a journey to various places (usually for pleasure, but also for presenting a series of entertainments, performances, etc. in different places)

tourist a person who travels around for pleasure

tournament (in mediaeval times) a jousting competition between knights on horseback; (nowadays) a contest or competition consisting of a series of games, athletic events, etc.

tourniquet *(say toornikay)* a bandage twisted tightly so as to bring pressure on a main artery, thus preventing great loss of blood

tousle to make untidy; to rumple; to tangle (especially hair)

tow 1 *(say toe)* to pull something (a car, a ship) along with a rope or cable □ a rope used for towing; the act of towing (as - He gave us a tow when the car broke down.)

tow 2 *(say toe)* the coarse part of hemp or flax
towheaded having very light-coloured (flaxen) hair

toward(s) in the direction of (as, to move towards a person, place); as part of, a share of (as, to save towards the cost of a holiday); near or close to (as - It is getting towards lunchtime.)

towel a piece of thick cloth, absorbent paper, etc., used for drying something wet (such as the face, hands, crockery, etc.)

tower a building or part of a building, higher than its width and length, usually rising above surrounding buildings; a fortress (as, the Tower of London); anything resembling a tower (as, a water tower) □ to rise or stand above surrounding buildings or people
towering rising high: very violent (as, a towering rage)

town a place with many buildings and houses, larger than a village; the people living in a town

town council the governing body in a town, elected by the ratepayers
town councillor a member of the town council
town hall the building where the official business of the town is carried on

toy a child's plaything; an article of no real value; a small or miniature object (such as a toy poodle, which is smaller than the ordinary type of poodle) □ to play with; to consider lightly (as - He toyed with the idea of growing a beard.)

trace 1 a mark or sign left behind by a person or thing; fragments, remains, etc. which are proof of something that has existed (as, traces of an ancient civilization; a small vestige or amount (as, a trace of perfume in the air) □ to copy (letters, a drawing) by putting transparent paper over the original and going over the lines with a pencil; to follow the track, course or development of something (as, to trace an animal trail, the course of a stream, the history of one's family)
tracery an ornamental design of lines (such as the delicate tracery of stonework which holds the glass in some church windows)
tracing a traced copy of something

trace 2 one of the straps, ropes, etc. by which a horse, donkey, etc. draws a cart or carriage

track a mark left (by a foot, tyre, hoofs, etc.); a path (through woods, fields, etc.); a course laid out for racing; a railway line □ to follow tracks (as, to track footprints in the sand)
trackless without a path (as, a trackless desert)

tract 1 a stretch or area of land, water, etc.

tract 2 a system of parts of the body that work together for a particular purpose (as, the digestive tract)

tractable easily managed or

handled; (of people) docile; easily led

traction the act of pulling or drawing (something along)

tractor a heavy motor vehicle that pulls something along (especially other vehicles or a farm implement such as a plough)

trade to buy and sell; to exchange; to deal (in goods) □ the kind of work or craft by which a person makes a living (as, the grocery trade, a carpenter's trade); the business of buying and selling; everyone in the same line of work or business (as - The motor show is of great interest to everyone in the automobile trade.)

trader a person whose job is buying and selling; a merchant ship

trademark a special mark, design, name, etc. belonging exclusively to one person or firm, put on goods or articles to show who made them

tradesman a shopkeeper

trade union a group of workers of the same trade who join together to bargain with employers for changes in wages, working conditions, etc.

trade wind a wind which blows steadily towards the equator

tradition the handing down of beliefs, customs, etc. from one generation to the next; a custom or practice passed on in this way **traditional** according to custom (as, a traditional Christmas dinner)

traffic the movement of people, vehicles, ships, aircraft, etc. using public roadways, waterways, airways; the people, vehicles, etc. moving along these routes; trade or commerce □ to trade or deal in

trafficking trading or dealing (often illegally, as trafficking in drugs)

tragedy a disaster; a very sad event; a play or opera with a tragic ending

tragic having to do with tragedy; very sad or terrible (often concerned with death)

trail to pull or drag along slowly; to lag behind; (of plants) to hang down (from a tree, window box, etc.) or creep along the ground; to hang down or float behind (as - Her wedding gown had a train that trailed on the floor, and her light veil trailed in the breeze.) □ a track or path (as, a trail followed by a hunter, or a trail through the forest); something left behind (as, a trail of smoke, a trail of destruction) **trailer** a person who trails; a climbing or creeping plant; a vehicle pulled behind another; a short film advertising a coming film or television programme

train 1 a number of connected railway carriages pulled by an engine; a part of a woman's formal dress that trails behind; attendants who follow an important person; a line or file of animals, vehicles, etc. moving along together; a line or series (of events, of thoughts)

train 2 to educate (in proper behaviour, etc.); (of animals) to tame and teach; to make (a plant) grow in a desired way or shape; to prepare by practice, study, etc. (for a profession, for a sport, for battle, etc.): to aim or point at (as, to train a gun on a target, to train a telescope on a mountain top) **trainee** a person who is being trained **trainer** a person who trains (athletes, race horses, etc.) **training** preparation for a sport, profession, craft, etc.

trait (*say trayt or tray*) a particular feature or quality of character or personality

traitor a person who betrays his friends or his country: see also **treason**

tram, tramcar a heavy passenger vehicle that runs on rails and is driven by electricity (usually in city streets and not in the open country)

tramp to travel on foot; to walk with heavy footsteps □ a hike or walk; a person who wanders from place to place with no permanent dwelling place (often sleeping out of doors and begging from other people); a small cargo boat that travels from port to port without a fixed schedule
trample to stamp on; to tread under foot roughly and heavily

trampoline a large piece of canvas or elastic material fastened by springs to a frame, used by gymnasts, acrobats, etc. for jumping on

trance a sleeplike state (but not natural sleep); a semi-conscious, dreamlike condition of mind

tranquil quiet; calm; peaceful
tranquillity a state of calm; peacefulness; quiet

transact to carry through or bring about a piece of business, a deal, etc.
transaction a business deal

transatlantic crossing, or on the other side of, the Atlantic ocean

transcend to rise above; to do or be (even) better than (as - The performance transcended her expectations.)

transcontinental crossing, or extending across, a continent

transfer to remove, carry, send, from one place to another; to give or hand over something to another person (especially legally, as, to transfer property); to move (oneself, one's business, etc.) from one place to another □ the act of transferring; a ticket that allows a person to leave one vehicle and continue his journey in another; a design that can be transferred from one surface to another

transfix to pierce through (as, with a spear); to make (a person) incapable of moving or thinking (because of terror, horror, surprise, etc.)
transfixed temporarily paralysed or incapable of thought;

thunderstruck (by wonder, fear, etc.)

transform to change the shape, appearance, nature, etc. of a person or thing
transformation a complete change (of character, appearance, etc.)
transformer a device for changing electrical energy from one voltage to another

transfusion the act of pouring or passing one thing into another (as, the transfusion of blood from one person's body into that of another)

transgress to go beyond (some limit); to break (a law, rule, etc.)
transgression the breaking of a law or rule; a sin
transgressor a person who breaks a law; a sinner

transient (say _transhent_) not lasting long; passing quickly (as, a transient mood)

transistor a very small electronic device used in television receivers, radio sets, computers, etc.; a small radio set which uses transistors instead of valves to detect and amplify radio signals

transit the carrying (of goods or passengers) from one place to another (as, a parcel lost in transit)
transition a change from one place or state to another (as, the transition from primary to secondary school)
transitory lasting only for a short time; transient

translate to put into another language (as, to translate from French into English)
translation the act of translating; something translated into another language
translator a person who translates

translucent allowing light to pass or show through, but not transparent

transmit to pass on (a message, etc.); to send out radio or television signals

transmission the act of transmitting; radio signals: the part of a motor car which connects the engine with the wheels

transmitter a radio set or station for sending out radio waves

transparent easily seen through (as, transparent glass, a transparent excuse)

transparency the quality of being transparent; a positive photograph which can be viewed by light shining through it

transpire to give off vapour or moisture (as - Leaves transpire.); (of a secret) to become known

transplant to remove and plant in another place; to replace a diseased organ (for example, a kidney) or diseased tissue by a healthy substitute

transport to carry from one place to another □ any means of transporting (as, rail transport, air transport)

transportation the act of transporting; means of transport

transverse lying across

trap a device for catching animals; a plan or trick for catching a person unawares □ to catch in a trap, or by a trick

trap-door a door in a floor

trapper someone who traps animals for their fur

trapeze *(say trapeez)* a swing with a bar for a seat (used by gymnasts and acrobats)

trapezium a figure with four unequal sides (especially one with two parallel sides)

trappings decorative clothes or ornaments (especially those put on horses for a parade)

trash something that is worthless; rubbish

trashy like trash; worthless

travail very hard work; pain in childbirth

travel to go on a journey, or from place to place □ the act of travelling (as, foreign travel)

traveller someone who travels; a travelling representative of a business firm

traverse to go across; to pass through (as, to traverse a wood)

trawl to fish by dragging a large net along the bottom of the sea □ a widemouthed net for large-scale fishing at sea

trawler a special fishing boat used for trawling

tray a flat receptacle (usually with a rim) made of wood, metal or plastic, for carrying food, dishes, cups, etc.

treachery *(say tretchery)* the act of betraying (a friend, etc.); disloyalty

treacherous likely to betray or be disloyal; dangerous (as, a treacherous bog)

treacle a dark sticky liquid left by crude sugar when it is refined; molasses

tread *(say tred)* to make steps (as, to tread heavily); to walk; to crush under foot (as - The peasants trod the grapes to make wine.) □ a person's step; the patterned part of a tyre that touches the ground

trod the past of tread

treadle a part of a machine moved by the foot

treadmill a big mill-wheel turned by the weight of persons or animals treading on steps fixed all round it (formerly used as a punishment for prisoners)

treason the giving of information about one's country to an enemy; disloyalty to a ruler or government

treasonable involving treason (as, a treasonable act)

treasure a store of riches (money, jewels, etc.); anything much valued □ to value greatly

treasurer someone who looks after money (as, the treasurer of a club)

treasure-trove treasure discovered hidden, whose owner is unknown

treasury the government department in charge of a country's financial affairs

treat to deal in a certain way with someone or something (as, to treat a horse kindly); to deal with an illness, etc. (as - The doctor treated her for influenza.); to pay for another person's meal, drink, etc. □ a free entertainment, outing, etc.

treatise (say _treetis_) a long essay treating a subject in a detailed formal way

treatment the act or manner of treating (as, hospital treatment for an illness)

treaty an agreement between countries about peace terms, etc.

treble triple or threefold: high in pitch □ to make, or become, three times as much □ the highest part in singing; a treble singer

tree a large plant with a woody trunk and branches

family tree a diagram like a tree showing the different branches of a family

trek a journey (especially by ox-wagon) □ to make such a journey

trellis many crossed strips of wood in the form of a lattice, used for holding up growing plants

tremble to shake or shiver (with fear, weakness, etc.)

tremor a quivering or shaking

tremulous trembling with fear, nervousness, etc. (as, a tremulous voice)

tremendous very large, great or powerful

tremor, tremulous see **tremble**

trench a long, deep ditch (often dug by soldiers as a shelter from enemy fire) □ to dig deeply with a spade

trenchant (of remarks, writing style, etc.) cutting deeply, vigorous

trend a slope; a general direction or tendency (as, an upward trend in prices, the trend of events, fashion, etc. - that is, the way things are going)

trepidation nervousness; alarm

trespass to go on someone's property unlawfully; to sin □ an act of trespassing; a sin (as - _Forgive us our trespasses._)

trespasser someone who trespasses

tress a plait or lock of hair (usually long)

trestle (say _tress'l_) a wooden support (usually a framework used to support planks, or a platform)

trial an act of trying or testing (as, a trial of strength); the judging of a prisoner in a court of law; a severe test or strain

triangle a figure with three angles and three sides; a small triangular musical instrument, played by striking with a small rod

triangular having three angles and three sides

tribe a group of families ruled by a chief

tribal having to do with tribes (as, tribal warfare)

tribulation great sorrow; hardship

tribunal a court of justice; a group of people specially appointed to give judgment in a difficult public matter

tributary a stream that flows into another larger one

tribute money paid by a defeated ruler or government to a conqueror or to another nation in return for peace and protection; an expression of praise, thanks, admiration, etc. (often in the form of gifts or honours)

trick a clever or skilful action intended to puzzle, amuse, surprise, etc.; an action intended to cheat, deceive or annoy; skill or knack (as, the trick of flipping over a pancake at the right moment) □ to cheat or deceive

trickery the use of tricks to cheat or deceive

tricky difficult to do or to handle

trickle to flow or drip in small amounts (as, water from a leaky tap) □ a small flow

tricycle a three-wheeled cycle

trident (say _triedent_) a three-pronged spear; any three-pronged instrument or weapon

trifle something small, of little value, unimportant; a small amount of money: a sweet food made of spongecake, jelly, cream or custard, fruit, etc. □ to act without proper respect, caution, etc. (as - People shouldn't trifle with weapons.); to amuse oneself in a lighthearted way
trifling small or insignificant (as, a trifling sum); frivolous

trigger a small lever which fires a gun when pulled or squeezed □ (usually with _off_) to start something (as - Her thoughtless remark triggered off a family row.)

trigonometry a branch of mathematics which studies the relationship between the sides and angles of triangles

trill to sing or play a quivering sound (produced by moving very quickly and repeatedly from one note to another and back again) □ the notes sung by some birds

trim to make something neat and shapely by cutting or clipping (hair, a hedge, etc.); to decorate (a hat, a Christmas tree); to arrange (sails, etc.) before sailing □ the act of trimming (as, to give his hair a trim); condition or state of readiness (as, to be in good trim before starting off)
trimming something added as a decoration (as, a trimming of lace for a blouse); (in plural) bits and pieces left over from anything that has been trimmed

trinket a small ornament or piece of jewellery (often of little value)

trio (say _tree-oe_) a set or group of three (as, a trio of friends); (in music) a composition for three instruments, voices, etc.; the three performers of such music

trip to stumble and fall (often caused by catching one's foot on something); to cause someone to make a mistake (as - I tripped him up on that point.); to move with quick, light steps □ a journey
tripper a person who goes on an outing or trip

tripe parts of the stomach of sheep and cattle, used for food

triple made up of three; multiplied by three (as, triple the usual amount) □ to make three times as large or as many, etc.; to treble
triplet three of a kind; one of three children born to the same mother at the same time; (in music) three notes played or sung in the same amount of time usually allowed for two notes
in triplicate in three exact copies

tripod a stand or rest on three legs or three feet (as, a camera tripod)

trite (of a saying, comment) used so often that it is boring or meaningless

triumph a great success or victory □ to win a great victory; to achieve a great success; to celebrate victory or success openly
triumphant victorious; successful; celebrating a victory or success

trivial unimportant; trifling

trod see **tread**

trolley, trolly a small cart or truck; a tray or set of trays on wheels; the wheel at the end of a pole on a tram, etc., that conducts electricity from overhead wires
trolleybus a bus that is powered by electricity from overhead wires

trombone a brass musical instrument with a long tube bent back on itself in two U curves, flaring into a trumpet shape at the end (The tube has a sliding part that changes the pitch of the notes being played.)

troop a crowd or collection of people, animals, etc.; a group of

Boy Scouts, Girl Guides, etc.; (in plural) armed forces; soldiers □ to move in a group or crowd (as - They all trooped in to lunch.)

trophy *(say troefee)* anything taken from an enemy, opponent, etc. as a memento of a victory or battle; a prize got by winning a competition; a display of antlers, etc., obtained from a hunting expedition

tropic either of two imaginary circles at equal distances north and south of the equator; (in plural) the hot countries in these regions
tropical (of climate) very hot; having to do with the tropics (as, tropical plants)

trot to move quickly, with short steps; (of a horse, donkey) to move quickly, using first one fore and opposite hind foot, then the other fore and opposite hind foot □ a gait or pace, between a walk and a run

troubadour *(say troobadoor)* a wandering poet or singer in mediaeval France

trouble to disturb or stir up (as, to trouble the surface of a pond etc.); to cause worry, sorrow, difficulties; to take great care; to make an effort □ a cause of worry, annoyance, unhappiness, etc.; an illness (as, heart trouble); care or pains taken in doing something
troublesome causing worry, difficulties, pain (as, a troublesome cough)

trough *(say troff)* a long open container used to hold animals' water, food, etc.; any long, narrow hollow or channel (as, a trough or dip between sea waves)

trounce to thrash or beat severely; to defeat

troupe a company of actors, singers, dancers, etc.

trousers a garment covering the body from the waist down, with separate sections for each leg

trousseau *(say troossoe)* a bride's outfit of clothes, etc.

trout a freshwater fish, valued for its delicate flavour

trowel a small hand spade, used in gardening and for spreading plaster, cement, etc.

truant a pupil who stays away from school without permission; anyone who stays away from work without good reason

truce a temporary stopping of fighting between armies, agreed to by both sides; an armistice

truck an open railway wagon or motor vehicle, used for carrying heavy goods; a two-wheeled hand barrow used for carrying luggage, etc.

truculent aggressive; bullying or fiercely threatening

trudge to walk along wearily, with heavy footsteps

true real; correct; agreeing with the facts; the opposite of false; loyal (as, a true friend)
truly really; faithfully; truthfully
truth a true statement; the actual facts; an accepted or proved principle
truthful correct; accurate (as, a truthful account); in the habit of telling the truth (as, a truthful child)

trumpet a brass musical instrument with a tube curved back on itself, widening into a cup or bell shape at the end; anything shaped or sounding like a trumpet □ to sound a trumpet; to make a sound like a trumpet (as - The elephants trumpeted loudly.)

truncheon a short heavy stick or baton (especially one carried by a policeman)

trundle to wheel or roll along (as, to trundle a hoop)

trunk the main stem of a tree; the body (but not head or limbs) of a person or animal: the long nose of an elephant: a big box or chest for holding clothing and other belongings (especially one used when travelling): (in plural) short, light-weight pants, worn for swimming, running, etc.

trunk call a long-distance telephone call, made by means of a trunk line

trunk line a main line of a railway, telephone system, etc., from which other lines branch out

trunk road a main road

truss a bundle (of hay or straw); a strong, rigid framework of beams, etc. to support a bridge, a roof, etc.; a bandage or device to support a weak part of the body □ to draw together and tie or bind; to skewer (as, to truss a chicken for cooking)

trust confidence or belief in the honesty, truth, goodness, etc. of a person, organization, government, etc.; a responsibility or duty (to care for or look after a person, charity funds, etc.); a number of business firms working under a central management □ to have belief or confidence in; to give into the care of another person; to hope or believe (as - I trust you are well.)

trustee a person who is entrusted with the care of property, money, etc., on behalf of another

trustful, trusting willing to trust others; the opposite of suspicious

trusty, trustworthy able to be trusted; honest; dependable

truth see **true**

try to make an effort or attempt to do something; to test or sample something (as, to try a new method, a new kind of food, etc.); to strain or annoy (as, to try one's eyes in a poor light, to try a person's patience by teasing); to attempt to use (as, to try a door); to put on trial in a court of law □ an attempt, an effort

trial see separate entry

trier a person who tries

tried the past tense of try □ tested; reliable

trying making an effort; test-

ing; hard to put up with; annoying

tsar, tzar, czar *(say tsahr or zahr)* the title given to Russian emperors in former times

tsarina, tzarina, czarina *(say tsahreena or zahreena)* the title given to Russian empresses in former times

tub a round, open wooden container; anything like a tub; a fixed sink or container for washing clothes, etc.; a bathtub

tubby round and plump; tub-shaped

tuba a large, trumpet-shaped musical instrument with very low-pitched tones

tube a long hollow cylindrical piece of metal, glass, wood, etc.; anything resembling a tube (as, bronchial tubes in the body); a round cylinder of soft metal, closed at one end, with a cap or stopper at the other, used to hold toothpaste, mustard, etc., which can be squeezed out; an underground railway in a tube-shaped tunnel

tubular tube-shaped

tuber the swollen underground stem of some plants (such as the potato)

tuberculosis an infectious disease mainly affecting the lungs

tuck to roll or fold up (sleeves, etc.); to press tightly in, around, etc. (as, to tuck a handkerchief in one's pocket, to tuck in the bedclothes); to begin to eat (to tuck in) □ a fold stitched in a piece of cloth (as, to take a tuck in a garment that is too large); sweets and chocolates, etc.

tuft a small cluster or bunch (of hair, feathers, grass, etc.)

tug to pull hard; to drag or haul along □ a strong pull; a tugboat

tugboat a small but powerful ship which tows larger ships

tug-of-war a contest of strength between two teams holding opposite ends of a rope and pulling against each other

tuition *(say tewishun)* teaching;

private teaching or coaching

tulip a spring garden plant with brightly coloured (usually single) flowers, which grow from a bulb

tulle *(say tool)* a material of thin silky net (often used in ballet and dance costumes)

tumble to fall down suddenly; to roll or toss about; to perform acrobatic tricks □ a fall
tumbler a tall drinking glass; an acrobat
tumbledown (of a house) falling down; dilapidated; shabby

tumour a swelling or growth in the body (usually not normal)

tumult *(say tewmult)* a loud noise made by a shouting crowd; confusion with uproar; excitement or disturbance
tumultuous noisy; excited; uproarious

tuna, tunny a very large sea-fish valued as a game fish and for food

tundra a level treeless plain in northern arctic regions

tune a melody; a series of musical notes arranged so as to be pleasing to hear, sing, etc.; correct pitch (as, to be in tune) □ to put a musical instrument in tune (by tightening and loosening strings, etc.)
tuning fork a metal instrument with two prongs which, when struck, gives out a musical sound of a certain pitch

tunic a tight-fitting jacket worn by soldiers, policemen, etc.; (in Roman times) a flowing garment reaching to the knees; (nowadays) a blouse-like garment (usually belted and extending below the hips)

tunnel an underground passage cut through a hill or mountain, or constructed under water □ to make a tunnel

tunny see **tuna**

turban a long piece of cloth wound round the head and worn by men in some Eastern countries; a similar headdress worn by women

turbine an engine powered by steam, gas, etc., which forces wheels (fitted with blades) to revolve continuously
turbo-jet a gas-turbine engine in which all the power is used to produce a jet of high-speed hot gas
turbo-prop a gas-turbine engine in which most of the power is used to drive a propeller, and the rest produces a jet of high-speed gas

turbot a large, flat sea-fish used as food

turbulent disturbed; restless and noisy

tureen a large, deep dish from which soup is served

turf short grass and the layer of soil just below the surface

turkey a large farmyard bird used for food

turmoil a state of disorder or commotion

turn to go, or move, round (as, a wheel turns, a car turns a corner); to go in a different direction (as, to turn right or left); to change (as - He turned his thoughts, or his attention, to a different subject.) □ the act of turning; a revolution (as, one turn of a wheel); a bend or turning-point; a chance to do something (as - It's your turn to bat.); a good or bad act towards someone (as - He did me a good turn.)
turncoat someone who deserts his side or party for the opposite one
turning the corner of a side-road or side-street
turning-point a point at which a turn, or important change, is made
turnout a crowd or gathering of people for a special purpose
turnover (in a business) the total amount of sales in a period (as, the yearly turnover)
turnstile a revolving gate which allows only one person through

at a time

turntable the revolving platform on a gramophone or record-player; a large circular platform for turning cars or railway engines round

to turn down to refuse (as, to turn down an offer, etc.)

to turn in to go to bed

to turn out to drive, or put, out (as, to turn somebody out of a house, to turn out a light); to go to, or gather for, a meeting, parade, etc.; to prove to be a fact (as - The story turned out to be true.)

to turn up to appear or arrive

turnip a vegetable with a large round root, which can be cooked and eaten or fed to farm animals

turpentine a colourless oil obtained from the resin of pine trees, mainly used in paint and varnish

turquoise *(say turkwahz or turk-woiz)* a greenish-blue stone, much used in jewellery

turret a small tower on a building; a revolving platform on a warship or a tank, with guns mounted on it

turtle 1 a large tortoise, especially one living in the sea

turtle 2, turtle-dove a handsome wild dove which makes a soft cooing noise

tusk one of the two large teeth which stick out of the mouths of elephants and walruses

tussle a struggle □ to struggle

tussock a tuft of grass

tutor a private teacher; a college supervisor □ to teach and direct studies

twang a sharp sound like that of a plucked banjo string; a sharp nasal tone of voice

tweak to pull sharply; to twitch (as, to tweak an ear)

tweed a rough woollen cloth, used (especially) for men's suits and sports jackets

tweezers small pincers (for pulling out hairs, holding small objects)

twelvemonth a year

twice two times

twig a small shoot or branch

twilight the time of faint light between day and night

twill a strong cloth, woven so as to show close diagonal lines

twin one of two children or animals born of the same mother at the same time (as, twin sisters); made up of two similar parts (as, twin-engined)

twine strong string made of twisted threads □ to wind round; to twist (threads, etc.) together

twinge a sudden, sharp pain

twinkle to shine or sparkle with a flickering light □ a blink or wink; an instant

twinkling a twinkle

twirl to turn round quickly; to whirl □ a whirl or spin

twist to wind one thing round another; to bend out of shape; to turn or wrench sharply (as, to twist a knob, an ankle) □ the act of twisting; a sharp turn or wrench

twit to taunt or tease a person

twitch to pull with a slight jerk (as, to twitch a friend's sleeve to get his attention); to move jerkily or spasmodically (as - His muscles twitched.) □ a quick pull or jerk; a slight spasm of the muscles

twitter to make small chirping noises; to tremble slightly from nervousness □ the noise made by twittering (as, the twitter or twittering of small birds); a nervous trembling

twofold double

type a letter, number, symbol, etc., moulded in metal, used for printing; a collection of such letters, etc. (as, the type on a typewriter or printing machine); a pattern or kind standing for a whole class of people or things (as, a type of person, of soldier, of book, of programme, etc.)

typewriter a machine which prints words on paper (It has different keys for the letters, which are tapped with the fingers.)

typical representing a certain type or kind (as, a typical English meal)

typist a person who uses a typewriter (usually as a job)

typhoid an infectious fever caused by a bacillus in bad food or impure drinking water

typhoon a violent storm in the seas around China

typhus a dangerous fever spread by rats

tyrant someone who rules, or uses his power, harshly or cruelly
tyrannical, tyrannous cruel
tyranny the rule, or behaviour, of a tyrant

tyre, tire the thick rubber cover fitted round the wheel of a cycle or motor car

tzar, tzarina see **tsar**

u

udder the milk bag of a cow, sheep, etc.

ugly unpleasant to look at; dangerous (as, an ugly situation)

ukelele *(say yewkalaylee)* an instrument like a small guitar (usually with four strings)

ulcer an open sore which is slow to heal

ulterior beyond what is seen or known; hidden (as, an ulterior motive)

ultimate farthest; last or final
ultimatum a final demand made by one country or party to another, threatening to break off peaceful discussion

ultramarine of a deep sky-blue colour □ a deep blue pigment

umber a brown pigment or colour

umbrage a suspicion of injury or offence (as - He took umbrage at my remarks.)

umbrella a folding covered framework for protection against the rain, carried in the hand

umpire someone called in to settle an argument or dispute; (in cricket, tennis, etc.) the person who acts as referee and decides doubtful points

un- a prefix usually meaning not or the opposite of (Examples are: **unanswerable, unapproachable, unaware, unbalanced unbeliever, unbend, unburden, uncertain, unclean, uncoil, uncomfortable, uncommon, uncompromising, unconcerned, unconscious, unconventional, undeniable, undeveloped, unemployed, unequal, uneven, unexpected, unfailing, unfair, unfasten, unfit, unflinching, unfortunate, ungrateful, unguarded, unhappy, unhealthy, unimportant, unintelligible, uninteresting, unkind, unlike, unload, unlucky, unnatural, unnecessary, unobservant, unorthodox, unpack, unpick, unpleasant, unprejudiced, unrelenting, unrequited, unsettle, unsteady, unsuccessful, unsuspecting, untidy, untimely, untrue, untruthful, unusual, unveil, unwell, unwrap**)

unaccountable not able to be accounted for or explained

unanimous *(say yewnanimus)* agreed to by all (as, a unanimous view or opinion)

unassuming modest

unawares without warning or off one's guard (as - He was caught unawares.)

unbecoming (of clothes) not suited to the wearer; (of behaviour) not to be expected from the person or in the particular circumstances

unbending not yielding; stiff and formal in attitude

unblushing without shame

unbridled not held in check

uncalled for quite unnecessary; rude (as - His remarks were uncalled for.)

uncanny strange; supernatural

uncle the brother of one's father or mother

unconscious not aware (of); senseless or stunned (as by an accident)

uncouth (say _uncooth_) clumsy; awkward; rude

undaunted not discouraged; fearless

undecided not having one's mind made up (as, undecided about choosing a present for a friend)

under, underneath beneath; below □ lower in position, rank, amount, etc.
under fire exposed to enemy fire
under one's breath in a low voice

under- a prefix usually meaning beneath, lower in position or rank, or too little (examples are: **underclothes, undercurrent, underestimate, underexposed, underfoot, undermentioned, undersigned, undersized, underskirt, underwear**)

underdog the loser in a struggle

underdone not completely cooked (as, an underdone steak)

undergo to endure or suffer

undergraduate a university student who has not yet taken a degree

underground under the ground; secret □ an underground railway

undergrowth shrubland; low plants growing among trees

underhand sly or mean

underline to draw a line under; to emphasize

undermine to weaken; to do damage to

underpass a road passing under another road, etc.

underrate to think too little of

understand to see the meaning of; to have a good knowledge of (as, to understand a subject); to take for granted; to appreciate another person's attitude, point of view, etc.
understanding the power of seeing the full meaning; an informal agreement; appreciation of another person's feelings, attitude, etc.

understate to state at less than the true value
understatement a statement (about something) expressing less than its true importance

understudy an actor who learns another actor's part so as to be able to take his place if needed □ to learn another's part in this way

undertake to take upon oneself (a duty, job, etc.)
undertaker someone who arranges and manages funerals
undertaking a project; a big job; a pledge or promise

undertone a low tone of voice

undertow a current below the surface of water that moves away from the shore, while the surface current moves towards the shore

underworld the gangs of lawbreakers in a city or country and the places frequented by them: (in mythology) the place of departed souls

undo to unfasten; to reverse, or spoil, the effect of what has been done (as, to undo someone's good work)
undoing ruin (as - This extravagance will be his undoing.)

undoubted not doubted or denied (as, the undoubted favourite)
undoubtedly without any

doubt; certainly

undress to take the clothes off

undue, unduly more than is necessary (as, undue worry, to worry unduly)

undulating wave-like; with hills and valleys (as, undulating country)

unearth to bring out from the earth, or from a hiding place
unearthly supernatural; very strange

uneasy not at ease; restless or anxious

unerring always accurate or right (as - William Tell took unerring aim.)

unfeeling hard-hearted

unfold to spread out; to give details of (a plan, etc.)

unfounded not based on facts; untrue

unfrequented not often visited (as, an unfrequented place)

ungainly awkward; clumsy

ungrudging given freely (as, ungrudging help)

uni- a prefix meaning one or single

unicorn (in old stories) an animal rather like a horse with one straight horn on its forehead

uniform having the same form, size, value, etc. (as, a uniform time for all shops to close); a standard dress worn by soldiers, sailors, etc.
uniformity the state of being uniform; sameness

unify to make into one (as, to unify the tribes of a backward country into one nation)
unification the act of unifying

union a joining together; the state of being united; marriage
trade union see **trade**
Union Jack the national flag of the United Kingdom

unique (*say yewneek*) without a like or equal

unison (in music) sounding at the same pitch; agreement

unit a single thing or person; a standard for measuring (as - The metre is a unit of length, the gramme is a unit of weight, the pound [£] a unit of currency, etc.)

unite to become one; to join or act together

unity the state of being one; complete agreement (as - There was a unity of purpose.); the number one (1)

universe all created things including the earth, the stars and everything out in space
universal having to do with all mankind; in general use
university a centre for higher education, having power to grant degrees

unkempt untidy

unless if not; except when (as - The dog is not allowed out unless he is on a lead.)

unmanly weak; cowardly

unmask to uncover; to expose or show up (a villain, etc.)

unmatched without an equal

unmistakable very clear or obvious

unmitigated complete; out-and-out (as, an unmitigated nuisance)

unmoved firm; calm

unpalatable not pleasing to the palate or taste

unparalleled having no parallel or equal

unqualified lacking the necessary qualifications (for a job, etc.): complete (as, an unqualified success)

unravel to disentangle; to solve (a mystery, etc.)

unremitting never ceasing (as, unremitting efforts)

unrest uneasiness; discontent (as, student unrest)

unruly ungovernable; disorderly (as, an unruly mob)

unsavoury tasteless; offensive

unsettled (of weather) changeable

unsightly ugly

unsophisticated simple; not experienced in life

unsound not in good condition; not correct (as, unsound reasoning); not sane (as, of unsound mind)

unsparing giving freely

unspeakable too bad to be put into words (as, an unspeakable action)

unthinkable too bad to be thought of; unimaginable

until up to the time of; till (as, no spare time until Saturday)

untold not told; too great to be counted

unwary not cautious

unwieldy awkward to handle

unwitting without knowing; unintentional

up towards a higher place; the opposite of down; at an end, to a finish (as - Time is up. He ate up his breakfast.)
uphill upwards; difficult (as, uphill work)
upland high ground
upper higher in position or rank
upmost, uppermost highest in position
uppercut a boxer's upward blow to the chin
upstairs in or to an upper storey
upstream towards the upper part of a stream
up-to-date new (as, up-to-date fashions)
upward(s) going, or directed, up

upbringing the bringing up, or training, of a child

upheaval a great disturbance; a violent shaking

uphold to support or maintain (a belief, a view, etc.)

upholster to fit (seats and settees) with springs, stuffing, covers, etc.

upholstery covers, cushions, etc.

upkeep the cost of keeping a house, a car, etc.

uplands high ground

upon on the top of

upright standing straight up; honest □ a vertical post

uproar noise and shouting

uproot to tear up by the roots

upset to overturn; to distress □ worried or anxious; unwell □ an overturning

upshot the final result or outcome

upside-down with the top part underneath; in confusion

upstart someone who has suddenly risen to wealth or power

uranium a radioactive metal

urban having to do with towns or cities; the opposite of rural
urbane courteous; smooth-mannered
urbanity highly civilized manners

urchin a small, mischievous boy

urge to drive (on); to try to persuade □ an impulse
urgency the state of being urgent
urgent requiring immediate attention or action (as, an urgent telegram)

urine the fluid produced by the kidneys which is passed out of the body as waste

urn a large metal container with a tap, for making tea, etc. in quantity; a vase for the ashes of the dead

us a pronoun standing for the persons who are speaking when they are the object, and not the subject, of a verb (as - Our parents met us at the station.)

use *(say yewz)* to employ something for a purpose (as, to use a knife and fork, to use one's brains at school); to spend or wear away (as, to use up one's pocket money); to have been in the habit of (as - He used to play golf.) □ *(say yewss)* the act of using; fitness for a purpose (as - It's of no use to me.)

usage *(say yewzij)* the manner of using; treatment (as, rough usage)

used *(say yewzd)* not new

useful *(say yewssful)* helpful; of practical use

useless *(say yewssless)* having no use or effect

usual done or happening, most often (as, our usual dinner on Sundays); customary (as, the usual annual outing)

usually on most occasions

usurp to take possession (of a throne or another's rights) by force or without right

usury *(say yewzhury)* the lending of money at a profit (usually by demanding a high rate of interest)

utensil an instrument or vessel used in everyday life (as, cooking utensils)

utilize to make use of (something that is available)

utility usefulness; a useful service (Bus services, water supplies, etc. are public utilities.)

utmost, uttermost greatest possible (as, the utmost care)

utter 1 to say or give out (words, cries, etc.)

utterance the act of uttering; something said

utter 2 extreme; complete (as, an utter failure)

utterly completely

uttermost see **utmost**

uvula *(say yewvewla)* the small tongue-like body which hangs down at the back of the throat

V

vacant *(say vaycant)* empty; not occupied; showing no intelligence (as, a vacant stare)

vacancy emptiness; an unfilled job (as - The factory has a number of vacancies for packers.)

vacate to leave empty; to move out of or cease to occupy (as, to vacate a flat, an office, etc.)

vacation a holiday

vaccinate *(say vaksinate)* to inject vaccine into the blood stream as a protection against serious diseases (such as smallpox)

vaccination the act of vaccinating

vaccine *(say vakseen)* a substance made from the virus or germs which cause a disease

vacuum *(say vakewum)* a space from which air and gas have been removed; empty space

vacuum cleaner a machine that cleans carpets, etc. by sucking up dust and dirt

vacuum flask a bottle with double walls, with a vacuum between them, which keeps liquids hot or cold

vagabond a wanderer; a person who has no permanent home; a rascal

vagrant *(say vaygrant)* having no settled home □ a wanderer; a tramp

vagrancy the state of being without a permanent home

vague not very clear or sure (as - His ideas on politics are rather vague.)

vain 1 having a very good opinion of one's own appearance, abilities, etc.

vanity foolish pride; conceit

vain 2 unsuccessful; useless; empty or worthless
vainly unsuccessfully; **in vain** without success or effect (as, to strive in vain)

vale a valley

valentine a card or greeting (affectionate or funny) sent on St Valentine's Day (February 14th); a sweetheart

valet *(say valet or valay)* a man-servant who looks after his employer's clothes, etc.

valiant brave; courageous; heroic in the face of danger

valid sound; reasonable; well-founded (as, a valid excuse for absence, valid argument); legally acceptable (as, a valid driving licence)

valley the low-lying land between hills or mountains
valleys the plural of valley

valour courage; bravery (especially in battle)
valorous brave; courageous

value worth (in money); price; importance (as, a speech of great value); a fair return or exchange (as, to get full value for what one has spent) □ to put a price on (as, to value a ring, a house, etc.); to think highly of or consider important (as, to value a friendship, to value an opportunity)
valuable having a high value □ (in plural) small objects worth a lot of money (jewellery, etc., often kept locked up)
valuation the act of valuing; the price or estimated worth of something

valve a device for controlling the flow of liquids, gases or steam: one of the two hinged shells of an oyster, clam, etc.: a glass bulb or tube used in some radio and television sets to detect or amplify radio signals
safety valve a valve which opens automatically to release pressure (as, a safety valve on a boiler, a pressure cooker, etc.)

vampire (in certain folklore and fiction) a dead person who is believed to rise at night to suck the blood of living people; a person who extorts money from others (by threats, blackmail, etc.)
vampire bat a blood-sucking bat

van 1 the front part or leaders in any action or movement (short for *van*guard)

van 2 a large covered wagon or vehicle used for carrying goods by road or rail (short for cara*van*)

vandal a person who carelessly or deliberately spoils, damages or destroys beautiful places, public buildings, works of art, etc.
vandalism the behaviour of a vandal

vane one of the blades of a windmill, propeller, etc.; a weathercock

vanguard the foremost part of an advancing army (going in front of the main part); the leaders in any movement

vanilla a flavouring for sweet foods that is obtained from the dried pod of a tropical climbing plant

vanish to go out of sight very suddenly; to disappear

vanity see **vain** 1

vanquish to conquer; to defeat

vapour *(say vaypor)* mist, steam or smoke floating in the air; the gas-like form of a substance that is usually liquid or solid
vaporize to change a liquid or a solid into vapour
vaporizer an apparatus for sending liquid out in a fine spray; an atomizer

variable, variation see **vary**

variegated marked with different colours (as, variegated foliage)

variety a collection or mixture of many kinds of things (as - This shop stocks a variety of goods.); kind or sort (as, a variety of rose, of ice cream)

various of different kinds or sorts; several (as - We considered various plans before deciding on this one.)

varnish a paint-like sticky liquid that hardens and gives a glossy finish to wood, metal, etc. □ to cover with varnish

vary to make different; to change about (as, to vary one's routine, one's eating habits); to disagree
varied of many kinds; of different sorts
variable changeable; able to be changed or altered
variance a difference; a lack of agreement (as - Their opinions were at variance.)
variation a varying or change (from what is usual, expected, regular, etc.); something that varies; the extent of change or difference (as - The variation of temperature in a day may be as much as 20 degrees.); (in music) a different way of presenting a basic melody or theme

vase a container, jar, etc. (usually rounded and taller than it is wide) used as an ornament or (mainly) for holding cut flowers

vassal (in feudal times) a person who held land belonging to an overlord and was therefore obliged to serve him; a dependant

vast of very great size or amount; immense; enormous

vat a large tub or tank used for fermenting liquor, dyeing, tanning, etc.

vaudeville a stage show with different kinds of entertainment (songs, dances, comic acts, etc.)

vault 1 an arched roof; a cellar or underground room (originally with an arched ceiling) used to store valuables (as, a bank vault), wine, etc.; a burial chamber
vaulted having an arched roof; resembling a vault

vault 2 to leap or leap over, using the hands, or (in athletics) a pole □ a leap

veal the meat from a calf

veer to change direction (as, the wind veered from east to northeast); to change course; to shift or turn

vegetable any plant which, as a whole or in part, is used as food □ of, or having to do with, plant life; obtained from vegetables (as, vegetable dyes, vegetable oils)
vegetarian made up of vegetables (as, a vegetarian diet) □ a person who eats vegetable foods only (refusing meat)
vegetate to grow as a plant does; (of people) to do little except grow and go on living
vegetation plant life (in general or of a particular region)
vegetable kingdom grasses, trees, plants as a whole

vehement (say *vee-iment*) forceful; passionate; full of enthusiasm, eagerness, etc. (as - He conducted a vehement argument on the subject of vegetarianism.)
vehemently violently; forcefully (as, to be vehemently in favour of prison reform)

vehicle (say *vee-ickl*) a means of transport (especially anything on wheels or runners); a means of conveying information (as, radio, newspapers); a medium (as - Language is a vehicle for communication, ideas, thoughts, etc.)

veil (say *vail*) a piece of thin netting or material worn by some women to hide their faces or to protect them from strong winds, hot sun, etc.; a nun's headdress; a bride's headdress □ to hide; to cover with, or as if with, a veil

vein one of the very thin long tubes that carry the blood round inside the body and back to the heart; one of the structural parts of the framework of a leaf, an insect wing, etc.; a thin streak or seam of mineral in rock; a streak of a different colour (as, a vein of white in green marble); a mood or personal quality (as, in sombre vein; a vein of humour)

veld, veldt *(say felt, velt)* (in South Africa) a grassy expanse of land with very few trees

vellum a fine quality parchment used for writing on or for binding special books; paper or material similar to parchment

velocity rate or speed of movement; swiftness

velvet a soft warm cloth made of silk, cotton, etc., with a furry surface
velvety soft and smooth like velvet
velveteen a cheaper material resembling velvet
velours *(say veloor)* a thick material similar to velvet, much used for hats

vend to sell
vendor, vender a person who sells
vending machine a slot machine for cigarettes, sweets, etc.

vendetta a bitter feud (usually started by a murder which the victim's family swears to avenge)

veneer to glue onto the surface of an article made of cheap wood, a thin covering of finer quality to give it a better appearance; to give an appearance of quality and worth to something that is basically not good □ a thin coating or surface covering (as, a veneer of good manners which is only for show)

venerable worthy of great respect because of age, long experience, good character of long standing, etc.
venerate to honour or respect; to revere

venetian blind a window blind or shade made of thin strips of wood, metal or plastic that can be moved to admit or exclude light

vengeance *(say venjans)* revenge: injury done in return for injury received
vengeful seeking revenge
with a vengeance with great force, energy, etc. (as, to set about a task with a vengeance)

venison the meat from deer

venom the poison secreted by some snakes and insects
venomous poisonous; spiteful

vent a small opening; a hole to let air, smoke, etc. pass out; a slit in the back of a coat; an outlet (as - She gave vent to her feelings.) □ to let out; to allow (smoke, gases, etc.) to escape
ventilate to allow fresh air to pass through: to talk about (as, to ventilate one's complaints)
ventilation the circulation of air (in a room, etc.)
ventilator a small grating or other device for introducing fresh air into a room

ventriloquist someone who can make his voice appear to come from a puppet or elsewhere

venture a journey, or any undertaking that involves some risks □ to risk; to dare
venturesome, venturous risky

veracity truthfulness

veranda(h) a kind of covered balcony along the front or side of a building (usually on the ground floor)

verb any word used to say what a person or thing does or experiences (examples are: to walk, talk, have, be, see, read, be equipped, etc.)
verbal in, or to do with, words: see also **oral**
verbatim *(say verbaytim)* word for word (as - He repeated the speech verbatim.)
verbose wordy
verbosity the use of more words than are necessary to convey what is meant

verdant green or fresh green (as, a verdant pasture)
verdure green vegetation

verdict the decision of a judge or finding of a jury at the end of a trial

verdigris *(say verdigrees)* a greenish coating formed on copper, brass and bronze by the action of the atmosphere

verge a border or edge

verger an attendant in a church

verify to prove to be true (by checking or by looking up all the facts)
verification the proving that something is true
veritable true; genuine
verity truthfulness; a truth

vermicelli *(say vermichelli)* a very thin kind of macaroni

vermilion a bright scarlet; a bright red pigment

vermin a name for all pests like rats, mice, fleas, bugs, etc.
verminous full of vermin

vernacular *(say vernakular)* the ordinary spoken language of a country (as, distinct from the literary language)

vernal having to do with spring

versatile able to turn easily from one subject or task to another; (of a material) useful for many different purposes
versatility the quality of being versatile

verse a line, or lines of poetry; a short division of a chapter in the Bible
version a translation into another language (as, the *Authorized Version* of the Bible); an account of something from one person's point of view (as - He gave his own version of how the accident happened.)

versed *(say verst)* skilled; knowledgeable (as, a person well versed in English history)

versus against (often shortened to v. or vs.)

vertebra one of the many bones in the spine
vertebrae the plural of vertebra
vertebrate an animal having a backbone

vertex the top corner or highest point
vertical standing upright; straight up and down
vertices *(say vertiseez)* the plural of vertex

vertigo giddiness

verve lively spirit; enthusiasm (as - The musicians played with verve.)

very in high degree (as, very good, very difficult) □ actual (as - That's the very present she wanted.)

vessel a ship; a container (usually for a liquid)
blood-vessel see **blood**

vest an undervest or undergarment worn next to the skin; a waistcoat

vestibule the part of a house or building just inside the entrance

vestige *(say vestij)* a trace; a track or footprint; (in plural) signs or marks of something that once existed

vestment a garment; (in plural) robes worn by clergymen during religious services

vestry a room (usually in a church) where vestments are kept

veteran old (as, a veteran car); experienced □ a person who has had long experience (especially a war veteran); an old soldier

veterinary having to do with the treatment of diseases and injuries of domesticated animals
veterinary surgeon, veterinarian (often abbreviated to **vet**) a doctor for animals
vet to check and pass as acceptable, correct

veto *(say veetoe)* the power or right to forbid or prevent □ to forbid; to reject or refuse consent to (as, to veto a proposed parliamentary bill, thus preventing it from becoming law)

vex to annoy; to make (someone) cross or irritable (by teasing, etc.)
vexation a feeling of annoyance; a cause of irritation

via *(say vie-a)* by way of (as, to go via the motorway)

viaduct a long bridge that carries a road or railway over a valley, etc.

vial a small bottle (especially one

used for medicine); a phial

vibrate to shake; to tremble; to swing or move to and fro rapidly
vibrant full of energy; thrilling (as, a vibrant singing voice)
vibration a rapid to-and-fro movement (as, the vibration of a guitar string); a trembling or shaking (as, the vibration from a ship's engine)

vicar a clergyman
vicarage the residence of a vicar

vice 1 a bad habit; evil conduct
vicious evil; malicious (as, to say vicious things about a person)

vice 2, vise an instrument for holding something tightly, by means of two metal jaws closed by a screw

vice versa *(say viesi-versah)* the other way round (as - *He has done me a few favours and vice versa*; that is to say, *I have also done him a few favours*.)

vice- a prefix added to a word, meaning a person who acts in place of another, or who is second in rank to another, taking his place when necessary (as, vice-admiral; vice-president; vice-chancellor)

vicinity nearness; the neighbourhood (as, to live in the vicinity of one's school)

vicious see **vice 1**

victim a person who is injured in some way or killed (either deliberately or accidentally)
victimize to cheat or swindle someone; to make an innocent person suffer

victor a person who wins a battle, a contest, etc.
victorious successful in a battle or contest
victory the winning of a battle or contest; the defeat of an enemy or competitor

victuals *(say vitt'lz)* food for human beings
victualler *(say vittler)* a person who sells provisions
licensed victualler an innkeeper

or publican who has a licence to sell beer, wines, etc.

vicuna *(say vikoonya)* a South American animal related to the llama, valued for its fine wool

videotape magnetic tape that reproduces recorded pictures and sounds when passed through a special machine

vie to compete or contend with someone in rivalry (as - They vied with each other in collecting for charity.)
vying competing; trying to be better than (someone else)

view a sight; that which is seen; a scene (as, a fine view of the countryside from a hilltop); opinion or idea (as, to give one's views on nature conservation; □ to look at; to watch (as, to view a television programme); to consider or think over (as, to view all sides of a problem)
viewpoint a place from which a fine view can be seen; a standpoint; a point of view, attitude or feelings about some subject, event, etc.

vigil a period of watching or keeping awake during the night (especially in connection with religious festivals, holy days, etc.)
vigilance alertness; watchfulness (especially against danger)
vigilant watchful; alert to danger
vigilante *(say vigilantee)* a member of a group of citizens who band together to protect the interests of a community against lawlessness (especially in unsettled territory)

vigour strength of body or mind; energy
vigorous strong; healthy and full of energy; (of plants) growing strongly

viking *(say vieking)* one of the pirates from northern Europe who raided western Europe in olden times

vile nasty; foul; wicked; very bad (as, vile conditions)
vilify to say evil things about

someone

villa a house (in former times, a rather grand house in the country or at the seaside, but nowadays applied to many houses with gardens in contrast to town houses or flats)

village a collection of houses and buildings in the country, not large enough to be called a town
villager a person who lives in a village

villain a wicked person; a rogue; a scoundrel; (jokingly) a rascal
villainous wicked; evil; very bad
villainy wickedness; an evil action

vindicate to defend successfully (a person, an action); to clear (of blame, suspicion, etc.)
vindication defence; justification or explanation (of some action)
vindictive spiteful; seeking revenge

vine a climbing or trailing plant (especially one that bears grapes)
vineyard (say vinyard) a field or plantation of grape vines (especially grapes for winemaking)

vinegar (say vinnigar) an acid-tasting liquid (made from cider, wine, etc.) used for flavouring salads, pickling foods, etc.

vintage the gathering of grapes in one season; wine produced in a particular year (as, the vintage of 1972) □ (of wine and some other things) of good quality; good and characteristic of its kind (as, vintage cars, which are old but still considered excellent of their type)

viola 1 a stringed instrument resembling, and played in the same way as, a violin, but larger and with a lower pitch

viola 2 a large family of plants, including the pansy and violet

violate to break or disregard an oath, a law, a treaty or agreement; to damage or treat with disrespect (as, to violate a church); to disturb or intrude on (a person's privacy; a country's boundaries)

violent moving or acting with great force (as, a violent storm, a violent outburst); caused by force or uncontrolled energy; great or uncontrollable (as, violent temper, pain, etc.)
violence great force; uncontrolled power

violet a small wild plant with purple or white flowers; a bluish-purple colour

violin a four-stringed musical instrument held under the chin and played with a bow
violinist a person who plays a violin

violoncello see **cello**

viper a poisonous snake

virgin a maiden; an unmated person □ pure; untouched or undisturbed (as, virgin forest, virgin snow)

virile strong and vigorous; manly; masculine
virility manliness; the quality of being masculine

virtue goodness; a good or excellent quality (as, truthfulness, kindness, patience)
virtually in effect; almost or practically (as, a virtually new car)
virtuous (of behaviour, character) good; without fault morally

virulent full of poison; bitter and dangerously spiteful (as, virulent remarks)

virus a minute organism (smaller than any bacteria) which causes some diseases

visa (say veeza) a country's official stamp put on a passport, which allows the bearer to travel in that country

visage the face (of a human being); the look or appearance of a face

viscount (say viekownt) a nobleman next in rank below an earl
viscountess the feminine of

viscount; a viscount's wife

viscous, viscid sticky (as, a viscous paste)

visible able to be seen
visibility the clearness with which things can be seen (as - Visibility is poor because of the fog.)

vision the ability to see; eyesight; the ability to foresee or imagine events in the future; a picture or dream in the mind; a ghostly image or apparition
visionary imagined (as, visionary dreams of becoming a film star); dreamy or fanciful ◻ a person who dreams or plans in an impractical way

visit to go to see (a person, a place); to call on ◻ a short stay; a brief call (as, a doctor's visit to a sick patient)
visitor a person who comes to call or stay as a house guest

visor *(say viezor)* the part of a helmet covering the face; a mask; an eyeshade; the peak of a cap that shades the eyes

vista a distant view (especially one seen at the end of a long avenue of trees)

visual having to do with sight or seeing
visualize to form a mental picture of something (as - He could visualize the way the garden would look in summer.)

vital *(say vietal)* having to do with life; necessary for life; essential (as - This work is vital to the success of our plans.)
vitality life; energy; ability to go on living
vitals the bodily organs necessary to life

vitamin one of a group of substances found in various natural foods (milk, fruit, vegetables, fish, etc.) necessary for good health and growth of all human beings

vivacious lively; sprightly
vivacity liveliness of behaviour

vivid life-like; striking; brilliant

vixen a female fox

viz. namely (as - Two languages are spoken in Belgium, viz., French and Flemish.)

vocabulary a selected list of words, usually in alphabetical order; all the words which a person knows and can use (as - He has a vocabulary of more than 10,000 words.)

vocal having to do with the voice; rather talkative
vocalist a singer

vocation a person's calling or profession (as - He is a teacher by vocation.)

vociferous *(say vosiferus)* loud-voiced; noisy

vodka a Russian alcoholic drink distilled from rye or potatoes

vogue the fashion at a particular time

voice the sound that comes from the mouth when speaking or singing; a say or opinion (as - He had no voice in selecting the team.) ◻ to give expression to (an opinion, etc.)

void empty; useless; not valid ◻ an empty space

volatile (of a liquid) easily turning into vapour (like petrol, which forms an explosive mixture with air); flighty or changeable in mood (as - That artist has a volatile nature.)

volcano a mountain, usually cone-shaped, with a crater from which molten rock and hot ashes are thrown out
volcanoes the plural of volcano
volcanic having to do with a volcano

vole a small gnawing animal (as, the water vole, often called the water rat)

volley a firing of many missiles at the same time; (in tennis) the return of a ball before it touches the ground ◻ to fire a volley; to return (a ball) before it bounces
volleys the plural of volley

volt the unit used for measuring the force of electricity

voltage electrical force measured in volts (as - A transistor radio has a very low voltage.)

voluble talkative; glib; (almost too) fluent
volubility talkativeness

volume a book; one of a series of related books (as, Volume 1, 2, 3, etc.); the amount of space occupied by anything (as, a volume of 75 cubic centimetres); fullness of sound (as, turning down the volume of a transistor radio)
voluminous filling much space; bulky

voluntary done by one's own choice and without any obligation (as, voluntary help in producing a school play) □ an organ solo
volunteer to offer to do something of one's own accord □ someone who offers himself for a task or service

vomit to throw up the contents of the stomach □ the matter thrown up when a person is sick

voodoo witchcraft of African origin; a person who believes in and practises such witchcraft

voracious very greedy (as, a voracious appetite); very eager (as, a voracious reader)

vortex a whirlpool; a whirlwind

vote to show one's support (for a candidate, a proposal, etc.) by putting a mark on a piece of paper or by raising one's hand (as, to vote for Mr. J. Smith as the new member of Parliament for a constituency) □ a person's formal opinion in an election, etc.
voter a person who votes

vouch (*say vowch*) to say that one is sure about something (as - The teacher vouched for the pupil's honesty.)
voucher a piece of paper with a money value for a certain purpose (as, a meals voucher, a gift voucher)

vow a solemn promise □ to make a solemn promise; to threaten (as - He vowed revenge.)

vowel a simple speech-sound made without moving the tongue, teeth or lips (that is, without using a consonant); one of the five letters (**a, e, i, o, u**) used either singly or together to represent a vowel sound

voyage a long journey (especially one by sea) □ to go on such a journey

vulgar commonplace; rude or coarse (as, a person with vulgar manners)
vulgarity rudeness; coarseness
vulgar fraction any fraction not written as a decimal fraction (such as, $\frac{1}{2}$ and $\frac{3}{4}$ and not ·5 or ·75)

vulnerable exposed to attack (as, a vulnerable enemy position); liable to be hurt or harmed in any way

vulture a large bird of prey which lives chiefly on dead animals

W

wad a mass of loose material (paper, cotton, wool, straw, etc.) used in packing, padding, stuffing cushions, etc.
wadding any soft material (such as cotton wool) used for padding garments, filling quilted bedcovers, etc.

waddle to walk with short steps, swaying from side to side as a duck does

wade to walk through water, snow, mud or other substance that offers some resistance; to make one's way with some difficulty or effort (as, to wade through a dull book); to cross or pass through (water) by wading

waders high waterproof boots worn by anglers

wafer a very thin biscuit

waffle a soft thick batter cake with an indented pattern, cooked in a hinged utensil of heavy metal (a waffle iron)

waft to move or carry gently and easily through the air or over water (as, a snatch of song wafted on the breeze)

wag 1 to move or be moved from side to side or to and fro □ a quick up and down or sideways movement (as, the wag of a tail)
wagged the past tense of wag

wag 2 a witty amusing person; someone who is always making jokes
waggish humorous; roguish

wage 1 to carry on (a war, a struggle against poor health, etc.)

wage 2 (often in plural) payment for work done

wager a bet □ to bet on the result of a race, a contest, etc.

waggle to wag (especially in an unsteady way)

wagon, waggon a four-wheeled vehicle (usually open) used for carrying heavy loads

wagtail a small wild bird with a long tail which it wags up and down

waif an uncared-for young child; a lost or strayed person or animal; a wanderer
waifs and strays people or animals without permanent homes

wail to make a long sad crying noise; to grieve or lament loudly □ a cry of grief

wainscot a wooden lining for the walls of a room

waist the narrow part of the body between ribs and hips
waistcoat a short (usually sleeveless) jacket, often worn under an outer jacket by men

wait to stay in the same place (until someone comes, some-

thing happens, etc.); to take no action (until receipt of further orders, information, etc.): to serve people at table □ a delay
waiter, waitress a person who serves food to people sitting at tables in cafes, restaurants, etc.
waiting list a list of people waiting for housing accommodation, medical attention, etc.
waiting room a place where people wait for buses, trains, aeroplanes, etc.
waits singers who go from house to house at Christmas time playing and singing carols

waive to give up a claim or right

wake 1 to be or become awake; to rouse a person from sleep □ an all-night watching and mourning for a dead person
waked, woke, woken the past forms of wake
wakeful not asleep; not able to sleep
waken to rouse (a person or animal) from sleep; to wake up or become awake

wake 2 the stream or track of foamy water left behind a moving vessel; any traces or track of something that has passed by (as, destruction in the wake of an advancing army)

walk (*say wawk*) to move along on foot (at a normal pace, not running) □ the act of walking; a person's gait or way of walking; a stroll or outing on foot, for pleasure (as, to go for a walk in the park); a place for walking; a person's usual place, occupation, rank, etc. (as - The army comprises people from all walks of life.)
walkie-talkie a small portable radio set (used by the police, army, etc.) for both sending and receiving messages
walkout a labour strike
walkover an easy victory
walking-stick a cane or light stick used for support in walking

wall (in olden times) the defending ramparts of a town or city; a structure of brick, stone, etc.,

erected to enclose private property (thus protecting it from intruders and separating it from other property); the side of a building, room, etc. between floor and roof or ceiling □ to protect or defend with a wall
wallflower a sweet-smelling flower that sometimes grows on old walls, but is usually grown in gardens
wallpaper paper used to decorate the walls of rooms in flats, houses, etc.

wallaby a small kind of kangaroo

wallet a small pocket-size case (usually of leather) used to carry paper money, tickets, stamps, personal papers, etc.

wallop to hit very hard

wallow to roll about in water, mud, etc. (usually enjoyably, as, hippopotomuses wallowing in muddy water): to enjoy living in a condition (as, to wallow in luxury, self-indulgence, etc.) □ a place where an animal wallows

walnut a tree valued for its nuts and its beautifully marked wood, much used for furniture and veneers

walrus a large sea animal, resembling a seal, with two large tusks

waltz a circling, gliding dance for two persons; music for such a dance (in triple time, with the emphasis on the first beat - **1**,2,3 **1**,2,3 etc.) □ to dance a waltz

wan pale and sickly; looking rather ill and weak

wand (in stories) a slender magic stick used by fairies, wizards, etc.; a stick used by conjurors when performing tricks

wander to roam about from place to place; to ramble or stroll about with no special purpose; to go astray or off the point (as, to wander from a path, to wander away from the topic of conversation)
wanderer a person who wanders, roams, etc.

wane to become smaller or weaker (as, when the full moon wanes); the opposite of wax; to lose power or importance
on the wane decreasing gradually

want to wish for or to be in need of something; to lack or be without □ scarcity; poverty; great need
wanting lacking; without; not good enough

wanton irresponsible; immoral; without cause or reason (as, wanton destruction of public property)

war a conflict between the armed forces of two or more countries □ to make war; to fight against
civil war an armed struggle between citizens of the same country
warring at war (as, warring nations)
warrior a skilled fighting man
warfare war; armed conflict; any continued struggle or campaign (as, to carry on warfare against disease)
warhead the part of a missile containing the explosive charge
warlike fond of war (as, a warlike nation); ready for or threatening war
warship a ship equipped with guns, etc. for war
on the warpath in fighting mood; ready for battle

warble to sing with trills, quavers, etc. (as birds do); to sing sweetly
warbler a singer; one of several kinds of small songbird (as, a reed warbler)

ward a large room in a hospital with a number of beds for patients: one of the sections into which a town or city is divided for elections, local government, etc.: a person (usually young) who is under the legal protection of a guardian □ to guard or take care of; to keep away (used with *off* - as, to ward off a cold, a blow)
warden a person who guards

or cares for (as, a game warden in a nature reserve); a person in charge of a hostel, a college, etc.
warder, wardress a guard (especially of prisoners)

wardrobe a cupboard or piece of furniture where clothes are kept; all the clothes belonging to a person; a collection of costumes and clothes used by a stage company

wardroom a room on a warship used by officers (for meals)

ware manufactured articles (especially of pottery, metal, etc.); (in plural) goods for sale
warehouse a building where goods are stored; a storehouse

warily see **wary**

warm fairly hot; more hot than cold; (of clothing, covers, etc.) protecting the body from cold by preventing loss of heat: friendly, welcoming, cordial (as, a warm handshake) □ to make or become warm
warmth moderate heat
warm-hearted affectionate; kindly

warn to tell a person that he should be on his guard against possible danger, trouble, etc.; to advise a person not to do something because it will result in punishment, pain, evil consequences, etc.; to give notice in advance (as, a bell that warns hospital visitors that visiting time is nearly up)
warning anything (such as a notice, a signpost, a spoken caution) that warns

warp to twist or become twisted out of shape □ (in weaving) the threads stretched lengthwise across the loom (in contrast to the weft or woof, which are the crosswise threads)
warped twisted out of shape; (of a person's outlook on life) embittered, soured

warrant something that guarantees or justifies; an authorization (as, a search warrant, a warrant for arrest) □ to guarantee; to justify (as - Such action

warrants a stiff punishment.)
warranted guaranteed as good (especially of goods for sale)

warren a place where many rabbits live together in a large number of burrows; a crowded slum area or building; a building or district with many narrow passages

wart a small hard lump on the skin (usually on the hands or face)

wary cautious; on one's guard against danger
warily cautiously
wariness watchfulness against danger

wash to clean with water, soap, etc.; to flow against (as, the waves washing rocks); to sweep (as - The flood washed away some farm land.) □ a washing; the disturbed water left behind a moving ship
washer someone who washes: a flat rubber or metal ring to keep a nut or joint tight
washing the act of cleaning with water; a bundle of clothes, etc. ready for washing
washhand basin a basin (usually fitted with taps) for washing the face and hands
washing machine a machine (usually driven by electricity) for washing clothes

wasp a stinging insect like a striped bee, with a very slender waist

waste to use up, or spend carelessly (as, to waste energy, money, time, etc.); to ruin or destroy □ thrown away as useless (as, waste paper, waste products); uncultivated or bare (as, waste ground) □ rubbish; an extravagant use or loss (as, a waste of money, of time, etc.); bare, empty land (as, the arctic wastes)
wastage loss by use, decay, etc.
wasteful causing waste; extravagant

watch to look at closely; to keep guard; to mind or look after □ the act of watching or keeping guard; a small timepiece worn on the wrist or carried in a pocket

watchful cautions; on the look-out

watchdog a dog kept to guard business premises, etc.

watchman a man who guards premises, etc., especially at night

watchword a maxim or motto (as - One of the party's watchwords was *Equal pay for women.*)

water a transparent liquid (without taste or smell when pure) which is a compound of hydrogen and oxygen (Rivers and most lakes consist of fresh water, the oceans and seas of salt water.) □ to supply or pour water on (as, to water the plants in the garden; to produce a watery liquid or tears (as - His mouth watered; his eyes watered.)

watery like water; full of water

water closet (or **W.C.**) a lavatory or toilet provided with a small cistern for flushing waste away through a pipe

water colour a paint made thinner with water instead of oil; a painting done in such colours

watercress a small green plant grown in fresh water and used in salads and garnishing

waterfall a fall of water from a height

water lily a pond plant with flat floating leaves and beautiful flowers with many petals

waterlogged soaked or filled with water

water main a large underground pipe carrying a water supply to houses, etc.

watermark a faint pattern in the texture of writing paper showing the maker's name or trademark

watermill a mill driven by water power

water polo a game played by swimmers (seven on each side) with a floating ball

waterproof not allowing water to pass through (as, a waterproof coat)

water rat a water vole

watershed a ridge of mountains or hills where rivers rise and flow away on either side

waterspout a pipe from which water spouts; a moving column of water caused by a whirlwind on the sea

waterworks the plant (machinery, filters, etc.) by which water is supplied to a town

watt a unit of electric power (named after James Watt)

wave a ridge or swell moving on the surface of the sea, a lake, etc.; anything that resembles a wave (as, waves in the hair); a vibrating disturbance travelling through the air or through space (as, sound waves, light waves); a surge or increase (as, a heat wave); a gesture with the hand □ to move (a hand, a flag, etc.) up and down, to and fro; to curve like a wave

wavy having, or resembling, waves

wavelength the distance between the crests of two waves, especially radio waves (as, a wavelength of 300 metres)

waver to be uncertain or undecided; to be unsteady

wax 1 to grow larger gradually (as — The moon appears to wax greater until it becomes a full moon.); the opposite of wane

wax 2 beeswax; any similar substance; sealing wax □ to smear, rub or polish with wax

waxen, waxy made of, or resembling, wax; (of a person's skin or complexion) pale and unhealthy-looking

waxwing a crested bird with red markings like sealing wax at the tips of the wing feathers

waxworks an exhibition of wax models of famous people

way a road, path, street, passage, etc.; direction (as - Which way shall we go?); distance (as, a long way); room or space (to move, to pass); manner (as, to handle a problem in an efficient way); means (as, the right way to do something); condition (as -

The accident left him in a bad way.); a person's own method or style (as - I prefer to do it my way.)

wayfarer a traveller (especially on foot)

waylay to lie in wait for a person in order to attack, rob, etc.; to wait for someone to pass by and stop him in order to speak, ask a favour, etc.

wayside the edge or side of a road, path, etc.

wayward wilful; capricious; irregular or changeable (as, a wayward breeze)

to give way see **give**

we the word used by two or more speakers, writers, etc. in referring to themselves; the plural of I

weak feeble, not strong; easily influenced; easily overcome (as, a weak opponent, a weak argument)
weakness lack of strength; a physical defect or character fault
weakling a person, animal, plant, etc. lacking strength
weaken to make, or become, weak or weaker

weal a raised mark on the skin, caused by a blow from a whip, a lash, a cane, etc.

wealth great riches; a great quantity of something (especially money)
wealthy rich

wean to train a young child or animal that has been living entirely on its mother's milk to eat solid food; to turn a person away from some habit or indulgence (as, to be weaned away from eating too many sweet foods)

weapon anything used to fight with (such as a gun, a sword, a spear, etc.)

wear *(say wair)* to be dressed in; to have or show on the face (as, to wear a smile, a sad expression); to last well through much use; to become damaged, fragile, rubbed into holes through much use □ damage by much use
wore the past tense of wear

worn showing signs of wear; exhausted
wearing tiring; annoying
to wear out to use up completely; to exhaust (as, to wear out a pair of shoes, to feel worn out after a tiring day)
wear and tear the gradual damage done to anything through constant wear and use

weary *(say weery)* tired; bored or impatient (as, weary of idle chatter); tiring or dreary (as, a weary task)
weariness exhaustion; tiredness
wearisome causing tiredness, boredom, etc.

weasel a small slender wild animal that lives on birds, mice, etc.

weather the state of the atmosphere (heat, coldness, sunshine, rain, etc., as, good weather, stormy weather) □ to be affected by exposure to all kinds of weather (as, a wooden fence weathered to a silvery grey colour); to last out or come through difficulties, a storm, etc.
weatherbeaten showing some change or damage as a result of exposure to weather
weathercock, weathervane a flat piece of metal (often in the shape of a cock) that turns with the wind, showing its direction

weave to make cloth on a loom by crossing threads over and under each other; to make something (such as a basket) by this method; to make, or construct a story, a play, etc. by working separate details and incidents into a whole □ a pattern or design of weaving
wove the past of weave
woven made by weaving (as, hand-woven tweed)

web a cobweb: a woven piece of cloth: the skin between the toes of ducks, geese, frogs, and other water birds and animals
webbed formed with a web; webfooted
webbing a strong, closely wov-

en fabric, used for belts, in upholstery, etc.

webfooted having toes connected by webs

wed to marry

wedded married; devoted to (as, wedded to music)

wedding marriage; the marriage ceremony

wedlock the state of being married; matrimony

wedge a triangular piece of metal, wood, etc., very thin at one end and thicker at the other, used in splitting wood, stone, etc. or for fixing something tightly (as, to keep a door open by putting a wedge under it); anything like a wedge (as, a wedge-shaped piece of cake) □ to split (as, though with a wedge); to fix firmly with a wedge; to press or squeeze in tightly (as, wedged in a football crowd)

wee very small; tiny

weed a wild plant that grows where it is not wanted in gardens or in cultivated fields □ to remove weeds; to remove or take out anything useless, unpleasant, etc.

weedy full of weeds; weed-like; (of a person) thin and lanky

week a period of seven days (especially from Sunday to Saturday); the six working days of the week

weekly happening or done once a week □ a magazine, newspaper, etc. published every week

weekday any day of the week except Sunday, and (sometimes) Saturday

weekend the days at the end of the week and the beginning of the next (usually Saturday and Sunday)

weep to shed tears; to show grief, joy, or some other emotion by shedding tears

weeping shedding tears; (of some trees) with drooping branches

wept the past tense of weep

weevil any of various kinds of small beetles that damage fruit, grain, nuts, etc.

weft (in weaving) the threads woven in and out across the warp

weigh *(say way)* to find out how heavy something is (usually by placing it on scales); to measure out a quantity (by weight) on scales; (of troubles, responsibilities, etc.) to press down on or burden; to consider carefully (as, to weigh both sides of an argument); to raise (a ship's anchor)

weight how much a thing or person weighs; heaviness (as, a measure of quantity - for example 2 kilos of sugar); a piece of metal of a standard heaviness (as, a weight of 100 grammes used in measuring out quantities of food); a burden or worry (as, a weight on one's mind)

weighty very heavy; important; serious (as, a weighty argument)

weir *(say weer)* a dam across a stream or river

weird strange and frightening; ghostly; supernatural

welcome to greet someone's arrival with pleasure; to accept gladly (as, a suggestion, an opportunity, an offer, etc.) □ a kindly greeting □ admitted freely or willingly (as - Visitors to the exhibition are welcome) □ a word used to express pleasure when a guest or caller arrives

weld to join pieces of metal together by heating and pressing together; to join closely (as, welded together by friendship)

welfare the condition of a person's health, general well-being, etc.; the general prosperity, etc. of the community or society as a whole

welfare state a nation which undertakes responsibility for the welfare of its citizens by means of a health service, unemployment insurance, retirement pensions, etc. (All citizens, including employers, make regular contributions to pay for these services.)

welfare work work concerned with the welfare of people in a country, state, community, etc.

well 1 a spring (of water, oil, etc.) gushing or bubbling up from the earth; a hole dug or drilled in the ground to reach such a spring; any structure resembling a well (as, the well of a staircase) □ to flow or gush (as - Tears welled up in her eyes at the sad news.)

well 2 in good health □ properly, thoroughly or successfully (as - She can ride well, but she can't dance very well.) □ an interjection expressing surprise, etc. (as - Well, I would never have believed it!)

well-advised wise
well-being welfare; comfort
well-bred having good manners
well-disposed favourable
well-informed having much, or reliable, information
well-known celebrated; familiar
well-off, well-to-do wealthy
well-read *(say well-red)* having read many good books
as well (as) in addition (to)

wellingtons long rubber boots (named after the Duke of Wellington)

welsh rabbit, rarebit melted and seasoned cheese on toast

welter to roll about or wallow □ a state of confusion
welter-weight (in boxing) a weight of $10^1/_2$ stones, between light and middle

west the direction in which the sun sets; the opposite of east
western, westward towards the west
westerly coming from the west (as, a westerly wind)

wet containing, or covered with, water; not dry; rainy (as, a wet day) □ to make wet □ wetness or rain (as - Come in out of the wet!)

whack to strike hard and sharply □ a loud slap or blow

whacking a beating

whale the largest sea mammal (not a fish)
whaling the catching of whales

wharf a landing place for loading and unloading ships
wharfs, wharves alternative plurals of wharf

what a pronoun or adjective used in questions (as - What is in your hand? What colour is it?); a pronoun meaning that which (as - He wants what you are holding.)
whatever anything that; no matter what (as - Whatever you do, don't forget to post that letter.)

wheat the kind of grain which is milled to produce flour for bread
wheaten made of wheat

wheedle to coax a person to do a favour, etc.

wheel a circular frame which turns on an axle (as, a bicycle wheel, a steering wheel) □ to move on wheels; to turn or move round in a curve (as - The soldiers wheeled to the left.)
wheelbarrow a handcart with one wheel in front and two handles and legs behind

wheeze to breathe with a hissing sound (and usually with difficulty) □ a sound of wheezing

whelk a kind of shellfish with a spiral shell (Some are edible.)

whelp a puppy; the young of certain animals, such as the lion, seal, fox, etc.

when at what time (as - When is he going?); at the time that (as, when the next term begins); while (as, when on holiday)
whence from what place or source
whenever at any, or every, time

where at, or in, what place (as - Where is your coat?); in, or to, which (as, the place where I lost it; the place where I go)
whereabouts the place where someone or something is (as - I don't know his whereabouts.)

whereas when in fact (as - He said he was at work, whereas we know he was elsewhere.)

whereby by which

whereupon after which

wherever no matter where (as - They will find him wherever he is.)

whet to sharpen the edge of a tool by rubbing; to make keen (as, to whet the appetite)

whetted the past tense of whet

whetstone a stone for sharpening knives, tools, etc.

whether if (as, to ask whether we should go); if or if not (as, to ask whether we should go to London or whether we should stay at home)

whey the watery part of milk when it is separated from the curd (the thick part)

which what one of two or more persons or things (as - Which friend will you ask? Which will you buy?); that (as, the plant which I bought; a dog which ran after me)

whichever any one (of a number, as, to choose whichever you like); no matter which (as - Whichever path you take, you will come out at the same place.)

whiff a sudden puff of fresh air, smoke, scent, etc.

while during the time that; as long as □ a space of time (as, to stay a while); time and trouble (as - It was worth your while to go to see them.) □ to pass the time agreeably, without boredom (as - He whiled away the time by listening to the radio.)

whilst *(say whielst)* during the time that; while

whim a sudden fancy or wish; a sudden change of mind; an odd idea

whimsical quaintly humorous; full of whims

whimper to cry in a low whining voice □ a whining cry

whine to make a low complaining sound; to complain in a whining voice, without real reason □ a low complaining cry

whinny (of horses) to neigh softly □ a soft neighing sound

whip a piece of thin strong cord or leather with a handle, used for punishing or driving □ to strike with a whip, lash, etc.: to beat eggs, cream, etc. into a froth with a beater or fork; to pull something out quickly (as, to whip out a gun); (with *up* or *away*) to snatch

whipping a beating or lashing with a whip

whiphand the hand that holds the whip in driving a coach, carriage, etc.; an advantage (as, to have the whiphand over a person in a fight or argument)

whippet a racing dog like a greyhound, but smaller

whir, whirr to move or turn rapidly with a buzzing sound □ a whirring sound

whirl to turn round and round very quickly; to move or carry something about rapidly (as - An autumn wind whirls dead leaves about.); to feel dizziness (as - My head is whirling.) □ a rapid turning round and round; noisy confusion, bustle, excitement, etc.

whirlpool a circular current in a river, sea, etc. which sucks nearby objects into its centre

whirlwind a violent whirling windstorm

whisk to move swiftly (as, to whisk something away, to whisk out of sight); to brush or sweep; to beat (eggs, cream, etc.) into a froth □ a quick brushing or sweeping movement (as, the whisk of a tail); a kitchen tool used for whipping up eggs, cream, etc.; a light brush to get rid of dust, flies, etc.

whisker (usually in plural) the hairs growing on the side of a man's face; one of the stiff hairs at the sides of the mouths of some animals (such as cats, lions, rabbits)

whisky a strong alcoholic drink distilled from grain

whisper to speak very softly without using the full voice; (of leaves in the trees, silk, etc.) to make a soft rustling sound; to spread rumours or tell secrets by whispering □ a soft sound uttered by using the breath and lips, but not the vocal cords

whist a card game played by four people (two against two)

whistle to make a shrill, high-pitched sound by blowing hard through nearly closed lips or teeth; to blow a whistle □ the sound made by whistling; an instrument which makes a whistling sound (as, a factory whistle, a police whistle)

white of the colour of pure snow; pale or light-coloured (wine, complexion) □ anything white (as, the white of an egg, whites of the eyes)
  whiten to make, or become, white or whiter
  white flag a sign of surrender or request for a truce
  white-hot at the degree of heat at which metals, etc. become white (even hotter than red-hot)
  whitewash a paint-like thin mixture of lime and water, used to whiten walls, etc. □ to cover with whitewash; to try to cover up or make excuses for wrong-doing

whither to what place?

whittle to pare or cut pieces, shavings, etc. from wood with a knife; to make something less, little by little (as, to whittle away a sum of money)

whiz, whizz to move, pass, etc. rapidly with a humming or hissing sound (as, racing cars whizzing by)

who, whom what or which person (as - Who is that? The man whom I saw. The man to whom I gave the message.); that (as - The girl who passed by. The girl whom you passed on your way here.)
  whose the possessive pronoun relating to who (as - Whose hat is this?)

whoever, whomever whatever or whichever person; anyone that (as - Will whoever wants to help please step forward?)

whole all; not a part; not divided or broken; complete; in sound and healthy condition
  wholly *(say holy)* completely
  wholesale the sale of goods in large quantities to retailers who then sell the goods in ordinary quantities to consumers □ on a large scale (as, wholesale destruction)
  wholesome healthy (as, wholesome exercise, wholesome food)

whoop a loud cry or shout (usually of joy, triumph, encouragement, etc.); the loud gasping sound of a person suffering from whooping cough
  whooping cough an infectious disease in which the patient has a cough with long loud whoops

whose see **who**

why for what reason or cause (as - Why did you go away?)

wick a strip or band of twisted thread in a candle, lamp, or oil stove which burns with a flame while supplied with melted grease or oil

wicked evil; sinful; very naughty or mischievous

wicker a flexible slender twig (such as willow) that can be bent and woven into baskets, light furniture, etc.
  wickerwork baskets, furniture, etc. made of wicker

wicket a small gate or door (especially one set in or near a larger one); (in cricket) a set of three upright stumps at which the bowler aims the ball; the pitch; (in croquet) one of the wire hoops through which the ball is driven

wide broad; the opposite of narrow; stretching far; completely open (as, wide-eyed with surprise, a wide-open window); measured across (as, material 36 inches wide, a room 10 feet wide); far apart; far from the point or target aimed at □ (in cricket) a ball bowled beyond the batsman's reach

widen to make, or become, wide or wider

width wideness or measurement across; the opposite of length

widespread extending over a large area; spread as wide as possible

widow a woman whose husband is dead

widower a man whose wife is dead

wield to use or manage (a weapon, a baton, etc.) with skill; to use power or authority to accomplish something

wife a married woman

wives the plural of wife

wig an artificial covering of real or imitation hair for the head

wiggle to move back and forth or from side to side in short jerky movements

wiggly wavy; not straight (as, a wiggly line)

wigwam (in former times) an American Indian hut (usually rounded or oval) made of hides, mats, etc. stretched over poles

wild not tamed or cultivated by people (as, wild animals, wild flowers); not civilized (as, a wild, primitive tribe); uncontrolled or violent (as, wild with anger, a wild and windy night); wide of the mark □ (in plural) an uninhabited, uncultivated area

wilderness a wild, uncultivated, uninhabited region

will 1 an auxiliary verb used to express determination, intention, or future action (as - I will finish this job tonight. I will go in spite of what you say. He will go with you next week.)

would the past tense of will (as - He said he would go.); a conditional form of will (as - I would like to go if the weather is fine.)

will 2 the power to choose or decide (how one acts, what one does, etc.) determination (as, the will to succeed); wish or desire: feeling towards a person or thing (as, good will): a legal document stating what is to happen to a person's property after his death □ to make a will or an act of will

wilful headstrong; wanting one's own way; stubborn

willing ready to do what is asked; not opposed; cheerful and helpful (as, a willing worker)

willow a tree or shrub with slender, pliable twigs used in basketwork; the wood of the willow tree; a cricket bat (made of willow)

weeping willow a kind of large willow tree with drooping branches

wilt (of flowers) to droop and become limp; to lose strength

wily crafty; sly

win to come first (in a race, etc.); to gain a victory through effort and skill (as, to win a contest, game, battle, etc.); to obtain by luck (as, to win a prize, a lottery, etc.); to obtain someone's support (as - We will try to win him over to our side of the argument.) □ a victory; a success

won the past tense of win

winning successful; victorious (as, the winning horse); charming; attractive (as, a winning manner)

winnings what is won (usually money from gambling)

wince to draw back quickly; to flinch (from sudden pain)

winch a crank or handle for turning a wheel on a machine, for winding a rope, cables, etc.; a hoisting machine

wind 1 *(rhymes with tinned)* air in motion; a strong current or movement of air (as, a wind of gale force); breath (as, to get one's wind back after running hard); flatulence; air carrying a scent (as, dogs following the scent of game) □ to cause a person to lose his breath (as, by punching him in the stomach)

winded out of breath

windy exposed to the wind (as, a windy hill); (of weather) with much wind blowing

windfall apples or other fruits blown down by the wind; any unexpected win, gift, etc.

wind instrument any musical instrument played by wind (especially the breath)

windmill a machine for pumping water, grinding grain, etc., worked by the wind turning sails

windpipe the tube-like passage for breathing that leads from the throat to the lungs

windscreen a transparent screen in a frame above the dashboard in a motor vehicle

windward towards the point from which the wind is blowing

second wind natural breathing restored after breathlessness from rapid running, etc.

wind 2 *(rhymes with kind)* to turn or twist (as, to wind a watch or clock); to coil (as, to wind up a ball of string); to make a way by turning and twisting (as - The river winds through the valley.)

winding curving; with many bends (as, a winding road)

to wind up to wind a watch or clock spring as far as it will go; to tighten; to bring to an end (as, to wind up a meeting, or a business)

wound 1 *(say wownd)* the past of wind (as - She wound the clock every night.)

windlass a winch

window an opening (usually glass-covered) in the wall of a building to let in light and air; a similar large opening in a shop (a shop window) where goods are displayed

window-pane, -sash, -sill see **pane, sash, sill**

wine an alcoholic drink made from the fermented juice of grapes

wing one of the arm-like parts of a bird, bat or insect with which it flies; one of the planes of an aeroplane; any side-piece or structure (as, the wing of a large house, the wings on a stage, etc.); a player (in football, etc.) whose position is at either end of the forward line

winged having wings; swift

wink to shut and open one eye quickly; (of lights) to twinkle □ an act of winking

winkle a small edible shellfish

to winkle out to extract gradually and with difficulty

winsome charming

winter the coldest season of the year □ to pass the winter □ suitable for winter (as, winter clothing)

wintry like winter, cold; stormy

winter sports skiing, tobogganing, etc.

wipe to clean or dry by rubbing □ the act of cleaning by rubbing

wiper someone who wipes; a moving arm which wipes the windscreen of a car

wire a metal thread or string (as, telephone wires): a telegram □ made of wire (as, a wire fence) □ to install or connect up electricity wires (in a building, etc.); to send a telegram

wireless another name for radio: see **radio**

wiry like wire; lean and strong (as, a wiry athlete)

wire-netting a network woven of thin wire in a wide mesh

wisdom see **wise**

wise 1 having much knowledge and experience in using that knowledge well; thoughtful or sensible (as, a wise decision)

wisdom *(say wizdom)* the quality of being wise

wisdom tooth one of four back teeth which usually appear in the late teens or early twenties

wise 2 way or manner (as, crosswise, in this wise)

wish to have, or to express, a desire □ a desire; a longing; desires expressed for another's good fortune or happiness (as, a message *Best Wishes* on a greetings card)

wishful thinking wishing for something that might happen but is unlikely to

wisp a small tuft (as, a wisp of hair, of hay, etc.)

wistful sadly thoughtful or yearning

wit understanding; common sense; the ability to express ideas in a clever, amusing way □ a person who can do this
witless stupid; foolish
witty clever and amusing
witticism a witty saying
wittingly knowingly

witch a woman supposed to have powers of magic to help or do harm to others; a sorcerer; a hag
witchcraft the power to practise magic; sorcery
witch doctor (in Africa) a member of a tribe who is believed to have magic powers to cure illnesses, keep evil spirits away, etc.

with near to or in the company of (as, to be with friends); against (as, to fight with an opponent); alongside or on the same side (as, to fight with the army of one's country); in the same direction as (as, to drift with the tide); by means of (as, to draw with a pencil); in possession of (as, a man with his own car, a girl with long black hair); in the care of (as, to leave the baby with a friend for an hour)

withdraw to move back or away; to take away (as, to withdraw an offer; to withdraw money from a bank account); to take back (an insulting remark, etc.)
withdrew the past tense of withdraw (as - The enemy fleet withdrew.)
withdrawal a withdrawing; a retreat
withdrawn (of a place) isolated; lonely; (of a person) not making friends easily

wither to become dry and faded; to shrivel; to lose freshness

withhold to keep back or refuse (as, to withhold permission)

within inside; in the limits of, or not going beyond (as, within one's rights, within the city limits); in the interior or inner part

without outside or in the outer part of (a place, etc.); not having (as, without money, without cares); in the absence of (as, to go somewhere without a companion)

withstand to oppose or resist (usually successfully)

witness a person who has seen something happen or who has personal knowledge of something; a person who gives evidence in a court □ to see or observe (some event); to sign one's name to a document (as proof that it is genuine); to give evidence; to be proof of

wizard a man supposed to have magic powers

wizened (*say wizz'nd*) dried up; shrivelled and wrinkled (as, a wizened face)

woad (*say wode*) a blue dye made from the leaves of the woad plant

wobble to rock unsteadily from side to side; to tremble or shake
wobbly shaky

woe grief; great unhappiness; deep sorrow; misery
woebegone looking sad and miserable (especially of expression or appearance)
woeful full of misery

wolf a dangerous dog-like wild animal
wolves the plural of wolf (as - Wolves hunt in packs for their prey.)
wolfish fierce; like a wolf

woman a female human being when she is grown up
women the plural of woman
womanhood the state of being a woman
womankind, womenfolk women in general; all women

womb (*say woom*) the organ inside a mother's body in which the young of mammals develop until they are ready to be born

wonder to be surprised or amazed at (something marvellous, unusual, unexpected, etc.); to feel curiosity about (as, to wonder why a person has done something); to have doubts about (as, to wonder whether a person will arrive on time) □ a feeling of surprise, awe, astonishment, reverence, etc. at some unusual happening, something marvellous, etc.; a strange or marvellous thing (as, *The Seven Wonders of the World*)

wonderful, wondrous marvellous; amazing; very good (as, wonderful news)

wonderland an imaginary place where wonderful things are supposed to happen

wonderment surprise; amazement

woo to try to gain the affections of (especially with a view to marriage); to try to win over a person's support; to seek to gain (success, wealth, etc.)

wood (often in plural) a group of growing trees; the hard part of a tree used for timber, firewood, etc. □ made of wood

wooded covered with trees (as, wooded hills)

wooden like, or made of, wood; (of a person's expression, movements, etc.) dull; stiff and awkward

woody like wood (as, a woody stem); having many woods (as, woody country)

woodcraft knowledge of forests and woods and how to live in them

woodcut a carved or engraved design on a block of wood (from which prints can be made); a print made from a woodcut

woodcutter a man who cuts and saws wood (especially as a job)

woodland land covered with trees; woods

woodpecker a wild bird having a hard sharp beak, with which it pecks holes in the bark of trees to find insects

wood pulp wood fibre reduced to pulp, used in making paper

woodwind one of the musical instruments made of wood and played by blowing (as, the clarinet, oboe, etc.); the section of an orchestra consisting of woodwind instruments

woodwork the wooden fittings for a building; carpentry

wool the thick warm hair covering sheep and some other animals; yarn made of wool (as, knitting wool); cloth made of wool; any light, fleecy material like wool

woollen made of wool; having to do with wool (as, the woollen industry)

woolly made of, or like, wool; covered with wool (as, a woolly lamb) □ a warm knitted garment (as, winter woollies)

word a spoken or written sign representing a thing, an idea, etc.; a group of letters which mean something when read or heard; something said (as, to have a word with someone); a promise (as, to keep one's word); a message or news (as, to bring word of a victory) □ to express in words

wordy using more words than are necessary; verbose

word for word in exactly the same words; verbatim

wording the way in which a thought is put into words

wore see **wear**

work the effort put into making or doing something; a task; labour; employment; anything made or done; any literary, musical, artistic, etc. production (as - The *Mona Lisa* is a work of art. The library has the complete works of Shakespeare.); a manner of working, quality of workmanship (as, good work, careless work); (in plural) a factory; the mechanism or working parts of a clock, etc. □ to put effort into doing or achieving something (as, to work for exams); to toil or labour (especially for money); to be employed; (of a machine, apparatus, etc.) to operate properly or efficiently; to make something work by managing, controlling, etc. (as, to work a machine)

worked the past tense of work: see also **wrought** - an old form of worked

workable able to be done, carried out, etc. (as, a workable plan)

working doing work; relating to work (as, working hours) □ (in plural) the parts of a mine where work is, or has been, done

working classes manual workers

workman a manual worker

workmanship skill in working or in doing a particular piece of work (as - This brooch is a beautiful piece of workmanship.)

world the earth, including everyone and everything on it and in it, as well as in the air around it; the universe; mankind or people in general; any planet or heavenly body; a state of existence (as, the world of the future); any particular part of the earth (as - Europe is in the Old World, North and South America in the New World); a particular area of activity, profession, etc. (as, the world of music, the gardening world)

worldly concerned with, or belonging to, this material world; not spiritual

world-wide extending, or found, all over the world

worm a small, wriggling animal without limbs or backbone; an earthworm: anything spiral (such as the thread of a screw); a mean, grovelling person; (in plural) a disease caused □ to worms in the intestines □ to move or work one's way slowly (as - He wormed his way into their confidence.)

worn, worn-out see **wear**

worry to be afraid something is going to go wrong, or that something bad may happen; to cause anxiety or trouble to someone: to shake and tear with the teeth (as, a puppy worries an old slipper) □ a trouble; an anxiety

worse not so well (as, a person who is more ill than he was before); the opposite of better; more bad (as - His behaviour is even worse than last time.)

worsen to make, or become, worse

worship to honour and respect (as, to worship God); to adore or greatly admire; to take part in a religious service □ respect and honour (especially for God); a religious service or ceremony; a title of respect used in addressing judges, mayors and other officials (as, Your Worship)

worst bad in the greatest degree; the least good; the opposite of best

worsted a firm, smooth fabric made from long, combed wool

worth value; price; importance □ equal in value to (as, worth 50 pence); meriting, or good enough for (as, an idea worth considering, a book worth reading)

worthless of no worth or value

worthy good or deserving (as, a worthy charity)

would see **will 1**

wound 1 *(say wownd)* see under **wind 2**

wound 2 *(say woond)* a deep cut or break in the skin caused by a weapon, an accident, etc.; a hurt or injury to the feelings (as, a wound to his pride) □ to make or cause a wound; to hurt someone's feelings

wounded hurt; injured □ a person or persons who have suffered wounds (especially soldiers after a battle)

wrangle to quarrel noisily □ an angry argument

wrap to cover by winding or folding round (as, to wrap up a parcel) □ a covering (such as a shawl)

wrapper a covering of some kind (such as a loose garment, paper wrapping, etc.)

wrath violent anger
wrathful very angry

wreath *(say reeth)* a garland of flowers or leaves (usually in the shape of a ring)

wreck a very badly damaged ship; the remains of anything destroyed (as, the wreck of a car); a person who is ruined in health or mind □ to destroy
wreckage the broken remains of a wrecked ship, car, etc.

wren a very small brown song-bird with a short erect tail

wrench to pull with a twist (usually with force) □ a violent twist; a tool like a spanner, for gripping and turning nuts, bolts, etc.

wrest to twist, or take away, by force

wrestle to struggle with an opponent and try to throw him down; to struggle (as, to wrestle with a problem)
wrestler someone who wrestles
wrestling a sport in which two persons wrestle against each other according to certain rules

wretch a miserable, unhappy person; a worthless person
wretched miserable; worthless; very unhappy (as - She was feeling wretched.)

wriggle to twist to and fro (as - A worm wriggles. The boy wriggled out of a tight corner.)

wring to twist or squeeze (so as to force water out of wet clothes, etc.); to force a person to say something (as, to wring a confession from a prisoner); to distress (as - The sad story wrung her heart.)
wrung the past tense of wring
wringer, wringing-machine a machine for forcing water from wet clothes

wrinkle a small crease or fold in material, paper, etc. or in the skin of older people □ to make wrinkles in

wrist the joint which joins the hand to the arm
wrist watch a watch worn on the wrist

writ a legal document ordering a person to do something (as, a writ to appear in court)

write to form letters and words with a pen or pencil; to write and post a letter (as - I wrote him a letter.); to compose or put into writing (as - He has written an essay, a book, a musical composition.)
writer someone who writes; an author
writing the act of a writer; something written; a literary composition or work (as, the writings of Charles Dickens)

writhe *(say rieth)* to twist violently; to squirm (as, to writhe in pain)

wrong not right; incorrect; not suitable; evil □ whatever is not right; an injustice to another person □ to do wrong to; to treat unfairly
wrongful unjust; unlawful
wrong-doer someone who does wrong; an offender
wrong-doing wrong or wicked conduct

wrought *(say rawt)* made, manufactured
wrought-iron iron which has been forged or rolled (used for ornamental gates, grilles, etc.)

wrung see **wring**

wry *(say rie)* twisted or turned to one side; expressing slight displeasure or mockery (as, a wry smile)
wryly in a wry manner

X

X-rays certain powerful rays which can pass through most things except metal and bone (Thus, an X-ray photograph of the body shows the bones clearly as dark shadows, and the surrounding parts much less clearly.)

xylophone *(say zielophone)* a horizontal musical instrument consisting of a number of narrow bars of varying lengths, which sound different notes when struck with two small wooden hammers

---

y

yacht *(say yot)* a sailing or motor vessel used for pleasure, racing, etc.
yachting the sport of sailing, racing, etc. in a yacht
yachtsman a person skilled in yachting; a yacht owner

yak a long-haired ox found in Tibet

yam a large potato-like tuber grown in tropical countries, where it is used for food

Yankee a person who comes from the north-eastern (New England) states of the U.S.A.; a person from the northern states, in contrast to one from the south; (in countries outside the U.S.A.) any American citizen

yap to bark sharply (as - The pekinese yapped at the postman.)

yard 1 a measurement (of 3 feet or 36 inches); a long beam on the mast of a ship for spreading sails
yard arm either end of a ship's yard

yard 2 a large space or area (usually enclosed by buildings, a fence, wall, etc.); such a space used for a special purpose (as, a shipyard, railway yard)

yarn thread spun from wool or cotton; one of the threads twisted into rope; a story (especially one told by someone, such as a sailor, who has travelled widely)

yarrow a strong-smelling wild plant with flat clusters of small white or pink flowers

yawn to open the mouth very wide and take a deep breath (as, to yawn from tiredness, boredom, etc.); to resemble a yawning mouth (as - The cave opening yawned ahead of them.)

ye an old form of you, no longer used, except in poetry, etc.

yea *(say yay)* an old form of yes (now mainly used in voting); the opposite of nay

year 365 days (except leap year which has 366); the time taken for the earth to go once round the sun 365$\frac{1}{4}$ days); the part of the year taken up by some work, activity, etc. (as, the school year, the gardening year)
yearling an animal a year old
yearly happening every year or once a year
yearbook a book appearing once a year (usually containing specialized information about what has happened during the past year)

yearn to have a great desire or longing for (a person, place, thing)
yearning a longing or desire (as, a yearning to visit one's old home)

yeast *(say yeest)* a substance causing fermentation, used in making bread, beer, etc.

yell to shout or call out loudly (in anger, fear, surprise, etc.)

yellow a bright colour like that of primroses or lemons □ of this colour (as - The canary is a yellow bird.)

yelp a short sharp cry or bark

□ to utter such a sound (as, a yelping puppy)

yen the unit of Japanese currency

yeoman a farmer or landowner having a small amount of land

yes a word showing agreement or consent; the opposite of no

yesterday the day before today

yet by now (as, not here yet); still (as, yet more difficult) □ however (as - Yet, I would like to go.)

yew a dark evergreen tree, often seen in country churchyards

yield to give in or give up; to produce or bring in (as - The orchard yielded a good crop.) □ the amount produced (as, a yield of 4 metric tons of wheat per hectare)
yielding giving way easily

yodel to sing by suddenly changing pitch from a natural voice to a high voice and back again

yogurt, yoghourt a dessert made of slightly sour, thickened milk (often flavoured)

yoke something that joins together; a wooden frame for carrying pails, or joining a pair of oxen □ to put a yoke on; to join together

yokel a country fellow

yolk the yellow part of an egg

yonder at a distance but within view (as, over yonder, yonder village)

you the pronoun which refers to any person(s) to whom one is speaking or writing
your, yours possessive forms of you (as, your hand, the book is yours)
yourself a reflexive pronoun used to emphasize you (as - You must do it yourself.)

young in the early part of life or growth; not old □ the offspring of animals
younger not as old as someone else
youngster a young person, not yet grown up

your(s), yourself see **you**

youth the state of being young, the early part of life; a young man; young people (as, the youth of today)
youthful young; fresh and vigorous

yo-yo a toy in the shape of a reel, which spins up and down on a string

Z

zeal great enthusiasm; keenness
zealot (say *zellot*) a person full of zeal; a fanatic
zealous (say *zellus*) full of zeal or enthusiasm

zebra an African wild animal like a small horse with stripes
zebra crossing a street crossing, marked with stripes for the use of pedestrians

zenith the point of the sky which is exactly overhead; the highest point reached (as, the zenith of an artist's career)

zephyr (say *zeffir*) a soft, gentle breeze

zero nothing; the figure 0; the point from which any scale begins (as, the 0 mark on a thermometer)

zest relish; keen enjoyment (as - They joined in the folk songs with zest.)

zigzag having short sharp turns like the letter Z □ to move forward in a side-to-side manner □ a path or road with many sharp angles

zinc a bluish-white, fairly soft metal

zinnia a summer garden plant

with stiff brightly-coloured flowers

zip a whizzing sound: a zip fastener □ to move with great speed and energy; to fasten with a zip fastener
zip fastener, zipper a long fastener for clothes, bags, etc., in which two sets of teeth are locked into each other by pulling a slide along them

zither a flat musical instrument with many metal strings, played by plucking

zodiac a large imaginary belt in the heavens, divided into twelve equal parts called *signs of the zodiac,* named (in olden times) after certain groups of stars

zone one of the five great belt-like areas into which the world is divided according to temperature (The north temperate zone includes nearly all of Europe and North America.); a region or area (as, a non-parking zone)

zoo, zoological garden a public park where wild animals are kept and exhibited
zoologist a person who studies animal life
zoology the science of animal life

zoom to make a loud, persistent, deep buzzing noise; (of an aircraft) to soar or climb sharply; to move along with a loud humming or buzzing noise

Appendix One

List of Verbs

Most verbs simply add -d or -ed in their past tenses. Here is a list of the verbs in this dictionary that do not form their past tenses regularly.

Present Tense	Past Tense	Past Participle
awake	awoke, awaked	awaked, awoke
bear	bore	borne, born
beat	beat	beaten
become	became	become
begin	began	begun
bend	bent	bent
bet	bet, betted	bet, betted
bind	bound	bound
bite	bit	bit, bitten
bleed	bled	bled
blow	blew	blown
break	broke	broken
breed	bred	bred
bring	brought	brought
broadcast	broadcast, broadcasted	broadcast, broadcasted
build	built	built
burn	burnt, burned	burnt, burned
burst	burst	burst
buy	bought	bought
cast	cast	cast
catch	caught	caught
choose	chose	chosen
cling	clung	clung
come	came	come
cost	cost	cost
creep	crept	crept
cut	cut	cut
deal	dealt	dealt
dig	dug	dug
do	did	done
draw	drew	drawn
dream	dreamed, dreamt	dreamed, dreamt

drink	drank	drunk
drive	drove	driven
eat	ate	eaten
fall	fell	fallen
feed	fed	fed
feel	felt	felt
fight	fought	fought
find	found	found
flee	fled	fled
fling	flung	flung
fly	flew	flown
forbid	forbade	forbidden
forecast	forecast, forecasted	forecast, forecasted
forego	forewent	foregone
foresee	foresaw	foreseen
foretell	foretold	foretold
forget	forgot	forgotten
forgive	forgave	forgiven
forsake	forsook	forsaken
freeze	froze	frozen
get	got	got
gild	gilded, gilt	gilded, gilt
give	gave	given
go	went	gone
grind	ground	ground
grow	grew	grown
hang	hung, hanged	hung, hanged
have	had	had
hear	heard	heard
hew	hewed	hewed, hewn
hide	hid	hidden, hid
hit	hit	hit
hold	held	held
hurt	hurt	hurt
inlay	inlaid	inlaid
keep	kept	kept
kneel	kneeled, knelt	kneeled, knelt
knit	knitted, knit	knitted, knit
know	knew	known

lay	laid	laid
lead	led	led
lean	leaned, leant	leaned, leant
leap	leaped, leapt	leaped, leapt
learn	learned, learnt	learned, learnt
leave	left	left
lend	lent	lent
let	let	let
lie	lay	lain
light	lighted, lit	lighted, lit
lose	lost	lost
make	made	made
mean	meant	meant
meet	met	met
mislay	mislaid	mislaid
mislead	misled	misled
mistake	mistook	mistaken
misunderstand	misunderstood	misunderstood
mow	mowed	mowed, mown
outdo	outdid	outdone
outrun	outran	outrun
overcome	overcame	overcome
overdo	overdid	overdone
overdraw	overdrew	overdrawn
overeat	overate	overeaten
overhang	overhung	overhung
overhear	overheard	overheard
oversee	oversaw	overseen
overtake	overtook	overtaken
overthrow	overthrew	overthrown
pay	paid	paid
put	put	put
read	read	read
repay	repaid	repaid
rid	rid	rid
ride	rode	ridden
ring	rang	rung
rise	rose	risen
run	ran	run
saw	sawed	sawed, sawn
say	said	said
see	saw	seen
seek	sought	sought

sell	sold	sold
send	sent	sent
set	set	set
sew	sewed	sewn, sewed
shake	shook	shaken
shear	sheared	shorn, sheared
shed	shed	shed
shine	shone	shone
shoe	shod	shod
shoot	shot	shot
show	showed	shown
shrink	shrank	shrunk
shut	shut	shut
sing	sang	sung
sink	sank	sunk
sit	sat	sat
sleep	slept	slept
slide	slid	slid
sling	slung	slung
slink	slunk	slunk
slit	slit	slit
smell	smelled, smelt	smelled, smelt
sow	sowed	sown, sowed
speak	spoke	spoken
speed	sped, speeded	sped, speeded
spell	spelled, spelt	spelled, spelt
spend	spent	spent
spill	spilled, spilt	spilled, spilt
spin	spun	spun
spit	spat	spat
split	split	split
spread	spread	spread
spring	sprang	sprung
stand	stood	stood
steal	stole	stolen
stick	stuck	stuck
sting	stung	stung
stink	stank, stunk	stunk
stride	strode	stridden
strike	struck	struck
string	strung	strung
strive	strove	striven
swear	swore	sworn
sweat	sweated, sweat	sweated, sweat
sweep	swept	swept
swell	swelled	swollen
swim	swam	swum
swing	swung	swung
take	took	taken
teach	taught	taught
tear	tore	torn
tell	told	told
think	thought	thought
thrive	throve, thrived	thriven
throw	threw	thrown
thrust	thrust	thrust

tread	trod	trodden, trod
undergo	underwent	undergone
understand	understood	understood
undertake	undertook	undertaken
upset	upset	upset
wake	woke, waked	waked, woken
wear	wore	worn
weave	wove	woven
weep	wept	wept
wet	wet, wetted	wet, wetted
win	won	won
wind	wound	wound
withdraw	withdrew	withdrawn
withhold	withheld	withheld
withstand	withstood	withstood
wring	wrung	wrung
write	wrote	written

Appendix Two

Common Prefixes and Suffixes

Prefixes

a-, an-	not, without
ab-	away from
ad-	to, at
ambi-	both, round about
an-	not, without
anglo-	English
ante-	before or ahead
anti-	against
aqu(a)-	water
auto-	self
bi-, bis-, bin-	twice, double
bio-	life
cent(i)-	the hundredth part of, a hundred
circum-	round about
com-, con-, co-	together, with, completely
contr(a)-	against
counter-	against
de-	down, away from, or the undoing of an action
demi-	half
di-	double
dia-	through
dis-	*reverses the meaning of the rest of the word*
en-, em-	in, on, into
equi-	equal
ex-, e-	out of, from
ex-	former
extra-	on the outside, beyond
for-	through, thorough, away
fore-	before

hemi-	half
hetero-	other
hom(o)-	same
hydro-	water
hyp(o)-	under
in-, im-	not, in, into
inter-	between, among
intro-	into, within
kilo-	a thousand
mal(e)-	badly, ill
micro-	little, small
mid-	at, in, in the middle of, with
mill(i)-	a thousand
mini-	small, miniature
mis-	wrong(ly) or bad(ly)
mono-	single
mult(i)-	many, much
non-	*reverses the meaning of the rest of the word*
off-	off
ortho-	straight, right, genuine
out-	away from, outwards, beyond
over-	above, across, upper, beyond
poly-	much, many
post-	after, behind
pre-	before
pro-	favouring, on the side of
proto-	first
pseudo-	false, sham
quad-	four
quin-	five
re-	again
retro-	back, backwards

semi-	half
sub-	under, below, lesser
super-	above, beyond, in addition, in excess
tele-	far
thermo-	heat
trans-	across, beyond
tri-	three
un-	not, the opposite of
under-	under, below, too little
vice-	in place of
with-	with, near, against, back

Suffixes

-able, -ible, -uble	capable of being
-ar	belonging to
-ary	place, person
-ble, -ple	number of times
-dom	dominion, power, state, act
-en	made of *(adjective suffix)*
-en	*(verb suffix)* to make
-ern	direction
-ern	belonging to
-erly	direction to or from
-ese	belonging to
-esque	having the quality of
-ess	feminine suffix
-et, -ette	small
-ful	full of, as much as will fill
-fy	to make
-hood	state, nature
-ible *see* **-able**	
-ic	of or belonging to
-ing	forming nouns from verbs
-ion, -sion,	
-tion, -son, -som	being, state of being
-ise, *see* **-ize**	
-ish	somewhat
-ism	system of belief or principles
-ist	denotes the person who holds a doctrine or practises an art
-itis	disease (usually inflammation)
-ize, -ise	*forming verbs from adjectives and nouns*

-lent	full of
-less	free from, lacking
-let	*diminutive*
-ling	*diminutive*
-ly	*adjective and adverb suffix*
-ment	*noun suffix*
-ness	*noun suffix denoting abstract idea*
-or, -er	denotes the person who does something
-our	*abstract noun*
-ous	*adjective suffix*
-ship	*noun suffix*
-sion *see* **-ion**	
-teen	ten to be added
-ty	being or state of being
-ty	ten to be multiplied
-uble *see* **-able**	
-ward(s)	indicates direction
-way, -ways	manner, direction
-wise	way, manner